RIPPLES OF HOPE

RIPPLES OF HOPE

Great American
Civil Rights Speeches

Edited by

JOSH GOTTHEIMER

Foreword by

PRESIDENT BILL CLINTON

Afterword by

MARY FRANCES BERRY

BASIC
CIVITAS
BOOKS

A Member of the
Perseus Books Group

Published by Basic *Civitas* Books,
A Member of the Perseus Books Group

Designed by Jeff Williams
Set in 11-point Bembo by the Perseus Books Group

Library of Congress Cataloging-in-Publication Data

Ripples of hope : great American civil rights speeches /
Josh Gottheimer, editor ; foreword by Bill Clinton ; afterword by Mary
Frances Berry.
    p. cm.
Includes index.
   ISBN 0-465-02752-0 (hardcover : alk. paper)
   1. Minorities—Civil rights—United States—History—Sources.
2. Civil rights movements—United States—History—Sources. 3. Civil rights—United
States—History—Sources. 4. United States—Race relations—Sources. 5. United States—
Ethnic relations—Sources. 6. United States—Social conditions—Sources. 7. Speeches,
addresses, etc., American. I. Gottheimer, Josh.

E184.A1 R53 2003
323.1'73—dc21
                                                                              2002152012

03 04/10 9 8 7 6 5 4 3 2 1

For my parents and sister,
who have always been there, and
my Uncle Barry, who was taken from us too soon.

Each time a man stands up for an ideal,
or acts to improve the lot of others,
or strikes out against injustice,
he sends forth a tiny ripple of hope,
and crossing each other from a million
different centers of energy and daring,
those ripples build a current which can sweep down
the mightiest walls of oppression and resistance.
—ROBERT F. KENNEDY

CONTENTS

MEASURED GAINS: TWO STEPS FORWARD, ONE STEP BACKWARD 1866–1949

THE CIVIL RIGHTS ERA: LIFT EVERY VOICE
1950–1969

THE CURRENT STRUGGLE:
SLOW BUT STEADY PROGRESS
1970–1998

FOREWORD

WILLIAM JEFFERSON CLINTON

If there is no struggle, there is no progress.
—FREDERICK DOUGLASS,
AUGUST 4, 1857

In the beginning was the word . . .

The most compelling force behind humanity's long and troubled march toward racial and social justice has been the power of the spoken word. From Jesus's miraculous Sermon on the Mount to Dr. Martin Luther King's historic moment on the Mall, generation after generation of freedom fighters, armed only with their eloquence and righteousness, have stoked the eternal fires of hope within the human soul.

This book celebrates that valiant journey. In it we hear the echoes of courageous voices that have risen from dimly lit slave huts, back-road churches, and street corners to lift the conscience of a nation. But the speeches in this volume are much more than exhortations from a near or distant past. They are living reminders of the challenges that remain and the work yet to be done.

As I was growing up in the segregated South, my low-grade fever for public service reached the boiling point under the influence of the speeches of Dr. King and John F. Kennedy. It wasn't long before I knew that I too wanted to serve my country and its highest ideals, none more important than racial reconciliation. I came of age at the height of the civil rights struggles of the sixties: the March on Washington, the passage of the Civil Rights Act and the Voting Rights Act. I will never forget that moment in 1965 when Lyndon Johnson, a white southerner, faced the Congress and the nation only a week after the tragedy of "Bloody Sunday." "At times," he said, "history and fate meet at a single time and place to shape a turning point in man's unending search for freedom. So it was at Lexington and Concord. So it was a century ago at Appomattox. So it was last week in Selma, Alabama."

On March 5, 2000, the thirty-fifth anniversary of Bloody Sunday, I had the privilege of returning to Selma with many of the original foot soldiers in that momentous moral confrontation. Before we retraced their steps across the Edmund Pettus Bridge, I told those gathered that, while we have come a long way since the bleakest days of the civil rights struggle, we still have many more bridges to cross in our journey toward becoming One America. These include the racial gaps in education, criminal justice, health, employment, and wealth. I dedicated much of my work as president to closing those gaps; but of course we have much more work to do if we are ever to eliminate discrimination based on race, ethnicity, gender, and sexual orientation. In that spirit, I recommend reading the speeches in this book not so much as an appreciation of history but as inspiration for the work that lies ahead.

I want to commend Josh Gottheimer for compiling this unprecedented collection of civil rights voices. As one of my presidential speechwriters, Mr. Gottheimer's passion for speaking truth to power was evident to me and to all who worked with him. I thank him for his enduring commitment to the cause of civil rights and social justice and for this important literary gift to America.

WILLIAM J. CLINTON

New York, New York

December 2002

INTRODUCTION

*No one can speak for him—no one knows
the thing as well as he does.*

—W. E. B. Du Bois,
on the consummate preacher

*[An orator] is a physician, who lifts men above themselves, and cre-
ates a higher appetite than he satisfies. [Oration] is the power to
translate a truth into language.*

—Ralph Waldo Emerson

The civil rights movements in America are ever evolving, with one generation of leaders building on the accomplishments—and the rhetoric—of
those before them.

Only a few miles from where I sit in Massachusetts, John Adams and his
founding brothers, in one of the earliest cries for equal opportunity, sounded
the trumpet for freedom. Adams's exhortation for independence in the late
eighteenth century paved the way for Thomas Jefferson's declaration of "life,
liberty, and the pursuit of happiness." Decades later, near the Charles River,
William Lloyd Garrison and Theodore Weld evoked Jefferson as they condemned slavery, and nearby, Angelina Grimké became the first woman to
speak out for abolition. To the north, in Vermont, Lucy Terry argued forcefully
for her right to property, becoming the first African-American woman to
speak before a court with a member of the U.S. Supreme Court on the bench.
In neighboring upstate New York, a carriage ride away, Elizabeth Cady
Stanton drew inspiration from the abolitionist cause as she delivered a stirring
address at the first women's rights conference.

Farther south, in Washington, D.C., Abraham Lincoln earned an indelible
place in history—and the ire of many—with his commanding excoriation of
slavery. Martin Luther King, Jr., a century later, echoed Lincoln's words when
he described his dream of equality to an audience of thousands. Several years
later, President Lyndon Johnson embraced King, Lincoln, and Scripture when,
in the face of race riots and segregation, he declared, "We shall overcome."

In San Francisco, gay activist Harry Hay recalled the social activists before him when he openly claimed at the height of the civil rights era that homosexuals were indeed a minority group deserving of equal opportunity. In another California city, César Chávez found inspiration from Dr. King and Mahatma Gandhi when he brought America's attention to centuries-old Chicano oppression. And Robert "Spark" Matsunaga, only a few years earlier, drew on his own heritage and the words of the earliest American settlers when he decried the overt discrimination practiced against Americans of Asian descent.

These towering figures, and others, embraced the power that Du Bois and Emerson described, that of dignity, self-reliance, and self-respect. As you will see in the following pages, the speakers whose words are included in this anthology shared strength, ideas, and even words with one another.

Reading great civil rights rhetoric will give you an appreciation for its convincing power and its purpose. The words will return you to the abolitionist protests of the 1840s and the internment camps of the 1940s; you will hear the roar of the audience; you will imagine men and women huddled around an itinerant abolitionist who, with each sentence, pumped life back into a weary community of slaves. His words transformed dismay into hope; his speech helped them believe that, with effort, persuasion, and unity, they could, as Dr. King later exhorted, overcome.

SPEAKING OUT: HOW EACH MOVEMENT LEARNED FROM THE PAST

At times when minorities were denied access to ballot boxes, lunch counters, or schoolhouses, the human voice was often their only tool of persuasion, and the church lectern their only platform for dissent. With the law and public institutions largely stacked against them, minorities, beginning in the nineteenth century, found that speech offered them a modicum of power in those systems designed to keep them silent. From one generation to the next, the steady calls for equality ultimately convinced crowds—and the nation—to rise up against discrimination.

African Americans were the first group in the United States to recognize their power by either speaking out themselves or through others. This revelation is not altogether surprising. With roots in African tribal culture, blacks placed great value on public speech, a reliance dating back to a time when many blacks could not read or write (for example, former slave Sojourner Truth was illiterate). Delivered by both men and women, African-American rhetoric evoked Scripture, tribal heritage, and the cadence of the slave song. This anthology, in part, traces blacks' oratorical path, beginning with the voice of a freed African American in the eighteenth century.

Lacking a formal education, slaves relied heavily on African oral tradition as a means of community building and social and political activism. Before the Civil War, in order to keep blacks from organizing, most were not permitted to read, write, or speak publicly. In the antebellum North, however, the African-American church was the one setting where blacks were permitted to congregate. Consequently, the first African-American leaders, and the earliest rhetoricians, were preachers who deftly used their pulpits as political cauldrons. Later, freed blacks in the North established fraternal organizations, like the Prince Hall Masonic Lodge, as venues for sermons and speeches.

Out of fear of being caught, most early African-American orators did not prepare their texts in advance but delivered them extemporaneously. Even those that were written down were frequently destroyed or misplaced. Such a fate also befell the texts of the early feminist, Asian-American, and Latino-American speeches. According to author Alice Moore Dunbar, "Most of the best [rhetoric] is lost; most of it is hidden away in forgotten places."

Like African Americans, white women were prohibited from speaking publicly in the nation's early years. Although female orators and activists did not face the same dire repercussions as their African-American counterparts (including lashings, hanging, and jail), women were nonetheless discouraged from adopting a public persona. A woman's role in society was considered a private one, and men cited the Bible as evidence that women should confine their speech to the home. Protesting this treatment, female activists began to organize and conduct meetings in favor of abolitionism. In the early 1830s, white women began comparing their own condition as second-class citizens to that of slaves. Gradually they garnered enough support to address mixed audiences of men and women, demanding equal rights, first for blacks and then for themselves. Even then, white women faced fierce opposition from husbands who still believed that female activism should be confined to the back bench of abolitionist meetings. This atmosphere changed markedly after the convention at Seneca Falls, New York, in 1848, in which sixty-eight women and thirty-two men signed the Declaration of Sentiments, demanding that the rights of women be respected by society.

Until the late twentieth century, many gay Americans were afraid to admit their sexual orientation, let alone stand at a microphone and tell the world that they deserved equal treatment. Even today, their public "coming out" has been measured and conducted largely in the face of a wary public, judiciary, and government. Likewise, most early Asian and Hispanic immigrants believed they would lose their jobs, citizenship rights, or even face deportation if they spoke out for their civil rights. When they finally did—in some instances with great fanfare—each group quickly learned the impact that speech could have in both advancing their agenda and protecting their communities from further discrimination.

Although no one leader changed the course of history, nor did one person spark the civil rights movement, each individual's work and speeches created "ripples of hope"—single waves of activism that together caused a grand wave of change. Those ripples brought progress to institutions once considered immutable, change to entrenched social and political norms, and enlightenment to the historically narrow-minded. As Senator Robert F. Kennedy explained in 1966 to a crowd of college activists in South Africa, "Crossing each other from a million different centers of energy and daring, those *ripples* built a current that can sweep down the mightiest walls of oppression and resistance."

King, Chávez, Stanton, and others who worked to overcome seemingly intractable barriers are now celebrated icons embedded in the American story. But in their day, civil rights leaders were viewed as deeply divisive figures whose radical approach threatened to splinter a peaceful, unified nation. They put their careers on hold, their reputations at risk, and often their lives on the line to eradicate inequality, bigotry, and injustice. Their work inspired the involvement of many more, who themselves went on to effect change.

This anthology is a collection of those ripples—a pooling of American civil rights history through the words of both the most-celebrated and less-recognized figures. The reader will have an opportunity to do what these leaders did: to study, distill, and employ the rhetoric of those before them—to understand the history of American civil rights through the delivered word. To see how Frederick Douglass and Eleanor Roosevelt swayed their audiences and how Lucretia Mott drew ideas and themes from Elizabeth Cady Stanton, allows us to understand how closely united their ideas and approaches were and how, over the years, they learned from and built on one another's hopes and accomplishments.

I urge you, when reading an individual speech, to consider its impact not only on an individual movement but also on the larger expanse of civil rights history.★ In compiling this collection, I was fascinated by how deeply interconnected the different movements were—in their objectives, their messages, and the words they delivered. Another unmistakable connection quickly became clear to me: In one way or another, the various civil rights movements had their roots in what I call the African-American or black movement, which at first encompassed the anti-slavery movement and later the struggle for equal rights and opportunity. The ripples from the abolitionist movement sparked the first women's movement, and the experiences and feats from the civil rights era in the 1950s and '60s led to the modern Asian-American, gay, Hispanic, and feminist movements. I draw these connections with great cau-

---

★Literally, the term "civil rights" connotes the rights of any citizen, no matter what his background; however, I use the term in reference to equal rights for minorities in the United States.

tion. As historians have rightly noted, each movement and group possesses a unique history and ideology with its own obstacles and agenda. The Asian- and Hispanic-American movements, for example, have been plagued by immigration discrimination, whereas immigration has never been a central issue for the women's, gay, or African-American movements. Still, whether for lessons on rhetoric, organizing marches, or lobbying Congress, all groups have looked expressly to the African-American movement for guidance in the steps they should take and the pitfalls they should avoid. Some have likened the civil rights struggle to a symphony: The black leadership conducted, but the opus would have fallen flat without the melody from each group.

The visibility of the African-American movement is partly a matter of timing, presence, and organization; it must be viewed in the larger historical context. African-American leaders sparked protests, outrage, and activism in early America, when the demands of the slave-driven economy undercut the original ideals of the Constitution's drafters and burrowed their way into the entrenched political and legal systems. Although blacks were the specific focus of segregation laws and race-driven violence in the antebellum and Jim Crow South, they still managed to galvanize the force necessary to fight prejudice, both in the judicial system and in the court of public opinion. With their vigorous leadership, African Americans were frequently the first to test civil rights strategies, which accounts for their having scored more public victories—as well as defeats—than any other minority group. Since abolition, the black movement has maintained a near monopoly about the literary and public debate about civil rights in the United States; it is often equated with the term "civil rights" despite the existence and overwhelming importance of several other struggles. As a result, more students are still taught the history of black civil rights than the story of Asian-American, Latino-American, or gay civil rights movements. Dr. King—not César Chávez—has a federal holiday named for him. But, as this book demonstrates, that trend is beginning to change, so that the progress of all movements is now celebrated.

Although the Hispanic and Asian-American movements have looked to the black civil-rights movement for guidance, they have not always agreed or followed the same tactical approaches or championed the same agenda. In the 1960s, for example, Asian and Hispanic Americans were often alienated from the mainstream civil rights movement, which centered on African-American concerns like desegregation and voting rights, not bilingual education or immigration barriers. Women working in the civil rights movement were also marginalized until the late 1960s, when they became a better-organized and more vocal community. These differences within and among minority groups—in ideology and approach—continue today. Segments of the contemporary Latino-American community, especially Cuban Americans, customarily take more conservative positions on social and economic issues than the left-leaning factions of the African-American and feminist communities. These differences have publicly divided what is traditionally perceived as "the civil rights community," and in many instances these divergent voices and missions, while inevitable and often valid, have weakened the larger cause.

This highlights a fundamental point. While the lessons from each civil rights movement have been instructive to others, we must remember, as I have mentioned, that there is no *one* civil rights history. Despite commonalities, each group has grappled with a unique set of experiences that have shaped its movement and, as importantly, the manner in which its leaders communicate. Cesar Chavez's rhetoric and style were not the same as abolitionist Frederick Douglass's. He may have drawn from Douglass's ideas and even his words, but his speaking method, language, cadence, and rhetorical flourishes were his own and were reflective of the Latino experience. Chavez's approach was also shaped by the context of his speech—the time period, the setting, and the audience.

In other words, each civil rights group possesses what historian John Hammerback describes as its own rhetorical conventions and history. The conventions are informed by cultural orientation and features, like the use of language, arguments, and organizational style, and help explain why Chavez's speeches were different from Dr. King's, even though the men shared similar principles (and a fund of common arguments). Moreover, these rhetorical conventions have shifted over time, along with the tides of history and reform, and have had a deep impact on speakers and speeches across all groups and causes.

THE AFRICAN-AMERICAN MOVEMENT

The enslavement of African Americans and the status of free and freed blacks were the first civil rights issues the United States grappled with in earnest; or rather, they were the first racial dilemmas the nation was *forced* to address.★ Slaves, aside from Native Americans, were the first minority group about which the Founders debated. Thomas Jefferson, George Washington, John Adams, and Thomas Paine all grappled with the propriety of slavery and, in many instances, chose to forgo their initial opposition in favor of a unified nation (the South, dependent on labor-intensive agriculture, insisted on slavery's continued exis-

---

★I use the terms "African American" and "black" interchangeably throughout the book. Not all blacks are native born, nor did their ancestors all emigrate from Africa. Many arrived in the United States from the West Indies and Europe. I should also add that many of the orators included in this anthology use what are now considered pejorative terms in referring to women, gays, and people of color. Over time, the terminology has changed; blacks are no longer referred to as Negroes. I urge you to cast aside what would be inappropriate by today's standards and seek out the spirit of the words.

tence).The "slave issue" eventually precipitated the United States's first and only civil war and continued to divide the nation under an umbrella of outright and de facto racial segregation. Over time, blacks fell victim to lynchings in the South and to the "separate but equal" policies of both the Jim Crow South and segregated northern cities. With the television cameras rolling, African Americans marched peacefully in their quest for equality, despite the oppressive force of violence, led by such men as Birmingham Public Safety Commissioner Bull Connor, who in 1963 wielded billy clubs and fire hoses to keep peaceful protestors in line.Today,African Americans remain at the center of hotly debated civil rights issues like affirmative action, criminal justice, and slave reparations.

Before the Civil War, the anti-slavery movement (composed predominantly of white abolitionists and Radical Republicans) was largely responsible for the major legislative accomplishments on both federal and state levels.The abolitionists, aided by the Civil War's effects, also led the charge for the Thirteenth, Fourteenth, and Fifteenth Amendments, which eliminated de jure slavery, guaranteed equal protection under the law (the equal protection clause has been one of the sharpest swords against discriminatory practices), and enfranchised the black male population. The Civil Rights Act of 1866 barred discrimination in contracts. Almost a century later, the Civil Rights Act of 1964 outlawed discrimination in property and employment and paved the way for affirmative action, which today is an endangered practice. The Voting Rights Act of 1965 banned discrimination in voter registration and at the polls—and the Great Society spurred investment in hard-pressed communities, education, healthcare, and job training. Landmark civil rights gains in the courts also involved African Americans, starting, most notably, with the 1954 *Brown v. Board of Education* decision, finding separate school facilities inherently unequal. Other civil rights movements have capitalized on these victories and others, including many of their own, rightly using the laws and court rulings—the "ripples of hope"—for their own advancement.

THE WOMEN'S MOVEMENT

The leaders of the early women's civil rights movement gained experience in the abolition effort, where their participation was, to a limited extent, tacitly accepted and even encouraged.* Although women could attend abolition rallies, American society in the early nineteenth century still frowned upon a woman publicly addressing an audience of both women and men.The attempt to silence women

---

*I use the terms "women's movement" and "feminist movement" interchangeably, both to describe the civil rights effort, even though the "feminist" movement often connotes a more radical approach.

at anti-slavery conventions in the United States and England led directly to Elizabeth Cady Stanton and Lucretia Mott's decision to hold the first Women's Rights Convention at Seneca Falls, New York, in June 1848. Among their many demands, these early feminists insisted on an immediate end to the domestic, economic, and social oppression that had "kept women down" for generations.

Until that point, married white women were largely prohibited from working outside the home (freed black women, in contrast, had worked for white families for years), and laws in most cities and states prevented them from owning land, signing contracts, or voting in elections. In essence, and commonly in the law, women were treated as the property of their fathers or husbands. The events at Seneca Falls began to change that, thus sparking the modern women's movement. With sixty-eight female delegates in attendance, this convention was the first public outcry from women (mostly white and middle class), and while their issues did not completely track, their tactics and rhetoric closely paralleled the group on whose behalf they had worked: African Americans. Ironically there were no African-American women present.* Drawing on tactics from the abolitionist movement and citing parallel forms of discrimination (including disenfranchisement and social and economic inequity), the early women activists argued vociferously for female suffrage. Yet, when their efforts repeatedly failed to win the vote in the late nineteenth century, many feminist leaders turned inward, abandoning the African-American civil rights movement that initially spurred their efforts. Once the black male population was enfranchised, many white feminists, who had fought tirelessly for emancipation, simply could not understand why they were still denied access to the ballot. The resulting rift between the black and women's movements set back the African-American cause and further alienated black women from the mainstream feminist movement.†

Years later, after finally winning suffrage in 1920, members of the women's movement divided into two distinct factions: one group intent on further expanding their legal rights through the Equal Rights Amendment (ERA), the

---

*There were also thirty-two male delegates in attendance at Seneca Falls; Frederick Douglass was the only black male delegate.

†This development was not surprising: Until recently, black women often lacked a seat at the table of the mainstream feminist movement; it was dominated by white middle-class women. The mainstream women's movement was concerned with its own issues (those concerning *white* women, like enfranchisement and temperance), not those affecting African Americans. Black women, in turn, had to straddle both the African-American and feminist movements, and they were often excluded from both. Additionally, in the workforce and in the home, black women historically assumed a much different role in their families and communities than white women did. As E. Franklin Frazier put it, "Neither economic necessity nor tradition . . . instilled in her the spirit of subordination to masculine authority." Maria W. Stewart, the first black female writer to gain prominence, urged black women in the early nineteenth century to exert themselves and lift "the rising generation."

other satisfied with certain legal "protections" (including limitations on professions women could enter, hours they could work, and organizations they could join). This latter group argued that a woman's primary role remained that of a traditional mother, not breadwinner. Led by political activist Phyllis Schlafly, they argued that women should not fight for legal equality, women's liberation, or the ERA.* However, both blocs did find some common cause in their demand for better education for women and stricter moral codes for men (like temperance) to help build stronger families and "a more virtuous state."

Despite their differences, when possible, the women's movement capitalized on black-won legal and political victories. In the mid-twentieth century, for example, women captured employment protection in Title VII of the 1964 Civil Rights Act—a bill championed by and introduced for African Americans. Organizers of the women's movement often took cues from the black movement in orchestrating protests for equal employment opportunity and economic independence; their own work in the African-American civil rights struggle—dating back to abolitionism—influenced their leadership styles and speaking skills when advocating their own agenda. The sit-ins of the 1960s influenced activities of women such as Betty Friedan, Gloria Steinem, and other female activists who were marginalized by the nearly all-male leadership in the black and anti-war movements. The feminists, of course, championed their own issues, independent from although not exclusive of the African-American agenda, including property rights, child care, suffrage, education, and sexual freedom. But undoubtedly their experience working for black rights helped them sharpen their leadership skills, inform their agenda, and first stump for a social cause.

The independence of the women's movement from the African-American civil rights movement should not be understated; in a struggle dominated by men, it simply took longer for the women's movement to develop this independence. Dating back to the nineteenth century, the feminist voice was a leading one, echoing loudly in Congress and on the national stage in successfully championing women's own issues, including suffrage, equal pay, and reproductive choice.

THE HISPANIC-AMERICAN MOVEMENT

The movement for Hispanic-American civil rights, as we perceive it today, did not gain its footing until the early 1960s. Before this time, the movement lacked a strong identity. It was composed of several independent, ad hoc

---

*Although I have included a sampling of speeches articulating this opinion, the majority of speeches I have included are by those who favored women's liberation.

movements of Latinos from different countries, backgrounds, and cultures, although most were of Mexican heritage. These groups were new to the United States, were geographically diverse, and feared deportation. The early movements began in the mid-nineteenth century in reaction to land disputes and discriminatory immigration policies, but unlike the early African-American and feminist movements, Latinos at first lacked a united, nationally recognizable message and leadership. Language posed a substantial barrier to broad acceptance, as civil rights speeches delivered in Spanish failed to capture the attention or empathy of the mainstream English-speaking press and politicians. Whether their grievances involved wage discrimination, worker standards, or basic xenophobia, the language barrier often posed an insurmountable hurdle. Beginning in the 1960s, however, the splintered movements succeeded in drawing together Hispanic Americans from different cultures, organizing a coordinated effort around common issues and, in English and Spanish, calling for far-reaching social and political change.*

The first phase of Latino protest emerged in 1848, after the Treaty of Guadalupe Hidalgo was signed, in which Mexico ceded upper California and New Mexico (including Arizona) to the United States and recognized U.S. claims over Texas, with the Rio Grande as its southern boundary. Although the pact guaranteed Mexican Americans living in these areas a right to their land and the legal protections of U.S. citizenship, this promise was largely an empty one. These new Americans quickly met with the same political, economic, and social bigotry that other minorities faced. By the 1860s, speculators and squatters used the 1862 Homestead Act illegally to strip Hispanic Americans of the land purportedly protected by the Hidalgo treaty. The U.S. federal government largely ignored these injustices, and as a whole, the language difference muffled the voices of dissent from within the Hispanic community.

In the meantime, the demand for inexpensive labor in California and the Southwest spiked, particularly to man farms and to build the transcontinental railroad. Further, with the Mexican Revolution forcing thousands more northward, the Mexican-American population continued to rise. By the mid- to late-nineteenth century, southwestern and far western farming and industry depended on Hispanic immigrants as the primary source of cheap labor. Like Asian Americans in California, Mexican Americans were denied the

---

*I use the terms "Hispanic American" and "Latino" to represent Americans descending from Mexico, Cuba, Puerto Rico, Latin America, and Europe. Over the years, Hispanic Americans, as a broad community, have also been referred to as "Chicanos," though that term was initially used in referencing "Mexican Americans." I use the three terms interchangeably in this book.

rights of citizenship, worker protections, and equal access to basic education and health care, in spite of the value of their labor. Many were "repatriated"— or deported—to Mexico, particularly in periods of economic downturn. Although some small civil rights groups spoke out and an occasional pro-Latino speech graced the floors of Congress, activists did not protest en masse until the late 1950s, under the leadership of men like Pablo De La Guerra. Those who did speak out were often ignored at the time and later excluded from historical accounts. In 1940 George I. Sánchez, a leading Mexican-American scholar, described his people as "the forgotten Americans . . . incapable of voicing their views and feelings."

Pointing to inhumane labor practices, poverty, educational inequity, and violated land treaties (stemming back to Guadalupe Hidalgo), a new guard of Chicano activist leaders came to power in the midtwentieth century. From Reies Tijerina to César Chávez, these leaders benefited from a growing Hispanic-American population, guidance from the black community, and a surge in national attention to labor abuses and civil rights. Historically marginalized and forgotten by the Anglo-American mainstream, the Latino community needed a nationwide civil rights effort to expose the inequities it faced—not just on the farm but in cities and suburban communities as well. Their words fell on a reinvigorated Hispanic populus which, at universities, in cities, and in small towns, had lost its patience with decades of "anti-brown" discrimination. Although some Latino leaders, like José Angel Gutiérrez, followed a radical approach akin to the black power movement (especially as the Vietnam War flared), Chávez and his compatriots pursued a path of nonviolent protest paved by Mahatma Gandhi, Martin Luther King, Jr., and others. The Latino community used boycotts and the media to bring attention to poverty, labor abuses (involving wages, hours, and union busting) and the closely connected issue of immigration. The immigration issue is a problem almost unique to Hispanic Americans—Asian Americans have also struggled with it. The civil rights implications involving farm and migrant labor were largely ignored until Chávez gained the attention of the American people. Although Chavez's approach and positions often varied from those of other Chicano leaders, his words, and especially the boycotts he organized, earned Chávez (and the Hispanic-American movement) the national spotlight. Hispanic Americans have since benefited from civil rights legislation initially passed for blacks and from legal protections earned by and distinctive to their cause. For example, in the 1970s, the Mexican American Legal Defense Fund was instrumental in promoting bilingual education efforts. And in 1994, when more than 60 percent of California citizens approved Proposition 187, prohibiting social services to aliens, the Hispanic-American outcry prompted a social debate—and ultimate repeal of this law. The Latino voice continues to grow stronger in the American polity and in the drive for equal opportunity.

THE ASIAN-AMERICAN MOVEMENT

Like Hispanic Americans, Asian Americans did not find a more unified voice until the late 1960s, following generations of silence and splintering caused largely by intimidation, cultural differences, and internal disorganization.* In the nineteenth century, Asian Americans organized to demand greater benefits for their community, and struck for higher wages and fair treatment on farms. But these activities were usually in response to individual incidents; their efforts never developed into a broad civil rights movement, with a defined agenda, akin to that of the anti-slavery effort. Today's Asian-American movement began in earnest at the height of the 1960s civil rights struggle, when Asian-American students organized for social justice, racial equality, and political empowerment. They also began to look to the courts to remedy discriminatory laws. In the forty years since, as the movement has become more organized, its influence has reached deeper into the political establishment, having widespread effects on contemporary civil rights and equal opportunity legislation.

Much like other immigrants who arrived in the mid-nineteenth century, Asian Americans were immediately victims of xenophobia, discriminatory laws, wage inequity, violence, and wretched work conditions. They were praised for their work ethic but blamed whenever the economy turned sour. An anti-Asian movement (often referring to Asians as a "Yellow Peril") spread like wildfire across the nation, particularly in the American West in heavily Asian pockets like San Francisco. School boards banned ethnic Asian children from public schools. Whites boycotted their stores, calling them disloyal and unproductive citizens. Although they occasionally spoke out, more often than not, language, cultural barriers, and fear of retaliation suppressed any coordinated Asian-American civil rights movement. Those who tried to protest discriminatory treatment often fell victim to violence. Aside from an occasional outburst, small community rally, or ephemeral movement for pro-immigration

---

*Like the term "Hispanic American," the phrase "Asian American" incorporates several immigrant groups of Asian descent, including but not limited to Chinese, Filipinos, Japanese, and Koreans. Each nation and its citizens have a unique relationship and history with the United States. Chinese Americans, for example, first arrived in California during the Gold Rush in the mid-1800s. In the early 1900s, the first group of Koreans came to Hawaii, and the first group of Filipino students came to study at American universities. For the most part, Asians who immigrated in the late eighteenth and nineteenth centuries migrated toward cities and agricultural communities in California. For example, most Japanese immigrants arrived in San Francisco, where they often worked on farms and in city stores. After arriving, Asian immigrants tended to settle into small enclaves composed of people from their homeland who shared similar customs and language. Those who did not settle in cities went to work on the transcontinental railroad, where they were a valuable source of inexpensive and hardworking labor.

legislation, ethnic Asians kept their heads down and their voices silent. This pattern continued deep into the twentieth century, even after scores of Asian Americans fought in World War I.

But that began to change during World War II, after President Franklin Roosevelt ordered the formation of Japanese-American internment camps, ostensibly to protect the nation from Japanese espionage or revolt. Thousands of Japanese Americans on the West Coast were torn from their homes, stripped of their possessions, and forced to live for years as outcasts behind barbed wire. Roosevelt's decision sparked a public outcry from those both within and outside the Japanese-American community, though many in Congress, the media, and the Supreme Court (in *Korematsu v. United States*) stood by the decision. But even that protest was measured; it was limited predominantly to a lone community rally, newspaper article, or liberal voice in Congress. After all, most Asian immigrants, though they had lived in the United States for decades, were not citizens because of a 1790 law restricting naturalization to whites; they could not vote, and most were still restricted in their employment opportunities. Others were forced to attend segregated schools and prevented from organizing labor unions.

With the rise of the black civil rights movement in the 1960s, which brought racial discrimination to center stage, Asian Americans began to think of themselves—and speak publicly—as a cohesive minority group. The first Asian-American civil rights organizations sprouted on college campuses, the very places where other oppressed groups had found their footing as a community, shortly after these minorities gained admission. Like Chicanos, Asian-American students, the sons and daughters of immigrants, became a presence on college campuses at the height of the civil rights era. They joined the New Left student movement to fight for black liberation and against the Vietnam War.

But Asian-American students soon found themselves marginalized, without a prominent voice on campus or a recognized agenda to advance. Although departments in women's and black studies flourished on college campuses, Asian Americans lacked their own academic programs. With the nation's attention on the black movement, civil rights leaders at universities—black, white, or other—focused their efforts on the African-American agenda, like voting rights and desegregation. The Asian-American message of discrimination against their community was drowned out and unable to compete for attention. Whereas King, Friedan, and Chávez articulated the concerns of their respective communities, they were without a leading national figure to define their issues and win the favor of politicians in Congress or reporters in the press. Only on rare occasions did a story about anti-Asian discrimination ever make the newspapers or an Asian-American activist get the attention of a United States senator.

This situation began to change as Asian-American students began to organize in large numbers. Taking cues from the black movement, they rallied against discrimination, labor abuses, anti-immigrant policies, and mainstream misgivings about their culture. Asian Americans were often the "forgotten" minority; it was always assumed that they were the "successful minority," in need of little assistance. This perception was a false one. Asian Americans remained marginalized in American cities, and in political circles and like other minority groups, they were victim to unequal treatment and opportunity. The students of the 1960s sought to change this misperception and fight the entrenched xenophobia that kept their people at the fringes. They demanded courses on Asian-American culture, language, and history, and a voice in the debate over civil rights. At the national level, they sought legal protections, such as affirmative action, that were afforded to other minority groups. In 1968, for example, Asian Americans joined other students of color to participate in the Third World Strike at San Francisco State College, which brought national attention to the educational and socioeconomic ills of Asian Americans in California. Since then, campaigns like this have flourished. Beginning in the 1970s, activists demanded and achieved reparations for the Japanese-American internment; others continue to decry discrimination in the media and public policy. Today, there are scores of leaders and organizations committed to addressing publicly the specific conditions of Asian Americans, whose voices have spurred an expansion of cultural pride and a defense of the Asian-American civil rights agenda. Asian Americans are not free from discrimination; the targeting of Korean-American store owners during the Los Angeles Riots in 1992 was a sign of that. But overall, the Asian-American community today is more accepted, assimilated, and successful, not just in its financial might but also in its presence and influence in neighborhoods nationwide.

THE GAY RIGHTS MOVEMENT

The gay rights movement did not find its voice in earnest until the mid- to late twentieth century, and even then, the community was noticeably divided over its agenda, tactics, and approach.* Years earlier, in 1924, German-born Henry Gerber founded the Society for Human Rights in Chicago, the first

---

*In discussing the gay rights movement, I use the terms "gay," "lesbian," and "homosexuals" interchangeably.

organization publicly committed to the goal of advancing equality for homosexuals. But, like others who tried before him, Gerber and his organization encountered two long-standing obstacles. First, on the law books and in the eyes of mainstream society, including the medical community, homosexuality was considered deviant behavior. Second, most gays and lesbians hid their own identity, in fear of embarrassment or marginalization at work, at home, and among friends. The reality of public condemnation and self-isolation limited their potential to mount public protest and kept gay men and women from advocating for their own civil rights.

These attitudes did not change until after World War II, with the release of the Kinsey Report on sexual behavior. Published in 1948, this report found the incidence of homosexuality to be much higher than previously suspected. Only a few years later, in 1950, pioneer activist Harry Hay identified homosexuals as a minority group. To advance his cause, Hay founded the Mattachine Society, which demanded for homosexuals the same civil rights granted to other minorities. Though at first cloaked in secrecy, the Mattachines later made their opinions heard through meetings and monthly newsletters, which eventually achieved wide circulation and reached previously isolated members of the gay community. Although Hay began his activities in Los Angeles, soon chapters of the Mattachine Society opened in cities across the country. And in San Francisco in 1955, a lesbian group founded the Daughters of Bilitis to fight discrimination against gay women.

From that point forward, gay activism assumed a public persona, particularly as the civil rights era of the 1960s unfolded. More gays and lesbians felt freer to go public with their homosexual identity, demanding their right to the same protections as other minorities. Citing a need to build on the efforts of oppressed groups, gay activists organized their own parades, lobbying efforts, education campaigns, and mass demonstrations. Drawing on the language, nonviolent tactics, and leadership styles of female and black leaders, the movement rallied large numbers of once-closeted gays to speak out. Activists in the community began to publish widely, teach others, and advance public understanding. In the summer of 1969, these activities reached an empowering, watershed moment at the Stonewall Inn, a club on Christopher Street in Greenwich Village, New York. In what has since become known as the Stonewall Riots, gays and lesbians sparked a spontaneous demonstration, awakening the nation—including the media and government—to the realities of homophobia, anti-gay discrimination, and police brutality. They also staked their claim as an oppressed minority in the larger civil rights movement. The word "Stonewall" entered the vocabulary of lesbians, gay men, bisexuals, and transgendered people everywhere as a potent emblem of how the gay community took a stand against oppression and demanded full equality. Because of this activism, which led to scientific discussion, the American Psychiatric Association eliminated homosexuality from its *Diagnostic and Statistical Manual of Mental Disorders* in 1973.

In 1979 more than 100,000 gays and lesbians marched on Washington demanding equal treatment under the law. Although much of their agenda remains unfulfilled, modern demands do not differ greatly from those of twenty-four years ago. The gay community still advocates equality and equal opportunity in family rights, employment, marriage, housing, the military service, and healthcare, especially in light of the HIV/AIDS crisis. Many of these objectives resonate with those of other minority groups, even though the exact approach or rhetoric may differ. Still, historically, African-American, feminist, and Hispanic-American organizations have included neither gay issues in their agendas nor openly gay people as partners in their efforts and vice versa. Legislation crafted to advance the civil rights agenda has generally failed to recognize gays as a protected group. For example, the Civil Rights Act of 1964 did not include "sexual orientation" as a protected class, and efforts to introduce new legislative protections—like the Employment Nondiscrimination Act in the late 1990s—have failed repeatedly. In the late 1990s, after a surge of hate crimes targeted gays, such as the 1998 murder of college student Matthew Shephard, Congress still refused to pass meaningful hate-crime legislation.

But the gay movement has not faltered. To the contrary, the movement has only grown more organized, more vocal, and more recognized in recent years. Despite criticism for his policy on gays in the military, Bill Clinton was the first president to attend fund-raisers and public events for gay organizations. And early in his tenure as president, George W. Bush followed suit. Additionally, mainstream civil rights organizations have started to take a more active role in including gay rights as part of their own agendas. With these developments—and a new public confidence—the gay and lesbian voice echoes loudly in what is now a more open civil rights movement.

LEARNING FROM OTHER VOICES: THE ROOTS OF THIS COLLECTION

My own interest in the power of words, the force of civil rights rhetoric, came to fruition while I was a speechwriter for President Bill Clinton. Clinton demonstrated this power of the bully pulpit—teaching me that with it, the president can help the people overcome. He helped me recognize that Dr. King's "I Have a Dream" address was not just a great civil rights speech but a great American speech. Before joining Clinton's team of speechwriters in

1998, I was a young politophile, just a spectator tracking Bill Clinton in the *New York Times* and on the Internet. I read speech after speech that he delivered, from the campaign trail and then from the White House. Clinton's candid approach to race and the level of trust he evoked from minority communities particularly impressed me. Since his days as governor of Arkansas, in his policies and rhetoric, he had urged Americans from all backgrounds to be more accepting of those unlike themselves—to reach across the lines that had historically divided Americans. From "mending, not ending," affirmative action to "building One America," Clinton often used his daily speaking opportunities to advance the civil rights agenda and to promote racial unity. Not until I joined the president in actually crafting those words did I fully understand the depth of consideration—and history—that went into every one of Clinton's civil rights addresses.* He urged his speechwriters to proceed cautiously, recognizing the potential power of his words, and always to train a keen eye on history.

Take, for example, Clinton's November 1998 speech at an awards ceremony for the Little Rock Nine. In 1957, under the protection of the National Guard, nine black children walked through the schoolhouse doors of Little Rock's Central High—overcoming threats of violence from the citizens of Arkansas and Governor Orval Faubus. These young heroes forced the integration of a school system long committed to segregation. Invoking themes from the civil rights movement, Clinton used his speech to celebrate their legacy and latest honor, the Congressional Gold Medal, which was bestowed as an expression of national appreciation for their distinguished achievement.

In preparing his remarks, Bill Clinton did what a good leader does when talking about race: He looked to the speeches of those who came before him. He urged us to draw on the examples of other orators—famous and obscure—who had embraced speech in pursuit of equality. Clinton himself, as a student of the civil rights movement, had read works by or about the most celebrated leaders. He had memorized King's March on Washington address and could recite parts of Lincoln and Kennedy speeches from memory.

The approach our office brought to crafting the president's words for the Little Rock Nine was similar to that used in other presidential speeches. We never delivered a draft of a civil rights speech to the president without first reading the texts of celebrated figures, whether that included Frederick Douglass, Susan B. Anthony, or César Chávez. Their words, and their approach, were more instrumental to our work than any briefing book or policy paper.

---

*In 1998, after having worked on the 1996 Clinton-Gore reelection team, I joined the White House Speechwriting Office, first as the staff director and then as a presidential speechwriter. I remained there for the remainder of Clinton's second term.

This compilation evolved from that process. While rummaging through the bookshelves of the White House Library, I discovered that few civil rights speech anthologies exist in print. I could not find one book to put on my office shelf, no single volume containing the fiery rhetoric of Du Bois, the drawling prose of Lyndon Johnson, and the measured verse of Betty Friedan. This collection was crafted to be a central source of civil rights speeches for writers, activists, and students of history.

HOW SPEECH HAS CHANGED

When the African-American civil rights leader Marcus Garvey spoke nearly a century ago, his followers and detractors scrutinized each word; they dissected, repeated, and memorized nearly every sentence. The early activists rarely spoke publicly, so when they did, people listened closely to every word. Before the advent of television and the modern media, the stakes for an individual speech were much higher, and each text was reprinted, circulated, and read widely. For example, when a freed slave addressed an audience, listeners published entire transcripts of his or her remarks and circulated them around abolitionist communities.

In contrast, in contemporary speeches the inevitable ten-second sound bites often drive the text. This is not of a leader's choosing but rather a recognition of the twenty-four-hour news cycle that supplies dozens of cable stations and the Internet. At the White House, the media's insatiable appetite for up-to-the-minute, "new" news has forced the office of the president to satiate them with endless events and sometimes warmed-over rhetoric. The press rarely airs a politician's entire speech—or even a five-minute story on its content. In fact, only a few lines dictate the success of even the most major speeches, like ones announcing a president's budget or the State of the Union address.

It is easy to forget that, until the advent of cable, whenever a major figure spoke, his or her words were not replayed over and over again on half a dozen news stations, as every speech—strong or flaccid—is today. In the 1960s, King delivered versions of his "I Have a Dream" speech at dozens of venues before perfecting it on national television. If he had spoken today, it is likely that portions of each one of his speeches would have been aired repeatedly, perhaps diminishing the value of his finale. The same could be said for any of the historic oratorical feats, from Abraham Lincoln to Elizabeth Cady Stanton to John F. Kennedy. Still, although television in the modern era has diminished the worth of an individual speech, it has also allowed for the success of struggles like the civil rights movement, whose progress depended on northerners' witnessing, firsthand, thousands of Freedom Riders physically being beaten as they attempted to ride a desegregated interstate bus through the segregated South. If television had not been there, King's dream sequence, Chávez's fasts, and Johnson's call for voting reforms might not carry the power they still do today.

In turn, today's speechwriter, including those at the White House, must speculate as to which line of any given speech the media will highlight. The speechwriter must adjust the tone of the text and the context of every phrase to accommodate this reality. When an orator is judged merely by a few words, his presentation is inevitably affected. A leader today has a very limited window in which to persuade a broad audience. He comes to recognize that what is important is not how he interacts with the audience directly in front of him but rather how he is judged by the millions perched in front of their televisions and computer screens at home. Because it is nearly impossible to produce poetic prose of historic worth several times a day, this new environment has often diminished the quality of the average speech.

Still, this modern environment does not mean that great civil rights speeches have vanished, particularly among preachers, activists, and civil rights leaders. It is just that the average text—at least in the political arena—is not consistently at the level of decades ago. But that may have been precipitated by the decline of the church, the dilution of civil rights movements, or the explosion of the mass media. Additionally, it can be argued that, overall, in light of these factors, the value of good rhetoric has waned. Still, there are several exceptions, and I have included many of them in this collection. They tend to be ones that were prepared to commemorate important occasions or milestones or to announce a new effort, like the recent debate over gay marriage or racial profiling. Although many of these selections were less recognized at the time they were delivered than they are now, they are equal in quality to their peers from different eras.

READING THIS COLLECTION

In any book, space is a limiting factor. There were simply not enough pages in a one-volume anthology to print every civil rights speech of historical and rhetorical significance, thus forcing reams of powerful and persuasive passages to the back shelf. I have included speeches, if available, from each movement and historical period. In some cases, for reasons discussed earlier, the pickings were slim. But in most cases, I struggled over what to exclude. For instance, although the 1960s were rife with superior African-American speeches, many made congruous points or were delivered to similar audiences. Similarly, for the abolitionist era, I could include only two of Frederick Douglass's speeches, though there were more than a dozen I would have liked to publish. Making the final selections was not an easy process, and I would therefore like to share my criteria.

First, I had to decide what came under the broad umbrella of "civil rights." I defined the category as any speech delivered with the express intent of advancing liberties for an oppressed group. I have conspicuously omitted what would today be construed as anti–civil rights rhetoric, although several important selections, such as those by Malcom X and Louis Farrakhan, are at times divisive and fueled by anger—not all of it righteous.

Second, I have included speeches from five distinct civil rights movements, dating from the colonial period to the present: African American, Asian American, Hispanic American, gay, and women. The rhetoric from other groups is equally rich and illuminating, but again, space forced me to narrow my focus. There remains a need for another collection of speeches given by Native Americans, people with disabilities, and white ethnic groups.

I have tried to include a balanced number of speeches from each movement, within the realities of each group's prominence on the public stage. This meant that I included more speeches by blacks and women than by Asians, gays, and Hispanics because of the relative depth and duration of each movement, as well as the sheer size of each group. Additionally, the availability of speech transcripts and other materials varied substantially for each group. Whereas there is an abundance of African-American transcripts in print, there is a dearth of those delivered by Asian and Hispanic Americans before the 1940s.

Third, within these confines, I have included what I view as the most important speeches in terms of rhetorical and historical significance. In some cases, a speech was selected primarily for its stirring language and lofty, vivid imagery. Others were chosen more for their importance to either the progress of a particular movement or to the larger civil rights struggle—even when the rhetoric itself was lacking. On the surface, not every speech is Churchillian in its verbiage or even evocative in a traditional sense. But each speech is significant in terms of the idea it addresses, the audience in attendance, the era in which it was given, or the person by whom it was delivered.

Fourth, I organized this collection chronologically and divided it into four sections to offer an historical—and a digestible—overview of the evolution of the American civil rights movement. The first section, "Early America: Early Dissent," spans the colonial period through 1865, the year that marked the end of the Civil War and de jure slavery. During this era, activists (particularly abolitionists) emerged and first found their public voice. Though dominated by the anti-slavery and women's movements, it also includes some of the rhetoric from the Hispanic- and Asian-American movements. The second section, "Measured Gains: Two Steps Forward, One Step Backward," covers the period 1866 through 1949, which marked the beginning of the American civil rights era. This section includes rhetoric from across the spectrum, with a focus on the black and early feminist civil rights movements. The third section, "The Civil Rights Era: Lift Every Voice," contains speeches from 1950 through 1969, the time during which the most significant gains were made among the public at large and on the legislative front. For the most part, every group represented in this anthology established its agenda and found its voice during this span of years. Finally, the fourth section, "The Current Struggle: Slow but Steady Progress," includes speeches from 1970 to 1998. This period has been a period of adjustment following the successful but stormy civil rights era, which began to lose momentum in the late 1960s. During this period, which extends until today, the agenda of all groups has shifted to some degree and many earlier legal and political gains have faltered.

Finally, before each speech and where possible, I have provided the reader with a sense of the speech's setting and historical time period, as well as a brief description of the orator's background. I encourage you to pay particular attention to the context. King's televised words before an audience of millions at the Lincoln Memorial differ greatly from those he delivered in a black church a decade earlier.

Many of the speeches are published in their entirety and their original form, with few omissions. Others have been edited for reasons of length and superfluous material, but hopefully not at the expense of quality or content. I have also provided titles for speeches that lacked them.

Plato once wrote, "He who would be a good orator ought to be just, and skilled in the knowledge of things just." My hope is that this anthology will serve as an inspiration for those seeking to be just—whether in the realm of civil rights, science, business, law, education, or entertainment. We are all students of history, and the courageous acts—and words—of those who came before us can prove inspirational, just as they do to leaders today.

I invite you to roll up your sleeves and dig through the speeches in this volume as you would through an old photo album. They are bursting with energy, wit, rebellious prose, innovative ideas, and allegories. In the field of rhetoric, it is only on rare occasion that we are blessed with gripping oration, with words that deserve a lasting place in the annals of history. But time and again, the civil rights movements in America have produced just that kind of powerful, purposeful rhetoric. This anthology includes what I believe to be the best of it.

Also, remember that speeches are unlike most other forms of writing. They are designed to be read aloud. You will not find perfect grammar; the periods and commas will not be where you would expect them in a Henry James novel. Speeches purposely include an abundance of dashes and fragments to help guide the speaker, and they are often full of run-on and choppy sentences. But therein lies their persuasive ability; their abrupt style is what allows them to come alive from the podium with language meant to be delivered to an audience.

That said, I hope you become an active participant in each speech, not only reading the words but experiencing and internalizing them. I encourage you to do exactly what my colleagues and I would do in the Clinton Speechwriting Office as we punched up the next assignment on our computer screens: picture the setting, read the text aloud, and imitate the orator's intonations (though I might avoid the southern drawl we northern writers acquired over the years). As you read, imagine yourself in the audience, brimming with hope and anticipation as your hero takes the podium and thunders away with an uncommon majesty and an electric passion. That was exactly my own experience as I pored over thousands of civil rights speeches. And it is exactly how I felt when I first read Robert F. Kennedy's Day of Affirmation address, which lends its words to the title of this collection and, in many ways, inspired its creation.

JOSH GOTTHEIMER
Cambridge, Massachusetts
January 2003

ACKNOWLEDGMENTS

I would like to begin by acknowledging the millions of fighters for freedom to whom this book belongs. These men and women are not always mentioned by name, and for the most part, their individual stories remain untold. But their collective voices are heard, loud and clear, in page after page of this anthology.

I apologize in advance to anyone whose contributions I have failed to note. All of the mistakes in this work are mine and mine alone.

A book of this nature is fundamentally about good research. I want to thank my research assistants at the University of Pennsylvania who, collectively, spent more than two years hunting for the gems in this book: Ari Alexander, Oliver Benn, Benjamin Berkowitz, William Groh, Nikki Cyter, Sarah Feuer, Julie Gerstein, Ofonedu Goodwyn, Dana Hersh, James Kim, Melissa La Vigne, Stephanie Lerman, Joshua Newcomer, Ilene Schneider, Lori Uscher, and Lynn Wu. A few went the extra mile, and I'd like to single them out: Liz Coopersmith, Seth Grossman, Vinay Harpalani, Scott Schreiber, and Julie Simons. Andrew Bushell, Adam Frankel, Jessie Grodstein, and Marc Lewis were also instrumental in the project's completion.

I am also grateful to three former White House colleagues—Terry Edmonds, Jeff Shesol, and Michael Waldman—for their thoughtful comments on several drafts; they have been good friends and important mentors. Michael and Jeff encouraged me to do this book years ago, and, as published authors themselves, have offered invaluable guidance at every step along the way.

Several others read all or part of the manuscript and offered vital suggestions: Kenneth Baer, Taylor Branch, Andrei Cherny, Stephanie Cutter, Robert Dallek, Christopher Edley, Lani Guinier, John Hammberback, Evelyn Higginbotham, Elena Kagan, Janis Kearny, Lazaro Lima, Martha Minow, David Mixner, Stacy Schneider, Ted Sorensen, and William Wei. Taylor Branch also shared several of his Martin Luther King, Jr. transcripts with me, several of which appear in this anthology. Doug Band, Julia Payne, Skip Rutherford, and Karen Tramontano generously helped with the presidential politics. Jonathan Aspatore, Paul Glastris, David Weinstein, and Wendy Weinstein offered critical advice throughout the process, and Ralph Alswang, as always, shot the perfect picture.

The History Department at the University of Pennsylvania provided a much-appreciated warm home for me during the spring of 2001. I want to thank the entire administrative staff of the department, and particularly the office director, Hannah Poole. I also want to acknowledge the helpful research staff at the Library of Congress and the Radcliff's Schlesinger Library in Cambridge, Massachusetts.

At Harvard, several of my classmates offered a keen eye and merited criticism on various drafts: Jason Bordoff, Deborah Gordon, and Anne Robinson, and especially Justin Driver, Sarah Hurwitz, Katherine Turner, and Andrew Goldsmith. Andrew has also had the unfortunate burden of being my roommate throughout the editing process, which he has handled with aplomb. I can't thank them enough for their intellectual support and friendship. Likewise, there are several old friends from Penn and Oxford who also provided their counsel and support along the way, especially Joshua Civin, Seth Fliegler, Ross Garland, Ben Harris, Adam Kupperman, Peter Levine, Justin Pope, Neil Sheth, and Jordan Zaken.

I am also deeply indebted to my dear friend and mentor Mary Frances Berry. She deserves special praise, as this book would not have been possible without her. I say that not just for her help in selecting particular speeches and in developing a publishable anthology. But, more importantly, for sparking my passion for civil rights history, and for bringing it to a necessary level of maturity. An activist, author, and academic, Dr. Berry has spent her lifetime fighting discrimination and injustice in the United States and abroad. She reminds all of us that what is right is not always what is popular, and that our movement for equality in America, though significantly more advanced than it was fifty years ago, is still nascent.

I would like to express my gratitude to former President Clinton. I first heard then-Governor Clinton speak when I was a high-school student, as I sat transfixed in front of my television set. No political figure in recent history has his ability on the stump—not just in the content of his message, or the power and ease with which he delivers it, but for his comfort with any audience, black or white, rich or poor, and his ability to reach across the lines that divide us. I am profoundly grateful for the opportunity I had to serve in his administration, for his guidance, and for his contribution to this work.

I would be remiss if I didn't acknowledge those who have helped me find my way in the political arena—Senator Hillary Rodham Clinton, Ambassador Thomas Foley, Senator Frank Lautenberg, Paul Begala, Jim Doyle, Ann Lewis, John Podesta, Stacie Spector, and Loretta Ucelli—and in academia—Robert Caruso, Richard Hochman, Tina Lane, Murray Murphey, Gillian Peele, and George Thomas. I would also like to recognize my colleagues in the Clinton speechwriting office for their friendship, support, and remarkable talent.

I would like to thank my agent, Wesley Neff, who believed in this project from moment one; Fred Courtright; Felicity Tucker and Steven Baker at Basic Books; and my editor, Vanessa Mobley, who poured her heart and intellect into every page. I was always told that your editor is either an ally or an obstacle in the creative process. Vanessa was not only my ally, she was also my most ardent advocate. She's been a wonderful partner and a thoughtful critic.

I want to thank my parents, Donald, Gwenn, and Harry; my sister Emily; and my grandparents, aunts and uncles, and cousins for all their support and love. Through storm and sunshine, they have always encouraged me to forge ahead, and, therefore, this work is theirs as much as it is mine.

Finally, I am grateful for the lessons this project, and each orator, has taught me—about the sheer power of community and the blessings of diversity, the value of finding strength in our differences, and the courage of pushing forward despite seemingly insurmountable obstacles. As Dr. King said more than thirty-five years ago, "How long? Not long, because the arm of the moral universe is long, but it bends toward justice."

EARLY AMERICA, EARLY DISSENT

1789–1865

A FREE NEGRO
(NAME UNKNOWN)

Blood and Slavery
1789

If you prick us, do we not bleed?

Contrary to popular perception today, many African Americans in the early colonial era never experienced the sting or indignity of slavery. Like Scottish and Irish immigrants, virtually all Africans coming to the colonies in the early 1600s arrived as bondsmen or indentured servants. After completing their terms of servitude, many northern blacks earned their freedom, and utilized the skills they had acquired in trade, publishing, or commerce to form strong communities with economic and social networks. Although freed blacks lacked the political and social standing of landowning whites, scores succeeded in lobbying for greater legal equality by learning to read and write and by publishing essays and letters in magazines. Others spoke out, albeit quietly, in opposition to the racist organizations that were flourishing in the North and South.

Over the years, as slavery replaced indentured servitude, courageous freedmen excoriated employment discrimination and the flourishing anti-black laws of the South. Even in the North, where the economy was not as dependent on manual labor, most whites became increasingly unsympathetic to the freedmen's cry. This shift did not prevent these free African Americans from taking the stump in protest.

Delivered by an unnamed "freed Negro," the raw power and emotion of this address testifies to just how effective freed blacks were in championing the abolitionist cause. A native of the West Indies, his remarks were published and read widely in liberal circles.

I AM ONE of that unfortunate race of men who are distinguished from the rest of the human species by a black skin and woolly hair—disadvantages of very little moment in themselves, but which prove to us a source of greatest misery, because there are men who will not be persuaded that it is possible for a human soul to be lodged within a sable body. The West Indian planters could not, if they thought us men, so wantonly spill our blood; nor could the natives of this land of liberty, deeming us of the same species with themselves, submit

3

to be instrumental in enslaving us, or think us proper subjects of a sordid commerce. Yet, strong as the prejudices against us are, it will not, I hope on this side of the Atlantic, be considered as a crime for a poor African not to confess himself a being of an inferior order to those who happen to be of a different color from himself, or be thought very presumptuous in one who is but a Negro to offer to the happy subjects of this free government some reflection upon the wretched condition of his countrymen. They will not, I trust, think worse of my brethren for being discontented with so hard a lot as that of slavery, nor disown me for their fellow-creature merely because I deeply feel the unmerited sufferings which my countrymen endure.

The first thing, then, which seems necessary in order to remove those prejudices which are so unjustly entertained against us is to prove that we are men—a truth which is difficult of proof only because it is difficult to imagine by what argument it can be combated. Can it be contended that a difference of color alone can constitute a difference of species? If not, in what single circumstance are we different from the rest of mankind? What variety is there in our organization? What inferiority of art in the fashioning of our bodies? What imperfection in the faculties of our minds? Has not a Negro eyes? has not a Negro hands, organs, dimensions, senses, affections, passions?—fed with the same food; hurt with the same weapons; subject to the same diseases; healed by the same means; warmed and cooled by the same summer and winter as a white man? If you prick us, do we not bleed? If you poison us, do we not die? Are we not exposed to all the same wants? Do we not feel all the same sentiments—are we not capable of all the same exertions—and are we not entitled to all the same rights as other men?

But I supplicate our enemies to be, though for the first time, just in their proceedings toward us, and to establish the fact before they attempt to draw any conclusions from it. Nor let them imagine that this can be done by merely asserting that such is our universal character. It is the character, I grant, that our inhuman masters have agreed to give us and which they have so industriously and too successfully propagated in order to palliate their own guilt by blackening the helpless victims of it and to disguise their own cruelty under the semblance of justice. Let the natural depravity of our character be proved— not by appealing to declamatory invectives and interest representations, but by showing that a greater proportion of crimes have been committed by the wronged slaves of the plantation than by the luxurious inhabitants of Europe, who are happily strangers to those aggravated provocations by which our passions are every day irritated and incensed. Show us that, of the multitude of Negroes who have within a few years transported themselves to this country, and who are abandoned to themselves; who are corrupted by example, prompted by penury, and instigated by the memory of their wrongs to the commission of crimes—show us, I say [and the demonstration, if it be possible, cannot be difficult], that a greater proportion of these than of white men have fallen under the animadversions of justice and have been sacrificed to your laws. . . .

Before so harsh a decision was pronounced upon our nature, we might have expected—if sad experience had not taught us to expect nothing but injustice from our adversaries—that some pains would have been taken to ascertain what our nature is; and that we should have been considered as we are found in our native woods and not as we now are—altered and perverted by an inhuman political institution. But instead of this, we are examined, not by philosophers, but by interested traders; not as nature formed us, but as man has depraved us—and from such an inquiry, prosecuted under such circumstances, the perverseness of our dispositions is said to be established. Cruel that you are! You make us slaves; you implant in our minds all the vices which are in some degree inseparable from that condition; and you then impiously impute to nature, and to God, the origin of those vices, to which you alone have given birth; and punish in us the crimes of which you are yourselves the authors.

The condition of the slave is in nothing more deplorable than in its being so unfavorable to the practice of every virtue. The surest foundation of virtue is love of our fellow-creatures; and that affection takes its birth in the social relations of men to one another. But to a slave these are all denied. He never pays or receives the grateful duties of a son—he never knows or experiences the fond solicitude of a father—the tender names of husband, of brother, and of friend, are to him unknown. He has no country to defend and bleed for— he can relieve no sufferings—for he looks around in vain to find a being more wretched than himself. He can indulge no generous sentiment—for he sees himself every hour treated with contempt and ridiculed, and distinguished from irrational brutes by nothing but the severity of punishment. Would it be surprising if a slave, laboring under all these disadvantages—oppressed, insulted, scorned, trampled on—should come at last to despise himself—to believe the calumnies of his oppressors—and to persuade himself that it would be against his nature to cherish any honorable sentiment or to attempt any virtuous action? Before you boast of your superiority over us, place some of your own color (if you have the heart to do it) in the same situation with us and see whether they have such innate virtue, and such unconquerable vigor of mind, as to be capable of surmounting such multiplied difficulties, and of keeping their minds free from the infection of every vice, even under the oppressive yoke of such a servitude.

But, not satisfied with denying us that indulgence, to which the misery of our condition gives us so just a claim, our enemies have laid down other and stricter rules of morality to judge our actions by than those by which the conduct of all other men is tried. Habits, which in all human beings except ourselves are thought innocent, are, in us, deemed criminal—and actions, which are even laudable in white men, become enormous crimes in Negroes. In proportion to our weakness, the strictness of censure is increased upon us; and as resources are withheld from us, our duties are multiplied. The terror of punishment is perpetually before our eyes; but we know not how to avert, what rules to act by, or what guides to follow. We have written laws, indeed, composed in a language we do not understand and never promulgated: but what avail written laws, when the supreme law, with us, is the capricious will of our overseers? To obey the dictates of our own hearts, and to yield to the strong propensities of nature, is often to incur severe punishment; and by emulating examples which we find applauded and revered among Europeans, we risk inflaming the wildest wrath of our inhuman tyrants.

To judge of the truth of these assertions, consult even those milder and subordinate rules for our conduct, the various codes of your West India laws—those laws which allow us to be men, whenever they consider us as victims of their vengeance, but treat us only like a species of living property, as often as we are to be the objects of their protection—those laws by which [it may be truly said] that we are bound to suffer and be miserable under pain of death. . . . And yet I learn from writers, whom the Europeans hold in the highest esteem, that treason is a crime which cannot be committed by a slave against his master; that a slave stands in no civil relation towards his master, and owes him no allegiance; that master and slave are in a state of war; and if the slave take up arms for his deliverance, he acts not only justifiably but in obedience to a natural duty, the duty of self-preservation. I read in authors whom I find venerated by our oppressors, that to deliver one's self and one's countrymen from tyranny is an act of the sublimest heroism. I hear Europeans exalted as the martyrs of public liberty, the saviors of their country, and the deliverers of mankind. I see other memories honored with statues, and their names immortalized in poetry—and yet when a generous Negro is animated by the same passion which ennobled them—when he feels the wrongs of his countrymen as deeply, and attempts to avenge them as boldly. I see him treated by those same Europeans as the most execrable of mankind, and led out, amidst curses and insults, to undergo a painful, gradual and ignominious death. And thus the same Briton, who applauds his own ancestors for attempting to throw off the easy yoke imposed on them by the Romans, punishes us, as detested parricides, for seeking to get free from the cruelest of all tyrannies, and yielding to the irresistible eloquence of an African Galgacus or Boadicea.

Are then the reason and morality, for which Europeans so highly value themselves, of a nature so variable and fluctuating as to change with the complexion of those to whom they are applied? Do rights of nature cease to be such when a Negro is to enjoy them? Or does patriotism in the heart of an African rankle into treason?

GOUVERNEUR MORRIS
(1752–1816)

The Curse of Slavery
MARCH 26, 1787

Are they men? Then make them citizens and let them vote.

The Constitutional Convention in 1787 was plagued by internal dissension—the debate over slavery was no exception. A decade earlier, when crafting the Declaration of Independence, Thomas Jefferson had considered language denouncing the practice. Abolition never found its way into the Declaration, but it remained a divisive topic in the early days of the republic.

In Philadelphia, after years of debate at the state level—particularly in the North, the slavery issue surfaced again in heated debate over drafting the Constitution. The dividing lines broke largely along geographic boundaries—northern delegates to the Constitutional Convention argued that slavery was "incompatible with the Republican values in which the American Revolution [had] been based," whereas southerners described slavery as a property right critical to the South's agrarian economy. In the end, neither side achieved its objective of gradual emancipation or permanent protection of the institution. The Constitution, instead, was a "prudent exercise in ambiguity," imposing an effective time limit on the slave trade and requiring a proportional count of slaves in each state. Additionally, an agreed upon "gag rule" would keep the topic of slavery off the agenda of the nascent United States Congress for years to come.

In this impassioned address to the Constitutional Convention, Gouverneur Morris, a New Yorker serving as a Pennsylvania delegate, decried the practice of slavery, its retarding effects, and its divisive impact on northern and southern states.

———

IT WAS A NEFARIOUS INSTITUTION—It was the curse of heaven on the States where it prevailed. Compare the free regions of the Middle States, where a rich & noble cultivation marks the prosperity & happiness of the people, with the misery & poverty which overspread the barren wastes of Va. Maryd. & the other States having slaves. Travel thro' ye whole Continent & you behold the prospect continually varying with the appearance & disappearance of slavery. The moment you leave ye E[astern] Sts. & enter N[ew] York, the effects of the institution become visible; Passing thro' the Jerseys and entering Pa.—every criterion of superior improvement witnesses the change. Proceed Southw[ar]dly, & every step you take thro' ye great regions of slaves, presents a desert increasing with ye increasing proportion of these wretched beings.

Upon what principle is it that the slaves shall be computed in the representation? Are they men? Then make them Citizens & let them vote. Are they property? Why then is no other property included? The Houses in this City (Philada.) are worth more than all the wretched slaves which cover the rice swamps of South Carolina. The admission of slaves into the Representation when fairly explained comes to this: that the inhabitant of Georgia and S. C. who goes to the Coast of Africa, and in defiance of the most sacred laws of humanity tears away his fellow creatures from their dearest connections & dam(n)s them to the most cruel bondages, shall have more votes in a Govt. instituted for protection of the rights of mankind, than the Citizen of Pa. or N[ew] Jersey who views with a laudable horror, so nefarious a practice. He would add that Domestic slavery is the most prominent feature in the aristocratic countenance of the proposed Constitution. The vassalage of the poor has ever been the favorite offspring of Aristocracy. And what is the proposed compensation to the Northern States for a sacrifice of every principle of right, of every impulse of humanity. They are to bind themselves to march their militia for the defence of the S.[outhern] States; for their defence ag[ain]st those very slaves of whom they complain. They must supply vessels & seamen, in case of foreign Attack. The Legislature will have indefinite power to tax them by excises, and duties on imports: both of which will fall heavier on them than on the Southern inhabitants; for the bohea tea used by a Northern freeman, will pay more tax than the whole consumption of the miserable slave, which consists of nothing more than his physical subsistence and the rag that covers his nakedness. On the other side the Southern States are not to be restrained from importing fresh supplies of wretched Africans, at once to increase the danger of attack, and the difficulty of defence; nay they are to be encouraged to it by an assurance of having their votes in the Natl Govt increased in proportion, and are at the same time to have their exports & their slaves exempt from all contributions for the public service. Let it not be said that direct taxation is to be proportioned to representation. It is idle to suppose that the Genl Govt. can stretch its hand directly into the pockets of the people scattered over so vast a Country. They can only do it through the medium of exports imports & excises. For what then are all these sacrifices to be made? He would sooner submit himself to a tax for paying for all the Negroes in the U[nited] States, than saddle posterity with such a Constitution.

Rev. Peter Williams, Jr.
(1780–1840)

This Is Our Country
July 4, 1830

We are natives of this country, we ask only to be
treated as well as foreigners.

In 1816 Robert Finley founded the American Colonization Society for the sole purpose of sending freed blacks "back" to their "African motherland." The society's mission—forced emigration—was part of a larger effort to resolve the poisonous black-white dichotomy in American society and to bring "liberty" to an oppressed group. The reality, however, was much more grim: Not only were the vast majority of African Americans shackled in the chains of slavery, but now freed blacks faced the real threat of forced "repatriation."

Rev. Peter Williams, Jr., was a leading voice in the chorus of those opposed to repatriation and the American Colonization Society. He believed that advocates of the Society sought to dispose of freed blacks in an effort to secure the institution of slavery, and, as historian Philip Foner argued, to promote the idea that African Americans were an "inferior, degraded class who should be removed from the United States." By encouraging anti-black bigotry, the Society was to blame for "depriving rights already enjoyed by free blacks." He was educated at the New York African Free School and the black Episcopalian church before pursuing a life in the church. Seven years after his consecration, Williams was ordained and installed as a minister at St. Philip's Protestant Episcopal Church.

This address, delivered from that pulpit, used Independence Day 1830 to expose the national hypocrisy of the colonizing movement, whose leadership often veiled its true objectives under false appeals to charity and religion. In 1834, under pressure from his white bishop, Williams was forced to resign his post on the Board of Managers of the New York Anti-Slavery Society.

~~~~~~

ON THIS DAY the fathers of this nation declared, "We hold these truths to be self-evident, that all men are created equal, that they are endowed by their Creator with certain unalienable rights, among which are life, liberty, and the pursuit of happiness."

These truly noble sentiments have secured to their author a deathless fame. The sages and patriots of the Revolution subscribed them with enthusiasm and "pledged their lives, their fortunes, and their sacred honour" in their support.

The result has been the freedom and happiness of millions, by whom the annual returns of this day are celebrated with the loudest and most lively expressions of joy.

But although this anniversary affords occasion of rejoicing to the mass of the people of the United States, there is a class, a numerous class, consisting of nearly three millions, who participate but little in its joys, and are deprived of their unalienable rights by the very men who so loudly rejoice in the declaration that "all men are born free and equal."

The festivities of this day serve but to impress upon the minds of reflecting men of colour a deeper sense of the cruelty, the injustice, and oppression, of which they have been the victims. While others rejoice in their deliverance from a foreign yoke, they mourn that a yoke a thousandfold more grievous is fastened upon them. Alas, they are slaves in the midst of freedom; they are slaves to those who boast that freedom is the unalienable right of all; and the clanking of their fetters, and the voice of their wrongs, make a horrid discord in the songs of freedom which resound through the land.

No people in the world profess so high a respect for liberty and equality as the people of the United States, and yet no people hold so many slaves, or make such great distinctions between man and man.

From various causes (among which we cheerfully admit a sense of justice to have held no inconsiderable rank) the work of emancipation has within a few years been rapidly advancing in a number of States. The State we live in, since the 4th of July, 1827, has been able to boast that she has no slaves, and other States where there still are slaves appear disposed to follow her example.

But, alas! the freedom to which we have attained is defective. Freedom and equality have been "put asunder." The rights of men are decided by the colour of their skin; and there is as much difference made between the rights of a free white man and a free coloured man as there is between a free coloured man and a slave.

Though delivered from the fetters of slavery, we are oppressed by an unreasonable, unrighteous, and cruel prejudice, which aims at nothing less than the forcing away of all the free coloured people of the United States to the distant shores of Africa. Far be it from me to impeach the motives of every member of the African Colonization Society. The civilizing and Christianizing of that vast continent, and the extirpation of the abominable traffic in slaves (which notwithstanding all the laws passed for its suppression is still carried on in all its horrors), are no doubt the principal motives which induce many to give it their support.

But there are those, and those who are most active and most influential in its cause, who hesitate not to say that they wish to rid the country of the free coloured population, and there is sufficient reason to believe, that with many, this is the principal motive for supporting that society; and that whether Africa is civilized or not, and whether the Slave Trade be suppressed or not, they would wish to see the free coloured people removed from this country to Africa.

Africa could certainly be brought into a state of civil and religious improvement without sending all the free people of colour in the United States there.

A few well-qualified missionaries, properly fitted out and supported, would do more for the instruction and improvement of the natives of that country than a host of colonists, the greater part of whom would need to be instructed themselves, and all of whom for a long period would find enough to do to provide for themselves instead of instructing the natives.

How inconsistent are those who say that Africa will be benefited by the removal of the free people of colour of the United States there, while they say they are the most vile and degraded people in the world. If we are as vile and degraded as they represent us, and they wish the Africans to be rendered a virtuous, enlightened and happy people, they should not think of sending us among them, lest we should make them worse instead of better.

The colonies planted by white men on the shores of America, so far from benefiting the aborigines, corrupted their morals, and caused their ruin; and yet those who say we are the most vile people in the world would send us to Africa to improve the character and condition of the natives. Such arguments would not be listened to for a moment were not the minds of the community strangely warped by prejudice.

Much has also been said by Colonizationists about improving the character and condition of the people of colour of this country by sending them to Africa. This is more inconsistent still. We are to be improved by being sent far from civilized society. This is a novel mode of improvement. What is there in the burning sun, the arid plains, and barbarous customs of Africa, that is so peculiarly favourable to our improvement? What hinders our improving here, where schools and colleges abound, where the gospel is preached at every corner, and where all the arts and sciences are verging fast to perfection? Nothing, nothing but prejudice. It requires no large expenditures, no hazardous enterprises to raise the people of colour in the United States to as highly improved a state as any class of the community. All that is necessary is that those who profess to be anxious for it should lay aside their prejudices and act towards them as they do by others.

We are natives of this country, we ask only to be treated as well as foreigners. Not a few of our fathers suffered and bled to purchase its independence; we ask only to be treated as well as those who fought against it. We have toiled to cultivate it, and to raise it to its present prosperous condition; we ask only to share equal privileges with those who come from distant lands, to enjoy the fruits of our labour. Let these moderate requests be granted, and we need not go to Africa nor anywhere else to be improved and happy. We cannot but doubt the purity of the motives of those persons who deny us these requests, and would send us to Africa to gain what they might give us at home.

The African Colonization Society is a numerous and influential body. Would they lay aside their own prejudices, much of the burden would be at once removed; and their example (especially if they were as anxious to have justice done us here as to send us to Africa) would have such an influence upon the community at large as would soon cause prejudice to hide its deformed head.

But, alas! the course which they have pursued has an opposite tendency. By the scandalous misrepresentations which they are continually giving of our character and conduct we have sustained much injury, and have reason to apprehend much more.

Without any charge of crime we have been denied all access to places to which we formerly had the most free intercourse; the coloured citizens of other places, on leaving their homes, have been denied the privilege of returning; and others have been absolutely driven out.

Has the Colonization Society had no effect in producing these barbarous measures?

They profess to have no other object in view than the colonizing of the free people of colour on the coast of Africa, with their own consent; but if our homes are made so uncomfortable that we cannot continue in them, or, if like our brethren of Ohio and New Orleans, we are driven from them, and no other door is open to receive us but Africa, our removal there will be anything but voluntary.

It is very certain that very few free people of colour wish to go to that land. The Colonization Society know this, and yet they do certainly calculate that in time they will have us all removed there.

How can this be effected but by making our situation worse here, and closing every other door against us?

MARIA W. STEWART
(1803–1879)

An Address at the African Masonic Hall
FEBRUARY 27, 1833

Give the man of color an equal opportunity. . . from the cradle to manhood, . . . and you would discover the dignified statesman.

On February 27, 1833, Maria W. Stewart addressed a crowd at the African Masonic Hall in Boston, Massachusetts, becoming the first native-born American woman—black or white—to "speak in public and to leave extant texts of her addresses."

Born a free black in 1803 in Hartford, Connecticut, Stewart was "bound out" to the family of a minister, where despite being denied a formal education, she learned the importance of the written and spoken word. Married at twenty-three, she was widowed three years later, at which point she launched her career as a pious, anti-slavery lecturer and teacher. Her now celebrated speeches and writings often focused on black education, abolition, and the issues of the nascent women's movement.

In these remarks, published in William Lloyd Garrison's abolitionist newspaper, the *Liberator,* Stewart repeatedly asserted that the intellectual capability and moral righteousness of African Americans would eventually force the white community to accept them. The address was the first part of a four-speech series delivered in Boston between 1832 and 1833. Soon after delivering it, however, and in response to public pressure from within the black community, due in part to the strong religious tone of her speeches, Stewart retired from the speaking circuit.

~~~~~~

AFRICAN RIGHTS and liberty is a subject that ought to fire the breast of every free man of color in these United States, and excite in his bosom a lively, deep, decided and heart-felt interest. When I cast my eyes on the long list of illustrious names that are enrolled on the bright annals of fame amongst the whites, I turn my eyes within, and ask my thoughts, "Where are the names of our illustrious ones?" It must certainly have been for the want of energy on the part of the free people of color that they have been long willing to bear the yoke of oppression. It must have been the want of ambition and force that has given the whites occasion to say, that our natural abilities are not as good, and our capacities by nature inferior to theirs. They boldly assert, that, did we possess a natural independence of soul, and feel a love for liberty within our breasts, some one of our sable race, long before this, would have testified it, notwithstanding the disadvantages under which we labor. We have made ourselves appear altogether unqualified to speak in our own defence, and are therefore looked upon as objects of pity and commiseration. We have been imposed upon, insulted and derided on every side; and now, if we complain, it is considered as the height of impertinence. We have suffered ourselves to be considered as dastards, cowards, mean, faint-hearted wretches; and on this account, (not because of our complexion), many despise us and would gladly spurn us from their presence.

These things have fired my soul with a holy indignation, and compelled me thus to come forward, and endeavor to turn their attention to knowledge and improvement; for knowledge is power. I would ask, is it blindness of mind, or stupidity of soul, or the want of education, that has caused our men who are 60 or 70 years of age, never to let their voices be heard nor their hands be raised in behalf of their color? Or has it been for the fear of offending the whites? If it has, O ye fearful ones, throw off your fearfulness, and come forth in the name of the Lord, and in the strength of the God of Justice, and make yourselves useful and active members in society; for they admire a noble and patriotic spirit in others—and should they not admire it in us? If you are men, convince them that you possess the spirit of men; and as your day, so shall your strength be. Have the sons of Africa no souls? Feel they no ambitious desires? Shall the chains of ignorance forever confine them? Shall the insipid appellation of "clever negroes," or "good creatures," any longer content them? Where can we find amongst ourselves the man of science, or a philosopher, or an able statesman, or a counsellor at law? Show me our fearless and brave, our noble and gallant ones. Where are our lecturers on natural history, and our critics in useful knowledge? There may be a few such men amongst us, but they are rare. It is true, our fathers bled and died in the revolutionary war, and others fought bravely under the command of Jackson, in defence of liberty. But where is the man that has distinguished himself in these modern days by acting wholly in the defence of African rights and liberty? There was one—although he sleeps, his memory lives.

I am sensible that there are many highly intelligent gentlemen of color in these United States, in the force of whose arguments, doubtless, I should discover my inferiority; but if they are blest with wit and talent, friends and fortune, why have they not made themselves men of eminence, by striving to take all the reproach that is cast upon the people of color, and in endeavoring to alleviate the woes of their brethren in bondage? Talk, without effort, is nothing; you are abundantly capable, gentlemen, of making yourselves men of distinction; and this gross neglect, on your part, causes my blood to boil within me. Here is the grand cause which hinders the rise and progress of the people of color. It is their want of laudable ambition and requisite courage.

Individuals have been distinguished according to their genius and talents, ever since the first formation of man, and will continue to be whilst the world stands. The different grades rise to honor and respectability as their merits may deserve. History informs us that we sprung from one of the most learned nations of the whole earth—from the seat, if not the parent of science; yes, poor, despised Africa was once the resort of sages and legislators of other nations, was esteemed the school for learning, and the most illustrious men in Greece flocked thither for instruction. But it was our gross sins and abominations that provoked the Almighty to frown thus heavily upon us, and give our glory unto others. Sin and prodigality have caused the downfall of nations, kings and emperors; and were it not that God in wrath remembers mercy, we might indeed despair; but a promise is left us;"Ethiopia shall again stretch forth her hands unto God."

But it is of no use for us to boast that we sprung from this learned and enlightened nation, for this day a thick mist of moral gloom hangs over millions of our race. Our condition as a people has been low for hundreds of years, and it will continue to be so, unless, by the true piety and virtue we strive, to regain that which we have lost. White Americans, by their prudence, economy and exertions, have sprung up and become one of the most flourishing nations in the world, distinguished for their knowledge of the arts and sciences, for their polite literature. Whilst our minds are vacant and starving for want of knowledge, theirs are filled to overflowing. Most of our color have been taught to stand in fear of the white man from their earliest infancy, to work as soon as they could walk, and call "master" before they scarce could lisp the name of mother. Continual fear and laborious servitude have in some degree lessened in us that natural force and energy which belong to man; or else, in defiance of opposition, our men, before this would have nobly and boldly contended for their rights. But give the man of color an equal opportunity with the white, from the cradle to manhood, and from manhood to the grave, and you would discover the dignified statesman, the man of science, and the philosopher. But there is no such opportunity for the sons of Africa, and I fear that our powerful ones are fully determined that there never shall be. Forbid, ye Powers on High, that it should any longer be said that our men possess no force. O ye sons of Africa, when will your voices be heard in our legislative halls, in defiance of your enemies, contending for equal rights and liberty? How can you, when you reflect from what you have fallen, refrain from crying mightily unto God, to turn away from us the fierceness of his anger, and remember our transgressions against us no more forever? But a God of infinite purity will not regard the prayers of those who hold religion in one hand, and prejudice, sin and pollution in the other; he will not regard the prayers of self-righteousness and hypocrisy. Is it possible, I exclaim, that for the want of knowledge, we have labored for hundreds of years to support others, and been content to receive what they chose to give us in return? Cast your eyes about—look as far as you can see—all, all is owned by the lordly white, except here and there a lowly dwelling which the man of color, midst deprivations, fraud and opposition, has been scarce able to procure. Like King Solomon, who put neither nail nor hammer to the temple, yet received the praise; so also have the white Americans gained themselves a name, like the names of the great men that are in the earth, whilst in reality we have been their principal foundation and support. We have pursued the shadow, they have obtained the substance; we have performed the labor, they have received the profits; we have planted the vines, they have eaten the fruits of them.

I would implore our men, and especially our rising youth, to flee from the gambling board and the dance hall; for we are poor, and have no money to throw away. I do not consider dancing as criminal in itself, but it is astonishing to me that our young men are so blind to their own interest and the future welfare of their children, as to spend their hard earnings for this frivolous amusement; for it has been carried on among us to such an unbecoming extent that it has become absolutely disgusting. "Faithful are the wounds of a friend, but the kisses of an enemy are deceitful." Had those men amongst us, who have had an opportunity, turned their attention as assiduously to mental and moral improvement as they have to gambling and dancing, I might have remained quietly at home, and they stood contending in my place. These polite accomplishments will never enroll your names on the bright annals of fame, who admire the belle void of intellectual knowledge, or applaud the dandy that talks largely on politics, without striving to assist his fellow in the revolution, when the nerves and muscles of every other man forced him into the field of action. You have a right to rejoice, and to let your hearts cheer you in the days of your youth; yet remember that for all these things God will bring you into judgment. Then, O ye sons of Africa, turn your mind from these perishable objects, and contend for the cause of God and the rights of man. Form yourselves into temperance societies. There are temperate men amongst you; then why will you any longer neglect to strive, by your example, to suppress vice in all its abhorrent forms? You have been told repeatedly of the glorious results arising from temperance, and can you bear to see the whites arising in honor and respectability, without endeavoring to grasp after that honor and respectability also?

But I forbear. Let our money, instead of being thrown away as heretofore, be appropriated for schools and seminaries of learning for our children and youth. We ought to follow the example of the whites in this respect. Nothing would raise our respectability, add to our peace and happiness and reflect so much honor upon us, as to be ourselves the promoters of temperance, and the supporters, as far as we are able, of useful and scientific knowledge. The rays of light and knowledge have been hid from our view; we have been taught to consider ourselves as scarce superior to the brute creation; and have performed the most laborious part of American drudgery. Had we as people received one half the early advantages the whites have received, I would defy the government of these United States to deprive us any longer of our rights.

I am informed that the agent of the Colonization Society has recently formed an association of young men, for the purpose of influencing those of us to go to Liberia who may feel disposed. The colonizationists are blind to their own interest, for should the nations of the earth make war with America, they would find their forces much weakened by our absence; or should we remain here, can our "brave soldiers" and "fellow citizens," as they were termed in time of calamity, condescend to defend the rights of the whites, and be again deprived of their own, or sent to Liberia in return? O, if the colonizationists are real friends to Africa, let them expend the money which they collect in erecting a college to educate her injured sons in this land of gospel light and liberty; for it would be most thankfully received on our part, and convince us of the truth of their professions, and save time, expense and anxiety. Let them place before us noble objects, worthy of pursuit, and see if we prove ourselves to be those unambitious negroes they term us. But ah! Methinks their hearts are so frozen towards us, they had rather their money should be sunk in the ocean than to administer it to our relief; and I fear, if they dared, like Pharaoh king of Egypt, they would order every male child amongst us to be drowned. But the most high God is still as able to subdue the lofty pride of these white Americans, as He was the heart of that ancient rebel. They say though we are looked upon as things, yet we sprang from a scientific people. Had our men the requisite force and energy, they would soon convince them, by their efforts both in public and private, that they were men, or things in the shape of men. Well may the colonizationists laugh us to scorn for our negligence; well may they cry, "Shame to the sons of Africa." As the burden of the Israelites was too great for Moses to bear, so also is our burden too great for our noble advocate to bear. You must feel interested, my brethren, in what he undertakes, and hold up his hands by your good words, or in spite of himself his soul will become discouraged, and his heart will die within him; for he has, as it were, the strong bulls of Bashan to contend with.

ANGELINA GRIMKÉ
(1792–1879)

Address to the Massachusetts Legislature
1838

It is often said that women rule the world,
through their influence over men.

The daughter of a South Carolinian slaveholder, Angelina Grimké has been called the first of the great female anti-slavery speakers. Along with her sister Sarah, Grimké rejected her life as a southern belle, converted to Quakerism, and joined the circuit of women influenced by abolitionist William Lloyd Garrison. In the North, Grimké soon became a regular speaker before female audiences that hailed her superior rhetorical ability. By June 1837 she crossed over into then-forbidden territory, speaking predominantly to audiences of both men and women.

In February 1838, the high point of her career, Grimké addressed members of the Massachusetts legislature—the first time a woman spoke before an American legislative body. Before a hall so packed that she was literally passed to the podium over the heads of spectators, Angela passionately demanded the immediate end of the slave trade in Washington, D.C. She then defended female political activism, pointing to the anti-slavery petition signed by more than 20,000 Massachusetts women. Months later, at the age of forty-two, Grimké married abolitionist Theodore Weld and retired from the lecture circuit.

<hr />

MR. CHAIRMAN—

More than 2,000 years have rolled their dark and bloody waters down the rocky, winding channel of time into the broad ocean of Eternity, since woman's voice was heard in the palace of an eastern monarch, and woman's petition achieved the salvation of millions of her race from the edge of the sword. The Queen of Persia, if Queen she might be called, who was but the mistress of her voluptuous lord, trained as she had been in the secret abominations of an oriental harem, had studied too deeply the character of Ahasuerus not to know that the sympathies of his heart could not be reached, except through the medium of his sensual appetites. Hence we find her arrayed in royal apparel, and standing in the inner court of the King's house, hoping by her personal charms to win the favor of her lord. And after the golden sceptre had been held out, and the inquiry was made, "What wilt thou, Queen Esther, and what is thy request? It shall be given thee to the half of the kingdom"—even then she dared not ask either for her own life, or that of her people. She *felt* that if her mission of mercy was to be successful, *his* animal propensities must be still more powerfully wrought upon—the luxurious feast must be prepared, the banquet of wine must be served up, and the favorable moment must be seized when, gorged with gluttony and intoxication, the king's heart was fit to be operated upon by the pathetic appeal. "If *I* have found favor in thy sight, O King, and if it please the King, let *my* life be given at my petition, and *my* people at my request." It was thus, through personal charms, and sensual gratification, and individual influence, that the Queen of Persia obtained the precious boon she craved—her own life, and the life of her beloved people. Mr. Chairman, it is my privilege to stand before you on a similar mission of life and love; but I thank God that we live in an age of the world too enlightened and too moral to admit of the adoption of the same *means* to obtain as holy an end. I feel that it would be an insult to this Committee, were I to attempt to win their favor by arraying my person in gold, and silver, and costly apparel, or by inviting them to partake of the luxurious feast, or the banquet of wine. I understand the spirit of the age too well to believe that *you* could be moved by such sensual means—means as unworthy of you, as they would be beneath the dignity of the cause of humanity. Yes, I feel that if you are reached at all, it will not be by me, but by the truths I shall endeavor to present to your understandings and your hearts. The heart of the eastern despot was reached through the lowest propensities of his animal nature; yours, I know, cannot be reached but through the loftier sentiments of the intellectual and moral feelings.

I stand before you as a citizen, on behalf of the 20,000 women of Massachusetts, whose names are enrolled on petitions which have been submitted to the Legislature of which you are the organ. These petitions relate to the great and solemn subject of American slavery—a subject fraught with the deepest interest to this republic, whether we regard it in its political, moral, or religious aspects. And because it is a *political* subject, it has often been tauntingly said, that *woman* has nothing to do with it. Are we aliens, because we are *women?* Are we bereft of citizenship, because we are the mothers, wives, and daughters of a mighty people? Have women *no* country—*no* interests staked in public weal—no liabilities in common peril—no partnership in a nation's guilt and shame? Let the history of the world answer these queries. Read the denunciations of Jehovah against the follies and crimes of Israel's daughters. Trace the influence of woman as a courtezan and a mistress in the destinies of nations, both ancient and modern, and see her wielding her power too often to debase and destroy, rather than to elevate and save. It is often said that women rule the world, through their influence over men. If so, then may we well hide our faces in the dust, and cover ourselves with sackcloth and ashes. It has not been by moral power and intellectual, but through the baser passions of man. *This* domination of women *must* be resigned—the sooner the better; in the age which is approaching, she should be something *more*—she should be a *citizen;* and this title, which demands an increase of knowledge and of reflection, opens before her a new empire! I hold, Mr. Chairman, that American women have to do with this subject, not only because it is moral and religious, but because it is *political,* inasmuch as we are citizens of this republic, and as such *our* honor, happiness, and well being, are bound up in its politics and government and laws.

I stand before you as a southerner, exiled from the land of my birth, by the sound of the lash, and the pitious cry of the slave. I stand before you as a repentant slaveholder. I stand before you as a moral being, endowed with precious and inalienable rights, which are correlative with solemn duties and high responsibilities; and as a moral being I feel that I owe it to the suffering slave, and to the deluded master, to my country and the world, to do all that I can to overturn a system of complicated crimes, built up upon the broken hearts and prostrate bodies of my countrymen in chains, and cemented by the blood and sweat and tears of my sisters in bonds. . . .

Sara T. Smith

Loosening the Bonds of Prejudice
May 17, 1838

The attentive consideration of what we owe to our colored brethren
will dispose us to manifest our sympathy with them.

On May 17, 1838, in Philadelphia, Pennsylvania, Sara T. Smith addressed the second Anti-Slavery Convention of American Women—an interracial meeting committed to the abolitionist movement. The meeting was scheduled to take place at the recently completed Pennsylvania Hall, a grand structure built by abolitionists after churches and other public buildings refused to rent them space. When the convention refused to heed the mayor's request to disband, an angry mob of men began to gather around the building, "prowling about the doors, examining the gas-pipes, and talking in an 'incendiary' manner." The crowd of protesters grew in size and strength, eventually breaking into the building, setting fires, and engulfing Pennsylvania Hall in flames. Refusing to bow to this onslaught, however, the women persevered, moving their meeting to a local member's house.

In her remarks to this gathering, Smith not only argued adamantly against violence in the anti-slavery movement but spoke at length about its morality, and the rights of women to publicly denounce the practice.

———

Dear Friends:—

In that love for our cause which knows not the fear of man, we address you, in confidence that our motives will be understood and regarded. . . .

We are told that it is not within the "province of woman," to discuss the subject of slavery; that it is a "political question," and we are "stepping out of our sphere," when we take part in its discussion. It is not true that it is *merely* a political question, it is likewise a question of justice, of humanity, of morality, of religion; a question which, while it involves considerations of immense importance to the welfare and prosperity of our country, enters deeply into the home-concerns, the every-day feelings of millions of our fellow beings. Whether the laborer shall receive the reward of his labor, or be driven daily to *unrequited* toil—whether he shall walk erect in the dignity of conscious manhood, or be reckoned among the beasts which perish—whether his bones and

sinews shall be his own, or another's—whether his child shall receive the protection of its natural guardian, or be ranked among the live-stock of the estate,
to be disposed of as the caprice or interest of the master may dictate—whether
the sun of knowledge shall irradiate the hut of the peasant, or the murky cloud
of ignorance brood darkly over it—whether "every one shall have liberty to
worship God according to the dictates of his own conscience," or man assume
the prerogative of Jehovah, and impiously seek to plant himself upon the
throne of the Almighty; these considerations are all involved in the question of
liberty or slavery.

And is a subject comprehending interests of such magnitude, merely a
"political question," and one in which woman "can take no part without losing something of the modesty and gentleness which are her most appropriate
ornaments"? May not the "ornament of a meek and quiet spirit" exist with an
upright mind and enlightened intellect, and must woman necessarily be less
gentle because her heart is open to the claims of humanity, or less modest
because she feels for the degradation of her enslaved sisters, and would stretch
forth her hand for their rescue?

By the Constitution of the United States, the whole physical power of the
North is pledged for the suppression of domestic insurrections, and should the
slaves, maddened by oppression, endeavor to shake off the yoke of the task-
master, the men of the North are bound to make common cause with the
tyrant, and put down, at the point of the bayonet, every effort on the part of
the slave, for the attainment of his freedom. And when the father, husband, son,
and brother shall have left their homes to mingle in the unholy warfare, "to
become the executioners of their brethren, or to fall themselves by their
hands," will the mother, wife, daughter, and sister feel that they have no interest in this subject? Will it be easy to convince them that it is no concern of
theirs, that their homes are rendered desolate, and their habitations the abodes
of wretchedness? Surely this consideration is of itself sufficient to arouse the
slumbering energies of woman, for the overthrow of a system which thus
threatens to lay in ruins the fabric of her domestic happiness; and she will not
be deterred from the performance of her duty to herself, her family, and her
country, by the cry of political question.

But admitting it to be a political question, have we no interest in the welfare of our country? May we not permit a thought to stray beyond the narrow limits of our own family circle, and of the present hour? May we not
breathe a sigh over the miseries of our countrymen, nor utter a word of
remonstrance against the unjust laws that are crushing them to the earth? Must
we witness "the headlong rage or heedless folly," with which our nation is
rushing onward to destruction, and not seek to arrest its downward course?
Shall we silently behold the land which we love with all the heart-warm affection of children, rendered a hissing and a reproach throughout the world, by

this system which is already tolling the death-bell of her decease among the nations? No: the events of the last two years have cast their dark shadows before, overclouding the bright prospects of the future, and shrouding the destinies of our country in more than midnight gloom, and we cannot remain inactive. Our country is as dear to us as to the proudest statesman, and the more closely our hearts cling to "our altars and our homes," the more fervent are our aspirations that every inhabitant of our land may be protected in his fireside enjoyments by just and equal laws; that the foot of the tyrant may no longer invade the domestic sanctuary, nor his hand tear asunder those whom God himself has united by the most holy ties. Let our course, then, still be *onward!* Justice, humanity, patriotism, every high and every holy motive urge us forward, and we dare not refuse to obey. The way of duty lies open before us, and though no pillar of fire be visible to the outward sense, yet an unerring light shall illumine our pathway, guiding us through the sea of persecution and the wilderness of prejudice and error, to the promised land of freedom where "every man shall sit under his own vine and under his own fig-tree, and none shall make him afraid."

The numerous small societies, scattered over the various districts of our extended country, we would greet with affectionate interest, with assured hope.

Though you are now only as glimmering lights on the hilltops, few and far between, yet if with all diligence these fires be kept burning, the surrounding country shall catch into flame—the chains fall from our brethren, and they unite with us in the jubilee song of thanksgiving. To bring about this glorious consummation of our hopes, we must be diligent in business, fervent in spirit; there must be the patient continuance in well doing of those who have been battling for the world's freedom, and who have counted nothing too near or too dear to sacrifice for their brethren in bonds; there must be an increase of energy and zeal in the many who have enlisted in the ranks of the friends of freedom. In joining an Anti-Slavery Society, we have set our names to no idle pledge. Let not any one member feel released from individual action; though by association we gain strength, yet it is strength to be used by each individual. The day, the hour calls imperatively for "doing with all our might" what our hands find to do; the means are various. To some among us may be given the head to devise, to others the hand to execute; one may have time to devote, another money; let each give liberally of that which he or she possesses. Time, talents, influence, wealth, all are required, all will aid in the great enterprise. Let each one seriously inquire how he or she can availingly promote the cause, and in that department faithfully work. Let the aged counsel, the young execute; plead not inability: we much fear that many among us rest satisfied with "the name to live and yet are dead." We give in our names as members of a society, pay a small annual subscription, and attend the meetings of the society. So far is well, but much more is needed for the accomplishment of our work. Ignorance yet remains to be enlightened, prejudice to be removed, injustice to be overthrown; and daily, almost hourly, opportunities may offer to exert our strength where it can be availingly applied; and in order to do this keep yourselves informed of every Anti-Slavery movement. The editor of the *Emancipator* says: "Other things being equal, those are the most efficient abolitionists who are the most intelligent; and, commonly, the most good is done in those places where our books and publications are most circulated and read."

The taunting question heard so long and so untiringly repeated, "What has the North to do with slavery?" is most triumphantly answered by the practice of any one active, consistent member of an Anti-Slavery Society, as "we remember them in bonds as bound with them." We find we have much to do, much even for ourselves. How slowly, yet how surely, do we feel the loosening of those bonds of prejudice wherewith we have been bound; how slow are we to feel the truth that all men are indeed "born free and equal?" How much do we find to do in acting up to this doctrine, in our closets, in our families, in our intercourse with the world, and by the wayside! The attentive consideration of what we owe to our colored brethren will dispose us to manifest our sympathy with them; and to show them by our conduct that we do not consider them as strangers and aliens; that we appreciate their manly struggles for the advancement of their race; and when favorable circumstances permit the escape of any beyond the prescribed length of the chain which has bound them, we cannot, we dare not join in the rude ridicule of the vulgar, the sneering contempt of the supercilious, or the mistaken kindness of the benevolent, who say that to awaken their sensibilities to their grievances would be cruelty in the extreme; that "where ignorance is bliss 'tis folly to be wise." We see the fallacy of this hackneyed sentiment. Ignorance is not bliss—insensibility is not enjoyment. The objector little knows how tightly these fetters of caste have been drawn around, how deeply they have scarred their victim! How bitterly the injustice has been felt, and the more intensely, as it has been borne in silence, without either the solace of sympathy or the hope of relief.

. . . While we thus labor to restore to our colored brethren the rights of which they have been so long and so unjustly deprived, let us endeavor to come to the work with pure hearts and clean hands. Let us refuse to participate in the guilt of him "who useth his neighbor's service without wages and giveth him not for his work." Whether we are guiltless of such participation while we continue to purchase and use the products of unrequited toil; becomes a question of serious import, and one which we recommend to your attentive consideration.

It is not necessary to enter into a labored argument to prove that one of the main props of the system of slavery is the price paid by the inhabitants of non-slaveholding states and countries for the productions of the states in which slavery prevails. This is so evident that we presume none will dispute it. Considering the fact, then, as admitted, we would ask, what is the slaveholder but our agent, holding and using his human chattels for our benefit? And if it be true that "what a man does by another, he does himself?" Are we not partners with him in guilt? With what consistency, then, can we demand that he "undo the heavy burdens, and let the oppressed go free," while we continue to pay him for retaining them in bondage?

Our inconsistency, in this respect, does not escape the vigilant eyes of our opponents. Said a slaveholder to an abolitionist, "we make the sugar, and you buy it," thus plainly intimating that if they were culpable, we were far from blameless. We feel that on this point we have been verily guilty, and though the scales are falling from the eyes of many, yet much remains to be done among ourselves. And what are the motives that restrain us from acting consistently on this subject?

Are we unwilling to forego a few sensual gratifications in such a cause? Will we not consent to be somewhat more coarsely clothed and to deny the palate some of its wonted gratifications, rather than contribute to swell the burden of sighs and groans which unceasingly ascend from breaking hearts to the throne of Him "who executeth righteousness and judgment for all that are oppressed?"

In presenting to your consideration a few remarks on the subject of peace, we would not be understood as wishing to identify the anti-slavery cause with that of peace. We no more desire that the Anti-Slavery Society should become a Peace Society, than we wish it to be a Temperance, Bible, or Missionary Society. We believe that each of these objects may be best promoted by a distinct organization of its friends. . . .

⁓

. . . We deem it very desirable and important that so powerful an influence should be enlisted in behalf of the anti-slavery cause. The work that we have to perform is a Herculean task, and we would gladly avail ourselves of all righteous means of hastening its accomplishment.

It is a universally admitted truth, that opposition strengthens human purpose, unless the judgment and conscience are convinced that the course pursued is wrong or inexpedient. Such conviction is not produced, is not designed to be produced, by the measures which we are discussing; therefore, they unfit the mind for the reception of truth, and the heart for righteous action. Thus the only influence which their use exerts upon the progress of anti-slavery principles, is deleterious. And even if it were admitted that they are sometimes necessary for the preservation of life, are there not those who love the cause of freedom and of God, with an ardor sufficient to induce them to suffer the loss of life, rather than injure the prosperity of that cause?

To pursue the discussion of this subject farther, would perhaps be to transcend our prescribed limits. We earnestly and respectfully commend it to the attention of our fellow laborers, especially to that portion of them who believe that Christianity justifies a resort to arms for self-preservation. Those who do not thus believe, of course, need not such arguments as we have presented.

Aware that a disposition to "prove all things," has ever been characteristic of abolitionists, we feel assured that by careful study, and fervent prayer, they will be enabled to choose right paths for their feet, and that, in the accomplishment of a work upon which God has so manifestly set his seal of approbation, his servants will not be left unaided by the illuminations of that Holy Spirit who was sent to guide them "into all truth."

In looking back on the past, have we not much to encourage us to persevere in the work set before us? For a long period a solitary voice was heard crying in the wilderness; now there is the shouting of a host. Then was demanded a little more sleep, a little more slumber; now there is the awakening of the nation; and though not yet sufficiently aroused to discern friends in those who have shaken this false rest, yet if we fail not in our duty, there can be no more "folding of the hands to sleep," but our country will arise and go forth, clothed with majesty, and girded with power.

JOHN QUINCY ADAMS
(1767–1848)

Defending the Amistad *Slaves*
FEBRUARY 24, 1841

In February 1839, violating all existing treaties, Portuguese slave hunters abducted a group of Africans from Sierra Leone and shipped them to Havana, Cuba, which at the time was a thriving center for the Atlantic slave trade. Britain, France, Portugal, and even the United States had outlawed the trade in slaves, and Spain had restricted the trade. A group of Spanish planters then purchased fifty-three of the abductees and shipped them to a Caribbean plantation. During the journey, however, the group of Africans, led by Joseph Cinqué, took control of the ship— the *Amistad*—killed the captain and the cook, and ordered the ship's crew to sail the vessel back to the slaves' homeland. But instead the Spanish crew steered the ship north toward America.

On August 24, 1839, a United States brig seized the *Amistad* off the coast of New York, freed the crew, and charged the Africans with murder. Although the murder charges were later dismissed, under pressure from President Martin Van Buren and the government of Spain, the Africans were held in confinement on violations of property rights and salvage claims.

With northern abolitionists funding the defense of the slaves, the *Amistad* case went to federal district court and then the United States Supreme Court. Former president John Quincy Adams was hired to defend the Africans, an unpopular position for any public figure at the time.

In one of the most famous cases before the highest court in the United States, Adams argued forcefully that the property and salvage charges were illegitimate and without any foundation. Adams, in the following excerpt from his argument, excoriated the practice of slavery and, with natural law on his side, demanded the Africans' immediate freedom. The Court found in their favor, and thirty-five men returned to Sierra Leone. Adams spent his remaining days in Congress fighting the gag rule on slavery, which precluded any petition against the practice from receiving legislative consideration.

THE TRUTH IS, that property in man has existed in all ages of the world, and results from the natural state of man, which is war. When God created the first family and gave them the fields of the earth as an inheritance, one of the number, in obedience to the impulses and passions that had been implanted in the human heart, rose and slew his brother. This universal nature of man is alone modified by civilization and law. War, conquest, and force have produced slavery, and it is state necessity and the internal law of self preservation, that will ever perpetuate and defend it.

There is the principle, on which a particular decision is demanded from this Court, by the Official Journal of the Executive, on behalf of the southern states. Is that a principle recognized by this Court? Is it the principle of that declaration? [Here Mr. Adams pointed to the Declaration of Independence, two copies of which hang before the eyes of the Judges on the bench.] It is alleged in the Official Journal, that war gives the right to take the life of our enemy, and that this confers a right to make him a slave, on account of having spared his life. Is that the principle on which these United States stand before the world? That declaration says that every man is "endowed by his Creator with certain inalienable rights," and that among these are life, liberty, and the pursuit of happiness." If these rights are inalienable, they are incompatible with the rights of the victor to take the life of his enemy in war, or to spare his life and make him a slave. If this principle is sound, it reduces to brute force all the rights of man. It places all the sacred relations of life at the power of the strongest. No man has a right to life or liberty, if he has an enemy able to take them from him. There is the principle. There is the whole argument of this paper.

Now I do not deny that the only principle upon which a color of right can be attributed to the condition of slavery is by assuming that the natural state of man is war. The bright intellect of the South clearly saw, that without this principle for a cornerstone, he had no foundation for his argument. He assumes it therefore without a blush, as Hobbes assumed it to prove that government and despotism are synonymous words. I will not here discuss the right or the rights of slavery, but I say that the doctrine of Hobbes, that War is the natural state of man, has for ages been exploded, as equally disclaimed and rejected by the philosopher and the Christian. That it is utterly incompatible with any theory of human rights, and especially with the rights which the Declaration of Independence proclaims as self-evident truths. The moment you come, to the Declaration of Independence, that every man has a right to life and liberty, an inalienable right, this case is decided. I ask nothing more in behalf of these unfortunate men, than this Declaration. The opposite principle is laid down, not by an unintelligent or unthinking man, but is given to the public and to this Court, as coming from one of the

brightest intellects of the South. Your Honors see what it comes to, when carried out. I will call the attention of the Court to one more paragraph [from
the district judge's opinion]:

> Instead of having the Negroes placed in a situation to receive punish-
> ment for what offenses they may have committed against their masters,
> those who have been in Cuba in undisputed possession of property
> under the Spanish flag were instantly deprived of that possession, and
> their final title to the property peremptorily decided upon by an
> American court, in defiance of the plainest treaty stipulations. Not only
> that, but Ruiz and Montes, Spanish citizens, thus forced into our terri-
> tory under appalling circumstances, where common humanity, inde-
> pendent of all law, demanded that they should be treated with hospital-
> ity as unfortunate guests, were actually thrown into prison under charges
> which the Negroes were instigated to make, for offenses committed
> against the Negroes while they were in Cuba, under the Spanish juris-
> diction. This is the justice of an American court, bowed down in dis-
> graceful subserviency before the bigoted mandates of that blind fanati-
> cism which prompted the Judge upon the bench to declare in his decree,
> in reference to one of these Negroes, that, "Although he might be stained
> with crime, yet he should not sigh in vain for Africa"; and all because his
> hands were reeking with the blood of murdered white men! It is a base
> outrage (I can use no milder language) upon all the sympathies of civi-
> lized life.

It is unnecessary further to repeat verbatim et literatim this argument of
the District judge to sustain his decree. Every word and letter of it teems with
anxiety to sustain the institution of Slavery, and to prostrate instead of enforcing the laws of the United States for the suppression of the slave trade. What
he calls certain restrictions placed on the trade by Spain, was the total prohibition of it north of the equator, even then stipulated by Spain in a treaty with
Great Britain, and enacted accordingly by her law. But what of that? The judge
admits that the trade is inhuman, that it is obnoxious to every benevolent feeling, but he is bound to consider it legal, notwithstanding its injustice, because
many years before it had been practiced by Great Britain, and not many years
before by the United States themselves. Is this reasoning for a Court of justice? When all the civilized nations of the earth shall have abolished the
African slave trade, the judge thinks that captured Africans would be considered free, unless proved to be slaves: and if Spain and Portugal should abolish
the slave trade, he thinks the burden of proof that Negroes captured in their
vessels were slaves, would rest upon their captors. In that case, the Court would
respect the rights of Africans as much as those of any other class of persons;

but, until then, how could the Court be permitted to examine into treaty stipulations of Spain, or into any restriction imposed by Spain upon the traffic of
her subjects in slaves?

Such was the reasoning of a slave-holding judge upon slavery and the slave
trade, and by such reasoning did he out of two hundred and twelve Africans,
forfeit to the United States, to receive from them the blessing of freedom, and
restoration to their native country, reduce the number who should enjoy that
privilege to seven individuals, consigning all the rest to perpetual, hopeless
Spanish and Portuguese slavery!

Henry Highland Garnet
(1815–1882)

An Address to the Slaves of the United States of America
1843

Let your motto be resistance! resistance! RESISTANCE! No oppressed people have ever secured their liberty without resistance.

Abolitionist and Presbyterian minister Henry Highland Garnet was born in 1815 to slave parents in New Market, Maryland. He attended the African Free School, the Phoenix High School for Colored Youth, and then the Noyes Academy in New Hampshire—before an anti-integrationist mob drove him from the school. At the age of nine, Garnet, his ten siblings, and their father escaped from slavery and fled to New York, where they met a wealth of new opportunity.

After studying at the Oneida Theological Institute, Garnet pursued a career as a scholar and clergyman, serving for several decades as a minister at the Liberty Street Presbyterian Church in Troy, New York. During this time, he also founded a school for black children in Geneva, New York.

In the 1850s, Garnet joined the Anti-Slavery Society, an organization that encouraged black missionary work and entrepreneurship in Africa. Known for his sharp tongue, Garnet quickly rose as a leading figure of the organization. During the Civil War, he helped organize black troops for the Union and later became the first African American to preach a sermon in the U.S. House of Representatives.

Garnet gained national prominence after delivering the following address to the 1843 National Convention of Colored Citizens in Buffalo, New York. His language was so extreme that the convention refused to adopt it, earning him a reputation as an unbridled radical. Six years later, John Brown had Garnet's address published at his own expense.

———

BRETHREN AND FELLOW CITIZENS: Years have rolled on, and tens of thousands have been borne on streams of blood and tears to the shores of eternity. While you have been oppressed, we have also been partakers with you; nor can we be free while you are enslaved. We, therefore, write to you as being bound with you.

Many of you are bound to us, not only by the ties of a common humanity, but we are connected by the more tender relations of parents, wives, husbands, and sisters, and friends. As such we most affectionately address you.

Slavery has fixed a deep gulf between you and us, and while it shuts out from you the relief and consolation which your friends would willingly render, it afflicts and persecutes you with a fierceness which we might not expect to see in the fiends of hell. But still the Almighty Father of mercies has left to us a glimmering ray of hope, which shines out like a lone star in a cloudy sky. Mankind are becoming wiser, and better—the oppressor's power is fading, and you, every day, are becoming better informed, and more numerous. Your grievances, brethren, are many. We shall not attempt, in this short address, to present to the world all the dark catalogue of the nation's sins, which have been committed upon an innocent people. Nor is it indeed necessary, for you feel them from day to day, and all the civilized world looks upon them with amazement.

Two hundred and twenty-seven years ago the first of our injured race were brought to the shores of America. They came not with glad spirits to select their homes in the New World. They came not with their own consent, to find an unmolested enjoyment of the blessings of this fruitful soil. The first dealings they had with men calling themselves Christians exhibited to them the worst features of corrupt and sordid hearts: and convinced them that no cruelty is too great, no villainy and no robbery too abhorrent for even enlightened men to perform, when influenced by avarice and lust. Neither did they come flying upon the wings of Liberty to a land of freedom. But they came with broken hearts, from their beloved native land, and were doomed to unrequited toil and deep degradation. Nor did the evil of their bondage end at their emancipation by death. Succeeding generations inherited their chains, and millions have come from eternity into time, and have returned again to the world of spirits, cursed and ruined by American slavery.

⌒

Nearly three millions of your fellow-citizens are prohibited by law and public opinion (which in this country is stronger than law) from reading the Book of Life. Your intellect has been destroyed as much as possible, and every ray of light they have attempted to shut out from your minds. The oppressors themselves have become involved in the ruin. They have become weak, sensual, and rapacious—they have cursed you—they have cursed themselves—they have cursed the earth which they have trod.

⌒

Slavery! How much misery is comprehended in that single word. . . .

To such degradation it is sinful in the extreme for you to make voluntary submission. . . . God will not receive slavery, nor ignorance, nor any other state of mind, for love and obedience to Him. Your condition does not absolve you from your moral obligation. The diabolical injustice by which your liberties are cloven down, neither God nor angels, or just men, command you to suffer for a single moment. Therefore it is your solemn and imperative duty to use every means, both moral, intellectual, and physical, that promises success. . . . The humblest peasant is as free in the sight of God as the proudest monarch that ever swayed a sceptre. Liberty is a spirit sent out from God, and like its great Author, is no respecter of persons.

Brethren, the time has come when you must act for yourselves. It is an old and true saying that, "if hereditary bondmen would be free, they must themselves strike the blow." You can plead your own cause, and do the work of emancipation better than any others. . . . The North has done much—her opinion of slavery in the abstract is known. But in regard to the South, we adopt the opinion of the *New York Evangelist*:"We have advanced so far, that the cause apparently waits for a more effectual door to be thrown open than has been yet." . . . Think how many tears you have poured out upon the soil which you have cultivated with unrequited toil and enriched with your blood; and then go to your lordly enslavers and tell them plainly, that you *are determined to be free*. Appeal to their sense of justice, and tell them that they have no more right to oppress you than you have to enslave them. Entreat them to remove the grievous burdens which they have imposed upon you, and to remunerate you for your labor. . . . If you would be free in this generation, here is your only hope. However much you and all of us may desire it, there is not much hope of redemption without the shedding of blood. If you must bleed, let it all come at once—rather *die freemen than live to be the slaves*. . . .

Fellowmen! patient sufferers! behold your dearest rights crushed to the earth! See your sons murdered, and your wives, mothers and sisters doomed to prostitution. In the name of the merciful God, and by all that life is worth, let it no longer be a debatable question, whether it is better to choose *liberty* or *death*.

Noble men! Those who have fallen in freedom's conflict, their memories will be cherished by the true-hearted and the God-fearing in all future generations; those who are living, their names are surrounded by a halo of glory.

Brethren, arise, arise! Strike for your lives and liberties. Now is the day and the hour. Let every slave throughout the land do this, and the days of slavery are numbered. You cannot be more oppressed than you have been—you cannot suffer greater cruelties than you have already. *Rather die freemen than live to be slaves.* Remember that you are four millions!

. . . In the name of God, we ask, are you men? Where is the blood of your fathers? Has it all run out of your veins? Awake, awake; millions of voices are calling you! Your dead fathers speak to you from their graves. Heaven, as with a voice of thunder, calls on you to arise from the dust.

Let your motto be resistance! *resistance!* RESISTANCE! No oppressed people have ever secured their liberty without resistance. What kind of resistance you had better make you must decide by the circumstances that surround you, and according to the suggestion of expediency. Brethren, adieu! Trust in the living God. Labor for the peace of the human race, and remember that you are four millions!

Elizabeth Cady Stanton
(1815–1902)

Address at Seneca Falls
July 19, 1848

*The right is ours. The question now is, how shall we
get possession of what rightfully belongs to us.*

Although others made important contributions, Elizabeth Cady
Stanton is often celebrated as the most important orator of the early
women's movement. Stanton was born into a prominent family of public servants, the daughter of a congressman who, against common practice, encouraged Elizabeth to follow her intellectual curiosity and pursue an education. Her local church minister, Simon Hosack, also
fostered Stanton's pursuit of intellectual and civic commitments. At a
young age, Stanton was sent to an all-boys school to study the classics
and mathematics; in her spare time, she read nearly all the books in her
father's law office. Despite being praised for her ambition, it was clear
to Elizabeth that as a woman she would never enjoy the full esteem of
her father, nor the respect of her male contemporaries. This reality
spurred her interest in following a career committed to equal opportunity for women—an idea antithetical to thinking of the time.

In 1840 Elizabeth married Henry B. Stanton, a friend and fellow
activist in the abolitionist movement. True to form, she had the word
"obey" excised from the wedding ceremony. That same year, Stanton
met Lucretia Mott, a fellow abolitionist, with whom she later joined
forces in presiding over Seneca Falls in 1848, the first women's rights
convention. With the Declaration of Independence as her guide,
Stanton crafted the Declaration of Sentiments, which submitted that
"all men and women were created equal," with a natural right to equality in all spheres.

This address to the convention, Stanton's first in a long and distinguished career, stressed the need for women to have their own voice and
identity—not to rely on their husbands and sons for financial, social, or
political advancement. Invoking the novel term "women's rights,"
Stanton also demanded the right for women to vote, a seminal moment
in the campaign for suffrage. Although she later called her remarks "diffident," there was nothing timid about their content or delivery. Instead,
Stanton argued repeatedly for women to reject the inferior role in soci-

ety and to recognize that, with the right opportunities, they could be equal to men—intellectually, physically, and morally.

———

I SHOULD FEEL exceedingly diffident to appear before you at this time, having never before spoken in public, were I not nerved by a sense of right and duty, did I not feel the time had fully come for the question of woman's wrongs to be laid before the public, did I not believe that woman herself must do this work; for woman alone can understand the height, the depth, the length, and the breadth of her own degradation. Man cannot speak for her, because he has been educated to believe that she differs from him so materially, that he cannot judge of her thoughts, feelings, and opinions by his own. Moral beings can only judge of others by themselves. The moment they assume a different nature for any of their own kind, they utterly fail. . . .

Among the many important questions which have been brought before the public, there is none that more vitally affects the whole human family than that which is technically called Woman's Rights. Every allusion to the degraded and inferior position occupied by women all over the world has been met by scorn and abuse. From the man of highest mental cultivation to the most degraded wretch who staggers in the streets do we meet ridicule, and coarse jests, freely bestowed upon those who dare assert that woman stands by the side of man, his equal, placed here by her God, to enjoy with him the beautiful earth, which is her home as it is his, having the same sense of right and wrong, and looking to the same Being for guidance and support. So long has man exercised tyranny over her, injurious to himself and benumbing to her faculties, that few can nerve themselves to meet the storm; and so long has the chain been about her that she knows not there is a remedy. . . .

As the nations of the earth emerge from a state of barbarism, the sphere of woman gradually becomes wider, but not even under what is thought to be the full blaze of the sun of civilization, is it what God designed it to be. In every country and clime does man assume the responsibility of marking out the path for her to tread. In every country does he regard her as a being inferior to himself, and one whom he is to guide and control. From the Arabian Kerek, whose wife is obliged to steal from her husband to supply the necessities of life; from the Mahometan who forbids pigs, dogs, women and other impure animals, to enter a Mosque, and does not allow a fool, madman or woman to proclaim the hour of prayer; from the German who complacently smokes his meerschaum, while his wife, yoked with the ox, draws the plough through its furrow; from the delectable carpet-knight, who thinks an inferior style of conversation adapted to woman; to the legislator, who considers her incapable of saying what laws shall govern her, is the same feeling manifested. . . .

Let us consider . . . man's superiority, intellectually, morally, physically.

Man's intellectual superiority cannot be a question until woman has had a fair trial. When we shall have had our freedom to find out our own sphere, when we shall have had our colleges, our professions, our trades, for a century, a comparison then may be justly instituted. When woman, instead of being taxed to endow colleges where she is forbidden to enter—instead of forming sewing societies to educate "poor, but pious," young men, shall first educate herself, when she shall be just to herself before she is generous to others; improving the talents God has given her, and leaving her neighbor to do the same for himself, we shall not hear so much about this boasted superiority. . . .

In consideration of man's claim to moral superiority, glance now at our theological seminaries, our divinity students, the long line of descendants from our Apostolic fathers, the immaculate priesthood, and what do we find there? Perfect moral rectitude in every relation of life, a devoted spirit of self-sacrifice, a perfect union of thought, opinion and feeling among those who profess to worship the one God, and whose laws they feel themselves called upon to declare to a fallen race? Far from it. . . . Is the moral and religious life of this class what we might expect from minds said to be fixed on such mighty themes? By no means. . . . The lamentable want of principle among our lawyers, generally, is too well known to need comment. The everlasting backbiting and bickering of our physicians is proverbial. The disgraceful riots at our polls, where man, in performing the highest duty of citizenship, ought surely to be sober-minded, the perfect rowdyism that now characterizes the debates in our national Congress—all these are great facts which rise up against man's claim for moral superiority. In my opinion, he is infinitely woman's inferior in every moral quality, not by nature, but made so by a false education. In carrying out his own selfishness, man has greatly improved woman's moral nature, but by an almost total shipwreck of his own. Woman has now the noble virtues of the martyr. She is early schooled to self-denial and suffering. But man is not so wholly buried in selfishness that he does not sometimes get a glimpse of the narrowness of his soul, as compared with woman. Then he says, by way of an excuse for his degradation, "God made woman more self-denying than man. It is her nature. It does not cost her as much to give up her wishes, her will, her life, even, as it does him. He is naturally selfish. God made him so."

No, I think not. . . . God's commands rest upon man as well as woman. It is as much his duty to be kind, self-denying and full of good works, as it is hers. As much his duty to absent himself from scenes of violence as it is hers. A place or position that would require the sacrifice of the delicacy and refinement of woman's nature is unfit for man, for these virtues should be as carefully guarded in him as in her. The false ideas that prevail with regard to the purity necessary to constitute the perfect character in woman, and that requisite for man, has done an infinite deal of mischief in the world. I would not have woman less pure, but I would have man more so. I would have the same code of morals for both. . . .

But there is a class of objectors who say they do not claim superiority, they merely assert a difference. But you will find by following them up closely, that they soon run this difference into the old groove of superiority. . . .

We have met here to-day to discuss our rights and wrongs, civil and political, and not, as some have supposed, to go into the detail of social life alone. We do not propose to petition the legislature to make our husbands just, generous and courteous, to seat every man at the head of a cradle, and to clothe every woman in male attire. None of these points, however important they may be considered by leading men, will be touched in this Convention. . . .

We are assembled to protest against a form of government, existing without the consent of the governed—to declare our right to be free as man is free, to be represented in the government which we are taxed to support, to have such disgraceful laws as give man the power to chastise and imprison his wife, to take the wages which she earns, the property which she inherits, and, in case of separation, the children of her love; laws which make her the mere dependent on his bounty. It is to protest against such unjust laws as these that we are assembled today, and to have them, if possible, forever erased from our statute-books, deeming them a shame and a disgrace to a Christian republic in the nineteenth century. . . .

And, strange as it may seem to many, we now demand our right to vote according to the declaration of the government under which we live. . . . We have no objection to discuss the question of equality, for we feel that the weight of argument lies wholly with us, but we wish the question of equality kept distinct from the question of rights, for the proof of the one does not determine the truth of the other. All white men in this country have the same rights, however they may differ in mind, body or estate. The right is ours. The question now is, how shall we get possession of what rightfully belongs to us. We should not feel so sorely grieved if no man who had not attained the full stature of a Webster, Clay, Van Buren, or Gerrit Smith could claim the right of the elective franchise. But to have drunkards, idiots, horse-racing, rumselling rowdies, ignorant foreigners, and silly boys fully recognized, while we ourselves are thrust out from all the rights that belong to citizens, it is too grossly insulting to the dignity of woman to be longer quietly submitted to. The right is ours. Have it we must. Use it we will. The pens, the tongues, the fortunes, the indomitable wills of many women are already pledged to secure this right.

The great truth, that no just government can be formed without the consent of the governed, we shall echo and re-echo in the ears of the unjust judge, until by continual coming we shall weary him. . . .

But what would woman gain by voting? Men must know the advantages of voting, for they all seem very tenacious about the right. Think you, if woman had a vote in this government, that all those laws affecting her interests would so entirely violate every principle of right and justice? Had woman a vote to give, might not the office-holders and seekers propose some change in her condition? Might not Woman's Rights become as great a question as free soil?

"But you are already represented by your fathers, husbands, brothers and sons?" Let your statute books answer the question. We have had enough of such representation. In nothing is woman's true happiness consulted. Men like to call her an angel—to feed her on what they think sweet food—nourishing her vanity; to make her believe that her organization is so much finer than theirs, that she is not fitted to struggle with the tempests of public life, but needs their care and protection!! Care and protection—such as the wolf gives the lamb—such as the eagle the hare he carries to his eyrie!! Most cunningly he entraps her, and then takes from her all those rights which are dearer to him than life itself—rights which have been baptized in blood—and the maintenance of which is even now rocking to their foundations the kingdoms of the Old World.

The most discouraging, the most lamentable aspect our cause wears is the indifference, indeed, the contempt, with which women themselves regard the movement. Where the subject is introduced, among those even who claim to be intelligent and educated, it is met by the scornful curl of the lip, and by expression of ridicule and disgust. But we shall hope better things of them when they are enlightened in regard to their present position. When women know the laws and constitutions under which they live, they will not publish their degradation by declaring themselves satisfied, nor their ignorance, by declaring they have all the rights they want. . . .

Let woman live as she should. Let her feel her accountability to her Maker. Let her know that her spirit is fitted for as high a sphere as man's, and that her soul requires food as pure and exalted as his. Let her live *first* for God, and she will not make imperfect man an object of reverence and awe. Teach her her responsibility as a being of conscience and reason, that all earthly support is weak and unstable, that her only safe dependence is the arm of omnipotence, and that true happiness springs from duty accomplished. Thus will she learn the lesson of individual responsibility for time and eternity. That neither father, husband, brother, or son, however willing they may be, can discharge her high duties of life, or stand in her stead when called into the presence of the great Searcher of Hearts at the last day. . . .

Let me here notice one of the greatest humbugs of the day, which has long found for itself the most valuable tool in woman—"The Education Society." The idea to me, is simply absurd, for women, in their present degradation and ignorance, to form sewing societies for the education of young men for the ministry. An order of beings above themselves, claiming to be gifted with superior powers, having all the avenues to learning, wealth and distinction thrown freely open to them, who, if they had but the energy to avail themselves of all these advantages, could easily secure an education for themselves, while woman herself, poor, friendless, robbed of all her rights, oppressed on all sides, civilly, religiously and socially, must needs go ignorant herself. Now, is not the idea preposterous, for such a being to educate a great, strong, lazy man, by working day and night with her needle, stitch, stitch, and the poor widow always throws in her mite, being taught to believe that all she gives for the decoration of churches and their black-coated gentry, is given unto the Lord. I think a man, who, under such conditions, has the moral hardihood to take an education at the hands of woman, and at such an expense to her, should, as soon as he graduates, with all his honors thick upon him, take the first ship for Turkey, and there pass his days in earnest efforts to rouse the inmates of the harems to a true sense of their degradation, and not, as is his custom, immediately enter our pulpits to tell us of his superiority to us, "weaker vessels,"—his prerogative to command, ours to obey, his duty to preach, ours to keep silence. . . . The last time when an appeal of this kind was made to me, I told the young girl that I would send her to school a year, if she would go, but I would never again give one red cent to the Education Society. And I do hope that every Christian woman, who has the least regard for her sex, will make the same resolve. We have worked long enough for man, and at a most unjust and unwarrantable sacrifice of self, yet he gives no evidence of gratitude, but has, thus far, treated his benefactors with scorn, ridicule and neglect. . . .

One common objection to this movement is, that if the principles of freedom and equality which we advocate were put into practice, it would destroy all harmony in the domestic circle. Here let me ask, how many truly harmonious households have we now? . . . The only happy households we now see are those in which husband and wife share equally in counsel and government. There can be no true dignity or independence where there is subordination to the absolute will of another, no happiness without freedom. Let us then have no fears that the movement will disturb what is seldom found, a truly united and happy family. . . .

There seems now to be a kind of moral stagnation in our midst. Philanthropists have done their utmost to rouse the nation to a sense of its sins. . . . Our churches are multiplying on all sides, our missionary societies, Sunday schools, and prayer meetings and innumerable charitable and reform organizations are all in operation, but still the tide of vice is swelling, and threatens the destruction of everything, and the battlements of righteousness are weak against the raging elements of sin and death. Verily, the world waits the coming of some new element, some purifying power, some spirit of mercy and love. The voice of woman has been silenced in the state, the church, and the home, but man cannot fulfill his destiny alone, he cannot redeem his race unaided. There are deep and tender chords of sympathy and love in the heart of the down-fallen and oppressed that woman can touch more skillfully than man. The world has never yet seen a truly great and virtuous nation, because in the degradation of woman the very fountains of life are poisoned at their source. It is vain to look for silver and gold from mines of copper and lead. It is the wise mother that has the wise son. So long as your women are slaves you may throw your colleges and churches to the winds. . . . Truly are the sins of the fathers visited upon the children to the third and fourth generation. God, in his wisdom, has so linked the whole human family together that any violence done at one end of the chain is felt throughout its length, and here, too, is the law of restoration, as in woman all have fallen, so in her elevation shall the race be recreated.

. . . We do not expect our path will be strewn with the flowers of popular applause, but over the thorns of bigotry and prejudice will be our way, and on our banners will beat the dark storm-clouds of opposition from those who have entrenched themselves behind the stormy bulwarks of custom and authority, and who have fortified their position by every means, holy and unholy. But we will steadfastly abide the result. Unmoved we will bear it aloft. Undaunted we will unfurl it to the gale, for we know that the storm cannot rend from it a shred, that the electric flash will but more clearly show to us the glorious words inscribed upon it, "Equality of Rights."

SOJOURNER TRUTH
(1797–1883)

Ar'n't I a Woman?
1851

When woman gets her rights, man will be right.

Born a slave in a Dutch settlement, Isabella Baumfee—later Sojourner Truth—received her emancipation in 1827 under New York state law. One of thirteen children, Isabella spoke Dutch until age eleven, when she was sold to a new master, who forced her to use English. Her Dutch, however, remained with her for the rest of her life.

In 1843, after working in several religious communities, Isabella officially adopted the name *Sojourner Truth*. She then embarked on a spiritual journey through New York and Connecticut, stopping to preach along the way, and eventually landed in Northampton, Massachusetts. There, she joined a utopian community and met abolitionists William Lloyd Garrison and Frederick Douglass. Truth soon added women's suffrage and abolition to her sermons, quickly earned a reputation for her powerful, public voice and for her firsthand and often gruesome accounts of slavery. Self-educated, most of her lectures were deeply influenced by her knowledge of Scripture. It was not long before she became one of the most powerful activists in the black, women's, and temperance movements.

As charismatic and persuasive as ever, Truth was nearly fifty-five years old when she delivered this celebrated speech to the 1851 Women's Rights Convention in Akron, Ohio. Speaking in colloquial language, she exposed the economic and social disadvantages suffered by women, including limited legal rights, occupational opportunities, and equal pay. She urged all women—black or white—to "be strong" in their quest for advancement and to join the abolitionist movement in its fight against slavery.

After the Civil War, Truth worked vigorously to aid newly freed southern slaves, continuing to lecture and preach until her retirement. In 1864 she was received at the White House by Abraham Lincoln and, shortly before her death, was appointed to the National Freedmen's Relief Association.

Harriet Beecher Stowe later described Truth: "I do not recall ever to have been conversant with anyone who had more of that silent and subtle power which we call personal presence than this person."

WELL, CHILDREN, where there is so much racket there must be something out o' kilter. I think that 'twixt the Negroes of the South and the women of the North all a-talking about rights, the white men will be in a fix pretty soon.

But what's all this here talking about? That man over there says that women need to be helped into carriages, and lifted over ditches, and to have the best place everywhere. Nobody ever helps me into carriages, or over mud puddles or gives me any best place *(and raising herself to her full height and her voice to a pitch like rolling thunder, she asked),* and aren't I a woman? Look at me! Look at my arm! *(And she bared her right arm to the shoulder, showing her tremendous muscular power.)* I have plowed, and planted, and gathered into barns, and no man could head me—and aren't I a woman? I could work as much and eat as much as a man (when I could get it), and bear the lash as well—and aren't I a woman? I have borne thirteen children and seen them almost all sold off into slavery, and when I cried out with a mother's grief, none but Jesus heard—and aren't I a woman? Then they talk about this thing in the head—what's this they call it? *("Intellect," whispered someone near.)* That's it, honey. What's that got to do with woman's rights or Negroes' rights? If my cup won't hold but a pint and yours holds a quart, wouldn't you be mean not to let me have my little half-measure full?

Then that little man in black there, he says women can't have as much rights as man, 'cause Christ wasn't a woman. Where did your Christ come from? *(Rolling thunder could not have stilled that crowd as did those deep, wonderful tones, as she stood there with outstretched arms and eye of fire. Raising her voice still louder, she repeated,)* Where did your Christ come from? From God and a woman. Man had nothing to do with him.

If the first woman God ever made was strong enough to turn the world upside down, all alone, these together ought to be able to turn it back and get it right side up again; and now they are asking to do it, the men better let them.

'Bliged to you for hearing on me, and now old Sojourner hasn't got anything more to say.

FREDERICK DOUGLASS
(1818–1895)

What to the Slave Is the Fourth of July?
JULY 5, 1852

*I hear the mournful wail of millions! whose chains . . . are today
rendered more intolerable by the jubilee shouts that reach them.*

One of the most distinguished figures in American history, Frederick
Douglass was born a slave on Holmes Hill Farm, near the town of
Easton on Maryland's Eastern Shore. In 1838, only months after escap-
ing bondage through the Underground Railroad, Douglass read his first
issue of William Lloyd Garrison's anti-slavery weekly, the *Liberator*.
Inspired by Garrison's activism, Douglass delivered his own abolitionist
orations three years later, speaking to the Convention of the
Massachusetts Anti-Slavery Society.

Hailed by the community as compelling and persuasive, Douglass
launched a career as arguably the most recognized and powerful of
black orators. In city after city, Douglass recounted his experiences with
slavery, decrying its practice, and demanding immediate abolition.
Later, during the war, he served as an adviser to President Abraham
Lincoln and fought for the adoption of the constitutional amendments
guaranteeing suffrage and civil liberties for all African-American men.

Douglass delivered the following remarks—the first of his celebrated Fourth of July speeches—to a predominantly white audience
at Corinthian Hall in Rochester, New York. Perhaps surprising his
audience, Douglass used the Independence Day theme to highlight
the inherent hypocrisy of American democracy, including its discriminatory legal and social institutions that unabashedly condoned and
even encouraged slavery. As was often the case, he took the strict line
that slavery was never the true intent of the Founders and argued
that, even if popular sentiment currently dictated otherwise, the inhumane institution of slavery was fundamentally un-American and
unpatriotic.

THE FACT IS, ladies and gentlemen, the distance between this platform and
the slave plantation, from which I escaped, is considerable—and the difficul-

ties to be overcome in getting from the latter to the former are by no means slight. That I am here today is, to me, a matter of astonishment as well as of gratitude. You will not, therefore, be surprised, if in what I have to say I evince no elaborate preparation, nor grace my speech with any high-sounding exordium. With little experience and with less learning, I have been able to throw my thoughts hastily and imperfectly together; and trusting to your patient and generous indulgence, I will proceed to lay them before you.

This, for the purpose of this celebration, is the Fourth of July. It is the birthday of your National Independence, and of your political freedom. This to you, is what the Passover was to the emancipated people of God. It carries your minds back to the day, and to the act of your great deliverance; and to the signs and to the wonders associated with that act and that day. . . .

Fellow citizens, I shall not presume to dwell at length on the associations that cluster about this day. The simple story of it is, that seventy-six years ago the people of this country were British subjects. The style and title of your "sovereign people" (in which you now glory) was not then born. You were under the British Crown. Your fathers esteemed the English government as the home government, and England as the fatherland. This home government, you know, although a considerable distance from your home, did, in the exercise of its parental prerogatives, impose upon its colonial children such restraints, burdens and limitations as, in its mature judgment, it deemed wise, right and proper.

⌒

Fellow citizens, pardon me, allow me to ask, why am I called upon to speak here today? What have I, or those I represent, to do with your national independence? Are the great principles of political freedom and of natural justice, embodied in that Declaration of Independence, extended to us? and am I, therefore, called upon to bring our humble offering to the national altar and to confess the benefits and express devout gratitude for the blessings resulting from your independence to us?

⌒

But such is not the state of the case. I say it with a sad sense of the disparity between us. I am not included within the pale of this glorious anniversary! Your high independence only reveals the immeasurable distance between us. The blessings in which you, this day, rejoice, are not enjoyed in common. The rich inheritance of justice, liberty, prosperity and independence, bequeathed by your fathers, is shared by you, not by me. The sunlight that brought light and healing to you, has brought stripes and death to me. This Fourth of July is *yours,* not *mine.* *You* may rejoice, *I* must mourn. To drag a man in fetters into the grand illuminated temple of liberty and call upon him to join you in joyous anthems were inhuman mockery and sacrilegious irony. Do you mean, citizens, to mock me, by asking me to speak today? If so, there is a parallel to your conduct. And let me warn you that it is dangerous to copy the example of a nation whose crimes, towering up to heaven, were thrown down by the breath of the Almighty, burying that nation in irrevocable ruin! I can today take up the plaintive lament of a peeled and woe-smitten people! . . .

Fellow citizens, above your national, tumultuous joy I hear the mournful wail of millions! whose chains, heavy and grievous yesterday, are today rendered more intolerable by the jubilee shouts that reach them. If I do forget, if I do not faithfully remember those bleeding children of sorrow this day, "may my right hand forget her cunning, and may my tongue cleave to the roof of my mouth!" To forget them, to pass lightly over their wrongs and to chime in with the popular theme would be treason most scandalous and shocking and would make me a reproach before God and the world. My subject, then, fellow citizens, is American slavery. I shall see this day and its popular characteristics from the slave's point of view. Standing there identified with the American bondman, making his wrongs mine, I do not hesitate to declare, with all my soul, that the character and conduct of this nation never looked blacker to me than on this Fourth of July. Whether we turn to the declarations of the past or to the professions of the present, the conduct of the nation seems equally hideous and revolting. America is false to the past, false to the present, and solemnly binds herself to be false to the future. Standing with God and the crushed and bleeding slave on this occasion, I will, in the name of humanity which is outraged, in the name of liberty which is fettered, in the name of the Constitution and the Bible which are disregarded and trampled upon, dare to call in question and to denounce, with all the emphasis I can command, everything that serves to perpetuate slavery—the great sin and shame of America! "I will not equivocate; I will not excuse"; I will use the severest language I can command; and yet not one word shall escape me that any man, whose judgement is not blinded by prejudice, or who is not at heart a slaveholder, shall not confess to be right and just.

But I fancy I hear some one of my audience say, "It is just in this circumstance that you and your brother abolitionists fail to make a favorable impression on the public mind. Would you argue more and denounce less, would you persuade more and rebuke less, your cause would be much more likely to succeed." But, I submit, where all is plain there is nothing to be argued. What point in the antislavery creed would you have me argue? On what branch of the subject do the people of this country need light? Must I undertake to prove that the slave is a man? That point is conceded already. Nobody doubts it. The slaveholders themselves acknowledge it in the enactments of laws for their government. They acknowledge it when they punish disobedience on the part of the slave. There are seventy-two crimes in the state of Virginia which, if committed by a black man (no matter how ignorant he be), subject him to the punishment of death; while only two of the same crimes will subject a white man to the like punishment. What is this but the acknowledgment that the slave is a moral, intellectual and responsible being? The manhood of the slave is conceded. It is admitted in the fact that Southern statute books are covered with enactments forbidding, under severe fines and penalties, the teaching of the slave to read or to write. When you can point to any such laws in reference to the beasts of the field, then I may consent to argue the manhood of the slave. When the dogs in your streets, when the fowls of the air, when the cattle on your hills, when the fish of the sea and the reptiles that crawl shall be unable to distinguish the slave from a brute, *then* will I argue with you that the slave is a man!

For the present, it is enough to affirm the equal manhood of the Negro race. Is it not astonishing that, while we are plowing, planting and reaping, using all kinds of mechanical tools, erecting houses, constructing bridges, building ships, working in metals of brass, iron, copper, silver and gold; that, while we are reading, writing and ciphering, acting as clerks, merchants and secretaries, having among us lawyers, doctors, ministers, poets, authors, editors, orators and teachers; that, while we are engaged in all manner of enterprises common to other men, digging gold in California, capturing the whale in the Pacific, feeding sheep and cattle on the hillside, living, moving, acting, thinking, planning, living in families as husbands, wives and children, and, above all, confessing and worshiping the Christian's God and looking hopefully for life and immortality beyond the grave, we are called upon to prove that we are men!

Would you have me argue that man is entitled to liberty? that he is the rightful owner of his own body? You have already declared it. Must I argue the wrongfulness of slavery? Is that a question for republicans? Is it to be settled by the rules of logic and argumentation, as a matter beset with great difficulty, involving a doubtful application of the principle of justice, hard to be understood? How should I look today, in the presence of Americans, dividing and subdividing a discourse, to show that men have a natural right to freedom, speaking of it relatively and positively, negatively and affirmatively? To do so would be to make myself ridiculous and to offer an insult to your understanding. There is not a man beneath the canopy of heaven that does not know that slavery is wrong *for him*.

What, then, remains to be argued? Is it that slavery is not divine; that God did not establish it; that our doctors of divinity are mistaken? There is blasphemy in the thought. That which is inhuman, cannot be divine! *Who* can reason on such a proposition? They that can, may; I cannot. The time for such argument is passed. . . .

⟿

What, to the American slave, is your Fourth of July? I answer: a day that reveals to him, more than all other days in the year, the gross injustice and cruelty to which he is the constant victim. To him, your celebration is a sham; your boasted liberty an unholy license; your national greatness swelling vanity; your sounds of rejoicing are empty and heartless; your denunciation of tyrants brass-fronted impudence; your shouts of liberty and equality hollow mockery; your prayers and hymns, your sermons and thanksgivings, with all your religious parade and solemnity, are to Him mere bombast, fraud, deception, impiety and hypocrisy—a thin veil to cover up crimes which would disgrace a nation of savages. There is not a nation on the earth guilty of practices more shocking and bloody than are the people of the United States at this very hour.

Go where you may, search where you will, roam through all the monarchies and despotisms of the Old World, travel through South America, search out every abuse, and when you have found the last, lay your facts by the side of the everyday practices of this nation, and you will say with me, that, for revolting barbarity and shameless hypocrisy, America reigns without a rival.

Take the American slave trade, which, we are told by the papers, is especially prosperous just now. Ex-Senator Benton tells us that the price of men was never higher than now. He mentions the fact to show that slavery is in no danger. This trade is one of the peculiarities of American institutions. It is carried on in all the large towns and cities in one half of this confederacy; and millions are pocketed every year by dealers in this horrid traffic. In several states this trade is a chief source of wealth. It is called (in contradistinction to the foreign slave trade) *"the internal slave trade."* It is probably called so, too, in order to divert from it the horror with which the foreign slave trade is contemplated. That trade has long since been denounced by this government as piracy. It has been denounced with burning words from the high places of the nation as an execrable traffic. To arrest it, to put an end to it, this nation keeps a squadron, at immense cost, on the coast of Africa. Everywhere in this country it is safe to speak of this foreign slave trade as a most inhuman traffic, opposed alike to the laws of God and of man. The duty to extirpate and destroy it is admitted even by our doctors of divinity. In order to put an end to it, some of these last have consented that their colored brethren (nominally free) should leave this country, and establish themselves on the western coast of Africa! It is, however, a notable fact that, while so much execration is poured out by Americans upon all those engaged in the foreign slave trade, the men engaged in the slave trade between the states pass without condemnation, and their business is deemed honorable.

Behold the practical operation of this internal slave trade, the American slave trade, sustained by American politics and American religion. Here you will see men and women reared like swine for the market. You know what is a swine-drover? I will show you a man-drover. They inhabit all our Southern states. They perambulate the country and crowd the highways of the nation with droves of human stock. You will see one of these human flesh jobbers, armed with pistol, whip and bowie knife, driving a company of a hundred men, women and children, from the Potomac to the slave market at New Orleans. These wretched people are to be sold singly or in lots, to suit purchasers. They are food for the cotton field and the deadly sugar mill. Mark the sad procession, as it moves wearily along, and the inhuman wretch who drives them. Hear his savage yells and his bloodcurdling oaths, as he hurries on his affrighted captives! There, see the old man with locks thinned and gray. Cast one glance, if you please, upon that young mother, whose shoulders are bare to the scorching sun, her briny tears falling on the brow of the babe in her arms. See, too, that girl of thirteen, weeping—*yes,* weeping—as she thinks of the mother from whom she has been torn! The drove moves tardily. Heat and sorrow have nearly consumed their strength; suddenly you hear a quick snap, like the discharge of a rifle; the fetters clank, and the chain rattles simultaneously; your ears are saluted with a scream, that seems to have torn its way to the center of your soul! The crack you heard was the sound of the slave whip; the scream you heard was from the woman you saw with the babe. Her speed had faltered under the weight of her child and her chains! That gash on her shoulder tells her to move on. Follow this drove to New Orleans. Attend the auction; see men examined like horses; see the forms of women rudely and brutally exposed to the shocking gaze of American slave buyers. See this drove sold and separated forever; and never forget the deep, sad sobs that arose from that scattered multitude. Tell me, citizens, where, under the sun, you can witness a spectacle more fiendish and shocking. Yet this is but a glance at the American slave trade, as it exists, at this moment, in the ruling part of the United States.

I was born amid such sights and scenes. To me the American slave trade is a terrible reality. When a child, my soul was often pierced with a sense of its horrors. I lived on Philpot Street, Fell's Point, Baltimore, and have watched from the wharves the slave ships in the Basin, anchored from the shore, with their cargoes of human flesh, waiting for favorable winds to waft them down the Chesapeake. There was at that time a grand slave mart kept at the head of Pratt Street by Austin Woldfolk. His agents were sent into every town and county in Maryland, announcing their arrival, through the papers, and on flaming *handbills* headed "Cash for Negroes." These men were generally well-dressed men, and very captivating in their manners; ever ready to drink, to treat and to gamble. The fate of many a slave has depended upon the turn of a single card; and many a child has been snatched from the arms of its mother by bargains arranged in a state of brutal drunkenness.

The flesh mongers gather up their victims by dozens, and drive them, chained, to the general depot at Baltimore. When a sufficient number has been collected here, a ship is chartered for the purpose of conveying the forlorn crew to Mobile, or to New Orleans. From the slave prison to the ship, they are usually driven in the darkness of night; for since the antislavery agitation a certain caution is observed.

~

But a still more inhuman, disgraceful and scandalous state of things remains to be presented. By an act of the American congress, not yet two years old, slavery has been nationalized in its most horrible and revolting form. By that act, Mason and Dixon's line has been obliterated; New York has become as Virginia; and the power to hold, hunt and sell men, women and children as slaves remains no longer a mere state institution, but is now an institution of the whole United States. The power is coextensive with the star-spangled banner and American Christianity. Where these go, may also go the merciless slave hunter. Where these are, man is not sacred. He is a bird for the sportsman's gun. By that most foul and fiendish of all human decrees, the liberty and person of every man are put in peril. Your broad republican domain is hunting ground for *men*. *Not* for thieves and robbers, enemies of society, merely, but for men guilty of no crime. Your lawmakers have commanded all good citizens to engage in this hellish sport. Your President, your Secretary of State, your *lords, nobles* and ecclesiastics enforce, as a duty you owe to your free and glorious country, and to your God, that you do this accursed thing. Not fewer than forty Americans have, within the past two years, been hunted down and, without a moment's warning, hurried away in chains and consigned to slavery and excruciating torture. Some of these have had wives and children, dependent on them for bread; but of this, no account was made. The right of the hunter to his prey stands superior to the right of marriage and to *all* rights in this republic, the rights of God included! For black men there is neither law nor justice, humanity nor religion. The Fugitive Slave Law makes mercy to them a crime; and bribes the judge who tries them. An American judge gets ten dollars for every victim he consigns to slavery, and five, when he fails to do so. The oath of any two villains is sufficient, under this hell-black enactment, to send the most pious and exemplary black man into the remorseless jaws of slavery! His own testimony is nothing. He can bring no witnesses for himself. The minister of American justice is bound by the law to hear but *one* side; and *that* side is the side of the oppressor. Let this damning fact be perpetually told.

Let it be thundered around the world that in tyrant-killing, king-hating, people-loving, democratic, Christian America the seats of justice are filled with judges who hold their offices under an open and palpable *bribe,* and are bound, in deciding the case of a man's liberty, *to hear only his accusers!*

In glaring violation of justice, in shameless disregard of the forms of administering law, in cunning arrangement to entrap the defenseless, and in diabolical intent, this Fugitive Slave Law stands alone in the annals of tyrannical legislation. I doubt if there be another nation on the globe having the brass and the baseness to put such a law on the statute book. If any man in this assembly thinks differently from me in this matter and feels able to disprove my statements, I will gladly confront him at any suitable time and place he may select.

I take this law to be one of the grossest infringements of Christian liberty, and if the churches and ministers of our country were not stupidly blind or most wickedly indifferent, they too would so regard it.

At the very moment that they are thanking God for the enjoyment of civil and religious liberty, and for the right to worship God according to the dictates of their own consciences, they are utterly silent in respect to a law which robs religion of its chief significance and makes it utterly worthless to a world lying in wickedness. Did this law concern the "*mint, anise and cumin,*" abridge the right to sing psalms, to partake of the sacrament or to engage in any of the ceremonies of religion, it would be smitten by the thunder of a thousand pulpits. A general shout would go up from the church demanding *repeal, repeal, instant repeal!* And it would go hard with that politician who presumed to solicit the votes of the people without inscribing this motto on his banner. Further, if this demand were not complied with, another Scotland would be added to the history of religious liberty, and the stern old covenanters would be thrown into the shade. A John Knox would be seen at every church door and heard from every pulpit, and Fillmore would have no more quarter than was shown by Knox to the beautiful, but treacherous, Queen Mary of Scotland. The fact that the church of our country (with fractional exceptions) does not esteem "the Fugitive Slave Law" as a declaration of war against religious liberty, implies that that church regards religion simply as a form of worship, an empty ceremony, and *not* a vital principle, requiring active benevolence, justice, love and good will towards man. It esteems sacrifice above mercy, psalm singing above right doing, solemn meetings above practical righteousness. A worship that can be conducted by persons who refuse to give shelter to the houseless, to give bread to the hungry, clothing to the naked, and who enjoin obedience to a law forbidding these acts of mercy is a curse, not a blessing to mankind. The Bible addresses all such persons as "scribes, pharisees, hypocrites, who pay tithe of *mint, anise* and *cumin,* and have omitted the weightier matters of the law, judgment, mercy and faith."

But the church of this country is not only indifferent to the wrongs of the slave, it actually takes sides with the oppressors. It has made itself the bulwark of American slavery and the shield of American slave hunters. Many of its most eloquent divines, who stand as the very lights of the church, have shamelessly given the sanction of religion and the Bible to the whole slave system. They have taught that man may, properly, be a slave; that the relation of master and slave is ordained of God; that to send back an escaped bondman to his master is clearly the duty of all the followers of the Lord Jesus Christ; and this horrible blasphemy is palmed off upon the world for Christianity.

For my part, I would say, Welcome infidelity! welcome atheism! welcome anything—in preference to the gospel, *as preached by those divines.* They convert the very name of religion into an engine of tyranny and barbarous cruelty, and serve to confirm more infidels, in this age, than all the infidel writings of Thomas Paine, Voltaire and Bolingbroke put together have done! These ministers make religion a cold and flinty-hearted thing, having neither principles of right action nor bowels of compassion. They strip the love of God of its beauty and leave the throne of religion a huge, horrible, repulsive form. It is a religion for oppressors, tyrants, man stealers, and *thugs.* It is not that "*pure and undefiled religion*" which is from above, and which is "*first pure, then peaceable, easy to be entreated,* full of mercy and good fruits, *without partiality and without hypocrisy,*" but a religion which favors the rich against the poor; which exalts the proud above the humble; which divides mankind into two classes, tyrants and slaves; which says to the man in chains, *stay there,* and to the oppressor, *oppress on;* it is a religion which may be professed and enjoyed by all the robbers and enslavers of mankind.

Americans! your republican politics, not less than your republican religion, are flagrantly inconsistent. You boast of your love of liberty, your superior civilization and your pure Christianity, while the whole political power of the nation (as embodied in the two great political parties) is solemnly pledged to support and perpetuate the enslavement of three millions of your countrymen. You hurl your anathemas at the crowned-headed tyrants of Russia and Austria and pride yourselves on your democratic institutions, while you yourselves consent to be the mere *tools* and *bodyguards* of the tyrants of Virginia and Carolina. You invite to your shores fugitives of oppression from abroad, honor them with banquets, greet them with ovations, cheer them, toast them, salute them, protect them, and pour out your money to them like water; but the fugitives from your own land you advertise, hunt, arrest, shoot and kill. You glory in your refinement and your universal education; yet you maintain a system as barbarous and dreadful as ever stained the character of a nation—a system begun in avarice, supported in pride, and perpetuated in cruelty. . . .

Fellow citizens, I will not enlarge further on your national inconsistencies. The existence of slavery in this country brands your republicanism as a sham, your humanity as a base pretense, and your Christianity as a lie. It destroys your moral power abroad; it corrupts your politicians at home. It saps the foundation of religion; it makes your name a hissing and a byword to a mocking earth. It is the antagonistic force in your government, the only thing that seriously disturbs and endangers your union. It fetters your progress; it is the enemy of improvement; the deadly foe of education; it fosters pride; it breeds insolence; it promotes vice; it shelters crime; it is a curse to the earth that supports it; and yet you cling to it as if it were the sheet anchor of all your hopes. Oh, be warned! Be warned! A horrible reptile is coiled up in your nation's bosom; the venomous creature is nursing at the tender breast of your youthful republic; *for the love of God, tear away* and fling from you the hideous monster, and *let the weight of twenty millions crush and destroy it forever!*

But it is answered in reply to all this, that precisely what I have now denounced is, in fact, guaranteed and sanctioned by the Constitution of the United States; that the right to hold and hunt slaves is part of that Constitution framed by the illustrious father of this republic.

Allow me to say, in conclusion, notwithstanding the dark picture I have this day presented, of the state of the nation, I do not despair of this country. There are forces in operation which must inevitably work the downfall of slavery. "The arm of the Lord is not shortened," and the doom of slavery is certain. I, therefore, leave off where I began, with hope. While drawing encouragement from "the Declaration of Independence," the great principles it contains and the genius of American institutions, my spirit is also cheered by the obvious tendencies of the age. Nations do not now stand in the same relation to each other that they did ages ago. No nation can now shut itself up from the surrounding world and trot round in the same old path of its fathers without interference. The time was when such could be done. Long-established customs of hurtful character could formerly fence themselves in and do their evil work with social impunity. Knowledge was then confined and enjoyed by the privileged few, and the multitude walked on in mental darkness. But a change has now come over the affairs of mankind. Walled cities and empires have become unfashionable. The arm of commerce has borne away the gates of the strong city. Intelligence is penetrating the darkest corners of the globe. It makes its pathway over and under the sea, as well as on the earth. Wind, steam, and lightning are its chartered agents. Oceans no longer divide, but link nations together. From Boston to London is now a holiday excursion. Space is comparatively annihilated. Thoughts expressed on one side of the Atlantic are distinctly heard on the other.

William Lloyd Garrison
(1805–1879)

No Compromise with the Evil of Slavery
1854

Every slave is a stolen man; every slaveholder is a man stealer.

For more than three decades—from the first issue of his weekly paper in 1831 until after the Civil War—William Lloyd Garrison excoriated slavery and espoused rights for African Americans.

Born in Newburyport, Massachusetts, the son of a merchant sailing master, Garrison was only a young boy when his father deserted his family. To help put food on the table, William sold homemade molasses and delivered food. In 1818, after several apprenticeships, Garrison began working for the *Newburyport Herald* as a writer and an editor, honing the skills he would utilize later in life.

At twenty-five Garrison joined the abolitionist movement, associating first with the American Colonization Society, an organization that supported the emigration of freed blacks to the west coast of Africa. By 1830, Garrison rejected the society's racist undertones and its lukewarm commitment to abolition. Two years later, he helped organize the New England Anti-Slavery Society and the American Anti-Slavery Society, the first organizations committed to the immediate emancipation of all slaves.

Garrison then returned to Massachusetts and began publishing an anti-slavery newspaper called the *Liberator.* Page after page, he promoted abolition and emancipation—going so far as to advocate northern secession from the Union because of southern slavery.

Garrison delivered this fiery address in 1854, the same year that the Kansas–Nebraska Act created the possibility that popular majorities in the territories carved out of the Louisiana Purchase could legalize slavery. In his characteristically blunt language, Garrison called for total abolition, urging his countrymen to stand with God against the "peculiar institution" of slavery.

LET ME DEFINE MY POSITIONS, and at the same time challenge anyone to show wherein they are untenable.

I am a believer in that portion of the Declaration of American Independence in which it is set forth, as among self-evident truths, "that all men are created equal; that they are endowed by their Creator with certain inalienable rights; that among these are life, liberty, and the pursuit of happiness." Hence, I am an abolitionist. Hence, I cannot but regard oppression in every form—and most of all, that which turns a man into a thing—with indignation and abhorrence. Not to cherish these feelings would be recreancy to principle. They who desire me to be dumb on the subject of slavery, unless I will open my mouth in its defense, ask me to give the lie to my professions, to degrade my manhood, and to stain my soul. I will not be a liar, a poltroon, or a hypocrite, to accommodate any party, to gratify any sect, to escape any odium or peril, to save any interest, to preserve any institution, or to promote any object. Convince me that one man may rightfully make another man his slave, and I will no longer subscribe to the Declaration of Independence. Convince me that liberty is not the inalienable birthright of every human being, of whatever complexion or clime, and I will give that instrument to the consuming fire. I do not know how to espouse freedom and slavery together. I do not know how to worship God and Mammon at the same time. If other men choose to go upon all fours, I choose to stand erect, as God designed every man to stand. If, practically falsifying its heaven-attested principles, this nation denounces me for refusing to imitate its example, then, adhering all the more tenaciously to those principles, I will not cease to rebuke it for its guilty inconsistency. Numerically, the contest may be an unequal one, for the time being; but the author of liberty and the source of justice, the adorable God, is more than multitudinous, and he will defend the right. My crime is that I will not go with the multitude to do evil. My singularity is that when I say that freedom is of God and slavery is of the devil, I mean just what I say. My fanaticism is that I insist on the American people abolishing slavery or ceasing to prate of the rights of man. . . .

The abolitionism which I advocate is as absolute as the law of God, and as unyielding as his throne. It admits of no compromise. Every slave is a stolen man; every slaveholder is a man stealer. By no precedent, no example, no law, no compact, no purchase, no bequest, no inheritance, no combination of circumstances, is slaveholding right or justifiable. While a slave remains in his fetters, the land must have no rest. Whatever sanctions his doom must be pronounced accursed. The law that makes him a chattel is to be trampled underfoot; the compact that is formed at his expense, and cemented with his blood, is null and void; the church that consents to his enslavement is horribly atheistical; the religion that receives to its communion the enslaver is the embodiment of all criminality. Such, at least, is the verdict of my own soul, on the supposition that I am to be the slave; that my wife is to be sold from me for the vilest purposes; that my children are to be torn from my arms, and disposed of to the highest bidder, like sheep in the market. And who am I but a man? What right have I to be free, that another man cannot prove himself to possess by nature? Who or what are my wife and children, that they should not be herded with four-footed beasts, as well as others thus sacredly related? . . .

If the slaves are not men; if they do not possess human instincts, passions, faculties, and powers; if they are below accountability, and devoid of reason; if for them there is no hope of immortality, no God, no heaven, no hell; if, in short, they are what the slave code declares them to be, rightly "deemed, sold, taken, reputed and adjudged in law to be chattels personal in the hands of their owners and possessors, and their executors, administrators and assigns, to all intents, constructions, and purposes whatsoever"; then, undeniably, I am mad, and can no longer discriminate between a man and a beast. But, in that case, away with the horrible incongruity of giving them oral instruction, of teaching them the catechism, of recognizing them as suitably qualified to be members of Christian churches, of extending to them the ordinance of baptism, and admitting them to the communion table, and enumerating many of them as belonging to the household of faith! Let them be no more included in our religious sympathies or denominational statistics than are the dogs in our streets, the swine in our pens, or the utensils in our dwellings. It is right to own, to buy, to sell, to inherit, to breed, and to control them, in the most absolute sense. All constitutions and laws which forbid their possession ought to be so far modified or repealed as to concede the right.

But, if they are men; if they are to run the same career of immortality with ourselves; if the same law of God is over them as over all others; if they have souls to be saved or lost; if Jesus included them among those for whom he laid down his life; if Christ is within many of them "the hope of glory"; then, when I claim for them all that we claim for ourselves, because we are created in the image of God, I am guilty of no extravagance, but am bound, by every principle of honor, by all the claims of human nature, by obedience to Almighty God, to "remember them that are in bonds as bound with them," and to demand their immediate and unconditional emancipation. . . .

These are solemn times. It is not a struggle for national salvation; for the nation, as such, seems doomed beyond recovery. The reason why the South rules, and the North falls prostrate in servile terror, is simply this: with the South, the preservation of slavery is paramount to all other considerations—above party success, denominational unity, pecuniary interest, legal integrity, and constitutional obligation. With the North, the preservation of the Union is placed above all other things—above honor, justice, freedom, integrity of soul, the Decalogue and the Golden Rule—the infinite God himself. All these she is ready to discard for the Union. Her devotion to it is the latest and the most terrible form of idolatry. She has given to the slave power a carte blanche, to be filled as it may dictate—and if, at any time, she grows restive under the yoke, and shrinks back aghast at the new atrocity contemplated, it is only necessary for that power to crack the whip of disunion over her head, as it has done again and again, and she will cower and obey like a plantation slave—for has she not sworn that she will sacrifice everything in heaven and on earth, rather than the Union?

What then is to be done? Friends of the slave, the question is not whether by our efforts we can abolish slavery, speedily or remotely—for duty is ours, the result is with God; but whether we will go with the multitude to do evil, sell our birthright for a mess of pottage, cease to cry aloud and spare not, and remain in Babylon when the command of God is "Come out of her, my people, that ye be not partakers of her sins, and that ye receive not of her plagues." Let us stand in our lot, "and having done all, to stand." At least, a remnant shall be saved. Living or dying, defeated or victorious, be it ours to exclaim, "No compromise with slavery! Liberty for each, for all, forever! Man above all institutions! The supremacy of God over the whole earth!"

LUCY STONE
(1818–1893)

Leave Women, Then, to Find Their Sphere
1855

*I am detaining you too long, many of you standing,
that I ought to apologize, but women have been wronged
so long that I may wrong you a little.*

A lecturer on women's suffrage, labor rights, and abolition, Lucy Stone gained recognition for retaining her family name after she married Harry Blackwell, and for her deep commitment to women's suffrage. Born near Brookfield, Massachusetts, Stone disobeyed her father's wishes as a child when she attended grade school, seminary, and then Oberlin College—paying her own way throughout.

The year she graduated from Oberlin, she delivered her first public address on abolition and women's rights, arguing that women should vote, run for public office, and pursue professional careers. She condemned the idea of a "separate sphere for women," damned the institution of marriage and its property regulations, and criticized the church for encouraging the subjugation of women. Stone even urged wives to refuse sex as a form of family planning.

A radical lecturer, Lucy Stone quickly became a controversial figure, attracting the approval and ire of thousands. Angry spectators burned her posters in protest and threw prayer books as she took the stage. After the Civil War, Stone and her husband formed the American Women Suffrage Association, which in 1887 merged with Susan B. Anthony and Elizabeth Cady Stanton's National Women Suffrage Association, creating the National American Women Suffrage Association.

In this 1855 address to the Women's Rights Convention, Stone argued that women should create their own spheres outside the home, independent of the financial and social burdens of marriage.

THE QUESTION OF WOMAN'S RIGHTS is a practical one. The notion has prevailed that it was only an ephemeral idea; that it was but women claiming the right to smoke cigars in the streets, and to frequent bar-rooms. Others have supposed it a question of comparative intellect; others still, of sphere. Too much has already been said and written about woman's sphere. Trace all the doctrines to their source and they will be found to have no basis except in the usages and prejudices of the age. This is seen in the fact that what is tolerated in woman in one country is not tolerated in another. In this country women may hold prayer-meetings, etc., but in Mohammaden countries it is written upon their mosques, "Women and dogs, and other impure animals, are not permitted to enter." Wendell Phillips says, "The best and greatest thing one is capable of doing, that is his sphere." I have confidence in the Father to believe that when He gives us the capacity to do anything He does not make a blunder. Leave women, then, to find their sphere. And do not tell us before we are born even, that our province is to cook dinners, darn stockings, and sew on buttons. We are told woman has all the rights she wants; and even women, I am ashamed to say, tell us so. They mistake the politeness of men for rights—seats while men stand in this hall to-night, and their adulations; but these are mere courtesies. We want rights. The flour-merchant, the house-builder, and the postman charge us no less on account of our sex; but when we endeavor to earn money to pay all these, then, indeed, we find the difference. Man, if he have energy, may hew out for himself a path where no mortal has ever trod, held back by nothing but what is in himself; the world is all before him, where to choose; and we are glad for you, brothers, men, that it is so. But the same society that drives forth the young man, keeps woman at home—a dependent—working little cats on worsted, and little dogs on punctured paper; but if she goes heartily and bravely to give herself to some worthy purpose, she is out of her sphere and she loses caste. Women working in tailor-shops are paid one-third as much as men. Some one in Philadelphia has stated that women make fine shirts for twelve and a half cents apiece; that no woman can make more than nine a week, and the sum thus earned, after deducting rent, fuel, etc., leaves her just three and a half cents a day for bread. Is it a wonder that women are driven to prostitution? Female teachers in New York are paid fifty dollars a year, and for every such situation there are five hundred applicants. I know not what you believe of God, but I believe He gave yearnings and longings to be filled, and that He did not mean all our time should be devoted to feeding and clothing the body. The present condition of woman causes a horrible perversion of the marriage relation. It is asked of a lady, "Has she married well?" "Oh, yes, her husband is rich." Woman must marry for a home, and you men are the sufferers by this; for a woman who loathes you may marry you because you have the means to get money which she can not have. But when a woman can enter the lists with you and make money for herself, she will marry you only for deep and earnest affection.

I am detaining you too long, many of you standing, that I ought to apologize, but women have been wronged so long that I may wrong you a little. [*Applause*]. A woman undertook in Lowell to sell shoes to ladies. Men laughed at her, but in six years she has run them all out, and has a monopoly of the

trade. Sarah Tyndale, whose husband was an importer of china, and died bankrupt, continued his business, paid off his debts, and has made a fortune and
built the largest china warehouse in the world. (Mrs. Mott here corrected
Lucy. Mrs. Tyndale has not the largest china warehouse, but the largest assortment of china in the world.) Mrs. Tyndale, herself, drew the plan of her warehouse, and it is the best plan ever drawn. A laborer to whom the architect
showed it, said: "Don't she know e'en as much as some men!" I have seen a
woman at manual labor turning out chair-legs in a cabinet-shop, with a dress
short enough not to drag in the shavings. I wish other women would imitate
her in this. It made her hands harder and broader, it is true, but I think a hand
with a dollar and a quarter a day in it, better than one with a crossed
ninepence. The men in the shop didn't use tobacco, nor swear—they can't do
those things where there are women, and we owe it to our brothers to go
wherever they work to keep them decent. The widening of woman's sphere is
to improve her lot. Let us do it, and if the world scoff, let it scoff—if it sneer,
let it sneer—but we will go on emulating the example of the sisters Grimké
and Abby Kelly. When they first lectured against slavery they were not listened
to as respectfully as you listen to us. So the first female physician meets many
difficulties, but to the next the path will be made easy. . . .

Pablo De La Guerra
On Seizing Land from Native Californians
April 1855

I say, sir, that. . . our property has been sacrificed.

The Hispanic-American civil rights struggle is rooted, in part, in the Mexican-American War and the resulting Treaty of Guadalupe Hidalgo (1848). The treaty was negotiated by the United States ostensibly to prevent American settlers moving West from seizing land that belonged to Mexicans before the war. With the gold rush in full throttle, however, the treaty was quickly abandoned, as pioneers seized land indiscriminately and without care for Mexican Americans.

In 1851, in direct violation of the treaty, Congress passed the Land Law, requiring all Latinos living in the "new" territories to provide proof of their land grants, a near impossibility considering the lack of documentation. In the meantime, while the courts discerned true ownership, the law allowed Anglo-Americans to seize and develop the disputed land. This mass confiscation later served as the root of the Chicano liberation movement and propelled the separatist ideas advanced by leaders like Reies López Tijerina. In the nineteenth century, however, most Mexican Americans struggled in virtual silence to maintain their land holdings.

Pablo De La Guerra, a prominent Mexican American, was a lone voice against this injustice. One of the few Mexican Americans in the California State Assembly and Senate during the 1850s, he was embraced by many Mexican Americans and whites as an ally and trustworthy citizen. Speaking passionately, De La Guerra succeeded in tabling one land seizure bill after another. A cascade of political pressure ultimately overwhelmed his cause, as more white settlers and miners moved to California and demanded to "reclaim" the land. After De La Guerra died, the Latino cause largely would be put on hold for another century.

I HOPE THE SENATE will allow me to offer a few remarks upon the merits of the bill, and to state why, upon the principles of reason and justice I consider that the bill should be indefinitely postponed. . . .

Well, sir, the war took place, and we, after doing our duty as citizens of Mexico, were sold like sheep—abandoned by our nation, and as it were, awoke from a dream, strangers on the very soil on which we were native and to the manor born. We passed from the hands of Mexico to that of the United States, but we had the consolation of believing that the United States, as a nation, were more liberal than our own. We had the greatest respect for an American. Every American who came to our country was held in higher estimation than even one of our own countrymen. And I call upon every American who visited us to bear testimony to this fact. And after being abandoned by our own country and annexed to the United States, we thought that we belonged to a nation the most civilized, the most humane—a nation that was the foremost in planting the banner of liberty on every portion of its dominions—a nation that was the most careful in protecting the just rights of its citizens. Well, sir, in 1849, a great many emigrated to California, not to settle upon the land or to cultivate the soil, but to work in the mines and go home; and from '49 to '52 they had no other object, but many finding that it was hard work in the mines, and being told that the land in the State had not been separated from the public domain, had no boundaries, and being probably further misled by lawyers, or interested persons, who stated that the land in this condition would never be confirmed to the owners by the Supreme Court of the United States, came and settled upon our lands. And I ask, are we to suffer for that?

I believe that I speak advisedly, when I say that three-fourths of the settlers upon the lands, have been aware that some one had a prior claim; they knew it by common report, that such a one and such a one had a claim upon the land; but they thought that even if it was confirmed to the owners, that the use of the land until the confirmation, would be worth more than the improvements that they would make. Perhaps one-fourth went upon the land in good faith. I do not know that such was the case, but I am willing to grant it; but now, when they find that it is probable that the Supreme Court of the United States will confirm these grants, and after deriving all the benefits for the use of the same, they apply to the Legislature, in order that a State Law may be set up as a bar against the action of the Court of the United States.

I say, sir, that already we have suffered deeply; our property has been sacrificed. The Bay of San Francisco alone, at one time, had more cattle than can now be found in the counties of Santa Clara, Monterey, Santa Cruz, San Luis Obispo, and Santa Barbara. Horses, at that time could be counted by thousands; and I believe that many settlers have settled upon lands for the purposes of stealing the cattle and sending them to the San Francisco market for sale.

Now, sir, of the 113 members in this Legislature, I am the only native of this State; and the native population expect from me, and through me, that in my place in this Legislative Hall, that I shall call the attention of this body to the facts I have now stated, and to tell you that badly treated as they have been in every respect, they look around them and find no other aid except in the mercy of Heaven, and the justice of this Legislature; and now, in their name, I call upon you, Senators, to consider that if they are deprived of what is left to them, they have no other place to go to. They have been rejected by the Mexicans; they know no other country but California, and by depriving them of their rights, they will be compelled to be beggars in the streets; and in order to prevent this terrible calamity from overtaking them, they, through me, throw themselves upon your mercy and clemency; and they ask and expect from you that protection that will justify before the eyes of the world the belief in the justice of the American people. If the American settlers are deprived of what they have expended for their improvements, they can go home and meet the aid and sympathies of their friends and countrymen; but the Californian, what prospect has he before him, or where shall he go.

I wish to make one remark about the expression, "settled in good faith," and I am done. Sir, if this bill has effect, it will be from the counties of Santa Clara upward, because in the south we have no settlers; but in those counties I am now referring to, the settlers greatly outnumber the land claimants, and it is useless to say that juries are incorruptible. We know that such is not the case from our daily experience. And these juries will be formed by whom? Sir, they will consist of those very settlers. The Sheriff will summon such a jury as will suit their views. I have seen a good deal of juries in California. I have seen where proof, as clear as noon day, would not alter the decision of a jury from their preconceived opinions. And I will affirm that I believe that out of one hundred cases tried between the settlers and the land owners, that ninety-nine will be given in favor of the settler.

And, sir, to conclude these remarks, permit me to assure you, upon my honor as a gentleman, that everything I have stated is true and as clear as conviction itself. I know that I am in the Senate chamber of California, where full liberty of speech is allowed, but if I were speaking to a barbarous people, I should still advocate the same sentiments, and even if I was killed for so doing, I should at least have the satisfaction of dying in a just cause, and should receive the reward from Him who has said, "Blessed are they who are persecuted, for righteousness sake, for of such is the kingdom of heaven."

Abraham Lincoln
(1809–1865)

A House Divided
June 16, 1858

A house divided against itself cannot stand.

The son of a Kentucky frontiersman, Abraham Lincoln struggled most of his early life to help make ends meet. In describing his childhood, he wrote, "My parents were . . . [from] undistinguished families. When I came of age I didn't know much. Still, somehow I could read, write, and cipher." Despite his humble upbringing, Lincoln possessed uncommon drive and intellect; while working on the farm, he made extraordinary efforts to educate himself by reading voraciously and even teaching himself the law. Lincoln used his experience as a lawyer and his service as a soldier in the Black Hawk War to win a seat in the Illinois State Legislature, where he spent eight years. In 1858, Lincoln captured the Republican nomination for the United States Senate. His law partner later said, "[Lincoln's] ambition was a little engine that knew no rest."

At 8 P.M. on June 16, 1858, only three hours after receiving that nomination, Abraham Lincoln addressed the delegates of the Illinois Republican State Convention in Springfield. Speaking to more than a thousand representatives in the statehouse, he boldly asserted that, with regard to slavery and its devisive effect on the nation, "a house divided against itself cannot stand." Evoking Jesus's words in the Synoptic Gospels, Lincoln's statement was far more radical than expected and, in the eyes of many, politically unsafe for a man with a calling for higher office.

Contrary to popular belief, however, Lincoln did not condemn slavery. Instead, he predicted that if the United States remained on its current course, it would ultimately face a choice between two stark and perilous paths: free nation or slave nation. Lincoln aligned himself with the former, condemning the 1854 Nebraska-Kansas Act, the 1857 *Dred Scott* decision, and the practice of "squatter sovereignty" that allowed pro-slavery settlers to migrate to the frontier in hope of upholding slavery. Lincoln's remarks were both direct—methodically outlining his opposition to Democratic candidate Stephen A. Douglas—and prophetic, foreshadowing the Union's staunch opposition to slavery. Lincoln lost the election, but his debate with Douglas—including his "house divided" line—earned him a national reputation and, in 1860, the Republican nomination for president.

MR. PRESIDENT, AND GENTLEMEN OF THE CONVENTION.

We are now far into the *fifth* year since a policy was initiated, with the *avowed* object, and *confident* promise, of putting an end to slavery agitation.

Under the operation of that policy, that agitation has not only, *not ceased,* but has *constantly augmented.*

In *my* opinion, it *will* not cease, until a *crisis* shall have been reached, and passed.

"A house divided against itself cannot stand."

I believe this Government cannot endure, permanently half *slave* and half *free.*

I do not expect the Union to be *dissolved*—I do not expect the house to *fall*—but I do expect it will cease to be divided.

It will become *all* one thing or *all* the other.

Either the *opponents* of slavery, will arrest the further spread of it, and place it where the public mind shall rest in the belief that it is in the course of ultimate extinction; or its *advocates* will push it forward, till it shall become alike lawful in *all* the States, *old* as well as *new*—*North* as well as *South.*

Have we no *tendency* to the latter condition?

Let any one who doubts carefully contemplate that now almost complete legal combination—piece of *machinery,* so as to speak—compounded of the Nebraska doctrine and the Dred Scott decision. . . .

The new year of 1854 found slavery excluded from more than half the States by State constitutions, and from most of the national territory by congressional prohibition. Four days later commenced the struggle which ended in repealing that congressional prohibition. This opened all the national territory to slavery, and was the first point gained.

But, so far, Congress only had acted, and an indorsement by the people, real or apparent, was indispensable, to save the point already gained and give chance for more.

This necessity had not been overlooked, but had been provided for, as well as might be, in the notable argument of "Squatter Sovereignty," otherwise called "sacred right of self-government," which latter phrase, though expressive of the only rightful basis of any government, was so perverted in this attempted use of it as to amount to just this: That if any one man choose to enslave another, no third man shall be allowed to object. That argument was incorporated into the Nebraska Bill itself, in the language which follows: "It being the true intent and meaning of this act not to legislate slavery into any Territory or State, nor to exclude it therefrom, but to leave the people thereof perfectly free to form and regulate their domestic institutions in their own way, subject only to the Constitution of the United States."

Then opened the roar of loose declamation in favor of "Squatter Sovereignty," and "sacred right of self-government." "But," said opposition members, "let us amend the bill so as to expressly declare that the people of the Territory may exclude Slavery." "Not we," said the friends of the measure; and down they voted the amendment.

While the Nebraska Bill was passing through Congress, a law case involving the question of a Negro's freedom, by reason of his owner having voluntarily taken him first into a Free State and then into a Territory covered by the congressional prohibition, and held him as a slave for a long time in each, was passing through the United States Circuit Court for the District of Missouri; and both Nebraska Bill and lawsuit were brought to a decision in the same month of May 1854. The Negro's name was "Dred Scott," which name now designates the decision finally made in the case. . . .

The several points of the Dred Scott decision, in connection with Senator Douglas's "care-not" policy, constitute the piece of machinery, in its present state of advancement. . . .

First, that no Negro slave, imported as such from Africa, and no descendant of such slave, can ever be a citizen of any State, in the sense of that term as used in the Constitution of the United States. This point is made in order to deprive the Negro, in every possible event, of the benefit of that provision of the United States Constitution, which declares that: "The citizens of each State shall be entitled to all privileges and immunities of citizens in the several States."

Second, that "subject to the Constitution of the United States," neither Congress nor a Territorial legislature can exclude slavery from any United States Territory. This point is made in order that individual men may fill up the Territories with slaves, without danger of losing them as property, and thus to enhance the chances of permanency to the institution through all the future.

Third, that whether the holding a Negro in actual slavery in a free State makes him free, as against the holder, the United States courts will not decide, but will leave to be decided by the courts of any slave State the negro may be forced into by the master. . . .

Auxiliary to all this, and working hand in hand with it, the Nebraska doctrine, or what is left of it, is to educate and mold public opinion, at least Northern public opinion, not to care whether slavery is voted down or voted up. This shows exactly where we now are; and partially, also, whither we are tending.

. . . In what cases the power of the States is so restrained by the United States Constitution is left an open question, precisely as the same question, as to the restraint on the power of the Territories, was left open in the Nebraska Act. Put this and that together, and we have another nice little niche which we may ere long see filled with another Supreme Court decision, declaring that the Constitution of the United States does not permit a State to exclude slavery from its limits. And this may especially be expected if the doctrine of "care not whether slavery be voted down or voted up," shall gain upon the public mind sufficiently to give promise that such a decision can be maintained when made.

Such a decision is all that slavery now lacks of being alike lawful in all the States. Welcome, or unwelcome, such decision is probably coming, and will soon be upon us, unless the power of the present political dynasty shall be met and overthrown. We shall lie down pleasantly dreaming that the people of Missouri are on the verge of making their State free, and we shall awake to the reality instead, that the Supreme Court has made Illinois a slave State. To meet and overthrow the power of that dynasty is the work now before all those who would prevent that consummation.

This is what we have to do.

But how can we best do it? There are those who denounce us openly to their own friends and yet whisper us softly, that Senator Douglas is the aptest instrument there is with which to effect that object. They wish us to infer all from the fact that he now has a little quarrel with the present head of the dynasty; and that he has regularly voted with us on a single point, upon which he and we have never differed. They remind us that he is a great man, and that the largest of us are very small ones. Let this be granted. But "a living dog is better than a dead lion." Judge Douglas, if not a dead lion for this work, is at least a caged and toothless one. How can he oppose the advances of slavery? He does not care anything about it. His avowed mission is impressing the "public heart" to care nothing about it. A leading Douglas Democratic newspaper thinks Douglas's superior talent will be needed to resist the revival of the African slave trade. Does Douglas believe an effort to revive that trade is approaching? He has not said so. Does he really think so? But if it is, how can he resist it? For years he has labored to prove it a sacred right of white men to take negro slaves into the new Territories. Can he possibly show that it is less a sacred right to buy them where they can be bought cheapest? And unquestionably they can be bought cheaper in Africa than in Virginia. He has done all in his power to reduce the whole question of slavery to one of a mere right of property; and as such, how can he oppose the foreign slave trade— how can he refuse that trade in that "property" shall be "perfectly free"—

unless he does it as a protection to the home production? And as the home producers will probably not ask the protection, he will be wholly without a ground of opposition.

Senator Douglas holds, we know, that a man may rightfully be wiser today than he was yesterday—that he may rightfully change when he finds himself wrong. But can we, for that reason, run ahead, and infer that he will make any particular change, of which he, himself, has given no intimation? Can we safely base our action upon any such vague inference? Now, as ever, I wish not to misrepresent Judge Douglas's position, question his motives, or do aught that can be personally offensive to him. Whenever, if ever, he and we can come together on principle so that our cause may have assistance from his great ability, I hope to have interposed no adventitious obstacle. But clearly, he is not now with us—he does not pretend to be—he does not promise to ever be.

Our cause, then, must be intrusted to, and conducted by, its own undoubted friends—those whose hands are free, whose hearts are in the work—who do care for the result. Two years ago the Republicans of the nation mustered over thirteen hundred thousand strong. We did this under the single impulse of resistance to a common danger, with every external circumstance against us. Of strange, discordant, and even hostile elements, we gathered from the four winds, and formed and fought the battle through, under the constant hot fire of a disciplined, proud, and pampered enemy. Did we brave all them to falter now?—*now*—when that same enemy is wavering, dissevered, and belligerent? The result is not doubtful. We shall not fail—if we stand firm, we shall not fail. Wise counsels may accelerate, or mistakes delay it, but, sooner or later, the victory is sure to come.

JOHN BROWN
(1800–1859)

No Consciousness of Guilt
NOVEMBER 2, 1859

I deny everything but what I have all along admitted:
of a design on my part to free slaves.

John Brown is often remembered as the most infamous abolitionist of the nineteenth century. Born into a deeply religious yet progressive family in Torrington, Connecticut, Brown spent his lifetime fighting slavery.

Although never a financial success, he still gave prodigiously to African Americans: He donated land to fugitive slaves, raised black youths in his own home, participated in the Underground Railroad, and founded organizations to protect fugitives from slave catchers. In 1849 he moved to Elba, New York, an African-American community, where he taught farming and organized a secret militia.

On October 16, 1859, Brown led twenty-one men in a raid of the federal arsenal at Harper's Ferry, Virginia, planning to arm slaves with the weapons he would steal. But Colonel Robert E. Lee, a group of Marines, and the local militia thwarted his plan. In the ensuing struggle, Brown lost ten men and killed five of Lee's before he was captured.

On November 2, a court in Charlestown, Virginia, condemned Brown to death. Following the verdict, Brown delivered the following address, in which he reiterated his continued belief in the freedom of slaves, without any "consciousness of guilt." He was hanged exactly one month later. Frederick Douglass later remarked, "Though a white gentleman, [Brown] is in sympathy a black man."

I HAVE, MAY IT PLEASE THE COURT, A FEW WORDS TO SAY.

In the first place, I deny everything but what I have all along admitted: of a design on my part to free slaves. I intended certainly to have made a clean thing of that matter, as I did last winter, when I went into Missouri and there took slaves without the snapping of a gun on either side, moving them through the country, and finally leaving them in Canada. I designed to have done the same thing again on a larger scale. That was all I intended. I never did intend murder, or treason, or the destruction of property, or to excite or incite slaves to rebellion, or to make insurrection.

I have another objection, and that is that it is unjust that I should suffer such a penalty. Had I interfered in the manner which I admit, and which I admit has been fairly proved—for I admire the truthfulness and candor of the greater portion of the witnesses who have testified in this case—had I so interfered in behalf of the rich, the powerful, the intelligent, the so-called great, or in behalf of any of their friends, either father, mother, brother, sister, wife or children, or any of that class, and suffered and sacrificed what I have in this interference, it would have been all right. Every man in this Court would have deemed it an act worthy of reward rather than punishment.

This Court acknowledges, too, as I suppose, the validity of the law of God. I see a book kissed, which I suppose to be the Bible, or at least the New Testament, which teaches me that all things whatsoever I would that men should do to me, I should do even so to them. It teaches me, further, to remember them that are in bonds as bound with them. I endeavored to act up to the instruction. I say I am yet too young to understand that God is any respecter of persons. I believe that to have interfered as I have done, as I have always freely admitted I have done, in behalf of His despised poor, I did not wrong, but right. Now, if it is deemed necessary that I should forfeit my life for the furtherance of the ends of justice, and mingle my blood further with the blood of my children and with the blood of millions in this slave country whose rights are disregarded by wicked, cruel, and unjust enactments, I say, let it be done.

Let me say one word further. I feel entirely satisfied with the treatment I have received on my trial. Considering all the circumstances, it has been more generous than I expected. But I feel no consciousness of guilt. I have stated from the first what was my intention, and what was not. I never had any design against the liberty of any person, nor any disposition to commit treason or incite slaves to rebel or make any general insurrection. I never encouraged any man to do so, but always discouraged any idea of that kind.

Let me say, also, in regard to the statements made by some of those who were connected with me, I hear it has been stated by some of them that I have induced them to join me. But the contrary is true. I do not say this to injure them, but as regretting their weakness. Not one but joined me of his own accord, and the greater part at his own expense. A number of them I never saw, and never had a word of conversation with, till the day they came to me, and that was for the purpose I have stated.

Now, I have done.

JONATHAN GIBBS
(c. 1827–1874)

A Day to Celebrate Emancipation
JANUARY 1, 1863

Give unto us the same guarantee of life, liberty and protection in the pursuit of happiness that you so cheerfully award to others.

On the day Abraham Lincoln signed the Emancipation Proclamation into law, January 1, 1863, scores of African Americans in the North congregated to celebrate the historic occasion. Amidst the fanfare, the Reverend Jonathan Gibbs delivered this speech, one of the day's more memorable addresses. After studying at Dartmouth College and Princeton Theological Seminary, Rev. Gibbs had risen to prominence in the black convention movement, becoming a leading figure in the abolitionist and Underground Railroad movements.

Before an overjoyed audience at the First African Presbyterian Church of Philadelphia, Gibbs honored the passage of the proclamation and praised African Americans for playing a critical role in the Civil War. That role, he argued, along with the successful resistance of past activists, like Crispus Attucks, earned blacks their freedom. Still, Gibbs warned presciently, the proclamation was but a "half measure" toward full equality; enfranchisement and equal opportunity still lay in the balance.

THE MORNING DAWNS! The long night of sorrow and gloom is past; rosy-fingered Aurora, early born of day, shows the first faint flush of her coming glory, low down on the distant horizon of Freedom's joyful day. O day, thrice blessed, that brings liberty to four million native-born Americans. O Liberty! O sacred rights of every human soul! O source of knowledge, of justice, of civilization, of Christianity, of strength, of power, bless us with the inspiration of thy presence. Today, standing on the broad platform of the common brotherhood of men, we solemnly appeal to the God of justice, our common Father, to aid us to meet manfully the new duties, the new obligations that this memorable day will surely impose.

The Proclamation has gone forth, and God is saying to this nation by its legitimate constitute head, Man must be free.

Scout, deride, malign this intimation, as the enemies of God and man will and may, the American people must yield to His inscrutable fiat, or the legacy of their fathers will be squandered 'midst poverty, ignorance, blood and shame. . . . The people must support this Proclamation, heartily, earnestly, strengthening the hands of our government by all the energies and resources they possess, or in a short time the question will not be whether black men are to be slaves, but whether white men are to be free! You had better a thousand times let us into the full light of liberty with yourselves, than that yourselves come into a condition equal to that of the slave at the South. We pray you this day, be just to yourselves, and then to us you *must* be true.

The black people of this country are thoroughly loyal. We are above disloyalty to the government. You may suspect a Garrisonian Abolitionist, but you cannot possibly suspect us. All our hopes and interests lie in the success of our government. We clearly discern that this is a contest between civilization and barbarism, two antagonistic systems of government, two fundamental principles that oppose each other. The black man is only a sort of accident connected with this struggle. The man who stoops to malign or abuse us as the cause of this war is, in point of intelligence, away down along the apes; he must be given up as a hopeless blockhead. If the same state of things existed in any country in the world, that exists in this, and all parties were white, or were black, just such a contest must come between these two antagonistic systems as we witness this day in our country, and one or the other of these systems must prevail. Which shall it be?

O, God, we appeal to *Thee*. Let this strife be so decided that justice, truth, honor may not be put to shame. You, my country, entered into a solemn covenant with God in 1776 and declared before highest Heaven that your first and only purpose was to foster and cherish the equality and fraternity of man. How have you kept this covenant? Let Dred Scott decisions, fugitive-slave laws, the judicial murders of Denmark Vesey, Nat Turner, John Brown, Gabriel and numerous others testify. . . .

Give unto us the same guarantee of life, liberty and protection in the pursuit of happiness that you so cheerfully award to others, and make the very same demands of us to support the government you make of others. In a word, enfranchise and arm the blacks North and South, and put them under the intelligent direction of a strong central government at New Orleans, or Charleston, South Carolina. Enfranchise and arm the black man. Let there be no half measures; half measures are dangerous measures in times like these. . . .

Many persons are asking, Will black men fight? That is not what they mean. The question they are asking is simply this: Have white men of the

North the same moral courage, the pluck, the grit, to lay down their foolish prejudice against the colored man and place him in a position where he can bear his full share of the toils and dangers of this war? That is the question that all such persons are asking, and no other. . . . We, the colored men of the North, put the laboring oar in your hands; it is for white men to show that they are equal to the demands of these times, by putting away their stupid prejudices. We are not children, but men, and are in earnest about the matter. There is not a battlefield throughout the country, from the days of '76 until now, but what our bones lie bleaching with yours. I *know* whereof I affirm, and I challenge contradiction. In the very first resistance that was made to British aggression in the Revolution of '76 was a black man, Crispus Attucks, who led the attack and was some of the first slain.

Did not a regiment of Rhode Island's freed blacks on the river Delaware at Red Bank, withstand three successive bayonet charges of British soldiers and finally wipe out the minions of British thralldom? What is the testimony of Andrew Jackson on this subject (a man who knew how to deal with traitors)? What has made the name of Haiti a terror to tyrants and slaveholders throughout the world, but the terrible fourteen years' fight of black men against some of the best troops of Napoleon—and the black men wiped them out. There are some fights that the world will never forget, and among them is the fight of black men for liberty on the Island of Haiti. . . .

Your destiny as white men and ours as black men are one and the same; we are all marching on to the same goal. If you rise, we will rise in the scale of being. If you fall, we will fall; but you will have the worst of it. . . .

Finally, let us offer the homage of grateful hearts to the friends of liberty and human progress the world over, for the hopes and prospects now before us, confidently predicting that the future will show that no efforts made in behalf of the bondman in this country were in vain. The sum of human happiness in this country will be increased, and God honored by the utter destruction of the hideous system of American slavery. . . .

ABRAHAM LINCOLN
(1809–1865)

Second Inaugural Address
MARCH 4, 1865

With malice for none, with charity for all . . . let us strive on to finish the work we are in, to bind up the nation's wounds, . . . and cherish a just and lasting peace among ourselves and with all nations.

Beginning his second term as president, Abraham Lincoln delivered this address to an embattled, war-torn nation yearning for peace. The Civil War was already four years old, and generals Robert E. Lee and Joseph E. Johnston would not surrender the Confederate flag for another month. In his first term Lincoln had governed a deeply divided country in a constant state of tumult. The cloud of slavery, secession, and the Emancipation Proclamation all weighed heavily on Lincoln's and the nation's conscience.

In his historic Second Inaugural Address—only 703 words, thirty-five sentences, and seven minutes in length—Lincoln conceded that there was little need for a lengthy discourse on his specific plans for office. Instead, with black leader Frederick Douglass watching on, he sought to "bind up the nation's wounds" by outlining the root causes of the Civil War, the injustices of slavery, and the desperate need for peace and reconstruction. Lincoln recognized that the nation's future lay in the balance; he needed to keep the United States looking forward to the resolution of a bloody, fractured era. Author Ronald C. White has called this address, which Lincoln handwrote, his "last will and testament to America."

FELLOW-COUNTRYMEN, at this second appearing to take the oath of the presidential office, there is less occasion for an extended address than there was at the first. Then a statement somewhat in detail of a course to be pursued seemed fitting and proper. Now, at the expiration of four years, during which public declarations have been constantly called forth on every point and phase of the great contest which still absorbs the attention and engrosses the energies of the nation, little that is new could be presented. The progress of our arms, upon which all else chiefly depends, is as well known to the public as to myself, and it is, I trust, reasonably satisfactory and encouraging to all. With high hope for the future, no prediction in regard to it is ventured.

On the occasion corresponding to this four years ago all thoughts were anxiously directed to an impending civil war. All dreaded it, all sought to avert it. While the inaugural address was being delivered from this place, devoted altogether to *saving* the Union without war, insurgent agents were in the city seeking to *destroy* it without war—seeking to dissolve the Union and divide effects by negotiation. Both parties deprecated war, but one of them would *make* war rather than let the nation survive, and the other would *accept* war rather than let it perish. And the war came.

One-eighth of the whole population was colored slaves, not distributed generally over the Union, but localized in the southern part of it. These slaves constituted a peculiar and powerful interest. All knew that this interest was somehow the cause of the war. To strengthen, perpetuate, and extend this interest was the object for which the insurgents would rend the Union even by war, while the Government claimed no right to do more than to restrict the territorial enlargement of it. Neither party expected for the war the magnitude or the duration which it has already attained. Neither anticipated that the *cause* of the conflict might cease with or even before the conflict itself should cease. Each looked for an easier triumph, and a result less fundamental and astounding. Both read the same Bible and pray to the same God, and each invokes His aid against the other. It may seem strange that any men should dare to ask a just God's assistance in wringing their bread from the sweat of other men's faces, but let us judge not, that we be not judged. The prayers of both could not be answered. That of neither has been answered fully. The Almighty has His own purposes. "Woe unto the world because of offenses; for it must needs be that offenses come, but woe to that man by whom the offense cometh." If we shall suppose that American slavery is one of those offenses which, in the providence of God, must needs come, but which, having continued through His appointed time, He now wills to remove, and that He gives to both North and South this terrible war as the woe due to those by whom the offense came, shall we discern therein any departure from those divine attributes which the believers in a living God always ascribe to Him? Fondly do we hope, fervently do we pray, that this mighty scourge of war may speedily pass away. Yet, if God wills that it continue until all the wealth piled by the bondsman's two hundred and fifty years of unrequited toil shall be sunk, and until every drop of blood drawn with the lash shall be paid by another drawn with the sword, as was said three thousand years ago, so still it must be said, "The judgments of the Lord are true and righteous altogether."

With malice toward none, with charity for all, with firmness in the right as God gives us to see the right, let us strive on to finish the work we are in, to bind up the nation's wounds, to care for him who shall have borne the battle and for his widow and his orphan, to do all which may achieve and cherish a just and lasting peace among ourselves and with all nations.

BOOKER T. WASHINGTON
(1856–1915)

In Praise of Labor
MARCH 4, 1895

We went into slavery pieces of property; we came out American citizens. We went into slavery with slave chains clanking around our wrists; we came out with the American ballot in our hands.

Booker T. Washington was born into slavery in Franklin County near Roanoke, Virginia, and moved with his family just after emancipation to Malden, West Virginia. At the age of nine, already a believer in hard work and endurance, he began work in a salt furnace and then a coal mine. Determined to get an education, he enrolled at the Hampton Normal and Agricultural Institute in Virginia, working as a janitor to help pay expenses. The institute's principal, Samuel Armstrong, an ardent opponent of slavery and former commander of African-American troops during the Civil War, was impressed with Washington's industriousness and arranged for a wealthy white man to pay his tuition.

In 1888, with the help of Armstrong and others, Washington built his own school for African Americans on an abandoned plantation near the outskirts of Tuskegee. The Tuskegee Institute taught academic subjects but emphasized a practical education—including farming, carpentry, printing, and cabinetmaking.

Washington believed that the road to black equality and advancement in the post-Reconstruction era was through pragmatic education in crafts and industrial skills and the cultivation of patience, enterprise, and thrift. He urged his fellow African Americans, most of whom were illiterate, impoverished farmhands, to abandon their efforts to win full civil rights and political power, and instead hone their industrial and farming skills in order to attain economic security. Moreover, Washington did not believe that African Americans should campaign for suffrage, claiming instead that they first needed to prove their loyalty to the United States by working hard without complaint. Blacks, he insisted, should temporarily accept segregation and discrimination; their eventual acquisition of wealth and culture would gradually lead to respect and acceptance from the white community, and in turn lead to the mitigation of prejudice. This path would eventually break down the divisions between the two races and, in the end, lead to equal citizenship for all blacks. Southern whites, who had previously opposed the education of African Americans, supported Washington's ideas, seeing them as a means of encouraging blacks to accept their inferior economic and social status.

Washington's ideas were deplored by critics like W. E. B. Du Bois, who derided their emphasis on vocational skills to the exclusion of academic development and civil rights. In the following address at Fisk University, Booker T. Washington outlined his highly controversial philosophy, highlighting its political, economic, and social implications.

I BELIEVE THAT we are going to reach our highest development largely along the lines of scientific and industrial education. For the last fifty years education has tended in one direction, the cementing of mind to matter.

Most people have the idea that industrial education is opposed to literary training, opposed to the highest development. I want to correct this error. I would choose the college graduate to receive industrial education. The more mind the subject has, the more satisfactory would be the results in industrial education. It requires as strong a mind to build a Corliss engine as it does to write a Greek grammar. Without industrial education, we are in danger of getting too many "smart men" scattered through the South. A young colored man in a certain town was pointed out to me as being exceedingly smart, and I have heard of him as being exceedingly smart and accomplished. Upon inquiry, however, I learned the young man applied his knowledge and training to no earthly good. He was just a "smart man," that was all.

... The old Negro woman and her washtub are fast being supplanted by the white man with his steam laundry, washing over a hundred shirts an hour. The many colored men who have formerly earned a living by cutting grass in the front yards and keeping the flower beds in trim are no competitors for the white man, who, bringing his knowledge of surveying and terracing and plotting land and his knowledge of botany and blending colors into active play, has dignified and promoted the work. He is not called a grass cutter or a yard cleaner, but a florist or a landscape gardener. The old black "mammy" could never again enter the sick room where she was once known as a peerless nurse. She has given place to the tidy little white woman, with her neat white cap and apron, her knowledge of physiology, bandaging, principles of diseases and the administration of medicine, who has dignified and glorified the art of nursing and has turned it into a profession.

I have been told that the young colored man is cramped, and that after he gets his education there are few chances to use it. I have little patience with such arguments. . . .

One trouble with the average Negro is that he is always hungry, and it is impossible to make progress along educational, moral, or religious lines while in that condition. It is a hard matter to make a Christian out of a hungry man. It has often been contended that the Negro needed no industrial education, because he already knew too well how to work. There never was a greater mistake.

MEASURED GAINS: TWO STEPS FORWARD, ONE STEP BACKWARD
1866–1949

FRANCES ELLEN WATKINS HARPER
(1825–1911)

We Are All Bound Up Together
MAY 1866

Society cannot trample on the weakest and feeblest of its members
without receiving the curse in its own soul.

A lecturer, author, and activist, Frances Ellen Watkins Harper was born
to free parents in Baltimore, Maryland, and later raised by her uncle, an
active abolitionist and friend of William Lloyd Garrison. At the age of
only twenty Harper published her first among many works of poetry,
helping land her a post teaching grade school. After Maryland passed
legislation enslaving freed northern Negroes, she became an outspoken
advocate of the anti-slavery movement, lending public support to the
Underground Railroad and anti-slavery societies. With a "clear, plaintive, and melodious" voice and often "without notes," Harper delivered
her first lecture in 1854 in New Bedford, Massachusetts, excoriating
discrimination against the "colored race" and reiterating the exigency
of education for both blacks and whites. Her speeches and remarkable
oratorical skill were hailed by abolitionists across the country. Boosted
by her emerging popularity, Harper's books of poetry soon became
best-sellers; in 1859 her open letter to the condemned John Brown was
read by tens of thousands of Americans. After the Civil War, Harper
addressed mixed audiences on reconstruction, temperance, and
women's suffrage. She also assumed leadership posts in several black and
white civil rights organizations.

In May 1866 Harper addressed the Eleventh National Women's
Rights Convention in New York, joining prominent white feminists,
including Elizabeth Cady Stanton and Susan B. Anthony. Harper described the dual burdens of racial and gender inequality.

———≈———

I FEEL I AM SOMETHING of a novice upon this platform. Born of a race whose
inheritance has been outrage and wrong, most of my life had been spent in
battling against those wrongs. But I did not feel as keenly as others, that I had
these rights, in common with other women, which are now demanded. About
two years ago, I stood within the shadows of my home. A great sorrow had
fallen upon my life. My husband had died suddenly, leaving me a widow, with

four children, one my own, and the others stepchildren. I tried to keep my children together. But my husband died in debt; and before he had been in his grave three months, the administrator had swept the very milk-crocks and wash tubs from my hands. I was a farmer's wife and made butter for the Columbus market; but what could I do, when they had swept all away? They left me one thing—and that was a looking glass! Had I died instead of my husband, how different would have been the result! By this time he would have had another wife, it is likely; and no administrator would have gone into his house, broken up his home, and sold his bed, and taken away his means of support.

I took my children in my arms, and went out to seek my living. While I was gone, a neighbor to whom I had once lent five dollars, went before a magistrate and swore that he believed I was a non-resident, and laid an attachment on my very bed. And I went back to Ohio with my orphan children in my arms, without a single feather bed in this wide world, that was not in the custody of the law. I say, then, that justice is not fulfilled so long as woman is unequal before the law.

We are all bound up together in one great bundle of humanity, and society cannot trample on the weakest and feeblest of its members without receiving the curse in its own soul. You tried that in the case of the Negro. You pressed him down for two centuries; and in so doing you crippled the moral strength and paralyzed the spiritual energies of the white men of the country. When the hands of the black were fettered, white men were deprived of the liberty of speech and the freedom of the press. Society cannot afford to neglect the enlightenment of any class of its members. At the South, the legislation of the country was in behalf of the rich slaveholders, while the poor white man was neglected. What is the consequence today? From that very class of neglected poor white men, comes the man who stands to-day, with his hand upon the helm of the nation. He fails to catch the watchword of the hour, and throws himself, the incarnation of meanness, across the pathway of the nation. My objection to Andrew Johnson is not that he has been a poor white man; my objection is that he keeps "poor whits" all the way through. [*Applause.*] That is the trouble with him.

This grand and glorious revolution which has commenced, will fail to reach its climax of success, until throughout the length and brea[d]th of the American Republic, the nation shall be so color-blind, as to know no man by the color of his skin or the curl of his hair. It will then have no privileged class, trampling upon and outraging the unprivileged classes, but will be then one great privileged nation, whose privilege will be to produce the loftiest manhood and womanhood that humanity can attain.

I do not believe that giving the woman the ballot is immediately going to cure all the ills of life. I do not believe that white women are dew-drops just exhaled from the skies. I think that like men they may be divided into three classes, the good, the bad, and the indifferent. The good would vote according to their convictions and principles; the bad, as dictated by preju[d]ice or malice; and the indifferent will vote on the strongest side of the question, with the winning party.

You white women speak here of rights. I speak of wrongs. I, as a colored woman, have had in this country an education which has made me feel as if I were in the situation of Ishmael, my hand against every man, and every man's hand against me. Let me go to-morrow morning and take my seat in one of your street cars—I do not know that they will do it in New York, but they will in Philadelphia—and the conductor will put up his hand and stop the car rather than let me ride.

Going from Washington to Baltimore this Spring, they put me in the smoking car. [*Loud Voices—"Shame."*] Aye, in the capital of the nation, where the black man consecrated himself to the nation's defence, faithful when the white man was faithless, they put me in the smoking car! They did it once; but the next time they tried it, they failed; for I would not go in. I felt the fight in me; but I don't want to have to fight all the time. Today I am puzzled where to make my home. I would like to make it in Philadelphia, near my own friends and relations. But if I want to ride in the streets of Philadelphia, they send me to ride on the platform with the driver. [*Cries of "Shame."*] Have women nothing to do with this? Not long since, a colored woman took her seat in an Eleventh Street car in Philadelphia, and the conductor stopped the car, and told the rest of the passengers to get out, and left the car with her in it alone, when they took it back to the station. One day I took my seat in a car, and the conductor came to me and told me to take another seat. I just screamed "murder." The man said if I was black I ought to behave myself. I knew that if he was white he was not behaving himself. Are there not wrongs to be righted?

In advocating the cause of the colored man, since the *Dred Scott* decision, I have sometimes said I thought the nation had touched bottom. But let me tell you there is a depth of infamy lower than that. It is when the nation, standing upon the threshold of a great peril, reached out its hands to a feebler race, and asked that race to help it, and when the peril was over, said, You are good enough for soldiers, but not good enough for citizens. . . .

We have a woman in our country who has received the name of "Moses," not by lying about it, but by acting it out [*applause*]—a woman who has gone down into the Egypt of slavery and brought out hundreds of our people into liberty. The last time I saw that woman, her hands were swollen. That woman who had led one of Montgomery's most successful expeditions, who was brave enough and secretive enough to act as a scout for the American army, had her hands all swollen from a conflict with a brutal conductor, who undertook to eject her from her place. That woman, whose courage and bravery won a recognition from our army and from every black man in the land, is excluded from every thoroughfare of travel. Talk of giving women the ballot-box? Go on. It is a normal school, and the white women of this country need it. While there exists this brutal element in society which tramples upon the feeble and treads down the weak, I tell you that if there is any class of people who need to be lifted out of their airy nothings and selfishness, it is the white women of America. [*Applause.*]

FREDERICK DOUGLASS
(1818–1895)

The Myth of "Yellow Peril"
DECEMBER 7, 1869

Repugnance to the presence and influence of foreigners is an ancient feeling among men. It is peculiar to no particular race or nation.

Frederick Douglass was perhaps the most prominent and visionary leader of the abolitionist movement in the nineteenth century, arguing vociferously against slavery decades before the Civil War even began. Although he recognized the societal distinctions between blacks and whites, Douglass argued that a "combination of races is always superior than any individual one." Unlike some of his contemporaries, Douglass carried that spirit to his view of all races. After the war ended, he became an outspoken advocate of equal rights for immigrant groups—particularly for Chinese laborers.

Between 1848 and 1882, with the California gold rush as a lure, more than 300,000 Chinese immigrants arrived in the United States, playing a vital role in American industrial development. But by 1869, after the transcontinental railroad was completed and the economy soured, thousands of Chinese workers were out of work and faced new, stringent immigration laws, mob violence, and other forms of discrimination tied to Anglo-American fears of a "Yellow Peril." One *New York Times* editorial reflected the mood of the time: "A floodtide of Chinese population . . . with all the social vices [and] with no knowledge."

Douglass delivered the following lecture in praise and defense of Chinese immigrants as part of the Parker Fraternity Course—a series of lectures in Boston, Massachusetts, established by the abolitionist minister Theodore Parker for men and women "who had something to say upon all great humane subjects of the day."

———

AM [HERE] TO SPEAK to you of the character and mission of the United States, with special reference to the question whether we are the better or the worse for being composed of different races of men. . . .

Without undue vanity or unjust depreciation of others, we may claim to be, in many respects, the most fortunate of nations. We stand in relation to all others, as youth to age. Other nations have had their day of greatness and glory; we are yet to have our day, and that day is coming. The dawn is already upon us. It is bright and full of promise. Other nations have reached their culminating point. We are at the beginning of our ascent. They have apparently exhausted the conditions essential to their further growth and extension, while we are abundant in all the material essential to further national growth and greatness.

We are a country of all extremes—ends and opposites; the most conspicuous example of composite nationality in the world. Our people defy all the ethnological and logical classifications. In races we range all the way from black to white, with intermediate shades which, as in the apocalyptic vision, no man can name a number.

In regard to creeds and faiths, the condition is no better, and no worse. Differences both as to race and to religion are evidently more likely to increase than to diminish.

We stand between the populous shores of two great oceans. Our land is capable of supporting one fifth of all the globe. Here, labor is abundant and here labor is better remunerated than any where else. All moral, social and geographical causes, conspire to bring to us the peoples of all other over populated countries.

Europe and Africa are already here, and the Indian was here before either He stands to-day between the two extremes of black and white, too proud to claim fraternity with either, and yet too weak to withstand the power of either. Heretofore the policy of our government has been governed by race pride rather than by wisdom. Until recently, neither the Indian nor the Negro has been treated as a part of the body politic. No attempt has been made to inspire either with a sentiment of patriotism, but the hearts of both races have been diligently sown with the dangerous seeds of discontent and hatred.

The policy of keeping the Indians to themselves, has kept the tomahawk and scalping knife busy upon our borders, and has cost us largely in blood and treasure. Our treatment of the negro has slacked humanity, and filled the country with agitation and ill-feeling and brought the nation to the verge of ruin.

Before the relations of these two races are satisfactorily settled, and in spite of all opposition, a new race is making its appearance within our borders, and claiming attention. It is estimated that not less than one-hundred thousand Chinamen, are now within the limits of the United States. Several years ago every vessel, large or small, of steam or sail, bound to our Pacific coast and hailing from the Flowery kingdom, added to the number and strength of this new element of our population.

Men differ widely as to the magnitude of this potential Chinese immigration. The fact that by the late treaty with China, we bind ourselves to receive immigrants from that country only as the subjects of the Emperor, and by the construction, at least, are bound not to [naturalize] them, and the further fact that Chinamen themselves have a superstitious devotion to their country and an aversion to permanent location in any other, contracting even to have their bones carried back, should they die abroad, and from the fact that many have returned to China, and the still more stubborn [fact] that resistance to their coming has increased rather than diminished, it is inferred that we shall never have a large Chinese population in America. This however is not my opinion.

It may be admitted that these reasons, and others, may check and moderate the tide of immigration; but it is absurd to think that they will do more than this. Counting their number now, by the thousands, the time is not remote when they will count them by the millions. The Emperor's hold upon the Chinamen may be strong, but the Chinaman's hold upon himself is stronger.

Treaties against naturalization, like all other treaties, are limited by circumstances. As to the superstitious attachment of the Chinese to China, that, like all other superstitions, will dissolve in the light and heat of truth and experience. The Chinaman may be a bigot, but it does not follow that he will continue to be one, to-morrow. He is a man, and will be very likely to act like a man. He will not be long in finding out that a country which is good enough to live in, is good enough to die in; and that a soil that was good enough to hold his body while alive, will be good enough to hold his bones when he is dead.

Those who doubt a large immigration, should remember that the past furnishes no criterion as a basis of calculation. We live under new and improved conditions of migration, and these conditions are constantly improving. America is no longer an obscure and inaccessible country. Our ships are in every sea, our commerce in every port, our language is heard all around the globe. Steam and lightning have revolutionized the whole domain of human thought, changed all geographical relations. Make a day of the present seem equal to a thousand years of the past, and the continent that Columbus only conjectured four centuries ago is now the centre of the world.

I believe that Chinese immigration on a large scale will yet be our irrepressible fact. The spirit of race pride will not always prevail. The reasons for this opinion are obvious; China is a vastly overcrowded country. Her people press against each other like cattle in a rail car. Many live upon the water, and have laid out streets upon the waves. Men, like bees, want elbow room. When the hive is overcrowded, the bees will swarm, and will be likely to take up their abode where they find the best prospect for honey. In matters of this sort, men are very much like bees. Hunger will not be quietly endured, even in the celestial empire, when it is once generally known that there is bread enough and to spare in America. What Satan said of Job is true of the Chinaman, as well as of other men, "All that a man hath will he give for his life." They will come here to live where they know the means of living are in abundance.

The same mighty forces which have swept to our shores the overflowing populations of Europe; which have reduced the people of Ireland three millions below its normal standard; will operate in a similar manner upon the hungry population of China and other parts of Asia. Home has its charms, and native land has its charms, but hunger, oppression, and destitution, will desolve these charms and send men in search of new countries and new homes.

Not only is there a Chinese motive behind this probable immigration, but there is also an American motive which will play its part, one which will be all the more active and energetic because there is in it an element of pride, of bitterness, and revenge.

Southern gentlemen who led in the late rebellion, have not parted with their convictions at this point, any more than at others. They want to be independent of the negro. They believed in slavery and they believe in it still. They believed in an aristocratic class and they believe in it still, and though they have lost slavery, one element essential to such a class, they still have two important conditions to the reconstruction of that class. They have intelligence and they have land. Of these, the land is the more important. They cling to it with all the tenacity of a cherished superstition. They will neither sell to the Negro, nor let the carpet baggers have it in peace, but are determined to hold it for themselves and their children forever. They have not yet learned that when a principle is gone, the incident must go also; that what was wise and proper under slavery, is foolish and mischievous in a state of general liberty; that the old bottles are worthless when the new wine has come; but they have found that land is a doubtful benefit where there are no hands to till it.

Hence these gentlemen have turned their attention to the Celestial Empire. They would rather have laborers who will work for nothing; but as they cannot get the Negroes on these terms, they want Chinamen who, they hope, will work for next to nothing.

Companies and associations may be formed to promote this Mongolian invasion. The loss of the negro is to gain them, the Chinese; and if the thing works well, abolition, in their opinion, will have proved itself to be another blessing in disguise. To the statesman it will mean Southern independence. To the pulpit it will be the hand of Providence, and bring about the time of the universal dominion of the Christian religion. To all but the Chinaman and the negro, it will mean wealth, ease and luxury.

But alas, for all the selfish inventions and dreams of men! The Chinaman will not long be willing to wear the cast off shoes of the Negro, and if he refuses, there will be trouble again. The negro worked and took his pay in religion and the lash. The Chinaman is a different article and will want the cash. He may, like the negro, accept Christianity, but unlike the Negro he will not care to pay for it in labor under the lash. He had the golden rule in substance, five hundred years before the coming of Christ, and has notions of justice that are not to be confused or bewildered by any of our *"Cursed be Canaan"* religion.

Nevertheless, the experiment will be tried. So far as getting the Chinese into our country is concerned, it will yet be a success. This elephant will be drawn by our southern brethren, though they will hardly know in the end what to do with him.

Appreciation of the value of Chinamen as laborers will, I apprehend, become general in this country. The North was never indifferent to Southern influence and example, and it will not be so in this instance.

The Chinese in themselves have first rate recommendations. They are industrious, docile, cleanly, frugal; they are dexterous of hand, patient of toil, marvelously gifted in the power of imitation, and have but few wants. Those who have carefully observed their habits in California, say they can subsist upon what would be almost starvation to others.

The conclusion of the whole will be that they will want to come to us, and as we become more liberal, we shall want them to come, and what we want will normally be done.

They will no longer halt upon the shores of California. They will b[u]rrow no longer in her exhausted and deserted gold mines where they have gathered wealth from bareness, taking what others left. They will turn their backs not only upon the Celestial Empire, but upon the golden shores of the Pacific, and the wide waste of waters whose majestic waves spoke to them of home and country. They will withdraw their eyes from the glowing west and fix them upon the rising sun. They will cross the mountains, cross the plains, descend our rivers, penetrate to the heart of the country and fix their homes with us forever.

Assuming then that this immigration already has a foothold and will continue for many years to come, we have a new element in our national composition which is likely to exercise a large influence upon the thought and the action of the whole nation.

The old question as to what shall be done with [the] Negro will have to give place to the greater question, "what shall be done with the mongolian" and perhaps we shall see raised one even still greater question, namely, what will the mongolian do with both the negro and the whites?

Already has the matter taken this shape in California and on the Pacific Coast generally. Already has California assumed a bitterly unfriendly attitude toward the Chinamen. Already has she driven them from her altars of justice. Already has she stamped them as outcasts and handed them over to popular contempt and vulgar jest. Already are they the constant victims of cruel harshness and brutal violence. Already have our Celtic brothers, never slow to execute the behests of popular prejudice against the weak and defenseless, recognized in the heads of these people, fit targets for their shilalahs. Already, too, are their associations formed in avowed hostility to the Chinese.

In all this there is, of course, nothing strange. Repugnance to the presence and influence of foreigners is an ancient feeling among men. It is peculiar to no particular race or nation. It is met with not only in the conduct of one nation toward another, but in the conduct of the inhabitants of different parts of the same country, some times of the same city, and even of the same village. "Lands intersected by a narrow frith, abhor each other. Mountains interposed, make enemies of nations." To the Hindoo, every man not twice born, is Mleeka. To the Greek, every man not speaking Greek, is a barbarian. To the Jew, every one not circumcised, is a gentile. To the Mahometan, every man not believing in the prophet, is a kaffe. I need not repeat here the multitude of reproachful epithets expressive of the same sentiment among ourselves. All who are not to the manor born, have been made to feel the lash and sting of these reproachful names.

For this feeling there are many apologies, for there was never yet an error, however flagrant and hurtful, for which some plausible defense could not be framed. Chattel slavery, king craft, priest craft, pious frauds, intolerance, persecution, suicide, assassination, repudiation, and a thousand other errors and crimes, have all had their defenses and apologies.

Prejudice of race and color has been equally upheld. The two best arguments in its defense are, first, the worthlessness of the class against which it is directed; and, second; that the feeling itself is entirely natural.

The way to overcome the first argument is, to work for the elevation of those deemed worthless, and thus make them worthy of regard and they will soon become worthy and not worthless. As to the natural argument it may be said, that nature has many sides. Many things are in a certain sense natural, which are neither wise nor best. It is natural to walk, but shall men therefore refuse to ride? It is natural to ride on horseback, shall men therefore refuse steam and rail? Civilization is itself a constant war upon some forces in nature; shall we therefore abandon civilization and go back to savage life?

Nature has two voices, the one is high, the other low; one is in sweet accord with reason and justice, and the other apparently at war with both. The more men really know of the essential nature of things, and of the true relation of mankind, the freer they are from prejudices of every kind. The child is afraid of the giant form of his own shadow. This is natural, but he will part with his fears when he is older and wiser. So ignorance is full of prejudice, but it will disappear with enlightenment. But I pass on.

I have said that the Chinese will come, and have given some reasons why we may expect them in very large numbers in no very distant future. Do you ask, if I favor such immigration, I answer *I would*. Would you have them naturalized, and have them invested with all the rights of American citizenship? *I would*. Would you allow them to vote? *I would*. Would you allow them to hold office? *I would*.

But are there not reasons against all this? Is there not such a law or principle as that of self preservation? Does not every race owe something to itself? Should it not attend to the dictates of common sense? Should not a superior race protect itself from contact with inferior ones? Are not the white people the owners of this continent? Have they not the right to say, what kind of people shall be allowed to come here and settle? Is there not such a thing as being more generous than wise? In the effort to promote civilization may we not corrupt and destroy what we have? Is it best to take on board more passengers than the ship will carry?

To all this and more I have one among many answers, altogether satisfactory to me, though I cannot promise that it will be so to you.

I submit that this question of Chinese immigration should be settled upon higher principles than those of a cold and selfish expediency.

There are such things in the world as human rights. They rest upon no conventional foundation, but are eternal, universal, and indestructible. Among these, is the right of locomotion; the right of migration; the right which belongs to no particular race, but belongs alike to all and to all alike. It is the right you assert by staying here, and your fathers asserted by coming here. It is this great right that I assert for the Chinese and the Japanese, and for all other varieties of men equally with yourselves, now and forever. I know of no rights of race superior to the rights of humanity, and when there is a supposed conflict between human and national rights, it is safe to go to the side of humanity. I have great respect for the blue eyed and light haired races of America. They are a mighty people. In any struggle for the good things of this world they need have no fear. They have no need to doubt that they will get their full share.

But I reject the arrogant and scornful theory by which they would limit migratory rights, or any other essential human rights to themselves, and which would make them the owners of this great continent to the exclusion of all other races of men.

I want a home here not only for the Negro, the mulatto, and the Latin races; but I want the Asiatic to find a home here in the United States, and feel at home here, both for his sake and for ours. Right wrongs no man. If respect is had to majorities, the fact that only one fifth of the population of the globe is white, the other four fifths are colored, ought to have some weight and influence in disposing of this and similar questions. It would be a sad reflection upon the laws of nature and upon the idea of justice, to say nothing of a common Creator, if four fifths of mankind were deprived of the rights of migration to make room for the one fifth. If the white race may exclude all other races from this continent, it may rightfully do the same in respect to all other lands, islands, capes and continents, and thus have all the world to itself. Thus what would seem to belong to the whole, would become the property only of a part. So much for what is right, now let us see what is wise.

And here I hold that a liberal and brotherly welcome to all who are likely to come to the United States, is the only wise policy which this nation can adopt.

It has been thoughtfully observed, that every nation, owing to its peculiar character and composition, has a definite mission in the world. What that mission is, and what policy is best adapted to assist in its fulfillment, is the business of its people and its statesmen to know, and knowing, to make a noble use of said knowledge.

I need not stop here to name or describe the missions of other and more ancient nationalities. Ours seems plain and unmistakable. Our geographical position, our relation to the outside world, our fundamental principles of Government, world embracing in their scope and character, our vast resources, requiring all manner of labor to develop them, and our already existing composite population, all conspire to one grand end, and that is to make us the most perfect national illustration of the unity and dignity of the human family, that the world has ever seen.

In whatever else other nations may have been great and grand, our greatness and grandeur will be found in the faithful application of the principle of perfect civil equality to the people of all races and of all creeds, and to men of no creeds. We are not only bound to this position by our organic structure and by our revolutionary antecedents, but by the genius of our people. Gathered here, from all quarters of the globe by a common aspiration for rational liberty as against caste, divine right Governments and privileged classes, it would be unwise to be found fighting against ourselves and among ourselves; it would be madness to set up any one race above another, or one religion above another, or proscribe any on account of race color or creed.

The apprehension that we shall be swamped or swallowed up by mongolian civilization; that the Caucasian race may not be able to hold their own against that vast incoming population, does not seem entitled to much respect. Though they come as the waves come, we shall be all the stronger if we receive them as friends and give them a reason for loving our country and our institutions. They will find here a deeply rooted, indigenous, growing civilization, augmented by an ever increasing stream of immigration from Europe; and possession is nine points of the law in this case, as well as in others. They will come as strangers, we are at home. They will come to us, not we to them. They will come in their weakness, we shall meet them in our strength. They will come as individuals, we will meet them in multitudes, and with all the advantages of organization. Chinese children are in American schools in San Francisco, none of our children are in Chinese schools, and probably never will be, though in some things they might well teach us valuable lessons. Contact with these yellow children of the Celestial Empire would convince us that the points of human difference, great as they, upon first sight, seem, are as nothing compared with the points of human agreement. Such contact would remove mountains of prejudice.

All great qualities are never found in any one man or in any one race. The whole of humanity, like the whole of everything else, is ever greater than a part. Men only know themselves by knowing others, and contact is essential to this knowledge. In one race we perceive the predominance of imagination; in another, like the Chinese, we remark its total absence. In one people, we have the reasoning faculty; in another, for music; in another, exists courage; in another, great physical vigor; and so on through the whole list of human qualities. All are needed to temper, modify, round and complete.

Not the least among the arguments whose consideration should dispose to welcome among us the peoples of all countries, nationalities and color, is the fact that all races and varieties of men are improvable. This is the grand distinguishing attribute of humanity and separates man from all other animals. If it could be shown that any particular race of men are literally incapable of improvement, we might hesitate to welcome them here. But no such men are anywhere to be found, and if there were, it is not likely that they would ever trouble us with their presence.

Now let me answer briefly some objections to the general scope of my arguments. I am told that science is against me; that races are not all of one origin, and that the unity theory of human origin has been exploded. I admit that this is a question that has two sides. It is impossible to trace the threads of human history sufficiently near their starting point to know much about the origin of races.

In disposing of this question whether we shall welcome or repel immigration from China, Japan, or elsewhere, we may leave the differences among the theological doctors to be settled by themselves.

Whether man originated at one time and one or another place; whether there was one Adam or five, or five hundred, does not affect the question.

The grand right of migration and the great wisdom of incorporating foreign elements into our body politic, are founded not upon any genealogical or archeological theory, however learned, but upon the broad fact of a common human nature.

Man is man, the world over. This fact is affirmed and admitted in any effort to deny it.

The sentiments we exhibit, whether love or hate, confidence or fear, respect or contempt, will always imply a like humanity.

A smile or a tear has no nationality; joy and sorrow speak alike to all nations, and they, above all the confusion of tongues, proclaim the brotherhood of man.

It is objected to the Chinaman that he is secretive and treacherous, and will not tell the truth when he thinks it for his interest to tell a lie.

There may be truth in all this; it sounds very much like the account of man's heart given in the creeds. If he will not tell the truth except when it is for his interest to do so, let us make it for his interest to tell the truth. We can do it by applying to him the same principle of justice that we apply to ourselves.

But I doubt if the Chinese are more untruthful than other people. At this point I have one certain test—mankind are not held together by lies. Trust is the foundation of society. Where there is no truth, there can be no trust, and where there is no trust there can be no society. Where there is society, there is trust, and where there is trust, there is something upon which it is supported. Now a people who have confided in each other for five thousand years; who have extended their empire in all direction till it embraces one fifth of the population of the globe; who hold important commercial relations with all nations; who are now entering into treaty stipulations with ourselves, and with all the great European powers, cannot be a nation of cheats and liars, but must have some respect for veracity. The very existence of China for so long a period, and her progress in civilization, are proofs of her truthfulness. But it is said that the Chinese is a heathen, and that he will introduce his heathen rights and superstitions here. This is the last objection which should come from those who profess the all conquering power of the Christian religion. If that religion cannot stand contact with the Chinese, religion or no religion, so much the worse for those who have adopted it. It is the Chinaman, not the Christian, who should be alarmed for his faith. He exposes that faith to great dangers by exposing it to the freer air of America. But shall we send missionaries to the heathen and yet deny the heathen the right to come to us? I think that a few honest believers in the teachings of Confucius would be well employed in expounding his doctrines among us.

The next objection to the Chinese is that he cannot be induced to swear by the Bible. This is to me one of his best recommendations. The American people will swear by anything in the heavens above or in the earth beneath.

We are a nation of swearers. We swear by a book whose most authoritative command is to swear not at all.

It is not of so much importance what a man swears by, as what he swears to, and if the Chinaman is so true to his convictions that he cannot be tempted or even coerced into so popular a custom as swearing by the Bible, he gives good evidence of his integrity and his veracity.

Let the Chinaman come; he will help to augment the national wealth. He will help to develop our boundless resources; he will help to pay off our national debt. He will help to lighten the burden of national taxation. He will give us the benefit of his skill as a manufacturer and tiller of the soil, in which he is unsurpassed.

Even the matter of religious liberty, which has cost the world more tears, more blood and more agony, than any other interest, will be helped by his presence. I know of no church, however tolerant; of no priesthood, however enlightened, which could be safely trusted with the tremendous power which universal conformity would confer. We should welcome all men of every shade of religious opinion, as among the best means of checking the arrogance and intolerance which are the almost inevitable concomitants of general conformity. Religious liberty always flourishes best amid the clash and competition of rival religious creeds.

To the minds of superficial men, the fusion of different races has already brought disaster and ruin upon the country. The poor Negro has been charged with all our woes. In the haste of these men they forgot that our trouble was not ethnographical, but moral; that it was not a difference of complexion, but a difference of conviction. It was not the Ethiopian as a man, but the Ethiopian as a slave and a coveted article of merchandise, that gave us trouble.

I close these remarks as I began. If our action shall be in accordance with the principles of justice, liberty, and perfect human equality, no eloquence can adequately portray the greatness and grandeur of the future of the Republic.

We shall spread the network of our science and civilization over all who seek their shelter whether from Asia, Africa, or the Isles of the sea. We shall mold them all, each after his kind, into Americans; Indian and Celt; negro and Saxon; Latin and Teuton; Mongolian and Caucasian; Jew and Gentile; all shall here bow to the same law, speak the same language, support the same Government, enjoy the same liberty, vibrate with the same national enthusiasm, and seek the same national ends.

SUSAN B. ANTHONY
(1820–1906)

Suffrage and the Working Woman
JULY 1871

A brain wasted because it happens to be a woman's. . . .
How will we remedy this?

Susan B. Anthony was born in 1820 in Adams, Massachusetts, the daughter of Quaker activists. From an early age, Anthony learned the importance of social and economic justice and moral righteousness. She brought that passion and commitment into the classroom, where she taught for fifteen years before becoming actively involved in the temperance movement and other women's causes. This experience, and her acquaintance with Elizabeth Cady Stanton, drew her to demand equal rights for women—concluding that only with full citizenship could women become effective workers for social betterment. Soon after, beginning at Seneca Falls Convention in 1848, Anthony dedicated her life entirely to the cause of women's suffrage.

Anthony delivered the following speech in 1871 but presented it in much the same form to audiences across the country from the 1860s until the early 1890s. In it, she passionately decried the low wages paid to women workers and the limits on their independence, citing her own experiences as a teacher earning one-third what her male counterparts did. Anthony argued that working meant more than financial survival—it symbolized independence.

With an inspirational tongue, she demanded equal opportunity, independence, and suffrage, pointing to African-American emancipation and enfranchisement to substantiate her case for women's equality. In 1872, in a test of women's suffrage under the Fourteenth Amendment, Susan B. Anthony became the first woman to cast a ballot in a presidential election. Two weeks later she was arrested for having violated the law.

I COME TO NIGHT . . . as a representative of the working women. I lay down my doctrine that the first step for the alleviation of their oppression is to secure to them pecuniary independence. Alexander Hamilton said 100 years ago "take my right over my subsistence and you possess absolute power over my moral being." That is applicable to the working women of the present day. Others possess the right over their subsistence. What is the cause of this? I will tell you. It is because of a false theory having been in the minds of the human family for ages that woman is born to be supported by man and to accept such circumstances as he chooses to accord to her. She not like him is not allowed to control her own circumstances. The pride of every man is that he is free to carve out his own destiny. A woman has no such pride.

A little circumstance happened at this hall last night which illustrates this. A mother and daughter came to the ticket office to purchase tickets, when they were confronted by a man who exclaimed, "Didn't I forbid you to come here to-night?" He had a heavy cane in his hand which he flourished over them, and finally drove them away from the hall.

I appeal to you men. If you were under such control of another man would you not consider it an absolute slavery? But you say that man was a brute. Suppose he is a brute, he is no more of a brute than the law permits him to be.

But to go back. Is it true that women are supported by men? If I was to go home with you all to-night, I should find ample proof of falsity. I should find among your homes many who support themselves. Then if I should go into your manufactories . . . I should find hundreds and thousands who support themselves by the industry of their own hands. In Boston there are 10,000 women engaged in shoemaking. You say these are extreme cases. So they are, but it is in these large cities that the hardship and wrong is most apparent. . . .

If you will take the stand with me on the main thoroughfares of New York, on the Bowery, at the ferries, you will see troops and troops of women going to their daily work. There are not quite so many as there are men, but the men think it is not disreputable to work. Not so with woman. If she makes an effort to support herself, she always makes an effort to conceal it. The young girl has her satchel as though going to the depot, or has her books as though going to school.

Some years ago we had a Woman's Benevolent Society in New York and appointed a committee to visit all over the city among the poor. The committee visited among others a family of rag pickers. . . . In one little garret was a mother and five little children. The committee appealed to the mother to allow them to put her in a way to support her children and send them to school. They pleaded with her for some time without avail and finally she straightened herself up and exclaimed, "No indeed, ladies. I'll have you to understand my husband is a gintleman and no gintleman allows his wife to go out to work." [Laughter]

That society is wrong which looks on labor as being any more degrading to woman than to man.

It was no more ridiculous for the rag picker's wife to scout the idea of going to work out than it is for the daughter of a well-to-do farmer to scout the idea of supporting herself. . . .

I am proud of San Francisco that she is an exception to the rule, and that she has raised a woman to the position of Principal of one of the cosmopolitan schools with a full salary of $1,200 a year. But if tomorrow, the same model girl, whom I have just referred to, were to marry a banker and live a life of idleness, with horses, carriages, and house finely furnished, able to take her trip to Europe and with all the advantages wealth could purchase, though her husband were a drunkard, a libertine and a vile and depraved wretch, the woman would never again receive pity. Now we want this rule changed.

The first result of this false theory is this: no woman is even educated to work. Sons are educated while daughters are allowed to grow up mere adornments, and when the hour of necessity comes, then comes cruelty in the extreme. The woman has to skill her hands for labor, and has to compete with men who have been skilled from boyhood; and not only this but when she has attained ability to compete with them and to do just as well in every respect she is placed at work, if at all, on half pay. Society dooms her always to a subordinate position, as an inferior. . . .

Nowhere can woman hold head offices and the reason is this, politicians can't afford to give an office to one who can't pay back in votes. If in New York the women could decide the fate of elections, don't you think they could afford to make women County Clerks or Surrogate Clerks or even Surrogate Judges? Said a Surrogate Judge to me, "Miss Anthony, I was almost converted by your lecture last night. I have one son and one daughter. The son is at college." I asked him, "Is your son possessed of the requisite ability to place him in your position?" "No," he replied; "he will spend his days in a garrett daubing paints on a canvass. But my daughter has a splendid legal mind, and understands already much of my duties. What a pity she was not a boy!" Only think, a brain wasted because it happens to be a woman's. For this reason one half the brain in the world remain undeveloped. How will we remedy this? Give woman an equal chance to compete with men, educate her and surround her with the same legal advantages. Every one knows that the great stimulus for activity is to be paid for in having that activity recognized by promotion.

How will the ballot cure the evil? You tell me the ballot is not going to alleviate this. I will tell you how it is going to alleviate it. Never have the disfranchised classes had equal chances with the enfranchised. What is the difference between the working classes of the United States and Europe? Simply that, here the workman has the ballot and there he has not. Here, if he has the brains or energy, his chances are quite equal with the son of the millionaire. That is American Republicanism—the ballot in the hand of every man. [*Applause*] . . . See how it works. Take the St. Crispins for example. . . . Well, these three hundred St. Crispins strike against a reduction of wages, and not only they, but twenty other St. Crispin Societies, and not only they but other workmen. Now, suppose the New York *World* denounced those men, and the Democratic party manifested prejudice, not only those 300 men would vote against the party but all the other societies: the hod carriers, brick layers, the masons, the carpenters and the tailors would vote solidly against the party which opposed them, and that party would go to the wall.

~~~

Now what do women want? Simply the same ballot. In this city, they, the women hat and cap makers, 2,000 of them, made a strike and held out three weeks, but finally they were forced to yield. Their employers said "Take that or nothing," and although "that" was *almost* "nothing" they had to take it or starve. Until two weeks ago I never heard of a successful strike among women. I'll tell you why this was successful. The employers of the Daughters of St. Crispin at Baltimore undertook to cut their wages down, and the Daughters struck. They were about to be defeated when the men St. Crispins came to the rescue and said to the employers, "If you don't accede we will strike," and they carried their point. How happened the workmen to do this? Because they are beginning to see that as long as women work, the capitalists are able to use them to undermine the workmen. . . .

~~~

Not long ago I met the President of the organization and I asked her "If you were men you would have won?" "O yes," she said, "the men always win when they strike." "What was the cause of your defeat?" She said: "I guess it was the newspapers. They said if the women were not satisfied, they had better get married." [*Laughter*] "What made the newspapers oppose you?" "I guess our employers paid them money." "How much?" "I think $10,000." I asked her if the five hundred collar workers had had votes, would the newspapers dared to have opposed them? She said they would not. When the men strike, the employers try to bribe the newspapers in just the same way, but the newspapers dare not sell. The political editor of a party paper puts the votes in one scale and the cash in the other, and the cash knocks the beam every time. [Laughter] Simply because those five hundred women were helpless and powerless and represented the whole half of a country who were helpless and powerless, they failed. . . .

Now let me give you an example for teachers. In a certain city in the East, the women teachers petitioned for an advance of salary. The School Board finding it necessary to retrench, instead of advancing their salaries deducted from the salaries of the women intermediate teachers $25 a month. They did not dare to reduce the salaries of the male teachers because they had votes.

I have a sister somewhat younger than I who has been in those schools for twenty years. [*Laughter*] Suppose six or seven women were members of the Board, do you believe the Board would have failed to receive that petition? . . .

A few years ago in this house a colored woman would not have been allowed a seat. Now the negro is enfranchised and what is the result? We see the black man walk the streets as proud as any man, simply because he has the ballot. Now black men are mayors of cities, legislators and office holders. Nobody dares to vent his spleen on Negroes today.

We always invite the mayor and governor to our conventions, but they always have important business which keeps them from attending. The Negro invites them and they come. Two years ago they did not. . . . Today the conservative Republicans bid the negro good morning, and even the Democrats look wistfully at him.

I visited last year the Legislature of Tennessee. I inquired, "Who is that negro member?" I was answered that it was the honorable gentleman of Lynchburg, and that is the honorable gentleman of Hampton County, and that is the honorable gentleman of somewhere else. There were 20 of them. They did not occupy the black man's corner. They were seated with the white members. One black member was sitting on the same cushion on which sat his master three or four years ago.

I thought it would be nice to ask this Legislative body to attend my lecture; and when I extended my invitation, a gentleman asked that the courtesy of the Legislature be extended to me, and that I be allowed the use of the Legislative Hall. This called forth derisive laughter. The question was put on a suspension of the rules and was lost by a vote of 18 to 38. For the benefit of the Democracy, I will state that the negroes voted in favor of the suspension. A man stood near, who, from his appearance, might have been a slave-driver, and he launched out in a tirade of oaths and ended with, "If that had been a damned nigger who wanted the House, he could have had it." [*Laughter*] And so he could. . . . I believe that women have now the legal right to vote, and I believe that they should go to the polls and deposit their ballot, and if refused carry the officers and inspectors before the Supreme Court.

When we get the ballot those men who now think we are angels just before election will actually see our wings cropping out. [*Laughter*]

You say the women and the negro are not parallel cases. The negro was a down trodden race, but for the women there is no such necessity for they are lovely and beloved, and the men will guard them from evil. I suppose they will guard their own wives and daughters and mothers and sisters, but is every man as careful to guard another man's wife, daughter, mother and sister? It is not a question of safety to women in general. It is simply "Is she *my* property?" . . . You women who have kind brothers and husband and sons, I ask you to join with us in this movement so that woman can protect herself.

James T. Rapier
(1839–1883)

Half Free, Half Slave
February 4, 1875

Either I am a man or I am not a man.

A labor leader, newspaper editor, and civil rights activist, James T. Rapier was sent to Congress from Alabama at the height of Reconstruction. The son of a white father and an African-American mother, Rapier matriculated at Montreal College in Canada and then at the University of Glasgow. Following the Civil War, he returned to the United States and, with his sharp tongue, noted wit, and the help of the Radical Republican Congress and Union Army, landed a seat in the House of Representatives. Within months, he became one of the most effective advocates for racial equality and, in particular, the Civil Rights Act of 1875, which granted all citizens, regardless of race or color, full access to public facilities and accommodations.

In this powerful address before the House of Representatives, Rapier described the experience of being a foreigner in his native country. He then questioned how a man could be elected to Congress, yet still be denied equal access to restaurants, inns, and schools. That, he argued, was what it meant to be "half free and half slave."

Mr. Speaker, I had hoped there would be no protracted discussion on the civil rights bill. It has been debated all over the country for the last seven years; twice it has done duty in our national political campaigns; and in every minor election during that time it has been pressed into service for the purpose of intimidating the weak white men who are inclined to support the republican ticket. I was certain until now that most persons were acquainted with its provisions, that they understood its meaning; therefore it was no longer to them the monster it had been depicted, that was to break down all social barriers, and compel one man to recognize another socially, whether agreeable to him or not.

I must confess it is somewhat embarrassing for a colored man to urge the passage of this bill, because if he exhibits an earnestness in the matter and expresses a desire for its immediate passage, straightway he is charged with a desire for social equality, as explained by the demagogue and understood by the ignorant white man. But then it is just as embarrassing for him not to do so, for, if he remains silent while the struggle is being carried on around, and for him, he is liable to be charged with a want of interest in a matter that concerns him more than any one else, which is enough to make his friends desert his cause. So in steering away from Scylla I may run upon Charybdis. But the anomalous and, I may add, the supremely ridiculous position of the Negro at this time, in this country, compels me to say something. Here his condition is without comparison, parallel alone to itself. Just that the law recognizes my right upon this floor as a lawmaker, but that there is no law to secure to me any accommodations whatever while traveling here to discharge my duties as a Representative of a large and wealthy constituency. Here I am the peer of the proudest, but on a steamboat or car I am not equal to the most degraded. Is not this most anomalous and ridiculous?

I wish to say in justice to myself that no one regrets more than I do the necessity that compels one to the manor born to come in these halls with hat in hand (so to speak) to ask at the hands of his political peers the same public rights they enjoy. And I shall feel ashamed for my country if there be any foreigners present who have been lured to our shores by the popular but untruthful declaration that this land is the asylum of the oppressed, to hear a member of the highest legislative body in the world declare from his place, upon his responsibility as a Representative, that, notwithstanding his political position, he has no civil rights that another class is bound to respect.

Here a foreigner can learn what he cannot learn in any other country, that it is possible for a man to be half free and half slave, or, in other words, he will see that it is possible for a man to enjoy political rights while he is denied civil ones; here he will see a man legislating for a free people, while his own chains of slavery hang about him and are far more galling than any the foreigner left behind him; here he will see and what is not to be seen elsewhere, that position is no mantle of protection in our "land of the free and home of the brave"; for I am subjected to far more outrages and indignities in coming to and going from this capital in discharge of my public duties than any criminal in the country provided he be white. Instead of my position shielding me for insult, it too often invites it.

I affirm, without the fear of contradiction, that any white ex-convict (I care not what may have been his crime, nor whether the hair on the shaven side of his head has had time to grow out or not) may start with me today to Montgomery, that all the way down he will be treated as a gentleman, while

I will be treated as the convict. He will be allowed a berth in a sleeping car with all its comforts, while I will be forced into a dirty, rough box with the drunkards, apple sellers, railroad hands, and next to any dead that be in transit, regardless of how far decomposition may have progressed. Sentinels are placed at the doors of the better coaches, with positive instructions to keep persons of color out; and I must do them the justice to say that they guard these sacred portals with a vigilance that would have done credit to the flaming swords at the gates of Eden. Tender, pure, intelligent young ladies are forced to travel in this way if they are guilty of the crime of color, the only unpardonable sin known in our Christian and Bible lands, where sinning against the Holy Ghost (whatever that may be) sinks into significance when compared with the sin of color. If from any cause we are compelled to lay over, the best bed in the hotel is his if he can pay for it, while I am invariably turned away, hungry and cold, to stand around the railroad station until the departure of the next train, it matters not how long, thereby endangering my health, while my life and property are at the mercy of any highwayman who may wish to murder and rob me.

And I state without the fear of being gainsaid, the statement of the gentleman from Tennessee to the contrary notwithstanding, that there is not an inn between Washington and Montgomery, a distance of more than a thousand miles, that will accommodate me to bed or meal. Now, then, is there a man upon this floor who is so heartless, whose breast is so void of the better feelings, as to say that this brutal custom needs no regulation? I hold that it does and that Congress is the body to regulate it. Authority for its action is found not only in the Fourteenth Amendment to the Constitution, but by virtue of that amendment (which makes all persons born here citizens) authority is found in Article 4, Section 2, of the federal Constitution, which declares in positive language that "the citizens of each state shall have the same rights as the citizens of the several states." Let me read Mr. Brightly's comment upon this clause; he is considered good authority, I believe. In describing the several rights he says they may all be comprehended under the following general heads: "Protection by the government; the enjoyment of life and liberty, with the right to acquire and possess property of every kind, and to pursue and obtain happiness and safety; the right of a citizen of one state to pass through or to reside in any other state for purposes of trade, agriculture, professional pursuits, or otherwise."

Sir, I submit that I am degraded as long as I am denied the public privileges common to other men, and that the members of this House are correspondingly degraded by recognizing my political equality while I occupy such humiliating position. What a singular attitude for lawmakers of this great nation to assume, rather come down to me than allow me to go up to them. Sir, did you ever reflect that this is the only Christian country where poor, finite man is held responsible for the crimes of the infinite God whom you profess to worship? But it is; I am held to answer for the crime of color, when I was not consulted in the matter. Had I been consulted, and my future fully described, I think I should have objected to being born in this Gospel land. The excuse offered for all this inhuman treatment is that they consider the Negro inferior to the white man, intellectually and morally. This reason might have been offered and probably accepted as truth some years ago, but not one now believes him incapable of a high order of culture, except someone who is himself below the average of mankind in natural endowments.

Mr. Speaker, time will not allow me to review the history of the American Negro, but I must pause here long enough to say that he has not been properly treated by this nation; he has purchased and paid for all, and for more than, he has yet received. Whatever liberty he enjoys has been paid for over and over again by more than two hundred years of forced toil; and for such citizenship as is allowed him he paid the full measure of his blood, the dearest price required at the hands of any citizen. In every contest, from the beginning of the Revolutionary struggle down to the War Between the States, has he been prominent. But we all remember in our late war when the government was so hard pressed for troops to sustain the cause of the Union, when it was so difficult to fill up the ranks that had been so fearfully decimated by disease and the bullet; when every train that carried to the front a number of fresh soldiers brought back a corresponding number of wounded and sick ones; when grave doubts as to the success of the Union arms had seized upon the minds of some of the most sanguine friends of the government; when strong men took counsel of their fears; when those who had all their lives received the fostering care of the nation were hesitating as to their duty in that trying hour, and others questioning if it were not better to allow the star of this Republic to go down and thus be blotted out from the great map of nations than to continue the bloodshed; when gloom and despair were widespread; when the last ray of hope had nearly sunk below our political horizon, how the Negro then came forward and offered himself as a sacrifice in the place of the nation, made bare his breast to the steel, and in it received the thrusts of the bayonet that were aimed at the life of the nation by the soldiers of that government in which the gentleman from Georgia figured as second officer.

Sir, the valor of the colored soldier was tested on many a battlefield, and today his bones lie bleaching beside every hill and in every valley from the Potomac to the Gulf; whose mute eloquence in behalf of equal rights for all before the law, is and ought to be far more persuasive than any poor language I can command.

⌐⌐

. . . Either I am a man or I am not a man. If one, I am entitled to all the rights, privileges and immunities common to any other class in this country; if not a man, I have no right to vote, no right to a seat here; if no right to vote, then 20 percent of the members on this floor have no right here, but, on the contrary, hold their seats in violation of the law. If the Negro has no right to vote, then one eighth of your Senate consists of members who have no shadow of a claim to the places they occupy; and if no right to vote, a half-dozen governors in the South figure as usurpers.

This is the legitimate conclusion of the argument, that the Negro is not a man and is not entitled to all the public rights common to other men, and you cannot escape it. But when I press my claims I am asked, "Is it good policy?" My answer is, "Policy is out of the question; it has nothing to do with it; that you can have no policy in dealing with your citizens; that there must be one law for all; that in this case justice is the only standard to be used, and you can no more divide justice than you can divide Deity." On the other hand, I am told that I must respect the prejudices of others. Now, sir, no one respects reasonable and intelligent prejudice more than I. I respect religious prejudices, for example, these I can comprehend. But how can I have respect for the prejudices that prompt a man to turn up his nose at the males of a certain race, while at the same time he has a fondness for the females of the same race to the extent of cohabitation? Out of four poor unfortunate colored women, who from poverty were forced to go to the lying-in branch of the Freedman's Hospital here in the District last year, three gave birth to children whose fathers were white men, and I venture to say that if they were members of this body, would vote against the civil-rights bill. Do you, can you wonder at my want of respect for this kind of prejudice? To make me feel uncomfortable appears to be the highest ambition of many white men. It is to them a positive luxury, which they seek to indulge at every opportunity.

Mr. Speaker, I trust this bill will become law, because it is a necessity, and because it will put an end to all legislation on this subject. It does not and cannot contemplate any such ideas as social equality; nor is there any man upon this floor so silly as to believe that there can be any law enacted or enforced that would compel one man to recognize another as his equal socially; if there be, he ought not to be here, and I have only to say that they have sent him to the wrong public building. I would oppose such a bill as earnestly as the gentleman from North Carolina, whose associations and cultivations have been of such a nature as to lead him to select the crow as his standard of grandeur and excellence in the place of the eagle, the hero of all birds and our national emblem of pride and power. I will tell him that I have seen many of his race to whose level I should object to being dragged.

Sir, it matters not how much men may differ upon the question of state and national rights; here is one class of rights, however, that we all agree upon, namely, individual rights, which include the right of every man to select associates for himself and family, and to say who shall and who shall not visit at his house. This right is God-given and custom-sanctioned, and there is, and there can be, no power overruling your decision in this matter. Let this bill become law, and not only will it do much toward giving rest to this weary country on this subject, completing the manhood of my race and perfecting his citizenship, but it will take him from the political arena as a topic of discussion where he has done duty for the last fifty years, and thus freed from anxiety respecting his political standing, hundreds of us will abandon the political fields who are there from necessity, and not from choice, and seek other and more pleasant ones; and thus relieved, it will be the aim of the colored man as well as his duty and interest, to become a good citizen, and to do all in his power to advance the interests of a common country.

Rev. L. T. Chamberlain
Unsung Heroes
March 2, 1879

*Do you imagine that men who . . . climbed the perilous heights
of the Sierra Nevada . . . are beneath our conception in
moral and social degradation?*

Invoking words like "peaceable, industrious, frugal, sober, and skilled,"
the Reverend L.T. Chamberlain thundered from the pulpit of his
Norwich, Connecticut, church in support of Chinese American civil
rights. Beginning in 1848, hundreds of thousands of Chinese immigrants
landed in San Francisco, at first in search of Sierra Nevada's gold, then
as a source of cheap labor for the transcontinental railroads, mines, farms,
canneries, and garment factories. These new Americans encountered
discrimination at ever turn, particularly in periods of economic downturn and struggle. In 1853, for example, California crippled Chinese
immigrants by imposing a foreign miner's tax; in 1859 San Francisco
banned immigrant children from its public schools; and by 1870, as
another recession roared, "cheap Chinese labor" once again became the
scapegoat for nationwide financial woes. Mobs and lynchings destroyed
Chinese communities in San Francisco and across California. In 1870,
playing off waves of jingoism, Congress passed the Naturalization Act,
which excluded Chinese immigrants from citizenship and prohibited
the entry of any new Chinese laborers. By 1879, the time of Rev. L.T.
Chamberlain's sermon, Congress was embroiled in debate over an
exclusion bill to further prohibit Chinese immigration and labor.

A respected member of his community and a leader in temperance
and education, Chamberlain debunked the commonly spoken claim that
Chinese labor in San Francisco caused unemployment, poverty—even the
national recession. Chamberlain also saluted the contributions of Chinese
workers and publicly excoriated the bigotry and xenophobia permeating
the American landscape. His words were far ahead of his time. Though
initially vetoed by President Rutherford B. Hayes, the Chinese Exclusion
Act eventually passed Congress in 1882. It was not repealed until 1943.

───≈───

Ah, do you comprehend the greatness of the issue? Do you begin to
realize how this is a thing in which the world is more than a spectator, and

humanity more than an incidental participant? Does it dawn on you, that, *prima facie,* the case is against the Republic? I will utter not one word in pre-judgment of the issue. I can understand that the act might be justifiable. I can imagine that circumstances might warrant the extent of the severity. It were possible that the seeming injustice should prove to be the truest Christian wis-dom. Yet this, my friends, is already clear; that the justifying reasons must be singularly urgent, must be supremely weighty, or the case will go against the western nation. From some source there must be brought considerations of most exceptional moment, or the Christian will be shamed in contrast with the Pagan. Yet the decree has been pronounced. We will search with care for the grounds on which it may be upheld. . . .

But, there must—one would say—be the reason somewhere, for the act before us; for Congress is not composed of either the demented or the wholly depraved. I cling to my faith in the general wisdom and integrity of our national legislature. I cannot readily believe that either party in Washington is predominantly corrupt. And, moreover, this Chinese legislation is supported by both parties, or at least by their distinguished leaders. May it not be, then, that the reason of the action taken is in the character of the emigrants them-selves? Certainly one might surmise that they were infectious persons, that they contaminated the common air, or that they were corrupters of the pop-ular morals! And that is not far from the allegation actually made. It is avowed by the supporters of the proscription, that the Chinese emigrant is uncleanly and immoral, to a degree of which the Anglo-Saxon mind cannot conceive; that he lives like the beast, and sets at naught every dictate of decency and health. And that statement is not simply by the low ruffians of the streets and sand-flats, it is repeated by many of the true and good. We must, accordingly, give it weight. If it is warranted, the case requires swift remedial treatment. It may require even the severity of excision, of absolute removal. But you will note one comprehensive, signal fact which, by somewhat and at once, rebuts the sweeping charge! It is universally admitted,—mark it, *universally* admit-ted—that the Chinaman is peaceable, patient, frugal, sober, industrious, apt at learning, successful in traffic, skilled in the arts requiring delicacy of manipu-lation, capable of great physical endurance, and especially fitted for resisting malarias. Do you suppose that such qualities are consistent with the abysmal pollution, the nameless, inconceivable beastliness in which the Chinaman is said to wallow? Do you not know that his vices must be somewhat less than are alleged? Do you think that such creatures of foulness physical and moral, could possibly excel as makers of cigars, boxes, sashes, doors, blinds, boots, shoes, bags, even ladies' and children's wear, and clothing generally? Would they excel in placer-mining, farming, fishing, gardening, fruit-picking, ped-dling, laundrying, and domestic service? And I have only named, word for word, the things which their enemies say they are monopolizing today on the

Pacific coast! Do you imagine that the men who, when Sacramento was menaced by a flood, faced the danger and raised the levee which saved the city; the men who climbed the perilous heights of the Sierra Nevada, and over ravines and through the living rock gave the Pacific railroad its path from the centre to the sea; do you imagine, I say, that those men are beneath our conception in moral and social degradation?

You may well shudder at what is the unquestionable condition of the Chinese quarter in San Francisco, but you may shudder also, and as well, at the condition of quarters in which their asserted superiors alone are found. Herded like beasts—a thing appalling and really unthinkable to the pure, immaculate Anglo-Saxon mind? Why I read but five days ago, of enormous, filthy, immoral, overcrowded, malarious, pestilential tenement-blocks in the very metropolis of America, containing each more than two thousand tenants, and not a Chinaman among them! Moreover, if San Francisco has within her municipality, as we are told, the "feculence and foulness of Sodom and Gomorrah," it is certainly her own shame as well as that of the Chinese which is attested. She has ample power to regulate the general conditions under which her inhabitants shall live. As she herself claims virtue and Christian wisdom, why doesn't she apply the ready remedy, instead of aspersing a whole race? Tell here, please, that she flaunts her own disgrace, when she testifies of her Chinese burrowing in the ground, and disregarding the common rules of civilized life. If such are the facts, she ought herself to be indicted for criminal, shameful neglect. The probable truth is that the average Chinaman in the United States, is of something like the average decency of his class! . . .

You know that hate begets hate. Do you think that with protection abrogated or surrendered, and proscription enacted, the Chinese will continue their past attention to our message from Christ? They will perceive, none more surely, that the word is gainsaid by deed. They may perhaps be tolerant in their own domain, and shame us by their forbearance, but their hearts must needs be hardened. They will be apt to turn, I think, from that Christ whose followers appear so unscrupulous, to that Confucius who taught them respect for pledges as one of the first principles of life. It were not, in justice, to be resented by us, should they take occasion to expel all our missionaries, as well as to close up their ports to our trade.

Let this hostile act become our veritable law, and the cause of Christ in China, so far as we are concerned with it, is apparently stricken to death. Aye, though it is prevented from becoming law, how shall we repair even the present loss? Who will restore that confidence which is so sensitive to wounds? . . .

P. B. S. PINCHBACK
(1837–1921)

The First African-American Governor
1880

I believe every pulsation of [Lincoln's] heart was honest and pure and that he was an ardent and devoted lover of universal liberty.

Pinckney Benton Stewart Pinchback, the nation's first African-American governor, was a lifelong champion of civil and political rights for blacks. The son of a white Mississippi planter and a former slave, Pinchback was born a free man, briefly attended school in Cincinnati, Ohio, and then worked as a cabin boy and steward on canal boats in Mississippi. During the Civil War, he volunteered to serve with the Union Army but quit in protest over rampant discrimination against black officers. Spurred by this experience, he began defending African-American civil rights, arguing publicly that blacks should not be drafted unless they could also vote. During Reconstruction, he helped found the Louisiana Republican Party and spoke out for universal suffrage, tax-supported schools, and equal opportunity.

With the party on his side, Pinchback was elected to the Louisiana state senate, where he was made president pro tempore, and then, after the governor was impeached, became acting governor of Louisiana. He served from December 9, 1872, until January 12, 1873. By the time Pinchback left office, Radical Republicans, especially blacks, became increasingly alarmed by the turn of events in the South. In Congress both Democrats and Republicans were developing plans to dismantle Reconstruction. In the Deep South, freed blacks increasingly fell subject to Jim Crow laws and intimidation tactics designed to suppress their rights.

Pinchback and his party compatriots would not capitulate without a fight. Many found an outlet for their frustration in the accommodationist philosophy preached by those like Booker T. Washington. Others continued their march for equal opportunity.

In the following speech, given in Indianapolis, Indiana during the presidential campaign of 1880, Pinchback extolled the role of African Americans in the Civil War, praised Lincoln's Emancipation Proclamation, and expounded on the importance of enfranchisement for all citizens, black and white.

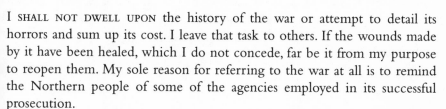

I SHALL NOT DWELL UPON the history of the war or attempt to detail its horrors and sum up its cost. I leave that task to others. If the wounds made by it have been healed, which I do not concede, far be it from my purpose to reopen them. My sole reason for referring to the war at all is to remind the Northern people of some of the agencies employed in its successful prosecution.

When it commenced, the principal labor element of the South—the source of its production and wealth—was the colored race. Four millions and a half of these unfortunate people were there, slaves and property of the men who refused to submit to the will of the people lawfully expressed through the ballot box. They were the bone and sinew of the Confederacy, tilling its fields and producing sustenance for its armies, while many of the best men of the North were compelled to abandon Northern fields to shoulder a musket in defense of the Union.

As a war measure and to deprive the South of such a great advantage, your president, the immortal Lincoln, issued a proclamation in September, 1862, in which he gave public notice that it was his purpose to declare the emancipation of the slaves in the States wherein insurrection existed on January 1, 1863, unless the offenders therein lay down their arms. That notice, thank God, was disregarded, and the proclamation of January 1, 1863, proclaiming universal emancipation followed. Had the requirements of the first proclamation been observed by the people to whom it was addressed who can doubt what would have been the fate of the colored people in the South? It is reasonable to assume, inasmuch as the war was waged to perpetuate the Union and not to destroy slavery—that they would have remained in hopeless bondage.

On more than one occasion President Lincoln officially declared that he would save the Union with slavery if he could, and not until it became manifest that slavery was the mainstay of the Confederacy, and the prosecution of the war to a successful close would be difficult without its destruction, did he dare touch it. I do not think that President Lincoln's hesitancy to act upon the question arose from sympathy with the accursed institution, for I believe every pulsation of his heart was honest and pure and that he was an ardent and devoted lover of universal liberty; but he doubted whether his own people would approve of his interference with it. Assured by the manner in which the people of the North received his first proclamation that they appreciated the necessity of destroying this great aid of the enemy, he went forward bravely declaring that, "possibly for every drop of blood drawn by the lash one might have to be drawn by the sword, but if so, as was said over eighteen hundred years ago, the judgments of the Lord are just and righteous altogether," and abolished human slavery from the land forever.

That this great act was a Godsend and an immeasurable blessing to the colored race, I admit, but I declare in the same breath that it was dictated and performed more in the interest of the white people of the North and to aid them in conquering the rebellion than from love of or a disposition to help the Negro. . . .

Alexander Crummell
(1819–1898)

The Queens of Womanhood
August 15, 1883

For, humble and benighted as she is, the black woman of the
South is one of the queens of womanhood.

Founder of the Union of Black Episcopalians and the Negro Academy and a graduate of Oxford, Alexander Crummell worked to strengthen black communities through worship, education, and social services provided by his church. Born in New York City, the son of a freedman, Crummell hoped to study for the priesthood, but was denied the opportunity at first because of his skin color. At twenty-five he was finally ordained in Massachusetts, though the diocese refused to admit him. Frustrated, Crummell left the United States for England and then Liberia.

In 1837, after years of experience abroad, Crummell returned to America, and began encouraging black ministers to join together in the fight against racism. He promoted black self-help, social assistance, and higher education for the African-American community—the last arguably the inspiration for W.E.B Du Bois's "talented tenth." The "missionary at large of the colored people" for the Episcopal Church, Crummell was also an outspoken abolitionist and supporter of rights for black women.

On August 15, 1883, he addressed the Freedman's Aid Society at the Methodist Episcopal Church in Ocean Grove, New Jersey. In this emotive and articulate speech, Crummell delineated the history of "the black woman of the South," urging his fellow clergymen to elevate African-American women, not just black men.

It is an age clamorous everywhere for the dignities, the grand prerogatives, and the glory of woman. There is not a country in Europe where she has not risen somewhat above the degradation of centuries, and pleaded successfully for a new position and a higher vocation. As the result of this new reformation we see her, in our day, seated in the lecture-rooms of ancient universities, rivaling her brothers in the fields of literature, the grand creators of ethereal art, the participants in noble civil franchises, the moving spirit in grand reformations, and the guide, agent, or assistant in all the noblest movements for the civilization and regeneration of man.

In these several lines of progress the American woman has run on in advance of her sisters in every other quarter of the globe. The advantage, she has received, the rights and prerogatives she has secured for herself, are unequaled by any other class of women in the world. It will not be thought amiss, then, that I come here to-day to present to your consideration the one grand exception to this general superiority of women, *the black woman of the South*.

～

The rural or plantation population of the South was made up almost entirely of people of pure Negro blood. And this brings out also the other disastrous fact, namely, that this large black population has been living from the time of their introduction into America, a period of more than two hundred years, in a state of unlettered rudeness. The Negro all this time has been an intellectual starveling. This has been more especially the condition of the black woman of the South. Now and then a black man has risen above the debased condition of his people. Various causes would contribute to the advantage of the *men:* the relation of servants to superior masters; attendance at courts with them; their presence at political meetings; listening to table-talk behind their chairs; traveling as valets; the privilege of books and reading in great houses, and with indulgent masters—all these served to lift up a black *man* here and there to something like superiority. But no such fortune fell to the lot of the plantation woman. The black woman of the South was left perpetually in a state of hereditary darkness and rudeness.

～

In her girlhood all the delicate tenderness of her sex was rudely outraged. In the field, in the rude cabin, in the press-room, in the factory, she was thrown into the companionship of coarse and ignorant men. No chance was given her for delicate reserve or tender modesty. From her girlhood she was the doomed victim of the grossest passions. All the virtues of her sex were utterly ignored. If the instinct of chastity asserted itself, then she had to fight like a tigress for the ownership and possession of her own person; and, ofttimes, had to suffer pains and lacerations for her virtuous self-assertion. When she reached maturity all the tender instincts of her womanhood were ruthlessly violated. At the age of marriage—always prematurely anticipated under slavery—she was mated, as the stock of the plantation were mated, *not* to be the companion of a loved and chosen husband, but to be the breeder of human cattle, for the field or the auction-block. With that mate she went out, morning after morning to toil, as a common field-hand. As it was *his,* so likewise was it her lot to wield the heavy hoe, or to follow the plow, or to gather in the crops. She was a "hewer of wood and a drawer of water." She was a common field-hand. She had to keep her place in the gang from morn till eve, under the burden of a heavy task, or under the stimulus or the fear of a cruel lash. She was a picker of cotton. She labored at the sugar-mill and in the tobacco-factory. When, through weariness or sickness, she has fallen behind her allotted task, there came, as punishment, the fearful stripes upon her shrinking, lacerated flesh.

Her home life was of the most degrading nature. She lived in the rudest huts, and partook of the coarsest food, and dressed in the scantiest garb, and slept, in multitudinous cabins, upon the hardest boards.

Thus she continued a beast of burden down to the period of those maternal anxieties which, in ordinary civilized life, give repose, quiet, and care to expectant mothers. But, under the slave system, few such relaxations were allowed. And so it came to pass that little children were ushered into this world under conditions which many cattle-raisers would not suffer for their flocks or herds. Thus she became the mother of children. But even then there was for her no suretyship of motherhood, or training, or control. Her own offspring were *not* her own. She and husband and children were all the property of others. All these sacred ties were constantly snapped and cruelly sundered. *This* year she had one husband; and next year, through some auction sale, she might be separated from him and mated to another. There was no sanctity of family, no binding tie of marriage, none of the fine felicities and the endearing affections of home. None of these things was the lot of Southern black women. Instead thereof, a gross barbarism which tended to blunt the tender sensibilities, to obliterate feminine delicacy and womanly shame, came down as her heritage from generation to generation; and it seems a miracle of providence and grace that, notwithstanding these terrible circumstances, so much struggling virtue lingered amid these rude cabins, that so much womanly worth and sweetness abided in their bosoms, as slave-holders themselves have borne witness to.

This is the state of black womanhood. Take the girlhood of this same region, and it presents the same aspect, save that in large districts the white man has not forgotten the olden times of slavery and with indeed the deepest sentimental abhorrence of "amalgamation," still thinks that the black girl is to be perpetually the victim of his lust! In the larger towns and in cities our girls in common schools and academies are receiving superior culture. Of the 15,000 colored school teachers in the South, more than half are colored young women, educated since emancipation. But even these girls, as well as their more ignorant sisters in rude huts, are followed and tempted and insulted by the ruffianly element of Southern society, who think that black *men* have no rights which white men should regard, and black *women* no virtue which white men should respect!

And now look at the *vastness* of this degradation. If I had been speaking of the population of a city, or a town, or even a village, the tale would be a sad and melancholy one. But I have brought before you the condition of millions of women. According to the census of 1880 there were, in the Southern States, 3,327,678 females of all ages of the African race. Of these there were 674,365 girls between twelve and twenty, 1,522,696 between twenty and eighty. "These figures," remarks an observing friend of mine, "are startling!" And when you think that the masses of these women live in the rural districts; that they grow up in rudeness and ignorance; that their former masters are using few means to break up their hereditary degradation, you can easily take in the pitiful condition of this population, and forecast the inevitable future to multitudes of females unless a mighty special effort is made for the improvement of the black womanhood of the South.

I should feel ashamed to allow these words to fall from my lips if it were not necessary to the lustration of the character of my black sisters of the South. I do not stand here to-day to plead for the black *man*. He is a man; and if he is weak he must go the wall. He is a man; he must fight his own way, and if he is strong in mind and body, he can take care of himself. But for the mothers, sisters, and daughters of my race I have a right to speak. And when I think of their sad condition down South; think, too, that since the day of emancipation hardly any one has lifted up a voice in their behalf, I feel it a duty and a privilege to set forth their praises and to extol their excellencies. For, humble and benighted as she is, the black woman of the South is one of the queens of womanhood. If there is any other woman on this earth who in native aboriginal qualities is her superior, I know not where she is to be found; for, I do say, that in tenderness of feeling, in genuine native modesty, in large disinterestedness, in sweetness of disposition and deep humility, in unselfish devotedness, and in warm, motherly assiduities, the Negro woman is unsurpassed by any other woman on this earth.

Ladies and gentlemen, since the day of emancipation millions of dollars have been given by the generous Christian people of the North for the intellectual training of the black race in this land. Colleges and universities have been built in the South, and hundreds of youth have been gathered within their walls. The work of your own Church in this regard has been magnificent and unrivaled, and the results which have been attained have been grand and elevating to the entire Negro race in America. The complement to all this generous and ennobling effort is the elevation of the black woman. Up to this day and time your noble philanthropy has touched, for the most part, the male population of the South, given them superiority, and stimulated them to higher aspirations. But a true civilization can only then be attained when the life of woman is reached, her whole being permeated by noble ideas, her fine taste enriched by culture, her tendencies to the beautiful gratified and developed, her singular and delicate nature lifted up to its full capacity; and then, when all these qualities are fully matured, cultivated and sanctified, all their sacred influences shall circle around ten thousand firesides, and the cabins of the humblest freedmen shall become the homes of Christian refinement and of domestic elegance through the influence and the charm of the uplifted and cultivated black woman of the South!

Elizabeth Cady Stanton
(1815–1902)

Man Cannot Speak for Her
January 18, 1892

We ask for woman a voice in the government under which she lives . . . because, as an individual, she must rely on herself.

At the frail age of seventy-six, after five decades of service to suffrage and equal opportunity, Elizabeth Cady Stanton delivered this address after stepping down as president of the National American Women Suffrage Association. In a trembling and emotive voice, she emphasized the importance of individual responsibility and women's rights, including female autonomy and, of course, the right to vote. Given on January 18, 1892, before the House Committee on the Judiciary and again on January 20 to the Senate Committee on Women Suffrage, Stanton's remarks signified a fitting conclusion to her public career. The Senate committee later published a favorable report of Stanton's speech, and the House distributed more than 10,000 copies of her remarks. Stanton herself called it "the best thing I have ever written . . . the strongest appeal ever made by mortal pen or tongue for the franchise." Even so, twenty-eight years elapsed before women finally secured the right to vote.

THE POINT I WISH plainly to bring before you on this occasion is the individuality of each human soul; our Protestant idea, the right of individual conscience and judgment—our republican idea, individual citizenship. In discussing the rights of woman, we are to consider, first, what belongs to her as an individual, in a world of her own, the arbiter of her own destiny, an imaginary Robinson Crusoe with her woman Friday on a solitary island. Her rights under such circumstances are to use all her faculties for her own safety and happiness.

Secondly, if we consider her as a citizen, as a member of a great nation, she must have the same rights as all other members, according to the fundamental principles of our Government.

Thirdly, viewed as a woman, an equal factor in civilization, her rights and duties are still the same—individual happiness and development. Fourthly, it is only the incidental relations of life, such as mother, wife, sister, daughter, tha may involve some special duties and training. In the usual discussion in regard to woman's sphere, . . . her rights and duties as an individual, as a citizen, as a woman, [are subordinated] to the necessities of these incidental relations, some of which a large class of woman may never assume. In discussing the sphere of man, we do not decide his rights as an individual, as a citizen, as a man by his duties as a father, a husband, a brother, or a son, relations some of which he may never fill. Moreover he would be better fitted for these very relations and whatever special work he might choose to do to earn his bread by the complete development of all his faculties as an individual.

Just so with woman. The education that will fit her to discharge the duties in the largest sphere of human usefulness will best fit her for whatever special work she may be compelled to do.

The isolation of every human soul and the necessity of self-dependence must give each individual the right to choose his own surroundings. The strongest reason for giving woman all the opportunities for higher education, for the full development of her faculties, forces of mind and body; for giving her the most enlarged freedom of thought and action; a complete emancipation from all forms of bondage, of custom, dependence, superstition; from all the crippling influences of fear, is the solitude and personal responsibility of her own individual life. The strongest reason why we ask for woman a voice in the government under which she lives; in the religion she is asked to believe; equality in social life, where she is the chief factor; a place in the trades and professions, where she may earn her bread, is because of her birthright to self-sovereignty; because, as an individual, she must rely on herself. No matter how much women prefer to lean, to be protected and supported, nor how much men desire to have them do so, they must make the voyage of life alone, and for safety in an emergency they must know something of the laws of navigation. . . . It matters not whether the solitary voyager is man or woman.

Nature having endowed them equally, leaves them to their own skill and judgment in the hour of danger, and, if not equal to the occasion, alike they perish. To appreciate the importance of fitting every human soul for independent action, think for a moment of the immeasurable solitude of self. We come into the world alone, unlike all who have gone before us; we leave it alone under circumstances peculiar to ourselves. . . . Seeing, then, what must be the infinite diversity in human character, we can in a measure appreciate the loss to a nation when any large class of the people uneducated and unrepresented in the government. We ask for the complete development of every individual, first, for his own benefit and happiness. In fitting out an army we give each soldier his own knapsack, arms, powder, his blanket, cup, knife, fork and spoon. We provide alike for all their individual necessities, then each man bears his own burden.

Again we ask complete individual development for the general good; for the consensus of the competent on the whole round of human interest; on all questions of national life, and here each man must bear his share of the general burden. It is sad to see how soon friendless children are left to bear their own burdens before they can analyze their feelings; before they can even tell their joys and sorrows, they are thrown on their own resources. The great lesson that nature seems to teach us at all ages is self-dependence, self-protection, self-support. . . .

In youth our most bitter disappointments, our brightest hopes and ambitions are known only to otherwise, even our friendship and love we never fully share with another; there is something of every passion in every situation we conceal. Even so in our triumphs and our defeats.

The successful candidate for Presidency and his opponent each have a solitude peculiarly his own, and good form forbid either to speak of his pleasure or regret. The solitude of the king on his throne and the prisoner in his cell differs in character and degree, but it is solitude nevertheless. We ask no sympathy from others in the anxiety and agony of a broken friendship or shattered love. When death sunders our nearest ties, alone we sit in the shadows of our affliction. Alike mid the greatest triumphs and darkest tragedies of life we walk alone. . . . In hours like these we realize the awful solitude of individual life, its pains, its penalties, its responsibilities; hours in which the youngest and most helpless are thrown on their own resources for guidance and consolation. Seeing then that life must ever be a march and a battle, that each soldier must be equipped for his own protection, it is the height of cruelty to rob the individual of a single natural right.

To throw obstacle in the way of a complete education is like putting out the eyes; to deny the rights of property, like cutting off the hands. To deny political equality is to rob the ostracized of all self-respect; of credit in the market place; of recompense in the world of work; of a voice among those who make and administer the law; a choice in the jury before whom they are tried, and in the judge who decides their punishment. . . .

❧

The young wife and mother, at the head of some establishment with a kind husband to shield her from the adverse winds of life, with wealth, fortune and position, has a certain harbor of safety, occurs against the ordinary ills of life. But to manage a household, have a detectable influence in society, keep her friends and the affections of her husband, train her children and servants well, she must have rare common sense, wisdom, diplomacy, and a knowledge of human nature. To do all this she needs the cardinal virtues and the strong points of character that the most successful statesman possesses.

An uneducated woman, trained to dependence, with no resources in herself must make a failure of any position in life. But society says women do not need a knowledge of the world, the liberal training that experience in public life must give, all the advantages of collegiate education; but when for the lack of all this, the woman's happiness is wrecked, alone she bears her humiliation; and the attitude of the weak and the ignorant is indeed pitiable. In the wild chase for the prizes of life, they are ground to powder.

The chief reason for opening to every soul the doors to the whole round of human duties and pleasures is the individual development thus attained, the resources thus provided under all circumstances to mitigate the solitude that at times must come to everyone....

Nothing strengthens the judgment and quickens the conscience like individual responsibility. Nothing adds such dignity to character as the recognition of one's self-sovereignty; the right to an equal place, every where conceded—a place earned by personal merit, not an artificial attainment by inheritance, wealth, family, and position. Conceding, then, that the responsibilities of life rest equally on man and woman, that their destiny is the same, they need the same preparation for time and eternity. The talk of sheltering woman from the fierce storms of life is the sheerest mockery, for they beat on her from every point of the compass, just as they do on man, and with more fatal results, for he has been trained to protect himself, to resist, to conquer. Such are the facts in human experience, the responsibilities of individual sovereignty. Rich and poor, intelligent and ignorant, wise and foolish, virtuous and vicious, man and woman, it is ever the same, each soul must depend wholly on itself.

But when all artificial trammels are removed, and women are recognized as individuals, responsible for their own environments, thoroughly educated for all the positions in life they may be called to fill; with all the resources in themselves that liberal thought and broad culture can give; guided by their own conscience and judgment; trained to self-protection by a healthy development of the muscular system and skill in the use of weapons of defense, and stimulated to self-support by the knowledge of the business world and the pleasure that pecuniary independence must ever give; when women are trained in this way they will, in a measure, be fitted for those hours of solitude that come alike to all, whether prepared or otherwise. We must depend on ourselves, the dictates of wisdom point of complete individual development. In talking of education how shallow the argument that each class must be educated for the special work it proposed to do, and all those faculties not needed in this special walk must lie dormant and utterly wither for want of use, when, perhaps, these will be the very faculties needed in life's greatest emerges. Some say, Where is the use of drilling in the languages, the sciences, in law, medicine, theology? As wives, mothers, housekeepers, cooks, they need a different curriculum from boys who are to fill all positions. The chief cooks in our great hotels and ocean steamers are men. In large cities men run the bakeries; they make our bread, cake and pies. They manage the laundries; they are now considered our best milliners and dressmakers. Because some men fill these departments of usefulness, shall we regulate the curriculum in Harvard and Yale to their present necessities? If not, why this talk in our best colleges of a curriculum for girls who are crowding into the trades and professions; teachers in all our public schools rapidly hiring many lucrative and honorable positions in life? . . .

. . . Women are already the equals of men in the whole realm of thought, in art, science, literature, and government. With telescopic vision they explore the starry firmament, and bring back the history of the planetary world. With chart and compass they pilot ships across the mighty deep, and with skillful finger send electric messages around the globe. . . .

. . . The poetry and novels of the century are theirs, and they have touched the keynote of reform in religion, politics, and social life. They fill the editor's and professor's chair, and plead at the bar of justice, walk the wards of the hospital, and speak from the pulpit and the platform; such is the type of womanhood that an enlightened public sentiment welcomes today, and such the triumph of the facts of life over the false theories of the past.

Whatever may be said of man's protecting power in ordinary conditions, mid all the terrible disasters by land and sea, in the supreme moments of danger, alone, woman must ever meet the horrors of the situation; the Angel of Death even makes no royal pathway for her. Man's love and sympathy enter only into the sunshine of our lives. In that solemn solitude of self, that links us with the immeasurable and the eternal, each soul lives alone forever. . . .

. . . There is a solitude, which each and every one of us has always carried with him, more inaccessible than the ice-cold mountains, more profound than the midnight sea; the solitude of self. Our inner being, which we call ourself, no eye nor touch of man or angel has ever pierced. It is more hidden than the caves of the gnome; the sacred adytum of the oracle; the hidden chamber of Eleusinian mystery, for to it only omniscience is permitted to enter.

Such is individual life. Who, I ask you, can take, dare take on himself the rights, the duties, the responsibilities of another human soul?

FRANCES ELLEN WATKINS HARPER
(1825–1911)

Women's Political Future
1893

*Men may boast of the aristocracy of blood, . . . but there is
one aristocracy which must ever outrank them all, and that is
the aristocracy of character, and it is the women . . .
who help to mold its character.*

In this address to the World Congress of Representative Women in
Chicago, more than 150,000 people, including Susan B. Anthony and
Lucy Stone, listened to Frances Ellen Watkins Harper discuss the
moral and civil obligations of women's suffrage. The first black
woman ever to address the convention, she called suffrage a means to
draw the national conscience back to African-American issues like
lynching and voter intimidation.

IF BEFORE SIN had cast its deepest shadows or sorrow had distilled its bitter-
est tears, it was true that it was not good for man to be alone, it is no less
true, since the shadows have deepened and life's sorrows have increased, that
the world has need of all the spiritual aid that woman can give for the social
advancement and moral development of the human race. The tendency of
the present age, with its restlessness, religious upheavals, failures, blunders,
and crimes, is toward broader freedom, an increase of knowledge, the emancipation of thought, and a recognition of the brotherhood of man; in this
movement woman as the companion of man, must be a sharer. So close is
the bond between man and woman that you can not raise one without lifting the other. The world can not move without woman's sharing in the
movement, and to help give a right impetus to that movement is woman's
highest privilege.

If the fifteenth century discovered America to the Old World, the nineteenth century is discovering woman to herself. Little did Columbus imagine,
when the New World broke upon his vision like a lovely gem in the coronet
of the universe, the glorious possibilities of a land where the sun should be our
engraver, the winged lightning our messenger, and steam our beast of burden.
But as mind is more than matter, and the highest ideal always the true reality,

so to woman comes the opportunity to strive for richer and grander discoveries than ever gladdened the eye of the Genoese mariner.

Not the opportunity of discovering new worlds, but that of filling this old world with fairer and higher aims than the greed of gold and the lust of power, is hers. Through weary, wasting years men have destroyed, dashed in pieces, and overthrown, but today we stand on the threshold of woman's era, and woman's work is grandly constructive. In her hand are possibilities whose use or abuse must tell upon the political life of the nation, and send their influence for good or evil across the track of unborn ages.

As the saffron tints and crimson flushes of morn herald the coming day, so the social and political advancement which woman has already gained bears the promise of the rising of the full-orbed sun of emancipation. The result will not be to make the home less happy, but society more holy; yet I do not think the mere extension of the ballot a panacea for all the ills of our national life. What we need today is not simply more voters, but better voters. Today there are red-handed men in our republic, who walk unwhipped of justice, who richly deserve to exchange the ballot of the freeman for the wristlets of the felon; brutal and cowardly men, who torture, burn, and lynch their fellow men, men whose defenselessness should be their best defense and their weakness an ensign of protection. More than the changing of institutions we need the development of a national conscience, and the upbuilding of national character. Men may boast of the aristocracy of blood, may glory in the aristocracy of talent, and be proud of the aristocracy of wealth, but there is one aristocracy which must ever outrank them all, and that is the aristocracy of character, and it is the women of a country who help to mold its character; and to influence if not determine its destiny; and in the political future of our nation woman will not have done what she could if she does not endeavor to have our republic stand foremost among the nations of the earth, wearing sobriety as a crown and righteousness a garment and a girdle. In coming into her political estate woman will find a mass of illiteracy to be dispelled. If knowledge is power, ignorance is also power. The power that educates wickedness may manipulate and dash against the pillars of any state when they are undermined and honeycombed by injustice.

<hr />

Today women hold in their hands influence and opportunity, and with these they have already opened doors which have been closed to others. By opening doors of labor woman has become a rival claimant for at least some of the wealth monopolized by her stronger brother. In the home she is the priestess, in society the queen, in literature she is a power, in legislative halls law-makers have responded to her appeals, and for her sake have humanized and liberalized their laws. The press has felt the impress of her hand. In the pews of the church she constitutes the majority; the pulpit has welcomed her, and in the school she has the blessed privilege of teaching children and youth. To her is apparently coming the added responsibility of political power; and what she now possesses should only be the means of preparing her to use the coming power for the glory of God and the good of mankind; for power without righteousness is one of the most dangerous forces in the world.

Political life in our country has plowed in muddy channels, and needs the infusion of clearer and cleaner waters. I am not sure that women are naturally so much better than men that they will clear the stream by the virtue of their womanhood; it is not through sex but through character that the best influence of women upon the life of the nation must be exerted.

I do not believe in unrestricted and universal suffrage for either men or women. I believe in moral and educational tests. I do not believe that the most ignorant and brutal man is better prepared to add value to the strength and durability of the government than the most cultured, upright, and intelligent woman. I do not think that willful ignorance should swamp earnest intelligence at the ballot-box, nor that educated wickedness, violence, and fraud should cancel the votes of honest men. The unsteady hands of a drunkard can not cast the ballot of a freeman. The hands of lynchers are too red with blood to determine the political character of the government for even four short years. The ballot in the hands of woman means power added to influence. How well she will use that power I can not foretell. Great evils stare us in the face that need to be throttled by the combined power of an upright manhood and an enlightened womanhood; and I know that no nation can gain its full measure of enlightenment and happiness if one-half of it is free and the other half fettered. China compressed the feet of her women and thereby retarded the steps of her men. The elements of a nation's weakness must ever be found at the hearthstone.

More than the increase of wealth, the power of armies, and the strength of fleets is the need of good homes, of good fathers, and good mothers.

. . . Woman coming into her kingdom will find enthroned three great evils, for whose overthrow she should be as strong in a love of justice and humanity as the warrior in his might. She will find intemperance sending its flood of shame, and death, and sorrow to the homes of men, a fretting leprosy in our politics, and a blighting curse in our social life; the social evil sending to our streets women whose laughter is sadder than their tears, who slide from the paths of sin and shame to the friendly shelter of the grave; and lawlessness enacting in our republic deeds over which angels might weep, if heaven knows sympathy.

O women of America! into your hands God has pressed one of the sublimest opportunities that ever came into the hands of the women of any race or people. It is yours to create a healthy public sentiment; to demand justice, simple justice, as the right of every race; to brand with everlasting infamy the lawless and brutal cowardice that lynches, burns, and tortures your own countrymen.

Let the hearts of the women of the world respond to the song of the herald angels of peace on earth and good will to men. Let them throb as one heart unified by the grand and holy purpose of uplifting the human race, and humanity will breathe freer, and the world grow brighter. With such a purpose Eden would spring up in our path, and Paradise be around our way.

Josephine St. Pierre Ruffin
(1842–1924)

A Call for Black Women
1895

We are women, American women, as intensely interested in all that pertains to us as such as all other American women.

Born into one of Boston's leading black families, Josephine St. Pierre Ruffin was a vocal proponent of civil rights for both blacks and women in the later nineteenth century. At the age of fifteen, she married George Lewis Ruffin, the first African American to graduate from Harvard Law School.

During the Civil War, Ruffin immersed herself in various civil rights causes, the women's suffrage movement, as well as charity work. Though they fought for similar causes, most black women were not welcome in white feminist organizations. Thus, between 1890 and 1920, African-American women like Ruffin formed their own segregated civic organizations to encourage camaraderie and "racial uplift."

From 1890 to 1897 Ruffin served as the editor and publisher of *Woman's Era,* the first newspaper published by and for African-American women. The paper served to highlight the achievements of African-American women and to champion their rights. In 1894 Ruffin organized the Women's Era Club, an African-American women's civic association. A year later, she assembled a conference of black women's clubs in Boston and organized the National Federation of Afro-American Women. This group joined forces with the Colored Women's League of Washington, D.C., to form the National Association of Colored Women, of which Ruffin was named vice president. Ruffin's philanthropic work brought her in contact with many eminent white and black leaders, including William Lloyd Garrison, Susan B. Anthony, Elizabeth Cady Stanton, and Booker T. Washington.

In this address to members of the Women's Era Club, Ruffin discussed the growing class of intelligent, modern black women, encouraging them to take action for the improvement and equality of all African Americans.

I HAVE LEFT the strongest reason for our conferring together until the last. All over America there is to be found a large and growing class of earnest, intelligent, progressive colored women, women who, if not leading full useful lives, are only waiting for the opportunity to do so, many of them warped and cramped for lack of opportunity, not only to do more but to *be* more; and yet, if an estimate of the colored women of America is called for, the inevitable reply, glibly given, is, "For the most part ignorant and immoral, some exceptions, of course, but these don't count."

Now for the sake of the thousands of self-sacrificing young women teaching and preaching in lonely southern backwoods, for the noble army of mothers who have given birth to these girls, mothers whose intelligence is only limited by their opportunity to get at books, for the sake of the fine cultured women who have carried off the honors in school here and often abroad, for the sake of our own dignity, the dignity of our race, and the future good name of our children, it is "mete, right and our bounden duty" to stand forth and declare ourselves and principles, to teach an ignorant and suspicious world that our aims and interests are identical with those of all good aspiring women. Too long have we been silent under unjust and unholy charges; we cannot expect to have them removed until we disprove them through *ourselves*. It is not enough to try to disprove unjust charges through individual effort, that never goes any further. Year after year southern women have protested against the admission of colored women into any national organization on the ground of the immorality of these women, and because all refutation has only been tried by individual work, the charge has never been crushed, as it could and should have been at the first. Now with an army of organized women standing for purity and mental worth, we in ourselves deny the charge and open the eyes of the world to a state of affairs to which they have been blind, often willfully so, and the very fact that the charges, audaciously and flippantly made, as they often are, are of so humiliating and delicate a nature, serves to protect the accuser by driving the helpless accused into mortified silence. It is to break this silence, not by noisy protestations of what we are not, but by a dignified showing of what we are and hope to become that we are impelled to take this step, to make of this gathering an object lesson to the world. For many and apparent reasons it is especially fitting that the *women* of the race take the lead in this movement, but for all this we recognize the necessity of the sympathy of our husbands, brothers and fathers.

Our woman's movement is [the] woman's movement in that it is led and directed by women for the good of women and men, for the benefit of *all* humanity, which is more than any one branch or section of it. We want, we ask the active interest of our men, and, too, we are not drawing the color line;

we are women, American women, as intensely interested in all that pertains to us as such as all other American women; we are not alienating or withdrawing, we are only coming to the front, willing to join any others in the same work and cordially inviting and welcoming any others to join us.

BOOKER T. WASHINGTON
(1856–1915)

The Atlanta Compromise
SEPTEMBER 18, 1895

In all things that are purely social we can be as separate as the fingers, yet one as the hand in all things essential to mutual progress.

In 1881, less than two decades after emancipation, Booker T. Washington became the first president of the Tuskegee Normal and Industrial Institute in Alabama. Over the next twenty years, he developed a strong belief in vocational training—not social equality or political advancement—as the best means for African-American progress. His writings and lectures, especially near the turn of the century, reflected this pronounced faith in industry to help southern blacks escape the endless cycle of sharecropping and debt.

In September 1895 Washington gained national recognition after this speech at the opening of the Cotton States and International Exposition in Atlanta, Georgia, was widely reported in American newspapers. In the now celebrated "Atlanta Compromise" address, Washington articulated his "accommodationist policy," urging blacks to concede disenfranchisement and segregation in exchange for white support for African-American progress in business and education. This arrangement would, he argued, help blacks be the "most useful and intellectual citizens."

Washington's conservative views brought him popularity with mainstream politicians who wanted Booker to become the new African-American leader. President William McKinley visited the Tuskegee Institute and praised Washington's achievements. In 1901 President Theodore Roosevelt invited Booker to visit him in the White House. But leaders in the black community, like W. E. B. Du Bois, attacked Washington's accommodationist views. One statement signed by twenty-three prominent African Americans claimed: "Mr. Washington's large financial responsibilities have made him dependent on the rich charitable public and . . . , for this reason, he has for years been compelled to tell, not the whole truth."

Mr. President and Gentlemen of the Board of Directors and Citizens: One-third of the population of the South is of the Negro race. No enterprise seeking the material, civil, or moral welfare of this section can disregard this element of our population and reach the highest success. I but convey to you, Mr. President and Directors, the sentiment of the masses of my race when I say that in no way have the value and manhood of the American Negro been more fittingly and generously recognized than by the managers of this magnificent Exposition at every stage of its progress. It is a recognition that will do more to cement the friendship of the two races than any occurrence since the dawn of our freedom.

Not only this, but the opportunity here afforded will awaken among us a new era of industrial progress. Ignorant and inexperienced, it is not strange that in the first years of our new life we began at the top instead of at the bottom; that a seat in Congress or the state legislature was more sought than real estate or industrial skill; that the political convention or stump speaking had more attractions than starting a dairy farm or truck garden.

A ship lost at sea for many days suddenly sighted a friendly vessel. From the mast of the unfortunate vessel was seen a signal: "Water, water; we die of thirst!" The answer from the friendly vessel at once came back, "Cast down your bucket where you are." A second time the signal, "Water, water; send us water!" ran up from the distressed vessel, and was answered: "Cast down your bucket where you are." And a third and fourth signal for water was answered, "Cast down your bucket where you are." The captain of the distressed vessel, at last heeding the injunction, cast down his bucket, and it came up full of fresh, sparkling water from the mouth of the Amazon River. To those of my race who depend on bettering their condition in a foreign land or who underestimate the importance of cultivating friendly relations with the Southern white man, who is their next door neighbor, I would say: "Cast down your bucket where you are"—cast it down in making friends in every manly way of the people of all races by whom we are surrounded.

Cast it down in agriculture, mechanics, in commerce, in domestic service, and in the professions. And in this connection it is well to bear in mind that whatever other sins the South may be called to bear, when it comes to business, pure and simple, it is in the South that the Negro is given a man's chance in the commercial world, and in nothing is this Exposition more eloquent than in emphasizing this chance. Our greatest danger is that in the great leap from slavery to freedom we may overlook the fact that the masses of us are to live by the productions of our hands, and fail to keep in mind that we shall prosper in proportion as we learn to dignify and glorify common labor, and put brains and skill into the common occupations of life; shall prosper in proportion as we learn to draw the line between the superficial and the substantial, the ornamental gewgaws of life and the useful. No race can prosper till it learns that there is as much dignity in tilling a field as in writing a poem. It is at the bottom of life we must begin, and not at the top. Nor should we permit our grievances to overshadow our opportunities.

To those of the white race who look to the incoming of those of foreign birth and strange tongue and habits for the prosperity of the South, were I permitted I would repeat what I say to my own race, "Cast down your bucket where you are." Cast it down among the eight millions of Negroes whose habits you know, whose fidelity and love you have tested in days when to have proved treacherous meant the ruin of your firesides. Cast down your bucket among these people who have, without strikes and labor wars, tilled your fields, cleared your forests, built your railroads and cities, and brought forth treasures from the bowels of the earth, and helped make possible this magnificent representation of the progress of the South. Casting down your bucket among my people, helping and encouraging them as you are doing on these grounds, and with education of head, hand, and heart, you will find that they will buy your surplus land, make blossom the waste places in your fields, and run your factories. While doing this, you can be sure in the future, as in the past, that you and your families will be surrounded by the most patient, faithful, law-abiding, and unresentful people that the world has seen. As we have proved our loyalty to you in the past, in nursing your children, watching by the sick bed of your mothers and fathers, and often following them with tear-dimmed eyes to their graves, so in the future, in our humble way, we shall stand by you with a devotion that no foreigner can approach, ready to lay down our lives, if need be, in defense of yours, interlacing our industrial, commercial, civil, and religious life with yours in a way that shall make the interests of both races one. In all things that are purely social we can be as separate as the fingers, yet one as the hand in all things essential to mutual progress.

There is no defense or security for any of us except in the highest intelligence and development of all. If anywhere there are efforts tending to curtail the fullest growth of the Negro, let these efforts be turned into stimulating, encouraging, and making him the most useful and intelligent citizen. Effort or means so invested will pay a thousand per cent interest. These efforts will be twice blessed—blessing him that gives and him that takes. There is no escape through law of man or God from the inevitable:

The laws of changeless justice bind
Oppressor with oppressed;
And close as sin and suffering joined
We march to fate abreast.

Nearly sixteen millions of hands will aid you in pulling the load upwards, or they will pull against you the load downward. We shall constitute one-third and more of the ignorance and crime of the South, or one-third [of] its intelligence and progress; we shall contribute one-third to the business and industrial prosperity of the South, or we shall prove a veritable body of death, stagnating, depressing, retarding every effort to advance the body politic.

. . . While we take pride in what we exhibit as a result of our independent efforts, we do not for a moment forget that our part in this exhibition would fall far short of your expectations but for the constant help that has come to our educational life, not only from the Southern states, but especially from northern philanthropists, who have made their gifts a constant stream of blessing and encouragement.

The wisest among my race understand that the agitation of questions of social equality is the extremest folly, and that progress in the enjoyment of all the privileges that will come to us must be the result of severe and constant struggle rather than of artificial forcing. No race that has anything to contribute to the markets of the world is long in any degree ostracized. It is important and right that all privileges of the law be ours, but it is vastly more important that we be prepared for the exercise of these privileges. The opportunity to earn a dollar in a factory just now is worth infinitely more than the opportunity to spend a dollar in an opera house.

In conclusion, may I repeat that nothing in thirty years has given us more hope and encouragement, and drawn us so near to you of the white race, as this opportunity offered by the Exposition; and here bending, as it were, over the altar that represents the results of the struggles of your race and mine, both starting practically empty-handed three decades ago, I pledge that in your effort to work out the great and intricate problem which God has laid at the doors of the South, you shall have at all times the patient, sympathetic help of my race; only let this be constantly in mind that, while from representations in these buildings of the product of field, of forest, of mine, of factory, letters, and art, much good will come, yet far above and beyond material benefits will be that higher good, that let us pray God, will come, in a blotting out of sectional differences and racial animosities and suspicions, in a determination to administer absolute justice, in a willing obedience among all classes to the mandates of law. This, coupled with our material prosperity, will bring into our beloved South a new heaven and a new earth.

W. E. B. Du Bois
(1868–1963)

Training Negroes for Social Power
1903

*The Negro problem, it has often been said, is largely a problem of
ignorance. . . . This can be gotten rid of only by training.*

Born in Great Barrington, Massachusetts, in 1868, W. E. B. Du Bois dedicated his life, through literature and the lectern, to the struggle for
African-American civil rights and equal opportunity. A true scholar, he
attended Fisk University and became the first African American to
receive a Ph.D. from Harvard University before joining the faculty at
Atlanta University, where he developed black sociology as a legitimate
field of study. While there, Du Bois founded an annual conference on
the plight of black Americans which brought him to the forefront of the
academy. He also developed a national reputation in the Pan-African
movement, which argued for a unified black front around the globe.

Early in the twentieth century, in an essay entitled "On Booker T.
Washington and Others," Du Bois broke with the accommodationist
philosophy of Booker T. Washington and the "Back to Africa" movement of Marcus Garvey—insisting instead that blacks should achieve
not only economic parity with whites but also full and immediate civil
and political equality. This division tipped off an intellectual feud
between Du Bois and Washington, both of whose arguments are still
debated today.

In 1903, as part of a lecture series against accommodation, Du Bois
delivered the following address on the exigency of educating black
youths, especially those with superior intellect—what Du Bois coined
the "talented tenth." In a fiery, fist-pounding speech, he decried the
long practice of segregation and demanded immediate suffrage, and
equality in both the school and workplace.

―――

THE RESPONSIBILITY for their own social regeneration ought to be placed
largely upon the shoulders of the Negro people. But such responsibility must
carry with it a grant of power; responsibility without power is a mockery and
a farce. If, therefore, the American people are sincerely anxious that the Negro

shall put forth his best efforts to help himself, they must see to it that he is not deprived of the freedom and power to strive. The responsibility for dispelling their own ignorance implies that the power to overcome ignorance is to be placed in black men's hands; the lessening of poverty calls for the power of effective work, and one responsibility for lessening crime calls for control over social forces which produce crime.

Such social power means, assuredly, the growth of initiative among Negroes, the spread of independent thought, the expanding consciousness of manhood; and these things today are looked upon by many with apprehension and distrust, and there is systematic and determined effort to avoid this inevitable corollary of the fixing of social responsibility. Men openly declare their design to train these millions as a subject caste, as men to be thought for, but not to think; to be led, but not to lead themselves. Those who advocate these things forget that such a solution flings them squarely on the other horn of the dilemma; such a subject child-race could never be held accountable for its own misdeeds and shortcomings; its ignorance would be part of the nation's design, its poverty would arise partly from the direct oppression of the strong and partly from thriftlessness which such oppression breeds; and, above all, its crime would be the legitimate child of that lack of self-respect which caste systems engender. Such a solution of the Negro problem is not one which the saner sense of the nation for a moment contemplates; it is utterly foreign to American institutions, and is unthinkable as a future for any self-respecting race of men. The sound afterthought of the American people must come to realize that the responsibility for dispelling ignorance and poverty and uprooting crime among Negroes cannot be put upon their own shoulders unless they are given such independent leadership in intelligence, skill, and morality as will inevitably lead to an independent manhood which cannot and will not rest in bonds.

Let me illustrate my meaning particularly in the matter of educating Negro youth.

The Negro problem, it has often been said, is largely a problem of ignorance—not simply of illiteracy, but a deeper ignorance of the world and its ways, of the thought and experience of men; an ignorance of self and the possibilities of human souls. This can be gotten rid of only by training; and primarily such training must take the form of that sort of social leadership which we call education. To apply such leadership to themselves, and to profit by it, means that Negroes would have among themselves men of careful training and broad culture, as teachers and teachers of teachers. There are always periods of educational evolution when it is deemed proper for pupils in the fourth reader to teach those in the third. Such a method, wasteful and ineffective at all times, is peculiarly dangerous when ignorance is widespread and when there are few homes and public institutions to supplement the work of the school. It is, therefore, of crying necessity among Negroes that the heads of their educational system—the teachers in the normal schools, the heads of high schools, the principals of public systems, should be unusually well-trained men; men trained not simply in common-school branches, not simply in the technique of school management and normal methods, but trained beyond this, broadly and carefully, into the meaning of the age whose civilization it is their peculiar duty to interpret to the youth of a new race, to the minds of untrained people. Such educational leaders should be prepared by long and rigorous courses of study similar to those which the world over have been designed to strengthen the intellectual powers, fortify character, and facilitate the transmission from age to age of the stores of the world's knowledge.

Not all men—indeed, not the majority of men, only the exceptional few among American Negroes or among any other people—are adapted to this higher training, as, indeed, only the exceptional few are adapted to higher training in any line; but the significance of such men is not to be measured by their numbers, but rather by the numbers of their pupils and followers who are destined to see the world through their eyes, hear it through their trained ears, and speak to it through the music of their words.

The very first step toward the settlement of the Negro problem is the spread of intelligence. The first step toward wider intelligence is a free public-school system; and the first and most important step toward a public-school system is the equipment and adequate support of a sufficient number of Negro colleges. These are first steps, and they involve great movements: first, the best of the existent colleges must not be abandoned to slow atrophy and death, as the tendency is today; secondly, systematic attempt must be made to organize secondary education. Below the colleges and connected with them must come the normal and high schools, judiciously distributed and carefully manned. In no essential particular should this system of common and secondary schools differ from educational systems the world over. Their chief function is the quickening and training of human intelligence; they can do much in the teaching of morals and manners incidentally, but they cannot and ought not to replace the home as the chief moral teacher; they can teach valuable lessons as to the meaning of work in the world, but they cannot replace technical schools and apprenticeship in actual life, which are the real schools of work. Manual training can and ought to be used in these schools, but as a means and not as an end—to quicken intelligence and self-knowledge and not to teach carpentry; just as arithmetic is used to train minds and not to make skilled accountants.

But spread of intelligence alone will not solve the Negro problem. If this problem is largely a question of ignorance, it is also scarcely less a problem of poverty. If Negroes are to assume the responsibility of raising the standards of living among themselves, the power of intelligent work and leadership toward proper industrial ideals must be placed in their hands. Economic efficiency depends on intelligence, skill, and thrift. The public-school system is designed to furnish the necessary intelligence for the ordinary worker, the secondary school for the more gifted worker, and the college for the exceptional few. Technical knowledge and manual dexterity in learning branches of the world's work are taught by industrial and trade schools, and such schools are of prime importance in the training of colored children. Trade-teaching cannot be effectively combined with the work of the common schools because the primary curriculum is already too crowded, and thorough common-school training should precede trade-teaching. It is, however, quite possible to combine some of the work of the secondary schools with purely technical training, the necessary limitations being matters of time and cost: the question whether the boy can afford to stay in school long enough to add parts of a high school course to the trade course, and particularly the question whether the school can afford or ought to afford to give trade-training to high-school students who do not intend to become artisans. A system of trade schools, therefore, supported by state and private aid, should be added to the secondary-school system.

But intelligence and skill alone will not solve the southern problem of poverty. With these must go that combination of homely habits and virtues which we may loosely call thrift. Something of thrift may be taught in school, more must be taught at home; but both these agencies are helpless when organized economic society denies to workers the just reward of thrift and efficiency. And this has been true of black laborers in the South from the time of slavery down through the scandal of the Freedman's Bank to the peonage and crop-lien system of today. If the southern Negro is shiftless, it is primarily because over large areas a shiftless Negro can get on in the world about as well as an industrious black man. This is not universally true in the South, but it is true to so large an extent as to discourage striving in precisely that class of Negroes who most need encouragement. What is the remedy? Intelligence—not simply the ability to read and write or to sew—but the intelligence of a society permeated by that larger division of life and broader tolerance which are fostered by the college and university. Not that all men must be college-bred, but that some men, black and white, must be, to leaven the ideals of the lump. Can any serious student of the economic South doubt that this today is her crying need?

Ignorance and poverty are the vastest of the Negro problems. But to these later years have added a third—the problem of Negro crime. That a great problem of social morality must have become eventually the central problem of emancipation is as clear as day to any student of history. In its grosser form as a problem of serious crime it is already upon us. Of course it is false and silly to represent that white women in the South are in daily danger of black assaulters. On the contrary, white womanhood in the South is absolutely safe in the hands of ninety-five percent of the black men—ten times safer than black womanhood is in the hands of white men. Nevertheless, there is a large and dangerous class of Negro criminals, paupers, and outcasts. The existence and growth of such a class, far from causing surprise, should be recognized as the natural result of that social disease called the Negro problem; nearly every untoward circumstance known to human experience has united to increase Negro crime: the slavery of the past, the sudden emancipation, the narrowing of economic opportunity, the lawless environment of wide regions, the stifling of natural ambition, the curtailment of political privilege, the disregard of the sanctity of black men's homes, and above all, a system of treatment for criminals calculated to breed crime far faster than all other available agencies could repress it. Such a combination of circumstances is as sure to increase the numbers of the vicious and outcast as the rain is to wet the earth. The phenomenon calls for no delicately drawn theories of race differences; it is a plain case of cause and effect.

Three things American slavery gave the Negro—the habit of work, the English language, and the Christian religion; but one priceless thing it debauched, destroyed, and took from him, and that was the organized home. For the sake of intelligence and thrift, for the sake of work and morality, this home life must be restored and regenerated with newer ideals. How? The normal method would be by actual contact with a higher home life among his neighbors, but this method the social separation of white and black precludes. A proposed method is by schools of domestic arts, but, valuable as these are, they are but subsidiary aids to the establishment of homes; for real homes are primarily centers of ideals and teaching and only incidentally centers of cooking. The restoration and raising of home ideals must, then, come from social life among Negroes themselves; and does that social life need no leadership? It needs the best possible leadership of pure hearts and trained heads, the highest leadership of carefully trained men.

Such are the arguments for the Negro college, and such is the work that Atlanta University and a few similar institutions seek to do. We believe that a rationally arranged college course of study for men and women able to pursue it is the best and only method of putting into the world Negroes with ability to use the social forces of their race so as to stamp out crime, strengthen the home, eliminate degenerates, and inspire and encourage the higher tendencies of the race not only in thought and aspiration, but in everyday toil. And we believe this, not simply because we have argued that such training ought to have these effects, or merely because we hoped for such results in some dim future, but because already for years we have seen in the work of our graduates precisely such results as I have mentioned: successful teachers of teachers, intelligent and upright ministers, skilled physicians, principals of industrial schools, businessmen, and, above all, makers of model homes and leaders of social groups, out from which radiate subtle but tangible forces of uplift and inspiration. The proof of this lies scattered in every state of the South, and, above all, in the half-unwilling testimony of men disposed to decry our work.

Between the Negro college and industrial school there are the strongest grounds for cooperation and unity. It is not a matter of mere emphasis, for we would be glad to see ten industrial schools to every college. It is not a fact that there are today too few Negro colleges, but rather that there are too many institutions attempting to do college work. But the danger lies in the fact that the best of the Negro colleges are poorly equipped, and are today losing support and countenance, and that, unless the nation awakens to its duty, ten years will see the annihilation of higher Negro training in the South. We need a few strong, well-equipped Negro colleges, and we need them now, not tomorrow; unless we can have them and have them decently supported, Negro education in the South, both common-school and the industrial, is doomed to failure, and the forces of social regeneration will be fatally weakened, for the college today among Negroes is, just as truly as it was yesterday among whites, the beginning and not the end of human training, the foundation and not the capstone of popular education.

Strange, is it not, my brothers, how often in America those great watchwords of human energy—"Be strong!" "Know thyself!" "Hitch your wagon to a star!"—how often these die away into dim whispers when we face these seething millions of black men? And yet do they not belong to them? Are they not their heritage as well as yours? Can they bear burdens without strength, know without learning, and aspire without ideals? Are you afraid to let them try? Fear rather, in this our common fatherland, lest we live to lose those great watchwords of liberty and opportunity which yonder in the eternal hills their fathers fought with your fathers to preserve.

Mary Church Terrell
(1863–1954)

The Progress of Colored Women
1904

*Not only are colored women with ambition and aspiration
handicapped on account of their sex, but they are almost
everywhere baffled and mocked because of their race.*

Mary Church Terrell, a suffragist and women's rights activist during the
late nineteenth century, was born the daughter of former slaves in
Memphis, Tennessee. After earning a degree from Oberlin College,
Terrell became a teacher at an all-black school in Washington, D.C.,
where she developed a deep interest in the rights and progress of
African-American women. With remarkable talent and drive, she took
the stump for black women, earning notoriety and praise. In 1896
Terrell was elected president of the National Association of Colored
Women. During her tenure she advocated reforms for women in aca-
demia and publicly decried lynching and segregation. A few years later,
she was appointed a charter member of the National Association for the
Advancement of Colored People (NAACP).

In this 1904 address Terrell discussed the specific disadvantages that
African-American women encounter, emphasizing education and religion as the primary solution to discrimination.

WHEN ONE CONSIDERS the obstacles encountered by colored women in
their effort to educate and cultivate themselves, since they became free, the
work they have accomplished and the progress they have made will bear favorable comparison, at least with that of their more fortunate sisters, from whom
the opportunity of acquiring knowledge and the means of self-culture have
never been entirely withheld. Not only are colored women with ambition and
aspiration handicapped on account of their sex, but they are almost everywhere baffled and mocked because of their race. Not only because they are
women, but because they are colored women, are discouragement and disappointment meeting them at every turn. But in spite of the obstacles encountered, the progress made by colored women along many lines appears like a
veritable miracle of modern times. Forty years ago for the great masses of col-

ored women, there was no such thing as home. Today in each and every section of the country there are hundreds of homes among colored people, the mental and moral tone of which is as high and as pure as can be found among the best people of any land.

To the women of the race may be attributed in large measure the refinement and purity of the colored home. The immorality of colored women is a theme upon which those who know little about them or those who maliciously misrepresent them love to descant. Foul aspersions upon the character of colored women are assiduously circulated by the press of certain sections and especially by the direct descendants of those who in years past were responsible for the moral degradation of their female slaves. And yet, in spite of the fateful heritage of slavery, even though the safeguards usually thrown around maidenly youth and innocence are in some sections entirely withheld from colored girls, statistics compiled by men not inclined to falsify in favor of my race show that immorality among the colored women of the United States is not so great as among women with similar environment and temptations in Italy, Germany, Sweden and France.

Scandals in the best colored society are exceedingly rare, while the progressive game of divorce and remarriage is practically unknown.

The intellectual progress of colored women has been marvelous. So great has been their thirst for knowledge and so Herculean their efforts to acquire it that there are few colleges, universities, high and normal schools in the North, East and West from which colored girls have not graduated with honor. In Wellesley, Vassar, Ann Arbor, Cornell and in Oberlin, my dear alma mater, whose name will always be loved and whose praise will always be sung as the first college in the country broad, just and generous enough to extend a cordial welcome to the Negro and to open its doors to women on an equal footing with the men, colored girls by their splendid records have forever settled the question of their capacity and worth. The instructors in these and other institutions cheerfully bear testimony to their intelligence, their diligence and their success.

As the brains of colored women expanded, their hearts began to grow. No sooner had the heads of a favored few been filled with knowledge than their hearts yearned to dispense blessings to the less fortunate of their race. With tireless energy and eager zeal, colored women have worked in every conceivable way to elevate their race. Of the colored teachers engaged in instructing our youth it is probably no exaggeration to say that fully eighty percent are women. In the backwoods, remote from the civilization and comforts of the city and town, colored women may be found courageously battling with those evils which such conditions always entail. Many a heroine of whom the world will never hear has thus sacrificed her life to her race amid surroundings and in the face of privations which only martyrs can bear.

Through the medium of their societies in the church, beneficial organizations out of it and clubs of various kinds, colored women are doing a vast amount of good. It is almost impossible to ascertain exactly what the Negro is doing in any field, for the records are so poorly kept. This is particularly true in the case of the women of the race. During the past forty years there is no doubt that colored women in their poverty have contributed large sums of money to charitable and educational institutions as well as to the foreign and home missionary work. Within the twenty-five years in which the educational work of the African Methodist Episcopal Church has been systematized, the women of that organization have contributed at least five hundred thousand dollars to the cause of education. Dotted all over the country are charitable institutions for the aged, orphaned and poor which have been established by colored women. Just how many it is difficult to state, owing to the lack of statistics bearing on the progress, possessions and prowess of colored women.

Up to date, politics have been religiously eschewed by colored women, although questions affecting our legal status as a race are sometimes agitated by the most progressive class. In Louisiana and Tennessee colored women have several times petitioned the legislatures of their respective states to repel the obnoxious Jim-Crow laws. Against the convict-lease system, whose atrocities have been so frequently exposed of late, colored women here and there in the South are waging a ceaseless war. So long as hundreds of their brothers and sisters, many of whom have committed no crime or misdemeanor whatever, are thrown into cells whose cubic contents are less than those of a good size grave, to be overworked, underfed and only partially covered with vermin-infested rags, and so long as children are born to the women in these camps who breathe the polluted atmosphere of these dens of horror and vice from the time they utter their first cry in the world till they are released from their suffering by death, colored women who are working for the emancipation and elevation of their race know where their duty lies. By constant agitation of this painful and hideous subject, they hope to touch the conscience of the country, so that this stain upon its escutcheon shall be forever wiped away.

Alarmed at the rapidity with which the Negro is losing ground in the world of trade, some of the farsighted women are trying to solve the labor question, so far as it concerns the women at least, by urging the establishment of schools of domestic science wherever means therefore can be secured. Those who are interested in this particular work hope and believe that if colored women and girls are thoroughly trained in domestic service, the boycott which has undoubtedly been placed upon them in many sections of the country will be removed. With so few vocations open to the Negro and with the labor organizations increasingly hostile to him, the future of the boys and girls of the race appears to some of our women very foreboding and dark.

The cause of temperance has been eloquently espoused by two women, each of whom has been appointed national superintendent of work among colored people by the Woman's Christian Temperance Union. In business, colored women have had signal success. There is in Alabama a large milling and cotton business belonging to and controlled by a colored woman, who has sometimes as many as seventy-five men in her employ. Until a few years ago the principal ice plant of Nova Scotia was owned and managed by a colored woman, who sold it for a large amount. In the professions there are dentists and doctors whose practice is lucrative and large. Ever since a book was published in 1773 entitled "Poems on Various Subjects, Religious and Moral by Phillis Wheatley, Negro Servant of Mr. John Wheatley," of Boston, colored women have given abundant evidence of literary ability. In sculpture we were represented by a woman upon whose chisel Italy has set her seal of approval; in painting by one of Bouguereau's pupils and in music by young women holding diplomas from the best conservatories in the land.

In short, to use a thought of the illustrious Frederick Douglass, if judged by the depths from which they have come, rather than by the heights to which those blessed with centuries of opportunities have attained, colored women need not hang their heads in shame. They are slowly but surely making their way up to the heights, wherever they can be scaled. In spite of handicaps and discouragements they are not losing heart. In a variety of ways they are rendering valiant service to their race. Lifting as they climb, onward and upward they go struggling and striving and hoping that the buds and blossoms of their desires may burst into glorious fruition ere long. Seeking no favors because of their color nor charity because of their needs they knock at the door of Justice and ask for an equal chance.

Carrie Chapman Catt
(1859–1947)

The Last, Hard Fight
1917

Woman suffrage is coming—you know it.

Born in Wisconsin, Carrie Chapman Catt attended preparatory school and graduated from Iowa State College at the top of her class, having worked her way through school washing dishes. In 1883 she became one of the first women appointed superintendent of schools, and in 1885, one of San Francisco's first female journalists.

After returning to Iowa, Catt gained a national reputation for speaking out for women's suffrage, which earned her the favor of feminists like Susan B. Anthony. With a sharp tongue and quick mind, she quickly ascended the ladder of the National American Women Suffrage Association. Anthony personally selected Catt to succeed her as president, an office she held from 1900 to 1904 and again from 1915 to 1920. Catt focused intently on women's suffrage and was willing to accommodate anyone, including southern racists, to accomplish this goal, unlike such feminists as Alice Paul, who took a more radical approach.

With victory in sight, and as part of a final push for suffrage, Catt addressed a U.S. Congressional committee in the winter of 1917, asking members to support the decades-old battle for a constitutional amendment. In 1918 Congress finally voted for the bill. Although it passed in the House, the legislation failed in the Senate, 62–34. A year later, however, the Nineteenth Amendment was finally submitted to the states for ratification; in 1920, it received the necessary state approval, securing a woman's right to vote.

<hr />

WOMAN SUFFRAGE IS INEVITABLE. . . .

First, the history of our country. Ours is a nation born of revolution, of rebellion against a system of government so securely entrenched in the customs and traditions of human society that in 1776 it seemed impregnable. From the beginning of things, nations had been ruled by kings and for kings, while the people served and paid the cost. The American Revolutionists boldly proclaimed the heresies: "Taxation without representation is tyranny.

Governments derive their just powers from the consent of the governed." The colonists won, and the nation which was established as a result of their victory has held unfailingly that these two fundamental principles of democratic government are not only the spiritual source of our national existence but have been our chief historic pride and at all times the sheet anchor of our liberties.

Eighty years after the Revolution, Abraham Lincoln welded those two maxims into a new one: "Ours is a government of the people, by the people, and for the people." Fifty years more passed and the president of the United States, Woodrow Wilson, in a mighty crisis of the nation, proclaimed to the world: "We are fighting for the things which we have always carried nearest to our hearts: for democracy, for the right of those who submit to authority to have a voice in their own government."

All the way between these immortal aphorisms political leaders have declared unabated faith in their truth. Not one American has arisen to question their logic in the 141 years of our national existence. However stupidly our country may have evaded the logical application at times, it has never swerved from its devotion to the theory of democracy as expressed by those two axioms. . . .

With such a history behind it, how can our nation escape the logic it has never failed to follow, when its last unenfranchised class calls for the vote? Behold our Uncle Sam floating the banner with one hand, "Taxation without representation is tyranny," and with the other seizing the billions of dollars paid in taxes by women to whom he refuses "representation." Behold him again, welcoming the boys of twenty-one and the newly made immigrant citizen to "a voice in their own government" while he denies that fundamental right of democracy to thousands of women public school teachers from whom many of these men learn all they know of citizenship and patriotism, to women college presidents, to women who preach in our pulpits, interpret law in our courts, preside over our hospitals, write books and magazines, and serve in every uplifting moral and social enterprise. Is there a single man who can justify such inequality of treatment, such outrageous discrimination? Not one. . . .

Second, the suffrage for women already established in the United States makes women suffrage for the nation inevitable. When Elihu Root, as president of the American Society of International Law, at the eleventh annual meeting in Washington, April 26, 1917, said, "The world cannot be half democratic and half autocratic. It must be all democratic or all Prussian. There can be no compromise," he voiced a general truth. Precisely the same intuition has already taught the blindest and most hostile foe of woman suffrage that our nation cannot long continue a condition under which government in half its territory rests upon the consent of half of the people and in the other half upon the consent of all the people; a condition which grants representation to the taxed in half of its territory and denies it in the other half; a condition which permits women in some states to share in the election of the president, senators, and representatives and denies them that privilege in others. It is too obvious to require demonstration that woman suffrage, now covering half our territory, will eventually be ordained in all the nation. No one will deny it. The only question left is when and how will it be completely established.

Third, the leadership of the United States in world democracy compels the enfranchisement of its own women. The maxims of the Declaration were once called "fundamental principles of government." They are now called "American principles" or even "Americanisms." They have become the slogans of every movement toward political liberty the world around, of every effort to widen the suffrage for men or women in any land. Not a people, race, or class striving for freedom is there anywhere in the world that has not made our axioms the chief weapon of the struggle. More, all men and women the world around, with farsighted vision into the verities of things, know that the world tragedy of our day is not now being waged over the assassination of an archduke, nor commercial competition, nor national ambitions, nor the freedom of the seas. It is a death grapple between the forces which deny and those which uphold the truths of the Declaration of Independence. . . .

Do you realize that in no other country in the world with democratic tendencies is suffrage so completely denied as in a considerable number of our own states? There are thirteen black states where no suffrage for women exists, and fourteen others where suffrage for women is more limited than in many foreign countries.

Do you realize that when you ask women to take their cause to state referendum you compel them to do this: that you drive women of education, refinement, achievement, to beg men who cannot read for their political freedom?

Do you realize that such anomalies as a college president asking her janitor to give her a vote are overstraining the patience and driving women to desperation?

Do you realize that women in increasing numbers indignantly resent the long delay in their enfranchisement?

Your party platforms have pledged women suffrage. Then why not be honest, frank friends of our cause, adopt it in reality as your own, make it a party program, and "fight with us"? As a party measure—a measure of all parties—why not put the amendment through Congress and the legislatures? We shall all be better friends, we shall have a happier nation, we women will be free to support loyally the party of our choice, and we shall be far prouder of our history.

"There is one thing mightier than kings and armies"—aye, than Congresses and political parties—"the power of an idea when its time has come to move." The time for woman suffrage has come. The woman's hour has struck. If parties prefer to postpone action longer and thus do battle with this idea, they challenge the inevitable. The idea will not perish; the party which opposes it may. Every delay, every trick, every political dishonesty from now on will antagonize the women of the land more and more, and when the party or parties which have so delayed woman suffrage finally let it come, their sincerity will be doubted and their appeal to the new voters will be met with suspicion. This is the psychology of the situation. Can you afford the risk? Think it over.

We know you will meet opposition. There are a few "women haters" left, a few "old males of the tribe," as Vance Thompson calls them, whose duty they believe it to be to keep women in the places they have carefully picked out for them. Treitschke, made world famous by war literature, said some years ago, "Germany, which knows all about Germany and France, knows far better what is good for Alsace-Lorraine than that miserable people can possibly know." A few American Treitschkes we have who know better than women what is good for them. There are women, too, with "slave souls" and "clinging vines" for backbones. There are female dolls and male dandies. But the world does not wait for such as these, nor does liberty pause to heed the plaint of men and women with a grouch. She does not wait for those who have a special interest to serve, nor a selfish reason for depriving other people of freedom. Holding her torch aloft, liberty is pointing the way onward and upward and saying to America, "Come."

To you and the supporters of our cause in Senate and House, and the number is large, the suffragists of the nation express their grateful thanks. This address is not meant for you. We are more truly appreciative of all you have done than any words can express. We ask you to make a last, hard fight for the amendment during the present session. Since last we asked a vote on this amendment, your position has been fortified by the addition to suffrage territory of Great Britain, Canada, and New York.

Some of you have been too indifferent to give more than casual attention to this question. It is worthy of your immediate consideration. A question big enough to engage the attention of our allies in wartime is too big a question for you to neglect.

Some of you have grown old in party service. Are you willing that those who take your places by and by shall blame you for having failed to keep pace with the world and thus having lost for them a party advantage? Is there any real gain for you, for your party, for your nation by delay? Do you want to drive the progressive men and women out of your party?

Some of you hold to the doctrine of states' rights as applying to woman suffrage. Adherence to that theory will keep the United States far behind all other democratic nations upon this question. A theory which prevents a nation from keeping up with the trend of world progress cannot be justified.

Gentlemen, we hereby petition you, our only designated representatives, to redress our grievances by the immediate passage of the Federal Suffrage Amendment and to use your influence to secure its ratification in your own state, in order that the women of our nation may be endowed with political freedom before the next presidential election, and that our nation may resume its world leadership in democracy.

Woman suffrage is coming—you know it. Will you, Honorable Senators and Members of the House of Representatives, help or hinder it?

Woodrow Wilson
(1856–1924)

A Moral Partnership Legitimized
September 30, 1918

We have made partners of the women in this war;
shall we admit them only to a partnership of suffering
. . . not to a partnership of privilege and right?

During the First World War, President Woodrow Wilson was the champion of policies that mixed moral purpose with informed pragmatism.
With regard to civil rights, Wilson was hardly a progressive—his friendship to African Americans was often marked by discrimination (among
other actions, he resegregated the White House). When it came to war,
however, his quest for victory colored his approach to equal opportunity for women; with domestic support for the war in question, Wilson
offered his imprimatur to a constitutional amendment for female suffrage, named in honor of Susan B. Anthony. In doing so, he reversed his
long-held opinion that each state—not the federal government—
should address the women's vote. Wilson depended on women for their
vote and support of the war, in the home, on the battlefield, and in the
workplace.

In this direct appeal, President Wilson asserted that the United
States would prove its commitment to freedom not only through its
support of democracies abroad but through its domestic policies. As he
noted, a vote for the Susan B. Anthony amendment was, "an act of right
justice to women of the country and the world." Despite his efforts, the
suffrage vote failed to pass in the Senate in 1918, but Wilson never abandoned his fight for women's rights.

In the darker days of the war, when asked how America's participa-
tion in the Great War would affect prosperity at home, Wilson replied,
"For our nation to advance materially, it must be redeemed spiritually."
The president's comment was taken by many as an oblique reference to
the struggle of American women. Lucy Anthony, niece of Susan B.
Anthony, demonstrated her support for Wilson, exclaiming to the *New
York Times,* "Washington, Lincoln, Wilson!"

THE UNUSUAL CIRCUMSTANCES of a world war in which we stand and are judged in the view not only of our own people and our own consciences but also in the view of all nations and peoples will, I hope, justify in your thought, as it does in mine, the message I have come to bring you. I regard the concurrence of the Senate in the constitutional amendment proposing the extension of the suffrage to women as vitally essential to the successful prosecution of the great war of humanity in which we are engaged. I have come to urge upon you the considerations which have led me to that conclusion. . . .

This is a people's war and the people's thinking constitutes its atmosphere and morale, not the predilections of the drawing room or the political considerations of the caucus. If we be indeed democrats and wish to lead the world to democracy, we can ask other people to accept in proof of our sincerity and our ability to lead them whither they wish to be led nothing less persuasive and convincing than our actions. . . . They are looking to the great, powerful, famous Democracy of the West to lead them to the new day for which they have so long waited; and they think, in their logical simplicity, that democracy means that women shall play their part in affairs alongside men and upon an equal footing with them. If we reject measures like this, . . . they will cease to believe in us; they will cease to follow or to trust us. They have seen their own Governments accept this interpretation of democracy,—seen old Governments like that of Great Britain, which did not profess to be democratic, promise readily and as of course this justice to women, though they had before refused it, the strange revelations of this war having made many things new and plain, to governments as well as to peoples.

Are we alone to refuse to learn the lesson? Are we alone to ask and take the utmost that our women can give,—service and sacrifice of every kind,—and still say we do not see what title that gives them to stand by our sides in the guidance of the affairs of their nation and ours? We have made partners of the women in this war; shall we admit them only to a partnership of suffering and sacrifice and toil and not to a partnership of privilege and right? . . .

. . . I tell you plainly, as the commander-in-chief of our armies and of the gallant men in our fleets, as the present spokesman of this people in our dealings with the men and women throughout the world who are now our partners, as the responsible head of a great government . . . I tell you plainly that this measure which I urge upon you is vital to the winning of the war and to energies alike of preparation and of battle.

And not to the winning of the war only. It is vital to the right solution of the great problems which we must settle, and settle immediately, when the war is over. We shall need then a vision of affairs, which is theirs, and, as we have never needed them before, the sympathy and insight and clear moral instinct of the women of the world. The problems of that time will strike to the roots of many things that we have not hitherto questioned, and I for one believe that our safety in those questioning days, as well as our comprehension of matters that touch society to the quick, will depend upon the direct and authoritative participation of women in our counsels. We shall need their moral sense to preserve what is right. . . .

John P. Irish

A Defense of Japanese Americans
November 10, 1919

Are there any Japanese anarchists? No.
Are there any Japanese bomb throwers?
No. . . . Then, what are they doing? They are at work.

Whereas Chinese laborers converged on California in the 1850s, Japanese immigrants did not arrive on the West Coast until the 1890s (the majority, in fact, landed in Hawaii, not in California). By the early twentieth century, Japanese Americans began converting the barren California interior into rich vineyards and truck farms. Despite their reputation for industriousness, Japanese immigrants, like the Chinese, encountered immediate xenophobia and legislative and economic dis-crimination—particularly in periods of economic downturn.

Bending to pressure from California and Washington, President Theodore Roosevelt concluded the Gentlemen's Agreement with Japan in 1907–08, limiting further Japanese immigration. Only a few years earlier, San Francisco had attempted to segregate ethnic Japanese children in the city's schools. In 1913 the Alien Land Act precluded noncitizens from owning farmland in California, and laws in most states banned interracial marriage.

Still, in face of those obstacles, Japanese Americans persevered by building stable businesses, farms, and communities—working tirelessly to assimilate into mainstream society. Pointedly, more than 29,000 Japanese Americans registered to fight in the First World War, a clear sign of patriotic support for their homeland.

In a rare event, Colonel John P. Irish, a leading white citizen and recognized orator, took to the podium in November 1919 to defend and praise Japanese Americans. His remarks were particularly poignant in light of the anti-Asian fervor then rampant in California.

Irish was in a uniquely influential position. Not only did he oper-ate the daily newspaper in Oakland and serve as the chief editor of one of San Francisco's dailies, he also knew that his audience, the California Fruit Growers and Farmers Convention, would be particularly recep-tive to his argument. Japanese Americans largely were responsible for the lucrative rice and strawberry farming the attendees profited from, and remained tireless farm hands despite the onslaught of bigotry.

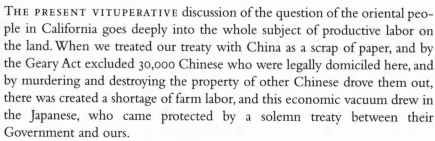

THE PRESENT VITUPERATIVE discussion of the question of the oriental people in California goes deeply into the whole subject of productive labor on the land. When we treated our treaty with China as a scrap of paper, and by the Geary Act excluded 30,000 Chinese who were legally domiciled here, and by murdering and destroying the property of other Chinese drove them out, there was created a shortage of farm labor, and this economic vacuum drew in the Japanese, who came protected by a solemn treaty between their Government and ours.

The Japanese now here constitute a fraction of one per cent of our population. Against this minute element many of our people are being lashed into a fury of apprehension, hatred, and rage. There may be left amongst us those who are capable of calm consideration, and to such I venture to address myself.

A little retrospection ought to calm the temper of this discussion and confine it to the truth. When San Francisco was shaken to its foundations and leveled by fire, and thousands of its people had no food or shelter, their cry for help went out to the world. The only country that heard and heeded was Japan. That Government immediately sent a quarter of a million in gold to the relief committee, of which Senator Phelan was a member. A few months later the San Francisco school board kicked all Japanese children out of the public schools, and its secretary gave as a reason that the Japanese children did nothing but study in school and in the examinations took the prizes and promotions that the white children ought to have.

We have now entered upon another phase of the anti-Japanese question: and in this phase the same old lies, refuted by that report, are in use once more, and the politicians, who eat their bread in the sweat of the taxpayers' face, are shouting them from the housetops.

Since that report was made what have the Japanese been doing? Nothing but working, and by their industry adding to the wealth of the State.

In our country the normal flux and change of affairs always following a war has been displaced by abnormal conditions. The hands of men are raised against our Government. Anarchists advocate destruction of our institutions. They destroy life and property by bombs. The I.W.W. [International Workers of the World] teach murder and arson as commendable occupations. Organized labor under this radical leadership strikes destructively. . . .

Are there any I.W.W.s amongst the Japanese? No. Are there any Japanese anarchists? No. Are there any Japanese bomb throwers? No. Are there any

Japanese mobs busy murdering men who want to work? No. Are there any Japanese groups teaching resistance to our laws and the destruction of our institutions? No. Then, what are they doing? They are at work. "But," cries the alarmist, "they should not be allowed on the land."

Why not? The Japanese have had but little independent access to the good lands of California. They found the sand and colloidal clays of Livingston cursed and barren as the fig tree of Bethany. On that infertile spot the Japanese wrought in privation and want for years, until they had charged the soil with humus and bacteria, and made it bear fruitful and profitable orchards and vineyards. Now, white men, led by these Japanese pioneers, pay high prices for land that was worthless, and grapes purple in the sun and peaches blush on the trees where all was a forbidding waste until Japanese skill, patience, and courage transformed it.

⌒

The anti-Japanese agitator represents that people as parasites. The fact is that wherever the Japanese has put his hand to the pruning hook and plow he has developed nobler uses of the soil, and land values have risen rapidly.

The statement is made, and was recently published in a *Chronicle* editorial, that when Japanese begin to settle in a farming district, that district is ruined for the occupation of whites, who get out of it as soon as they can. Of course that is a falsehood. . . .

⌒

Now it is proposed to expel them, not for their vices but for their virtues, and every Japanese oppressed by brutal legislation and expelled can hold his head high erect in his own country and say, "I was excluded from California for my virtues, my industry, my skill, and the benefit I was to the land and its production."

The Japanese with wives are all married according to our laws. The women are amiable, good wives, mothers, and housekeepers. It is false that they work in the fields. Their children, admitted to our schools, will make good and useful Americans. But the cry is raised that though only about one per cent of our population, they will outbreed, outwork, and outdo the other 99 per cent of white people. If this be true it proves a degeneracy of the whites which would be a just cause of alarm. The field is open. Economic law repeals all statutes. The way to combat the Japanese is not by lying about them and depriving them of the common, primitive rights of humanity, but excelling them in industry, in foresight and enterprise.

MARGARET SANGER
(1879–1966)

Crusade for Women's Birth Control
DECEMBER 8, 1920

We object . . . to the state or the Church which appoints itself as arbiter and dictator in [the sexual] sphere and attempts to force unwilling women into compulsory maternity.

A pioneer of sexual freedom, Margaret Sanger founded the United States' first birth control clinic and the American Birth Control League, which in 1942 became Planned Parenthood.

Born in Corny, New York, one of eleven children of Irish-American parents, Sanger attributed her mother's early death to overwork and the burden of a large family. From that moment forward, she fought for feminist progress: first as a nursing student, then in the Socialist Party, and finally in the movement for sexual and reproductive freedom.

In 1912 she became an outspoken advocate for birth control, publishing family planning pamphlets with explicit instructions on contraception. After Sanger inevitably violated New York's Comstock Law preventing the trade of "obscene literature" and "immoral articles," she fled to Europe, only to return in 1915 in the midst of a nationwide birth control movement. Seeking the support of physicians, eugenicists, and other women reformers, Sanger continued to lead her single-issue campaign for family planning. By the 1960s, with overpopulation a growing concern, most states legalized contraception, more as a medical necessity than a woman's right.

In the following address, which she delivered regularly in the 1920s, Sanger criticized the Catholic Church for its attempted authority over a woman's body and for deeming sex a lewd activity.

———

RELIGIOUS PROPAGANDA against birth control is crammed with contradiction and fallacy. It refutes itself. Yet it brings the opposing views into vivid contrast. In stating these differences we should make clear that advocates of birth control are not seeking to attack the Catholic Church. We quarrel with that Church, however, when it seeks to assume authority over non-Catholics and to dub their behavior immoral because they do not conform to the dictatorship of Rome. The question of bearing and rearing children we hold is the concern of the mother and the potential mother. If she delegates the responsibility, the ethical education, to an external authority, that is her affair. We object, however, to the state or the Church which appoints itself as arbiter and dictator in this sphere and attempts to force unwilling women into compulsory maternity. . . .

The sex instinct in the human race is too strong to be bound by the dictates of any church. The Church's failure, its century after century of failure is now evident on every side. For having convinced men and women that only in its baldly propagative phase is sexual expression legitimate, the teachings of the Church have driven sex underground into secret channels, strengthened the conspiracy of silence, concentrated men's thoughts upon the "lusts of the body," have sown, cultivated, and reaped a crop of bodily and mental diseases, and developed a society congenitally and almost hopelessly unbalanced. How is any progress to be made, how is any human expression or education possible when women and men are taught to combat and resist their natural impulses and to despise their bodily functions? . . .

More than ever in history, women need to realize that nothing can ever come to us from another. Everything we attain we must owe to ourselves. Our own spirit must vitalize it. Our own heart must feel it. For we are not passive machines. We are not to be lectured, guided, and molded this way or that. We are alive and intelligent, we women, no less than men, and we must awaken to the essential realization that we are living beings, endowed with will, choice, comprehension, and that every step in life must be our own initiative.

Moral and sexual balance in civilization will only be established by the assertion and expression of power on the part of women. This power will not be found in any futile seeking for economic independence or in the aping of men in industrial or business pursuits, nor by joining the so-called "single standard." Woman's power can only be expressed and make itself felt when she refuses the task of bringing unwanted children into the world to be exploited in industry and slaughtered in wars. When we refuse to produce battalions of babies to be exploited, when we declare to the nation, "Show us that the best possible chance in life is given to every child now brought into the world before you cry for more! At present our children are a glut on the market. You hold infant life cheap. Help us to make the world a fit place for our children. When you have done this, we will bear you children. Then we shall be true women." The new morality will express this power and responsibility on the part of women. . . .

Birth control is an ethical necessity for humanity today because it places in our hands a new instrument of self-expression and self-realization. It gives us control over one of the primordial forces of nature, to which in the past the majority of mankind have been enslaved, and by which it has been cheapened and debased. It arouses us to the possibility of newer and greater freedom. It develops the power, the responsibility, and intelligence to use this freedom in living a liberated and abundant life. It permits us to enjoy this liberty without danger of infringing upon the similar liberty of our fellow men, or of injuring and curtailing the freedom of the next generation. It shows us that we need not seek in the amassing of worldly wealth, nor in the illusion of some extraterrestrial heaven or earthly utopia of a remote future, the road to human development. The kingdom of heaven is in a very definite sense within us. Not by leaving our body and our fundamental humanity behind us, not by aiming to be anything but what we are, shall we become ennobled or immortal. By knowing ourselves, by expressing ourselves, by realizing ourselves more completely than has ever before been possible, not only shall we attain the kingdom ourselves but we shall hand on the torch of life undimmed to our children and the children of our children.

ALONSO S. PERALES
(1898–1960)

Defending Mexican Americans
1921

*I feel it my duty to deny most emphatically that the
Mexican race is inferior to any other race.*

Between 1910 and 1917 the Mexican Revolution sparked a massive
social upheaval, prompting nearly one-tenth of the Mexican population to seek refuge in the United States. Poor and uneducated, the
majority of these new immigrants sought low-wage jobs in the farming, mining, herding, and railroad industries. By 1908 more than
16,000 of them were working on railroads in the West and Southwest.
They quickly settled in large colonies near urban centers, held
together in part by the Spanish language and patriotic icons like the
Catholic Church.

Immigrant nationalism was no match for burgeoning Anglo-
American racism. Although some whites tolerated Mexican immigrants
as a necessary economic evil, for the most part, Mexican Americans fell
under the contempt of segregation, police brutality, workplace abuse,
and overall rejection by the mainstream society. The sustained and hostile abuse of their civil rights provoked some of the first efforts to
organize among Mexican Americans, but with the language and economic barriers, most still relied on the Mexican government for assistance—an increasingly untenable recourse. With violence escalating as
the U.S. economy soured following the First World War, thousands of
immigrants were forced to "repatriate" to Mexico without any formal
deportation process.

When the U.S. Congress ordered hearings on immigration in 1921,
only a handful of activists testified in support of Mexican immigrants.
Alonso S. Perales, a native Texan, lawyer, veteran of the First World War,
and founder of the League of United Latin American Citizens
(LULAC), defended Mexican Americans living in the United States as
legal citizens and decried the extreme racial prejudice they faced. Still,
like many other "old Mexican immigrants"—those Americanized
under the Treaty of Guadalupe Hidalgo in 1848—Perales had assimilated to Anglo norms, and for this reason, refused to encourage further

Mexican immigration. His testimony instead took a rather measured approach to the increasingly perilous environment for Mexican Americans still living in the United States.

AT THE OUTSET, Mr. Chairman and members of the committee, I want to state that I am not here to oppose the Box bill or the Johnson bill or any other bill, but to promote the welfare of Texas—of the American people. Therefore I am not going to discuss the economic phases of this problem.

However, I do wish to refer to the statements made by some sponsors of this quota bill, to the effect that the Mexican people is an inferior and degenerate race. Being a Mexican by blood, and being just as proud of my racial extraction as I am of my American citizenship, I feel it my duty to deny most emphatically that the Mexican race is inferior to any other race, and I have quoted authorities here in support of my statement.

The charge is also made that Mexicans ought to be restricted because they do not become American citizens. I am one of the founders of what is known in Texas as the League of United Latin American Citizens. . . .

The main objects of this organization are to develop within the members of our race the best, purest, and most perfect type of a true and loyal citizen of the United States of America; and to define with absolute and unmistakable clearness our unquestionable loyalty to the ideals, principles, and citizenship of the United States of America.

The acquisition of the English language, which is the official language of our country, being necessary for the enjoyment of our rights and privileges, we declare it to be the official language of this organization, and we pledge ourselves to learn, and speak, and teach the same to our children.

We shall oppose any radical and violent demonstration which may tend to create conflicts and disturb the peace and tranquility of our country.

Now, gentlemen, the question is also asked that, if we are not an inferior race, why is it that we have not produced outstanding men? Well, if I may answer that in a general way, I will say that we have, despite our handicap as a race, produced a few outstanding men. I will quote, for instance, Doctor Maca, one of the outstanding statesmen of the world.

I will also refer to another Mexican, who is now in Europe, an outstanding European lawyer, now serving as umpire on several international claims commissions.

Why have we not produced outstanding men in Texas? Gentlemen, the problem in Texas has been mostly one of racial prejudice, with us. We have received very little encouragement to forge ahead and become useful

American citizens. On the other hand, attempts have been made to keep us down. Therefore, our effort here to organize ourselves into this organization known as the League of United Latin American Citizens, to the end that we may become better citizens, seems to me to be all the more commendable.

That is all I wish to say, and I will be very glad to answer any questions.

MARCUS GARVEY
(1887–1940)

A Separate Nation
NOVEMBER 25, 1922

The Universal Negro Improvement Association seeks independence
of government, while the other organizations seek to make the
Negro a secondary part of existing governments.

In the early years of the twentieth century, Marcus Moziah Garvey became the first civil rights leader to encourage blacks around the world to view themselves as a united people, sharing a common heritage, pride, and agenda. Having failed to attract a following in his native country, Jamaica, he settled in Harlem and founded the Universal Negro Improvement Association (UNIA), a black-governed nationalist movement. By 1919, after establishing branches of the UNIA throughout the North, Garvey's popularity burgeoned in the black world, with a following of more than 2 million. He called on all blacks to return to Africa, where they could create a motherland free from oppression and racial bigotry. By outlining his plan to build an African nation-state, Garvey attracted popular support, and thousands enrolled in the UNIA, heeding its motto: "One God, One Aim, One Destiny."

From the platform of the association's Liberty Hall and in his newspaper, the *Negro World,* Garvey spoke of a "new Negro," proud of being black. He thundered his famous battle cry: "Up, you mighty race! You can accomplish what you will." Known as "Black Moses," Garvey preached that African Americans would be respected only when they were economically strong, with an independent black economy structured within the framework of white capitalism. To this end, he established the Negro Factories Corporation, the transatlantic Black Star Line, a chain of restaurants and grocery stores, laundries, a hotel, and a printing press.

Garvey also embraced the disenchanted spirit of black veterans returning home from the First World War when their accomplishments on the front lines in Europe failed to earn them equal opportunity in the United States. He encouraged these veterans, and all blacks, to be proud of their color and find solace in their African roots. Reaching the apogee of his power in 1920, Garvey presided over a 50,000-person parade through Harlem.

On November 25, 1922, Marcus Garvey spoke to a crowd of thousands in New York City under the banner "Africa for Africans," and described the principles of UNIA and its separatist movement. Drawing on the accommodationist message of Booker T. Washington, Garvey promoted a "new line of thought" among civil rights activists, calling on fellow blacks to repatriate to Africa or seek independence in a unified black front.

OVER FIVE YEARS AGO the Universal Negro Improvement Association placed itself before the world as the movement through which the new and rising Negro would give expression of his feelings. This Association adopts an attitude not of hostility to other races and peoples of the world, but an attitude of self-respect, of manhood rights on behalf of 400,000,000 Negroes of the world.

We represent peace, harmony, love, human sympathy, human rights and human justice, and that is why we fight so much. Wheresoever human rights are denied to any group, wheresoever justice is denied to any group, there the U.N.I.A. finds a cause. And at this time among all the peoples of the world, the group that suffers most from injustice, the group that is denied most of those rights that belong to all humanity, is the black group of 400,000,000. Because of that injustice, because of that denial of our rights, we go forth under the leadership of the One who is always on the side of right to fight the common cause of humanity; to fight as we fought in the Revolutionary War, as we fought in the Civil War, as we fought in the Spanish-American War, and as we fought in the war between 1914–18 on the battle plains of France and Flanders. As we fought up the heights of Mesopotamia; even so under the leadership of the U.N.I.A., we are marshaling the 400,000,000 Negroes of the world to fight for the emancipation of the race and for the redemption of the country of our fathers.

We represent a new line of thought among Negroes. Whether you call it advanced thought or reactionary thought, I do not care. If it is reactionary for people to seek independence in government, then we are reactionary. If it is advanced thought for people to seek liberty and freedom, then we represent the advanced school of thought among the Negroes of this country. We of the U.N.I.A. believe that what is good for the other fellow is good for us. If government is something that is worth while; if government is something that is appreciable and helpful and protective to others, then we also want to experiment in government. We do not mean a government that will make us citizens without rights or subjects without consideration. We mean the kind of government that will place our race in control, even as other races are in control of their own governments.

That does not suggest anything that is unreasonable. It was not unreasonable for George Washington, the great hero and father of the country, to have fought for the freedom of America giving to us this great republic and this great democracy; it was not unreasonable for the Liberals of France to have fought against the Monarchy to give to the world French Democracy and French Republicanism; it was no unrighteous cause that led in giving to the world the social democracy of Russia, an experiment that will probably prove to be a boon and a blessing to mankind. If it was not an unrighteous cause that led Washington to fight for the independence of this country, and led the Liberals of France to establish the Republic, it is therefore not an unrighteous cause for the U.N.I.A. to lead 400,000,000 Negroes all over the world to fight for the liberation of our country.

⁓

In advocating the principles of this Association we find we have been very much misunderstood and very much misrepresented by men from within our own race, as well as others from without. Any reform movement that seeks to bring about changes for the benefit of humanity is bound to be misrepresented by those who have always taken it upon themselves to administer to, and lead the unfortunate, and to direct those who may be placed under temporary disadvantages. It has been so in all other movements whether social or political; hence those of us in the Universal Negro Improvement Association who lead, do not feel in any way embarrassed about this misrepresentation, about this misunderstanding as far as the aims and objects of the Universal Negro Improvement Association go. But those who probably would have taken kindly notice of this great movement, have been led to believe that this movement seeks, not to develop the good within the race, but to give expression to that which is most destructive and most harmful to society and to government.

I desire to remove the misunderstanding that has been created in the minds of millions of peoples throughout the world in their relationship to the organization. The Universal Negro Improvement Association stands for the Bigger Brotherhood; the Universal Negro Improvement Association stands for human rights, not only for Negroes, but for all races. The Universal Negro Improvement Association believes in the rights of not only the black race, but the white race, the yellow race and the brown race. The Universal Negro Improvement Association believes that the white man has as much right to be considered, the yellow man has as much right to be considered, the brown man has as much right to be considered as well as the black man of Africa. In view of the fact that the black man of Africa has contributed as much to the world as the white man of Europe, and the brown man and yellow man of Asia, we of the Universal Negro Improvement Association demand that the white, yellow and brown races give to the black man his place in the civilization of the world. We ask for nothing more than the rights of 400,000,000 Negroes. We are not seeking, as I said before, to destroy or disrupt the society or the government of other races, but we are determined that 400,000,000 of us shall unite ourselves to free our motherland from the grasp of the invader. We of the Universal Negro Improvement Association are determined to unite 400,000,000 Negroes for their own industrial, political, social and religious emancipation.

We of the Universal Negro Improvement Association are determined to unite the 400,000,000 Negroes of the world to give expression to their own feeling; we are determined to unite the 400,000,000 Negroes of the world for the purpose of building a civilization of their own. And in that effort we desire to bring together the 15,000,000 of the United States, the 180,000,000 in Asia, the West Indies and Central and South America, and the 200,000,000 in Africa. We are looking toward political freedom on the continent of Africa, the land of our fathers.

The Universal Negro Improvement Association is not seeking to build up another government within the bounds or borders of the United States of America. The Universal Negro Improvement Association is not seeking to disrupt any organized system of government, but the Association is determined to bring Negroes together for the building up of a nation of their own. And why? Because we have been forced to it. We have been forced to it throughout the world; not only in America, not only in Europe, not only in the British Empire, but wheresoever the black man happens to find himself, he has been forced to do for himself.

⌒

You and I fare no better in America, in the British Empire, or in any other part of the white world; we fare no better than any black man wheresoever he shows his head. And why? Because we have been satisfied to allow ourselves to be led, educated, to be directed by the other fellow, who has always sought to lead in the world in that direction that would satisfy him and strengthen his position. We have allowed ourselves for the last 500 years to be a race of followers, following every race that has led in the direction that would make them more secure.

The U.N.I.A. is reversing the old-time order of things. We refuse to be followers any more. We are leading ourselves. That means, if any saving is to be done, later on, whether it is saving this one nation or that one government, we are going to seek a method of saving Africa first. Why? And why Africa? Because Africa has become the grand prize of the nations. Africa has become the big game of the nation hunters. Today Africa looms as the greatest commercial, industrial and political prize in the world.

The difference between the Universal Negro Improvement Association and the other movements of this country, and probably the world, is that the Universal Negro Improvement Association seeks independence of government, while the other organizations seek to make the Negro a secondary part of existing governments. We differ from the organization in America because they seek to subordinate the Negro as a secondary consideration in a great civilization, knowing that in America the Negro will never reach his highest ambition, knowing that the Negro in America will never get his constitutional rights. All those organizations which are fostering the improvement of Negroes in the British Empire know that the Negro in the British Empire will never reach the height of his constitutional rights.

What do I mean by constitutional rights in America? If the black man is to reach the height of his ambition in this country—if the black man is to get all of his constitutional rights in America—then the black man should have the same chance in the nation as any other man to become president of the nation, or a street cleaner in New York. If the black man in the British Empire is to have all his constitutional rights it means that the Negro in the British Empire should have at least the same right to become premier of Great Britain as he has to become street cleaner in the city of London. Are they prepared to give us such political equality? You and I can live in the United States of America for 100 more years, and our generations may live for 200 years or for 5,000 more years, and so long as there is a black and white population, when the majority is on the side of the white race, you and I will never get political justice or get political equality in this country.

Then why should a black man with rising ambition, after preparing himself in every possible way to give expression to that highest ambition, allow himself to be kept down by racial prejudice within a country? If I am as educated as the next man, if I am as prepared as the next man, if I have passed through the best schools and colleges and universities as the other fellow, why should I not have a fair chance to compete with the other fellow for the biggest position in the nation? I have feelings, I have blood, I have senses like the other fellow; I have ambition, I have hope. Why should he, because of some racial prejudice, keep me down and why should I concede to him the right to rise above me, and to establish himself as my permanent master? That is where the U.N.I.A. differs from other organizations. I refuse to stultify my ambition, and every true Negro refuses to stultify his ambition to suit any one, and therefore the U.N.I.A. decides if America is not big enough for two presidents, if England is not big enough for two kings, then we are not going to quarrel over the matter; we will leave one president in America, we will leave one king in England, we will leave one president in France and we will have one president in Africa. Hence, the Universal Negro Improvement Association does not seek to interfere with the social and political systems of France, but by the arrangement of things today the U.N.I.A. refuses to recognize any political or social system in Africa except that which we are about to establish for ourselves.

We are not preaching a propaganda of hate against anybody. We love the white man; we love all humanity, because we feel that we cannot live without the other. The white man is as necessary to the existence of the Negro as the Negro is necessary to his existence. There is a common relationship that we cannot escape. Africa has certain things that Europe wants, and Europe has certain things that Africa wants, and if a fair and square deal must bring white and black with each other, it is impossible for us to escape it. Africa has oil, diamonds, copper, gold and rubber and all the minerals that Europe wants, and there must be some kind of relationship between Africa and Europe for a fair exchange, so we cannot afford to hate anybody.

The question often asked is what does it require to redeem a race and free a country? If it takes man power, if it takes scientific intelligence, if it takes education of any kind, or if it takes blood, then the 400,000,000 Negroes of the world have it.

It took the combined man power of the Allies to put down the mad determination of the Kaiser to impose German will upon the world and upon humanity. Among those who suppressed his mad ambition were two million Negroes who have not yet forgotten how to drive men across the firing line. Surely those of us who faced German shot and shell at the Marne, at Verdun, have not forgotten the order of our Commander-in-Chief. The cry that caused us to leave America in such mad haste, when white fellow citizens of America refused to fight and said, "We do not believe in war and therefore, even though we are American citizens, and even though the nation is in danger, we will not go to war." When many of them cried out and said, "We are German-Americans and we can not fight," when so many white men refused to answer to the call and dodged behind all kinds of excuses, 400,000 black men were ready without a question. It was because we were told it was a war of democracy; it was a war for the liberation of the weaker peoples of the world. We heard the cry of Woodrow Wilson, not because we liked him so, but because the things he said were of such a nature that they appealed to us as men. Wheresoever the cause of humanity stands in need of assistance, there you will find the Negro ever ready to serve.

⌒

. . . A few months after our appearance in France and on the various battle fronts, we succeeded in driving the German hordes across the Rhine, and driving the Kaiser out of Germany, and out of Potsdam into Holland. We have not forgotten the prowess of war. If we have been liberal minded enough to give our life's blood in France, in Mesopotamia and elsewhere, fighting for the white man, whom we have always assisted, surely we have not forgotten to fight for ourselves, and when the time comes that the world will again give Africa an opportunity for freedom, surely 400,000,000 black men will march out on the battle plains of Africa, under the colors of the red, the black and the green.

We shall march out, yes, as black American citizens, as black British subjects, as black French citizens, as black Italians or as black Spaniards, but we shall march out with a greater loyalty, the loyalty of race. We shall march out in answer to the cry of our fathers, who cry out to us for the redemption of our own country, our motherland, Africa.

We shall march out, not forgetting the blessings of America. We shall march out, not forgetting the blessings of civilization. We shall march out with a history of peace before and behind us, and surely that history shall be our breastplate, for how can man fight better than knowing that the cause for which he fights is righteous? How can man fight more gloriously than by knowing that behind him is a history of slavery, a history of bloody carnage and massacre inflicted upon a race because of its inability to protect itself and fight? Shall we not fight for the glorious opportunity of protecting and forever more establishing ourselves as a mighty race and nation, never more to be disrespected by men? Glorious shall be the battle when the time comes to fight for our people and our race.

We should say to the millions who are in Africa to hold the fort, for we are coming 400,000,000 strong.

MARCUS GARVEY
(1887–1940)

A Last Word Before Incarceration
JUNE 17, 1923

In laying the Negro low you but bring down the pillars of creation.

As much as he preached African-American unity, Marcus Garvey created great division among black civil rights leaders with his question-
able business methods and doctrines of racial purity and separatism.
Both A. Phillip Randolph and W.E.B. Du Bois denounced Garvey's
"jingoism." His influence declined rapidly after 1922, when he and
other UNIA members were indicted and imprisoned for mail fraud in
connection with the sale of stock for the Black Star Line, a company
with ships that were supposed to transport blacks back to Africa. In
1927 Calvin Coolidge commuted Garvey's sentence but deported him
as an undesirable alien. He was never able to revive his movement
abroad, and died penniless in virtual obscurity.

Shortly before going to prison, Garvey delivered this address at
Liberty Hall in New York City. He highlighted the central themes of
economic empowerment, separatism, and black pride—which were
hallmarks of his political career. It was the last speech he delivered to
any sizeable crowd.

———

AMONG THE MANY NAMES by which I have been called, I was dubbed by
another name a couple days ago. The District Attorney, with whom I have
been contesting the case for my liberty and for the existence of the Universal
Negro Improvement Association, in his fervid appeal, in his passionate appeal,
to the gentlemen of the jury last Friday cried out: "Gentlemen, will you let
the tiger loose?"

The tiger is already loose, and he has been at large for so long that it is no
longer one tiger, but there are many tigers. The spirit of the Universal Negro
Improvement Association has, fortunately for us, made a circuit of the world, to
the extent that harm of injury done to any one, will in no way affect the great
membership of this association or retard its great program. The world is ignorant of the purpose of this association. The world is ignorant of the scope of this
great movement, when it thinks that by laying low any one individual it can

permanently silence this great spiritual wave, that has taken hold of the souls and the hearts and minds of 400,000,000 Negroes throughout the world. We have only started; we are just on our way; we have just made the first lap in the great race for existence, and for a place in the political and economic sun of men.

Those of you who have been observing events for the last four or five weeks with keen eyes and keen perceptions will come to no other conclusion than this—that through the effort to strangle the Universal Negro Improvement Association—through the effort to silence Marcus Garvey—there is a mad desire, there is a great plan to permanently lay the Negro low in this civilization and in future civilizations. But the world is sadly mistaken. No longer can the Negro be laid low; in laying the Negro low you but bring down the pillars of creation, because 400,000,000 Negroes are determined to [be] a man, to take a place in the world and to hold that place. The world is sadly mistaken and rudely shocked at the same time. They thought that the new Negro would bend; they thought that the new Negro was only bluffing and would exhibit the characteristic of the old Negro when pushed to the corner or pushed to the wall. If you want to see the new Negro fight, force him to the wall, and the nearer he approaches the wall the more he fights, and when he gets to the wall he is even more desperate.

What does the world think . . . that we are going back to sixty years ago in America . . . going back to eighty-five years ago in the West Indies . . . going back to 300 years ago in Africa? The world is crazy if they indulge that thought. We are not going back; we are going forward . . . forward to the emancipation of 400,000,000 oppressed souls; forward to the redemption of a great country and the re-establishment of a greater government.

Garvey has just started to fight; Garvey has not given his first exhibition of his fighting prowess yet. Men, we want you to understand that this is the age of men, not of pigmies, not of serfs and peons and dogs, but men and we who make up the membership of the Universal Negro Improvement Association reflect the new manhood of the Negro. No fear, no intimidation, nothing can daunt the courage of the Negro who affiliates himself with the Universal Negro Improvement Association. The Universal Negro Improvement Association is light, and we have entered into light and shall not go back into darkness. We have entered into the light of a new day; we have seen the light of a new creation; we have seen the light of a new civilization, and we shall follow where that light leads.

I was amused when my friend, the District Attorney, said that he was more interested in Negroes than Marcus Garvey. They are so accustomed to the old camouflage that they believe they can plead it everywhere to the satisfaction of every Negro, and to everyone who comes in contact with them. That is the old camouflage that made them our missionaries sixty years ago; it is the same camouflage that will not stand today. It is impossible for a Negro to be more interested in a Jew than a Jew is interested in himself. It is impossible for an Englishman to be more interested in an Irishman than that Irishman is in himself. It is a lie for any Jew to say he is more interested in Negroes than Negroes are in themselves. It is an unnatural lie to talk about one race being more interested in another race than that race is interested in itself. But that only shows how desperate they are. Sometimes we have to beware of Greeks bearing gifts. Unfortunately, I did not have the last word and therefore I was silenced after I placed my defense in; but, nevertheless, the world will know tomorrow the outcome of this case wherein Marcus Garvey and the Universal Negro Improvement Association is involved. One way or the other, the world will not be disappointed. There is no verdict that would disappoint me. I tell you this, that there is to be no disappointment; if they were to give any other verdict than guilty, Marcus Garvey will be very much disappointed; Marcus Garvey knows them so well that Marcus Garvey will expect anything from them; so, whether they give a verdict of guilty or not guilty, it is immaterial to Marcus Garvey; the fight will just then be starting.

Now, understand this is a fight to the finish. We are not fighting this great government, because all Negroes in America—all Negroes all over the world—know that the greatest democracy in the world is the American democracy, the greatest government in the world is the American republic. We are not fighting America; we are fighting hypocrisy and lies, and that we are going to fight to the bitter end. Now, understand me well, Marcus Garvey has entered the fight for the emancipation of a race; Marcus Garvey has entered the fight for the redemption of a country. From the graves of millions of my forebears at this hour I hear the cry, and I am going to answer it even though hell is cut loose before Marcus Garvey. From the silent graves of millions who went down to make me what I am, I shall make for their memory this fight that shall leave a glaring page in the history of man.

They do not know what they are doing. They brought millions of black men from Africa who never disturbed the peace of the world, and they shall put up a constitutional fight, that shall write a page upon the history of human affairs that shall never be effaced until the day of judgement. I did not bring myself here; they brought me from my silent repose in Africa 300 years ago, and this is only the first Marcus Garvey. They have thought that they could for 300 years brutalize a race. They have thought that they could for 300 years steep the soul of a race in blood and darkness and let it go at that. They make a terrible mistake. Marcus Garvey shall revenge the blood of his sires. So don't be afraid of Marcus Garvey. When Marcus Garvey goes to jail the world of Negroes will know. They have come at the wrong time.

I appreciate the splendid way in which you have behaved and conducted yourselves during the trial. We shall observe to the letter the laws of the great country, but Africa shall tell the tale. Marcus Garvey has no fear about going to jail. Like Mac-Swiney or like Carson, like Roger Casement, like those who have led the fight for Irish freedom, so Marcus Garvey shall lead the fight for African freedom.

I repeat that if they think they can stamp out the souls of 400,000,000 black men, they make a tremendous and terrible mistake. We are no longer dogs; we are no longer peons; we are no longer serfs—we are men. The spirit that actuated George Washington in founding this great republic—the spirit that actuated the fathers of this great nation, is the spirit that actuates 6,000,000 black men who are at the present time members of the Universal Negro Improvement Association; it is the spirit that will actuate 400,000,000 Negroes in the redemption of their motherland, Africa. Tell us about fear; we were not born with fear. Intimidation does not drive fear into the soul of Marcus Garvey. There is no fear, but the fear of God. Man cannot drive fear into the heart of man, because man is but the equal of man. The world is crazy and foolish if they think that they can destroy the principles, the ideals of the Universal Negro Improvement Association.

W. E. B. DU BOIS
(1868–1963)

A Negro Nation Within a Nation
JUNE 26, 1934

*The colored people of America are coming to face the fact quite
calmly that most white Americans do not like them.*

Although W. E. B. Du Bois was a fierce champion of racial integration,
there were periods in his career when he favored economic and political separatism as the best means to African-American dignity and
equality. By the late 1920s, he called not only for economic, political,
and educational parity, but also a separate Negro "nation within a
nation"—a marked departure from statements and remarks made earlier in his life. In fact, Du Bois's call for "race pride" has been credited
by some as the forerunner to the Black Power movement.

On June 26, 1934, Du Bois resigned from the NAACP—which he
had helped found in 1909—and delivered the following address, in
which he advocated voluntary racial segregation—a common theme of
many of his later speeches. During the 1950s, he became an ardent supporter of communism and the Soviet Union. In 1961 Du Bois left the
United States for Ghana, where he died two years later on the eve of
the historic March on Washington. The author August Meier later
described the formidable Du Bois: "Scholar and prophet; mystic and
materialist; ardent agitator for political rights . . . a Marxist who was
fundamentally a middle-class intellectual."

NO MORE CRITICAL SITUATION ever faced the Negroes of America than
that of today—not in 1830, nor in 1861, nor in 1867. More than ever the appeal
of the Negro for elementary justice falls on deaf ears.

Three-fourths of us are disfranchised; yet no writer on democratic reform,
no third-party movement says a word about Negroes. The Bull Moose crusade
in 1912 refused to notice them; the La Follette uprising in 1924 was hardly
aware of them; the Socialists still keep them in the background. Negro children are systematically denied education; when the National Educational
Association asks for federal aid to education it permits discrimination to be
perpetuated by the present local authorities. Once or twice a month Negroes

convicted of no crime are openly and publicly lynched, and even burned; yet a National Crime Convention is brought to perfunctory and unwilling notice of this only by mass picketing and all but illegal agitation. When a man with every qualification is refused a position simply because his great-grandfather was black, there is not a ripple of comment or protest.

Long before the depression Negroes in the South were losing "Negro" jobs, those assigned them by common custom—poorly paid and largely undesirable toil, but nevertheless life-supporting. New techniques, new enterprises, mass production, impersonal ownership and control have been largely displacing the skilled white and Negro worker in tobacco manufacturing, in iron and steel, in lumbering and mining, and in transportation. Negroes are now restricted more and more to common labor and domestic service of the lowest paid and worst kind. In textile, chemical and other manufactures Negroes were from the first nearly excluded, and just as slavery kept the poor white out of profitable agriculture, so freedom prevents the poor Negro from finding a place in manufacturing. The worldwide decline in agriculture has moreover carried the mass of black farmers, despite heroic endeavor among the few, down to the level of landless tenants and peons.

The World War and its wild aftermath seemed for a moment to open a new door; two million black workers rushed North to work in iron and steel, make automobiles and pack meat, build houses and do the heavy toil in factories. They met first the closed trade union which excluded them from the best-paid jobs and pushed them into the low-wage gutter, denied them homes and mobbed them. Then they met the depression.

Since 1929 Negro workers, like white workers, have lost their jobs, have had mortgages foreclosed on their farms and homes, have used up their small savings. But, in the case of the Negro worker, everything has been worse in larger or smaller degree; the loss has been greater and more permanent. Technological displacement, which began before the depression, has been accelerated, while unemployment and falling wages struck black men sooner, went to lower levels and will last longer.

The colored people of America are coming to face the fact quite calmly that most white Americans do not like them, and are planning neither for their survival, nor for their definite future if it involves free, self-assertive modern manhood. This does not mean all Americans. A saving few are worried about the Negro problem; a still larger group are not ill-disposed, but they fear prevailing public opinion. The great mass of Americans are, however, merely representatives of average humanity. They muddle along with their own affairs and scarcely can be expected to take seriously the affairs of strangers or people whom they partly fear and partly despise.

For many years it was the theory of most Negro leaders that this attitude was the insensibility of ignorance and inexperience, that white America did not know of or realize the continuing plight of the Negro. Accordingly, for the last two decades, we have striven by book and periodical, by speech and appeal, by various dramatic methods of agitation, to put the essential facts before the American people. Today there can be no doubt that Americans know the facts; and yet they remain for the most part indifferent and unmoved.

~~~

The peculiar position of Negroes in America offers an opportunity. Negroes today cast probably 2,000,000 votes in a total of 40,000,000, and their vote will increase. This gives them, particularly in northern cities, and at critical times, a chance to hold a very considerable balance of power, and the mere threat of this being used intelligently and with determination may often mean much. The consuming power of 2,800,000 Negro families has recently been estimated at $166,000,000 a month—a tremendous power when intelligently directed. Their manpower as laborers probably equals that of Mexico or Yugoslavia. Their illiteracy is much lower than that of Spain or Italy. Their estimated per capita wealth about equals that of Japan.

For a nation with this start in culture and efficiency to sit down and await the salvation of a white God is idiotic. With the use of their political power, their power as consumers, and their brainpower, added to that chance of personal appeal which proximity and neighborhood always give to human beings, Negroes can develop in the United States an economic nation within a nation, able to work through inner cooperation, to found its own institutions, to educate its genius, and at the same time, without mob violence or extremes of race hatred, to keep in helpful touch and cooperate with the mass of the nation. This has happened more often than most people realize, in the case of groups not so obviously separated from the mass of people as are American Negroes. It must happen in our case, or there is no hope for the Negro in America.

Any movement toward such a program is today hindered by the absurd Negro philosophy of Scatter, Suppress, Wait, Escape. There are even many of our educated young leaders who think that because the Negro problem is not in evidence where there are few or no Negroes, this indicates a way out! They think that the problem of race can be settled by ignoring it and suppressing all reference to it. They think that we have only to wait in silence for the white people to settle the problem for us; and finally and predominantly, they think that the problem of twelve million Negro people, mostly poor, ignorant workers, is going to be settled by having their more educated and wealthy classes gradually and continually escape from their race into the mass of the American people, leaving the rest to sink, suffer and die.

Proponents of this program claim, with much reason, that the plight of the masses is not the fault of the emerging classes. For the slavery and exploitation that reduced Negroes to their present level or at any rate hindered them from rising, the white world is to blame. Since the age-long process of raising a group is through the escape of its upper class into welcome fellowship with risen peoples, the Negro intelligentsia would submerge itself if it bent its back to the task of lifting the mass of people. There is logic in this answer, but futile logic.

If the leading Negro classes cannot assume and bear the uplift of their own proletariat, they are doomed for all time. It is not a case of ethics; it is a plain case of necessity. The method by which this may be done is, first, for the American Negro to achieve a new economic solidarity.

. . . It may be said that this matter of a nation within a nation has already been partially accomplished in the organization of the Negro church, the Negro school and the Negro retail business, and, despite all the justly due criticism, the result has been astonishing. The great majority of American Negroes are divided not only for religious but for a large number of social purposes into self-supporting economic units, self-governed, self-directed. The greatest difficulty is that these organizations have no logical and reasonable standards and do not attract the finest, most vigorous and best educated Negroes. When all these things are taken into consideration it becomes clearer to more and more American Negroes that, through voluntary and increased segregation, by careful autonomy and planned economic organization, they may build so strong and efficient a unit that twelve million men can no longer be refused fellowship and equality in the United States.

JAMES OMURA
(1912–)

Fighting Words
1942

*Our citizenship has even been attacked as an evil cloak
under which we expect immunity for the nefarious purpose of
conspiracy to destroy the American way of life.*

At the apogee of the Second World War, journalist James Omura spoke
out against the mass expulsion and internment of Japanese Americans
from the West Coast. To help assist those displaced in resettlement, he
created the Pacific Coast Evacuee Placement Bureau in Denver,
Colorado. Omura was also the only journalist at the time to write
about the growing draft resistance among the Nisei (Japanese American
citizens born in the United States), and the public outcry against discriminatory practices against Japanese-American enlistees in the Armed
Forces.

His support of the Fair Play Committee (FPC)—a group leading
the Japanese-American effort against conscription—landed him in
court along with seven others for conspiracy to counsel draft evasion.
Since the mainstream Japanese-American community, including members of the Japanese American Citizens League, favored strict cooperation with evacuation, Omura and his FPC compatriots were deemed
traitors and ostracized by their own ethnic group. Citing freedom of
the press, Omura fought for and later gained his release, the only defen-
dant to be acquitted. The other FPC leaders were later exonerated after
a lengthy appeal and pardoned by President Truman in 1947. In 1989,
the Asian American Journalists Association (AAJA) recognized Omura
for his lifelong activism and commitment to civil rights.

Omura delivered this statement in 1942 before the Tolan Committee,
a select body of the U.S. House of Representatives soliciting testimony
on how the evacuations of Japanese Americans should be conducted.

═══

I REQUESTED TO BE HEARD here due largely to the fact that I am strongly
opposed to mass evacuation of American-born Japanese. It is my honest belief
that such an action would not solve the question of Nisei loyalty. If any such

action is taken, I believe that we would be only procrastinating on the question of loyalty, that we are afraid to deal with it, and that at this, our first opportunity, we are trying to strip the Nisei of their opportunity to prove their loyalty.

I do not believe there has ever been, or ever could be again, a situation of this kind where the Nisei can prove their loyalty.

I specifically refer to the J. A. C. L. It is a matter of public record among the Japanese community that I have been consistently opposed to the Japanese-American Citizen League. I have not been opposed to that organization primarily in regards to its principles, but I have felt that the leaders were leading the American-born Japanese along the wrong channels, and I have not minced words in saying so publicly.

I do not know what else I could say, except that I desire to have an unpublished editorial of *Current Life* read into the record. . . .

Promoters of racialism—the gulf which seems to eternally divide oriental Americans from fellow Americans of Caucasian ancestry—have enjoyed a virtual field day to date in their vigorous campaign to oust resident Japanese, including bona fide citizens, from their hard-won economic niche. . . . The theory of racial "divine creation" is a theory which gains greater and more ominous impetus with the progress of war in the Pacific, especially intensified at the current hour by virtue of repeated Allied losses in the Far East.

The Nisei Americans, the unfortunate children of destiny in this Pacific war, are mere stepping stones for political aspirants and self-seekers. They are being utilized today as political footballs for ambitious officeholders and aspiring demagogs who find it quite opportune to grind their personal axes on the fate of these oft-vilified and persecuted voiceless Americans. The extent to which bigotry and racial antipathy can go in denying civil liberties—a vital cornerstone of democracy—to a segment of the population is witnessed in the summary dismissal of Nisei civil-service employees in the city and county of Los Angeles.

Racialism doubtlessly will play a significant and important role in the war over the Pacific. And the brunt of the guilt for the criminal act of December 7, at Pearl Harbor seems destined to fall upon the guiltless brow of the poor, hapless Nisei—merely because they wear the outward features of the race whose people committed the now historic crime. For that act, the Caucasian population on the Pacific coast will find fiendish glee in exacting punishment upon citizen Americans with Japanese faces. What could be more unjust and un-American?

The future of Nisei Americans is indeed dark. They walk through life in fear, dreading that with each passing moment new restrictions and edicts, disrupting the normal conduct of their daily lives will be adopted.

They have watched with saddening brows the pathos and confusion of their alien parents being uprooted forcefully from the homes which took some of the best years of their oppressed lives to build commanded by the stern measures of a nation at war to go elsewhere in some distant alien surroundings to build anew. Will the hour arrive when they, too, must unwillingly follow after?

Should that hour come, the history of our American Republic will never again stand high in the council chambers of justice and tolerance. Democracy will suffer deeply by it. The forceful evacuation of citizen Americans on the synthetic theory of racial fidelity—"Once a Jap, always a Jap"—would be an indictment against every racial minority in the United States. It would usher in the bigoted and misguided belief that Americanism is a racial attribute and not a national symbol. The scar that will be left will be broad and deep—a stigma of eternal shame.

We must stand shoulder to shoulder in these critical hours. National unity is not best served by discriminating against a segment of the citizenry merely because of physical differences. It would be well to remember that the Nisei Americans and their alien parents have contributed generously and are continuing to contribute in like fashion to the cause of national defense. In spirit, we are Americans. . . .

It is doubtlessly rather difficult for Caucasian Americans to properly comprehend and believe in what we say. Our citizenship has even been attacked as an evil cloak under which we expect immunity for the nefarious purpose of conspiring to destroy the American way of life. To us—who have been born, raised, and educated in American institutions and in our system of public schools, knowing and owing no other allegiance than to the United States—such a thought is manifestly unfair and ambiguous.

I would like to ask the committee: Has the Gestapo come to America? Have we not risen in righteous anger at Hitler's mistreatments of the Jews? Then, is it not incongruous that citizen Americans of Japanese descent should be similarly mistreated and persecuted? I speak from a humanitarian standpoint and from a realistic and not a theoretical point of view. This view, I believe, does not endanger the national security of this country nor jeopardize our war efforts. . . .

Are we to be condemned merely on the basis of our racial origin? Is citizenship such a light and transient thing that that which is our inalienable right in normal times can be torn from us in times of war? We in America are intensely proud of our individual rights and willing, I am sure, to defend those rights with our very lives. I venture to say that the great majority of Nisei Americans, too, will do the same against any aggressor nation—though that nation be Japan. Citizenship to us is no small heritage; it is a very precious and jealous right. You have only to look back on our records in social welfare and community contributions to understand that.

May I ask the committee members if any or all of you are acquainted with the Nisei? I believe that much of this distrust of citizen Japanese is based on ignorance. It would seem more compatible in the sense of fair play and justice that we should not be prejudged and that racialism should not be the yardstick by which our loyalty is measured. Our words, in current times, have no meaning, and so I ask you to examine our records, for there I believe that to a large measure, if not necessarily so, lies the true determination of our oft-questioned loyalty.

It seems to me that we are less fortunate than our alien parents. They, at least, are subjects of Japan and are entitled to recourse and redress through the Japanese Government. Not so is our case. We are but children of destiny—citizens by birth but citizens in virtually name only.

A. Philip Randolph
(1889–1979)

Desegregating the Military
September 27, 1942

Some of us will be put in jail, and court battles may ensue, but this will give the Negro masses a sense of their importance.

In the first half of the twentieth century, A. Philip Randolph became one of America's foremost labor leaders, fighting discrimination in industry, unions, and the armed forces.

A native of Crescent City, Florida, Randolph attended the state's first black high school before moving to Harlem, New York, where he began organizing unions and challenging the practices of big business. This proved unpopular with his employers, as did his involvement with socialism and active opposition to American entry in the First World War. But Randolph continued blasting the United States' policy of claiming to make "the world safe for democracy" while tolerating "undemocratic" treatment of blacks at home.

Randolph then focused his attention on the Brotherhood of Sleeping Car Porters (BSCP)—the first serious effort to organize the African-American workers of the Pullman Company, a mighty railroad conglomerate. In 1925, despite vigorous opposition, the BSCP was officially launched, and its immediate success in attracting members drew the ire of Pullman, which decried the union as "communist" and "benefactors of the Negro race." After years of courageous battles, the porters eventually won the support of black churches, the NAACP, and even the American Federation of Labor. In 1937 the BSCP negotiated a contract with Pullman—the first labor contract ever between a company and a black union.

In 1941, as part of his continued effort against racist intolerance, Randolph began planning the "March on Washington" rally, an all-black protest of the discrimination and segregation in the military and defense industry. Fearing global backlash in the midst of the Second World War, President Franklin D. Roosevelt urged Randolph to call off the July 1 rally and, with it, the 50,000 African Americans who planned to march. Randolph refused to budge.

On June 25, 1941, FDR signed Executive Order 8802, which prohibited racial discrimination in the hiring of defense industry workers, and established the Fair Employment Practices Committee to monitor unequal treatment. Randolph, in turn, canceled the demonstration.

Months later, on September 27, 1942, A. Philip Randolph addressed a conference of supporters in Detroit, Michigan, where in the following speech, he celebrated the executive order and outlined the future goals of the civil rights movement. Twenty years later, Randolph joined Dr. Martin Luther King, Jr. and 200,000 other civil rights activists in the historic March on Washington.

FELLOW MARCHERS and delegates to the Policy Conference of the March on Washington Movement and friends: We have met at an hour when the sinister shadows of war are lengthening and becoming more threatening. As one of the sections of the oppressed darker races, and representing a part of the exploited millions of the workers of the world, we are deeply concerned that the totalitarian legions of Hitler, Hirohito and Mussolini do not batter the last bastions of democracy. We know that our fate is tied up with the fate of the democratic way of life. And so, out of the depth of our hearts, a cry goes up for the triumph of the United Nations. But we would not be honest with ourselves were we to stop with a call for a victory of arms alone. We know this is not enough. We fight that the democratic faiths, values, heritages and ideals may prevail.

Unless this war sounds the death knell to the old Anglo-American empire systems, the hapless story of which is one of exploitation for the profit and power of a monopoly-capitalist economy, it will have been fought in vain. Our aim, then, must not only be to defeat Nazism, fascism and militarism on the battlefield but to win the peace, for democracy, for freedom and the Brotherhood of Man without regard to his pigmentation, land of his birth or the God of his fathers.

We therefore sharply score the Atlantic Charter as expressing a vile and hateful racism and a manifestation of the tragic and utter collapse of an old, decadent democratic political liberalism which worshiped at the shrine of a world-conquering monopoly capitalism. This system grew fat and waxed powerful off the flesh, blood, sweat and tears of the tireless toilers of the human race and the sons and daughters of color in the underdeveloped lands of the world.

When this war ends, the people want something more than the dispersal of equality and power among individual citizens in a liberal, political, democratic system. They demand with striking comparability the dispersal of equality and power among the citizen-workers in an economic democracy that will make certain the assurance of the good life—the more abundant life—in a warless world.

But, withal this condition of freedom, equality and democracy is not the gift of the Gods. It is the task of men—yes, men—brave men, honest men, determined men.

This is why we have met in Detroit in this Policy Conference of the March on Washington Movement. We have come to set forth our goals, declare our principles, formulate our policies, plan our program and discuss our methods, strategy, and tactics. This is the job of every movement which seeks to map out clearly the direction in which it is going as well as build up and strengthen the motivations.

Now our goals are what we hope to attain. They are near and remote, immediate and ultimate. This requires the long and short range program.

Thus our feet are set in the path toward equality—economic, political and social and racial. Equality is the heart and essence of democracy, freedom and justice. Without equality of opportunity in industry, in labor unions, schools and colleges, government, politics and before the law, without equality in social relations and in all phases of human endeavor, the Negro is certain to be consigned to an inferior status. There must be no dual standards of justice, no dual rights, privileges, duties or responsibilities of citizenship. No dual forms of freedom.

If Negroes are not the equal of white citizens, then they are unequal, either above or below them. But if they are to set the standards, Negroes will be below them. And if Negroes are considered unequal on a sub-standard basis, then they will receive unequal or inferior treatment.

Justice for the slave is not the same justice for the freeman. Treatment of a thoroughbred is not the same as the treatment of a workhorse.

But our nearer goals include the abolition of discrimination, segregation and Jim Crow in the government, the Army, Navy, Air Corps, U.S. Marine, Coast Guard, Women's Auxiliary Army Corps and the Waves, and defense industries; the elimination of discrimination in hotels, restaurants, on public transportation conveyances, in educational, recreational, cultural, and amusement and entertainment places such as theaters, beaches and so forth.

We want the full works of citizenship with no reservations. We will accept nothing less.

As to the composition of our movement. Our policy is that it be all-Negro, and pro-Negro but not anti-white, or anti-Semitic or anti-labor, or anti-Catholic. The reason for this policy is that all oppressed people must assume the responsibility and take the initiative to free themselves. Jews must wage their battle to abolish anti-Semitism. Catholics must wage their battle to abolish anti-Catholicism. The workers must wage their battle to advance and protect their interests and rights.

But this does not mean that because Jews must take the responsibility and initiative to solve their own problems that they should not seek the cooperation and support of Gentiles, or that Catholics should not seek the support of Negroes, or that the workers should not attempt to enlist the backing of Jews, Catholics, and Negroes in their fight to win a strike; but the main reliance must be upon the workers themselves. By the same token because Negroes build an all-Negro movement such as the March, it does not follow that our movement should not call for the collaboration of Jews, Catholics, trade unions and white liberals to help restore the President's Fair Employment Practice Committee to its original status of independence, with responsibility to the President. That was done. William Green, President of the AF of L and Philip Murray, President of CIO were called upon to send telegrams to the President to restore the Committee to its independence. Both responded. Their cooperation had its effects. Workers have formed citizens committees to back them while on strike, but this does not mean that they take those citizens into their unions as members. No, not at all.

And while the March on Washington Movement may find it advisable to form a citizens committee of friendly white citizens to give moral support to a fight against the poll tax or white primaries, it does not imply that these white citizens or citizens of any racial group should be taken into the March on Washington Movement as members. The essential value of an all-Negro movement such as the March on Washington is that it helps to create faith by Negroes in Negroes. It develops a sense of self-reliance with Negroes depending on Negroes in vital matters. It helps to break down the slave psychology and inferiority complex in Negroes which comes and is nourished with Negroes relying on white people for direction and support. This inevitably happens in mixed organizations that are supposed to be in the interest of the Negro.

The problem of lynching is a specialized one and Negroes must take the responsibility and initiative to solve it, because Negroes are the chief victims of low wages and must act to change and raise them.

But the problems of taxation, sanitation, health, a proper school system, an efficient fire department, and crime are generalized problems. They don't only concern the workers or Jews or Negroes or Catholics, but everybody and hence it is sound and proper social strategy and policy for all of these groups in the community to form a generalized or composite movement, financed by all, to handle these problems that are definitely general in nature. Neither group can depend upon the other in dealing with a general social problem. No one group can handle it properly. But this same general organization could not be depended upon to fight for the abolition of segregation of Negroes in the government, or to abolish company unionism in the interest of the workers, or to fight anti-Semitism. Its structure is too general to qualify it to attempt to solve a special problem. And, by the same logic, the Zionist Movement, or the Knights of Columbus, or the Longshoremen's Union is too special in structure and purpose to be qualified to deal with such a general problem as crime, or health, or education in a community.

Therefore, while the March on Washington Movement is interested in the general problems of every community and will lend its aid to help solve them, it has as its major interest and task the liberation of the Negro people, and this is sound social economy. It is in conformity with the principle of the division of labor. No organization can do everything. Every organization can do something, and each organization is charged with the social responsibility to do that which it can do, is built to do.

<div align="center">~~~</div>

Hence, it is apparent that the Negro needs more than organization. He needs mass organization with an action program, aggressive, bold and challenging in spirit. Such a movement is our March on Washington.

Our first job, then, is actually to organize millions of Negroes, and build them into block systems, with captains, so that they may be summoned to action overnight and thrown into physical motion. Without this type of organization, Negroes will never develop mass power, which is the most effective weapon a minority people can wield. Witness the strategy and maneuver of the people of India with mass civil disobedience and noncooperation and the marches to the sea to make salt. It may be said that the Indian people have not won their freedom. This is so, but they will win it. The central principle of the struggle of oppressed minorities like the Negro, labor, Jews, and others is not only to develop mass-demonstration maneuvers, but to repeat and continue them. The workers don't picket firms today and quit. They don't strike today and fold up. They practice the principle of repetition. . . .

We must develop huge demonstrations, because the world is used to big dramatic affairs. They think in terms of hundreds of thousands and millions and billions. Millions of Germans and Russians clash on the Eastern Front. Billions of dollars are appropriated at the twinkling of an eye. Nothing little counts.

<div align="center">~~~</div>

Our Movement must be blueprinted. Our forces must be marshaled, with block captains to provide immediate and constant contact. Our block captains must hold periodic meetings for their blocks to develop initiative and the capacity to make decisions and move in relation to direction from the central organization of the division.

Our educational program must be developed around the struggle of the Negro masses.

This can be done by developing mass plans to secure mass registration of the Negro people for the primaries and elections. Through this program the Negro masses can be given a practical and pragmatic view of the mechanics and function of our government and the significance of mass political pressure.

Plans should be mapped by the various divisions to fight for Negro integration in the public utilities as motormen and conductors. During the war women may be placed on these jobs. We must make a drive now to see to it that Negro men and women receive their appropriate consideration in every important field of American industry from which Negroes are now generally barred.

Our day-to-day exercise of our civil rights is a constant challenge. In theaters, hotels, restaurants, amusement places, even in the North, now there is discrimination against Negroes. This is true in every large city. Negroes have the moral obligation to demand the right to enjoy and make use of their civil and political privileges. If we don't, we will lose the will to fight for our citizenship rights, and the public will consider that we don't want them and should not have them. This fight to break down these barriers in every city should be carefully and painstakingly organized. By fighting for these civil rights the Negro masses will be disciplined in struggle. Some of us will be put in jail, and court battles may ensue, but this will give the Negro masses a sense of their importance and value as citizens and as fighters in the Negro liberation movement and the cause for democracy as a whole. It will make white people in high places and the ordinary white man understand that Negroes have rights that they are bound to respect.

The giant public protest meetings must continue. They are educative and give moral strength to our movement and the Negro masses.

For this task we need men and women who will dedicate and consecrate their life, spirit, mind and soul to the great adventure of Negro freedom and justice.

Our divisions must serve as Negro mass parliaments where the entire community may debate the day-to-day issues such as police brutality, high rents, and other questions and make judgments and take action in the interest of the community. These divisions should hold meetings at least twice a month. In them every Negro should be made to feel his importance as a factor in the Negro liberation movement. We must have every Negro realize his leadership ability, the educated and uneducated, the poor and wealthy. In the March on Washington Movement the highest is as low as the lowest and the lowest is as high as the highest. Numbers in mass formation is our key, directed, of course, by the collective intelligence of the people.

Let us put our weight behind the fight to abolish the poll tax. This will give the black and white workers of the South new hope. But the Negro people are not the only oppressed section of mankind. India is now waging a world-shaking, history-making fight for independence. India's fight is the Negro's fight.

Now, let us be unafraid. We are fighting for big stakes. Our stakes are liberty, justice and democracy. Every Negro should hang his head in shame who fails to do his part now for freedom. This is the hour of the Negro. It is the hour of the common man. May we rise to the challenge to struggle for our rights. Come what will or may, let us never falter.

CAREY MCWILLIAMS
(1905–1980)

A Cloud of Suspicion
JULY 15, 1943

*If we permit the concept of citizenship to be broken down
at one point for one group, we're undermining the
very structure of American citizenship.*

For more than fifty years, the leftist writer, political activist, and labor lawyer Carey McWilliams fought against discrimination and racial inequality. In the 1930s, as a young lawyer in California, he defended striking Mexican citrus workers. McWilliams later supported studio workers in Hollywood struggling to save their union from the forceful ways of organized crime.

From 1939 to 1942, under Culbert Olson, California's first Democratic governor, McWilliams served as the chief of the Immigration and Housing Division, where he actively supported farm workers— winning the admiration of Chicano leaders including César Chávez. After Earl Warren defeated Olson in the next governor's race, he unsurprisingly fired McWilliams, freeing him to focus full-time on fighting the relocation and internment of Japanese Americans (a policy Warren favored, along with most Californians on the left and right).

McWilliams delivered this address at a town meeting in Santa Barbara, California. His brazen remarks, which were broadcast widely, rebuked a House Un-American Activities Committee (HUAC) member in attendance, and encouraged the immediate release of interned Japanese Americans.

THE PRESENT AGITATION against the return of any evacuees is, in fact, being conducted with primary regard to nonmilitary considerations. No attempt is made to disguise the fact that this agitation has for its real purpose the permanent exclusion of all Japanese from the west coast. [*Applause and cries of "Sure" and "Why not?"*] Its avowed purposes include such objectives as stripping the American-born Japanese of their American citizenship, establishing rigid economic barriers against them, and laying the foundation for their eventual deportation. If this emerging pattern is permitted to take form now, it is likely to result in the indefinite postponement of the restoration of full citizenship even to those who have never been suspected of disloyalty.

Since this was not our intention in ordering mass evacuation, we should either promptly restore full citizenship rights or give an immediate guarantee of such restoration the moment the military emergency terminates. We cannot ignore the fact that this current agitation is being largely predicated, now as in the past, upon dangerously irrelevant so-called racial considerations, unsupported by a shred of scientific evidence.

To make a race issue of this problem is to do precisely what Tojo is trying to do: namely, to convince the colored peoples of the Far East that this is a race war. How we handle the evacuee problem is, therefore, one measure to our intention to apply the four freedoms to all peoples regardless of color. The peoples of India and China, as well as our own colored minorities, are watching the development of race feeling in the United States with the deepest concern. There can be no doubt but that the manner in which the evacuee problem is being discussed on the west coast today has tended to heighten race tension in a dangerously irresponsible fashion. Since race agitation seems to be cumulative in its intensity, scope, and consequences, any attempt to appease race bigotry can only result in stimulating further aggressions, not merely against the particular minority, but against all minorities.

As a Nation, we stand firmly committed to the great ideal that distinctions based upon race, color, or creed have no place in American life in peace or in war. [*Applause.*] If we permit the concept of citizenship to be broken down at one point for one group, we're undermining the very structure of American citizenship. We have never tolerated the notion that there could be different levels of citizenship with rights withheld from some citizens which were freely granted others. Political subdivisions of the Nation, therefore, should not be encouraged in the arrogant assumption that they can set up their own canons of citizenship. As I recall, there are forty-eight States in the Union. Not forty-five, and certainly not forty-seven.

Once investigated and released, no cloud of suspicion should follow the evacuees. Unity is imperative in the war effort, but unity cannot be achieved if we listen to those who believe that loyalty is only skin deep. In the relocation centers today there are men who are veterans of the first World War. Today, also, several thousand citizens of Japanese descent are serving with the armed forces of this Nation. When on furlough, these soldiers are now permitted to visit the west coast on military passes. They are to me, as I am sure they are to most Americans, living symbols of the greatness and strength of American democracy. To suggest that race can be a test of loyalty is as insulting to these soldiers and to their families as it is to some sixteen million other American citizens whose skins happen to be red or black, yellow or brown.

Such a suggestion is utterly at variance with American ideals and is well cal-culated to jeopardize America's magnificent opportunity for world leadership in an unprecedented crisis in human affairs. As President Roosevelt has reminded us, Americanism is a matter of the mind and heart. Americanism is not, and never has been a matter of race or ancestry.

BAYARD RUSTIN
(1910–1987)

Jim Crow Army
APRIL 11, 1948

*Segregation in the military must be resisted
if democracy and peace are to survive.*

An able lieutenant to A. Philip Randolph and, later, Dr. Martin Luther King, Jr., Bayard Rustin was a powerful agent of the civil rights, socialist, and anti-war movements. Raised in a Quaker household in West Chester, Pennsylvania, Rustin studied at Wilberforce College and then City College, singing in nightclubs to support himself.

In 1941 he met A. Philip Randolph, an event that had a profound and lasting impact on his personal and professional development. In short order, Rustin was assigned to head the youth arm of Randolph's emerging March on Washington movement. Like Randolph, he embraced socialism and nonviolent protest and sought an active role in the budding civil rights, labor, and anti-war movements. In fact, during the second World War, Rustin served two years in prison as a conscientious objector to the draft.

Rustin joined and quickly rose through the ranks of the newly formed Congress of Racial Equality (CORE), becoming its first field secretary. In 1955 he helped Dr. King organize the Montgomery bus boycott. Later, as King's special assistant in the Southern Christian Leadership Conference, Rustin played a critical role in 1963 organizing the historic March on Washington.

A member of the "old guard," Rustin went on to direct the A. Philip Randolph Institute, taking a public stance against black separatism and working to build "coalitions with white and black liberals." Despite these achievements, Rustin, according to his partner, Walter Naegle, was silenced, threatened, beaten, and fired from important leadership positions throughout his career largely because he was an openly gay man in a homophobic era.

On April 11, 1948, a decade before Rosa Parks refused to surrender her seat on a Montgomery bus, Rustin delivered this address to the Council Against Intolerance in America. He urged young African Americans to engage in civil disobedience against segregation in the U.S. military, encouraging them to refuse to serve if drafted.

IT IS A REAL OPPORTUNITY to speak with American citizens who seriously seek to remove racial and religious intolerance from our national life, for recent history amply reveals that America cannot gain moral leadership in the world until intolerance of minority groups has been eliminated at home. The Journey of Reconciliation was organized not only to devise techniques for eliminating Jim Crow in travel, but also as a training ground for similar peaceful projects against discrimination in such major areas as employment and in the armed services.

The use of these methods against Jim Crow military service is a regrettable necessity. Today no single injustice more bitterly stands out in the hearts and minds of colored people the world over, or continues more successfully to frustrate the United States' efforts abroad, than the continuation of discrimination and segregation in our military forces.

As a follower of the principles of Mahatma Gandhi, I am an opponent of war and of war preparations and an opponent of universal military training and conscription; but entirely apart from that issue, I hold that segregation in any part of the body politic is an act of slavery and an act of war. Democrats will agree that such acts are to be resisted, and more and more leaders of the oppressed are responsibly proposing nonviolent civil disobedience and noncooperation as the means.

On March 22, 1948, A. Philip Randolph and Grant Reynolds, trusted Negro leaders, told President Truman that Negroes "do not propose to shoulder another gun for democracy abroad while they are denied democracy here at home." A few days later, when Mr. Randolph testified before the Senate Armed Services Committee, he declared that he openly would advise and urge Negro and white youth not to submit to Jim Crow military institutions. At this statement, Senator Wayne Morse interrupted and warned Mr. Randolph that "the Government would apply the legal doctrine of treason to such conduct."

This is a highly regrettable statement for a United States senator to make. Certainly throughout Asia and Africa millions must have agreed with the lovers of freedom here who reasoned that if treason is involved, it is the treason practiced by reactionaries in the North and South who struggle to maintain segregation and discrimination and who thus murder the American creed. The organizers and perpetuators of segregation are as much the enemy of America as any foreign invader. The time has come when they are not merely to be protested. They must be resisted.

The world and the United States should know that there are many younger leaders, both black and white, in positions of responsibility who, not wishing to see democracy destroyed from within, will support Mr. Randolph and Mr. Reynolds.

We know that men should not and will not fight to perpetuate for themselves caste and second-class citizenship. We know that men cannot struggle for someone else's freedom in the same battle in which they fasten semi-slavery more securely upon themselves. While there is a very real question whether any army can bring freedom, certainly a Jim Crow army cannot. On the contrary, to those it attempts to liberate, it will bring discrimination and segregation such as we are now exporting to Europe and to South America. To subject young men at their most impressionable age to a forced caste system, as now outlined in the Universal Military Training and Selective Service bills, is not only undemocratic but will prove to be suicidal.

Segregation in the military must be resisted if democracy and peace are to survive. Thus civil disobedience against caste is not merely a right but a profound duty. If carried out in the spirit of good will and nonviolence, it will prick the conscience of America as Gandhi's campaigns stirred the hearts of men the world over.

Therefore, in the future I shall join with others to advise and urge Negroes and white people not to betray the American ideal by accepting Jim Crow in any of our institutions, including the armed services. Further, I serve notice on the government that, to the extent of my resources, I shall assist in the organization of disciplined cells across the nation to advise resistance and to provide spiritual, financial, and legal aid to resisters.

If Senator Morse and the government believe that intimidation, repression, prison, or even death can stop such a movement, let them examine past struggles for freedom. If the government continues to consider such action treason, let it recall the advice that Justice Jackson gave the German people at the opening of the Nuremberg trials: "Men," he said, "are individually responsible for their acts, and are not to be excused for following unjust demands made upon them by governments." Failure of the German citizens to resist antisocial laws from the beginning of the Hitler regime logically ended in their placing Jews in gas furnaces and lye pits. Justice Jackson indicated in conclusion that individual resistance to undemocratic laws would have been a large factor in destroying the unjust Nazi state.

I believe that American citizens would do well to ponder Mr. Jackson's remarks. Civil disobedience is urged not to destroy the United States but because the government is now poorly organized to achieve democracy. The aim of such a movement always will be to improve the nature of the government, to urge and counsel resistance to military Jim Crow in the interest of a higher law—the principle of equality and justice upon which real community and security depend.

I sincerely hope that millions of Negroes and white people who cherish freedom will pledge themselves now to resist Jim Crow everywhere, including the military establishments. Thereby the United States may, in part, achieve the moral leadership in world affairs for which we so vigorously strive. I urge you to register this intention now with your Senators and Congressmen.

It is my supreme desire that those who resist will do so in that spirit which is without hatred, bitterness, or contention. I trust that all resisters will hold firm to the true faith that only good-will resistance, in the end, is capable of overcoming injustice.

HUBERT HUMPHREY
(1927–1993)

No Compromises
JULY 14, 1948

I do not believe that there can be any compromise
on the guarantee of civil rights.

With the Civil War and Reconstruction long past and the influence of southerners strong, civil rights was not often the topic of discussion in the Democratic Party. That was, at least, until then-mayor of Minneapolis Hubert Humphrey took his seat on the 119-member Democratic Platform Committee at the 1948 Democratic National Convention in Philadelphia. At 98 degrees, it would be the last non-air-conditioned convention ever held by either party.

Although he later served as a U.S. senator, as vice president, and presidential nominee, Humphrey was in 1948 a relatively unknown figure until, in the face of opposition from within his own party, he brought a strong civil rights plank to the convention floor—calling it a "matter of conscience and an imperative of political pragmatism." As mayor, Humphrey had secured passage of the nation's first effective fair employment practices ordinance and worked tirelessly to rid Minneapolis of its anti-Semitic reputation.

Unwilling to compromise, the thirty-seven-year-old Humphrey decided to challenge the Democratic Party's old guard, despite warnings that such defiance could potentially ruin his political future "in a crackpot crusade" and antagonize the Old Confederacy (votes which the splintered party desperately needed). Humphrey's proposed platform outlined four objectives for President Truman: abolition of poll taxes in federal elections, a national law against lynching, creation of a permanent fair employment commission, and integration of the armed services.

According to historian Robert Caro, for two days and nights Humphrey fought in committee with the party elders to bring his liberal plank to the floor, helping, he argued, to secure the black vote which was becoming pivotal in northern cities. After losing in committee to "sellouts to states rights," Humphrey brought the civil rights plank right to the convention floor himself.

With sweat glistening on his brow, Humphrey delivered this speech to a packed, sweltering hall on the convention's third night, only hours before President Truman would accept the party's nomination. After a passionate and courageous oration, interrupted by a standing ovation and waves of banners, Humphrey's civil rights plank passed 651 1/2 to 582 1/2, to the great shock of political commentators and the party faithful. As suspected, the plank's adoption resulted in what would be a permanent rift between northern liberals and southern Democrats over the issue of civil rights. In fact, right after the vote, thirty-five southern delegates, led by Governor Strom Thurmond of South Carolina, stormed out of the hall in protest. That November, Thurmond's newly formed Dixiecrat Party gave the former democrat thirty-eight electoral votes from the Deep South. Illinois senator Paul Douglass captured the moment: "No braver David ever faced a more powerful Goliath."

Months after his speech in Philadelphia, Humphrey won a seat in the Senate, marking the start of his lifelong career as a champion of civil rights, both in Congress and as vice president. He later recalled, "I knew that the traditional thing to do was to make a gesture toward what was right in terms of civil rights, but not so tough a gesture that the south would leave the Democratic coalition."

FELLOW DEMOCRATS, FELLOW AMERICANS:

I realize that in speaking in behalf of the minority report on civil rights as presented by Congressman DeMiller of Wisconsin that I am dealing with a charged issue—with an issue which has been confused by emotionalism on all sides of the fence. I realize that there are here today friends and colleagues of mine—many of them—who feel just as deeply and keenly as I do about this issue and who are yet in complete disagreement with me.

My respect and admiration for these men and their views was great when I came to this convention. It is now far greater because of the sincerity, the courtesy, and the forthrightness with which many of them have argued in our prolonged discussions in the platform committee.

Because of this very great respect—and because of my profound belief that we have a challenging task to do here—because good conscience, decent morality, demands it—I feel I must rise at this time to support a report—the minority report—a report that spells out our democracy, a report that the people of this country can and will understand and a report that they will enthusiastically acclaim on the great issue of civil rights!

Now let me say at the outset that this proposal is made with no single region. Our proposal is made for no single class, for no single racial or religious groups in mind.

All of the regions of this country, all of the states have shared in the precious heritage of American freedom. All the states and all the regions have seen at least some infringements of that freedom—all people—get this—all people, white and black, all groups, all racial groups have been the victims at times in this nation of—let me say—vicious discrimination.

The masterly statement of our keynote speaker, the distinguished United States Senator from Kentucky, Alben Barkley, made that point with great force. Speaking of the founder of our party, Thomas Jefferson, he said this, and I quote from Alben Barkley:

> He did not proclaim that all the white, or the black, or the red, or the yellow men are equal; that all Christian or Jewish men are equal; that all Protestant and all Catholic men are equal; that all rich or poor men are equal; that all good and bad men are equal.
>
> What he declared was that all men are equal; and the equality which he proclaimed was the equality in the right to enjoy the blessings of free government in which they may participate and to which they have given their support.

Now these words of Senator Barkley's are appropriate to this convention—appropriate to this convention of the oldest, the most truly progressive political party in America. From the time of Thomas Jefferson, the time of that immortal American doctrine of individual rights, under just and fairly administered laws, the Democratic party has tried hard to secure expanding freedoms for all citizens. Oh, yes, I know, other political parties may have *talked* more about civil rights, but the Democratic party has surely *done* more about civil rights.

We have made progress, we have made great progress, in every part of this country. We've made great progress in the South, we've made it in the West, in the North, and in the East, but we must now focus the direction of that progress towards the realization of a full program of civil rights for all. This convention must set out more specifically the direction in which our party efforts are to go.

We can be proud that we can be guided by the courageous trail blazing of two great Democratic presidents. We can be proud of the fact that our great and beloved immortal leader Franklin Roosevelt gave us guidance. And we be proud of the fact—we can be proud of the fact—that Harry Truman has had the courage to give to the people of America the new emancipation proclamation!

It seems to me, it seems to me, that the Democratic party needs to make definite pledges of the kinds suggested in the minority report to maintain the trust and the confidence placed in it by the people of all races and all sections of this country.

Sure, we're here as Democrats. But my good friends, we're here as Americans—we're here as the believers in the principle and the ideology of democracy, and I firmly believe that as men concerned with our country's future, we must specify in our platform the guarantees which we have mentioned in the minority report.

Yes, this is far more than a party matter. Every citizen has a stake in the emergence of the United States as a *leader* in a free world. That world is being challenged by the world of slavery. For us to play our part effectively, we must be in a morally sound position.

We can't use a double standard—there's no room for double standards in American politics—for measuring our own and other people's policies. Our demands for democratic practices in other lands will be no more effective than the guarantees of those practiced in our own country.

Friends, delegates, I do not believe that there can be any compromise on the guarantee of civil rights which I have mentioned in the minority report.

In spite of my desire for unanimous agreement on the entire platform, in spite of my desire to see everybody here in honest and unanimous agreement, there are some matters which I think must be stated clearly and without qualification. There can be no hedging—the newspaper headlines are wrong! There will be no hedging, and there will be no watering down—if you please—of the instruments and the principles of the civil-rights program!

To those who say, my friends, to those who say, that we are rushing this issue of civil rights, I say to them we are 172 years late! To those who say, to those who say that this civil-rights program is an infringement on states' rights, I say this: the time has arrived in America for the Democratic party to get out of the shadow of state's rights and walk forthrightly into the bright sunshine of human rights!

People, people—human beings—this is the issue of the twentieth century. People of all kinds, all sorts of people, and these people are looking to America for leadership, and they're looking to America for precept and example.

My good friends—my fellow Democrats—I ask you for calm consideration of our historic opportunity.

Let us not forget—let us do forget—the evil passions, the blindness of the past. In these times of world economic, political, and spiritual—above all spiritual—crisis, we cannot—we must not—turn from the path so plainly before us. That path has already led us though many valleys of the shadow of death. Now is the time to recall those who were left on that path of American freedom.

For all of us here, for the millions who have sent us, for the whole two-billion members of the human family—our land is now, more than ever before, the last best hope on earth. I know that we can—I know that we shall—begin here the fuller and richer realization of that hope—that promise of a land where all men are truly free and equal, and each man uses his freedom and equality wisely and well.

My good friends, I ask my party, I ask the Democratic party, to march down the *high* road of progressive democracy. I ask this convention, I ask this convention, to say in unmistakable terms that we proudly hail, and we courageously support, our President and leader Harry Truman in his great fight for civil rights in America!

ELEANOR ROOSEVELT
(1884–1962)

The Universal Declaration of Human Rights
DECEMBER 9, 1948

Man's desire for peace lies behind this declaration.

First lady from 1933 to 1945 and the wife of the thirty-second president of the United States, Eleanor Roosevelt was a noted humanitarian, an advocate for women and the disenfranchised, and a delegate to the United Nations.

The daughter of Elliott Roosevelt and Anna Hall Roosevelt and niece of President Theodore Roosevelt, Eleanor grew up in a wealthy family that attached great value to civic and public service. She became one of the world's most widely admired and influential women in the twentieth century.

In the White House, Eleanor Roosevelt instituted regular press conferences for women correspondents, forcing wire services that had not employed women to hire and train female correspondents. In 1939, when the Daughters of the American Revolution refused to let Marian Anderson, an African-American opera singer, perform in Constitution Hall, Mrs. Roosevelt resigned her membership and arranged to hold the concert at the Lincoln Memorial. Her defense of African Americans, youth, and the poor helped bring groups into government that were formerly alienated from the political process.

In 1946, President Harry Truman appointed Eleanor as a delegate to the United Nations, where she served as chair of the Commission on Human Rights and played a major role in the drafting and adoption of the 1948 Universal Declaration of Human Rights. Her celebrated address before the plenary committee of the United Nations showcased her concern and care for minorities of all backgrounds and from all nations. In it, Mrs. Roosevelt discussed the urgency of social and economic rights around the world.

———

THE LONG AND METICULOUS study and debate of which this Universal Declaration of Human Rights is the product means that it reflects the composite views of the many men and governments who have contributed to its formulation. Not every man nor every government can have what he wants in a document of this kind. There are of course particular provisions in the declaration before us with which we are not fully satisfied. I have no doubt this is true of other delegations, but taken as a whole the Delegation of the United States believes that this is a good document—even a great document—and we propose to give it our full support. The position of the United States on the various parts of the declaration is a matter of record in the Third Committee. I shall not burden the Assembly, and particularly my colleagues of the Third Committee, with a restatement of that position here.

Certain provisions of the declaration are stated in such broad terms as to be acceptable only because of the limitations in article 29 providing for limitation on the exercise of the rights for the purpose of meeting the requirements of morality, public order, and the general welfare. An example of this is the provision that everyone has the right of equal access to the public service in his country. The basic principle of equality and of nondiscrimination as to public employment is sound, but it cannot be accepted without limitations. My Government, for example, would consider that this is unquestionably subject to limitation in the interest of public order and the general welfare. It would not consider that the exclusion from public employment of persons holding subversive political beliefs and not loyal to the basic principles and practices of the constitution and laws of the country would in any way infringe upon this right.

Likewise, my Government has made it clear in the course of the development of the declaration that it does not consider that the economic and social and cultural rights stated in the declaration imply an obligation on governments to assure the enjoyment of these rights by direct governmental action. This was made quite clear in the Human Rights Commission text of article 23 which served as a so-called "umbrella" article to the articles on economic and social rights. We consider that the principle has not been affected by the fact that this article no longer contains a reference to the articles which follow it. This in no way affects our whole-hearted support for the basic principles of economic, social, and cultural rights set forth in these articles.

In giving our approval to the declaration today, it is of primary importance that we keep clearly in mind the basic character of the document. It is not a treaty; it is not an international agreement. It is not and does not purport to be a statement of law or legal obligation. It is a declaration of basic principles of human rights and freedoms, to be stamped with the approval of the General Assembly by formal vote of its members, and to serve as a common standard of achievement for all peoples of all nations.

We stand today at the threshold of a great event both in the life of the United Nations and in the life of Mankind, that is the approval by the General Assembly of the Universal Declaration of Human Rights recommended by the Third Committee. This declaration may well become the international

Magna Carta of all men everywhere. We hope its proclamation by the General Assembly will be an event comparable to the proclamation of the Declaration of the Rights of Man by the French people in 1789, the adoption of the Bill of Rights by the people of the United States and the adoption of comparable declarations at different times in other countries.

At a time when there are so many issues on which we find it difficult to reach a common basis of agreement, it is a significant fact that 58 states have found such a large measure of agreement in the complex field of human rights. This must be taken as testimony of our common aspiration first voiced in the Charter of the United Nations to lift men everywhere to a higher standard of life and to a greater enjoyment of freedom. Man's desire for peace lies behind this declaration. The realization that the flagrant violation of human rights by Nazi and Fascist countries sowed the seeds of the last world war has supplied the impetus for the work which brings us to the moment of achievement here today.

In a recent speech in Canada, Gladstone Murray said:

The central fact is that man is fundamentally a moral being, that the light we have is imperfect does not matter so long as we are always trying to improve it . . . we are equal in sharing the moral freedom that distinguishes us as men. Man's status makes each individual an end in himself. No man is by nature simply the servant of the state or of another man . . . the ideal and fact of freedom—and not technology—are the true distinguishing marks of our civilization.

This declaration is based upon the spiritual fact that man must have freedom in which to develop his full stature and through common effort to raise the level of human dignity. We have much to do to fully achieve and to assure the rights set forth in this declaration. But having them put before us with the moral backing of 58 nations will be a great step forward.

As we here bring to fruition our labors on this Declaration of Human Rights, we must at the same time rededicate ourselves to the unfinished task which lies before us. We can now move on with new courage and inspiration to the completion of an international covenant on human rights and of measures for the implementation of human rights.

In conclusion I feel that I cannot better than to repeat the call to action by Secretary Marshall in his opening statement to this Assembly:

"Let this third regular session of the General Assembly approve by an overwhelming majority the Declaration of Human Rights as a standard of conduct for all; and let us, as Members of the United Nations, conscious of our own shortcomings and imperfections, join our effort in good faith to live up to this high standard."

THE CIVIL RIGHTS ERA:
LIFT EVERY VOICE
1950–1969

Thurgood Marshall
(1908–1993)

Dismantling Segregation:
Brown v. Board of Education
December 8, 1953

*It makes no great difference whether we say that the
Negro is wronged because he is segregated, or that he
is wronged because he received unequal treatment.*

On the long road from his childhood home in Baltimore, Maryland,
Thurgood Marshall vaulted economic and social barriers to become
one of the most celebrated lawyers in American history. After graduating with honors from Howard University Law School in 1920, Marshall
began a twenty-year tenure with the NAACP Legal Defense Fund.
With mentor Charles Hamilton Houston, Marshall attacked the primary root of racial disparity, America's education system, by organizing
a long-term legal campaign to eradicate segregation in the nation's
schools. Marshall and Houston concentrated first on graduate and professional schools, hoping that white judges would be more sympathetic
to these plaintiffs. After several legal victories, they turned to segregation in elementary and secondary schools. This strategy culminated in
the 1954 landmark Supreme Court decision *Brown v. Board of Education,*
which deemed segregation in public schools illegal; in an oft-quoted
decision, the court ruled that "separate education facilities are inherently unequal."

In 1961, in the face of strong southern opposition, President John F.
Kennedy appointed Marshall to the Second Circuit of the U.S. Court
of Appeals, where he wrote 112 opinions between 1961 and 1965—
none of which were overturned. Then, in 1967, after Marshall served as
Solicitor General, Lyndon Johnson named him to the United States
Supreme Court, calling the nomination "the right thing to do, the right
time to do it, the right man and the right place." Justice Marshall served
with distinction until he retired in 1993, after penning scores of widely
praised opinions championing equal opportunity.

On December 8, 1953, while still an NAACP lawyer, Marshall delivered these remarks before the U.S. Supreme Court during oral argu-

ments in the *Brown* case. He urged the justices to sustain the organization's position that segregation, on its face, relied on the fundamentally flawed principle that blacks were inherently inferior to whites.

IT FOLLOWS THAT with education, this Court has made segregation and inequality equivalent concepts. They have equal rating, equal footing, and if segregation thus necessarily imports inequality, it makes no great difference whether we say that the Negro is wronged because he is segregated, or that he is wronged because he received unequal treatment. . . .

I would like to say that each lawyer on the other side has made it clear as to what the position of the state was on this, and it would be all right possibly but for the fact that this is so crucial. There is no way you can repay lost school years.

These children in these cases are guaranteed by the states some twelve years of education in varying degrees, and this idea, if I understand it, to leave it to the states until they work it out—and I think that is a most ingenious argument—you leave it to the states, they say, and then they say that the states haven't done anything about it in a hundred years, so for that reason this Court doesn't touch it.

The argument of judicial restraint has no application in this case. There is a relationship between federal and state, but there is no corollary or relationship as to the Fourteenth Amendment.

The duty of enforcing, the duty of following the Fourteenth Amendment, is placed upon the states. The duty of enforcing the Fourteenth Amendment is placed upon this Court, and the argument that they make over and over again to my mind is the same type of argument they charge us with making, the same argument Charles Sumner made. Possibly so.

And we hereby charge them with making the same argument that was made before the Civil War, the same argument that was made during the period between the ratification of the Fourteenth Amendment and the *Plessy* v. *Ferguson* case.

And I think it makes no progress for us to find out who made what argument. It is our position that whether or not you base this case solely on the intent of Congress or whether you base it on the logical extension of the doctrine as set forth in the *McLaurin* case, on either basis the same conclusion is required, which is that this Court makes it clear to all of these states that in administering their governmental functions, at least those that are vital not to the life of the state alone, not to the country alone, but vital to the world in general, that little pet feelings of race, little pet feelings of custom—I got the feeling on hearing the discussion yesterday that when you put a white child in a school with a whole lot of colored children, the child would fall apart or something. Everybody knows that is not true.

Those same kids in Virginia and South Carolina—and I have seen them do it—they play in the streets together, they play on their farms together, they go down the road together, they separate to go to school, they come out of school and play ball together. They have to be separated in school.

There is some magic to it. You can have them voting together, you can have them not restricted because of law in the houses they live in. You can have them going to the same state university and the same college, but if they go to elementary and high school, the world will fall apart. And it is the exact same argument that has been made to this Court over and over again, and we submit that when they charge us with making a legislative argument, it is in truth they who are making the legislative argument.

They can't take race out of this case. From the day this case was filed until this moment, nobody has in any form or fashion, despite the fact I made it clear in the opening argument that I was relying on it, done anything to distinguish this statute from the Black Codes, which they must admit, because nobody can dispute, say anything anybody wants to say, one way or the other, the Fourteenth Amendment was intended to deprive the states of power to enforce Black Codes or anything else like it.

We charge that they are Black Codes. They obviously are Black Codes if you read them. They haven't denied that they are Black Codes, so if the Court wants to very narrowly decide this case, they can decide it on that point.

So whichever way it is done, the only way that this Court can decide this case in opposition to our position, is that there must be some reason which gives the state the right to make a classification that they can make in regard to nothing else in regard to Negroes, and we submit the only way to arrive at that decision is to find that for some reason Negroes are inferior to all other human beings.

Nobody will stand in the Court and urge that, and in order to arrive at the decision that they want us to arrive at, there would have to be some recognition of a reason why of all of the multitudinous groups of people in this country you have to single out Negroes and give them this separate treatment.

It can't be because of slavery in the past, because there are very few groups in this country that haven't had slavery some place back in history of their groups. It can't be color because there are Negroes as white as the drifted snow, with blue eyes, and they are just as segregated as the colored man.

The only thing can be is an inherent determination that the people who were formerly in slavery, regardless of anything else, shall be kept as near that stage as is possible, and now is the time, we submit, that this Court should make it clear that that is not what our Constitution stands for.

Thank you, sir.

MARTIN LUTHER KING, JR.
(1929–1968)

Montgomery Bus Boycott
DECEMBER 5, 1955

*There comes a time when people get tired of
being trampled over by the iron feet of oppression.*

Like African-American leaders before him, Martin Luther King, Jr., was, above all, "fundamentally a clergyman." His great grandfather, Willis Williams, preached in antebellum Georgia; his grandfather led Ebenezer Baptist Church, a bedrock institution in Atlanta; his father, "Daddy King," guided that church through trying times and later shared the pulpit with his son, Martin Luther.

Martin Luther King, Jr., realized at an early age that the pulpit was one of the few places African Americans could speak out publicly on political and social matters and, as he once said, "touch every phase of community life." In preparation, Dr. King attended Morehouse College, in Atlanta, then studied at Crozer Theological Seminary in Chester, Pennsylvania, and finally at Boston University—where he received a doctorate in systematic theology. In 1954, when he arrived in Montgomery, Alabama, to deliver his first sermon as the new pastor of Dexter Avenue Baptist Church, King planned to preach for only a few years before returning to academia.

Although like his father and grandfather King was active in the local chapter of the NAACP, it was not until the Montgomery bus boycott that he moved to the forefront of the burgeoning civil rights movement. By January 1957, Dr. King led the Montgomery Improvement Association (MIA) and founded the Southern Christian Leadership Conference—two roles in which he displayed his exceptional leadership abilities.

It was not long before he drew an onslaught of white hatred, leading to the 1956 bombing of his house. He found recourse by attacking Montgomery's racist laws and prompting the MIA to file a federal suit attacking the laws establishing bus segregation.

Although Dr. King spoke out on secular issues, he never abandoned his Christian principles of nonviolence and a "beloved community," with integration and equality as the ultimate goal. His secular addresses, like his sermons, incorporated biblical texts and were often given in churches.

King delivered these remarks, the first of his major public addresses, at the opening meeting of the Montgomery Improvement Association. Before nearly 5,000 people at the packed Holt Street Baptist Church in Montgomery—many of whom had traveled from other Alabama cities—King derided the continued mistreatment of African-American bus passengers and praised the civil disobedience of Rosa Parks. Four days earlier, Parks had been arrested for refusing to comply with a city ordinance requiring black passengers to ride in the rear of city buses.

In what marked the beginning of the Montgomery Bus Boycott, and has since been called the first event in the civil rights era, the assembled group voted overwhelmingly to "refrain from riding buses . . . until the arrangement has been worked out with the bus company." The *New York Times* reported the incident as a small item in the back of its National section.

King later commented on his own apprehensions that day: "What could I say to keep [my people] courageous and prepared for positive action and yet devoid of hate and resentment? Could the militant and the moderate be combined in a single speech?"

MY FRIENDS, we are certainly very happy to see each of you out this evening. We are here this evening for serious business. [*Audience: Yes*] We are here in a general sense because first and foremost we are American citizens [*That's right*] and we are determined to apply our citizenship to the fullness of its meaning. [*Yeah, That's right*] We are here also because of our love for democracy [*Yes*], because of our deep-seated belief that democracy transformed from thin paper to thick action [*Yes*] is the greatest form of government on earth. [*That's right*]

But we are here in a specific sense, because of the bus situation in Montgomery. [*Yes*] We are here because we are determined to get the situation corrected. This situation is not at all new. The problem has existed over endless years. [*That's right*] For many years now Negroes in Montgomery and so many other areas have been inflicted with the paralysis of crippling fears [*Yes*] on buses in our community. [*That's right*] On so many occasions, Negroes have been intimidated and humiliated and impressed—oppressed—because of the sheer fact that they were Negroes. [*That's right*] I don't have time this evening to go into the history of these numerous cases. Many of them now are lost in the thick fog of oblivion [*Yes*], but at least one stands before us now with glaring dimensions. [*Yes*]

Just the other day, just last Thursday to be exact, one of the finest citizens in Montgomery [*Amen*]—not one of the finest Negro citizens [*That's right*], but one of the finest citizens in Montgomery—was taken from a bus [*Yes*] and carried to jail and arrested [*Yes*] because she refused to get up to give her seat to a white person. [*Yes, That's right*] Now the press would have us believe that she refused to leave a reserved section for Negroes [*Yes*], but I want you to know this evening that there is no reserved section. [*All right*] The law has never been clarified at that point. [*Hell no*] Now I think I speak with, with legal authority—not that I have any legal authority, but I think I speak with legal authority behind me [*All right*]—that the law, the ordinance, the city ordinance has never been totally clarified. [*That's right*]

Mrs. Rosa Parks is a fine person. [*Well, well said*] And, since it had to happen, I'm happy that it happened to a person like Mrs. Parks, for nobody can doubt the boundless outreach of her integrity. [*Sure enough*] Nobody can doubt the height of her character [*Yes*], nobody can doubt the depth of her Christian commitment and devotion to the teachings of Jesus. [*All right*] And I'm happy since it had to happen, it happened to a person that nobody can call a disturbing factor in the community. [*All right*] Mrs. Parks is a fine Christian person, unassuming, and yet there is integrity and character there. And just because she refused to get up, she was arrested.

And you know, my friends, there comes a time when people get tired of being trampled over by the iron feet of oppression. [*thundering applause*] There comes a time, my friends, when people get tired of being plunged across the abyss of humiliation, where they experience the bleakness of nagging despair. [*Keep talking*] There comes a time when people get tired of being pushed out of the glittering sunlight of life's July and left standing amid the piercing chill of an alpine November. [*That's right*] [*applause*] There comes a time. [*Yes sir, Teach*] [*applause continues*]

We are here, we are here this evening because we're tired now. [*Yes*] [*applause*] And I want to say that we are not here advocating violence. [*No*] We have never done that. [*Repeat that, Repeat that*] [*applause*] I want it to be known throughout Montgomery and throughout this nation [*Well*] that we are Christian people. [*Yes*] [*applause*] We believe in the Christian religion. We believe in the teachings of Jesus. [*Well*] The only weapon that we have in our hands this evening is the weapon of protest. [*Yes*] [*applause*] That's all.

And certainly, certainly, this is the glory of America, with all of its faults. [*Yeah*] This is the glory of our democracy. If we were incarcerated behind the iron curtains of a Communistic nation we couldn't do this. If we were dropped in the dungeon of a totalitarian regime we couldn't do this. [*All right*] But the great glory of American democracy is the right to protest for right. [*That's right*] [*applause*] My friends, don't let anybody make us feel that we are to be compared in our actions with the Ku Klux Klan or with the White Citizens Council. [*applause*] There will be no crosses burned at any bus stops in Montgomery. [*Well, That's right*] There will be no white persons pulled out of their homes and taken out on some distant road and lynched for not cooperating. [*applause*] There will be nobody amid, among us who will stand up and defy the Constitution of this nation. [*applause*] We only assemble here because of our desire to see right exist. [*applause*] My friends, I want it to be known that we're going to work with grim and bold determination to gain justice on the buses in this city. [*applause*]

And we are not wrong, we are not wrong in what we are doing. [*Well*] If we are wrong, the Supreme Court of this nation is wrong. [*Yes sir*] [*applause*] If we are wrong, the Constitution of the United States is wrong. [*Yes*] [*applause*] If we are wrong, God Almighty is wrong. [*That's right*] [*applause*] If we are wrong, Jesus of Nazareth was merely a utopian dreamer that never came down to earth. [*Yes*] [*applause*] If we are wrong, justice is a lie [*Yes*]. Love has no meaning. [*applause*] And we are determined here in Montgomery to work and fight until justice runs down like water [*Yes*] [*applause*], and righteousness like a mighty stream. [*Keep talking*] [*applause*]

I want to say that in all of our actions we must stick together. [*That's right*] [*applause*] Unity is the great need of the hour [*Well, That's right*], and if we are united we can get many of the things that we not only desire but which we justly deserve. [*Yeah*] And don't let anybody frighten you. [*Yeah*] We are not afraid of what we are doing [*Oh no*], because we are doing it within the law. [*All right*] There is never a time in our American democracy that we must ever think we're wrong when we protest. [*Yes sir*] We reserve that right. When labor all over this nation came to see that it would be trampled over by capitalistic power, it was nothing wrong with labor getting together and organizing and protesting for its rights. [*That's right*]

We, the disinherited of this land, we who have been oppressed so long, are tired of going through the long night of captivity. And now we are reaching out for the daybreak of freedom and justice and equality. [*applause*] May I say to you my friends, as I come to a close, and just giving some idea of why we are assembled here, that we must keep—and I want to stress this, in all of our doings, in all of our deliberations here this evening and all of the week and while—whatever we do, we must keep God in the forefront. [*Yeah*] Let us be Christian in all of our actions. [*That's right*] But I want to tell you this evening that it is not enough for us to talk about love, love is one of the pivotal points of the Christian face, faith. There is another side called justice. And justice is really love in calculation. [*All right*] Justice is love correcting that which revolts against love. [*Well*]

The Almighty God himself is not the only, not the, not the God just standing out saying through Hosea, "I love you, Israel." He's also the God that stands up before the nations and said: "Be still and know that I'm God [*Yeah*], that if you don't obey me I will break the backbone of your power [*Yeah*] and slap you out of the orbits of your international and national relationships." [*That's right*] Standing beside love is always justice, and we are only using the tools of justice. Not only are we using the tools of persuasion, but we've come to see that we've got to use the tools of coercion. Not only is this thing a process of education, but it is also a process of legislation. [*applause*]

As we stand and sit here this evening and as we prepare ourselves for what lies ahead, let us go out with a grim and bold determination that we are going to stick together. [*applause*] We are going to work together. [*applause*] Right here in Montgomery, when the history books are written in the future [*Yes*], somebody will have to say, "There lived a race of people [*Well*], a *black* people [*Yes sir*], 'fleecy locks and black complexion' [*Yes*], a people who had the moral courage to stand up for their rights. [*applause*] And thereby they injected a new meaning into the veins of history and of civilization." And we're gonna do that. God grant that we will do it before it is too late. [*Oh yeah*] As we proceed with our program let us think of these things. [*Yes*] [*applause*]

But just before leaving I want to say this. I want to urge you. You have voted [for this boycott], and you have done it with a great deal of enthusiasm, and I want to express my appreciation to you, on behalf of everybody here. Now let us go out to stick together and stay with this thing until the end. [*applause*] Now it means sacrificing, yes, it means sacrificing at points. But there are some things that we've got to learn to sacrifice for. [*Yeah*] And we've got to come to the point that we are determined not to accept a lot of things that we have been accepting in the past.

So I'm urging you now. We have the facilities for you to get to your jobs, and we are putting, we have the cabs there at your service. Automobiles will be at your service, and don't be afraid to use up any of the gas. If you have it, if you are fortunate enough to have a little money, use it for a good cause. Now my automobile is gonna be in it, it has been in it, and I'm not concerned about how much gas I'm gonna use. [*That's right*] I want to see this thing work.

And we will not be content until oppression is wiped out of Montgomery, and really out of America. We won't be content until that is done. We are merely insisting on the dignity and worth of every human personality. And I don't stand here, I'm not arguing for any selfish person. I've never been on a bus in Montgomery. But I would be less than a Christian if I stood back and said, because I don't ride the bus, I don't have to ride a bus, that it doesn't concern me. [*applause*] I will not be content. I can hear a voice saying, "If you do it unto the least of these, my brother, you do it unto me." [*applause*]

And I won't rest, I will face intimidation, and everything else, along with these other stalwart fighters for democracy and for citizenship. We don't mind it, so long as justice comes out of it. And I've come to see now that as we struggle for our rights, maybe some of them will have to die. But somebody said, if a man doesn't have something that he'll die for, he isn't fit to live. [*enthusiastic applause*]

KEN BURNS

The Homosexual Faces a Challenge
1956

When will the homosexual ever realize that social reform, to be
effective, must be preceded by personal reform?

In the 1950s, fearing persecution in a dominant heterosexual culture, many leaders in the gay movement elected to follow a strategy of assimilation. This path was in opposition to the "minority group concept," and the vision of other homosexual leaders, like the founders of the Mattachine Society, who favored unmasking gay life.

Ken Burns, one of its leaders, delivered this speech to the Mattachine Society's Third Annual Convention. Advocating a more accomodationist view, he addressed the challenge of promoting gay and lesbian liberation through legal and medical means and offered his view on the "religious problem of the homosexual." He also challenged gays and lesbians to consider their public image, criticized the notion of the homosexual superiority, and highlighted the need for pragmatic "personal reform" within the oppressive circumstances of American society.

———

LET US LOOK for a few moments at some of the problems which face the homosexual and cause him to be set apart or feel that he is set apart, from society and his family. In reviewing these problems it is not my desire to emphasize differences in principle, but rather to emphasize differences of approach which I feel have done much to continue this segregation of man. And, let me add, these problems are not subject to the homosexual alone. They are, as well, the problems of society—every individual in it—for each of us is interdependent on the other in this complex civilization in which we live. Our social order is based on the principle that each of us shall be our brother's keeper. It is tragic that this has not been universally accepted and practiced not only by Mr. Average Citizen, but by those in authority as well.

But to get back to the problems which the Mattachine Society must meet. One which has seemed to me at times to be definitely over-rated because of the unusual amount of emphasis placed on it is the problem of the law. I sometimes wonder if some homosexuals don't desire a carte blanche to carry on their activities "anywhere, anytime, anybody." This is regarded as a right. To those individuals I would say, "Come down from your marble pillar and begin to live. This Utopia is neither constructive nor productive." We do not enact laws just to have laws—there is a reason—good or bad—behind each law. Laws are made for the protection of man, and, when these laws are broken, the consequences must be expected and accepted. This is not to say, however, that we must agree with the suitability of the law. We must test it on the basis of whether the law accomplishes the purpose for which it became statute. Has it impelled those for whom it was intended to act differently? Does it serve the principles of society and our social order?

In the case of the homosexual, it would seem that law has had little or no effect on his activities. Yet, to prove that all law accomplishes that for which it was designed—and incidentally, to prove that all human problems can be solved by law—it is the custom for some enforcement agencies to hide behind their authority using techniques of harassment, blackmail, and entrapment and to assume the role of judge and jury in the interpretation and application of law. Some are no better than male prostitutes themselves in their role of agent provocateurs. Society seems to have taken theory, or the explanation of some phenomenon which exists in someone's mind and which has not yet been demonstrated by scientific measurement, and made it into law which is a summary of the truth supported by facts which no one can dispute, and expressed in terms of a sound working principle which can safely be used as a guide. The basic theory seems not to prevent trouble but to punish it. Is it a case of reforming or getting even? Yes, it would seem that the law dealing with homosexual practices has had much more effect on the activities of some law enforcement officers and those in the legal field.

. . . What consenting adults do in private, however, is their own business as long as they don't injure themselves or others. Maybe you don't agree with what they do; maybe they don't agree with what you do. If that is so, then it is a matter of education, not law. These are principles fundamental to our democracy.

The Mattachine Society is prepared to sit down with legislators, law enforcement officers, judges and others in the legal field to work out an objective program to meet the legal problems affecting homosexuality and to constructively administer to the causes and not the symptoms of the problem. We do not say that our judgement is sound and the judgement of others unwise. We do say, however, that "if you want to build a bridge, go to an engineer"; if you have a problem with homosexuals go to an organization that can help you. This offer is also open to others interested in the homosexual.

Let us look for a moment at the religious or spiritual problem of the homosexual. In my opinion this is a subject which needs more emphasis. All of us have a spiritual side to our nature. This cannot be divorced from the material, for only through the spiritual does the material have meaning and value. Some would deny this, but I believe they do so as a defense against the teachings—or what they believe to be the teachings—of particular faiths. We have only to look around us and within us to discern a force, a spirit, God— call this what you will. There is a plan in this great universe and you and I— every single person and thing—is an integral part of that plan.

There are those who profess to minister to us on behalf of God, however, who would deny the homosexual any part in this universal plan. "The church is no place for this filth, he is anathema," they would say. I submit to you that the church if it truly be the representative of God, must be always open to the creatures of God no matter what they may think, say, or do. God is not exclusive. He does not create only to reject and forget. Neither does he create scapegoats. These are the results of fearful men who because of this fear are unable to comprehend love—not only love of their fellow-man, but love of God, also.

The results of this rejection by ministers has caused them to deviate from their role as leaders toward a fuller spiritual life for everyone. Both religion and homosexuality are emotional subjects and they have been played to the hilt in creating and maintaining strife among groups. Sodom and Gomorrah have been twisted all out of proportion to their original intent and meaning. . . . It is high time that all of us got back on the path toward a richer and more satisfying life. A life in which we will welcome all people, leaving it to God to judge their intentions.

We have seen that the law cannot legislate morals. Morals are the result of ethical values. These values are the result of tradition and education to a large extent. These interpretations must be constantly reexamined in order to give meaning to this modern day. We have advanced measurably since the middle ages and our philosophy of life must be vitalized if the brotherhood of man is to be accomplished. We must mean what we say and practice what we preach.

Now, what about the medical problem of the homosexual. Generally, this is a field which has been most progressive in its attitudes. Psychiatry especially has made great strides forward in its analysis and comprehension of homosexuality. Medical people, schooled as they are in the objective approach to research, however, would be the first subject. They have only scratched the surface. Most of the questions still remain to be answered accurately through recognized research methods.

But what is being done by the medical profession to determine the answers and thereby, partially at least, release the homosexual from this dark age of ignorance of a problem affecting untold millions throughout the world? I know of no concerted effort being made by any professional group to conduct research into the psychic, physical, or social reaches of homosexuality. True, some individuals have conducted research into various phases of the subject and this is certainly a beginning. But, there has been no attempt to correlate these findings and exhibit them into the entire picture of the individual. We are composed of arms, legs, a trunk and a head. Yet, there is a correlation and interdependence of these members. Without this, there is little meaning. The problems involved are, of course, much more complex than I can describe. I doubt if man will ever be able to truly understand and evaluate either himself, another individual, or mankind. This is always the constant challenge which has urged man on to greater feats.

If professional people, most particularly those in the medical profession, determine to undertake the task of meeting and solving this unknown—homosexuality and its many facets—this nation would literally experience a rebirth. One person is born every second of the day and night in the U.S. Of those that survive every fifth person may become homosexually inclined temporarily, and every tenth person permanently. There are few things which are termed problems which have greater incidence. And as long as we continue in this twilight of comparative inactivity it shall continue to be so. But, does it have to be? The homosexual is accused of attempting to create a homosexual society. Yet it is the homosexual himself who cries out for help in controlling this continuous cycle by constructive means. Castigating homosexuals now living is sheer stupidity. The solution of the problems of persons yet to be born who will become homosexual—who are maybe even destined to be homosexual—lies in preventive means.

This brings us to the problem the homosexual encounters in his home, with his family and those who are nearest and dearest to him. Love and companionship contribute much to our inner security and much to our outward attitudes. They are essential to life and its adjustments. They are so important that individuals feel forced to lie and lead double existences to keep them. These most precious things—so fleeting and elusive they seem at times. We seem to be inadequate to their meaning and potential—and perhaps we are.

⟶

Fortunately, some families have faced the situation and do everything possible to understand. People who love for the joy they receive rather than hate that which life contains. Others, however, resign themselves only to hate. They must punish themselves to remove this stain. Tragic!

⟶

Society has often spoken out to control the "homosexual menace." Yet today it cannot recognize and evaluate homosexuality. Until it can do this, society must grope blindly in the dark—continually knocking the periphery and never getting at the core. A good example of this and its consequences is the problem the homosexual faces in employment.

Business, taking its lead from the federal government to a large extent, has denied employment to homosexuals. This has been found expedient because they are "security risks." I would remind you of the hundreds of thousands of homosexuals who served this country and still serve it well. I know no homosexual who would not lay down his life for the security of all the people in this nation and the ideals on which this nation was built. We, perhaps more than most, know the value of security. But what is this "risk"? Is it the risk of homosexuals because of their acts? Or is it the risk of blackmailing which some homosexuals may be subject to? Is it because some are more talkative, less adequately adjusted, or more willing to submit to blackmail than all other individuals?

The federal government more and more, has spoken out against unequal rights for groups. Yet, here are individuals given the status of a group to be judged and condemned as a group. This nation was founded on individual rights, individual freedoms and individual responsibility. The destiny of the individual was to be protected. We have strayed far when every man does not recognize this devaluation of the individual—his cherished heritage to be judged on his own merits. The federal government has afforded sanctuary to those who would make all men the same. It has encouraged the blackmailer and given protection to his practices. It has pronounced a sentence of guilty until proven innocent on the homosexual.

Compliance with this has permeated every branch of the government and seeped down into private enterprise, sometimes at the direction of the government. Today, the homosexual is the victim—the scapegoat. Tomorrow, unless we are vigilant and unless this practice is ended, we may see further inroads into the basic freedom of the individual.

Now we come to perhaps the greatest problem of all—the homosexual's relationship with himself and his surroundings. We can never adequately solve the problems which face us without first facing and seeking solutions to the problems within us. Pressures from without are often the reaction to pressures within. We must blame ourselves for much of our plight. When will the homosexual ever realize that social reform, to be effective, must be preceded by personal reform? People who are non-homosexual usually get their knowledge of homosexuality by the education given them by homosexuals. And what an education it has been at times.

In his efforts to be recognized, the homosexual has channeled his actions into super-colossal productions to demonstrate and accentuate differences. The result has been an ever widening chasm based on a premise that there is a difference. If we are to publicly act different than accepted standards we must be certain that our differences will be recognized as superior. There are some who would say that homosexuals are superior, "the chosen of God." But I say, show me the facts. I am not interested in your egotism. Look beyond your self-interest and emotions. You are different only in that way you think you are different. Stop being afraid of yourself and use fear as an aid to growth and not as a form of escape. Yes, it is time that all of us took an agonizing reappraisal of our personal and social relationships. Do we truly contribute [to the] welfare of others? There is no place for complacency in the answer. None of us are so good that we can't be better.

I do not mean to infer that what I have said is the official position of the Mattachine Society; I have spoken only for myself, nor do I wish to give you the impression that I am bitter or have a chip on my shoulder. I am not fighting against the situation which exists. Rather, I am fighting for all of us to undertake the responsibility of being citizens in a nation which still gives us the right to disagree. Uniformity is not demanded of us—but unity of all of our people is required to meet and solve the problems of our environment. There need be no fear, for all of us together are adequate and equal to the problems. I am reminded of Justice Holmes's statement: "The inevitable comes to pass through effort." Greater effort is needed on the part of all of us. . . .

All who join the ranks of this crusade can feel justly proud. We must never falter in the principles on which Mattachine was organized. We must continue to serve, to face the world boldly, unafraid, with faith in the future and say, "This I believe. This I have done."

DWIGHT D. EISENHOWER
(1890–1969)

Federal Court Orders Must Be Upheld
SEPTEMBER 24, 1957

We are a nation in which laws, not men, are supreme.
I regret to say that this truth—the cornerstone of our liberties—
was not observed in this instance.

After the U.S. Supreme Court declared segregation illegal in the 1954 *Brown v. Board of Education* decision, scores of southerners continued to resist integration. In one of the more incendiary occurrences, Arkansas governor Orval Faubus attempted to block the integration of the Little Rock public school system by sending the Arkansas National Guard to Central High School. Ostensibly, the troops were deployed to "maintain order," but their real purpose was to prevent a group of black students—the Little Rock Nine—from entering the school.

The Guard's presence provoked violence in Little Rock and caused a national social crisis; conservatives lined up behind Faubus and the militia, while civil rights activists rallied behind the young students. The previous July, President Dwight D. Eisenhower had stated that he could not "imagine any set of circumstances that would ever induce [him] to send in federal troops." Even when the crisis erupted, Ike remained reluctant to intervene, falling back on the conservative axiom that it was impossible to legislate morality, and that time would be the best remedy. But the daily barrage of media reports from the school, including images of children surrounded by men in army fatigues, heightened political pressure on the White House, generating sympathy for black children from the international community, including the United Nations and the Soviet Union, which used it as a propaganda tool. Feeling pressure, President Eisenhower finally responded by publicly calling for peace and strongly urging the governor to give up his "disgraceful" effort to prevent desegregation. When Faubus refused, the president took to the airwaves.

In a cautiously worded evening address delivered from the Oval Office over radio and television, President Eisenhower announced his decision to federalize the Arkansas National Guard and dispatch 1,000 paratroopers to escort the black students to class and control the mob. His actions marked the first occasion since Reconstruction that federal forces were deployed to guarantee the equal treatment of African

Americans in the South. Faubus eventually capitulated, and the Little Rock Nine were peacefully admitted to Central High School. Southern conservatives like Senator Richard Russell compared the federal soldiers to "Hitler's storm troopers"; President Eisenhower immediately took steps to "play down the incident" and the imposition on state authority. Long after the crisis, Eisenhower offered a window into his decision, writing, "If the day comes when we can obey the order of our courts only when we personally approve of them, the end of the American system, as we know it, will not be far off."

GOOD EVENING, MY FELLOW CITIZENS:

For a few minutes this evening I want to speak to you about the serious situation that has arisen in Little Rock. To make this talk I have come to the President's office in the White House. I could have spoken from Rhode Island, where I have been staying recently, but I felt that, in speaking from the house of Lincoln, of Jackson and of Wilson, my words would better convey both the sadness I feel in the action I was compelled today to take and the firmness with which I intend to pursue this course until the orders of the Federal court at Little Rock can be executed without unlawful interference.

In that city, under the leadership of demagogic extremists, disorderly mobs have deliberately prevented the carrying out of proper orders from a Federal court. Local authorities have not eliminated that violent opposition and, under the law, I yesterday issued a Proclamation calling upon the mob to disperse.

This morning the mob again gathered in front of the Central High School of Little Rock, obviously for the purpose of again preventing the carrying out of the Court's order relating to the admission of Negro children to that school.

Whenever normal agencies prove inadequate to the task and it becomes necessary for the Executive Branch of the Federal Government to use its powers and authority to uphold Federal courts, the President's responsibility is inescapable.

In accordance with that responsibility, I have today issued an Executive Order directing the use of troops under Federal authority to aid in the execution of Federal law at Little Rock, Arkansas. This became necessary when my Proclamation of yesterday was not observed, and the obstruction of justice still continues.

It is important that the reasons for my action be understood by all our citizens.

As you know, the Supreme Court of the United States has decided that separate public educational facilities for the races are inherently unequal and therefore compulsory school segregation laws are unconstitutional.

Our personal opinions about the decision have no bearing on the matter of enforcement; the responsibility and authority of the Supreme Court to interpret the Constitution are very clear. Local Federal courts were instructed by the Supreme Court to issue such orders and decrees as might be necessary to achieve admission to public schools without regard to race—and with all deliberate speed.

During the past several years, many communities in our Southern states have instituted public school plans for gradual progress in the enrollment and attendance of school children of all races in order to bring themselves into compliance with the law of the land.

They thus demonstrated to the world that we are a nation in which laws, not men, are supreme. I regret to say that this truth—the cornerstone of our liberties—was not observed in this instance.

It was my hope that this localized situation would be brought under control by city and state authorities. If the use of local police powers had been sufficient, our traditional method of leaving the problem in those hands would have been pursued. But when large gatherings of obstructionists made it impossible for the decree of the Court to be carried out, both the law and the national interest demanded that the President take action.

Here is the sequence of events in the development of the Little Rock school case.

In May of 1955, the Little Rock School Board approved a moderate plan for the gradual desegregation of the public schools in that city. It provided that a start toward integration would be made at the present term in the high school, and that the plan would be in full operation by 1963. Here I might say that in a number of communities in Arkansas integration in the schools has already started and without violence of any kind. Now this Little Rock plan was challenged in the courts by some who believed that the period of time as proposed in the plan was too long.

The United States Court at Little Rock, which has supervisory responsibility under the law for the plan of desegregation in the public schools, dismissed the challenge, thus approving a gradual rather than an abrupt change from the existing system. The court found that the school board had acted in good faith in planning for a public school system free from racial discrimination.

Since that time, the court has on three separate occasions issued orders directing that the plan be carried out. All persons were instructed to refrain from interfering with the efforts of the school board to comply with the law.

Proper and sensible observance of the law then demanded the respectful obedience which the nation has a right to expect from all its people. This, unfortunately, has not been the case at Little Rock. Certain misguided persons, many of them imported into Little Rock by agitators, have insisted upon defying the law and have sought to bring it into disrepute. The orders of the court have thus been frustrated.

The very basis of our individual rights and freedoms rests upon the certainty that the President and the Executive Branch of Government will support and insure the carrying out of the decisions of the Federal Courts, even, when necessary, with all the means at the President's command.

Unless the President did so, anarchy would result.

There would be no security for any except that which each one of us could provide for himself.

The interest of the nation in the proper fulfillment of the law's requirements cannot yield to opposition and demonstrations by some few persons.

Mob rule cannot be allowed to override the decisions of our courts.

Now, let me make it very clear that Federal troops are not being used to relieve local and state authorities of their primary duty to preserve the peace and order of the community. Nor are the troops there for the purpose of taking over the responsibility of the School Board and the other responsible local officials in running Central High School. The running of our school system and the maintenance of peace and order in each of our states are strictly local affairs and the Federal Government does not interfere except in a very few special cases and when requested by one of the several states. In the present case the troops are there, pursuant to law, solely for the purpose of preventing interference with the orders of the court.

The proper use of the powers of the Executive Branch to enforce the orders of a Federal court is limited to extraordinary and compelling circumstances. Manifestly, such an extreme situation has been created in Little Rock. This challenge must be met and with such measures as will preserve to the people as a whole their lawfully-protected rights in a climate permitting their free and fair exercise.

The overwhelming majority of our people in every section of the country are united in their respect for observance of the law—even in those cases where they may disagree with that law.

They deplore the call of extremists to violence.

The decision of the Supreme Court concerning school integration, of course, affects the South more seriously than it does other sections of the country. In that region I have many warm friends, some of them in the city of Little Rock. I have deemed it a great personal privilege to spend in our Southland tours of duty while in the military service and enjoyable recreational periods since that time.

So from intimate personal knowledge, I know that the overwhelming majority of the people in the South—including those of Arkansas and of Little

Rock—are of good will, united in their efforts to preserve and respect the law even when they disagree with it.

They do not sympathize with mob rule. They, like the rest of our nation, have proved in two great wars their readiness to sacrifice for America.

A foundation of our American way of life is our national respect for law.

In the South, as elsewhere, citizens are keenly aware of the tremendous disservice that has been done to the people of Arkansas in the eyes of the nation, and that has been done to the nation in the eyes of the world.

At a time when we face grave situations abroad because of the hatred that communism bears toward a system of government based on human rights, it would be difficult to exaggerate the harm that is being done to the prestige and influence, and indeed to the safety, of our nation and the world.

Our enemies are gloating over this incident and using it everywhere to misrepresent our whole nation. We are portrayed as a violator of those standards of conduct which the peoples of the world united to proclaim in the Charter of the United Nations. There they affirmed "faith in fundamental human rights" and "in the dignity and worth of the human person" and they did so "without distinction as to race, sex, language or religion."

And so, with deep confidence, I call upon the citizens of the state of Arkansas to assist in bringing to an immediate end all interference with the law and its processes. If resistance to the Federal court orders ceases at once, the further presence of Federal troops will be unnecessary and the city of Little Rock will return to its normal habits of peace and order and a blot upon the fair name and high honor of our nation will be removed.

Thus will be restored the image of America and of all its parts as one nation, indivisible, with liberty and justice for all.

Good night, and thank you very much.

JOHN F. KENNEDY
(1917–1963)

Civil Rights Message
JUNE 11, 1963

Every American ought to have the right to be treated as he would wish to be treated, as one would wish his children to be treated.

Although black leaders were initially skeptical of candidate John F. Kennedy's commitment to equal opportunity, including his endorsement of a civil rights platform at the Democratic National Convention, his public praise of Martin Luther King, Jr., convinced a significant number of blacks to support him. The youngest man ever elected to the presidency and the first Roman Catholic, Kennedy won the election of November 1960 by a razor-thin margin.

As president, Kennedy was at first reluctant to pursue an active civil rights agenda, sparking an onslaught of criticism from African-American leaders. By 1962, however, following the Freedom Rides, sit-ins, and a rash of racial violence in the South, the president was no longer satisfied with an incrementalist approach.

In 1963, when Governor George Wallace, flouting federal law and direction, refused to admit two black students to the University of Alabama, Kennedy decided to take action. Surrounded by television cameras and soldiers, decrying what he called Kennedy's "central government," Wallace literally stood in the doorway of Foster Auditorium, where the black students had hoped to register. Despite opposition from his most trusted aides, Kennedy staged a showdown with Wallace, knowing that a broad endorsement of civil rights might cost him reelection.

On the evening of June 11, Kennedy addressed the nation from the Oval Office, declaring that the United States faced a "moral crisis" because of growing and justified discontent among blacks. He also used this speech to announce his decision to federalize the Alabama National Guard and to send strengthened civil rights legislation to Congress. Privately, as historian Richard Reeves later reported, Kennedy supported a civil rights package that would not alienate southerners and risk his tax bill. The president described the perfect bill: "The minimum we can ask for and the maximum we can stand behind."

According to the president's speechwriter, Ted Sorensen, Kennedy had been honing his ideas for several months, but had not elected to deliver his June 11 speech until 5 P.M. that night, only three hours before the networks would carry his speech live. The president dispatched Sorensen, Attorney General Robert Kennedy, and Assistant Attorney General Burke Marshall to work out the details and direction of his text. Then Sorensen returned to his West Wing office, where he huddled over his signature yellow legal pad, handing page after page to his secretary to type up. The president kept the pressure on Sorensen, walking in and out of his office to check on his young writer's progress. At eight o'clock, as he sat down in front of the cameras, he was still scribbling his own edits to Sorensen's draft, forcing him to ad-lib a portion of his eighteen-minute address.

The president's powerful remarks ignited a fiery battle over civil rights legislation, which ultimately led to the passage of the landmark 1964 Civil Rights Act. Though Kennedy was assassinated before the bill became a law, many historians have argued that without the sympathy for Kennedy's death and the political acumen of his successor, Lyndon B. Johnson, the bill would have perished at the hands of conservative legislators.

<hr/>

GOOD EVENING, MY FELLOW CITIZENS:

This afternoon, following a series of threats and defiant statements, the presence of Alabama National Guardsmen was required on the University of Alabama to carry out the final and unequivocal order of the United States District Court of the Northern District of Alabama. That order called for the admission of two clearly qualified young Alabama residents who happened to have been born Negro.

That they were admitted peacefully on the campus is due in good measure to the conduct of the students of the University of Alabama, who met their responsibilities in a constructive way.

I hope that every American, regardless of where he lives, will stop and examine his conscience about this and other related incidents. This Nation was founded by men of many nations and backgrounds. It was founded on the principle that all men are created equal, and that the rights of every man are diminished when the rights of one man are threatened.

Today we are committed to a worldwide struggle to promote and protect the rights of all who wish to be free. And when Americans are sent to Viet-Nam or West Berlin, we do not ask for whites only. It ought to be possible, therefore, for American students of any color to attend any public institution they select without having to be backed up by troops.

It ought to be possible for American consumers of any color to receive equal service in places of public accommodation, such as hotels and restaurants and theaters and retail stores, without being forced to resort to demonstrations in the street, and it ought to be possible for American citizens of any color to register and to vote in a free election without interference or fear of reprisal.

It ought to be possible, in short, for every American to enjoy the privileges of being American without regard to his race or his color. In short, every American ought to have the right to be treated as he would wish to be treated, as one would wish his children to be treated. But this is not the case.

The Negro baby born in America today, regardless of the section of the Nation in which he is born, has about one-half as much chance of completing a high school as a white baby born in the same place on the same day, one-third as much chance of completing college, one-third as much chance of becoming a professional man, twice as much chance of becoming unemployed, about one-seventh as much chance of earning $10,000 a year, a life expectancy which is 7 years shorter, and the prospects of earning only half as much.

This is not a sectional issue. Difficulties over segregation and discrimination exist in every city, in every State of the Union, producing in many cities a rising tide of discontent that threatens the public safety. Nor is this a partisan issue. In a time of domestic crisis men of good will and generosity should be able to unite regardless of party or politics. This is not even a legal or legislative issue alone. It is better to settle these matters in the courts than on the streets, and new laws are needed at every level, but law alone cannot make men see right.

We are confronted primarily with a moral issue. It is as old as the scriptures and is as clear as the American Constitution.

The heart of the question is whether all Americans are to be afforded equal rights and equal opportunities, whether we are going to treat our fellow Americans as we want to be treated. If an American, because his skin is dark, cannot eat lunch in a restaurant open to the public, if he cannot send his children to the best public school available, if he cannot vote for the public officials who represent him, if, in short, he cannot enjoy the full and free life which all of us want, then who among us would be content to have the color of his skin changed and stand in his place? Who among us would then be content with the counsels of patience and delay?

One hundred years of delay have passed since President Lincoln freed the slaves, yet their heirs, their grandsons, are not fully free. They are not yet freed from the bonds of injustice. They are not yet freed from social and economic oppression. And this Nation, for all its hopes and all its boasts, will not be fully free until all its citizens are free.

We preach freedom around the world, and we mean it, and we cherish our freedom here at home, but are we to say to the world, and much more importantly, to each other that this is a land of the free except for the Negroes; that we have no second-class citizens except Negroes; that we have no class or caste system, no ghettoes, no master race except with respect to Negroes?

Now the time has come for this Nation to fulfill its promise. The events in Birmingham and elsewhere have so increased the cries for equality that no city or State or legislative body can prudently choose to ignore them.

The fires of frustration and discord are burning in every city, North and South, where legal remedies are not at hand. Redress is sought in the streets, in demonstrations, parades, and protests which create tensions and threaten violence and threaten lives.

We face, therefore, a moral crisis as a country and as a people. It cannot be met by repressive police action. It cannot be left to increased demonstrations in the streets. It cannot be quieted by token moves or talk. It is a time to act in the Congress, in your State and local legislative body and, above all, in all of our daily lives.

It is not enough to pin the blame on others, to say this is a problem of one section of the country or another, or deplore the fact that we face. A great change is at hand, and our task, our obligation, is to make that revolution, that change, peaceful and constructive for all.

Those who do nothing are inviting shame as well as violence. Those who act boldly are recognizing right as well as reality.

Next week I shall ask the Congress of the United States to act, to make a commitment it has not fully made in this century to the proposition that race has no place in American life or law. The Federal judiciary has upheld that proposition in a series of forthright cases. The executive branch has adopted that proposition in the conduct of its affairs, including the employment of Federal personnel, the use of Federal facilities, and the sale of federally financed housing.

But there are other necessary measures which only the Congress can provide, and they must be provided at this session. The old code of equity law under which we live commands for every wrong a remedy, but in too many communities, in too many parts of the country, wrongs are inflicted on Negro citizens and there are no remedies at law. Unless the Congress acts, their only remedy is in the street.

I am, therefore, asking the Congress to enact legislation giving all Americans the right to be served in facilities which are open to the public—hotels, restaurants, theaters, retail stores, and similar establishments.

This seems to me to be an elementary right. Its denial is an arbitrary indignity that no American in 1963 should have to endure, but many do.

I have recently met with scores of business leaders urging them to take voluntary action to end this discrimination and I have been encouraged by their response, and in the last 2 weeks over 75 cities have seen progress made in desegregating these kinds of facilities. But many are unwilling to act alone

Susan B. Anthony and Elizabeth Cady Stanton

Library of Congress

Sojourner Truth

Library of Congress

W. E. B. Du Bois on the lecture tour.

Special Collections and Archives, W. E. B. Du Bois Library,
University of Massachusetts–Amherst.

*Booker T. Washington addresses a crowd at the
dedication of a cotton seed mill in Mississippi.*

Bettmann/CORBIS

Eleanor Roosevelt broadcasts from New York in 1947.

Bettmann/CORBIS

Hubert H. Humphrey speaking at the 1948 Democratic National Convention in Philadelphia, Pennsylvania.

International News, Minnesota Historical Society

Malcolm X speaks at a rally in Harlem, New York, in June 1963.

Bettmann/CORBIS

Martin Luther King, Jr., addresses a group of Watts residents only weeks after the week-long rampage of the 1965 Watts Riots.

Bettmann/CORBIS

FK addresses a civil rights rally in June 1963 outside the Department of Justice.

AP/Wide World Photos

President John F. Kennedy delivers a live civil rights address to the nation from the Oval Office in June 1963.

John F. Kennedy Library

(Above) President Lyndon B.
Johnson, with his daughter,
Lynda Bird, delivers a
civil rights speech in
May 1964 to a crowd
in Gainesville, Georgia.

Lyndon B. Johnson Library

(Above) Senator Daniel Inouye of Haw
prepares to deliver the keynote address
delegates at the Democratic National
Convention in Chicago, Illinois, in
August 1968.

AP/Wide World Photos

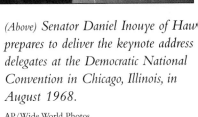

(Left) César Chávez speaks at a news
conference in Miami, Florida, in Marc
1972, at the end of a labor dispute
between Coca-Cola and citrus harveste

AP/Wide World Photos

Betty Friedan speaking in October 1975 at a
NOW Conference in Philadelphia, Pennsylvania.

Bettye-Lane

Harvey Milk delivers a speech at a Union Square rally in
Miami on the evening of Anita Bryant's victory in 1977.

Jerry Pritikin

*Jesse Jackson, Jr.,
addresses a crowd on the
Mall in Washington,
D.C. in 1968.*

Washington, D.C., Public Library

*President Clinton speaks to the annual convocation of the Church of
God in Christ in Memphis, Tennessee, on November 13, 1993,
from the same pulpit that Dr. King delivered his last sermon.*

AP/Wide World Photos

and for this reason, nationwide legislation is needed if we are to move this problem from the streets to the courts.

I am also asking Congress to authorize the Federal Government to partici-pate more fully in lawsuits designed to end segregation in public education. We have succeeded in persuading many districts to desegregate voluntarily. Dozens have admitted Negroes without violence. Today a Negro is attending a State-supported institution in every one of our 50 States, but the pace is very slow.

Too many Negro children entering segregated grade schools at the time of the Supreme Court's decision 9 years ago will enter segregated high schools this fall, having suffered a loss which can never be restored. The lack of an ade-quate education denies the Negro a chance to get a decent job.

The orderly implementation of the Supreme Court decision, therefore, cannot be left solely to those who may not have the economic resources to carry the legal action or who may be subject to harassment.

Other features will be also requested, including greater protection for the right to vote. But legislation, I repeat, cannot solve this problem alone. It must be solved in the homes of every American in every community across our country.

In this respect, I want to pay tribute to those citizens North and South who have been working in their communities to make life better for all. They are acting not out of a sense of legal duty but out of a sense of human decency.

Like our soldiers and sailors in all parts of the world they are meeting free-dom's challenge on the firing line, and I salute them for their honor and their courage.

My fellow Americans, this is a problem which faces us all—in every city of the North as well as the South. Today there are Negroes unemployed, two or three times as many compared to whites, inadequate in education, moving into the large cities, unable to find work, young people particularly out of work without hope, denied equal rights, denied the opportunity to eat at a restau-rant or lunch counter or go to a movie theater, denied the right to a decent education, denied almost today the right to attend a State university even though qualified. It seems to me that these are matters which concern us all, not merely Presidents or Congressmen or Governors, but every citizen of the United States.

This is one country. It has become one country because all of us and all the people who came here had an equal chance to develop their talents.

We cannot say to ten percent of the population that you can't have that right; that your children can't have the chance to develop whatever talents they have; that the only way that they are going to get their rights is to go into the streets and demonstrate. I think we owe them and we owe ourselves a better country than that.

Therefore, I am asking for your help in making it easier for us to move ahead and to provide the kind of equality of treatment which we would want ourselves; to give a chance for every child to be educated to the limit of his talents.

As I have said before, not every child has an equal talent or an equal ability or an equal motivation, but they should have the equal right to develop their talent and their ability and their motivation, to make something of themselves.

We have a right to expect that the Negro community will be responsible, will uphold the law, but they have a right to expect that the law will be fair, that the Constitution will be color blind, as Justice Harlan said at the turn of the century.

This is what we are talking about and this is a matter which concerns this country and what it stands for, and in meeting it I ask the support of all our citizens.

Thank you very much.

Martin Luther King, Jr.
(1929–1968)

I Have a Dream
August 28, 1963

I have a dream that my four little children will one day
live in a nation where they will not be judged by the color of
their skin but by the content of their character.

On August 28, 1963, before a crowd of nearly 300,000, Dr. Martin Luther King, Jr., delivered what is arguably the most celebrated civil rights speech in American history. Forming a half-mile blanket over both sides of the Lincoln Memorial, singing "We Shall Overcome," crowds flocked in trains and buses from all over the country for the historic March on Washington—"the first and essentially last mass meeting to ever reach the national airwaves."

King biographer Taylor Branch described the scene: "The gathering sea of placards and faces produced the most brain-numbing sights since the first ghost fleet of empty buses chugged through Montgomery." Washington, D.C., was on high alert. For the first time since prohibition liquor sales were banned in the entire city; the Washington Senators canceled two games; and 15,000 army paratroopers were placed on standby.

An idea first conceived by A. Philip Randolph in 1941, the march, which followed on the heels of the Birmingham riots, was held to protest a nation unresponsive to worsening conditions for African Americans. Although the Supreme Court had ruled separate was inherently unequal in its 1954 decision *Brown v. Board of Education,* most blacks still lived in segregated communities lacking the vote and equal economic, social, and political opportunity. Dr. King and the mainstream civil rights movement continued to favor a course of nonviolent protest—a path that would slowly come undone over the next two years.

Despite last-minute dissent over the order of speakers, the text of Student Nonviolent Coordinating Committee president John Lewis's remarks, and the exclusion of women on the dais, the day's events were a remarkable success: no rioting, violent confrontations, or bloodshed. After nearly a minute-long ovation, with the television networks carrying him live, Dr. King delivered the final address of the afternoon.

Until the peroration, King recited his text nearly verbatim, urging the black and white audience to keep fighting for justice in a land where all men were purportedly "created equal." But then, "with no alternative but to preach," Dr. King suddenly departed from his text, from his "dream sequence" to the old Negro spiritual "free at last," offering the most memorable lines of the day.

I AM HAPPY TO JOIN with you today in what will go down in history as the greatest demonstration for freedom in the history of our nation. [*Applause*]

Fivescore years ago, a great American, in whose symbolic shadow we stand today, signed the Emancipation Proclamation. This momentous decree came as a great beacon light of hope to millions of Negro slaves who had been seared in the flames of withering injustice. It came as a joyous daybreak to end the long night of their captivity.

But one hundred years later, the Negro still is not free. [*Audience:*] [*My Lord*] One hundred years later, the life of the Negro is still sadly crippled by the manacles of segregation and the chains of discrimination. One hundred years later, the Negro lives on a lonely island of poverty in the midst of a vast ocean of material prosperity. One hundred years later [*My Lord*] [*Applause*], the Negro is still languished in the corners of American society and finds himself an exile in his own land. And so we've come here today to dramatize a shameful condition.

In a sense we've come to our nation's capital to cash a check. When the architects of our republic wrote the magnificent words of the Constitution and the Declaration of Independence [*Yeah*], they were signing a promissory note to which every American was to fall heir. This note was a promise that all men, yes, black men as well as white men, would be guaranteed the "unalienable Rights of Life, Liberty, and the pursuit of Happiness." It is obvious today that America has defaulted on this promissory note insofar as her citizens of color are concerned. Instead of honoring this sacred obligation, America has given the Negro people a bad check, a check which has come back marked "insufficient funds." [*Sustained applause*]

But we refuse to believe that the bank of justice is bankrupt. [*My Lord*] [*Laughter*] [*Sure enough*] We refuse to believe that there are insufficient funds in the great vaults of opportunity of this nation. And so we've come to cash this check [*Yes*], a check that will give us upon demand the riches of freedom [*Yes*] and the security of justice. [*Applause*]

We have also come to this hallowed spot to remind America of the fierce urgency of now. This is no time [*My Lord*] to engage in the luxury of cooling off or to take the tranquilizing drug of gradualism. [*Applause*] Now is the time to make real the promises of democracy. [*My Lord*] Now is the time to rise from the dark and desolate valley of segregation to the sunlit path of racial justice. Now is the time [*Applause*] to lift our nation from the quicksands of racial injustice to the solid rock of brotherhood. Now is the time [*Applause*] to make justice a reality for all of God's children.

It would be fatal for the nation to overlook the urgency of the moment. This sweltering summer of the Negro's legitimate discontent will not pass until there is an invigorating autumn of freedom and equality. Nineteen sixty-three is not an end, but a beginning. And those who hope that the Negro needed to blow off steam and will now be content will have a rude awakening if the nation returns to business as usual. [*Applause*] There will be neither rest nor tranquillity in America until the Negro is granted his citizenship rights. The whirlwinds of revolt will continue to shake the foundations of our nation until the bright day of justice emerges.

But there is something that I must say to my people, who stand on the warm threshold which leads into the palace of justice: In the process of gaining our rightful place, we must not be guilty of wrongful deeds. Let us not seek to satisfy our thirst for freedom by drinking from the cup of bitterness and hatred. [*My Lord*] [*Applause*] We must forever conduct our struggle on the high plane of dignity and discipline. We must not allow our creative protest to degenerate into physical violence. Again and again, we must rise to the majestic heights of meeting physical force with soul force. The marvelous new militancy which has engulfed the Negro community must not lead us to a distrust of all white people, for many of our white brothers, as evidenced by their presence here today, have come to realize that their destiny is tied up with our destiny. [*Applause*] And they have come to realize that their freedom is inextricably bound to our freedom. We cannot walk alone.

And as we walk, we must make the pledge that we shall always march ahead. We cannot turn back. There are those who are asking the devotees of civil rights, "When will you be satisfied?" [*Never*]

We can never be satisfied as long as the Negro is the victim of the unspeakable horrors of police brutality. We can never be satisfied [*Applause*] as long as our bodies, heavy with the fatigue of travel, cannot gain lodging in the motels of the highways and the hotels of the cities. [*Applause*] We cannot be satisfied as long as the Negro's basic mobility is from a smaller ghetto to a larger one. We can never be satisfied as long as our children are stripped of their selfhood and robbed of their dignity by signs stating "for whites only." [*Applause*] We cannot be satisfied as long as a Negro in Mississippi cannot vote and a Negro in New York believes he has nothing for which to vote. [*Yes*] [*Applause*] No, no, we are not satisfied and we will not be satisfied until justice rolls down like waters and righteousness like a mighty stream. [*Applause*]

I am not unmindful that some of you have come here out of great trials and tribulations. [*My Lord*] Some of you have come fresh from narrow jail cells. Some of you have come from areas where your quest for freedom left you battered by the storms of persecution [*Yes*] and staggered by the winds of police brutality. You have been the veterans of creative suffering. Continue to work with the faith that unearned suffering is redemptive. Go back to Mississippi [*Yes*], go back to Alabama, go back to South Carolina, go back to Georgia, go back to Louisiana, go back to the slums and ghettos of our northern cities, knowing that somehow this situation can and will be changed. [*Yes*] Let us not wallow in the valley of despair.

I say to you today, my friends [*Applause*], so even though we face the difficulties of today and tomorrow, I still have a dream. [*Yes*] It is a dream deeply rooted in the American dream.

I have a dream that one day [*Yes*] this nation will rise up and live out the true meaning of its creed: "We hold these truths to be self-evident, that all men are created equal." [*Yes*] [*Applause*]

I have a dream that one day on the red hills of Georgia, the sons of former slaves and the sons of former slave owners will be able to sit down together at the table of brotherhood.

I have a dream that one day even the state of Mississippi, a state sweltering with the heat of injustice [*Well*], sweltering with the heat of oppression, will be transformed into an oasis of freedom and justice.

I have a dream [*Well*] [*Applause*] that my four little children will one day live in a nation where they will not be judged by the color of their skin but by the content of their character. [*My Lord*] I have a dream today. [*Applause*]

I have a dream that one day down in Alabama, with its vicious racists, with its governor having his lips dripping with the words of "interposition" and "nullification" [*Yes*], one day right there in Alabama little black boys and black girls will be able to join hands with little white boys and white girls as sisters and brothers. I have a dream today. [*Applause*]

I have a dream that one day every valley shall be exalted [*Yes*], and every hill and mountain shall be made low; the rough places will be made plain, and the crooked places will be made straight [*Yes*]; and the glory of the Lord shall be revealed, and all flesh shall see it together. [*Yes*]

This is our hope. This is the faith that I go back to the South with. [*Yes*] With this faith we will be able to hew out of the mountain of despair a stone of hope. [*Yes*] With this faith we will be able to transform the jangling discords of our nation into a beautiful symphony of brotherhood. [*Talk about it*] With this faith [*My Lord*] we will be able to work together, to pray together, to struggle together, to go to jail together, to stand up for freedom together, knowing that we will be free one day. [*Applause*] This will be the day [*Applause continues*], this will be the day when all of God's children [*Yes*] will be able to sing with new meaning:

My country, 'tis of thee [*Yes*], sweet land of liberty, of thee I sing.

Land where my fathers died, land of the pilgrim's pride [*Yes*],

From every mountainside, let freedom ring!

And if America is to be a great nation, this must become true.

And so let freedom ring [*Yes*] from the prodigious hilltops of New Hampshire.

Let freedom ring from the mighty mountains of New York.

Let freedom ring from the heightening Alleghenies of Pennsylvania. [*Yes, That's right*]

Let freedom ring from the snowcapped Rockies of Colorado. [*Well*]

Let freedom ring from the curvaceous slopes of California. [*Yes*]

But not only that: Let freedom ring from Stone Mountain of Georgia. [*Yes*]

Let freedom ring from Lookout Mountain of Tennessee. [*Yes*]

Let freedom ring from every hill and molehill of Mississippi. [*Yes*]

From every mountainside, let freedom ring. [*Applause*]

And when this happens [*Applause continues*], when we allow freedom ring, when we let it ring from every village and every hamlet, from every state and every city [*Yes*], we will be able to speed up that day when all of God's children, black men and white men, Jews and Gentiles, Protestants and Catholics, will be able to join hands and sing in the words of the old Negro spiritual:

Free at last! [*Yes*] Free at last!

Thank God Almighty, we are free at last! [*Applause*]

JOHN LEWIS
(1940–)

We Must Free Ourselves
AUGUST 28, 1963

We will not wait for the President, the Justice Department, nor Congress, but we will take matters into our own hands.

John Lewis is one of the few leaders from the 1960s civil rights movement who remains an active and vocal force today. For more than forty years, he has been on the front lines of the struggle for equal opportunity in the United States, advancing the formation of what he calls "the Beloved Community."

Lewis was born the son of sharecroppers outside Troy, Alabama, where he was raised on a farm, and attended segregated public schools. Lewis found his calling in the civil rights movement as a student at American Baptist Theological Seminary. He participated in Freedom Rides, marches, and sit-ins, earning a reputation for his implacable commitment to nonviolent protest. Lewis's devotion to equal opportunity was sharpened by his participation in the Student Nonviolent Coordinating Committee (SNCC). Lewis quickly ascended the ranks of that organization, serving as its leader from 1963 until 1966. Lewis capitalized on his experience, and in 1981 was elected to the Atlanta city council. Five years later, he upset political favorite Julian Bond for a seat in the U.S. House of Representatives, in which he continues to serve today.

With millions watching live, within yards of the Lincoln Memorial or from their home televisions, Lewis delivered a version of this address at the historic March on Washington. Only minutes earlier, in arguably his most famous speech, Dr. Martin Luther King, Jr., delivered his "I Have a Dream" address.

Lewis, who represented the movement's "new guard," had planned to give a speech that was critical of the Kennedy Administration and of "old guard" incrimentalist tactics. Many, including King, argued that the march should serve as a sign of support for the civil rights legislation Kennedy had recently submitted to Congress. John Lewis disagreed. Despite protest from elder leaders—including Roy Wilkins, Patrick O'Boyle, and Walter Fauntroy—Lewis was determined to use his speech, and its "inflammatory tone," as an opportunity to criticize the president and vocalize the growing impatience among mainstream activists.

The heated conflict continued backstage until only moments before Lewis approached the rostrum. The elder leader A. Philip Randolph pleaded with Lewis one more time to temper his remarks. Lewis later recalled his words, "I've waited all my life for this opportunity. Please don't ruin it. We've come this far together. Let us stay together." Lewis reluctantly agreed.

The following text is the original, unedited version of Lewis's draft, not the speech he actually delivered.

WE MARCH TODAY for jobs and freedom, but we have nothing to be proud of. For hundreds and thousands of our brothers are not here. They have no money for their transportation, for they are receiving starvation wages . . . or no wages, at all.

In good conscience, we cannot support the administration's civil rights bill, for it is too little, and too late. There's not one thing in the bill that will protect our people from police brutality.

This bill will not protect young children and old women from police dogs and fire hoses, [for] engaging in peaceful demonstrations. . . .

The voting section of this bill will not help thousands of black citizens who want to vote. It will not help the citizens of Mississippi, of Alabama, and Georgia, who are qualified to vote, but lack a 6th Grade education. "One man, one vote," is the African cry. It is ours, too. (It must be ours.)

We are now involved in . . . revolution. This nation is still a place of cheap political leaders who build their careers on immoral compromise and ally themselves with open forms of political, economic and social exploitation. What political leader here can stand up and say, "My party is the party of principles"? The party of Kennedy is also the party of Eastland. The party of Javits is also the party of Goldwater. Where is *our* party?

In some parts of the South we work in the fields from sun-up to sun-down for $12 a week. In Albany, Georgia, nine of our leaders have been indicted not by Dixiecrats but by the Federal Government for peaceful protest. But what did the Federal Government do when Albany's Deputy Sheriff beat Attorney C. B. King and left him half dead? What did the Federal Government do when local police officials kicked and assaulted the pregnant wife of Slater King, and she lost her baby?

It seems to me that the Albany indictment is part of a conspiracy on the part of the Federal Government and local politicians in the interest of expediency.

I want to know, which side is the Federal Government on?

The revolution is at hand, and we must free ourselves of the chains of political and economic slavery. The non-violent revolution is saying, "We will not wait for the courts to act, for we have been waiting for hundreds of years. We will not wait for the President, the Justice Department, nor Congress, but we will take matters into our own hands and create a source of power, outside any national structure that could and would assure us a victory." To those who have said, "Be Patient and Wait," we must say that, "Patience is a dirty and nasty word." We cannot be patient, we do not want to be free gradually, we want our freedom, and we want it now. We cannot depend on any political party, for both the Democrats and the Republicans have betrayed the basic principles of the Declaration of Independence.

We all recognize the fact that if any radical social, political and economic changes are to take place in our society, the people, the masses, must bring them about. In the struggle we must seek more than civil rights; we must work for the community of love, peace and true brotherhood. Our minds, souls, and hearts cannot rest until freedom and justice exist for *all the people*.

The revolution is a serious one. Mr. Kennedy is trying to take the revolution out of the street and put it in the courts. Listen, Mr. Kennedy, listen, Mr. congressman, listen, fellow citizens, the black masses are on the march for jobs and freedom, and we must say to the politicians that there won't be a "cooling-off" period.

⌐

We won't stop now. All of the forces of Eastland, Barnett, Wallace, and Thurmond won't stop this revolution. The time will come when we will not confine our marching to Washington. We will march through the South, through the Heart of Dixie, the way Sherman did. We shall pursue our own "scorched earth" policy and burn Jim Crow to the ground—nonviolently. We shall fragment the South into a thousand pieces and put them back together in the image of democracy. We will make the action of the past few months look petty. And I say to you, WAKE UP AMERICA!

HOWARD "JUDGE" SMITH
(1883–1976)

Sex Discrimination in the Civil Rights Act
FEBRUARY 8, 1964

This amendment is offered . . . to prevent discrimination against
another minority group, the women, . . . in the absence of which
the majority group would not be here today.

Born in Broad Run, Virginia, Howard Worth Smith studied law, served
as a local judge, and was, from 1931 to 1967, one of the most influential
conservative Democrats in the U.S. Congress.

In January 1964, as the debate over what became the Civil Rights
Act heated up, Smith offered an amendment to the legislation, inserting
the word "sex" into the description of those groups protected under the
bill's Title VII employment provisions. This section explicitly prohibited
discrimination in employment on the basis of race, color, religion,
national origin—and now gender.

It is widely argued that Smith, a lifelong opponent of civil rights legislation, introduced the "sex" amendment to derail the bill's legitimacy
and ultimate passage. This tactic was not uncommon in Congress. In the
past, civil rights opponents had regularly used the amendment process to
dilute legislation. With that in mind, proponents of women's rights,
including those in the Johnson administration, opposed the amendment,
believing that it would "overburden the legislation" introduced to protect African-American civil rights. In fact, congresswoman and feminist
Martha Wright Griffiths later recalled that Smith admitted to her that
the amendment was indeed offered in jest. Even so, Smith argued
ardently for the amendment, claiming that white women deserved the
same protections as black women.

To the surprise of everyone, the "sex" amendment passed. By that
point, President Johnson and the women's groups realized that the
larger bill could pass with the "sex" addition; in turn, they stood firmly
behind the amendment.

In a speech from the House floor on February 8, 1964, excerpted
here from the *Congressional Record,* Smith highlighted his reasoning for
adding "sex" to the civil rights bill. Congressman Emanuel Celler from
New York, a strident proponent of the legislation, questioned Smith's

intentions and the legitimacy of his amendment, fearing that it would hinder passage of the bill and the rights of women.

———

MR. SMITH OF VIRGINIA. Mr. Chairman, this amendment is offered to the fair employment practices title of this bill to include within our desire to prevent discrimination against another minority group, the women, but a very essential minority group, in the absence of which the majority group would not be here today.

Now, I am very serious about this amendment. It has been offered several times before, but it was offered at inappropriate places in the bill. Now, this is the appropriate place for this amendment to come in. I do not think it can do any harm to this legislation; maybe it can do some good. I think it will do some good for the minority sex.

I think we all recognize and it is indisputable fact that all throughout industry women are discriminated against in that just generally speaking they do not get as high compensation for their work as do the majority sex. Now, if that is true, I hope that the committee chairman will accept this amendment. . . .

I want to read you an extract from a letter that I received the other day. This lady has a real grievance on behalf of the minority sex. She said that she had seen that I was going to present an amendment to protect the most important sex, and she says:

> I suggest that you might also favor an amendment or a bill to correct the present "imbalance" which exists between males and females in the United States.
>
> Just why the Creator would set up such an imbalance of spinsters, shutting off the "right" of every female to have a husband of her own, is, of course, known only to nature.
>
> But I am sure you will agree that this is a grave injustice—

And I do agree, and I am reading you the letter because I want all the rest of you to agree, you of the majority—

> But I am sure you will agree that this is a grave injustice to womankind and something the Congress and President Johnson should take immediate steps to correct—

I am serious about this thing. I just hope that the committee will accept it. Now, what harm can you do this bill that was so perfect yesterday and is so imperfect today—what harm will this do to the condition of the bill?

⟜

Mr. CELLER. Mr. Chairman, I rise in opposition to the amendment.

Mr. SMITH of Virginia. Oh, no.

Mr. CELLER. Mr. Chairman, I heard with a great deal of interest the statement of the gentleman from Virginia that women are in the minority. Not in my house. I can say as a result of 49 years of experience—and I celebrate my 50th wedding anniversary next year—that women, indeed, are not in the minority in my house. As a matter of fact, the reason I would suggest that we have been living in such harmony, such delightful accord for almost half a century is that I usually have the last two words, and those words are, "Yes, dear." Of course, we all remember the famous play by George Bernard Shaw, "Man and Superman"; and man was not the superman, the other sex was.

⟜

. . . At first blush it seems fair, just, and equitable to grant these equal rights. But when you examine carefully what the import and repercussions are concerning equal rights throughout American life, and all facets of American life you run into a considerable amount of difficulty.

You will find that there are in the equality of sex that some people glibly assert, and without reason, serious problems. I have been reluctant as chairman of the Committee on the Judiciary to give favorable consideration to that constitutional amendment.

⟜

Imagine the upheaval that would result from adoption of blanket language requiring total equality. Would male citizens be justified in insisting that women share with them the burdens of compulsory military service? What would become of traditional family relationships? What about alimony? Who would have the obligation of supporting whom? Would fathers rank equally with mothers in the right of custody to children? What would become of the crimes of rape and statutory rape? Would the Mann Act be invalidated? Would the many State and local provisions regulating working conditions and hours of employment for women be struck down?

You know the biological differences between the sexes. In many States we have laws favorable to women. Are you going to strike those laws down? This is the entering wedge, an amendment of this sort. The list of foreseeable consequences, I will say to the committee, is unlimited.

What is more, even conceding that some degree of discrimination against women obtains in the area of employment, it is contrary to the situation with respect to civil rights for Negroes. Real and genuine progress is being made in discrimination against women. . . .

It is a little surprising to find the gentleman from Virginia offering the language he does offer as an amendment to the pending measure. The House knows that this is the language of a proposed constitutional amendment introduced in the House.

~

It is rather anomalous that two men of our age should be on the opposite sides of this question.

Mr. SMITH of Virginia. I am sure we are not. But I know the gentleman is under obligation not to submit any amendments other than those that are agreed upon between the coalition of the Republicans and Democrats that is controlling the movement of the committee. I wanted to ask the gentleman to clarify what he said. I did not exactly get what he stated about Negroes. He said he was surprised.

Mr. CELLER. I was a little surprised at your offering the amendment.

Mr. SMITH of Virginia. About what?

Mr. CELLER. Because I think the amendment seems illogical, ill timed, ill placed, and improper. I was of that opinion, the amendment coming from the astute and very wise gentleman from Virginia.

Mr. SMITH of Virginia. Your surprise at my offering the amendment does not nearly approach my surprise, amazement, and sorrow at your opposition to it.

MALCOLM X
(1925–1965)

The Ballot or the Bullet
APRIL 3, 1964

*I'm speaking as a victim of this American system.
And I see America through the eyes of the victim. I don't see
any American dream; I see an American nightmare.*

Born Malcolm Little, Malcolm X was raised in a hard-pressed Michigan family. He graduated from junior high school at the top of his class, only to lose interest after a favorite teacher told him that his dream of becoming a lawyer was "no realistic goal for a nigger." After the Ku Klux Klan murdered his father, Malcolm went to work as a small-time hustler and drug dealer.

In 1946, while imprisoned for robbery, Malcolm X converted to the Black Muslim faith and, within years of his release, rose up the ranks as a minister in the Nation of Islam. He claimed that his new name, "Malcolm X," embodied his life: ex-drinker, ex-Christian, ex-smoker, ex-slave; the "X" signified his lost tribal name. "Malcolm Little," in contrast, was nothing more than a slave name.

Under the tutelage of Elijah Muhammad, the flamboyant Nation of Islam minister and propagator of black separatism, Malcolm quickly became the leading voice of black nationalism. He achieved national prominence when a fissure developed in the civil rights movement between traditional leaders, who favored integration, and the new guard, who advocated separatism as the true means toward equality.

In his travels across the country, Malcolm preached vengeance against the "white devil," advocating a mixture of violence, independence, and black pride. He successfully used newspaper columns, radio, and television to communicate these ideas and the tenets of the Nation of Islam. His conviction, charisma, and drive added to his allure, attracting an astounding number of new members to the organization.

As Malcolm X's popularity grew, leaders in the Nation of Islam, including Elijah Muhammad, felt threatened to the point that they organized an effort to expel him. Malcolm was eventually silenced by Muhammad for his inappropriate comment on the assassination of President John F. Kennedy. (Kennedy "never foresaw that the chickens would come home to roost so soon.") In retaliation, Malcolm left the Nation to form his own Muslim organization.

Shortly after the split, Malcolm X delivered this speech, often considered his most famous, to the Cory Methodist Church in Cleveland, Ohio. At the event, sponsored by the Congress of Racial Equality, he decried the white political leadership, including liberal Democrats, for its failure to sufficiently help African Americans. Repeating the mantra "black is beautiful," he urged blacks to promote separatism and violent aggression, and to embrace his revolutionary approach.

———

IF WE DON'T DO SOMETHING real soon, I think you'll have to agree that we're going to be forced either to use the ballot or the bullet. It's one or the other in 1964. It isn't that time is running out—time has run out! 1964 threatens to be the most explosive year America has ever witnessed. The most explosive year. Why? It's also a political year. It's the year when all of the white politicians will be back in the so-called Negro community jiving you and me for some votes. The year when all of the white political crooks will be right back in your and my community with their false promises, building up our hopes for a letdown, with their trickery and their treachery, with their false promises which they don't intend to keep. As they nourish these dissatisfactions, it can only lead to one thing, an explosion; and now we have the type of black man on the scene in America today . . . who just doesn't intend to turn the other cheek any longer.

———

No, I'm not an American. I'm one of the twenty-two million black people who are the victims of Americanism. One of the twenty-two million black people who are the victims of democracy, nothing but disguised hypocrisy. So, I'm not standing here speaking to you as an American, or a patriot, or a flag-saluter, or a flag-waver—no, not I. I'm speaking as a victim of this American system. And I see America through the eyes of the victim. I don't see any American dream; I see an American nightmare.

———

In this present administration they have in the House of Representatives 257 Democrats to only 177 Republicans. They control two-thirds of the House vote. Why can't they pass something that will help you and me? In the Senate, there are 67 senators who are of the Democratic Party. Only 33 of them are Republicans. Why, the Democrats have got the government sewed up, and you're the one who sewed it up for them. And what have they given you for it? Four years in office, and just now getting around to some civil rights leg-islation. Just now, after everything else is gone, out of the way, they're going to sit down now and play with you all summer long—the same old giant con game that they call filibuster. All those are in cahoots together. Don't you ever think they're not in cahoots together, for the man that is heading the civil rights filibuster is a man from Georgia named Richard Russell. When Johnson became president, the first man he asked for when he got back to Washington, D.C., was "Dicky"—that's how tight they are. That's his boy, that's his pal, that's his buddy. But they're playing that old con game. One of them makes believe he's for you, and he's got it fixed where the other one is so tight against you, he never has to keep his promise.

So it's time in 1964 to wake up. And when you see them coming up with that kind of conspiracy, let them know your eyes are open. And let them know you got something else that's wide open too. It's got to be the ballot or the bullet. The ballot or the bullet. If you're afraid to use an expression like that, you should get on out of the country, you should get back in the cotton patch, you should get back in the alley. They get all the Negro vote, and after they get it, the Negro gets nothing in return. All they did when they got to Washington was give a few big Negroes big jobs. Those big Negroes didn't need big jobs, they already had jobs. That's camouflage, that's trickery, that's treachery, window-dressing. I'm not trying to knock out the Democrats for the Republicans, we'll get to them in a minute. But it is true—you put the Democrats first and the Democrats put you last.

Look at it the way it is. What alibis do they use, since they control Congress and the Senate? What alibi do they use when you and I ask, "Well, when are you going to keep your promise?" They blame the Dixiecrats. What is a Dixiecrat? A Democrat. A Dixiecrat is nothing but a Democrat in disguise. The titular head of the Democrats is also the head of the Dixiecrats, because the Dixiecrats are a part of the Democratic Party. The Democrats have never kicked the Dixiecrats out of the party. The Dixiecrats bolted themselves once, but the Democrats didn't put them out. Imagine, these lowdown Southern segrega-tionists put the Northern Democrats down. But the Northern Democrats have never put the Dixiecrats down. No, look at that thing the way it is. They have got a con game going on, a political con game, and you and I are in the mid-dle. It's time for you and me to wake up and start looking at it like it is, and trying to understand it like it is; and then we can deal with it like it is.

The Dixiecrats in Washington, D.C., control the key committees that run the government. The only reason the Dixiecrats control these committees is because they have seniority. The only reason they have seniority is because they come from states where Negroes can't vote. This is not even a govern-ment that's based on democracy. It is not a government that is made up of rep-resentatives of the people. Half of the people in the South can't even vote.

Eastland is not even supposed to be in Washington. Half of the senators and congressmen who occupy these key positions in Washington, D.C., are there illegally, are there unconstitutionally.

These senators and congressmen actually violate the constitutional amendments that guarantee the people of that particular state or county the right to vote. And the Constitution itself has within it the machinery to expel any representative from a state where the voting rights of the people are violated. You don't even need new legislation. Any person in Congress right now, who is there from a state or a district where the voting rights of the people are violated, that particular person should be expelled from Congress. And when you expel him, you've removed one of the obstacles in the path of any real meaningful legislation in this country. In fact, when you expel them, you don't need new legislation, because they will be replaced by black representatives from counties and districts where the black man is in the majority, not in the minority.

If the black man in these Southern states had his full voting rights, the key Dixiecrats in Washington, D.C., which means the key Democrats in Washington, D.C., would lose their seats. The Democratic Party itself would lose its power. It would cease to be powerful as a party. When you see the amount of power that would be lost by the Democratic Party if it were to lose the Dixiecrat wing, or branch, or element, you can see where it's against the interests of the Democrats to give voting rights to Negroes in states where the Democrats have been in complete power and authority ever since the Civil War. You just can't belong to that party without analyzing it.

I say again, I'm not anti-Democrat, I'm not anti-Republican, I'm not anti-anything. I'm just questioning their sincerity, and some of the strategy that they've been using on our people by promising them promises that they don't intend to keep. When you keep the Democrats in power, you're keeping the Dixiecrats in power. . . . A vote for a Democrat is a vote for a Dixiecrat. That's why, in 1964, it's time now for you and me to become more politically mature and realize what the ballot is for, what we're supposed to get when we cast a ballot; and that if we don't cast a ballot, it's going to end up in a situation where we're going to have to cast a bullet. It's either a ballot or a bullet.

In the North, they do it a different way. They have a system that's known as gerrymandering, whatever that means. It means when Negroes become too heavily concentrated in a certain area, and begin to gain too much political power, the white man comes along and changes the district lines. You may say, "Why do you keep saying white man?" Because it's the white man who does it. I haven't ever seen any Negro changing any lines. They don't let him get near the line. It's the white man who does this. And usually, it's the white man who grins at you the most, and pats you on the back, and is supposed to be your friend. He may be friendly, but he's not your friend.

So, what I'm trying to impress upon you, in essence, is this: You and I in America are faced not with a segregationist conspiracy, we're faced with a government conspiracy. Everyone who's filibustering is a senator—that's the government. Everyone who's finagling in Washington, D.C., is a congressman—that's the government. You don't have anybody putting blocks in your path but people who are a part of the government. The same government that you go abroad to fight for and die for is the government that is in a conspiracy to deprive you of your voting rights, deprive you of your economic opportunities, deprive you of decent housing, deprive you of decent education. You don't need to go to the employer alone, it is the government itself, the government of America, that is responsible for the oppression and exploitation and degradation of black people in this country. And you should drop it in their lap. This government has failed the Negro. This so-called democracy has failed the Negro. And all these white liberals have definitely failed the Negro.

So, where do we go from here? First, we need some friends. We need some new allies. The entire civil rights struggle needs a new interpretation, a broader interpretation. We need to look at this civil rights thing from another angle—from the inside as well as from the outside. To those of us whose philosophy is black nationalism, the only way you can get involved in the civil rights struggle is give it a new interpretation. That old interpretation excluded us. It kept us out. So, we're giving a new interpretation to the civil rights struggle, an interpretation that will enable us to come into it, take part in it. And these handkerchief-heads who have been dillydallying and pussyfooting and compromising—we don't intend to let them pussyfoot and dillydally and compromise any longer.

How can you thank a man for giving you what's already yours? How then can you thank him for giving you only part of what's already yours? You haven't even made progress, if what's being given to you, you should have had already. That's not progress. . . . We're behind where we were in 1954. There's more segregation now than there was in 1954. There's more racial animosity, more racial hatred, more racial violence today in 1964, than there was in 1954. Where is the progress?

And now you're facing a situation where the young Negro's coming up. They don't want to hear that "turn-the-other-cheek" stuff, no. In Jacksonville, those were teenagers, they were throwing Molotov cocktails. Negroes have never done that before. But it shows you there's a new deal coming in. There's new thinking coming in. There's new strategy coming in. It'll be Molotov cocktails this month, hand grenades next month, and something else next month. It'll be ballots, or it'll be bullets. It'll be liberty, or it will be death. The only difference about this kind of death—it'll be reciprocal. You know what is meant by "reciprocal"? That's one of Brother Lomax's words, I stole it from him. I don't usually deal with those big words because I don't usually deal with big people. I deal with small people. I find you can get a whole lot of small people and whip hell out of a whole lot of big people. They haven't got anything to lose, and they've got everything to gain. And they'll let you know in a minute: "It takes two to tango; when I go, you go."

The black nationalists, those whose philosophy is black nationalism, in bringing about this new interpretation of the entire meaning of civil rights, look upon it as meaning, as Brother Lomax has pointed out, equality of opportunity. Well, we're justified in seeking civil rights, if it means equality of opportunity, because all we're doing there is trying to collect for our investment. Our mothers and fathers invested sweat and blood. Three hundred and ten years we worked in this country without a dime in return—I mean without a dime in return. You let the white man walk around here talking about how rich this country is, but you never stop to think how it got rich so quick. It got rich because you made it rich.

You take the people who are in this audience right now. They're poor, we're all poor as individuals. Our weekly salary individually amounts to hardly anything. But if you take the salary of everyone in here collectively it'll fill up a whole lot of baskets. It's a lot of wealth. If you can collect the wages of just these people right here for a year, you'll be rich—richer than rich. When you look at it like that, think how rich Uncle Sam had to become, not with this handful, but millions of black people. Your and my mother and father, who didn't work an eight-hour shift, but worked from "can't see" in the morning until "can't see" at night, and worked for nothing, making the white man rich, making Uncle Sam rich.

This is our investment. This is our contribution—our blood. Not only did we give of our free labor, we gave of our blood. Every time he had a call to arms, we were the first ones in uniform. We died on every battlefield the white man had. We have made a greater sacrifice than anybody who's standing up in America today. We have made a greater contribution and have collected less. Civil rights, for those of us whose philosophy is black nationalism, means: "Give it to us now. Don't wait for next year. Give it to us yesterday, and that's not fast enough."

I might stop right here to point out one thing. Whenever you're going after something that belongs to you, anyone who's depriving you of the right to have it is a criminal. Understand that. Whenever you are going after something that is yours, you are within your legal rights to lay claim to it. And anyone who puts forth any effort to deprive you of that which is yours, is breaking the law, is a criminal. And this was pointed out by the Supreme Court decision. It outlawed segregation. Which means segregation is against the law. Which means a segregationist is breaking the law. A segregationist is a criminal. You can't label him as anything other than that. And when you demonstrate against segregation, the law is on your side. The Supreme Court is on your side.

Now, who is it that opposes you in carrying out the law? The police department itself. With police dogs and clubs. Whenever you demonstrate against segregation, whether it is segregated education, segregated housing, or anything else, the law is on your side, and anyone who stands in the way is not the law any longer. They are breaking the law, they are not representatives of the law. Any time you demonstrate against segregation and a man has the audacity to put a police dog on you, kill that dog, kill him, I'm telling you, kill that dog. I say it, if they put me in jail tomorrow, kill—that—dog. Then you'll put a stop to it. Now, if these white people in here don't want to see that kind of action, get down and tell the mayor to tell the police department to pull the dogs in. That's all you have to do. If you don't do it, someone else will.

If you don't take this kind of stand, your little children will grow up and look at you and think "shame." If you don't take an uncompromising stand— I don't mean go out and get violent; but at the same time you should never be nonviolent unless you run into some nonviolence. I'm nonviolent with those who are nonviolent with me. But when you drop that violence on me, then you've made me go insane, and I'm not responsible for what I do. And that's the way every Negro should get. Any time you know you're within the law, within your legal rights, within your moral rights, in accord with justice, then die for what you believe in. But don't die alone. Let your dying be reciprocal. This is what is meant by equality. What's good for the goose is good for the gander.

When we begin to get in this area, we need new friends, we need new allies. We need to expand the civil rights struggle to a higher level—to the level of human rights. Whenever you are in a civil rights struggle, whether you know it or not, you are confining yourself to the jurisdiction of Uncle Sam. No one from the outside world can speak out in your behalf as long as your struggle is a civil rights struggle. Civil rights comes within the domestic affairs of this country. All of our African brothers and our Asian brothers and our Latin American brothers cannot open their mouths and interfere in the domestic affairs of the United States. And as long as it's civil rights, this comes under the jurisdiction of Uncle Sam.

But the United Nations has what's known as the charter of human rights; it has a committee that deals in human rights. You may wonder why all of the atrocities that have been committed in Africa and in Hungary and in Asia and in Latin America are brought before the UN, and the Negro problem is never brought before the UN. This is part of the conspiracy. . . . They keep you wrapped up in civil rights. And you spend so much time barking up the civil rights tree, you don't even know there's a human rights tree on the same floor.

When you expand the civil rights struggle to the level of human rights, you can then take the case of the black man in this country before the nations in the UN. You can take it before the General Assembly. You can take Uncle Sam before a world court. But the only level you can do it on is the level of human rights. Civil rights keeps you under his restrictions, under his jurisdiction. Civil rights keeps you in his pocket. Civil rights means you're asking Uncle Sam to treat you right. Human rights are something you were born with. Human rights are your God-given rights. Human rights are the rights that are recognized by all nations of this earth. And any time any one violates your human rights, you can take them to the world court. Uncle Sam's hands are dripping with blood, dripping with the blood of the black man in this country. He's the earth's number-one hypocrite. He has the audacity—yes, he has—imagine him posing as the leader of the free world. The free world!—and you over here singing "We Shall Overcome." Expand the civil rights struggle to the level of human rights, take it into the United Nations, where our African brothers can throw their weight on our side, where our Asian brothers can throw their weight on our side, where our Latin American brothers can throw their weight on our side, and where eight hundred million Chinamen are sitting there waiting to throw their weight on our side.

Let the world know how bloody his hands are. Let the world know the hypocrisy that's practiced over here. Let it be the ballot or the bullet. Let him know that it must be the ballot or the bullet.

When you take your case to Washington, D.C., you're taking it to the criminal who's responsible; it's like running from the wolf to the fox. They're all in cahoots together. They all work political chicanery and make you look like a chump before the eyes of the world. Here you are walking around in America, getting ready to be drafted and sent abroad, like a tin soldier, and when you get over there, people ask you what are you fighting for, and you have to stick your tongue in your cheek. No, take Uncle Sam to court, take him before the world.

By ballot I only mean freedom. Don't you know—I disagree with Lomax on this issue—that the ballot is more important than the dollar? Can I prove it? Yes. Look in the UN. There are poor nations in the UN; yet those poor nations can get together with their voting power and keep the rich nations from making a move. They have one nation—one vote, everyone has an equal vote. And when those brothers from Asia and Africa and the darker parts of this earth get together, their voting power is sufficient to hold Sam in check Or Russia in check. Or some other section of the earth in check. So, the ballot is most important.

Right now, in this country, if you and I, twenty-two million African Americans—that's what we are—Africans who are in America. You're nothing but Africans. Nothing but Africans. In fact, you'd get farther calling yourself African instead of Negro. Africans don't catch hell. You're the only one catching hell. They don't have to pass civil rights bills for Africans. An African can go anywhere he wants right now. All you've got to do is tie your head up. That's right, go anywhere you want. Just stop being a Negro. Change your name to Hoogagagooba. That'll show you how silly the white man is. You're dealing with a silly man. A friend of mine who's very dark put a turban on his head and went into a restaurant in Atlanta before they called themselves desegregated. He went into a white restaurant, he sat down, they served him, and he said, "What would happen if a Negro came in here?" And there he's sitting, black as night, but because he had his head wrapped up the waitress looked back at him and says, "Why, there wouldn't no nigger dare come in here."

So, you're dealing with a man whose bias and prejudice are making him lose his mind, his intelligence, every day. He's frightened. He looks around and sees what's taking place on this earth, and he sees that the pendulum of time is swinging in your direction. The dark people are waking up. They're losing their fear of the white man. No place where he's fighting right now is he winning. Everywhere he's fighting, he's fighting someone your and my complexion. And they're beating him. He can't win any more. He's won his last battle. He failed to win the Korean War. He couldn't win it. He had to sign a truce. That's a loss. Any time Uncle Sam, with all his machinery for warfare, is held to a draw by some rice-eaters, he's lost the battle. He had to sign a truce. America's not supposed to sign a truce. She's supposed to be bad. But she's not bad any more. She's bad as long as she can use her hydrogen bomb, but she can't use hers for fear Russia might use hers. Russia can't use hers, for fear that Sam might use his. So, both of them are weaponless. They can't use the weapon because each's weapon nullifies the other's. So the only place where action can take place is on the ground. And the white man can't win another war fighting on the ground. Those days are over. The black man knows it, the brown man knows it, the red man knows it, and the yellow man knows it. So they engage him in guerrilla warfare. That's not his style. You've got to have heart to be a guerrilla warrior, and he hasn't got any heart. I'm telling you now.

The political philosophy of black nationalism means that the black man should control the politics and the politicians in his own community; no more. The black man in the black community has to be re-educated into the science of politics so he will know what politics is supposed to bring him in return. Don't be throwing out any ballots. A ballot is like a bullet. You don't throw your ballots until you see a target, and if that target is not within your reach, keep your ballot in your pocket. The political philosophy of black nationalism is being taught in the Christian church. It's being taught in the NAACP. It's being taught in CORE meetings. It's being taught in SNCC meetings. It's being taught in Muslim meetings. It's being taught where nothing but atheists and agnostics come together. It's being taught everywhere. Black people are fed up with the dillydallying, pussyfooting, compromising approach that we've been using toward getting our freedom. We want freedom now, but we're not going to get it saying "We Shall Overcome." We've got to fight until we over-come.

The economic philosophy of black nationalism is pure and simple. It only means that we should control the economy of our community. Why should white people be running all the stores in our community? Why should white people be running the banks of our community? Why should the economy of our community be in the hands of the white man? Why? If a black man can't move his store into a white community, you tell me why a white man should move his store into a black community. The philosophy of black nationalism involves a reeducation program in the black community in regards to economics. Our people have to be made to see that any time you take your dollar out of your community and spend it in a community where you don't live, the community where you live will get poorer and poorer, and the community where you spend your money will get richer and richer. Then you wonder why where you live is always a ghetto or a slum area. And where you and I are concerned, not only do we lose it when we spend it out of the community, but the white man has got all our stores in the community tied up; so that though we spend it in the community, at sundown the man who runs the store takes it over across town somewhere. He's got us in a vise.

So the economic philosophy of black nationalism means in every church, in every civic organization, in every fraternal order, it's time now for our people to become conscious of the importance of controlling the economy of our community. If we own the stores, if we operate the businesses, if we try and establish some industry in our own community, then we're developing to the position where we are creating employment for our own kind. Once you gain control of the economy of your own community, then you don't have to picket and boycott and beg some cracker downtown for a job in his business.

The social philosophy of black nationalism only means that we have to get together and remove the evils, the vices, alcoholism, drug addiction, and other evils that are destroying the moral fiber of our community. We ourselves have to lift the level of our community, the standard of our community to a higher level, make our own society beautiful so that we will be satisfied in our own social circles and won't be running around here trying to knock our way into a social circle where we're not wanted.

So I say, in spreading a gospel such as black nationalism, it is not designed to make the black man re-evaluate the white man—you know him already—but to make the black man re-evaluate himself. Don't change the white man's mind—you can't change his mind, and that whole thing about appealing to the moral conscience of America—America's conscience is bankrupt. She lost all conscience a long time ago. Uncle Sam has no conscience. They don't know what morals are. They don't try and eliminate an evil because it's evil, or because it's illegal, or because it's immoral; they eliminate it only when it threatens their existence. So you're wasting your time appealing to the moral conscience of a bankrupt man like Uncle Sam. If he had a conscience, he'd straighten this thing out with no more pressure being put upon him. So it is not necessary to change the white man's mind. We have to change our own mind. You can't change his mind about us. We've got to change our own minds about each other. We have to see each other with new eyes. We have to see each other as brothers and sisters. We have to come together with warmth so we can develop unity and harmony that's necessary to get this problem solved ourselves. How can we do this? How can we avoid jealousy? How can we avoid the suspicion and the divisions that exist in the community? I'll tell you how.

Our gospel is black nationalism. We're not trying to threaten the existence of any organization, but we're spreading the gospel of black nationalism. Anywhere there's a church that is also preaching and practicing the gospel of black nationalism, join that church. If the NAACP is preaching and practicing the gospel of black nationalism, join the NAACP. If CORE is spreading and practicing the gospel of black nationalism, join CORE. Join any organization that has a gospel that's for the uplift of the black man. And when you get into it and see them pussyfooting or compromising, pull out of it because that's not black nationalism. We'll find another one.

It's time for you and me to stop sitting in this country, letting some cracker senators, Northern crackers and Southern crackers, sit there in Washington, D.C., and come to a conclusion in their mind that you and I are supposed to have civil rights. There's no white man going to tell me anything about my rights. Brothers and sisters, always remember, if it doesn't take senators and congressmen and presidential proclamations to give freedom to the white man, it is not necessary for legislation or proclamation or Supreme Court decisions to give freedom to the black man. You let that white man know, if this is a country of freedom, let it be a country of freedom; and if it's not a country of freedom, change it.

We will work with anybody, anywhere, at any time, who is genuinely interested in tackling the problem head-on, nonviolently as long as the enemy is nonviolent, but violent when the enemy gets violent. We'll work with you on the voter-registration drive, we'll work with you on rent strikes, we'll work with you on school boycotts—I don't believe in any kind of integration; I'm not even worried about it because I know you're not going to get it anyway;

you're not going to get it because you're afraid to die; you've got to be ready to die if you try and force yourself on the white man, because he'll get just as violent as those crackers in Mississippi, right here in Cleveland. But we will still work with you on the school boycotts because we're against a segregated school system. A segregated school system produces children who, when they graduate, graduate with crippled minds. But this does not mean that a school is segregated because it's all black. A segregated school means a school that is controlled by people who have no real interest in it whatsoever.

. . . When you're under someone else's control, you're segregated. They'll always give you the lowest or the worst that there is to offer, but it doesn't mean you're segregated just because you have your own. You've got to control your own. Just like the white man has control of his, you need to control yours.

You know the best way to get rid of segregation? The white man is more afraid of separation than he is of integration. Segregation means that he puts you away from him, but not far enough for you to be out of his jurisdiction; separation means you're gone. And the white man will integrate faster than he'll let you separate. So we will work with you against the segregated school system because it's criminal, because it is absolutely destructive, in every way imaginable, to the minds of the children who have to be exposed to that type of crippling education.

Last but not least, I must say this concerning the great controversy over rifles and shotguns. The only thing that I've ever said is that in areas where the government has proven itself either unwilling or unable to defend the lives and the property of Negroes, it's time for Negroes to defend themselves. Article number two of the constitutional amendments provides you and me the right to own a rifle or a shotgun. It is constitutionally legal to own a shotgun or a rifle. This doesn't mean you're going to get a rifle and form battalions and go out looking for white folks, although you'd be within your rights—I mean, you'd be justified; but that would be illegal and we don't do anything illegal. If the white man doesn't want the black man buying rifles and shotguns, then let the government do its job. That's all. And don't let the white man come to you and ask you what you think about what Malcolm says—why, you old Uncle Tom. He would never ask you if he thought you were going to say, "Amen!" No he is making a Tom out of you.

So, this doesn't mean forming rifle clubs and going out looking for people, but it is time, in 1964, if you are a man, to let that man know. If he's not going to do his job in running the government and providing you and me with the protection that our taxes are supposed to be for, since he spends all those billions for his defense budget, he certainly can't begrudge you and me spending $12 or $15 for a single-shot, or double-action. I hope you understand. Don't go out shooting people, but any time, brothers and sisters, and especially the men in this audience—some of you wearing Congressional Medals of Honor, with shoulders this wide, chests this big, muscles that big— any time you and I sit around and read where they bomb a church and mur- der in cold blood, not some grownups, but four little girls while they were praying to the same god the white man taught them to pray to, and you and I see the government go down and can't find who did it.

Why, this man—he can find Eichmann hiding down in Argentina some- where. Let two or three American soldiers, who are minding somebody else's business way over in South Vietnam, get killed, and he'll send battleships, stick- ing his nose in their business. He wanted to send troops down to Cuba and make them have what he calls free elections—this old cracker who doesn't have free elections in his own country. No, if you never see me another time in your life, if I die in the morning, I'll die saying one thing: the ballot or the bullet, the ballot or the bullet.

If a Negro in 1964 has to sit around and wait for some cracker senator to filibuster when it comes to the rights of black people, why, you and I should hang our heads in shame. You talk about a march on Washington in 1963, you haven't seen anything. There's some more going down in '64. And this time they're not going like they went last year. They're not going singing "We Shall Overcome." They're not going with white friends. They're not going with placards already painted for them. They're not going with round-trip tickets. They're going with one-way tickets.

And if they don't want that non-nonviolent army going down there, tell them to bring the filibuster to a halt. The black nationalists aren't going to wait. Lyndon B. Johnson is the head of the Democratic Party. If he's for civil rights, let him go into the Senate next week and declare himself. Let him go in there right now and declare himself. Let him go in there and denounce the Southern branch of his party. Let him go in there right now and take a moral stand—right now, not later. Tell him, don't wait until election time. If he waits too long, brothers and sisters, he will be responsible for letting a condition develop in this country which will create a climate that will bring seeds up out of the ground with vegetation on the end of them looking like some- thing these people never dreamed of. In 1964, it's the ballot or the bullet. Thank you.

Martin Luther King, Jr.
(1929–1968)

A Long, Long Way to Go
January 25, 1965

There are dark moments in this struggle, but . . . often the darkest
hour . . . appears before the dawn of a new fulfillment.

Although six months earlier Lyndon B. Johnson had signed the 1964
Civil Rights Act guaranteeing equal opportunity for minorities, in
truth, as the president himself emphasized, it "was only the beginning
of a new day . . . not the end of a journey." African Americans were still
at the bottom of the economic ladder, living in poverty, and largely
excluded from public office. Most glaringly, despite all federal action to
date, an alarming number of blacks remained locked out of voting
booths across the South. That, more than anything, drew Martin Luther
King, Jr., to Selma, Alabama, in January 1965 to join others in beginning what would be a seven-month protest of the harassment, intimidation, and arrest of blacks attempting to register to vote.

Selma had long been a hotbed of racial apartheid, and those in power
were not interested in yielding to federal law, outside pressure, or the
direct protest of African Americans. Dallas County's population was
almost 60 percent African American, yes in 1965, because the county had
resisted a federal court injunction to end voter discrimination, only 335
of the 10,000 registered voters were black. African Americans could register only after completing a form with more than fifty blanks, including writing passages and complex questions about the Constitution and
federal government. As part of an ongoing campaign, every morning
hundreds of blacks lined up outside the Dallas County Courthouse and
attempted to register to vote. By day's end, usually less than a dozen were
given the voting test. The intimidation didn't stop there. To keep pro-
tester organization to a minimum, the mayor obtained a court order
providing that no one "outside the [voting] line" could "interfere . . .
[or] even talk to . . . those in the line."

On January 25, 1965, Jim Clark, the billy club–wielding sheriff of
Dallas County, accosted Dr. King when he "stepped close to the line,"
provoking several protesters, including Annie Lee Cooper, an African-
American woman waiting to register. When Cooper lunged out of line
to protect King, Sheriff Clark and three other police officers "over-

powered" her with their nightsticks, repeatedly clubbing and kicking her as she lay prostrate on the street. After charging her with assault, the sheriff reported to the press that he had been "smashed in the face," causing a "reddened and swelled left eye."

That evening King, with thunder in his voice, delivered this address to a restless crowd of nearly 1,000. With Rev. Ralph David Abernathy at his side, he urged activists in Selma to remain committed to nonviolent protest and continue their registration drive and stand against segregation. Drawing on a familiar refrain, Dr. King reminded his compatriots that the struggle for civil rights would be a "long one," but "morning" would come soon enough. Seven months later, after a bloody march from Selma to Montgomery, Congress passed the Voting Rights Act of 1965.

In describing the progress of Dr. King, historian Gary Wills wrote, "The orator's first test is his ability to create heroes in response to his call. The orator's final test is his ability to create heroism in himself to match what he has been preaching."

King biographer Taylor Branch supplied these remarks from a police surveillance tape; this is their first time in print.

THANK YOU SO MUCH, MY DEAR FRIENDS. . . .

It's great to be back with you and to see you tonight in such large numbers and with such overflowing enthusiasm. You will remember that it was on a beautiful afternoon in June of 1963 that a brilliant, dedicated, youthful president appeared on television and spoke to our nation in eloquent terms. He said the civil rights issue is not merely a political issue, it is not merely a matter of economics, it is at bottom a moral issue. He went on to say it is as old as the Scriptures. And as modern as the Constitution. It is a question of whether we will treat our Negro brothers as we ourselves would like to be treated.

On the heels of that eloquent speech, that great young president went and offered to the Congress of our United States the most comprehensive civil rights bill we've had in our nation.

Not too many months after that, our nation experienced a dark and desolate night. Even though it was afternoon, it was still midnight. That same young president was cut down by an assassin's bullet on Elm Street in Dallas, Texas. But after months of debate and at points months of delay, that civil rights bill was passed, and it will remain an eternal tribute to the memory and the work and the vision of President John F. Kennedy. [*Applause*]

It was on the second of July that President Johnson signed that bill into law, last year. But the interesting thing is that many people felt that after the passage of the civil rights bill, we had accomplished everything. We didn't have anything else to do. There were some people who thought that the civil rights organizations could now go out of business because the millennium had come. Some unforeseen utopia had developed on the American shores, and that we would miraculously move into a new era of freedom.

But when we opened our eyes, we came to see that the civil rights bill, as marvelous as it is, is only the beginning of a new day and not the end of a journey. [*Applause*]

If this bill is not implemented in all of its dimensions, it will mean nothing, and all of its eloquent words will be as sounding brass on a tinkling cymbal. We must take this bill and lift it from thin paper to thick action. And go all out all over this nation to implement it.

So I come to you tonight to remind you once more that we still have a long, long way to go. Even though we have a civil rights bill, the Negro is still at the bottom of the economic ladder. Even though we have a civil rights bill, the Negro is still smothering in an air-tight cage of poverty in the midst of an affluent society. Even though we have a civil rights bill, our little children still grow up with clouds of inferiority in their little mental skies. Even though we have a civil rights bill, the Negro is still confined to slums and ghettoes. Even though we have a civil rights bill, 83 percent of the Negro families of Selma, Alabama still earn less than $2,000 a year. We still have a long, long way to go. [*Applause*]

Now, the way we're going to change these things, the way you're going to get this street out here paved and all of the other streets where Negroes live that are unpaved, the way you're going to get better salaries, the way you will have better homes, will be to engage in a vigorous, nonviolent struggle to get the ballot and put people like Sheriff Clark out of office. [*Cheering*]

So our job now is much bigger than integrating a lunch counter. As important as this happens to be, the civil rights movement must move into the realm of political action, and we've got to get political power in order to bring about the kind of political reforms that will make for change all over the South and all over the nation.

Now, on the voting front, on the political action front, we still have a big job. We've done a fairly good job and I'm thankful that in the civil rights organizations, we've united and worked hard over the last four years. We had about a million, two hundred thousand Negroes register to vote in the South in 1960. When we went into the election the other day, that number had leaped to a little better than 2 million.

So we have more than 2 million Negroes eligible to vote now in the South, who are registered voters. That sounds pretty fair, but let me give you the other side. There are still more than 10 million Negroes living in the

South. More than 6 million are of voting age. This means that we still have about 4 million Negroes in the South who are not registered to vote.

All types of conniving methods are still being used to keep the Negro from becoming a registered voter. They give us these complex literacy tests that a Ph.D. in any field or a person with a law degree from any great university in our country couldn't answer to the even more difficult questions of how many bubbles do you find in a bar of soap. They ask questions like this down in Mississippi every now and then.

The process is so structured that only a few people can register. Now, take in Mississippi, you have about 28,000 Negroes registered to vote. There are 970-some-odd-thousand Negroes in Mississippi, 465,000 are eligible to vote in that they're of voting age, and yet only 28,000 are registered. I checked it the other day, on the basis that they are registering Negroes in Mississippi now, it will take exactly 132 years to get half of the Negroes eligible to vote registered. And I don't believe we're going to wait that long.

So you see the job that we have to do. It's a big job, my friends, it's a job that will take perseverance, it's a job that will take commitment, it's a job that will take sacrifice, it's a job that means going down over and over and over again, letting the power structure of this city know that we aren't going to stop marching to the courthouse until we can register and vote as any other citizen in the white community of Dallas County.

Now, Selma is something of the proving ground, so to speak, of a larger campaign for the whole state of Alabama. We will be going not only into Dallas County, we'll be going into Perry County, we're going into Maringo County, we're going into Wilcox County, we're going into Lowns County, we're going into Barber County, we're going to every hamlet and village in this state where the Negro is denied the right to vote, and we're going to dramatize this issue and make a plea to the nation to do something about conditions in Alabama and conditions in Mississippi, because without the ballot, we aren't going to be able to change many of the things that we are facing, and many of the conditions that we face all over these sections and all over these black belt counties.

I want to urge you to be back tomorrow morning. Not in numbers of one or two here and there, but we want you there by the hundreds. We will go right back to the courthouse. Now, as you know, that is an injunction, and I want to just make a brief report on that. We went into court through our lawyers, seeking an injunction against the harassing, intimidating, arresting methods of Sheriff Clark. This was in the federal district court in Mobile, Alabama, presided over by Judge Thomas. Judge Thomas did issue that injunction. We've had our lawyers working on it and giving us an interpretation of it most of the afternoon so that we could see exactly what the injunction meant and what it will mean for the movement.

Now, there's nothing in that injunction that tells us or says to us that we must stop our activity. It isn't as clear as we would like to see it. But there is nothing in that injunction that tells us that we cannot engage in peaceful assembly. In fact, the injunction specifically states that over and above the 100 people who can line up to register, people have a legitimate right to be there to encourage other people or to serve as vouchers.

Now, we are not going to allow Sheriff Clark to harass us. We are not going to allow him to intimidate us. Our lawyer said to us this afternoon that he is absolutely convinced and of the legal opinion that Sheriff Clark has already violated that injunction. [*Applause*]

The thing I want to get over to you is that we must have the vote. We're going to march down to the courthouse, orderly, peacefully, nonviolently. We are willing to say, and I believe you would follow me in saying it, that if something isn't done and if they start arresting people, we will fill up the jails of Dallas County. [*Applause*]

This is our opportunity to continue a great movement. Now, it's obvious to me, and I believe you've noticed it, when the opposition gets pushed up against the wall, whether it's legally or morally, they react in strange ways. You know, I have a psychological theory about the violence that white people on the lunatic fringe and on other levels take out against us and inflict upon us in this struggle. Now, I feel that the white South has a deep sense of guilt about how it's treated the Negro. A deep sense of guilt, a haunting, agonizing guilt.

But you know, guilt does two things to you. It has a constructive angle, and that is, it causes you to repent. It makes you penitent, and you go on and mend your evil and unjust ways. But you know, another thing that guilt does, I saw the other day. I was counseling a young man who had become an alcoholic. We were talking about this problem and I was saying to him that he had gotten in the rut of feeling a deep sense of guilt which was good about his alcoholism. He needed to feel a sense of guilt, because when he would come back to the level of sobriety almost, the guilt feeling would agonize him even more. In order to drown the guilt, he'd go right back to drinking. So he was trying to drown the guilt by engaging more in the very act that brought on the guilt.

That's what's happening to some of our white brothers. You see, they tried to drown their guilt about how they treated the Negro by engaging more in the guilt-producing act. So they are pushed up against the wall with these nagging guilt feelings, and people do strange things. They get violent and they begin to beat on you. They begin to shoot at you, and do strange and terrible things.

Now, their backs are against the wall. And they're going to try to provoke violence within us. They're going to try through brutal language and through brutal methods and outright physical violence inflicted upon us, to arouse us to the point that we will retaliate with violence.

This is what happened today. Mrs. Cooper was down in that line, and they haven't told the press the truth about it. Mrs. Cooper wouldn't have turned around and hit Sheriff Clark just to be hitting. And of course, as you know, we teach a philosophy of not retaliating and not hitting back, but the truth of the situation is that Mrs. Cooper, if she did anything, was provoked by Sheriff Clark. At that moment, he was engaging in some very ugly business-as-usual action. This is what brought about that scene there.

Now, we're going to get more of that. They're going to try to provoke violence, because their backs are against the wall. But if we will keep on in the spirit of love and nonviolence, we can change this thing.

Now, I want to say just a few words, because somebody asked me the other night, "You talk so much about love, how in the world can you love these people who are beating on you and who are oppressing you and who are doing all of these things to stand in the way of progress? How can you love them? What do you mean?"

Now, let me assure you that I'm not talking about emotional bosh. I'm not talking about some sentimental or affectionate emotion. It would be nonsense to urge oppressed people to love their violent oppressors in an affectionate sense. I'm talking about something much deeper.

Fortunately, the Greek language comes to our aid when we try to determine the meaning of love here. There are three words in Greek for love. One is the word "eros." Plato uses it a great deal in his dialogues as a journey of the soul for the realm of the divine. It has come to us to mean a sort of romantic love. And so in this sense, we all know about eros, because we have experienced it and read about it in all of the beauties of literature. In a sense, Edgar Allan Poe was talking about eros when he talked about his beautiful Annabelle Lee with a love surrounded by the halo of eternity. In a sense, Shakespeare was talking about eros when he said love is not love which alters when it alterations finds, it bends with the remover to remove, it is an ever-fixed mark that looks on ... and is never shaken. It is a star to every wandering voyage. You know, I can remember this because I used to quote it to my wife when we were courting. That's eros, from the Greek language.

The Greek language comes out with the word "fileo," which is another level of love. It is a sort of intimate affection between personal friends. This is a reciprocal love. You love the people that you like, that you get along with, whose ways appeal to you. This is friendship.

Then the Greek language comes out with the word "agape." Agape is more than romantic love, agape is more than friendship. Agape is understanding, creative, redemptive goodwill for all men. It is an overflowing love which seeks nothing in return. Theologians would say it is a love of God operating in the human heart, and when you rise to love on this level, you love every man. Not because you like him. You love every man not because his ways appeal to you. You love every man because God loves him and you come to see that Christ died for the segregationists as well as the integrationists.

So you rise to the level of loving the person who does the evil deed, while hating the deed that the person does. I think this is what Jesus meant when he said "Love your enemies." And I'm so happy that he didn't say "Like your enemies," because it's pretty difficult to like some people. I must confess that I find it difficult to like the things that Brother Wallace and Brother Thurmond and Brother Eastland and Brother Stennis are doing. I really find it difficult. But Jesus said, "Love them," and love is greater than like. Love is understanding, creative, redemptive goodwill for all men.

If we would get this kind of love, we will be able to inject new meaning into the veins of our nation's history. If we get this kind of love, we will be able to transform dark yesterdays into bright tomorrows. If we get this kind of love, we will be able to tell the world something that it needs to know, and that it needs to hear. If we get this kind of love, we will speed up the days. There will be the day not of the white man, not of the black [man], but the day of man as man.

I'm sure that I want to say don't despair. I know we get very upset and resentful about things that happen to us. We are still the victims of man's inhumanity to man. To see four police officers brutalizing and beating a woman as they did this morning, to see them dragging a young man across the street as if he is some wayward animal, causes us to rise up deep down within and say, "Why? My God, my God, why?"

I know we ask that question over and over again, and there are dark moments in this struggle, but I want to tell you that I've seen it over and over again, that so often the darkest hour is that hour that just appears before the dawn of a new fulfillment.

———

So I'm here to tell you tonight, don't despair. I must admit that there are some difficult days ahead. It's still midnight in Selma. But the psalmist is right Weeping may tarry for a night, but joy cometh in the morning.

Centuries ago, a great prophet by the name of Jeremiah raised a great agonizing question. He looked out and he noticed the evil people off and prospering, and the good and righteous people off and suffering. He wondered about the injustices of life and he raised the question, "Is there no balm in Gilead? Is there no physician there?"

Centuries later, our slave forefathers came along. They had nothing to look forward to morning after morning but the sizzling heat, the rawhide whip of the overseer and long rows of cotton. They too knew about the injustices of life, but they did an amazing thing. They looked back across the centuries, and took Jeremiah's question mark and straightened it into an exclamation point, and in one of their spirituals they could sing "There is a balm in Gilead that makes the wounded whole. There is a balm in Gilead that heals the sin-sick soul." They had another verse.

Sometimes I must confess that I have to sing it. Sometimes I feel discouraged in Alabama. Sometimes I feel discouraged in Mississippi. Sometimes I feel discouraged in this struggle. Sometimes I feel my work's in vain, but then the Holy Spirit revives my soul again. There is a balm in Gilead that makes the wounded whole. [*Applause*]

MALCOLM X
(1925–1965)

Brotherhood Among Ourselves
FEBRUARY 14, 1965

Let us practice brotherhood among ourselves, and then if
others want to practice brotherhood with us, we're
for practicing it with them also.

In April 1964 Malcolm X departed on a pilgrimage to Mecca, an obligatory trip for orthodox Muslims at least once in their lifetime. He then traveled to Africa and the Middle East, where, contrary to his expectations, he observed people from different classes, and from different racial and ethnic backgrounds, unified by their common Islamic faith. When he returned to the United States, Malcolm X publicly declared his abandonment of the Nation of Islam's militant, separatist approach to civil rights, converted to orthodox Islam, and changed his name to El-Hajj Malik El-Shabazz.

To the surprise of many, Malcolm X reached out to those he had earlier condemned, including moderate blacks and sympathetic whites, endorsing the possibility of a brotherhood between the two groups. In speech after speech, he reiterated his new philosophy: a more pragmatic black nationalism devoid of a call for strict separatism. He also urged blacks to control the problems within their own communities before protesting those raging on the national stage, and founded the Organization of Afro-American Unity to promote political justice for blacks of all faiths.

Malcolm's conversion had a deep impact on his relationship with the Nation of Islam. His former supporters delivered threats of violence against their old leader, forcing Malcolm X to seek refuge and armed protection.

On February 14, 1965, angry about his reformed views, a group of Black Muslims bombed Malcolm X's home, nearly killing his wife and children. The very next day, he delivered this speech to the Afro-American Broadcasting Congress in Detroit, Michigan, in which he discussed the relationships among the civil rights struggles in America, and described the tenets of his new philosophy. One week later, Malcolm was assassinated during a rally in Harlem, New York.

WHY SHOULD THE BLACK MAN in America concern himself since he's been away from the African continent for three or four hundred years? Why should we concern ourselves? What impact does what happens to them have upon us? Number one, you have to realize that up until 1959 Africa was dominated by the colonial powers. Having complete control over Africa, the colonial powers of Europe projected the image of Africa negatively. They always project Africa in a negative light: jungle savages, cannibals, nothing civilized. Why then, naturally it was so negative that it was negative to you and me, and you and I began to hate it. We didn't want anybody telling us anything about Africa, much less calling us Africans. In hating Africa and in hating the Africans, we ended up hating ourselves, without even realizing it. Because you can't hate the roots of a tree, and not hate the tree. You can't hate your origin and not end up hating yourself. You can't hate Africa and not hate yourself.

You show me one of these people over here who has been thoroughly brainwashed and has a negative attitude toward Africa, and I'll show you one who has a negative attitude toward himself. You can't have a positive attitude toward yourself and a negative attitude toward Africa at the same time. To the same degree that your understanding of and attitude toward Africa becomes positive, you'll find that your understanding of and your attitude toward yourself will also become positive. And this is what the white man knows. So they very skillfully make you and me hate our African identity, our African characteristics.

You know yourself that we have been a people who hated our African characteristics. We hated our heads, we hated the shape of our nose, we wanted one of those long doglike noses, you know; we hated the color of our skin, hated the blood of Africa that was in our veins. And in hating our features and our skin and our blood, why, we had to end up hating ourselves. And we hated ourselves. Our color became to us a chain—we felt that it was holding us back; our color became to us like a prison which we felt was keeping us confined, not letting us go this way or that way. We felt that all of these restrictions were based solely upon our color, and the psychological reaction to that would have to be that as long as we felt imprisoned or chained or trapped by black skin, black features, and black blood, that skin and those features and that blood holding us back automatically had to become hateful to us. And it became hateful to us.

It made us feel inferior; it made us feel inadequate, made us feel helpless. And when we fell victims to this feeling of inadequacy or inferiority or helplessness, we turned to somebody else to show us the way. We didn't have confidence in another black man to show us the way, or black people to show us the way. In those days we didn't. We didn't think a black man could do anything except play some horns—you know, make some sound and make you happy with some songs and in that way. But in serious things, where our food, clothing, shelter, and education were concerned, we turned to the man. We never thought in terms of bringing these things into existence for ourselves, we never thought in terms of doing things for ourselves. Because we felt helpless. What made us feel helpless was our hatred for ourselves. And our hatred for ourselves stemmed from our hatred for things African. . . .

One of the things that made the Black Muslim movement grow was its emphasis upon things African. This was the secret to the growth of the Black Muslim movement. African blood, African origin, African culture, African ties. And you'd be surprised—we discovered that deep within the subconscious of the black man in this country, he is still more African than he is American. He thinks that he's more American than African, because the man is jiving him, the man is brainwashing him every day. He's telling him, "You're an American, you're an American." Man, how could you think you're an American when you haven't ever had any kind of an American treat over here? You have never, never. Ten men can be sitting at a table eating, you know, dining, and I can come and sit down where they're dining. They're dining; I've got a plate in front of me, but nothing is on it. Because all of us are sitting at the same table, are all of us diners? I'm not a diner until you let me dine. Just being at the table with others who are dining doesn't make me a diner, and this is what you've got to get in your head here in this country.

Just because you're in this country doesn't make you an American. No, you've got to go farther than that before you can become an American. You've got to enjoy the fruits of Americanism. You haven't enjoyed those fruits. You've enjoyed the thorns. You've enjoyed the thistles. But you have not enjoyed the fruits, no sir. You have fought harder for the fruits than the white man has, but you've enjoyed less. When the man put the uniform on you and sent you abroad, you fought harder than they did. Yes, I know you—when you're fighting for them, you can fight. . . .

Brothers and sisters, let me tell you, I spend my time out there in the streets with people, all kinds of people, listening to what they have to say. And they're dissatisfied, they're disillusioned, they're fed up, they're getting to the point of frustration where they begin to feel, "What do we have to lose?" When you get to that point, you're the type of person who can create a very dangerously explosive atmosphere. This is what's happening in our neighborhoods, to our people.

I read a poll taken by *Newsweek* magazine this week saying that Negroes are satisfied. Oh, yes, *Newsweek,* you know, supposed to be a top magazine with a top pollster, talking about how satisfied Negroes are. Maybe I haven't met the Negroes he met. Because I know he hasn't met the ones that I've met. And this is dangerous. This is where the white man does himself the most harm. He invents statistics to create an image, thinking that that image is going to hold things in check. You know why they always say Negroes are lazy? Because they want Negroes to be lazy. They always say Negroes can't unite, because they don't want Negroes to unite. And once they put this thing in the Negro's mind, they feel that he tries to fulfill their image. If they say you can't unite black people, and then you come to them to unite them, they won't unite, because it's been said that they're not supposed to unite. It's a psycho that they work, and it's the same way with these statistics.

When they think that an explosive era is coming up, then they grab their press again and begin to shower the Negro public, to make it appear that all Negroes are satisfied. Because if you know you're dissatisfied all by yourself and ten others aren't, you play it cool; but if you know that all ten of you are dissatisfied, you get with it. This is what the man knows. The man knows that if these Negroes find out how dissatisfied they really are—even Uncle Tom is dissatisfied, he's just playing his part for now—this is what makes the man frightened. It frightens them in France and frightens them in England, and it frightens them in the United States.

And it is for this reason that it is so important for you and me to start organizing among ourselves, intelligently, and try to find out: "What are we going to do if this happens, that happens or the next thing happens?" Don't think that you're going to run to the man and say, "Look, boss, this is me." Why, when the deal goes down, you'll look just like me in his eyesight; I'll make it tough for you. Yes, when the deal goes down, he doesn't look at you in any better light than he looks at me. . . .

I say again that I'm not a racist, I don't believe in any form of segregation or anything like that. I'm for brotherhood for everybody, but I don't believe in forcing brotherhood upon people who don't want it. Let us practice brotherhood among ourselves, and then if others want to practice brotherhood with us, we're for practicing it with them also. But I don't think that we should run around trying to love somebody who doesn't love us.

Lyndon B. Johnson
(1908–1973)

We Shall Overcome
March 15, 1965

There is no Negro problem. There is no Southern problem. There is no Northern problem. There is only an American problem.

Born in Stonewall, Texas, to a family of teachers, preachers, and politicians, Lyndon Johnson, the thirty-fifth president, was raised in the segregated South, where he grew up among impoverished Mexican-Americans and a marginalized African-American community. Johnson's first campaigns, for the U.S. House of Representatives and Senate, were laden with thinly-veiled appeals to racist whites; his voting record on matters of race was hardly exemplary. In fact, until Johnson turned his ambitions toward national public office, steering the 1957 Civil Rights Act to passage, he had never voted in favor of any piece of civil rights legislation. Over time, however, Johnson became one of the—if not the—greatest presidential champions of equal opportunity.

In the 1964 presidential election, Johnson defeated Barry Goldwater by one of the largest margins in political history. Just a year earlier, with the assassination of President Kennedy, Johnson had inherited a deeply divided nation, one embroiled in racial and social upheaval. Despite his efforts in passing the 1964 Civil Rights Act and promoting equality from the bully pulpit, African Americans still languished in segregation and continued to suffer the sting of voting inequity.

In reaction, civil rights groups organized voting rights protests in towns across the country, including, most famously, a march from Montgomery to Selma, Alabama. On March 7, with John Lewis at the helm, police brutally attacked the protestors with tear gas, whips, and clubs as they crossed the Edmund Pettus Bridge in Selma, hospitalizing more than eighty people. In a seminal moment for the movement, the major television networks all broadcast the event—later dubbed "Bloody Sunday"—to homes and living rooms across the nation.

On March 15, 1965, with the images from Selma still fresh, President Johnson addressed a joint session of Congress about the insufficiencies of the 1964 Civil Rights Act, and the pressing need for voting rights legislation. Speechwriter Richard Goodwin had only eight hours to write a first and final draft of Johnson's remarks. According to Goodwin, presidential aide Jack Valenti initially assigned another writer to pen LBJ's speech, but when Johnson found out, he declared, "Don't you know a liberal Jew has his hand on the pulse of America?" As Goodwin completed each page, it was immediately taken to the president for his edits; there was not even enough time to type the speech into the teleprompter.

Declaring "we shall overcome," a line from an old Negro spiritual, Johnson's ringing oration before the roomful of lawmakers received critical acclaim and a wave of support. On the House floor, congressmembers and senators gasped and then applauded as Johnson invoked the civil rights protest hymn. In living rooms across the nation, Americans—including Martin Luther King, Jr.—wept as their southern president took the moral high ground. The *New York Times* dubbed it, "the deepest commitment to the Negro cause of any American president."

Only a few months later, Congress passed the 1965 Voting Rights Act, affording the federal government new enforcement power to protect African-American enfranchisement.

I SPEAK TONIGHT for the dignity of man and the destiny of democracy.

I urge every member of both parties, Americans of all religions and of all colors, from every section of this country, to join me in that cause.

At times, history and fate meet at a single time in a single place to shape a turning-point in man's unending search for freedom.

So it was at Lexington and Concord. So it was a century ago at Appomattox. So it was last week in Selma, Alabama.

There, long suffering men and women peacefully protested the denial of their rights as Americans. Many were brutally assaulted. One good man—a man of God—was killed.

There is no cause for pride in what has happened in Selma. There is no cause for self-satisfaction in the long denial of equal rights of millions of Americans. But there is cause for hope and for faith in our democracy in what is happening here tonight.

For the cries of pain and the hymns of oppressed people have summoned into convocation all the majesty of great Government—the Government of the greatest nation on earth.

Our mission is at once the oldest and the most basic of this country—to right wrong, to do justice, to serve man.

In our time we have come to live with the moments of great crisis. Our lives have been marked with debate about great issues, issues of war and peace, issues of prosperity and depression.

But rarely in any time does an issue bare the secret heart of America itself. Rarely are we met with a challenge, not to our growth or abundance, or our welfare or our security, but rather to the values and the purposes and the meaning of our beloved nation.

The issue of equal rights for American Negroes is such an issue.

And should we defeat every enemy, and should we double our wealth and conquer the stars, and still be unequal to this issue, then we will have failed as a people and as a nation.

For, with a country as with a person, "What is a man profited if he shall gain the whole world, and lose his own soul?"

There is no Negro problem. There is no Southern problem. There is no Northern problem. There is only an American problem.

And we are met here tonight as Americans—not as Democrats or Republicans; we're met here as Americans to solve that problem.

This was the first nation in the history of the world to be founded with a purpose. The great phrases of that purpose still sound in every American heart, North and South:

"All men are created equal." "Government by consent of the governed." "Give me liberty or give me death."

And those are not just clever words, and those are not just empty theories.

In their name Americans have fought and died for two centuries and tonight around the world they stand there as guardians of our liberty risking their lives.

Those words are promised to every citizen that he shall share in the dignity of man. This dignity cannot be found in a man's possessions. It cannot be found in his power or in his position: It really rests on his right to be treated as a man equal in opportunity to all others.

It says that he shall share in freedom. He shall choose his leaders, educate his children, provide for his family according to his ability and his merits as a human being.

To apply any other test, to deny a man his hopes because of his color or race or his religion or the place of his birth is not only to do injustice, it is to deny America and to dishonor the dead who gave their lives for American freedom.

Our fathers believed that if this noble view of the rights of man was to flourish it must be rooted in democracy. The most basic right of all was the right to choose your own leaders.

The history of this country in large measure is the history of expansion of that right to all of our people. Many of the issues of civil rights are very complex and most difficult. But about this there can and should be no argument: every American citizen must have an equal right to vote.

There is no reason which can excuse the denial of that right. There is no duty which weighs more heavily on us than the duty we have to insure that right. Yet the harsh fact is that in many places in this country men and women are kept from voting simply because they are Negroes.

Every device of which human ingenuity is capable has been used to deny this right. The Negro citizen may go to register only to be told that the day is wrong, or the hour is late, or the official in charge is absent.

And if he persists and if he manages to present himself to the registrar, he may be disqualified because he did not spell out his middle name, or because he abbreviated a word on the application. And if he manages to fill out an application, he is given a test.

The registrar is the sole judge of whether he passes this test. He may be asked to recite the entire Constitution, or explain the most complex provisions of state law.

And even a college degree cannot be used to prove that he can read and write. For the fact is that the only way to pass these barriers is to show a white skin.

Experience has clearly shown that the existing process of law cannot overcome systematic and ingenious discrimination. No law that we now have on the books, and I have helped to put three of them there, can insure the right to vote when local officials are determined to deny it. In such a case, our duty must be clear to all of us.

The Constitution says that no person shall be kept from voting because of his race or his color. We have all sworn an oath before God to support and to defend that Constitution. We must now act in obedience to that oath.

On Wednesday, I will send to Congress a law designed to eliminate illegal barriers to the right to vote. . . .

Outside this chamber is the outraged conscience of a nation, the grave concern of many nations and the harsh judgement of history on our acts.

But even if we pass this bill the battle will not be over.

What happened in Selma is part of a far larger movement which reaches into every section and state of America. It is the effort of American Negroes to secure for themselves the full blessings of American life.

Their cause must be our cause too. Because it's not just Negroes but really it's all of us who must overcome the crippling legacy of bigotry and injustice. And we shall overcome.

As a man whose roots go deeply into Southern soil, I know how agonizing racial feelings are. I know how difficult it is to reshape the attitudes and the structure of our society. But a century has passed—more than one hundred years—since the Negro was freed.

And he is not fully free tonight.

It was more than one hundred years ago that Abraham Lincoln—a great President of another party—signed the Emancipation Proclamation. But emancipation is a proclamation and not a fact.

A century has passed—more than one hundred years—since equality was promised, and yet the Negro is not equal.

A century has passed since the day of promise, and the promise is unkept. The time of justice has now come, and I tell you that I believe sincerely that no force can hold it back. It is right in the eyes of man and God that it should come, and when it does, I think that day will brighten the lives of every American.

For Negroes are not the only victims. How many white children have gone uneducated? How many white families have lived in stark poverty? How many white lives have been scarred by fear, because we wasted energy and our substance to maintain the barriers of hatred and terror?

And so I say to all of you here and to all in the nation tonight that those who appeal to you to hold on to the past do so at the cost of denying you your future. This great rich, restless country can offer opportunity and education and hope to all—all, black and white, all, North and South, sharecropper and city dweller.

These are the enemies: poverty, ignorance, disease. They are our enemies, not our fellow man, not our neighbor. And these enemies too—poverty, disease and ignorance—we shall overcome.

Lyndon B. Johnson
(1908–1973)

To Fulfill These Rights
June 4, 1965

*You do not take a person who, for years, has been hobbled by
chains and liberate him, bring him up to the starting line of a race
and then say, "you are free to compete with all the others."*

President Lyndon Johnson delivered this historic commencement
address at Howard University on the heels of a major legislative victory
in the struggle for civil rights: the Civil Rights Act of 1964.

Despite progress in Congress, racial unrest continued to plague
America's cities. Johnson feared that sharp economic and social barriers
fueled the violence, and stood firmly in the way of African-
American progress and equality. A report drafted by Assistant Secretary
of Labor Daniel Patrick Moynihan in 1965 added to the president's
concerns. The Moynihan Report argued that the "deteriorating black
family" and the "systematic weakening of the Negro male" would continue
to stifle minority achievement and perpetuate the cycle of
poverty. Johnson responded by arguing that new jobs and programs
were the only true solution to this problem.

Before a predominantly African-American audience of nearly 5,000,
the president cited the burgeoning economic disparity between blacks
and whites and offered a plan for "affirmative action" as the best means
to remedy the continuing crisis. Under Johnson's directive, Moynihan
and speechwriter Dick Goodwin penned the draft for the president;
African-American leaders Martin Luther King, Jr., Roy Wilkins, Whitney
Young, and A. Philip Randolph added their imprimatur.

The speech garnered near-universal praise in the press and from civil
rights leaders. The following day, Dr. King sent Johnson a telegram stating,
"Never before has a president articulated the depths and dimensions
of the problem of racial injustice more eloquently and profoundly."

⸻

I am delighted at the chance to speak at this important [occasion]
and this historic institution. Howard has long been an outstanding center for
the education of Negro Americans. Its students are of every race and color and

they come from many countries of the world. It is truly a working example of democratic excellence.

Our earth is the home of revolution. In every corner of every continent men charged with hope contend with ancient ways in the pursuit of justice. They reach for the newest of weapons to realize the oldest of dreams, that each may walk in freedom and pride, stretching his talents, enjoying the fruits of the earth.

Our enemies may occasionally seize the day of change, but it is the banner of our revolution they take. And our own future is linked to this process of swift and turbulent change in many lands in the world. But nothing in any country touches us more profoundly, and nothing is more freighted with meaning for our own destiny than the revolution of the Negro American.

In far too many ways American Negroes have been another nation: deprived of freedom, crippled by hatred, the doors of opportunity closed to hope.

In our time change has come to this Nation, too. The American Negro, acting with impressive restraint, has peacefully protested and marched, entered the courtrooms and the seats of government, demanding a justice that has long been denied. The voice of the Negro was the call to action. But it is a tribute to America that, once aroused, the courts and the Congress, the President and most of the people, have been the allies of progress.

Thus we have seen the high court of the country declare that discrimination based on race was repugnant to the Constitution, and therefore void. We have seen in 1957, and 1960, and again in 1964, the first civil rights legislation in this Nation in almost an entire century.

As majority leader of the United States Senate, I helped to guide two of these bills through the Senate. And, as your President, I was proud to sign the third. And now very soon we will have the fourth—a new law guaranteeing every American the right to vote.

The voting rights bill will be the latest, and among the most important, in a long series of victories. But this victory—as Winston Churchill said of another triumph for freedom—"is not the end. It is not even the beginning of the end. But it is, perhaps, the end of the beginning."

That beginning is freedom; and the barriers to that freedom are tumbling down. Freedom is the right to share, share fully and equally, in American society—to vote, to hold a job, to enter a public place, to go to school. It is the right to be treated in every part of our national life as a person equal in dignity and promise to all others.

But freedom is not enough. You do not wipe away the scars of centuries by saying: Now you are free to go where you want, and do as you desire, and choose the leaders you please.

You do not take a person who, for years, has been hobbled by chains and liberate him, bring him up to the starting line of a race and then say, "you are free to compete with all the others," and still justly believe that you have been completely fair.

Thus it is not enough just to open the gates of opportunity. All our citizens must have the ability to walk through those gates.

This is the next and the more profound stage of the battle for civil rights. We seek not just freedom but opportunity. We seek not just legal equity but human ability, not just equality as a right and a theory but equality as a fact and equality as a result.

For the task is to give 20 million Negroes the same chance as every other American to learn and grow, to work and share in society, to develop their abilities—physical, mental and spiritual, and to pursue their individual happiness.

To this end equal opportunity is essential, but not enough, not enough. Men and women of all races are born with the same range of abilities. But ability is not just the product of birth. Ability is stretched or stunted by the family that you live with, and the neighborhood you live in—by the school you go to and the poverty or the richness of your surroundings. It is the product of a hundred unseen forces playing upon the little infant, the child, and finally the man.

This graduating class at Howard University is witness to the indomitable determination of the Negro American to win his way in American life.

The number of Negroes in schools of higher learning has almost doubled in 15 years. The number of nonwhite professional workers has more than doubled in 10 years. The median income of Negro college women tonight exceeds that of white college women. And there are also the enormous accomplishments of distinguished individual Negroes—many of them graduates of this institution, and one of them the first lady ambassador in the history of the United States.

These are proud and impressive achievements. But they tell only the story of a growing middle class minority, steadily narrowing the gap between them and their white counterparts.

But for the great majority of Negro Americans—the poor, the unemployed, the uprooted, and the dispossessed—there is a much grimmer story. They still, as we meet here tonight, are another nation. Despite the court orders and the laws, despite the legislative victories and the speeches, for them the walls are rising and the gulf is widening.

Moreover, the isolation of Negro[es] from white communities is increasing, rather than decreasing as Negroes crowd into the central cities and become a city within a city.

Of course Negro Americans as well as white Americans have shared in our rising national abundance. But the harsh fact of the matter is that in the battle for true equality too many—far too many—are losing ground every day.

We are not completely sure why this is. We know the causes are complex and subtle. But we do know the two broad basic reasons. And we do know that we have to act.

First, Negroes are trapped—as many whites are trapped—in inherited, gateless poverty. They lack training and skills. They are shut in, in slums, without decent medical care. Private and public poverty combine to cripple their capacities.

We are trying to attack these evils through our poverty program, through our education program, through our medical care and our other health programs, and a dozen more of the Great Society programs that are aimed at the root causes of this poverty.

We will increase, and we will accelerate, and we will broaden this attack in years to come until this most enduring of foes finally yields to our unyielding will.

But there is a second cause—much more difficult to explain, more deeply grounded, more desperate in its force. It is the devastating heritage of long years of slavery; and a century of oppression, hatred, and injustice.

For Negro poverty is not white poverty. Many of its causes and many of its cures are the same. But there are differences—deep, corrosive, obstinate differences—radiating painful roots into the community, and into the family, and the nature of the individual.

These differences are not racial differences. They are solely and simply the consequence of ancient brutality, past injustice, and present prejudice. They are anguishing to observe. For the Negro they are a constant reminder of oppression. For the white they are a constant reminder of guilt. But they must be faced and they must be dealt with and they must be overcome, if we are ever to reach the time when the only difference between Negroes and whites is the color of their skin.

Nor can we find a complete answer in the experience of other American minorities. They made a valiant and a largely successful effort to emerge from poverty and prejudice.

The Negro, like these others, will have to rely mostly upon his own efforts. But he just can not do it alone. For they did not have the heritage of centuries to overcome, and they did not have a cultural tradition which had been twisted and battered by endless years of hatred and hopelessness, nor were they excluded—these others—because of race or color—a feeling whose dark intensity is matched by no other prejudice in our society.

Nor can these differences be understood as isolated infirmities. They are a seamless web. They cause each other. They result from each other. They reinforce each other.

Much of the Negro community is buried under a blanket of history and circumstance. It is not a lasting solution to lift just one corner of that blanket. We must stand on all sides and we must raise the entire cover if we are to liberate our fellow citizens.

One of the differences is the increased concentration of Negroes in our cities. More than 73 percent of all Negroes live in urban areas compared with less than 70 percent of the whites. Most of these Negroes live in slums. Most of these Negroes live together—a separated people.

Men are shaped by their world. When it is a world of decay, ringed by an invisible wall, when escape is arduous and uncertain, and the saving pressures of a more hopeful society are unknown, it can cripple the youth and it can desolate the men.

There is also the burden that a dark skin can add to the search for a productive place in our society. Unemployment strikes most swiftly and broadly at the Negro, and this burden erodes hope. Blighted hope breeds despair. Despair brings indifferences to the learning which offers a way out. And despair, coupled with indifferences, is often the source of destructive rebellion against the fabric of society.

There is also the lacerating hurt of early collision with white hatred or prejudice, distaste or condescension. Other groups have felt similar intolerance. But success and achievement could wipe it away. They do not change the color of a man's skin. I have seen this uncomprehending pain in the eyes of the little, young Mexican-American schoolchildren that I taught many years ago. But it can be overcome. But, for many, the wounds are always open.

Perhaps most important—its influence radiating to every part of life—is the breakdown of the Negro family structure. For this, most of all, white America must accept responsibility. It flows from centuries of oppression and persecution of the Negro man. It flows from the long years of degradation and discrimination, which have attacked his dignity and assaulted his ability to produce for his family.

This, too, is not pleasant to look upon. But it must be faced by those whose serious intent is to improve the life of all Americans.

Only a minority—less than half—of all Negro children reach the age of 18 having lived all their lives with both of their parents. At this moment, tonight, little less than two-thirds are at home with both of their parents. Probably a majority of all Negro children receive federally-aided public assistance some-time during their childhood.

The family is the cornerstone of our society. More than any other force it shapes the attitude, the hopes, the ambitions, and the values of the child. And when the family collapses it is the children that are usually damaged. When it happens on a massive scale the community itself is crippled.

So, unless we work to strengthen the family, to create conditions under which most parents will stay together—all the rest: schools, and playgrounds, and public assistance, and private concern, will never be enough to cut completely the circle of despair and deprivation.

There is no single easy answer to all of these problems.

Jobs are part of the answer. They bring the income which permits a man to provide for his family.

Decent homes in decent surroundings and a chance to learn—an equal chance to learn—are part of the answer.

Welfare and social programs better designed to hold families together are part of the answer.

Care for the sick is part of the answer.

An understanding heart by all Americans is another big part of the answer.

And to all of these fronts—and a dozen more—I will dedicate the expanding efforts of the Johnson administration.

But there are other answers that are still to be found. Nor do we fully understand even all of the problems. Therefore, I want to announce tonight that this fall I intend to call a White House conference of scholars, and experts, and outstanding Negro leaders—men of both races—and officials of Government at every level.

This White House conference's theme and title will be "To Fulfill These Rights."

Its object will be to help the American Negro fulfill the rights which, after the long time of injustice, he is finally about to secure.

To move beyond opportunity to achievement.

To shatter forever not only the barriers of law and public practice, but the walls which bound the condition of many by the color of his skin.

To dissolve, as best we can, the antique enmities of the heart which diminish the holder, divide the great democracy, and do wrong—great wrong—to the children of God.

And I pledge you tonight that this will be a chief goal of my administration, and of my program next year, and in the years to come. And I hope, and I pray, and I believe, it will be a part of the program of all America.

For what is justice?

It is to fulfill the fair expectations of man.

Thus, American justice is a very special thing. For, from the first, this has been a land of towering expectations. It was to be a nation where each man could be ruled by the common consent of all—enshrined in law, given life by institutions, guided by men themselves subject to its rule. And all—all of every station and origin—would be touched equally in obligation and in liberty.

Beyond the law lay the land. It was a rich land, glowing with more abundant promise than man had ever seen. Here, unlike any place yet known, all were to share the harvest.

And beyond this was the dignity of man. Each could become whatever his qualities of mind and spirit would permit—to strive, to seek, and, if he could, to find his happiness.

This is American justice. We have pursued it faithfully to the edge of our imperfections, and we have failed to find it for the American Negro.

So, it is the glorious opportunity of this generation to end the one huge wrong of the American Nation and, in so doing, to find America for ourselves, with the same immense thrill of discovery which gripped those who first began to realize that here, at last, was a home for freedom.

All it will take is for all of us to understand what this country is and what this country must become.

The Scripture promises: "I shall light a candle of understanding in thine heart, which shall not be put out."

Together, and with millions more, we can light that candle of understanding in the heart of all America.

And, once lit, it will never again go out.

ROBERT F. KENNEDY
(1925–1968)

Day of Affirmation Address
JUNE 7, 1966

Only those who dare to fail greatly can ever achieve greatly.

In what many have called his most significant speech, Robert F. Kennedy, then the junior U. S. senator from New York, addressed the National Union of South African Students on June 7, 1966, the Day of Affirmation in South Africa.

Dating back to his tenure as U.S. attorney general, Kennedy had been an ardent champion of civil rights, the rural poor, and migrant workers. Concerned about his message, the South African government did everything in its power to undermine Kennedy's attendance, refusing to grant him a visa for five months, banishing the students who invited him, and declining to grant travel permits for sixty foreign journalists. According to authors Edwin Guthman and Richard Allen, Kennedy spent months preparing for his journey: He read widely and attended congressional hearings on U.S.–South African relations; he scheduled regular briefing sessions with academics at his home, Hickory Hill; and he toiled tirelessly with his speechwriters on the draft, including Adam Walinsky, Dick Goodwin, and Allard Lowenstein.

The pro-apartheid South African newspapers brimmed with speculation on Kennedy's visit, calling him a troublemaker seeking to partner with "a breeding nest of vipers." The *Rand Daily Mail* claimed Kennedy was taking the trip "purely to advance his political ambitions [for president] at home . . . [and] to capture the Negro vote." Nonetheless, despite these political daggers and the bitter cold, more than 18,000 cheering people awaited Kennedy's arrival outside Cape Town University's Jameson Hall. The *Cape Times* noted that Kennedy was quickly "engulfed" by the dense crowd and that he "had to wait half an hour before a way was cleared." Tickets to the 1,600-seat hall were sold out, but thousands listened via loudspeaker from a neighboring lawn. Once inside, the senator joined a procession of students and school officials, led by a student carrying an extinguished torch, representing the state of academic freedom in South Africa.

In his address, Kennedy eloquently described the struggle for freedom in South Africa and the battle for equality being fought around the globe, including in the United States. With tears in his eyes, Kennedy applauded the world's youth, exhorting them to carry on the movement against discrimination, and to heed the words of his brother, the late president, in the tireless fight for freedom.

I CAME HERE BECAUSE of my deep interest and affection for a land settled by the Dutch in the mid-seventeenth century, then taken over by the British, and at last independent; a land in which the native inhabitants were at first subdued, but relations with whom remain a problem to this day; a land which defined itself on a hostile frontier; a land which has tamed rich natural resources through the energetic application of modern technology; a land which once imported slaves, and now must struggle to wipe out the last traces of that former bondage. I refer, of course, to the United States of America.

This is a Day of Affirmation, a celebration of liberty. We stand here in the name of freedom.

At the heart of that Western freedom and democracy is the belief that the individual man, the child of God, is the touchstone of value, and all society, groups, the state, exist for his benefit. Therefore the enlargement of liberty for individual human beings must be the supreme goal and the abiding practice of any Western society.

The first element of this individual liberty is the freedom of speech: the right to express and communicate ideas, to set oneself apart from the dumb beasts of field and forest; to recall governments to their duties and obligations; above all, the right to affirm one's membership and allegiance to the body politic—to society—to the men with whom we share our land, our heritage, and our children's future.

Hand in hand with freedom of speech goes the power to be heard, to share in the decisions of government which shape men's lives. Everything that makes man's life worthwhile—family, work, education, a place to rear one's children and a place to rest one's head—all this depends on decisions of government; all can be swept away by a government which does not heed the demands of its people. Therefore, the essential humanity of men can be protected and preserved only where government must answer—not just to the wealthy, not just to those of a particular religion, or a particular race, but to all its people.

And even government by the consent of the governed, as in our own Constitution, must be limited in its power to act against its people; so that there may be no interference with the right to worship, or with the security of the home; no arbitrary imposition of pains or penalties by officials high or low; no restrictions on the freedom of men to seek education or work or opportunity of any kind, so that each man may become all he is capable of becoming.

These are the sacred rights of Western society. These were the essential differences between us and Nazi Germany, as they were between Athens and Persia.

They are the essence of our differences with communism today. I am unalterably opposed to communism because it exalts the state over the individual and the family, and because of the lack of freedom of speech, of protest, of religion, and of the press, which is the characteristic of totalitarian states. The way of opposition to communism is not to imitate its dictatorship, but to enlarge individual freedom, in our own countries and all over the globe. There are those in every land who would label as Communist every threat to their privilege. But as I have seen on my travels in all sections of the world, reform is not communism. And the denial of freedom, in whatever name, only strengthens the very communism it claims to oppose.

Many nations have set forth their own definitions and declarations of these principles. And there have often been wide and tragic gaps between promise and performance, ideal and reality. Yet the great ideals have constantly recalled us to our duties. And—with painful slowness—we have extended and enlarged the meaning and the practice of freedom for all our people.

For two centuries, my own country has struggled to overcome the self-imposed handicap of prejudice and discrimination based on nationality, social class, or race—discrimination profoundly repugnant to the theory and command of our Constitution. Even as my father grew up in Boston, signs told him that No Irish Need Apply. Two generations later President Kennedy became the first Catholic to head the nation; but how many men of ability had, before 1961, been denied the opportunity to contribute to the nation's progress because they were Catholic, or of Irish extraction? How many sons of Italian or Jewish or Polish parents slumbered in slums—untaught, unlearned, their potential lost forever to the nation and human race? Even today, what price will we pay before we have assured full opportunity to millions of Negro Americans?

In the last five years we have done more to assure equality to our Negro citizens, and to help the deprived both white and black, than in the hundred years before. But much more remains to be done.

For there are millions of Negroes untrained for the simplest of jobs, and thousands every day denied their full equal rights under the law; and the violence of the disinherited, the insulted and injured, looms over the streets of Harlem and Watts and South Side Chicago.

But a Negro American trains as an astronaut, one of mankind's first explorers into outer space; another is the chief barrister of the United States government, and dozens sit on the benches of court; and another, Dr. Martin Luther King, is the second man of African descent to win the Nobel Peace Prize for his nonviolent efforts for social justice between races.

We have passed laws prohibiting discrimination in education, in employment, in housing, but these laws alone cannot overcome the heritage of centuries—of broken families and stunted children, and poverty and degradation and pain.

So the road toward equality of freedom is not easy, and great cost and danger march alongside us. We are committed to peaceful and nonviolent change, and that is important for all to understand—though all change is unsettling. Still, even in the turbulence of protest and struggle is greater hope for the future, as men learn to claim and achieve for themselves the rights formerly petitioned from others.

And most important of all, all the panoply of government power has been committed to the goal of equality before the law, as we are now committing ourselves to the achievement of equal opportunity in fact.

We must recognize the full human equality of all of our people before God, before the law, and in the councils of government. We must do this, not because it is economically advantageous, although it is; not because the laws of God command it, although they do; not because people in other lands wish it so. We must do it for the single and fundamental reason that it is the right thing to do.

We recognize that there are problems and obstacles before the fulfillment of these ideals in the United States, as we recognize that other nations, in Latin America and Asia and Africa, have their own political, economic, and social problems, their unique barriers to the elimination of injustices.

In some, there is concern that change will submerge the rights of a minority, particularly where the minority is of a different race from the majority. We in the United States believe in the protection of minorities; we recognize the contributions they can make and the leadership they can provide; and we do not believe that any people—whether minority, majority, or individual human beings—are "expendable" in the cause of theory or policy. We recognize also that justice between men and nations is imperfect, and that humanity sometimes progresses slowly.

All do not develop in the same manner, or at the same pace. Nations, like men, often march to the beat of different drummers, and the precise solutions of the United States can neither be dictated nor transplanted to others. What is important is that all nations must march toward increasing freedom; toward justice for all; toward a society strong and flexible enough to meet the demands of all its own people, and a world of immense and dizzying change.

In a few hours, the plane that brought me to this country crossed over oceans and countries which have been a crucible of human history. In minutes we traced the migration of men over thousands of years; seconds, the briefest glimpse, and we passed battlefields on which millions of men once struggled and died. We could see no national boundaries, no vast gulfs or high walls dividing people from people; only nature and the works of man—homes and factories and farms—everywhere reflecting man's common effort to enrich his life. Everywhere new technology and communications bring men and nations closer together, the concerns of one inevitably becoming the concerns of all. And our new closeness is stripping away the false masks, the illusion of difference which is at the root of injustice and hate and war. Only earthbound man still clings to the dark and poisoning superstition that his world is bounded by the nearest hill, his universe ended at river shore, his common humanity enclosed in the tight circle of those who share his town and views and the color of his skin.

It is your job, the task of the young people of this world, to strip the last remnants of that ancient, cruel belief from the civilization of man.

Each nation has different obstacles and different goals, shaped by the vagaries of history and of experience. Yet as I talk to young people around the world I am impressed not by the diversity but by the closeness of their goals, their desires and their concerns and their hope for the future. There is discrimination in New York, the racial inequality of apartheid in South Africa, and serfdom in the mountains of Peru. People starve in the streets of India, a former Prime Minister is summarily executed in the Congo, intellectuals go to jail in Russia, and thousands are slaughtered in Indonesia; wealth is lavished on armaments everywhere in the world. These are differing evils; but they are the common works of man. They reflect the imperfections of human justice, the inadequacy of human compassion, the defectiveness of our sensibility toward the sufferings of our fellows; they mark the limit of our ability to use knowledge for the well-being of our fellow human beings throughout the world. And therefore they call upon common qualities of conscience and indignation, a shared determination to wipe away the unnecessary sufferings of our fellow human beings at home and around the world.

It is these qualities which make of youth today the only true international community. More than this I think that we could agree on what kind of a world we would all want to build. It would be a world of independent nations, moving toward international community, each of which protected and respected the basic human freedoms. It would be a world which demanded of each government that it accept its responsibility to insure social justice. It would be a world of constantly accelerating economic progress—not material welfare as an end in itself, but as a means to liberate the capacity of every human being to pursue his talents and to pursue his hopes. It would, in short, be a world that we would be proud to have built.

Just to the north of here are lands of challenge and opportunity rich in natural resources, land and minerals and people. Yet they are also lands confronted by the greatest odds—overwhelming ignorance, internal tensions and strife, and great obstacles of climate and geography. Many of these nations, as colonies, were oppressed and exploited. Yet they have not estranged themselves from the broad traditions of the West; they are hoping and gambling their progress and stability on the chance that we will meet our responsibilities to help them overcome their poverty.

In the world we would like to build, South Africa could play an outstanding role in that effort. This is without question a preeminent repository of the wealth and knowledge and skill of the continent. Here are the greater part of Africa's research scientists and steel production, most of its reservoirs of coal and electric power. Many South Africans have made major contributions to African technical development and world science; the names of some are known wherever men seek to eliminate the ravages of tropical diseases and pestilence. In your faculties and councils, here in this very audience, are hundreds and thousands of men who could transform the lives of millions for all time to come.

But the help and the leadership of South Africa or the United States cannot be accepted if we—within our own countries or in our relations with others—deny individual integrity, human dignity, and the common humanity of man. If we would lead outside our borders, if we would help those who need our assistance, if we would meet our responsibilities to mankind, we must first, all of us, demolish the borders which history has erected between men within our own nations—barriers of race and religion, social class and ignorance.

Our answer is the world's hope; it is to rely on youth. The cruelties and obstacles of this swiftly changing planet will not yield to obsolete dogmas and outworn slogans. It cannot be moved by those who cling to a present which is already dying, who prefer the illusion of security to the excitement and danger which comes with even the most peaceful progress.

This world demands the qualities of youth; not a time of life but a state of mind, a temper of the will, a quality of the imagination, a predominance of courage over timidity, of the appetite for adventure over the love of ease. It is a revolutionary world we live in, and thus, as I have said in Latin America and Asia, in Europe and in the United States, it is young people who must take the lead. Thus you, and your young compatriots everywhere, have had thrust upon you a greater burden of responsibility than any generation that has ever lived.

"There is," said an Italian philosopher, "nothing more difficult to take in hand, more perilous to conduct, or more uncertain in its success than to take the lead in the introduction of a new order of things." Yet this is the measure of the task of your generation, and the road is strewn with many dangers.

First, is the danger of futility: the belief there is nothing one man or one woman can do against the enormous array of the world's ills—against misery and ignorance, injustice and violence. Yet many of the world's greatest movements, of thought and action, have flowed from the work of a single man. A young monk began the Protestant Reformation, a young general extended an empire from Macedonia to the borders of the earth, and a young woman reclaimed the territory of France. It was a young Italian explorer who discovered the New World, and the thirty-two-year-old Thomas Jefferson who proclaimed that all men are created equal.

"Give me a place to stand," said Archimedes, "and I will move the world." These men moved the world, and so can we all. Few will have the greatness to bend history itself, but each of us can work to change a small portion of events, and in the total of all those acts will be written the history of this generation. Thousands of Peace Corps volunteers are making a difference in isolated villages and city slums in dozens of countries. Thousands of unknown men and women in Europe resisted the occupation of the Nazis and many died, but all added to the ultimate strength and freedom of their countries. It is from numberless diverse acts of courage and belief that human history is shaped. Each time a man stands up for an ideal, or acts to improve the lot of others, or strikes out against injustice, he sends forth a tiny ripple of hope, and crossing each other from a million different centers of energy and daring, those ripples build a current which can sweep down the mightiest walls of oppression and resistance.

"If Athens shall appear great to you," said Pericles, "consider then that her glories were purchased by valiant men, and by men who learned their duty." That is the source of all greatness in all societies, and it is the key to progress in our time.

The second danger is that of expediency; of those who say that hopes and beliefs must bend before immediate necessities. Of course, if we would act effectively we must deal with the world as it is. We must get things done. But if there was one thing President Kennedy stood for that touched the most profound feelings of young people around the world, it was the belief that idealism, high aspirations, and deep convictions are not incompatible with the most practical and efficient of programs—that there is no basic inconsistency between ideals and realistic possibilities, no separation between the deepest desires of heart and of mind and the rational application of human effort to human problems. It is not realistic or hardheaded to solve problems and take action unguided by ultimate moral aims and values, although we all know some who claim that it is so. In my judgment, it is thoughtless folly. For it ignores the realities of human faith and of passion and of belief—forces ultimately more powerful than all of the calculations of our economists or of our generals. Of course to adhere to standards, to idealism, to vision in the face of immediate dangers takes great courage and takes self-confidence. But we also know that only those who dare to fail greatly, can ever achieve greatly.

It is this new idealism which is also, I believe, the common heritage of a generation which has learned that while efficiency can lead to the camps at Auschwitz, or the streets of Budapest, only the ideals of humanity and love can climb the hills of the Acropolis.

A third danger is timidity. Few men are willing to brave the disapproval of their fellows, the censure of their colleagues, the wrath of their society. Moral courage is a rarer commodity than bravery in battle or great intelligence. Yet it is the one essential, vital quality of those who seek to change a world which yields most painfully to change. Aristotle tells us that "at the Olympic games it is not the finest and the strongest men who are crowned, but they who enter the lists. . . . So too in the life of the honorable and the good it is they who act rightly who win the prize." I believe that in this generation those with the courage to enter the moral conflict will find themselves with companions in every corner of the world.

For the fortunate among us, the fourth danger is comfort, the temptation to follow the easy and familiar paths of personal ambition and financial success so grandly spread before those who have the privilege of education. But that is not the road history has marked out for us. There is a Chinese curse which says "May he live in interesting times." Like it or not we live in interesting times. They are times of danger and uncertainty; but they are also more open to the creative energy of men than any other time in history. And everyone here will ultimately be judged—will ultimately judge himself—on the effort he has contributed to building a new world society and the extent to which his ideals and goals have shaped that effort.

So we part, I to my country and you to remain. We are—if a man of forty can claim that privilege—fellow members of the world's largest younger generation. Each of us have our own work to do. I know at times you must feel very alone with your problems and difficulties. But I want to say how impressed I am with what you stand for and the effort you are making; and I say this not just for myself, but for men and women everywhere. And I hope you will often take heart from the knowledge that you are joined with fellow young people in every land, they struggling with their problems and you with yours, but all joined in a common purpose; that, like the young people of my own country and of every country I have visited, you are all in many ways more closely united to the brothers of your time than to the older generations of any of these nations; and that you are determined to build a better future. President Kennedy was speaking to the young people of America, but beyond them to young people everywhere, when he said that "the energy, the faith, the devotion which we bring to this endeavor will light our country and all who serve it—and the glow from that fire can truly light the world."

And, he added, "With a good conscience our only sure reward, with history the final judge of our deeds, let us go forth to lead the land we love, asking His blessing and His help, but knowing that here on earth God's work must truly be our own."

Franklin Kameny

(1925–)

Furthering the Homophile Movement

August 25, 1966

*Much too much of the efforts of the movement over the past decade
and a half have consisted of homosexuals talking about
homosexuality to homosexuals.*

A native of New York with a doctorate in astronomy, Frank Kameny dedicated his life to the gay rights movement after he was discharged from the United States Army Map Service because of his sexual orientation.

In 1955, Kameny helped found the Mattachine Society, an organization committed to educating the public about homosexuality, helping gays cope with discrimination, and lobbying for the repeal of discriminatory housing and employment laws. Deriving its name from the Italian "Mattachino," a court jester who dared tell the truth to the king, the society embodied the idea that for too long "gays [had been] a masked people, unknown and anonymous."

Under Kameny's direction, the Mattachines abandoned the traditional accommodationist, closeted approach of previous leaders, ushering the gay movement into the 1960s under a banner of public activism. Kameny demanded social change rooted in an independent gay movement. Gays, he insisted, no longer needed the imprimatur of heterosexuals. Thanks to his bold tactics, many in the homosexual community felt comfortable declaring publicly that "gay is good."

In this address before the National Planning Conference of Homophile Organizations in San Francisco, Kameny articulated the long- and short-range strategy for the gay civil rights movement.

═══

WE HAVE MANY PEOPLE in the movement who feel a deep concern and who are sincerely distressed at the present plight of the homosexual, and who want to do something, but who, when you examine their efforts, quite clearly aren't really sure of what needs to be done, or how to do it, or why or why not to do what should or should not be done. Our movement has shown too little concern with long-range strategy and tactics, and too much with an opportunistic, moment to moment, ad hoc attempt to find ways to remedy case-by-case situations.

But no plan of concerted, meaningful action, with long-range implications is going to be possible without a firm, solidly constructed, internally self-consistent intellectual basis. This we do not have as a movement. What we hear, from time to time, from the movement, ranges from the occasionally good through the frequently mediocre, to the appallingly bad.

Much of it contains, implicitly, the negative attitude of society-at-large toward the homosexual and his homosexuality—a negativism which has a way of showing itself in most unexpected places—often subtly and perniciously so—in the movement's statements and publications. There has been a tendency in the past to view as virtuous an impartial position, expressing all views and ideas on homosexuality—a practice which has often degenerated into our having no views and positions of our own, but becoming merely a passive battlefield for conflicting—often half-baked—ideas on homosexuals and homosexuality. This may have been appropriate at one time, but that time is now past. As a movement, we should have a viewpoint, and that alone should be propagandized. We are not properly neutral on most of the various questions raised about homosexuality. The Republicans do not present the viewpoints of the Democrats, except in order to refute them.

So, without belaboring the point further, we need—first—a clear, consistent, coordinated, positive philosophy and ideology, vigorously and actively propounded publicly at every opportunity.

This is not the place to go into the details of that philosophy, but a few general facts should be mentioned. First, we must start off as the prime foundation, with the assumption of complete and precise equality, in terms of value judgments, between homosexuality and heterosexuality, between the homosexual and the heterosexual, without the implication of inferiority and undesirability of homosexuality which so often appears, even in the enlightened discussions of the subject, and even in some of our publications. Second, and most important in a practical sense, in determining our directions and our emphasis, we must keep firmly in mind that in the last analysis, the problems of the homosexual—in their entirety—are, or stem from the prejudice and discrimination directed against him by the heterosexual majority around him, and it is there that our efforts must be directed if we are to accomplish any lasting good, or achieve any long-range goals—and, in fact, those long-range goals must be formulated with this precept in mind.

The burdens of blame, culpability, adaptation, change, adjustment, must not be directed upon the homosexual in the mass. They rarely belong there, and, in fact, fundamentally, they never belong there.

Third, what should our long range goals be? Here again, this is not the place for a detailed analysis or discussion of those goals. In brief, however, as I see them, they should be the complete integration of the homosexual—as a homo-sexual—into society at large. Our movement must be integrationist and assim-ilationist, and must take great care lest it develop segregationist and separatist tendencies. We must avoid "ghettoization"—a pitfall all too easy to stumble into. Fourth, basically the purpose of the movement, if it is to achieve any real, lasting, meaningful success, should be to look after the interests of homosexuals in the aggregate, rather than to minister to the needs of the homosexual indi-vidually. Thus—and I very explicitly am not prescribing methods here, nor excluding any area of endeavor—the point at which the balance is struck between social service on the one hand, and information, education, and civil liberties on the other hand, will determine the degree to which the results of our efforts will be ephemeral, transitory, and evanescent on the one hand, and permanent and meaningful on the other. Fifth—and this point needs much less to be made now than it did a very few years ago—much too much of the efforts of the movement over the past decade and a half have consisted of homosexu-als talking about homosexuality to homosexuals, or heterosexuals talking about homosexuality to homosexuals, and all too little of homosexuals talking about homosexuality to heterosexuals. We have been talking to ourselves.

We must get our position before the public, but we have to have a well and properly formulated [position] first. Next we must take specific positive steps to cultivate a good public image for the movement. If we wish to be heard and to have our views listened to and considered, the views and those presenting them must be packaged in a form as acceptable as possible to those to whom they are directed. I know this raises some peoples' hackles. In our movement, as in many others, one hears a great deal of maundering and fuzzy thinking about our being engaged in a battle for all personal freedoms, and rights, etc., etc. This is all well and good, and what we are engaged in certainly ties in with that, but that is not what we are actually engaged in. If you try to fight for everything, you end up spreading yourself so thin that you are fighting effec-tively for nothing. This is the homophile movement, not the conformophobic movement.

As the homophile movement, we are not fighting for sexual freedom, nor trying to solve the problems of all of those who have problems in sexual areas, nor fighting against conformity per se, nor any of a number of other things. We are, or should be, working in the manner most effective for achieving rights and equality for homosexuals, specifically and narrowly. Let us not mix causes! And let us remember that the purpose of the movement is to improve the status of the homosexual in the aggregate, not to provide an opportunity for particular homosexuals to assert their personalities or publicly to exercise their freedom and individuality.

It is necessary, if we are to accomplish lasting results, where those results are meaningful, that we carefully cultivate a high, professional type of image. One factor which can tear down such an image—irreparably—and this is my next point—is public internecine warfare. There is absolutely no excuse for an attack in any movement publication generally available by one homophile organization against another or against any of its personnel. One of our organizations stresses it well and properly. Such attacks are utterly irresponsible, and viciously so.

Certainly private discussion—orally or in letter, and as vigorously as strongly held convictions and feelings may make appropriate—is quite in order. But publicly? Never! At most, then only after very careful consideration, and only in the most carefully and temperately worded fashion, a disavowal of, or disaffiliation from a particular action or position taken by another organization may be in order—and this only rarely and in clearly important cases. A public image of basic movement unity is critically important. We are few, and we are likely to remain few. If we appear fragmented, we will be discounted utterly.

Next—for all of the growing militancy, overtness, openness and directness of our movement, there is still a subtle tendency toward an odd kind of covertness, indirection and evasion. This, too, may have been in order at one time, but is hardly so now. . . .

~~~

. . . The controversy over the use of the word "homophile" is an example of an illogical and strangely Victorian evasion of realities—an attempt to cater to an oddly misplaced romanticism. Homosexual means "same gender." That is what we are dealing with; that is what we are; let's say so.

~~~

Next—there is still too much tendency in our movement to defer to so-called authorities; to hide behind them; to let them—in all the magnificent splendor of their ignorance and misinformation—speak for and about us, and for us to defer to their opinion. We print and endorse their often fundamentally disparaging views in our publications, if they've thrown us a few crumbs of charity by not being totally hostile. In the last analysis, again, we know homosexuality as they cannot; we know our situation, our complaints, our grievances, and the abuses directed against us, as they cannot possibly know them. True—in many instances, we will have to educate ourselves, and develop our own philosophy—back to my first point again—but still, homosexuals—avowedly as such—should speak for homosexuals. A beautiful example—one of many examples—occurred at the Kansas City conference. With all due respect to Dr. Colwell, and then some respect beyond what is merely due, and with no slightest intent to slur, or adverse reflection of any sort upon him—here we had a conference of the national leadership of the homophile movement—of those who are most open, outspoken, militant and insistent upon rights, equality, dignity, full human and personal status for the homosexual. And who spoke for us to the newspapers—an avowed heterosexual. Ridiculous, and a bit sad.

Fifteen minutes is a very short time in which to develop ideas. . . . While I have intended offense to no one, I have not totally blunted adverse criticism either.

Basically, my suggestions boil down to the establishment of a theoretically well based, unified movement, presenting a carefully calculated public image, knowing where it's going, in some detail, and how it's going to get there, in some detail, and using homosexuals as their own agents for the determination of their own fate.

STOKELY CARMICHAEL
(1941–1998)

Black Power
OCTOBER 1966

*People ought to understand . . . we were never fighting for the right
to integrate, we were fighting against white supremacy.*

Stokely Carmichael was already a dominant figure in the civil rights
movement when he ascended to the helm of the Student Nonviolent
Coordinating Committee (SNCC) in 1966. By this point, after leading
voter registration drives, Freedom Rides, and nonviolent protests,
Carmichael had lost faith in the "old guard" leadership and nonviolent
tactics of the civil rights movement. As chair of SNCC, he joined in the
rising chorus of young blacks who questioned the very premise of
peaceful integration. In contrast to Dr. Martin Luther King, Jr.,
Carmichael called on blacks to create their own political, economic,
and social systems separate from those of white society.

In June 1966, while incarcerated in a Greenwood, Mississippi, jail,
Carmichael popularized a new, arguably prescient battle cry for the
civil rights movement: "We want black power." Though the phrase
"black power" was not new—both author Richard Wright and
Congressman Clayton Powell had used it earlier—it was Carmichael
who brought it front and center as the theme of a more confronta-
tional approach to African-American equality. Some viewed black
power as a call for solidarity; others saw it as an effort to wrest power
from whites; and some believed it signified a power play within the
black community.

Whenever he spoke, Carmichael faced a barrage of questions as to
the phrase's meaning. He tried, therefore, to explain the idea in several
speeches delivered to predominantly white audiences. This address at
the University of California at Berkeley was one of his first attempts.

In his remarks, Carmichael emphasized the inherently racist nature
of the United States, arguing passionately for a black movement toward
equality without the direct assistance of whites. His call to "black
power" encouraged a number of preeminent young leaders to adopt a
more militant position.

IT'S A PRIVILEGE and an honor to be in the white intellectual ghetto of the West. This is a student conference, as it should be, held on a campus, and we'll never be caught up in intellectual masturbation on the question of Black Power. That's a function of the people who are advertisers but call themselves reporters. Incidentally, for my friends and members of the press, my self-appointed white critics, I was reading Mr. Bernard Shaw two days ago, and I came across a very important quote that I think is most apropos to you. He says, "All criticism is an autobiography." Dig yourself. OK.

The philosophers Camus and Sartre raise the question of whether or not a man can condemn himself. The black existentialist philosopher who is pragmatic, Frantz Fanon, answered the question. He said that man could not. Camus and Sartre don't answer the question. We in SNCC tend to agree with Fanon—a man cannot condemn himself. If he did, he would then have to inflict punishment upon himself. An example is the Nazis. Any of the Nazi prisoners who, after he was caught and incarcerated, admitted that he committed crimes, that he killed all the many people he killed, had to commit suicide. The only ones able to stay alive were the ones who never admitted that they committed a crime against people—that is, the ones who rationalized that Jews were not human beings and deserved to be killed, or that they were only following orders. There's another, more recent example provided by the officials and the population—the white population—of Neshoba County, Mississippi (that's where Philadelphia is). They could not condemn Sheriff Rainey, his deputies, and the other fourteen men who killed three human beings. They could not because they elected Mr. Rainey to do precisely what he did; and condemning him would be condemning themselves.

In a much larger view, SNCC says that white America cannot condemn herself for her criminal acts against black America. So black people have done it—you stand condemned. The institutions that function in this country are clearly racist; they're built upon racism. The questions to be dealt with then are: How can black people inside this country move? How can white people who say they're not part of those institutions begin to move? And how then do we begin to clear away the obstacles that we have in this society, to make us live like human beings?

Several people have been upset because we've said that integration was irrelevant when initiated by blacks, and that in fact it was an insidious subterfuge for the maintenance of white supremacy. In the past six years or so, this country has been feeding us a "thalidomide drug of integration," and some Negroes have been walking down a dream street talking about sitting next to white people. That does not begin to solve the problem. We didn't go to Mississippi to sit next to Ross Barnett [former Governor of Mississippi], we did not go to sit next to Jim Clark [sheriff of Selma, Alabama], we went to get them out of our way. People ought to understand that; we were never fighting for the right to integrate, we were fighting against white supremacy. In order to understand white supremacy we must dismiss the fallacious notion that white people can give anybody his freedom. A man is born free. You may enslave a man after he is born free, and that is in fact what this country does. It enslaves blacks after they're born. The only thing white people can do is stop denying black people their freedom.

I maintain that every civil rights bill in this country was passed for white people, not for black people. For example, I am black. I know that. I also know that while I am black I am a human being. Therefore I have the right to go into any public place. White people didn't know that. Every time I tried to go into a public place they stopped me. So some boys had to write a bill to tell that white man, "He's a human being; don't stop him." That bill was for the white man, not for me. I knew I could vote all the time and that it wasn't a privilege but my right. Every time I tried I was shot, killed or jailed, beaten or economically deprived. So somebody had to write a bill to tell white people, "When a black man comes to vote, don't bother him." That bill was for white people. I know I can live anyplace I want to live. It is white people across this country who are incapable of allowing me to live where I want. You need a civil rights bill, not me. The failure of the civil rights bill isn't because of Black Power or because of the Student Nonviolent Coordinating Committee or because of the rebellions that are occurring in the major cities. That failure is due to the whites' incapacity to deal with their own problems inside their own communities.

We are now engaged in a psychological struggle in this country about whether or not black people have the right to use the words they want to use without white people giving their sanction. We maintain the use of the words Black Power—let them address themselves to that. We are not going to wait for white people to sanction Black Power. We're tired of waiting; every time black people try to move in this country, they're forced to defend their position beforehand. It's time that white people do that. They ought to start defending themselves as to why they have oppressed and exploited us. A man was picked as a slave for one reason—the color of his skin. Black was automatically inferior, inhuman, and therefore fit for slavery, so the question of whether or not we are individually suppressed is nonsensical, and it's a downright lie. We are oppressed as a group because we are black, not because we are lazy or apathetic, not because we're stupid or we stink, not because we eat watermelon or have good rhythm. We are oppressed because we are black.

In order to escape that oppression we must wield the group power we have, not the individual power that this country sets as the criterion under which a man may come into it. That's what is called integration. "You do what

I tell you to do and we'll let you sit at the table with us." Well, if you believe in integration, you can come live in Watts, send your children to the ghetto schools. Let's talk about that. If you believe in integration, then we're going to start adopting us some white people to live in our neighborhoods. So it is clear that this question is not one of integration or segregation. We cannot afford to be concerned about the 6 per cent of black children in this country whom you allow to enter white schools. We are going to be concerned about the 94 per cent. You ought to be concerned about them too. But are we willing to be concerned about the black people who will never get to Berkeley, never get to Harvard, and cannot get an education, the ones you'll never get a chance to rub shoulders with and say, "Why, he's almost as good as we are; he's not like the others"? The question is, How can white society begin to move to see black people as human beings? I am black, therefore I am. Not: I am black and I must go to college to prove myself. I am black, therefore I am. And don't deprive me of anything and say to me that you must go to college before you gain access to X, Y, and Z. That's only a rationalization for suppression.

⌐⌐

We have found all the myths of the country to be nothing but downright lies. We were told that if we worked hard we would succeed, and if that were true we would own this country lock, stock, and barrel. We have picked the cotton for nothing; we are the maids in the kitchens of liberal white people; we are the janitors, the porters, the elevator men; we sweep up your college floors. We are the hardest workers and the lowest paid. It is nonsensical for people to talk about human relationships until they are willing to build new institutions. Black people are economically insecure. White liberals are economically secure. Can you begin to build an economic coalition? Are the liberals willing to share their salaries with the economically insecure black people they so much love? Then if you're not, are you willing to start building new institutions that will provide economic security for black people? That's the question *we* want to deal with!

American students are perhaps the most politically unsophisticated students in the world. Across every country of the world, while we were growing up, students were leading the major revolutions of their countries. We have not been able to do that. They have been politically aware of their existence. In South America our neighbors have one every 24 hours just to remind us that they are politically aware. But we have been unable to grasp it because we've always moved in the field of morality and love while people have been politically jiving with our lives. You can't move morally against men like Brown and Reagan. You can't move morally against Lyndon Baines Johnson because he is an immoral man. He doesn't know what it's all about. So you've got to move politically. We have to develop a political sophistication that doesn't parrot, "The two-party system is the best system in the world." We have to raise questions about whether we need new types of political institutions in this country, and we in SNCC maintain that we need them now. Any time Lyndon Baines Johnson can head a party that has in it Bobby Kennedy, Wayne Morse, Eastland, Wallace, and all those other supposed-to-be-liberal cats, there's something wrong with that party. They're moving politically, not morally. If that party refuses to seat black people from Mississippi and goes ahead and seats racists like Eastland and his clique, it's clear to me that they're moving politically, and that one cannot begin to talk morality to people like that.

We must question the values of this society, and I maintain that black people are the best people to do that since we have been excluded from that society. We ought to think whether or not we want to become a part of that society. That's precisely what the Student Nonviolent Coordinating Committee is doing. We are raising questions about this country. I do not want to be a part of the American pie. The American pie means raping South Africa, beating Vietnam, beating South America, raping the Philippines, raping every country you've been in. I don't want any of your blood money. I don't want to be part of that system. We are the generation who has found this country to be a world power and the wealthiest country in the world. We must question whether or not we want this country to continue being the wealthiest country in the world at the price of raping everybody else. And because black people are saying we do not now want to become a part of you, we are called reverse racists. Ain't that a gas?

White society has caused the failure of nonviolence. I was always surprised at Quakers who came to Alabama and counseled me to be nonviolent, but didn't have the guts to tell James Clark to be nonviolent. That's where nonviolence needs to be preached—to Jim Clark, not to black people. White people should conduct their nonviolent schools in Cicero where they are needed, not among black people in Mississippi. Six-foot-two men kick little black children in Grenada—can you conduct nonviolent schools there? Can you name one black man today who has killed anybody white and is still alive? Even after a rebellion, when some black brothers throw bricks and bottles, ten thousand of them have to pay the price. When the white policeman comes in, anybody who's black is arrested because we all look alike.

The youth of this country must begin to raise those questions. We are going to have to change the foreign policy of this country. One of the problems with the peace movement is that it is too caught up in Vietnam, and if America pulled out the troops from Vietnam this week, next week you'd have to get another peace movement for Santo Domingo. We have to hook up with black people around the world; and that hookup must not only be psychological, but real. If South America were to rebel today, and black people were to shoot the hell out of all the white people there, as they should, Standard Oil would crumble tomorrow. If South Africa were to go today, Chase Manhattan Bank would crumble tomorrow. If Zimbabwe, which is called Rhodesia by white people, were to go tomorrow, General Electric would cave in on the East Coast. How do we stop those institutions that are so willing to fight against "Communist aggression" but close their eyes against racist oppression? We're not talking about a policy of aid or sending Peace Corps people in to teach people how to read and write and build houses while we steal their raw materials from them. Because that's all this country does. What underdeveloped countries need is information about how to become industrialized, so they can keep their raw materials where they have them, produce goods, sell them to this country for the price it's supposed to pay. Instead, America keeps selling goods back to them for a profit and keeps sending our modern day missionaries there, calling them the sons of Kennedy. And if the youth are going to participate in that program, how do you begin to control the Peace Corps?

This country assumes that if someone is poor, they are poor because of their own individual blight, or because they weren't born on the right side of town, or they had too many children, or went in the army too early, or because their father was a drunk, or they didn't care about school—they made a mistake. That's a lot of nonsense. Poverty is well calculated in this country, and the reason why the poverty program won't work is because the calculators of poverty are administering it.

How can you, as the youth in this country, move to start carrying those things out? Move into the white community. We have developed a movement in the black community. The white activist has miserably failed to develop the movement inside of his community. Will white people have the courage to go into white communities and start organizing them? That's the question for the white activist. We won't get caught up in questions about power. This country knows what power is. It knows what Black Power is because it deprived black people of it for over four hundred years. White people associate Black Power with violence because of their own inability to deal with blackness. If we had said "Negro power" nobody would get scared. Everybody would support it. If we said power for colored people, everybody'd be for that, but it is the word "black" that bothers people in this country, and that's their problem, not mine. That's the lie that says anything black is bad.

You're all a college and university crowd. You've taken your basic logic course. You know about major premise, minor premise. People have been telling you anything all black is bad. Let's make that our major premise.

Major premise: Anything all black is bad.

Minor premise or particular premise: I am all black.

Therefore . . . I'm never going to be put in that bag; I'm all black and I'm all good. Anything all black is not necessarily bad. Anything all black is only bad when you use force to keep whites out. Now that's what white people have done in this country, and they're projecting their same fears and guilt on us, and we won't have it. Let them handle their own affairs and their own guilt. Let them find their own psychologists. We refuse to be the therapy for white society any longer. We have gone stark, raving mad trying to do it.

I look at Dr. King on television every single day, and I say to myself: "Now there is a man who's desperately needed in this country. There is a man full of love. There is a man full of mercy. There is a man full of compassion." But every time I see Lyndon on television, I say, "Martin, baby, you got a long way to go."

If we were to be real and honest, we would have to admit that most people in this country see things black and white. We live in a country that's geared that way. White people would have to admit that they are afraid to go into a black ghetto at night. They're afraid because they'd be "beat up," "lynched," "looted," "cut up," etc. It happens to black people inside the ghetto every day, incidentally. Since white people are afraid of that, they get a man to do it for them—a policeman. Figure his mentality. The first time a black man jumps, that white man's going to shoot him. Police brutality is going to exist on that level. The only time I hear people talk about nonviolence is when black people move to defend themselves against white people. Black people cut themselves every night in the ghetto—nobody talks about nonviolence. White people beat up black people every day—nobody talks about nonviolence. But as soon as black people start to move, the double standard comes into being. You can't defend yourself. You show me a black man who advocates aggressive violence who would be able to live in this country. Show him to me. Isn't it hypocritical for Lyndon to talk about how you can't accomplish anything by looting and you must accomplish it by the legal ways? What does he know about legality? Ask Ho Chi Minh.

We must wage a psychological battle on the right for black people to define themselves as they see fit, and organize themselves as they see fit. We don't know whether the white community will allow for that organizing, because once they do they must also allow for the organizing inside their own community. It doesn't make a difference, though—we're going to organize our way. The question is how we're going to organize our way. The question is how we're going to facilitate those matters, whether it's going to be done with a thousand policemen with submachine guns, or whether it's going to be done in a context where it's allowed by white people warding off those policemen. Are white people who call themselves activists ready to move into the white communities on two counts, on building new political institutions to destroy the old ones that we have, and to move around the concept of white youth refusing to go into the army? If so, then we can start to build a new world. We must urge you to fight now to be the leaders of today, not tomorrow. This country is a nation of thieves. It stands on the brink of becoming a nation of murderers. We must stop it. We must stop it. We must stop it.

We are on the move for our liberation. We're tired of trying to prove things to white people. We are tired of trying to explain to white people that we're not going to hurt them. We are concerned with getting the things we want, the things we have to have to be able to function. The question is, Will white people overcome their racism and allow for that to happen in this country? If not, we have no choice but to say very clearly, "Move on over, or we're going to move on over you."

Joseph M. Montoya

(1915–1978)

The Silent People No Longer

November 17, 1967

No longer are they the silent people. No longer are they content to labor silently in a million fields.

A moderate and committed Democrat, Joseph Montoya fulfilled the dual roles of congressman and champion of the Latino community.

Born in New Mexico, the son of Spanish immigrants, Montoya at the age of twenty-two became the youngest man in the state's history to be elected to the New Mexico House of Representatives. From there, like a lightning bolt, he shot into the national arena, where he served eighteen years in U. S. Congress, first in the House and then in the Senate. During his decades of service, Montoya championed civil rights, education, and health care for all Americans, while always ensuring that government programs were accessible to all Mexican Americans.

In November 1967 Montoya testified before Congress in support of the Interagency Committee on Mexican-American Affairs, declaring that the Latino community could no longer afford to be silent on the issue of civil rights. In an oblique criticism of the increasingly militant Chicano youth movement, Montoya advocated nonviolent protest as the ultimate means of progress.

———

Mr. President, for these many years the Spanish-speaking people of our Nation have been silent. Although they have cried out in their own way, they were not heard. Yet by their very silence, they spoke volumes.

Now, throughout our Nation, and particularly in the southwestern part of the country, our Spanish-speaking citizens are moving forward. Their voices are often heard after all these years. Sometimes they are heard in protest against injustice. Always they are raised in favor of self-help and progress.

There is a stirring among them that is unique in their history. It comes like a ground swell, and is irresistible in its force, as it reaches out to and carries along almost all our young people. Suddenly they are aware that what suited the people of yesterday need not suit them today, and surely not tomorrow. It is as if a curtain had been brushed aside, and an entire new world had been revealed to them.

No longer are they "the silent people." No longer are they content to labor silently in a million fields. The time is forever past when they were content to stand silent at thousands of back doors. A time will never return when they are willing to wait silently at thousands of store counters.

Their eyes look up or forward, rather than down. Their hats remain on their heads, instead of being in their hands. Truly, a new age is upon us.

Throughout the area they are participating in new, vital programs that have brought so much new awareness to so many of them.

Many of these programs are successful. Some have had limited success. But most important of all, they have made them aware of themselves as people, and given them a new pride in an old heritage. It is enhancing their ability to contribute to this Nation. I take pardonable pride in their awakening. I seek to give impetus to their strivings. I wish to hasten them on their road to accomplishment.

These vast movings are all the more significant because our American dream has become even more meaningful to them. Their faith is deep and gives all the more impetus to their seeking. But it also carries within it the seeds of their frustration.

We must meet them halfway. We must let them know our land keeps faith with them, and will never turn its back on their just requests.

Reies López Tijerina
(1926–)

The Land Grant Question
NOVEMBER 20, 1967

*I only stand as . . . an American citizen, for those rights that truth-
fully, constitutionally belong to the Spanish American.*

Arguably the most militant Chicano activist of his time, Reies López
Tijerina grew up in the deprived world of impoverished immigrant
workers. Years before he was born, Reies's father, like thousands of
Mexican Americans at the time, had lost his land to duplicitous Anglo
landowners.

At nineteen, Tijerina attended bible college in Texas and quickly
earned a reputation as a fiery, persuasive orator who, with clapping hands
and waving arms, invoked New Testament parables and an "actor's shift-
ing of emotional levels." By the late 1950s, he applied social and community activism and to the controversial land grant issue. Prey to legal
technicalities, swindlers, and government taxes, New Mexicans alone by
1958 had lost 3.7 million acres of grazing and crop land that Tijerina
argued was rightly theirs under the 1848 Treaty of Guadalupe Hidalgo.
The loss of land and pervasive discrimination resulted in poverty, malnutrition, welfare dependence, and unemployment. In response, Tijerina
launched a militant social campaign in 1963—dubbed "Alianza Federal
de Mercedes"—to reclaim the lost land through the courts and demand
cultural, political, and educational rights for all Hispanic Americans, especially those he represented in rural New Mexico.

Although Tijerina gained recognition through his radio, television,
and newspaper campaigns, he catapulted to national prominence in the
mid-1960s after he was arrested and imprisoned for shooting up a courthouse in Tierra Amarilla. *Newsweek* reported that a growing number of
Latinos openly attacked Tijerina and his "racist" ways. Still, the Chicano
leader with "the tongue of a Latin Moses" remained front and center in
the Hispanic American civil rights movement in the 1960s.

On November 20, 1967, Tijerina delivered this speech to a predominantly Anglo audience at the University of Colorado at Denver, not
long after he was released from prison.

THANK YOU, LADIES AND GENTLEMEN. It's a pleasure to be here. I'd like to thank the student body or whoever invited me to be here.

I'd like to take advantage of the opportunity in order to destroy certain lies, fabricated, calculated with evil intentions by the press, especially UPI who gave me the new name of "King Tiger."

—————

Ladies and gentlemen, it is my privilege to, to explain the historical, organized crimes of federal government through its agencies. To explain the truth, constitutional, legal and international laws that have been frozen completely—with evil intentions. I will try to explain why they froze those truths, those laws. Even though United States prides itself in the, being the ruler and referee, umpire throughout the world through international commitments, treaties. Through a treaty he keeps a foot in Guantanamo Base. Through a treaty he keeps a foot in Vietnam and throughout the whole world. Yet I will call your attention at this time [to] what finger or foot he is keeping on the Treaty of Guadalupe Hidalgo.

A life of a nation, of a people, depends on this treaty; therefore we feel that it's very much important to us. It is our Constitution. If you read Article Two, Section—Article Six, Section Two of the Constitution of the United States, you will read that all the treaties made by the authority of the United States become the supreme law of the land.

When I came to New Mexico twenty-five years ago, nobody there—not even the politicians—knew that Article Two, Section Five of the constitution of New Mexico existed, which stipulated that all the rights, privileges and immunities—civil, political or religious—guaranteed to the people of New Mexico by the Treaty of Guadalupe Hidalgo were, shall be preserved inviolate. Yet they were not only violated but all those privileges, immunities and rights were frozen completely and wrecked.

Ladies and gentlemen, we must learn to distinguish between the reality and discrimination, between reality and nationalism, between the reality and isolation. I'm not against any nation or race or creed or religion or political philosophies, but I only stand as a citizen, as an American citizen, for those rights that truthfully, constitutionally belong to the Spanish American.

Many who have heard and read what has been happening in New Mexico the last two or three years only know that they are some "rebels" and some people trying to claim land. They have no rights. And some have, go as far as to say that if we are to return land, well let's return it to the Indians. Those narrow and stupid opinions and statements will not hold water in the light of law and order, constitutional and international law.

I'd like to explain the background of our claims in order to help those that truly want to understand because we—like the black man and like the

Indian—are here to stay, and we don't intend to allow anybody from here on to tamper and fool around with our cultural rights and our property. The world has developed. Science has developed. And while some are dedicated and spending millions of dollars to discover techniques, science and elements to make bombs and subdue other people, we are dedicated to justice—that hidden element, that potential, hidden potential that has been left aside and it has been used only the name.

Before going into the land grant question, ladies and gentlemen, I'd like to for the benefit as I said of those who really want to understand because we are part of America. We belong here and there is much more connected to the land grants and to the Spanish language. This is an educational institution and writers and historians are like architects. They build, they coin, they frame the history; they write it. They either irritate, incite hatred or harmonize and bring synchronization between languages, races and creeds. So I'd like to state clear to the student body: I think you should be interested in knowing the facts. In order to understand the, or to find a medicine for the illness we must discover first what is the kind of disease, what is the ailment, what is the, how the illness or disease developed.

~

We must know these facts, ladies and gentlemen, in order to understand who we are. Where does the United States stand and will stand twenty, thirty years from now when there will be six hundred million Castilian, Spanish speaking, Latin American or Spanish Americans throughout the continent? Where will the United States be when he loses every friend around the world? It is proven and we are seeing that fact. Eventually we're cutting and breaking friendships and every neighbor, every friend around throughout the world with our million soldiers scattered throughout forty countries, tampering and fooling around with the constitution and rights of every country in the world because we feel that God has commanded us to tell everybody what to do. There is, there is *no* reason, as holy as it might be, that might give us the right to tamper and fool around with the destiny of other nations. So we must understand these facts, ladies and gentlemen, because now you are dealing and we are Spanish Americans, not Spaniards. We are a new breed, a new people developed in the last four hundred and fifty-three years last October the nineteenth.

~

God told Abraham when Abraham said, "Where is my people? Where is my nation? You promised me a nation, where is it?" He said, "Four hundred and thirty years from now you will have one. But it is necessary for you people to be slaves, servants in Egypt. But after four hundred years I will get them out of

Egypt, and they will be a great nation and I will give them this land that is now inhabited by the Canaanites." After four hundred odd years it was fulfilled.

Why four hundred and thirty years, ladies and gentlemen? That's how much it takes for a race, a new breed, to develop. Did you know that time is the most important element in nations, and breeds and individuals? It is very important, the time, the years for an individual, on the individual life and also on the nation. In order for a child when he goes to school he knows not history. He begans—four, five or six-year-old child—he goes to school. There he meets with other young ones that are already in the third grade and the fourth grade. They know more so they take advantage of that poor child. But eventually he goes through the same experiences and developing and then learns and learns to compete and then he graduates and then he becomes a young man. And he goes to the world to face the life.

That's just the way it is with nations, ladies and gentlemen. Don't overlook that. You are in an educational institution. You are in a place where you can learn it. Sociology. Anthropology. The Anglo is two thousand, five hundred years old; that's equivalent of a young man of twenty-five years old. The Jew is from five to six thousand years old so that makes him an old man of sixty years old worth plenty of intelligence accumulated. But the Spanish American—the new breed—is only four years and some days and months old. So we just have hit the stage, the time when we now have found ourselves. We now know that this continent has breed, brewed a new breed, a new people.

———

Ladies and gentlemen, it is from this standpoint of view that I would like to speak to you tonight. Every nation has the date of birth, every nation, even the Anglo. There was a time when two races got together and mixed and out came another race, which is now known as the Anglo race. The Italian, the Frenchman, the Jew, the Egyptian, the Arab—we all had our dates of birth. October the nineteenth, one thousand, five hundred and fourteen, according to Law Two, Title One, Book Four of the Laws of the Indies, this new breed was born, ladies and gentlemen. I am proud to say that I know the day, I know the year and I know the law that, through which we were born. Born out of law. And we are not bastards, as some people call us in Texas. Bastards! No, we were born by Law Two, Title One, Book Four of the Law of the Indies. What was the date? And to what law the Anglo was born? Do I see somebody lifting his fingers or hand? Does he know the date, the year, the law? Were they born in lock, in law, or were they born out of law, out?

Ladies and gentlemen, it might sound funny because, of course, you have no point. But I have it. It is my privilege to sound, make noise, yes, ring the bells around these facts. There is no citizen of the United States that has the right to condemn nor curse or say, "Baloney, to hell with your dates and laws, etc." I'm sorry.

Ladies and gentlemen, United States has a role to play in this continent, a temporary role. Let's not overlook it. God has been keeping up with the conduct of this nation ever since 1776. . . .

We are not asking for something that does not belong to us legally, constitutionally, ladies and gentlemen. The land grant question is a part of this continent, part of the Constitution and is part of our language and our face. So please endure, allow us to establish our side. There is a hidden side, a dark side of the moon, a dark side of the history of the United States—a hidden side, ladies and gentlemen—that has been kept frozen and hidden. But I would bring it partly out tonight, if you allow me. You have this hidden side. That's why they murdered, they destroyed, they killed sixty million buffaloes. Something that no savage nation, not even Genghis Khan had done—to whip the Indians because they couldn't whip them face to face. Every chief— Crazyhorse, Cochise, Vittorio, every one of them were murdered in the conference table, except Geronimo. But because, like he said, because he learned to lie, he stayed around by lying like the Anglo, or the white man as he used to call him.

Ladies and gentlemen, why am I talking this way? Am I anti-Anglo? No, sir. No. I like to stay alive and I like to help the Anglo. He's my older brother because he's twenty-five years old and—but I must help him. He needs me and I need him. If we are to survive we must come face to face and face our sins and our crimes and confess them. Just like we have the courts and the police. They enforce the law with the force, with guns, with a badge. Well, just as history, facts and the power of justice is catching up with this nation, is catching up with Uncle Sam, ladies and gentlemen, that is why, that is why Uncle Sam is afraid of Alianza Federal of Free City States. That is why they are afraid of Tijerina. Not because he believes in violence. No, sir. On the contrary, this nation likes violence. Yes, throughout the whole world he's engulfed in violence. He likes violence. That's what he's doing in Vietnam. And that's what he wants me to do so he can destroy me immediately. But why then, if he likes violence and he's not afraid of having me commit violence, why is he preaching in the newspaper across the nation that Tijerina and the Alianza is violent and using violence in New Mexico? Why? It's too easy to understand it. They're afraid of their own sins, their own crimes, historical crimes that were kept on the hidden, dark side of the moon and now they are coming out. The flame, the spark, the spirit of justice in the stream of blood of this new breed is bringing the whole thing to the surface, ladies and gentlemen.

That is why this nation, especially the executive department, the President, who knows very well. Maybe you read the papers. I don't know whether you got it here when Hubert Humphrey in El Paso, speaking to the Spanish

Americans in the all–Spanish American executive-level meeting, he said: "The Spanish Americans have top priority because their fore-fathers were driven out of their Spanish and Mexican land grants." For the first time we got him to confess it publicly. It's on the record, on the newspaper, on the front page of the Albuquerque General. The Alianza is not a trouble-maker, ladies and gentlemen. Tijerina is not a trouble-maker.

Now what about these land grants? What are the land grants? What's in it for us? Does the destiny of the United States depend on these land grants? Or is it just a minor problem, ladies and gentlemen? There are seventeen hundred and fifteen land grants in the United States of America, an area of over one hundred million acres, all covered by international law in the Treaty of Guadalupe Hidalgo. The Anglo and company; remember, remember that Spain ruled the continent for three hundred years. They had accumulated plenty of hatred, as you can see in the books written by the experts. Haters. Expert writers, who saw nothing in Spain but bad, evil: "Catholicism is a devil religion, so let's rid them out. Let's get rid of them!"

Ladies and gentlemen, that is why we have to stop hate. The historians have been building up hate through the writing, writings, through their books. That is why we were robbed of our land, of our culture because of the hate that the U.S. had against Spain, ladies and gentlemen. Let's face it. I'm not lying. The history is full of those repetitions: one nation taking revenge against the other nation because the other nation had built up an empire. Now when they got him down, they retaliate. Just like they did with the Roman empire, the Egyptian empire, the Grecian empire, the Assyrian empire, Babylonian empire and now this great empire, ladies and gentlemen. Like they all did with Spain and succeeded they will do with this great power, ladies and gentlemen.

With power you cannot reason. That's why the Monroe Doctrine says, "Out! America for the Americans." But on the street we were called "Mexicans." Then James Monroe, what he meant was that America for the Anglo, the English speaking people. But he used the term psychologically, diplomatically—"America for the Americans." But they had something hidden. Ladies and gentlemen, we have suffered for the crimes and sins of Spain. We have suffered, we the Spanish Americans. That's why our culture was not respected nor protected, even though the Constitution provides for it. Now the Anglo, the Italian, the French and company, they have finished the job so now they no longer hate us; now they want to live like brothers. Now they want to preach the Bible: "Thou shalt not kill. Thou shalt not steal—not even land grants. Thou shalt not take these." But, what do we see on the TV? The Bible in one hand, the rifle in another hand: stealing, burning and destroying and murdering, ladies and gentlemen.

These land grants are scattered throughout South America. And as our land grants were taken away here in New Mexico, in Mexico were taken away from the Indians and the new breed by blue-eyed Spaniards, rich millionaires from Mexico. In Argentina the same, in Brazil, in Chile, Peru—all throughout South America, ladies and gentlemen. And, it will be a chain reaction. Let's not fool ourselves. It will come to surface because science and power have balanced the whole thing between the rich and the poor, the powerful and the weak. It's catching up. That is why the government, the federal government is trying to brand me as a "rebel, criminal" and send me to the penitentiary. That is why, because he's afraid to face these facts; the hidden, dark side of the moon of the United States has come to the open, ladies and gentlemen.

These common lands, these lands that we are claiming belong, not to individuals, they belong to the pueblos, town councils, villas and cities. . . .

Ladies and gentlemen, we cannot swallow it. We cannot live with this kind of destruction, fake, hypocrisy, murdering, killing, destroying. That is why they want to, they have frozen the Spanish American education in schools. They don't want our children to know about the treaty, about the land grants, about the historical background, about the dates of our birth. They don't want our children to know the facts because then they will have pride.

Everyone in America has the right to state their beliefs, ladies and gentlemen. This Constitution does not say that only English shall be spoken. This Constitution does not limit the rights, protection for the rights of the Anglos, or the Italians or the Jews. It involves, especially Article Nine of the Amendments to the Constitution of the United States. Read the history of the Supreme Court and you will find that Article Nine has never been invoked by any court of the United States of America. Did you know that? Ask a lawyer. Why? Because it says the enumeration of certain rights in this Constitution shall not be construed to deprive the people, deprive other rights retained by the people. You got it? The enumeration of certain rights in this Constitution shall not be construed to deprive other rights retained by the people. Now, what are those other rights retained by the people? It already mentions the elaboration of certain rights. What are those other rights retained by the people? That's where the Laws of the Indies and the original rights of the Spanish Americans had retained for three hundred years. We were promised protection for those rights, ladies and gentlemen. That's why they have never invoked, have never made use of Article Nine of the Amendments to the Constitution of the United States. They have no use for it. But we have. The Spanish Americans. We do have.

So, ladies and gentlemen, I thank you for your attention, and I hope you got part of the picture. It's too long; it's too large to bring it out and condense it in forty-five minutes clear enough for you to get it and understand it. Even myself, when I came to this law, these facts, they didn't attract my attention. But the more I thought about it they became a reality, serious. And then I found out that we could not survive, we could not be heard without focusing the attention of the world on to these facts and these laws and these rights, ladies and gentlemen.

So, we will prove in the courts, and if the United Nations come in and investigate the whole thing, we will show the proof, facts, evidence. How our leaders were murdered. How our documents were destroyed. How Congress enacted laws to rape our cities, our villages and our language. How the United States has been violating the Constitution made by its own founders.

So you see, ladies and gentlemen, now why, why the Spanish American is speaking out. The Spanish American—as poor as he is—he can see through the future and see that we're running out of time and out of friends. Eventually only Latin America, South America will come to the rescue of the Anglo, that's what John F. Kennedy said before he died. And, of course, that was too bitter for the proudful and the bad part—the bad Anglos—for the good ones are always with the Constitution and with the truth and justice. But the bad ones, they couldn't swallow that; to hear President and Robert Kennedy saying that Texas and the War of Texas was a shame, was a dark, dirty page in the history of [the] United States.

So, ladies and gentlemen, you can see we are needed. We have a role to play in this continent in the future. Not right now. Right now we look like a cricket. What is a cricket? King of the insects; a little, tiny animal. All the cricket can do is just "cricket, cricket, cricket." Just a noise, that's all. But you know, if that cricket gets in the eye and the ear of the lion and scratches the inside, there is nothing the lion can do. There is nothing; there is no way the lion can use his claws and tooth and jaws to destroy the cricket because, because he's way deep in the structure inside. The more the lion scratches himself the more deeper the cricket goes inside and scratches. We are a cricket, but we are too deep inside of this continent, of this country, ladies and gentlemen. And the lion, the greatest giant ever built by taxpayers, Uncle Sam. There's nothing he can do to destroy us. Let's face it. Let's come to a table. Let's confer. Let's talk. Let's come to an understanding.

———⌐

Now you understand that it's not something rare that we are preaching the land grants, invoking them, proclaiming, protesting them, demanding. Now you know why. This is the era of justice and claims. The Indian is doing it. The black man is doing it—in his own way. And he's succeeding. Small nations are getting independence, such as Africa. Twenty years ago Africa was nothing but colonies of white nations. Now there are more than thirty-four all-African, nationalist, independent nations. Why? Did they use atom bombs to secure their independence? No, ladies and gentlemen. The pressure of justice. The pressure of mankind. The pressure of humanity and the pressure of mankind will deliver the land grants, liberate these land grants. The pressure of mankind, ladies and gentlemen.

So now we have spoken. We invite all good Anglos, Italians, Jews, et cetera, et cetera, to help us with our struggle. We will help you with your struggle, whatever it might be. But let's not turn our backs to history, to facts, to law, to the Constitution. You claim your rights under the Constitution; we claim our land grants under the Constitution, Article Six, Section Two. So it's nothing new; it's just that you didn't know about it. This great giant didn't want it preached in school, that's all. So how could you know? It's not discrimination. Let's face it. Spain, sure, Spain made her mistakes and crimes and whatever you want to call them. But it was not the new breed. Why should we pay for the crimes of Spain? We are true Americans. Did you know that we are the only—speaking politically, constitutionally, grass-roots from bottom—did you know that we are one of the only breeds, off-spring of the continent? We are not descendants of immigrants; we are not descendants of wetbacks. No. We were born from the native Indian, ladies and gentlemen. Yes. The rulers in Spain are sprinkled with blood, yes, and he left his Castilian language. But the tortilla, the chili he didn't give us. Those are our original fruits, fruits of the new breed, the tortilla.

～～

Ladies and gentlemen, behold our country coming to nothing just like all the empires. Let's help. Let's come in and help, but it's going to be a little bitter because we got some land coming and you have to help us. We'll help you. This country can be inhabited by Indians because, let me tell you, that this document that will be presented to the United Nations will be signed by the Spanish Americans, by the black man and by the Indians. Because we have all been hurt, oppressed and deprived of certain rights—the black man, the Indian and the Spanish American, the new breed.

We'll ask the United Nations to investigate. Only for the survival of the United States, ladies and gentlemen, not because we hold any hatred. Hatred is not mobilized in our hearts and spirits. It's just that new potential that has been discovered in New Mexico: Justice—not communism—justice. Communism does not stand a chance in New Mexico. No, only justice. But not that justice written in the books by historians, ladies, no. Justice—that virgin element, potential created by God—that synchronizes, harmonizes all the elements of the world and brings about peace. Thank you very much.

CÉSAR CHÁVEZ
(1927–1993)

Breaking Bread for Progress
MARCH 10, 1968

It is my deepest belief that only by giving our lives do we find life.

Born in 1927 on a farm near Yuma, Arizona, César Chávez, with his constant yet "quiet intensity and charisma," became one of the most celebrated leaders of nonviolent protest and civic activism. In 1939 Chávez's parents lost their farm in a bank foreclosure, forcing them into the life of migrant agricultural workers. César soon experienced firsthand the mistreatment and injustice migrant laborers in his community withstood on a daily basis. It was then that he decided to dedicate his life to organizing and protecting farmhands and harvest workers. In 1962 he formed the National Farm Workers Association, which later became the United Farm Workers branch of the AFL-CIO. Mainstream magazines quickly labeled Chávez "a folk legend" and "one of the best-known American labor leaders, and probably the most controversial." Although celebrated, he often clashed with other Latino leaders over his positions on unions and immigration, as well as his rhetorical approach and manner.

In 1965, protesting low wages for grape harvesters, Chávez organized a strike against the San Joaquin Valley, California, grape growers. Supported by multiple organizations, this one protest grew into a widespread crusade for civil rights and human dignity that lasted late into the decade.

In 1968, with Gandhi and King as his guides, Chávez undertook a twenty-five-day fast to promote nonviolent protest and equal opportunity in the San Joaquin Valley and beyond. The strike drew attention and support from all corners of the country, particularly in the media and the halls of Congress. Upon its completion, Chávez broke bread with Senator Robert Kennedy, who flew to California to join him at the celebratory mass.

On March 10, 1968, scores of workers gathered in Delano, the center of the strike, to receive a message from Chávez, who was too weak to speak himself. Read by Rev. James Drake, Chávez's words commemorated the grape growers and their remarkable harmony and fidelity; he urged them to maintain their enthusiasm and commitment to nonviolent protest.

I HAVE ASKED the Rev. James Drake to read this statement to you because my heart is so full and my body too weak to be able to say what I feel.

My warm thanks to all of you for coming today. Many of you have been here before, during the Fast. Some have sent beautiful cards and telegrams and made offerings at the Mass. All of these expressions of your love have strengthened me and I am grateful.

We should all express our thanks to Senator Kennedy for his constant work on behalf of the poor, for his personal encouragement to me, and for taking the time to break bread with us today.

I do not want any of you to be deceived about the Fast. The strict Fast of water only which I undertook on February 15 ended after the 21st day because of the advice of our doctor, James McKnight, and other physicians. Since that time I have been taking liquids in order to prevent serious damage to my kidneys.

We are gathered here today not so much to observe the end of the Fast but because we are a family bound together in a common struggle for justice. We are a Union family celebrating our unity and the non-violent nature of our movement. Perhaps in the future we will come together at other times and places to break bread and to renew our courage and to celebrate important victories.

The Fast has had different meanings for different people. Some of you may still wonder about its meaning and importance. It was not intended as a pressure against any growers. For that reason we have suspended negotiations and arbitration proceedings and relaxed the militant picketing and boycotting of the strike during this period. I undertook this Fast because my heart was filled with grief and pain for the sufferings of farm workers. The Fast was first for me and then for all of us in this Union. It was a Fast for non-violence and a call to sacrifice.

Our struggle is not easy. Those who oppose our cause are rich and powerful and they have many allies in high places. We are poor. Our allies are few. But we have something the rich do not own. We have our own bodies and spirits and the justice of our cause as our weapons.

When we are really honest with ourselves, we must admit that our lives are all that really belong to us. So, it is how we use our lives that determines what kind of men we are. It is my deepest belief that only by giving our lives do we find life. I am convinced that the truest act of courage, the strongest act of manliness is to sacrifice ourselves for others in a totally non-violent struggle for justice.

To be a man is to suffer for others. God help us to be men!

MARTIN LUTHER KING, JR.
(1929–1968)

I've Been to the Mountaintop
APRIL 3, 1968

I'm not worried about anything. I'm not fearing any man.
Mine eyes have seen the glory of the coming of the Lord.

By the late 1960s, as with other early activists, Martin Luther King, Jr.'s nonviolent, incrementalist approach to civil rights fell under the harsh criticism of those in the black power movement. Despite Dr. King's successes, de facto discrimination remained a bitter reality, even for those in the "old guard." At the risk of being marginalized, King responded by expanding his scope of issues to include economic—not just racial—discrimination and inequality. His Poor People's Movement joined in common cause with hard-pressed Americans of all races and backgrounds, from African-American custodians to Hispanic migrant workers.

On April 3, 1968, King spoke to nearly 3,000 striking sanitation workers at the Masonic Temple in Memphis, Tennessee. In his remarks, King exhorted his audience to continue along the path of nonviolent resistance, particularly in the struggle against economic apartheid, the next step in the march for equal rights.

An eerie prescience of his death, King explained in this well-known passage that he had "been to the mountaintop [and] seen the promised land." The next day, while standing on the balcony of a Memphis hotel, Reverend King was assassinated by James Earl Ray.

───

WELL, I DON'T KNOW what will happen now. We've got some difficult days ahead. But it doesn't matter with me now. Because I've been to the mountaintop. And I don't mind. Like anybody, I would like to live a long life. Longevity has its place. But I'm not concerned about that now. I just want to do God's will. And He's allowed me to go up to the mountain. And I've looked over. And I've seen the promised land. I may not get there with you. But I want you to know tonight, that we, as a people, will get to the promised land. And I'm happy, tonight. I'm not worried about anything. I'm not fearing any man. Mine eyes have seen the glory of the coming of the Lord.

Robert F. Kennedy
(1925–1968)

On Martin Luther King's Death
April 4, 1968

What we need in the United States is . . . love and wisdom
and compassion toward one another, and a feeling of justice
toward those who still suffer within our country, whether
they be white or they be black.

Amid the tragedy of the assassination of Rev. Martin Luther King, Jr.,
Robert F. Kennedy, younger brother of slain president John F. Kennedy,
happened to be scheduled to address a large gathering of African-
American supporters in Indianapolis, Indiana. Police had advised
Kennedy, who was in the midst of his own campaign to win the 1968
Democratic nomination for president, not to make this campaign stop,
which was in a part of the city considered to be a dangerous ghetto.
But Kennedy insisted on going.

Just after he arrived by plane at Indianapolis, Kennedy was told of
King's death. He arrived to find the people in an upbeat mood, anticipating the excitement of a Kennedy appearance. He climbed onto the
platform and, realizing they did not know, broke the news. Just two
months after this speech, Kennedy himself was assassinated on June 5,
1968.

⸻

I HAVE BAD NEWS for you, for all of our fellow citizens, and people who love
peace all over the world, and that is that Martin Luther King was shot and
killed tonight.

Martin Luther King dedicated his life to love and to justice for his fellow
human beings, and he died because of that effort.

In this difficult day, in this difficult time for the United States, it is perhaps
well to ask what kind of a nation we are and what direction we want to move
in. For those of you who are black—considering the evidence there evidently
is that there were white people who were responsible—you can be filled with
bitterness, with hatred, and a desire for revenge. We can move in that direction
as a country, in great polarization—black people amongst black, white people
amongst white, filled with hatred toward one another.

Or we can make an effort, as Martin Luther King did, to understand and to comprehend, and to replace that violence, that stain of bloodshed that has spread across our land, with an effort to understand with compassion and love.

For those of you who are black and are tempted to be filled with hatred and distrust at the injustice of such an act, against all white people, I can only say that I feel in my own heart the same kind of feeling. I had a member of my family killed, but he was killed by a white man. But we have to make an effort in the United States, we have to make an effort to understand, to go beyond these rather difficult times.

My favorite poet was Aeschylus. He wrote: "In our sleep, pain which cannot forget falls drop by drop upon the heart until, in our own despair, against our will, comes wisdom through the awful grace of God."

What we need in the United States is not division; what we need in the United States is not hatred; what we need in the United States is not violence or lawlessness; but love and wisdom, and compassion toward one another, and a feeling of justice toward those who still suffer within our country, whether they be white or they be black.

So I shall ask you tonight to return home, to say a prayer for the family of Martin Luther King, that's true, but more importantly to say a prayer for our own country, which all of us love—a prayer for understanding and that compassion of which I spoke.

We can do well in this country. We will have difficult times; we've had difficult times in the past; we will have difficult times in the future. It is not the end of violence; it is not the end of lawlessness; it is not the end of disorder.

But the vast majority of white people and the vast majority of black people in this country want to live together, want to improve the quality of our life, and want justice for all human beings who abide in our land.

Let us dedicate ourselves to what the Greeks wrote so many years ago: to tame the savageness of man and make gentle the life of this world.

Let us dedicate ourselves to that, and say a prayer for our country and for our people.

DANIEL INOUYE
(1924–)

From Expatriation to Emancipation
AUGUST 29, 1968

Let us reject violence as a means of protest, and let us reject those who preach violence. But let us not tempt those who would hide the evil face of racism behind the mask of law and order.

Until the bombing of Pearl Harbor, Daniel Inouye dreamed of pursuing a career in medicine. But in December 1941, like other Japanese Americans, his life was uprooted. Inouye and his family were classified as "enemy aliens" and marginalized as traitors living on American soil.

Undeterred by this scarlet letter, Inouye enlisted in the military, choosing to fight as an American in World War II, for which he earned fifteen medals as a member of the 442nd Regimental Combat Team. After the war, he returned to Honolulu where he enrolled in law school before pursuing a career in Democratic politics. Inouye has since represented Hawaii in the U.S. House of Representatives and Senate, where he has championed civil rights legislation, including the Civil Rights Act of 1964 and President Lyndon Johnson's Great Society.

Daniel Inouye delivered this keynote address to the Democratic National Convention in Chicago in 1968, at the height of the tumultuous civil rights era. That summer, the nation was still reeling from race riots in its cities, the assassinations of Dr. Martin Luther King, Jr., and Robert F. Kennedy, and the rash of anti-war demonstrations at universities across America. In his stirring remarks, Senator Inouye criticized those attempting to divide the nation and called on all Americans to unite in this time of despair. His words drew widespread approval, launching him onto the short list of vice presidential candidates.

~~~~~

MY FELLOW AMERICANS: This is my country. Many of us have fought hard for the right to say that. Many are struggling today from Harlem to Danang so that they may say it with conviction.

This is our country.

And we are engaged in a time of great testing—testing whether this nation, or any nation conceived in liberty and dedicated to opportunity for all its citizens, can not only endure but continue to progress. The issue before all of us in such a time is how shall we discharge, how shall we honor our citizenship.

—⁀—

I believe the real reason we are here is that there is a word called "commitment," because we are committed to the future of our country and all our people, and because for that future, hope and faith are more needed now than pride in our party's past.

For even as we emerge from an era of unsurpassed social and economic progress, Americans are clearly in no mood for counting either their blessings or their bank accounts.

We are still embarked on the longest unbroken journey of economic growth and prosperity in our history. Yet we are torn by dissension, and disrespect for our institutions and leaders is rife across the land.

In at least two of our greatest universities, learning has been brought to a halt by student rebellions; others of the student revolution have publicly burned draft cards and even the American flag.

Crime has increased so that we are told one out of every three Americans is afraid to walk in his own neighborhood after dark.

Riot has bludgeoned our cities, laying waste our streets, our property and, most important, human lives. The smoke of destruction has even shrouded the dome of our Capitol, and in Washington the task of restoring order drew more than twice as many federal troops as were involved in the defense of Khesanh in Vietnam.

Voices of angry protest are heard throughout the land, crying for all manner of freedoms. Yet our political leaders are picketed and some who cry loudest for freedom have sought to prevent our president, our vice president and cabinet officers from speaking in public.

None go so far as publicly to condone a politics of assassination. Yet assassins' bullets have robbed our country of three great leaders within the last five years.

Why? . . . Why—when we have at last had the courage to open up an attack on the age-old curses of ignorance and disease and poverty and prejudice—why are the flags of anarchism being hoisted by leaders of the next generation? Why, when our maturing society welcomes and appreciates art as never before, are poets and painters so preponderantly hostile? Some conveniently blame all our ills and agonies on a most difficult and unpopular commitment overseas. The Vietnam war must end, they say, because it is an immoral war.

Of course, the war in Vietnam must be ended. But it must be ended, as President Johnson said last March, by patient political negotiation rather than through the victorious force of arms—even though this may be unpalatable for those raised in the tradition of glorious military victories.

But like our other complex problems, this one must also be solved responsibly. Just as we shun irresponsible calls for total and devastating military victory, so must we guard against the illusion of an instant peace that has no chance of permanence.

Of course, the Vietnam war is immoral. Whether by the teachings of Moses or by the teachings of Christ or by the teachings of Buddha, I believe that wars are immoral. During the Crusades, Christians in the name of Jesus Christ slaughtered innocent men, women and children and plundered their cities—because they were of another faith. These were immoral wars.

In Vietnam we build schools across the countryside and feed the hungry in the cities. And our president has pledged massive sums in aid to all Vietnamese as an incentive to peace. And yet this is an immoral war.

Perhaps by the time my four-year-old son is grown, men will have learned to live by the Ten Commandments. But men have not yet renounced the use of force as a means to their objectives.

And until they do, are we more immoral—if there be such a degree—to fracture our solemn commitments and then see our word doubted, not only by our friends abroad, but by our enemies?

Knowing that this could lead to tragic miscalculations, is it less immoral now to take the easier course, and gamble the lives of our sons and grandsons on the outcome?

These are not easy questions and perhaps there are no certain answers.

But when young people have rioted in China and Czechoslovakia as well as at Columbia, and in Paris and Berlin as well as in Berkeley, I doubt that we can blame all the troubles of our time on Vietnam.

Other critics tell us of the revolution of rising expectations. They charge that it has reached such proportions that men now take it as an insult when they are asked to be reasonable in their desires and demands.

If this is too often true as a generalization, it is all too frequently aimed particularly at our fellow citizens of African ancestry, whose aspirations have burst full-blown on us after more than one hundred years of systematic racist deprivation.

As an American whose ancestors came from Japan, I have become accustomed to a question most recently asked by a very prominent businessman who was concerned about the threat of riots and the resultant loss in life and property. "Tell me," he said, "why can't the Negro be like you?"

First, although my skin is colored, it is not black. In this country, the color of my skin does not ignite prejudice that has smoldered for generations.

Second, although my grandfather came to this country in poverty, he came without shackles; he came as a free man enjoying certain constitutional rights under the American flag.

Third, my grandfather's family was not shattered as individual members of it were sold as chattel or used as security on loans. And fourth, although others of my ancestry were interned behind barbed wires during World War II, neither my parents nor I were forced by covenants and circumstances to live in ghettos.

Unlike those of my ancestry, the Negro's unemployment rate is triple the national average. The mortality rate of his children is twice that of white children.

He often pays more for his miserable tenement than comparable space will cost in the white suburbs. He is likely to pay more for his groceries, more for his furniture, more for his liquor and more for his credit.

And, my fellow Americans, today many thousands of black Americans return from Vietnam with medals of valor, some of them have been crippled in the service of their country. But too often they return to economic and social circumstances that are barely, if at all, improved over those they left.

Is it any wonder that the Negro questions whether his place in our country's history books will be any less forgotten than were the contributions of his ancestors? Is it any wonder that the Negroes find it hard to wait another one hundred years before they are accepted as full citizens in our free society?

Of course, expectations are rising—and they are rising faster than we in our imperfect world can fulfill them.

The revolution we in the United States are experiencing was born of Democratic processes that not only accommodate economic progress and social mobility, but actively encourage them.

But it is important to remember that these expectations are the children of progress and that today's restlessness has been nurtured by our very real achievements. Out of these should emerge a brighter and better society than we have known.

Nowhere is this clearer than in the situation of our young people today. The success of our economic system has freed them in ever-increasing numbers from the tragedies of premature mortality and early labor.

It has built the schools in which they are being educated to higher levels than ever in our nation's history. And this progress has been achieved in a political system that not only admits but safeguards the right of dissent.

So it should hardly surprise us when the children of such progress demand to be heard when they become aware of inequities still to be corrected. Neither should we fear their voices. On the contrary, whether we know it or not, the marching feet of youth have led us into a new era of politics and we can never turn back.

But what should concern us is something far more fundamental. The true dimension of the challenge facing us is a loss of faith. I do not mean simply a loss of religious faith, although this erosion is a major contributor to our unease. I mean a loss of faith in our country, in its purposes and its institutions. I mean a retreat from the responsibilities of citizenship.

The plain fact is that in the face of complexity and frustration, too many Americans have drifted into the use of power for purely destructive purposes. Too many Americans have come to believe it is their right to decide as individuals which of our laws they will obey and which they will violate.

I do not mean to say that all our laws are just. They're not, and I don't mean to suggest that protest against unjust laws is not proper. Performed in an orderly manner, the right to protest is a cornerstone of our system.

Men must have the opportunity to be heard even when their views are extreme and in a lesser democratic country, dangerous. I, too, have spoken against laws which I considered wrong and unjust, and I am sure I will speak—and vote—against many, many more.

But my fellow Americans, I have not burned my birth certificate, and I will not renounce my citizenship.

Those who would do such things are relatively few. But there is a much larger number who in the face of change and disorder have retreated into disengagement and quiet despair. Less destructively but not less surely, such men are also retreating from the responsibilities of citizenship.

Now let us not deceive ourselves about the consequences of such abdication. It is anarchy. It is a state in which each individual demands instant compliance with his own desires, and from there it is but a short step to the assumption by each individual of the right to decide which of his neighbors shall live and which shall not, and so accelerate the sickening spiral of violence which has already cost us our beloved John F. Kennedy, our great leader Martin Luther King Jr. and the voice of this decade, Senator Robert F. Kennedy.

We have been told that the revolts are against the system, and that Establishment must be torn down. But my fellow Americans, in Paris recently, students cut down hundred-year-old trees to erect temporary street barricades. Those trees had lived through two world wars. Some of them had even survived the revolution of 1848.

Were the goals of these students served by the destruction of those trees? How long will it take for their beauty and the vitality they symbolized to grow again? What trees did the students plant in their place?

If we cut down our institutions, public and private, and with indifference starve the systems which have given us our achievements, who will feed the hungry? Who will train the unskilled?

Who will supply the jobs that mean opportunity for the generation whose voices are not yet heard? And who will launch the much-needed Marshall Plan to rebuild our cities and open opportunity for all Americans? These undertakings are too great for individuals going their separate ways.

Finally, my fellow Americans, let us remember that even anarchy is only a way station. Man, the social animal, has always craved order. He has made the most essential function of his government the maintenance of some level of order.

Chaos and anarchy have never been more than preludes to totalitarianism. Tyrants like Adolph Hitler have taught this before.

So, my fellow Americans, let us reject violence as a means of protest, and let us reject those who preach violence. But let us not tempt those who would hide the evil face of racism behind the mask of law and order.

To permit violence and anarchy to destroy our cities is to spark the beginning of a cancerous growth of doubt, suspicion, fear and hatred that will gradually infect the whole nation.

Poverty, discrimination, deprivation, as evil as they are, do not justify violence or anarchy, do not justify looting or burning and do not justify murder or assassination. Law and order must be respected and maintained to protect the rights—yes, the civil rights—of all our citizens.

But let us resist also the temptation to apathy because we can never cure the causes of violence with indifference. And, my fellow Americans, in the last analysis law and order can only rest securely with justice and its foundation.

The last eleven years have seen the passage of the five civil rights laws passed during the entire history of the United States, and I might note in passing that Lyndon Baines Johnson is the author, chief architect or primary sponsor of each of the civil rights laws.

When all summers are long and hot, it is well to remember that the one hundred years of the Emancipation Proclamation is finally but slowly but becoming a reality, and the occupants of some of our highest offices are testimony that black talent is just as important as white talent.

Working together, we have done much. We can and we must do much, much more.

The need for new ideas and improved institutions should not deter us now— we have long been a party of new ideas.

So let us go forward with programs responsive to the needs of today and responsive to the needs of tomorrow.

And as we all know, we have much to do. Putting aside hatred on the one hand and timidity on the other, let us grow fresh faith in our purpose and new vigor in our citizenship.

In closing I wish to share with you a most sacred word of Hawaii. It is "aloha." To some of you who visited us it may have meant hello. To others "aloha" may have meant good-bye. But to those of us who have been privileged to live in Hawaii, "aloha" means "I love you."

So to all of you, my fellow Americans, aloha.

BETTY FRIEDAN
(1921–)

The Real Sexual Revolution
1969

*Motherhood is a bane almost by definition, or at least
partly so, as long as women are forced to be mothers—
and only mothers—against their will.*

Betty Friedan was born in Peoria, Illinois, in 1921, one year after
women won the right to vote. The daughter of a Russian Jewish immigrant and a former newspaperwoman, Betty was encouraged by her
parents to strive for excellence in her every endeavor. After excelling at
Smith College, she moved to New York City and became a reporter for
the Workers Press and then an outspoken activist in the feminist movement. In 1949, after becoming pregnant with her second child, Friedan
was fired from her job in journalism, sparking her lifelong career as an
advocate of women's rights both in and outside the home.

In 1963 Friedan published *The Feminine Mystique*, a controversial
book which argued that generations of social and economic barriers
had left women in a "housewife trap"—a perpetual, vicious, and often
discriminatory cycle. She called the suburban home a "comfortable
concentration camp." Friedan's book ignited a wave of controversy and
catapulted the forty-two-year-old mother of three to the center of the
civil rights movement.

A critical voice for equal pay, bodily choice, and affirmative action,
Friedan then helped found the National Organization for Women
(NOW) and the National Women's Political Caucus. Her work con-
tributed to the adoption of seminal civil rights legislation, including the
Civil Rights Act of 1964 and the Equal Pay Act.

In 1969, at the First National Conference for the Repeal of
Abortion Laws in Chicago, Illinois, Friedan declared in this speech that
women could achieve liberation only through individual responsibility
and contended that abortion and reproduction were civil rights to be
enjoyed by all women.

WOMEN, EVEN THOUGH they're almost too visible as sex objects in this country, are invisible people. As the Negro was the invisible man, so women are the invisible people in America today: women who have a share in the decisions of the mainstream of government, of politics, of the church—who don't just cook the church supper, but preach the sermon; who don't just look up the zip codes and address the envelopes, but make the political decisions; who don't just do the housework of industry, but make some of the executive decisions. Women, above all, who say what their own lives and personalities are going to be, and no longer listen to or even permit male experts to define what "feminine" is or isn't.

The essence of the denigration of women is our definition as sex object. To confront our inequality, therefore, we must confront both society's denigration of us in these terms and our own self-denigration as people.

Am I saying that women must be liberated from sex? No. I am saying that sex will only be liberated to be a human dialogue, sex will only cease to be a sniggering, dirty joke and an obsession in this society, when women become active self-determining people, liberated to a creativity beyond motherhood, to a full human creativity.

Am I saying that women must be liberated from motherhood? No. I am saying that motherhood will only be a joyous and responsible human act when women are free to make, with full conscious choice and full human responsibility, the decisions to become mothers. Then, and only then, will they be able to embrace motherhood without conflict, when they will be able to define themselves not just as somebody's mother, not just as servants of children, not just as breeding receptacles, but as people for whom motherhood is a freely chosen part of life, freely celebrated while it lasts, but for whom creativity has many more dimensions, as it has for men.

The hostility between the sexes has never been worse. The image of women in avant-garde plays, novels and movies, and behind the family situation comedies on television is that mothers are man-devouring, cannibalistic monsters, or else Lolitas, sex objects—and objects not even of heterosexual impulse, but of sadomasochism. That impulse—the punishment of women—is much more of a factor in the abortion question than anybody ever admits.

Motherhood is a bane almost by definition, or at least partly so, as long as women are forced to be mothers—and only mothers—against their will. Like a cancer cell living its life through another cell, women today are forced to live too much through their children and husbands (they are too dependent on them, and therefore are forced to take too much varied resentment, vindictiveness, inexpressible resentment and rage out on their husbands and children).

Perhaps it is the least understood fact of American political life: the enormous buried violence of women in this country today. Like all oppressed people, women have been taking their violence out on their own bodies, in all the maladies with which they plague the MDs and the psychoanalysts. Inadvertently, and in subtle and insidious ways, they have been taking their violence out, too, on their children and on their husbands, and sometimes they're not so subtle.

Am I saying that women have to be liberated from men? That men are the enemy? No. I am saying the *men* will only be truly liberated to love women and to be fully themselves when women are liberated to have a full say in the decisions of their lives and their society.

Until that happens, men are going to bear the guilty burden of the passive destiny they have forced upon women, the suppressed resentment, the sterility of love when it is not between two fully active, joyous people, but has in it the element of exploitation. And men will not be free to be all they can be as long as they must live up to an image of masculinity that disallows all the tenderness and sensitivity in a man, all that might be considered feminine. Men have enormous capacities in them that they have to repress and fear in order to live up to the obsolete, brutal, bear-killing, Ernest Hemingway, crew-cut Prussian, napalm-all-the-children-in-Vietnam, bang-bang-you're-dead image of masculinity. Men are not allowed to admit that they sometimes are afraid. They are not allowed to express their own sensitivity, their own need to be passive sometimes and not always active. Men are not allowed to cry. So they are only half-human, as women are only half-human, until we can go this next step forward. All the burdens and responsibilities that men are supposed to shoulder alone makes them, I think, resent women's pedestal, much as that pedestal may be a burden for women.

This is the real sexual revolution. Not the cheap headlines in the papers about at what age boys and girls go to bed with each other and whether they do it with or without the benefit of marriage. That's the least of it. The real sexual revolution is the emergence of women from passivity, from the point where they are the easiest victims for all the seductions, the waste, the worshiping of false gods in our affluent society, to full self-determination and full dignity. And it is the emergence of men from the stage where they are inadvertent brutes and masters to sensitive, complete humanity.

If we are finally allowed to become full people, not only will children be born and brought up with more love and responsibility than today, but we will break out of the confines of that sterile little suburban family to relate to each other in terms of all of the possible dimensions of our personalities—male and female, as comrades, as colleagues, as friends, as lovers. And without so much hate and jealousy and buried resentment and hypocrisies, there will be a whole new sense of love that will make what we call love on Valentine's Day look very pallid.

It's crucial, therefore, that we see this question of abortion as more than a quantitative move, more than a politically expedient move. Abortion repeal is not a question of political expediency. It is part of something greater. It is historic that we are addressing ourselves this weekend to perhaps the first national confrontation of women and men. Women's voices are finally being heard aloud, saying it the way it is about the question of abortion both in its most basic sense of morality and in its new political sense as part of the unfinished revolution of sexual equality.

In this confrontation, we are making an important milestone in this marvelous revolution that began long before any of us here were born and which still has a long way to go. As the pioneers from Mary Wollstonecraft to Margaret Sanger gave us the consciousness that brought us from our several directions here, so we here, in changing the very terms of the debate on abortion to assert woman's right to choose, and to define the terms of our lives ourselves, move women further to full human dignity. Today, we moved history forward. . . .

Henry B. González
1916–2000

This Is No Land of Cynics
April 3, 1969

*These few are themselves becoming the purveyors
of the hate they denounce.*

In the late 1960s, with the rise of the black power movement, the young leaders of the Mexican-American "movimiento" also took a turn toward radicalism and militancy. Groups like La Causa and the Mexican American Youth Organization (MAYO), under the direction of José Angel Gutiérrez, attacked Anglo culture and embraced firebrand slogans like "*malos gringos* [bad gringos]" and "Kill the gringos."

Founded in 1969, MAYO called for the formation of aggressive Chicano political power to achieve immediate social change. Members of the Mexican-American old guard, like Texas congressman Henry B. González, attacked the radical groups and their message of violence, saying they epitomized reverse discrimination. Although González championed equal opportunity, above all he believed in cooperation and nonviolence.

The son of Mexican immigrants, Henry González rose through the ranks of the political establishment—first in the Texas statehouse and then the United States Congress. Feisty and unpredictable, he was a lifelong critic of special interests and an unflagging supporter of civil rights. In 1963, for example, González spearheaded the attack on the Bracero Bill, which allowed the importation of temporary, low-wage workers into the United States from Mexico. These workers were often exploited and denied labor protections. González also lent a loud voice in support of the Civil Rights Act of 1964. Journalist Christopher Hitchens called him "one of the few just men to have spent time on the Hill."

In this speech on the floor of the House of Representatives, González denounced MAYO's radical approach and urged Mexican Americans to pursue instead a path of "decency" and civil disobedience.

———

MR. SPEAKER, there is no greater poison of mind and spirit than race hate. There is no greater evil among men than the irrational antipathy that is based in race and race alone. There is no greater injustice than to be labeled "inferior" or "undeserving" or "subhuman" or "second class" solely on account of race or descent; and there is no greater evildoer than the spreader of race hate. My colleagues know well the number of times I have spoken out against those who would discover some nonexistent plot among minority groups, or those who automatically assume that Negroes, or Jews, or Indians, or Mexicans are somehow sinister influences. My colleagues know all too well the sorrows visited on this House and this Nation because of the messages of hate. It is because I oppose this irrational, this pervasive, this debasing hate that I have joined my colleagues against it, and for human decency.

All my political life I have asked only that I be judged for my qualifications, for my policies, for my proposals, not on what I am, or what my name may be. I ask for every man that he be given that same privilege. Throughout my career I have been attacked repeatedly by right-wing extremists because I stand for equality for all men before God, before man, and before the law. I have been called a Communist, my life has been threatened. I have been castigated as a "nigger lover," and I am certain, denounced as a "dirty meskin." I have been branded a Fabian Socialist, denounced as a hater, and denigrated as a wrecker of stability and destroyer of harmony. Yet, I do not regret it; the people of San Antonio and Bexar County have repeatedly demonstrated that they do not care what I am or what I am called, as long as I make an honest effort to be an honest Representative. My faith has been affirmed time and again in the basic decency and integrity of the vast and overwhelming majority of the people of this land. I have seen it proved all over the country that there is far more decency than indecency, far more tolerance than intolerance, and far more honor than dishonor. That has made it worthwhile; that has removed the sting from the barbs of haters both professional and amateur alike; and that has enabled me to say truthfully that the haters are a small and contemptible minority.

Ironically, I now find myself assaulted from the left as well as from the right. Yet I do not hesitate to say now, as before, that evil is evil, that it is just as wrong for a member of an ethnic minority to succumb to hate and fear as it is for any one else to do so. A racist is no good either to himself or to his fellow man, be he black, white, brown, red, or yellow. I believe in decency, and I denounce indecency; and I serve public notice that my policy will not change.

Mr. Speaker, I have watched with alarm as new Mexican-American militant groups have formed, not because they have formed, but because some of them no matter how worthy their ideals may be, have fallen into the spell and trap of reverse racism. These few are themselves becoming the purveyors of the hate they denounce; they are themselves the personification of the unspeakable evils they declaim against; and they are themselves the ultimate tragedy of racism. If there can be no moral justification for racial antipathy on one side, neither can there be on the other; yet tragically these new racists seem utterly convinced of their moral rectitude.

I have heard and read and been shocked by violent denouncements of the so-called establishment and now of gringos and even of yankee imperialists. Whatever the title may be, the result is the same argument: the majority, the Anglo-Saxon American, is joined in a fantastic plot to subjugate and hold in poverty the Mexican-American citizen of this land. This new dogma is just as fantastic as the old cries about "Wall Street imperialists" of years back, and as xenophobic as the know-nothings of a century gone by. It is as evil as the deadly hatred of the Nazis, and as terrible in its implications as the rantings of demagogs warning against "mongrelization of the races" by white suprema-cists. I do not know, and defy anyone to find, any one race, any one ethnic group that is the personification and embodiment of evil; neither do I know of any that is the incarnation of good. Neither racism nor reverse racism is defensible.

I cannot stand silently by if an organization like the Mexican-American Youth Organization, or MAYO, as it is known, publishes hate sheets contain-ing statements like:

> The gringo took your grandfather's land, he took your father's job, and now he's sucking out your soul. There is no such thing as *"mala suerte"* (bad luck): there is only *malos gringos* (bad gringos).

MAYO styles itself the embodiment of good and the Anglo-American as the incarnation of evil. That is not merely ridiculous; it is drawing fire from the deepest wellsprings of hate. The San Antonio leader of MAYO, José Angel Gutiérrez, may think himself something of a hero, but he is, in fact, only a benighted soul if he believes that in the espousal of hatred he will find love. He is simply deluded if he believes that the wearing of fatigues and a beard makes his followers revolutionaries, or that the genius of revolution is in slogans.

As for the so-called older radicals who lend their assent and even support of the orators of race and hate, they need not wonder why their integrity is questioned. They cannot claim the support of all men, or the right to just con-sideration, if they denounce some men irrationally; one cannot espouse evil and not expect the favor to be returned. One cannot fan the flames of emo-tion, or turn on the streams of bigotry one moment and expect them to dis-appear the next.

I cannot accept the argument that this is an evil country or that our sys-tem does not work, or that it is foolish to expect redress of a just grievance. It may be wrong to expect miracles, but it is also wrong to expect no progress at all. I have seen too much proof that there is a residue of good will in this country, that there is a determination for progress, and I have seen, taken part in, and been the beneficiary of too much progress to deny its existence, or to say that we are incapable of it. I cannot find evidence that there is any country in the world that matches the progress of this one. For all our inequity, for all our admitted failings, for all the urgent unmet needs, this country is the living embodiment of a revolution that the so-called militants only play at. They may proclaim the romance of heroes dead and gone, but they do not know what the realities of those men were. The wearing of a Zapata moustache today does not mean that his "*pan y tierra*" ever came into being; and the bitter truth is that the true revolution is here, not somewhere else.

Mr. Speaker, this is not the time to despair, and it is not the time to give over to hate; it is still the time for faith. I believe that the majority of people in this land agree with me. I take my stand here, and against . . . nihilism.

RODOLFO "CORKY" GONZALES
(1929–)

Chicano Nationalism: Fighting for La Raza
NOVEMBER 13, 1969

Nationalism comes first out of the family, then into tribalism,
and then into the alliances that are necessary to lift the
burden of all suppressed humanity.

Blending "compassion and rage" with "idealism and realism," Rodolfo
"Corky" Gonzales emerged as one of the leading militant Chicano
leaders in the 1960s. The son of a migrant agricultural worker, Gonzales
spent his winters in Denver, Colorado, and his summers working in
sugar-beet fields.

By the age of sixteen, when he graduated from high school,
Gonzales was already suspicious of Anglo institutions. He found his first
escape from white culture in professional boxing. In 1950, after rising
to the top ten in the featherweight division, Gonzales retired from the
ring and turned his attention toward political and social activism, public speaking, and poetry. Capitalizing on his boxing fame, he served in
the Kennedy administration and later the Johnson administration, in its
War on Poverty.

But in 1965, aggravated and alienated, he broke away from mainstream politics and founded the Crusade for Justice, an organization
offering educational, legal, medical, and financial services for Chicanos
in the barrio. Under the banner of Hispanic ethnic nationalism, separatism, and self-determination, Gonzales hosted the first Chicano Youth
Conference, led the Colorado La Raza Unida, and eventually published
his poem "Yo Soy Joaquin." Part of his larger rhetorical campaign,
Gonzales's poem became a standard rallying point in the movement,
serving as both a social statement and historical essay for Mexican
Americans.

In this speech, during a symposium on "Chicano liberation" in
Haywood, California, Gonzales announced his frustration at operating
"within the [Anglo] system," opting instead for an independent
Chicano political organization.

WHAT ARE THE COMMON DENOMINATORS that unite the people? The key
common denominator is nationalism. When I talk about nationalism, some
people run around in their intellectual bags, and they say this is reverse racism.
The reverse of a racist is a humanitarian. I specifically mentioned what I felt
nationalism was. Nationalism becomes *la familia*. Nationalism comes first out
of the family, then into tribalism, and then into the alliances that are necessary
to lift the burden of all suppressed humanity.

Now, if you try to climb up a stairway, you have to start with the first step.
You can't jump from the bottom of this floor to the top of those bleachers. If
you can, then you must be "super-*macho.*" (I don't talk about super-man.) But,
you can't, so you start using those tools that are necessary to get from the bottom to the top. One of these tools is nationalism. You realize that if Chávez,
or any popular figure in the Mexicano scene decides to run, and if he ran for
any party, as popular as he is, then out of nationalism we would even vote for
an idiot. If his name was Sanchez, if his name was González, you would walk
in and vote for him, whether you know him or not, because you are nation-
alistic. And we have elected too many idiots in the past out of nationalism,
right?

Now, let's take that common denominator, that same organizing tool of
nationalism, and utilize it to work against the system. Let's use it to work
against the two parties that I say are like an animal with two heads eating out
of the same trough, that sits on the same boards of directors of the banks and
corporations, that shares in the same industries that make dollars and profits
off wars. To fight this thing, you look for the tools.

Now, if Tony is a socialist, if my brother here is an independent, if my sister is a Republican—she might hit me later—if one of the others is a
Democrat and one is a communist, and one from the Socialist Labor Party,
what do we have in common politically? Nothing. We've been fighting over
parties across the kitchen table, wives are Republicans and husbands are
Democrats, sometimes, and we argue over a bunch of garbage. And the same
Republicans and Democrats are having cocktails together at the same bar and
playing golf together and kissing each other behind the scenes.

So you tell me then, what is the common denominator that will touch the
barrio, the *campos* and the *ranchitos?* Are we going to go down there with some
tremendous words of intellectualism which they cannot relate to, when they
relate on the level of, "We need food. We need health care for our children. I
need someone to go down to juvenile court with my son. There is no job for
my husband." And the revolution of 15 or 20 years from now is not going to
feed a hungry child today. . . .

All right, how do we start this? We start it and call it an independent
Chicano political organization. . . .

We must start off by creating the structure—the *concilio*—by calling a congress sometime this spring, bringing together all those people that believe that it can be done. We understand that when we organize in an area where we are a majority, we can control. Where we are a minority, we will be a pressure group. And we will be a threat.

We understand the need to take action in the educational system. We understand that we need actions such as the "blow-outs," because the youth are not afraid of anything. Because the youth are ready to move. The whole party will be based on the actions of the young, and the support of the old.

Secondly, in the communities where we are a majority, we can then control and start to reassess taxes, to start charging the exploiters for what they have made off our people in the past. You can also incorporate the community to drive out the exploiters, to make them pay the freight for coming into the community, and sign your own franchises. You can de-annex a community as easily as they annex a *barrio* and incorporate it. You can create your own security groups, and place a gun here to protect the people, not to harass them, but to protect them from the Man who is going to come in from the outside. You can also create your own economic base by starting to understand that we can share instead of cut each others' throats.

Now what are the tools? We said nationalism, which means that we have to be able to identify with our past, and understand our past, in order that we can dedicate ourselves to the future, dedicate ourselves to change. And we have to understand what humanism really is. We can tie the cultural thing into it, but we also have to tie in the political and the economic. We tie these things together, and we start to use the common denominator of nationalism.

Now for those Anglo supporters, don't get up-tight. For the Black brothers, they are practicing the same thing right now. And we understand it and respect it. And we are for meaningful coalitions with organized groups.

We have to start to consider ourselves as a nation. We can create a congress or a *concilio*. We can understand that we are a nation of *Aztlan*. We can understand and identify with Puerto Rican liberation. We understand and identify with Black liberation. We can understand and identify with white liberation from this oppressing system once we organize around ourselves.

⟶

Where they have incorporated themselves to keep us from moving into their neighborhoods, we can also incorporate ourselves to keep them from controlling our neighborhoods. We have to also understand economic revolution, of driving the exploiter out. We have to understand political change. And we have to understand principle. And the man who says we can do it within the system—who says, "Honest, you can, look at me, I have a $20,000-a-year job"—

he's the man who was last year's militant and this year's OEO employee [Office of Economic Opportunity]. And now he's keeping his mouth shut and he ain't marching any more. We have to understand that he is not a revolutionary, that he's a counter-revolutionary. He's not an ally, he becomes an enemy because he's contaminated.

You can't walk into a house full of disease with a bottle full of mercurochrome and cure the disease without getting sick yourself. That's what we say about the lesser of the two evils. If four grains of arsenic kill you, and eight grains of arsenic kill you, which is the lesser of two evils? You're dead either way.

We have to understand that liberation comes from self-determination, and to start to use the tools of nationalism to win over our *barrio* brothers, to win over the brothers who are still believing that *machismo* means getting a gun and going to kill a communist in Vietnam because they've been jived about the fact that they will be accepted as long as they go get themselves killed for the *gringo* captain; who still think that welfare is giving them something and don't understand that the one who is administering the welfare is the one that's on welfare, because about 90 percent of the welfare goes into administration; and who still do not understand that the war on poverty is against the poor, to keep them from reacting.

We have to win these brothers over, and we have to do it by action. Whether it be around police brutality, the educational system, whether it be against oppression of any kind—you create an action, you create a blow-out, and you see how fast those kids get politicized. Watch how fast they learn the need to start to take over our own communities. And watch how fast they learn to identify with ourselves, and to understand that we need to create a nation.

We can create a thought, an idea, and we can create our own economy. You don't hear of any "yellow power" running around anywhere. Because they base their power around their church, their house, their community. They sell Coca Cola, but their profits go to their own people, you see, so that they have an economic base. We are strangers in our own church. We have got *gachupin* [traditional term of contempt for Spaniards who ruled Mexico for 400 years] priests from Spain in our communities, telling us *vamos a hechar unos quatros pesos en la canasta* [let's throw four pesos in the collection dish]. And then he tells you, "I'm your religious leader," and he tries to tell you how to eat, where to go, who to sleep with and how to do it right—while he's copping everything else out. You know, we're tired of this kind of leadership.

⌒

You have to understand that we can take over the institutions within our community. We have to create the community of the Mexicano here in order to have any type of power. As much as the young ladies have created power in their own community. But they have to share it with the rest of us. They have to be able to bring it together. And we are glad when they sit down instead of retreating. It means that we're all one people. It means that we're all one *Raza* and that we will work together and we will walk out of here in a positive fashion.

KARLA JAY
(1947–)

Take Destiny into Your Own Hands
JUNE 26, 1977

No matter how comforting that darkness was, that closet was, . . .
it's no match for the light ahead of us, for the freedom ahead of us.

A radical gay rights activist, academic, and writer, Karla Jay was born in Brooklyn, New York, and graduated from Barnard College with a degree in French. While at Columbia University in 1968, she joined the notorious student civil rights demonstrations and, a year later, the Redstockings, a leftwing feminist group. That year, the Redstockings—including Jay—were on the frontlines of the gay liberation movement, which swelled in the wake of the Stonewall Riots.

After a stint as a graduate student at New York University, where she studied comparative literature, Kay packed up her banners and began putting her views on paper, publishing several works, including *Out of the Closets: Voices of Gay Liberation* (1972) and *Dyke Life: A Celebration of the Lesbian Experience* (1995), which won a Lambda Literary Award.

In this 1977 speech at a gay pride rally in New York, Jay traced the struggles of the gay and lesbian movements, highlighting the events at Stonewall and the scores of human rights abuses inflicted by law enforcement officials against homosexuals. Jay urged gays and lesbians to "take destiny into [their] own hands" through activism and open pride.

———

THIS IS THE FIRST TIME I've ever been asked to speak at a gay pride rally here in New York. I think it's because I'm one of those radical dykes some people have been trying to keep away from the media. But here I am, and I'm going to presume that I'm here because now you also are too radical! Thank you for inviting me.

There are lots of things I could talk to you about today, but I want to talk to you about *today,* about this week, Gay Pride Week. This week is crucial for us, for we will never be a people until we establish a culture, and a culture is what has been denied to us. We have been shoved into the dark by our oppressors, who allowed us to have a subculture in their bars, in their baths, in their tearooms, as long as we didn't show our faces in the light of day. They quashed our history, denied us our rights, took our heroines and heroes as theirs, have tried to obliterate us, tried to exterminate us, and then to claim that we hardly exist, that we are a minute minority.

At the Stonewall Riots, a group of people rose up against that oppression, rose up to say that we would not be kept in the darkness of the bars, we would not be kept in the darkness of their ignorance and/or our own ignorance about ourselves, that we would no longer be silenced, no longer be brutalized by the police departments of this country, of this world.

And part of that enlightening about ourselves lets us know that those brothers and sisters who fought at the Stonewall bar in Greenwich Village were not the first to fight our struggle. They were the heirs of the Amazons and matriarchs whose cultures all around this world were subjugated under the yoke of the patriarchy, of the witches and faggots who were burned at the stake for adhering to the Dianic cult, to the matriarchal religion, or who were simply different. They were the heirs of Verlaine who languished in a Swiss prison, of Oscar Wilde put in jail and driven in disrepute from England, of Radclyffe Hall forced to flee England because of the *Well of Loneliness,* of the hundreds of thousands of homosexuals and lesbians murdered in concentration camps by Stalin and later by the Nazis, of the gays in concentration camps in countries around the world even today or locked in city ghettos, of the countless gay men murdered in parks or brutally run over like Pasolini, of women shot and killed because we have dared to look different, to be different.

And if the rising of our sisters and our brothers at the Stonewall has been part of that tradition, it has not been the end. Oppression has not ceased despite small and almost meaningless gains in state legislatures, for the quality of life is not better in Connecticut than in Virginia. . . . So we must never relax our vigilance lest we, like the Trojans, accept a token horse from our oppressors, only to find it filled with swords to slay us.

Let us also remember the ideas of the early movement after the Stonewall. We knew then that we are allied to other groups, and that the sexism that oppresses straight and lesbian women is at the root of what oppresses all gay people, that the racism at the root of this culture is the pyramidic discrimination which oppresses us too, and that we will never be free until we all are free. Let us not do what the liberals are doing to us. Let us not permit gay men to sell out lesbians, so that they can have their male privilege, let us not attack all women because Anita Bryant is a woman, because "ain't I a woman too?" Let us not sell out our Third-World sisters and brothers so that we can retain our white skin privilege. Let us not sell out teachers or transvestites, lesbian mothers and faggot fathers so that the rest can be free. For some of us have forgotten those ties.

Let us also remember our early goals. Ours was a movement of gay people, by gay people, for *all* people. The early groups, such as the gay liberation fronts and radical lesbians learned from the women's liberation movement that we are equal, that we have *all* suffered as gay people, that we are *all* experts at being gay. We also knew that legislation was only the outward tool used on us by a society which is fatally sexist at its roots, and that we will never be free until that basic, cancerous sexism is uprooted from this country, from the twisted sexual minds of the heterosexist male oppressors. Now we are being told that we are no longer experts on our own oppression, that we should sit back and raise money for a handful of experts who will explain our oppression for us, who will beg for a few legislative crumbs from the very people who created sexist laws to begin with. And so we have moved from an angry people creating important social change to the legislative equivalent of a sugar lobby, an oil lobby. We have turned over our destiny to a few experts, experts who lead us back into the bars to raise money for them, when originally one of our first struggles was against the bars who did and still charge extravagant prices for poorly ventilated hellholes. The Stonewall was such a bar, and it was torn down, but now not only are there newer, more expensive bars, but we have to come out of that darkness, provide alternatives for our people. But that can't happen as long as you only come out for one rally a year, as long as your only contribution to the movement is one of money given at the door of a bar or at a fund-raiser for a good time, as long as you allow a few people to control your destiny in your name.

And so in this year of seeming defeat, I ask you to take your destiny into your own hands, to create your own projects, to actively support those which exist, and not to go back into the darkness of the bars and your closets until next rally. Do not go back into that spiritual darkness, but work to stay in the sunlight, for we are barely emerging now into that light. So no matter how comforting that darkness was, that closet was, no matter how protective it was like a womb, it's no match for the light ahead of us, for the freedom ahead of us, for the new lives ahead of us. For ourselves and for our spiritual and actual daughters and sons. And if we truly remember this, the spirit of Stonewall, we will never be thrust back in the dark, we will never be thrust back into ignorance, we will never allow that oppression to happen again, and we and our children will find ourselves in a new age where sexism has no place.

THE CURRENT STRUGGLE:
SLOW BUT STEADY PROGRESS
1970–1998

JOSÉ ANGEL GUTIÉRREZ
(1949–)

A Chicano Defined
NOVEMBER 12, 1970

We believe that by virtue of birth we're entitled to dignity,
to respect, to a free, clean environment and the opportunity
to make oneself worth something.

An accomplished student, champion debater, and president of his high-school class, José Angel Gutiérrez was the type of student Anglo-Americans in his community cited as an "example of how a bright and ambitious Mexican American could get ahead." Bright he was, and growing up the son of a medical doctor in Crystal City, Texas, Gutiérrez realized at an early age the extent of discrimination he faced.

In 1963, after attending St. Mary's University, Gutiérrez used his rhetorical ability to help elect five Mexican Americans to the city council, in a town where Anglos had dominated politics and the city government—but not the population—for generations. These victories didn't come easily. On the campaign trail, Texas Rangers, an arm of the city's Department of Public Safety, beat Gutiérrez time and again. But that didn't stop him from taking the stump on the issues of housing, poverty, and education.

In college, Gutiérrez also helped found the Mexican American Youth Organization (MAYO), an "active and aggressive" Latino organization committed to social change. Joined by other activists, including Carlos René Guerra, Gutiérrez's group criticized the accommodationist approach of their Chicano elders and other mainstream civil rights leaders. They instead encouraged "confrontation of the gringo"—or Anglo—and direct action in the fields of education, economic parity, and equal employment opportunity. MAYO also supported the formulation of an independent third political party.

In 1970 Gutiérrez formed the Chicano Political Party, called "La Raza Unida." La Raza soon elected several members to the Crystal City council, a majority to the local school board, and eventually Gutiérrez himself to a county judgeship. From the bench, as a leading political voice, Gutiérrez thundered against Anglo discrimination, linked Mexican-American poverty to education and corporate exclusion, and promulgated—under the term "Chicano"—the right to

Spanish culture and language. Gutiérrez's speaking style varied greatly depending on the composition of his audience—whether it was Latino or not—and he often adopted a forthright tone in communicating with his young listeners.

On November 12, 1970, after yet another successful election for La Raza candidates, Gutiérrez addressed a crowd of students at the University of Texas. Throughout the speech, he abandoned his familiar style and use of Spanish in an effort to reach the mostly white audience and educate them about the Chicano movement.

<hr/>

I WAS ASKED to come and speak at the university, and I had quite a bit of trouble trying to make up my mind as to what to say. . . .

<hr/>

. . . We're really talking about two things here—the definition [of "Chicano"] and we're talking about identity, of trying to identify what is what. And that's the same thing that the black brothers have gone through. They always ask about their black power . . . soul . . . Will the SNCC-ers [Student Non-Violent Coordinating Committee] become violent? . . . whether the Panthers are really going to do this or that or the other . . . And you never can satisfy anybody. And with the Chicanos the same thing.

And I can't think of a better description than to just, you know, give a flat answer that we know what a Chicano is because we are one. But when you explain it to a Gringo who doesn't know what the hell's going on . . .

<hr/>

. . . It gets to be a very difficult thing in that we take the attitude that being in this society in this country and being deprived of many of the so-called opportunities that this makes us somewhat of a bastard community in that we are not Mexicans from Mexico; we are not Americans in terms of treatment and in terms of things that we receive. Consequently we get to be very demanding and very militant about what it is that we want. Because our land—this part here and throughout the Southwest; it is occupied Mexico—is ours. We get very militant and very adamant about the fact that education—the institutions, the teachers, the curriculum—is all designed for Gringos. It's making the mexicano a pushout. Consequently we have such a low median grade level of attainment. It means that regardless of what you do to get better employment, to get better education, the vast majority of mexicanos are still denied adequate housing, equal wages or fair wages, denied the right of due process. You know, one fellow said that when he experienced going to the courthouse to hear all these different things said about justice, and he always ended up getting the shaft, that he finally came to the conclusion that justice meant "Just Us Gringos."

We also get upset and we are very upset at the fact that we are the ones who have to join the armed forces of this country in order to get education, in order to get housing, in order to get benefits. So we're being used by this country to wage war on people who suffer the same kind of treatment and abuse as we do. We're also forced under the guise of an open society, of a competitive society to act and behave as animals, of trying to outdo and destroy the other or make it at the expense of others.

In religion, which you know is a very, very big factor in the attitude of the Chicano—particularly with the Catholic dogma—you have a variety of saints that are the object of our veneration. One of them is black and nobody has hangups about that. It's interesting to note that when Dr. King was slain and there was talk about making him a saint, just talking about it, that the white community was the one that got uptight. I never heard any comments from Chicanos.

In architecture, in design of homes, of landscapes, you find another kind of objection. When a housing project was being promoted and advocated in San Antonio of placing middle-class homes in a middle-class white community and moving Chicanos in there and blacks, the objections by the white community were not along the racist lines of "devaluating our property and our schools are going to go to pot or we're going to have junkyards in our block." They made such comments as "Mexicanos don't have these crewcut lawns. They have no sense of balance and color. They throw all kinds of psychedelic flowers out there." And you go into one of these homes in suburbia and see a *molcajete*—maybe you got one in your home—we use a *molcajete* to make *chili;* you guys use it for an ash tray.

So we get to the question of making money. It's only those Chicanos who because the movement now has status, who are really "white" Mexicans, all they're doing is playing Mexican. These are the guys who are materialistic. But the average Chicano is misunderstood. When a Chicano says, "That will be enough, you know. I don't need a second car, especially a Volkswagen. I don't need an air conditioner. I don't need my wife to take pills." You got something that strikes at the very heart of the nature of a Chicano in that we will not compromise the human worth of another child for a vacation in the Bahamas or a Las Vegas weekend. We won't compromise another pay raise or going to college an extra year or getting an extra degree or taking a second job to get into a higher income bracket and planning to have kids at the right time to qualify for a tax deduction.

These are things that . . . there's many, many other things that we can talk about. But these are things that are real, that are very much appreciated, very much a part of a mexicano, a Chicano, and misunderstood by the white community. We're called apathetic, disorganized. We drink beer. Like to make babies. That we fight. That we're slow learners. That we're not—in the words of the Gringo mayor of San Antonio [W. W. McAllister]—not as "ambitiously motivated" as an Anglo. That we're weird in terms of art and music. And everything that is applied to us is really a commentary on society, the Gringo. The problem is not us. The problem is the white society. It's the kind of problem that we have, we're going to have, for two more years.

Under, under the flag of this country and under the doctrines of this country it talks about wonderful things. And when they picture a good American they see speaking Spanish as being un-American. They see having a purple house as being cheap. . . .

The same thing goes on with the redistricting of counties, with the federal programs that are implemented. Take the case of VISTA [the Volunteers in Service to America program]. These people get assigned to different counties. And whenever they're good they might last four or five months, and if they're lucky they might last a year. And this is ironic because there's been only one program that has been relevant to the Chicano community. These are mostly white kids, students, who've come in believing all that garbage they learned in college and believing all that stuff they read in books. And they go down there and try to match wits with people who don't have any wits. For all they do is react out of, you know, gut ignorance. "Mexicans don't have problems. We've always got along fine with them. They're good people. They're happy people. Some of my best friends are Mexican" . . .

And this goes back to the thing about identity. You ask a Chicano in Spanish "What are you?" He's either mexicano, Chicano or *la raza*. You ask in English and he begins to explain, "I'm Spanish American. I'm Latin American. I'm American with Spanish surname. I'm Mexican American." Because the system really operates on two levels. If you want to be far out and want to do and get in with all the kinds of crap that they do, then you're "all right," you're a "good boy." But the minute you try to assert yourself for your own self-interest and self-determination then "you're a trouble-maker. You're a rebel. You're a militant. You're a communist. You're a hippie. You're a subversive." And in many cases "you're just plain dumb. You don't know what's happening. You're misinformed." And these things have been a part of the mexicano community for so long that now you can see—in spite of the media and mistreatment of events—that the Chicano community is radicalizing and politicizing itself to a degree that on other occasions has been equal but not on as large a scale as it is now. Chicanos are not going to put up with this kind of treatment.

But there is one thing that's being done and that is trying to work—and we're doing this in Crystal City—trying to work within the framework of the system—as a last kind of attempt. We've had over forty-nine school strikes by Chicanos across this state. We've had I don't know how many labor strikes. We've had arrests constantly by police, particularly in urban centers. You have Gringos engaging in slavery in trading of humans from Mexico here. The young Chicano is becoming aware of the fact that he is being used as a weapon for the foreign policy and the internal policy of this country. These things are part and parcel of our entire history in the struggle.

———

The Chicano community has a very un-American attitude about the worth of an individual. There's very few Chicanos—I haven't met one yet, in fact—who can make a case that rights are given by government or by Gringos. The Chicano is very heavily, heavily committed to the idea that an individual has certain birthrights as a human being. . . .

This is the same attitude Chicanos have today when you talk to them in Spanish, not in English. We believe that by virtue of birth we're entitled to dignity, to respect, to a free, clean environment and the opportunity to make oneself worth something so he can handle his mind or his mouth or whatever talent he possesses to the full development of his talent. And believe very strongly also in the preservation of our culture and our conditioning and our folkways and mores.

———

And the attitude of the Gringos is not changing whatsoever. There is a tremendous amount of interest in many of the white people to understand. But we find that this kind of understanding still comes under the heading of paternalism. Because understanding is only part of it. You got to accept the differences of mexicanos and attribute to us as much value as your own personal lifestyle or hangups or whatever you got. A commitment has to be made to the self-determination of the Chicano, as the Chicanos see it, by methods that they see.

And all these communities in south Texas, they are losing population to the urban areas. But they're also gaining population in terms of the young Chicano who has gone to read the white man's books and has come back to the community to organize the mexicano. There is no longer concern for earning the title "All-American Boy" or "Good Boy." We're not going to accept anything less than complete liberation and complete control of the resources and the government and the educational institutions that are in this area. And this is going to make for a very radical transition.

The minute the 18, 19 and 20-year-old is entitled to vote it's going to change at least half of this state to a degree that won't be recognized. The median age of the Chicano is sixteen or seventeen years old. And the activity, the intensity of feeling and the commitments that are being made by the young Chicanos today is such that the political turning point and the experiences that we are learning in the Winter Garden area about this kind of machine or system is unidirectional. The way things are structured is such that it cannot be dismantled. It cannot be slowed down. It cannot be reversed. It can only go forward.

And there is so much to be changed and made up for. That's why the Gringos are so uncomfortable about being fired in Crystal City and the surrounding areas. When you start altering and, in fact, changing the method of instruction and the curriculum you're producing a different kind of individual. When you reinforce what's natural in the Chicano community about birthrights and reinforcing his attitude about self-respect and the music and the food and the architecture, and all the other symbols, he starts following no matter what. And when these things become a part of his life the Chicano—most of the time—will identify with the changes that are being made because now they are legitimate and now they are effective and now they are tasting for the first time these kinds of victories. And he can nurture the spirit to fight again and to fight alone and export the struggle to the surrounding communities and expand.

⤙

As in the words of Bob Dylan in that song about "something's happening; we don't know what it is," there's something happening in Chicanos. There's something happening in the Chicano community. There's something happening in Chicano country, in *Aztlán,* in the Southwest that many people don't know about. And the kinds of situations that are exploding daily across *Aztlán* only indicate the one thing, that this decade is going to be a very violent one in terms of change because the Chicano is very serious that the struggle is not only his. But these things that I talked about. But it's a struggle for survival, survival as a people. But that's the situation that we find ourselves in economics and in political power, in wealth, and the status of society.

And the grip of the Gringo is such that the mexicano will not engage in any destruction in this decade. We will end up in the same situation as the Indian. We will become showcased on reservations or museums because there'll be no room for a Chicano with a Gringo education. There'll be no room for a twenty-year veteran in the armed forces who knows nothing but to kill. There'll be no room for the unskilled laborer who has been doing farm work all this time. Mechanization has already passed him by. There will be no room in the border areas when this country is actively industrializing the Mexican side of the border.

There will be no room for an open election by Chicanos in this country because the Gringo is afraid to give democracy and a voice to the people because this is exactly what was learned by La Raza Unida in the recent election. The only way the Gringos could win because they recognize their old pride and their ignorance. The only way to win was to be on the ballot by themselves. The only way they could keep a Chicano community in line is to bring in the Department of Public Safety and the Rangers and to turn loose the other law enforcement agencies, such as the Game Warden and the Border Patrol. And the constant harassment and embarrassment and humiliation by the other semi-police agencies, such as Welfare, Unemployment Commission, Family Planning, [and] the War on Poverty Program. . . .

And let me get off this serious tone with one of my standard jokes about the Gringo who was having a big ball to announce the eligibility of his daughter for marriage. He only had a girl, and he wanted a grandson. And he had this huge barbecue, and the musicians were playing and all the neighbors were there. He told them what the occasion was and that he had a beautiful young daughter and he wanted to marry her off. But he wanted to marry her to a real stud. And this guy—to prove he was a man and so on—had to swim in this swimming pool full of alligators. And about that time there was a splash and all you could see were arms and legs. And then on the other side out popped a Chicano dripping wet, shaking like a leaf. And the neighbors all turned to their host and said, "What are you going to do now?" And the guy said, "Well, let's talk to this Mexican." So he called him over and said, "Hey, I said that anybody that could do this kind of thing would get my daughter's hand in marriage, or since you're such a bright man, I'll give you a million dollars. Which would you want?" He said, "Ask whoever pushed me in the pool."

And that is what I'm trying to tell you. That is no longer the case; we know who pushed us in the swimming pool. And now that we have the answer we're going to do something about it.

SARAH WEDDINGTON
(1945–)

Roe v. Wade: *Legalizing Abortion*
DECEMBER 13, 1971

I think one of the purposes of the Constitution was to guarantee to individuals the right to determine the course of their own lives.

On January 22, 1973, the U.S. Supreme Court announced its decision in *Roe v. Wade,* one of the most controversial rulings in contemporary social and legal history. The case involved a challenge to a Texas statute making it a crime to perform an abortion unless a woman's life was at stake. Initially filed by "Jane Roe," an unmarried woman who sought to legally and safely terminate her pregnancy, the case was appealed all the way to the Supreme Court.

Twenty-five-year-old attorney Sarah Weddington represented Roe, arguing that, under the constitutional guarantee to privacy, a woman possessed the right to decide whether or not to terminate her own pregnancy. A former teacher, Weddington was born in the small town of Abilene, Texas, the daughter of a Methodist minister. She graduated from the University of Texas Law School.

Siding with Roe in a 7–2 decision, the Court ultimately struck down the Texas law, recognizing for the first time that the constitutional right to privacy "is broad enough to encompass a woman's decision whether or not to terminate her pregnancy." Roe has come to be known as *the* case that legalized abortion nationwide. At the time the decision was handed down, nearly two-thirds of the states had outlawed abortion except when necessary to save a woman's life. *Roe v. Wade* rendered these laws unconstitutional, setting a legal precedent that has affected dozens of subsequent Supreme Court cases involving abortion.

In this excerpt from her argument before the Supreme Court, Sarah Weddington challenged the existing Texas law, arguing that, because a pregnancy has the potential to disrupt women's lives, denial of an abortion can severely limit their freedom.

MR. CHIEF JUSTICE, AND MAY IT PLEASE THE COURT: . . .

In Texas, the woman is the victim. The state cannot deny the effect that this law has on the women of Texas. Certainly there are problems regarding even the use of contraception. Abortion now, for a woman, is safer than childbirth. In the absence of abortions—or, legal, medically safe abortions—women often resort to the illegal abortions, which certainly carry risks of death, all the side effects such as severe infections, permanent sterility, all the complications that result. And, in fact, if the woman is unable to get either a legal abortion or an illegal abortion in our state, she can do a self-abortion, which is certainly, perhaps, by far the most dangerous. And that is no crime.

Texas, for example, it appears to us, would not allow any relief at all, even in situations where the mother would suffer perhaps serious physical and mental harm. There is certainly a great question about it. If the pregnancy would result in the birth of a deformed or defective child, she has no relief. Regardless of the circumstances of conception, whether it was because of rape, incest, whether she is extremely immature, she has no relief.

I think it's without question that pregnancy to a woman can completely disrupt her life. Whether she's unmarried, whether she's pursuing an education, whether she's pursuing a career, whether she has family problems—all of the problems of personal and family life for a woman are bound up in the problem of abortion.

~~~~~

There is no duty for employers to rehire women if they must drop out to carry a pregnancy to term. And, of course, this is especially hard on the many women in Texas who are heads of their own households and must provide for their already existing children. And, obviously, the responsibility of raising a child is a most serious one, and at times an emotional investment that must be made cannot be denied.

So a pregnancy to a woman is perhaps one of the most determinative aspects of her life. It disrupts her body. It disrupts her education. It disrupts her employment. And it often disrupts her entire family life. And we feel that, because of the impact on the woman, this certainly—in as far as there are any rights which are fundamental—is a matter which is of such fundamental and basic concern to the woman involved that she should be allowed to make the choice as to whether to continue or to terminate her pregnancy.

I think the question is equally serious for the physicians of our state. They are seeking to practice medicine in what they consider the highest methods of practice. We have affidavits in the back of our brief from each of the heads of public—of heads of obstetrics and gynecology departments from each of our public medical schools in Texas. And each of them points out that they were willing and interested to immediately begin to formulate methods of providing care and services for women who are pregnant and do not desire to continue the pregnancy. They were stopped cold in their efforts, even with the declaratory judgment, because of the DA's position that they would continue to prosecute. . . .

[Concerning the constitutionality of the case], in the lower court, as I'm sure you're aware, the court held that the right to determine whether or not to continue a pregnancy rested upon the Ninth Amendment—which, of course, reserves those rights not specifically enumerated to the government to the people. I think it is important to note, in a law review article recently submitted to the Court and distributed among counsel by Professor Cyril Means Jr. entitled "The Phoenix of Abortional Freedom," that at the time the Constitution was adopted there was no common-law prohibition against abortions, that they were available to the women of this country. . . .

[And] insomuch as members of the Court have said that the Ninth Amendment applies to rights reserved to the people, and those which were most important—and certainly this is—that the Ninth Amendment is the appropriate place insofar as the Court has said that life, liberty, and the pursuit of happiness involve the most fundamental things of people; that this matter is one of those most fundamental matters. I think, in as far as the Court has said there is a penumbra that exists to encompass the entire purpose of the Constitution, I think one of the purposes of the Constitution was to guarantee to individuals the right to determine the course of their own lives. . . .

Patricia Schroeder

(1940–)

You Can Do It

February 9, 1973

You can do the job—but first, you have to get the job.

A former congresswoman and the current president of the Association of American Publishers, Patricia Schroeder first ran for the House of Representatives only eight years after graduating from Harvard Law School. Born in Portland, Oregon, she relocated to Colorado after receiving her law degree in 1964.

The first woman ever elected to the U.S. House of Representatives from Colorado, Schroeder was well aware of entrenched attitudes against women in Congress. When a colleague asked her how she, a mother of two small children, could be both a parent and a legislator at the same time, she responded, "I have a brain and a uterus, and I use them both."

During twenty-five years in Congress, Schroeder championed education, abortion, and civil rights and was the first woman to serve on the House Armed Services Committee. The "dean" of congressional women, she worked tirelessly to recruit women to run for public office, claiming the "only way [we] will get a higher quality of life is if everyone participates."

In this February 9, 1973, speech to the National Women's Political Caucus in Houston, Texas, Schroeder offered her suggestions on how women could play an active role in the political process.

———

Senator Robert Kennedy once said of his brother, John, after the President's assassination, "If there is a lesson from his life and death, it is that in this world of ours, we can no longer be satisfied with being mere spectators, critics on the sidelines."

And surely that must be the continuing message for all of us here today. Women especially can no longer be mere spectators of the political process, critics on the sidelines; but active participants, playing an important and vital role out on the field.

By your presence here today, each of you is demonstrating her interest in the political process. Many of you have no doubt taken active roles in community and civic organizations, political activities and campaigns, or business and professional activities. You can *do* the job—but first, you have to *get* the job. For those of you, and I hope there are many, who may be contemplating a run for office—whether it be party, city, state, judicial, or federal—let me offer a few suggestions from my own experience.

First: Assess critically your own qualifications. It is probably fair to say—although certainly unfair in practice—that a woman running for public office should be "overqualified." Having been chairman of your church's women's club may not carry the same clout as being program chairman of the local Rotary Club.

It is interesting to note that all five of this year's new congresswomen are lawyers. Perhaps this is because, as lawyers, we have necessarily been thrust into an adverse, and often competitive, role with members of the male establishment. Furthermore, we have come into constant contact with many of the problems that face our communities, and worked on possible legislative solutions.

Second: Examine carefully the real base of your support. The support of one's family, close friends, and associates is indispensable. But what contacts, or qualifications do you have that will enable you to gain the confidence and backing of other groups and allies? In my own case, an extensive labor law background was valuable in helping eventually obtain both organizational and financial support from many labor unions. Teaching contacts with three major colleges in Denver were also important. Finally, it is essential to take the pulse, and constantly stroke the brows of many of the key party leaders and workers in your area. Many of these veterans of the political wars often will make astute judgements about prospective candidates. Every candidate honestly believes he or she is in fact the best candidate. If none of the pros agree, best reexamine your position.

Third: Build credibility. Because you are a woman, you will constantly confront the attitude that you are not "a serious candidate." At our County nominating convention it is customary for candidates to have booths, give away courtesy coffee, distribute literature, placard the walls with posters, etc. I had a basic feeling of aversion to that sort of thing; but we decided it was probably more important that I do some of the traditional things, simply because I was the untraditional candidate.

Because you are a woman you may have the ability to gain more than your fair share of press and media coverage, because you are the different candidate. But the other side of the coin is that you will often be more severely cross-examined on your views and statements by newspeople than is the average male candidate.

Fourth: Develop a strong "grassroots" organization. You will find that there are great reservoirs of dedicated, talented women who will really work for another woman. This is especially true of many older, retired women; and many younger gals, such as students and working girls.

You will probably have a very hard time raising money. My husband often said that the money "is controlled by male chauvinist pigs." Organization and union money is controlled by men, and they will usually have little confidence in the chances of a woman candidate. Hence, the bigger and better volunteer group you can muster, the better chance you will have of putting your scarce dollars into essential items like printed materials and media time.

Fifth: Use innovative and hard-hitting media. Because a woman candidate is "different," don't be afraid to run a different kind of campaign, utilizing original and different media techniques and content. Let me give you one example: the standard political brochure. You know what I am talking about—the picture of the candidate with family, with coat over the shoulder, in front of the Capitol, etc. with the standard one-liners: "X is honest; X is against pollution; X is for fiscal responsibility." We were able to achieve real impact—and also ruffle some feathers—with colorful miniposters.

And finally, Sixth: Be issue-oriented. Running for public office is too time-consuming and too expensive to embark on such a venture merely for the experience, or for the ego satisfaction. If you run, take a stand. Get out front on the issues that concern you, your family, your community, and the nation. The risk, of course, is great; but so are the rewards.

And again, being a woman has both its advantages and disadvantages. I think a woman can more easily take a strong position on the war, on gun control, or education, than perhaps can a man. Isn't a mother going to be against wholesale bombing, for tougher gun control, for better schools? However, you must also guard against being pushed into unreasonable or irresponsible extreme positions by your erstwhile supporters. I was the only major candidate running in Denver last fall who would attend and speak at an abortion panel hearing held at a local college. But I was criticized by some women there when I tried to emphasize my support for birth control and family planning programs, rather than an "abortion on demand" policy. It is all too easy to become a "Kamikaze candidate"—crashing and burning on one or two emotionally packed issues.

So, it can be done. Women can run. And win. "You can do it!" I hope there will be questions later, and I look forward to talking with many of you individually later on today. Thank you.

PHYLLIS LYON
(1924–)

Recognition NOW
MAY 25, 1974

*We want the language and behavior of every person
to bespeak a consciousness about, and an affirmation of,
lesbians' existence as lesbians.*

In 1955, with only eight members, Del Martin and Phyllis Lyon founded the Daughters of Bilitis (DOB) in San Francisco, the first lesbian civil rights organization in the United States. They also were perhaps the first lesbian couple to gain national attention through their public activism. DOB quickly grew into a major social and political force, helping lesbians meet outside bars, promoting gay civil rights, and publishing the *Ladder,* a national newsletter for lesbians. Del and Phyllis—the first openly gay couple to join the National Organization for Women—have written extensively together on the lesbian experience in America.

On May 25, 1974, after more than four decades fighting for lesbian rights, Lyon delivered the keynote address at NOW's national conference in Houston, Texas. Representing the San Francisco chapter, she delivered a history of the women's movement and lesbians' long involvement with the feminist cause. She also addressed a widespread concern that NOW was slowly being transformed into an organization of "special interest" lesbians. Lyon had quit the organization in protest of its homophobia in the late 1970s, only to rejoin a decade later.

———

MOST PEOPLE THINK of the second wave of feminism as having started in the late 1960s. Few realize that there was already a group of women who had organized around feminist issues as early as the mid-1950s. These were Lesbian women who had banded together to fight for their own rights. It is true that originally these women identified themselves as homosexuals, and their struggle as one for sexual freedom. But as they developed educational programs on homosexuality, inevitably they found themselves dealing with the whole spectrum of human sexuality. The only model lesbians had at that time was a heterosexual one—Mom and Dad, dominant-passive sex roles.

They began to question this pattern, began to drop ill-fitting sex roles and to develop more egalitarian relationships. They wrote papers on the oppression of sex role stereotypes and they protested inequities in employment and educational opportunities for women. And the more they worked with gay men, the more feminist they became, the more they wished more women would get involved.

So, when the National Organization for Women came along in 1966, there was already an army of women—an army of lovers, if you will—ready to join in battle for the rights of all women. Few of them identified themselves openly as Lesbians, however, lest they embarrass the new feminist movement. For the media tried to perform a D&C on the early women's liberationists (that's the old Divide and Conquer technique) by calling them "a bunch of man-hating dykes."

Some of these gay women had already had a taste of freedom, had already come out of the closet, and it was difficult to start playing the dual role again, difficult to pretend to be heterosexual. But they bided their time, waiting for the women's movement to take hold and to become strong enough to deal with another dimension in the liberation of woman—woman not as sex object, but as sexual being.

By 1970 some feminists were beginning to make noises like they understood the solidarity of all women and that women as a class could not be divided into Lesbian and non-Lesbian any more than they could be divided by ethnic background, race or religion. All women come from the same cultural pool, are subject to the same conditioning from birth and are victims of the same oppression. NOW's recent ventures into international feminism have produced even further evidence of our sameness rather than our difference.

Having survived their first major philosophical differences over abortion and the Equal Rights Amendment, NOW members decided to move into the next phase of the women's revolution and take on the so-called Lesbian "issue" at the 1971 Los Angeles conference. Everyone was geared for the big battle—the battle that never took place. It wasn't exactly like the fantasy about "the war that was called and nobody came." Everybody came—together—to publicly declare that NOW "recognizes the double oppression of women who are Lesbians and affirms that a woman's right to her own person includes the right to define and express her own sexuality and to choose her own life style." NOW also resolved to support Lesbian mothers in their struggle for custody of their children.

At the 1973 conference in Washington, D.C., the Image of Women in the Media Task Force pledged to undertake an active campaign against the media where they misinformed, misrepresented, manipulated or ignored issues of concern to Lesbians. NOW also promised to "actively introduce and support civil rights legislation to end discrimination based on sexual orientation."

Everyone rejoiced that at long last the Lesbian "issue" had been resolved. What more could the Lesbians in NOW possibly ask for? Well, the answer is simple and is best expressed in two words: implementation and personhood. Resolutions passed in the conference atmosphere of solidarity and sisterhood are one thing—living up to these lofty ideals quite another. It is time for a reality check.

A National Task Force on Sexuality and Lesbianism has at long last been established, although not without some struggle and strife. It is coordinated by two very able women, Sidney Abbott and Jayne Vogan, to develop a sex education program and to effect necessary remedial legislation. Some NOW chapters and some state organizations have already set up task forces to work on these same programs at the local level.

In some chapters Lesbians are made to feel welcome, to feel free enough to come out if they wish and to be an integral part of the organization. In other chapters they are deliberately denied participation in the speakers bureau or at a press conference, presumably because they just might talk about Lesbian concerns—concerns to which NOW is supposed to be committed.

Only a few chapters have actively worked for gay civil rights legislation, though there are many such bills being introduced all over the country at state and municipal levels. Many NOW chapters have been all too willing to allow "sex *and* sexual orientation" clauses in such legislation to be divided into two separate bills so as not to jeopardize passage of the safe one, the one which prohibits discrimination because of sex.

There have been accusations about "special interest" chapters because a Lesbian happened to be the convenor of a new chapter. There has been no concern about "special interests," however, when the convenor happened to be white, married and middle class.

There have been accusations of a Lesbian conspiracy or takeover if Lesbian or their sympathizers run for office in a chapter. On the other hand, some chapters have elected Lesbian presidents—sometimes knowingly and sometimes unknowingly.

There have been disputes over inclusion of educational material on Lesbianism in chapter newsletters, and over the appropriateness of having a Lesbian/Feminist rock band entertain at a regional conference. Several hundred women met on the lawn and held an unscheduled Lesbian workshop because it had been omitted from a NOW regional conference schedule for lack of interest.

Some chapters have indicated that they just know they must have some Lesbians in their membership, but they don't know who they are. Is it any wonder? There is no excuse for ignorance about Lesbianism in today's feminist movement. Where such ignorance exists it can only be regarded as heterosexist. And NOW is in the business of eliminating sexism.

Lesbianism is not just "an aspect of human sexuality" or "an alternative lifestyle." Nor can Lesbianism any longer be categorized as a mental disorder according to a two-thirds vote of the American Psychiatric Association. And that's a political statement if I ever heard one.

Lesbians want to be understood for who they are—real women—alive, strong, energetic, caring, loving. We are women fighting for recognition of our whole existence. We are Lesbians—that is a fundamental way of being in the world. It does not attach itself as a qualifier or as an afterthought to the terms "homosexual" or "woman." It is an identity in and of itself.

What do Lesbians want? We want to be an assumption. We want the language and behavior of every person to bespeak a consciousness about, and an affirmation of, Lesbians' existence as Lesbians. That means NOW, in NOW, and at every level of NOW.

ROBERT "SPARK" MATSUNAGA
(1916–1990)

America Should Admit Its Guilt
JANUARY 25, 1978

Of the 120,000 Americans of Japanese ancestry . . . placed in
detention camps, . . . not one was convicted or tried
for or even charged with the commission of a crime.

After graduating from the University of Hawaii, Spark Matsunaga deferred Harvard Law School so that he could enlist in the United States Army as a second lieutenant. Only six months later, with the Second World War underway, Matsunaga was dismissed because he was Japanese American. Within weeks, the former soldier and his family were interned in an internment camp on the West Coast. In 1943, however, after nearly a year behind barbed wire, Matsunaga was released in order to join the 442nd Regimental Combat Team, a newly created unit composed of nearly 1,500 Japanese American volunteers. While on the front lines of the European theater, Matsunaga was wounded twice, becoming one of the war's most decorated infantrymen.

Matsunaga returned to Hawaii after the war and soon became active in local Democratic politics. After Hawaii became a state in 1959, he was elected to its state senate, then to the U.S. House of Representatives, and eventually, in 1976, to the U.S. Senate.

There, he devoted himself unfailingly to issues of national defense. In 1980 Senator Matsunaga cosponsored legislation to examine the injustices inflicted upon Japanese Americans during the Second World War (what he called "one great blot on the Constitution"), and explore the possibility of reparations. In his remarks before the Senate Governmental Affairs Committee, he brought his personal experience to bear on the indignities suffered by his people.

~~~~~

MR. CHAIRMAN, I welcome this opportunity to join such a distinguished panel of witnesses in urging that early and favorable consideration of S[enate bill] 1647. S. 1647 provides for the establishment of a federal commission to study, in an impartial and unbiased manner, the detention of civilians under the provisions of Executive Order 9066 during World War II.

Some of those who are here today will recall with great clarity the atmosphere which prevailed in the United States following the attack on Pearl Harbor on December 7, 1941. Rumors were rampant that Japanese warplanes had been spotted off the west coast, and erroneous reports of followup attacks on the U.S. mainland abounded. A great wave of fear and hysteria swept the United States, particularly the west coast.

Some two months after the attack on Pearl Harbor, in February 1942, President Franklin D. Roosevelt issued Executive Order 9066. The Executive Order gave to the Secretary of War the authority to designate "military areas" and to exclude "any or all" persons from such areas. Penalties for the violation of such military restrictions were subsequently established by Congress in Public Law 77–503, enacted in March of that year.

Also in March, the military commander of the western district—General John L. DeWitt—issued four public proclamations, and it was under those proclamations that the first civilian order was issued by the general on March 24, 1942, which marked the beginning of the evacuation of some 120,000 Japanese Americans and their parents from the west coast.

It is significant to note that the military commander of the then-territory of Hawaii, which had actually suffered an enemy attack, did not feel it was necessary to evacuate all individuals of Japanese ancestry from Hawaii—although it is true that a number of leaders in the Japanese American community in Hawaii were sent to detention camps on the mainland.

Moreover, no military commander felt that it was necessary to evacuate from any area of the country all Americans of German or Italian ancestry, although the United States was also at war with Germany and Italy.

FBI Director J. Edgar Hoover, who could hardly be accused of being soft on suspected seditionists, opposed the evacuation of Japanese Americans from the west coast, pointing out that the FBI and other law enforcement agencies were capable of apprehending any suspected saboteurs or enemy agents.

I might point out that whenever I criticized the FBI, the late J. Edgar Hoover was quick on the telephone to remind me that he opposed the evacuation of Japanese Americans from the west coast.

Indeed, martial law was never declared in any of these western states, and the federal courts and civilian law enforcement agencies continued to function normally.

You will be interested to know, Mr. Chairman, as a senator from the state of Washington, that one of the real strong defenders of the Japanese Americans during this distressing period in their lives was the mayor of Tacoma, Washington, the Honorable Harry Cain. One western governor, the Honorable Ralph Carr of Colorado, was willing to accept Americans of Japanese ancestry as residents of his state and undertook to guarantee their constitutional rights.

Of the 120,000 Americans of Japanese ancestry and their parents who were evacuated from the west coast and placed in detention camps, about one-half were under the age of twenty-one; about one-quarter were young children; many were elderly immigrants prohibited by law from becoming naturalized citizens, who had worked hard to raise their American-born children to be good American citizens. Not one, I repeat, not one, was convicted or tried for or even charged with the commission of a crime.

As a consequence of their evacuation, they lost their homes, jobs, businesses, and farms. More tragically the American dream was snuffed out of them and their faith in the American system was severely shaken. Reportedly, one of the evacuees, a combat veteran of World War I, who fervently believed that his own U.S. government would never deprive him of his liberty without due process of law, killed himself when he discovered that he was wrong.

In retrospect, the evacuation of Japanese Americans from the west coast and their incarceration in what can only be properly described as concentration camps is considered by many historians as one of the blackest pages in American history. It remains the single most traumatic and disturbing experience in the lives of many Nisei.

Some, now middle-aged and older, still weep when they think about it. Some become angry. And some still consider it such a degrading experience that they refuse to talk about it. More importantly, their children have started to ask questions about the internment of their parents and grandparents. Why didn't they "protest?" Did they commit any crimes that they are ashamed of? If the government was wrong, why hasn't the wrong been admitted and laid to rest forever?

No branch of the federal government has ever undertaken a comprehensive examination of the actions taken under Executive Order 9066. In 1943 and 1944, the U.S. Supreme Court did hear three cases involving the violation of the Executive Order. In *Hirabayashi v. United States* (1943) and *Korematsu v. United States* (1944), the Court ruled that an American citizen could be restrained by a curfew and could be excluded from a defined area.

However, in *Ex parte Endo* (1944), the Court held that neither the Executive Order nor act of Congress authorized the detention of an American citizen against her will in a relocation camp.

In 1972, the Congress repealed the Emergency Detention Act, a repugnant law enacted in 1950 which provided a procedural means of incarcerating Americans suspected of espionage or sabotage during an internal security emergency in camps similar to those established for Japanese Americans in World War II.

In 1975, President Ford revoked Executive Order 9066, and Congress repealed Public Law 77–503, and a host of other outmoded emergency war powers granted to the president on a temporary basis since the Civil War.

Despite these commendable actions, many unanswered questions remain about the detention of Japanese Americans during World War II, and there remains an unfinished chapter in our national history.

In recent years, the issue of how to write the end to this sad and unsavory episode has been widely discussed in the Japanese American community. From time to time, reports that the Japanese Americans might be preparing to request monetary reparations have been floated in the national press.

Some members of the Japanese-American community do believe that the federal government should provide some form of monetary compensation to redress them for the injustice they suffered. However, members of this committee ought to know that an almost equal number maintain that no amount of money can ever compensate them for the loss of their inalienable right to life, liberty, and the pursuit of happiness, or the loss of their constitutional rights.

The proposed bill is not a redress bill. Should the Commission authorized to look into the matter decide that some form of compensation should be provided, the Congress would still be able to consider the question and make the final decision. Whether or not redress is provided, the study undertaken by the Commission will be valuable in and of itself, not only for Japanese Americans, but for all Americans.

Passage of S. 1647 will be just one more piece of evidence ours is a nation great enough to recognize and rectify its mistakes.

Thank you.

HARVEY MILK
(1930–1978)

Tired of the Silence
JUNE 25, 1978

I'm tired of the conspiracy of silence.

Born into a wealthy family in Long Island, New York, Harvey Milk served in the Korean War and, after returning home, became an investment banker. Bored with his Wall Street career, Milk moved to California in the early 1970s. In 1973 he ran for city supervisor of San Francisco, as an openly gay man, but lost that race and three subsequent attempts.

Despite the hostile climate for homosexuals in the 1970s, Milk continued to campaign with clever grassroots devices, like human billboards along the major streets in San Francisco. He argued that invisibility was the gay community's greatest obstacle, prompting hundreds of people to "out" themselves in his support. In 1977, Milk finally won a seat on the Board of Supervisors. During his brief tenure, Milk regularly repeated, "The story doesn't center on me being gay. It's just about a gay person who is doing this job."

This address at City Hall in San Francisco was the cornerstone event of the 1978 Gay Freedom Day Parade. Energizing the assembled 375,000 men and women against Anita Bryant, a devout Baptist, Miss America runner-up, and anti-gay campaigner, Milk's message focused on equal opportunity for gays and the exigency of their public presence.

Only months later, on November 27, 1978, fueled by anti-gay sentiment, fellow supervisor Daniel White assassinated Harvey Milk. Lawyers for White relied on homophobia as a defense by packing the jury with anti-gay members; his lawyers also called on a psychologist to testify that "junk food" had exacerbated White's insanity (the so-called Twinkie defense). White only received a five-year sentence with parole, a pittance for the crime committed. After the verdict, the city erupted in riots; more than 160 people were hospitalized.

MY NAME IS HARVEY MILK—and I want to recruit you. I want to recruit you for the fight to preserve your democracy from the John Briggs and the Anita Bryants who are trying to constitutionalize bigotry.

We are not going to allow that to happen. We are not going to sit back in silence as 300,000 of our gay brothers and sisters did in Nazi Germany. We are not going to allow our rights to be taken away and then march with bowed heads into the gas chambers. On this anniversary of Stonewall I ask my gay sisters and brothers to make the commitment to fight. For themselves. For their freedom. For their country.

Here, in San Francisco, we recently held an election for a judgeship. An anti-gay smear campaign was waged against a presiding judge because she was supported by lesbians and gay men. Here, in so-called liberal San Francisco, an anti-gay smear campaign was waged by so-called liberals.

And here, in so-called liberal San Francisco, we have a columnist for the *San Francisco Examiner,* a columnist named Kevin Starr, who has printed a number of columns containing distortions and lies about gays. He's getting away with it.

These anti-gay smear campaigns, these anti-gay columns, are laying the groundwork for the Briggs initiative. We had better be prepared for it.

In the *Examiner,* Kevin Starr defames and libels gays. In the *San Francisco Chronicle,* Charles McCabe warns us to be quiet, that talking about gay rights is counter-productive. To Mr. McCabe I say that the day he stops talking about freedom of the press is the day he no longer has it.

The blacks did not win their rights by sitting quietly in the back of the bus. They got off!

Gay people, we will not win their rights by staying quietly in our closets. . . . We are coming out! We are coming out to fight the lies, the myths, the distortions! We are coming out to tell the truth about gays!

For I'm tired of the conspiracy of silence.

I'm tired of listening to the Anita Bryants twist the language and the meaning of the Bible to fit their own distorted outlook. But I'm even more tired of the silence from the religious leaders of this nation who know that she is playing fast and loose with the true meaning of the Bible. I'm tired of their silence more than of her biblical gymnastics!

And I'm tired of John Briggs talking about false role models. He's lying in his teeth and he knows it. But I'm even more tired of the silence from educators and psychologists who know that Briggs is lying and yet say nothing. I'm tired of their silence more than of Briggs' lies!

I'm tired of the silence. So I'm going to talk about it. And I want *you* to talk about it.

Gay people, we are painted as child molesters. I want to talk about that. I want to talk about the *myth* of child molestations by gays. I want to talk about the fact that in this state some 95 percent of child molestations are heterosexual and usually the parent. . . .

I want to talk about the fact that all child abandonments are heterosexual.

I want to talk about the fact that all abuse of children is by their heterosexual parents.

I want to talk about the fact that some 98 percent of the six million rapes committed annually are heterosexual.

I want to talk about the fact that one out of every three women who will be murdered in this state this year will be murdered by their husbands.

I want to talk about the fact that some 30 percent of all marriages contain domestic violence.

And finally, I want to tell the John Briggs and the Anita Bryants that you talk about the myths of gays but today I'm talking about the facts of heterosexual violence and what the hell are you going to do about that?

Clean up your own house before you start telling lies about gays. Don't distort the Bible to hide your own sins. Don't change facts to lies. Don't look for cheap political advantage in playing upon people's fears! Judging by the latest polls, even the youth can tell you're lying!

[calmer] Anita Bryant, John Briggs: Your unwillingness to talk about your own house, your deliberate lies and distortions, your unwillingness to face the truth, chills my blood—it reeks of madness!

And like the rest of you, I'm tired of our so-called friends who tell us that we must set standards.

What standards?

The standards of the rapists? The wife beaters? The child abusers? The people who ordered the bomb to be built? The people who ordered it to be dropped? The people who pulled the trigger? The people who gave us Vietnam? The people who built the gas chambers? The people who built the concentration camps—right here, in California, and then herded all the Japanese-Americans into them during World War II? . . . The Jew baiters? The nigger knockers? The corporate thieves? The Nixons? The Hitlers?

What standards do you want us to set? Clean up your act, clean up your violence before you criticize lesbians and gay men because of their sexuality. . . . It is madness to glorify killing and violence on one hand and be ashamed of the sexual act, the act that conceived you, on the other . . .

There is a difference between morality and murder. The fact is that more people have been slaughtered in the name of religion than for any other single reason. That, that, my friends, that is true perversion! For the standards that we should set, should we read your next week's headlines? . . .

Well, I'm tired of the lies of the Anita Bryants and the John Briggs.

I'm tired of their myths.

I'm tired of their distortions.

I'm speaking out about it.

Gay brothers and sisters, what are you going to do about it? You must come out. Come out . . . to your parents. . . . I know that it is hard and will hurt them but think about how they will hurt you in the voting booth! Come out . . . to your relatives. I know that is hard and will upset them but think of how they will upset you in the voting booth. Come out to your friends . . . if they indeed they are your friends. Come out to your neighbors . . . to your fellow workers . . . to the people who work where you eat and shop. . . . Come out only to the people you know, and who know you. Not to anyone else. But once and for all, break down the myths, destroy the lies and distortions.

For your sake.

For their sake.

For the sake of the youngsters who are becoming scared by the votes from Dade to Eugene.

If Briggs wins he will not stop. They never do. Like all mad people, they are forced to go on, to prove they were right!

There will be no safe "closet" for any gay person.

So break out of yours today—tear the damn thing down once and for all!

And finally

Most of all

I'm tired of the silence from the White House.

Jimmy Carter: You talked about human rights a lot . . . In fact, you want to be the world's leader for human rights. Well, damn it, lead!!! There are some fifteen to twenty million lesbians and gay men in this nation listening and listening very carefully.

Jimmy Carter: When are you going to talk about *their* rights?

You talk a lot about the Bible. . . . But when are you going to talk about that most important part: "Love thy neighbor?" After all, she may be gay.

Jimmy Carter: The time has come for lesbians and gay men to come out— and they are. Now the time has come for you to speak out. When are you?

Until you speak out against hatred, bigotry, madness, you are just Jimmy Carter. When you do, then and only then, will some twenty million lesbians and gay men be able to say Jimmy Carter is *our* president, too!

Jimmy Carter, you have the choice: How many more years?

How much more damage?

How much more violence?

How many more lives?

History says that, like all groups seeking their rights, sooner or later we will win.

The question is: When?

Jimmy Carter, you have to make the choice—it's in your hands: Either years of violence . . . or you can help turn the pages of history that much faster.

It is up to you. And now, before it becomes too late, come to California and speak out against Briggs. . . .

If you don't—then we will come to you!!!

If you do not speak out, if you remain silent, if you do not lift your voice against Briggs, then I call upon lesbians and gay men from all over the nation . . . your nation . . . to gather in Washington . . . one year from now . . . on that national day of freedom, the Fourth of July . . . the Fourth of July, 1979 . . . to gather in Washington on that very same spot where over a decade ago Dr. Martin Luther King spoke to a nation of his dreams . . . dreams that are fast fading, dreams that to many millions in this nation have become nightmares rather than dreams. . . .

I call upon all minorities and especially the millions of lesbians and gay men to wake up from their dreams . . . to gather on Washington and tell Jimmy Carter and their nation: "Wake up . . . wake up, America . . . no more racism, no more sexism, no more ageism, no more hatred . . . no more!"

On the Statue of Liberty it says: "Give me your tired, your poor, your huddled masses yearning to be free. . . . " In the Declaration of Independence it is written: "All men are created equal and they are endowed with certain inalienable rights. . . . " And in our national anthem it says: "Oh, say does that star-spangled banner yet wave o'er the land of the free."

For Mr. Briggs and Mrs. Bryant and Mr. Starr and all the bigots out there: That's what America is. No matter how hard you try, you cannot erase those words from the Declaration of Independence. No matter how hard you try, you cannot chip those words from off the base of the Statue of Liberty. And no matter how hard, you cannot sing the "Star Spangled Banner" without those words.

That's what America is.

Love it or leave it.

CLIFFORD UYEDA
(1920–)

That a Past Wrong Be Admitted
JULY 20, 1979

If we continue to ignore the past because it was unpleasant, . . .
then the experience emasculates the entire
Japanese Americans as a group.

As president of the Japanese American Citizens League (JACL), Clifford Uyeda led twin campaigns, one for an apology and reparations for Japanese-American internment, and the other for the pardon of Iva Toguri, better known as "Tokyo Rose." Popular sentiment held that Toguri was unjustly convicted of treason in 1949 for broadcasting Japanese propaganda to troops in the Pacific region.

Even after President Gerald Ford pardoned Toguri, affording credibility to Asian-American activists, Uyeda's drive for reparations was a lonely one. Many Japanese Americans wanted the memories of the war, including Toguri, behind them. In their eyes, reparations were a form of welfare that would only further unearth unpleasant vestiges of the past.

A native of Washington State, Uyeda studied medicine at Tulane University in New Orleans, Louisiana, and practiced pediatrics in San Francisco before becoming immersed in the movement for Asian-American civil rights and equal opportunity. In this speech to the Twin Cities JACL chapter in Minneapolis, Minnesota, Uyeda outlined his reasoning behind his fight for reparations—a measure he believed critical to preventing future injustice.

———

I APPRECIATE THIS OPPORTUNITY to appear before you tonight. I believe you will want me to speak out on the subject of redress which Japanese Americans seek for the injustices suffered as an official act of our own United States government. It happened in our lifetime. It is not an ancient wrong of the dim past.

There was no evidence or record of sabotage or espionage. There was no charge or indictment made against us. The [Supreme] Court, however, upheld the proposition that all persons of Japanese ancestry were enemies, that the war was not directed against Japan but at the Japanese race.

Losses sustained by the evacuees were far reaching. Property losses alone were estimated by the Federal Reserve Bank of San Francisco to be in excess of $400 million in 1942.

For those who point to the Evacuation Claims Act of 1948, remind them that the amount returned was less than a single year's interest on the original sum. [That] $400 million would, in thirty-seven years, accumulate in interest alone billions of dollars.

For those who point to $25,000 per individual as too large a redress, ask them if they would be willing to be uprooted from their homes and without a charge be incarcerated in a desert camp for years with complete uncertainty about their future for a mere $25,000.

⁓

Loss of freedom or injustice can never be equated monetarily. A meaningful redress, however, is a tangible expression of our own government's acknowledgment of the injustice and wrong committed against her own people.

Many fear backlash. It is fear of what their non-Japanese friends would say or think. There is also fear of reawakening in them their own feelings which had been so long suppressed.

Such fears may be well founded, but they are inappropriate in a responsible citizen. If we continue to ignore the past because it was unpleasant, and never even ask for a just restitution because it is not popular, then the experience emasculates the entire Japanese Americans as a group. To continue this submissive stance is tantamount to saying: "We prefer to be second class. Let someone else take the risk and the responsibility of a first-class citizenship."

If there are those amongst us who have achieved decent income, there are also others who have not. Let us not forget them.

Then there is the plight of the Japanese elderly. One out of five has income less than poverty level. According to the latest available national statistics, the Japanese 65 years and over have a lower median income than that of the total elderly population. It was $2,400 a year for males and $1,300 a year for females. Forty percent of the males and sixty-three percent of the females had income less than $2,000 a year.

In spite of the lower income the elderly Japanese received lower Social Security benefits than families of other races.

Therefore, many elderly Japanese Americans have very low median income on which to subsist, many are below poverty level, and many live alone.

Much of this was due to their having been expelled from the West Coast at the height of their productive years. They not only could not save for old age, they had lost everything they worked for.

It is the height of insensitivity to ignore our own people who must live in poverty because some of us are not in want.

We hear that because there will be recipients who are not at poverty level, redress is not justified. Since when has wealth or poverty of an individual had anything to do with one's right to be free from false imprisonment, his right to constitutional safeguards, and his right to redress the wrong committed against him?

We are talking about the fundamental rights guaranteed all Americans by our own Constitution. Are the guarantees of the Bill of Rights absolute, or are we free to suspend them at anytime according to the whims of those in power or the mood of hysteria which may prevail? We must take responsibility for what we do as a nation. We readily take credit for what our past generations have accomplished in the name of humanity. Can we so easily exclude ourselves then from our past national mistakes? Japanese Americans were deprived of liberty and property without criminal charges, and without a trial of any kind.

We must not be intimidated by irrational statements from the public, or even by some amongst us. What are some of the major backlashes being heard in America?

[First] that those other Americans drafted to fight in the war were also uprooted from their homes, lived in camps, suffered deprivations, pain and even death on the battlefields.

Japanese American soldiers—there were 33,000 of them during World War II—also went through the same sacrifices common to all citizens during wartime, and we seek no redress for such deprivations and sufferings.

Yes, there was a war going on. But to be regarded and treated as an enemy by one's own government without a shred of evidence, stripped of all constitutional and human rights, and then be told that your suffering is no different from those of any other American—any other American subjected to similar treatment by one's own government would have been equally outraged.

[Second] that if Japanese Americans seek redress, all Americans who suffered under enemy actions should be compensated. What about Americans who died at Pearl Harbor, and what about the sufferings of the POWs, they say.

The plain answer is that Japanese Americans had nothing to do with Pearl Harbor. We were also the victims on that tragic day. The POWs were under the control of the Japanese military government, not Japanese Americans.

These are the very reasons why we must speak about the evacuation and the need for redress. The very fact that so many Americans associate Japanese Americans with Pearl Harbor and the sufferings of the POWs clearly indicates that America still does not see us as Americans but as former enemies.

Jesse Jackson
(1941–)

Our Time Has Come:
1984 Democratic Convention Speech
July 17, 1984

Our flag is red, white, and blue, but our nation is a rainbow.

Jesse Louis Jackson arguably has been the leading voice for civil rights in the last quarter century. Born in Greenville, South Carolina, Jackson attended the University of Illinois and North Carolina Agricultural and Technical College. In 1965 he joined the Southern Christian Leadership Conference (SCLC) and served as the executive director of its Operation Breadbasket program, putting pressure on corporations to hire blacks and support black businesses. In that capacity, Jackson befriended and marched alongside Dr. Martin Luther King, Jr. He has carried Dr. King's mantle since his assassination.

After being ordained as a Baptist minister in 1971, Jackson resigned from the SCLC and founded Operation PUSH (People United to Save Humanity)—later renamed the Rainbow PUSH Coalition. Through PUSH, Jackson continues to pursue the economic objectives of Operation Breadbasket, but with expanded reach into areas of social and political underdevelopment. Under Reverend Jackson's direction, the organization has developed into a vehicle for protesting racial conflict and apartheid in communities in the United States and around the globe, from the streets of Harlem to the capitol of Nigeria.

In 1984 Jesse Jackson became the first black American to run a serious campaign for president. Though he finished behind Democrats Walter Mondale and Gary Hart, Jackson succeeded in advancing his "people's platform," thereby establishing a base of support among minority groups in a true "rainbow coalition."

In his fifty-minute address at the Democratic National Convention in San Francisco, Jackson delivered an impassioned plea for party and racial unity. Although his speech did not air until 11 P.M., more than 33 million viewers tuned in, more than at any other time during the entire convention. Then–Florida governor Bob Graham proclaimed, "If you are a human being and weren't affected by what you heard, you may be beyond redemption." Jackson ran for president again in 1988; although unsuccessful, he furthered his role as an international figure.

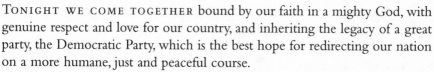

TONIGHT WE COME TOGETHER bound by our faith in a mighty God, with genuine respect and love for our country, and inheriting the legacy of a great party, the Democratic Party, which is the best hope for redirecting our nation on a more humane, just and peaceful course.

This is not a perfect party. We are not a perfect people. Yet, we are called to a perfect mission: our mission to feed the hungry; to clothe the naked; to house the homeless; to teach the illiterate; to provide jobs for the jobless; and to choose the human race over the nuclear race. [*Applause*]

We are gathered here this week to nominate a candidate and adopt a platform which will expand, unify, direct and inspire our Party and the Nation to fulfill this mission.

My constituency is the desperate, the damned, the disinherited, the disrespected, and the despised. They are restless and seek relief. They've voted in record numbers. They have invested faith, hope and trust that they have in us. The Democratic Party must send them a signal that we care. I pledge my best to not let them down.

There is the call of conscience, redemption, expansion, healing and unity. Leadership must heed the call of conscience, redemption, expansion, healing and unity, for they are the key to achieving our mission. Time is neutral and does not change things. With courage and initiative, leaders can change things. No generation can choose the age or circumstance in which it is born, but through leadership it can choose to make the age in which it is born an age of enlightenment, an age of jobs and peace and justice. [*Applause*]

Only leadership—that intangible combination of gifts, the discipline, information, circumstance, courage, timing, will and divine inspiration—can lead us out of the crisis in which we find ourselves. The leadership can mitigate the misery of our nation. Leadership can part the waters and lead our nation in the direction of the Promised Land. Leadership can lift the boats stuck at the bottom.

I've had the rare opportunity to watch seven men, and then two, pour out their souls, offer their service and heal—and heed the call of duty to direct the course of our Nation. There is a proper season for everything. There is a time to sow, a time to reap. There is a time to compete, and a time to cooperate.

I ask for your vote on the first ballot as a vote for a new direction for this Party and this Nation. [*Applause*] A vote of conviction, a vote of conscience. [*Applause*]

But I will be proud to support the nominee of this convention for the Presidency of the United States of America. [*Applause*] Thank you.

This campaign has taught me much; that leaders must be tough enough to fight, tender enough to cry, human enough to make mistakes, humble enough to admit them, strong enough to absorb the pain and resilient enough to bounce back and keep on moving. [*Applause*]

For leaders, the pain is often intense. But you must smile through your tears and keep moving with the faith that there is a brighter side somewhere.

I went to see Hubert Humphrey three days before he died. He had just called Richard Nixon from his dying bed, and many people wondered why. I asked him. He said, "Jesse, from this vantage point, with the sun setting in my life, all of the speeches, the political conventions, the crowds and the great fights are behind me now. At a time like this you are forced to deal with your irreducible essence, forced to grapple with that which is really important to you. And what I have concluded about life," Hubert Humphrey said, "when all is said and done, we must forgive each other, and redeem each other, and move on."

Our party is emerging from one of its most hard fought battles for the Democratic Party's presidential nomination in our history. But our healthy competition should make us better, not bitter. [*Applause*]

We must use the insight, wisdom, and experience of the late Hubert Humphrey as a balm for the wounds in our Party, this Nation and the world. We must forgive each other, redeem each other, regroup and move on.

Our flag is red, white and blue, but our nation is a rainbow—red, yellow, brown, black and white—and we're all precious in God's sight.

America is not like a blanket—one piece of unbroken cloth, the same color, the same texture, the same size. America is more like a quilt—many patches, many pieces, many colors, many sizes, all woven and held together by a common thread. The white, the Hispanic, the black, the Arab, the Jew, the woman, the native American, the small farmer, the businessperson, the environmentalist, the peace activist, the young, the old, the lesbian, the gay and the disabled make up the American quilt. [*Applause*]

Even in our fractured state, all of us count and all of us fit somewhere. We have proven that we can survive without each other. But we have not proven that we can win and progress without each other. We must come together. [*Applause*]

From Fannie Lou Hamer in Atlantic City in 1964 to the Rainbow Coalition in San Francisco today; from the Atlantic to the Pacific, we have experienced pain but progress as we ended American apartheid laws, we got public accommodation, we secured voting rights, we obtained open housing, as young people got the right to vote. We lost Malcolm, Martin, Medgar, Bobby, John and Viola. The team that got us here must be expanded, not abandoned. [*Applause*]

Twenty years ago, tears welled up in our eyes as the bodies of Schwerner, Goodman and Chaney were dredged from the depths of a river in Mississippi. Twenty years later, our communities, black and Jewish, are in anguish, anger and pain. Feelings have been hurt on both sides.

There is a crisis in communications. Confusion is in the air. But we cannot afford to lose our way. We may agree to agree; or agree to disagree on issues; we must bring back civility to these tensions.

We are co-partners in a long and rich religious history—the Judeo-Christian traditions. Many blacks and Jews have a shared passion for social justice at home and peace abroad. We must seek a revival of the spirit, inspired by a new vision and new possibilities. We must return to higher ground. [*Applause*]

Twenty years later, we cannot be satisfied by just restoring the old coalition. Old wine skins must make room for new wine. We must heal and expand. The Rainbow Coalition is making room for Arab Americans. They, too, know the pain and hurt of racial and religious rejection. They must not continue to be made pariahs. The Rainbow Coalition is making room for Hispanic Americans who this very night are living under the threat of the Simpson-Mazzoli bill. [*Applause*]

And farmworkers from Ohio who are fighting the Campbell Soup Company with a boycott to achieve legitimate workers' rights. [*Applause*]

The Rainbow is making room for the Native American, the most exploited people of all, a people with the greatest moral claim amongst us. We support them as they seek the restoration of their ancient land and claim amongst us. We support them as they seek the restoration of land and water rights, as they seek to preserve their ancestral homelands and the beauty of a land that was once all theirs. They can never receive a fair share for all they have given us. They must finally have a fair chance to develop their great resources and to preserve their people and their culture.

The Rainbow Coalition includes Asian Americans, now being killed in our streets, scapegoats for the failures of corporate, industrial and economic policies. The Rainbow is making room for the young Americans. Twenty years ago, our young people were dying in a war for which they could not even vote. Twenty years later, young America has the power to stop a war in Central America and the responsibility to vote in great numbers. [*Applause*] Young America must be politically active in 1984. The choice is war or peace. We must make room for young America.

The Rainbow includes disabled veterans. The color scheme fits in the Rainbow. The disabled have their handicap revealed and their genius concealed; while the able-bodied have their genius revealed and their disability concealed. But ultimately, we must judge people by their values and their contribution. Don't leave anybody out. I would rather have Roosevelt in a wheelchair than Reagan on a horse. *[Applause]*

The Rainbow includes for small farmers. They have suffered tremendously under the Reagan regime. They will either receive 90 percent parity or 100 percent charity. We must address their concerns and make room for them.

The Rainbow includes lesbians and gays. No American citizen ought to be denied equal protection from the law.

We must be unusually committed and caring as we expand our family to include new members. All of us must be tolerant and understanding as the fears and anxieties of the rejected and of the party leadership express themselves in so many different ways. Too often what we call hate—as if it were some deeply rooted philosophy or strategy—it is simply ignorance, anxiety, paranoia, fear and insecurity. *[Applause]*

To be strong leaders, we must be long-suffering as we seek to right the wrongs of our Party and our Nation. We must expand our Party, heal our Party and unify our Party. That is our mission in 1984. *[Applause]*

We are often reminded that we live in a great nation—and we do. But it can be greater still. The Rainbow is mandating a new definition of greatness. We must not measure greatness from the mansion down, but from the manger up. Jesus said that we should not be judged by the bark we wear but by the fruit that we bear. Jesus said that we must measure greatness by how we treat the least of these.

President Reagan says the nation is in recovery. . . .

The big corporations and rich individuals who received the bulk of a three-year, multibillion [dollar] tax cut from Mr. Reagan are recovering. But no such recovery is under way for the least of these. Rising tides don't lift all boats, particularly those stuck at the bottom.

For the boats stuck at the bottom there's a misery index. This Administration has made life more miserable for the poor. Its attitude has been contemptuous. Its policies and programs have been cruel and unfair to working people. . . .

Mr. Reagan will ask us to pray, and I believe in prayer. I have come to this way by power of prayer. But then, we must watch false prophecy. He cuts energy assistance to the poor, cuts breakfast programs from children, cuts lunch programs from children, cuts job training from children, and then says to an empty table, "Let us pray." *[Applause]* Apparently he is not familiar with the structure of prayer. You thank the Lord for the food that you are about to receive, not the food that just left. *[Laughter and applause]* I think that we should pray, but don't pray for the food that left. Pray for the man that took the food—to leave.

We need a change. We need a change in November. *[Applause]*

Under Mr. Reagan, the misery index has risen for the poor. The danger index has risen for everybody. Under this administration, we have lost the lives of our boys in Central America and Honduras, in Grenada, in Lebanon, in a nuclear standoff in Europe. Under this Administration, one-third of our children believe they will die in a nuclear war. The danger index is increasing in this world.

⌒

. . . We have a challenge as Democrats to point a way out. Democracy guarantees opportunity, not success. Democracy guarantees the right to participate, not a license for either a majority [or minority] to dominate. The victory for the Rainbow Coalition in the Platform debates today was not whether we won or lost, but that we raised the right issues.

We could afford to lose the vote; issues are non-negotiable. We could not afford to avoid raising the right questions. Our self-respect and our moral integrity were at stake. Our heads are perhaps bloody, but not bowed. Our back is straight. We can go home and face our people. Our vision is clear. *[Applause]*

When we think, on this journey from slave ship to championship, that we have gone from the planks of the Boardwalk in Atlantic City in 1964 to fighting to help write the planks in the platform in San Francisco in 1984, there is a deep and abiding sense of joy in our souls in spite of the tears in our eyes. Though there are missing planks, there is a solid foundation upon which to build. Our party can win, but we must provide hope, which will inspire people to struggle and achieve; provide a plan that shows a way out of our dilemma and then lead the way.

In 1984, my heart is made to feel glad because I know there is a way out— justice. The requirement for rebuilding America is justice. The linchpin of progressive politics in our nation will not come from the North; they in fact will come from the South.

⌒

It is not enough to hope that ERA will pass. How can we pass ERA? If Blacks vote in great numbers, progressive Whites win. It is the only way progressive Whites win. If Blacks vote in great numbers, Hispanics win. When Blacks, Hispanics and progressive Whites vote, women win. When women win, children win. When women and children win, workers win. We must all come together. We must come together. *[Spontaneous demonstration]* Thank you.

I tell you, in all our joy and excitement, we must not save the world and lose our souls. We should never short-circuit enforcing the Voting Rights Act at every level. When one of us rises, all of us will rise. Justice is the way out. Peace is the way out. We should not act as if nuclear weaponry is negotiable and debatable. In this world in which we live, we dropped the bomb on Japan and felt guilty, but in 1984 other folks have also got bombs. This time, if we drop the bomb, six minutes later we, too, will be destroyed. It is not about dropping the bomb on somebody. It is about dropping the bomb on everybody. We must choose to develop minds over guided missiles, and then think it out and not fight it out. It is time for a change. *[Applause]*

With all this confusion in this Convention, the bright lights and parties and big fun, we must raise up the single proposition: If we lift up a program to feed the hungry, they will come running; if we lift up a program to start a war no more, our youth will come running; if we lift up a program to put America back to work, and an alternative to welfare and despair, they will come running.

If we cut that military budget without cutting our defense, and use that money to rebuild bridges and put steel workers back to work, and use that money and provide jobs for our cities, and use that money to build schools and pay teachers and educate our children, and build hospitals, and train doctors and train nurses, the whole nation will come running to us. *[Applause]*

As I leave you now, we vote in this convention and get ready to go back across this nation in a couple of days, in this campaign I tried to be faithful to my promise. I lived in old barrios, ghettos and in reservations and housing projects. I have a message for our youth. I challenge them to put hope in their brains and not dope in their veins. *[Applause]* I told them that like Jesus, I, too, was born in the slum, and just because you're born in a slum does not mean the slum is born in you, and you can rise above it if your mind is made up. *[Applause]* I told them in every slum there are two sides. When I see a broken window, that's the slummy side. Train some youth to become a glazier; that is the sunny side. When I see a missing brick, that is the slummy side. Let that child in a union and become a brick mason and build; that is the sunny side. When I see a missing door, that is the slummy side. Train some youth to become a carpenter; that is the sunny side. When I see the vulgar words and hieroglyphics of destitution on the walls, that is the slummy side. Train some youth to be a painter and artist; that is the sunny side.

We leave this place looking for the sunny side because there's a brighter side somewhere. I am more convinced than ever that we can win. We will vault up the rough side of the mountain. We can win. I just want young America to do me one favor, just one favor.

Exercise the right to dream. You must face reality, that which is. But then dream of a reality that ought to be, that must be. Live beyond the pain of reality with the dream of a bright tomorrow. Use hope and imagination as weapons of survival and progress. Use love to motivate you and obligate you to serve the human family.

Young America, dream. Choose the human race over the nuclear race. Bury the weapons and don't burn the people. Dream—dream of a new value system. Teachers who teach for life and not just for a living; teach because they can't help it. Dream of lawyers more concerned about justice than a judgeship. Dream of doctors more concerned about public health than personal wealth. *[Applause]*

Dream of preachers and priests who will prophesy and not just profiteer. Preach and dream! Our time has come. Our time has come.

Suffering breeds character. Character breeds faith, and in the end faith will not disappoint. Our time has come. Our faith, hope and dreams have prevailed. Our time has come. Weeping has endured for nights but that joy cometh in the morning.

Our time has come. No grave can hold our body down. Our time has come. No lie can live forever. Our time has come. We must leave the racial battle ground and come to the economic common ground and moral higher ground. America, our time has come.

We come from disgrace to amazing grace. Our time has come. Give me your tired, give me your poor, your huddled masses who yearn to breathe free and come November, there will be a change because our time has come.

Thank you and God bless you.

CÉSAR CHÁVEZ
(1927–1993)

We Organized
NOVEMBER 9, 1984

*You cannot humiliate the person who feels pride. You cannot
oppress the people who are not afraid anymore.*

César Chávez delivered this address to the Commonwealth Club of
California more than two decades after his successful Table-Grape
Growers Boycott, which ended in the ratification of union contracts
between farmhands and farm owners. Three years later, Chávez instituted
a second boycott after the grape growers failed to renew their contracts.
Nearly 17 million Americans participated in that protest, forcing growers
to capitulate to a California state law allowing workers to engage in collective bargaining.

In the following years, the United Farm Workers Union wrestled
with financial and political problems, and Chávez himself came under
criticism for his apparent dominance of the UFW. Still, farm workers
continued to draw on his wisdom and infinite fortitude. Chicano activist
José Angel Gutiérrez described his commitment to farm workers as "total
and complete . . . [and] the embodiment of a Chicano."

In 1982 Chávez was called upon again, when the California government, under the leadership of George Dukmejian, took steps to curtail
the gains made for farm workers under the 1975 Agricultural Labor
Relations Act. Under Dukmejian, the farm labor board ceased to enforce
the legislation, which included higher pay, family health coverage, and
pension benefits for farmworkers. By 1984, it was clear that the gains
growers achieved in the 1960s and '70s were unraveling. Chávez called
for a third boycott, reminding participants that they were fighting for
their freedom and the future of their children.

This speech came on the cusp of that boycott and was framed in the
broader accomplishments of the Latino movement—from gains in voter
registration and farm conditions to child labor provisions and political
representation. It was Chávez's last major address; he died nine years later.*

---

*Chávez often delivered his speeches in Spanish, unless, as in this case, he was
addressing non-Hispanic audiences, reporters, or staff. In some cases, he alternated
between the two languages.

As was customary, his remarks were "simple," "plain spoken," and "mon-otone." He "rarely raised his voice to make a point."

TWENTY-ONE YEARS AGO last September, on a lonely stretch of railroad track paralleling U.S. Highway 101 near Salinas, 32 Bracero farmworkers lost their lives in a tragic accident.

The Braceros had been imported from Mexico to work on California farms. They died when their bus, which was converted from a flatbed truck, drove in front of a freight train.

Conversion of the bus had not been approved by any government agency. The driver had "tunnel" vision.

Most of the bodies lay unidentified for days. No one, including the grower who employed the workers, even knew their names.

Today, thousands of farmworkers live under savage conditions—beneath trees and amid garbage and human excrement—near tomato fields in San Diego County, tomato fields which use the most modern farm technology.

Vicious rats gnaw on them as they sleep. They walk miles to buy food at inflated prices. And they carry in water from irrigation pumps.

Child labor is still common in many farm areas.

As much as 30 percent of Northern California's garlic harvesters are under-aged children. Kids as young as six years old have voted in state-conducted union elections since they qualified as workers.

Some 800,000 under-aged children work with their families harvesting crops across America. Babies born to migrant workers suffer 25 percent higher infant mortality than the rest of the population.

Malnutrition among migrant worker children is 10 times higher than the national rate.

Farmworkers' average life expectancy is still 49 years—compared to 73 years for the average American.

All my life, I have been driven by one dream, one goal, one vision: To over-throw a farm labor system in this nation which treats farmworkers as if they were not important human beings.

Farmworkers are not agricultural implements. They are not beasts of bur-den—to be used and discarded.

That dream was born in my youth. It was nurtured in my early days of organizing. It has flourished. It has been attacked.

I'm not very different from anyone else who has ever tried to accomplish something with his life. My motivation comes from my personal life—from watching what my mother and father went through when I was growing up; from what we experienced as migrant farmworkers in California.

That dream, that vision, grew from my own experience with racism, with hope, with the desire to be treated fairly and to see my people treated as human beings and not as chattel.

It grew from anger and rage—emotions I felt forty years ago when people of my color were denied the right to see a movie or eat at a restaurant in many parts of California.

It grew from the frustration and humiliation I felt as a boy who couldn't understand how the growers could abuse and exploit farmworkers when there were so many of us and so few of them.

Later, in the '50s, I experienced a different kind of exploitation. In San Jose, in Los Angeles and in other urban communities, we—the Mexican American people—were dominated by a majority that was Anglo.

I began to realize what other minority people had discovered: That the only answer—the only hope—was in organizing. More of us had to become citizens. We had to register to vote. And people like me had to develop the skills it would take to organize, to educate, to help empower the Chicano people.

I spent many years—before we founded the union—learning how to work with people.

We experienced some successes in voter registration, in politics, in battling racial discrimination—successes in an era when Black Americans were just beginning to assert their civil rights and when political awareness among Hispanics was almost non-existent.

But deep in my heart, I knew I could never be happy unless I tried organizing the farmworkers. I didn't know if I would succeed. But I had to try.

All Hispanics—urban and rural, young and old—are connected to the farmworkers' experience. We had all lived through the fields—or our parents had. We shared that common humiliation.

How could we progress as a people, even if we lived in the cities, while the farmworkers—men and women of our color—were condemned to a life without pride?

How could we progress as a people while the farmworkers—who symbolized our history in this land—were denied self-respect?

How could our people believe that their children could become lawyers and doctors and judges and business people while this shame, this injustice was permitted to continue?

Those who attack our union often say, "It's not really a union. It's something else: A social movement. A civil rights movement. It's something dangerous."

They're half right. The United Farm Workers is first and foremost a union. A union like any other. A union that either produces for its members on the bread and butter issues or doesn't survive.

But the UFW has always been something more than a union—although it's never been dangerous if you believe in the Bill of Rights.

The UFW was the beginning! We attacked that historical source of shame and infamy that our people in this country lived with. We attacked that injustice, not by complaining; not by seeking hand-outs; not by becoming soldiers in the War on Poverty.

We organized!

Farmworkers acknowledged we had allowed ourselves to become victims in a democratic society—a society where majority rule and collective bargaining are supposed to be more than academic theories or political rhetoric. And by addressing this historical problem, we created confidence and pride and hope in an entire people's ability to create the future.

The UFW's survival—its existence—was not in doubt in my mind when the time began to come—after the union became visible—when Chicanos started entering college in greater numbers, when Hispanics began running for public office in greater numbers—when our people started asserting their rights on a broad range of issues and in many communities across the country.

The union's survival—its very existence—sent out a signal to all Hispanics that we were fighting for our dignity, that we were challenging and overcoming injustice, that we were empowering the least educated among us—the poorest among us.

The message was clear: If it could happen in the fields, it could happen anywhere—in the cities, in the courts, in the city councils, in the state legislatures.

I didn't really appreciate it at the time, but the coming of our union signaled the start of great changes among Hispanics that are only now beginning to be seen.

I've traveled to every part of this nation. I have met and spoken with thousands of Hispanics from every walk of life—from every social and economic class.

One thing I hear most often from Hispanics, regardless of age or position—and from many non-Hispanics as well—is that the farmworkers gave them hope that they could succeed and the inspiration to work for change.

From time to time you will hear our opponents declare that the union is weak, that the union has no support, that the union has not grown fast enough. Our obituary has been written many times.

How ironic it is that the same forces which argue so passionately that the union is not influential are the same forces that continue to fight us so hard.

The union's power in agriculture has nothing to do with the number of farmworkers under union contract. It has nothing to do with the farmworkers' ability to contribute to Democratic politicians. It doesn't even have much to do with our ability to conduct successful boycotts.

The very fact of our existence forces an entire industry—unionized and non-unionized—to spend millions of dollars year after year on improved wages, on improved working conditions, on benefits for workers.

If we're so weak and unsuccessful, why do the growers continue to fight us with such passion?

Because so long as we continue to exist, farmworkers will benefit from our existence—even if they don't work under union contract.

It doesn't really matter whether we have 100,000 members or 500,000 members. In truth, hundreds of thousands of farmworkers in California—and in other states—are better off today because of our work.

And Hispanics across California and the nation who don't work in agriculture are better off today because of what the farmworkers taught people about organization, about pride and strength, about seizing control over their own lives.

Tens of thousands of the children and grandchildren of farmworkers and the children and grandchildren of poor Hispanics are moving out of the fields and out of the barrios—and into the professions and into business and into politics. And that movement cannot be reversed!

Our union will forever exist as an empowering force among Chicanos in the Southwest. And that means our power and our influence will grow and not diminish.

Two major trends give us hope and encouragement.

First, our union has returned to a tried and tested weapon in the farmworkers' non-violent arsenal—the boycott!

After the Agricultural Labor Relations Act became law in California in 1975, we dismantled our boycott to work with the law.

During the early- and mid-'70s, millions of Americans supported our boycotts. After 1975, we redirected our efforts from the boycott to organizing and winning elections under the law.

The law helped farmworkers make progress in overcoming poverty and injustice. At companies where farmworkers are protected by union contracts, we have made progress in overcoming child labor, in overcoming miserable wages and working conditions, in overcoming sexual harassment of women workers, in overcoming dangerous pesticides which poison our people and poison the food we all eat.

Where we have organized, these injustices soon pass into history.

But under Republican governor George Dukmejian, the law that guarantees our right to organize no longer protects farmworkers. It doesn't work anymore.

In 1982, corporate growers gave Dukmejian one million dollars to run for governor of California. Since he took office, Dukmejian has paid back his debt to the growers with the blood and sweat of California farmworkers.

Instead of enforcing the law as it was written against those who break it, Dukmejian invites growers who break the law to seek relief from the governor's appointees.

What does all this mean for farmworkers?

It means that the right to vote in free elections is a sham. It means that the right to talk freely about the union among your fellow workers on the job is a cruel hoax. It means the right to be free from threats and intimidation by growers is an empty promise.

It means the right to sit down and negotiate with your employer as equals across the bargaining table—and not as peons in the field—is a fraud. It means that thousands of farmworkers—who are owed millions of dollars in back pay because their employers broke the law—are still waiting for their checks.

It means that, for farmworkers, child labor will continue. It means that infant mortality will continue. It means malnutrition among our children will continue. It means the short life expectancy and the inhuman living and working conditions will continue.

Are these make-believe threats? Are they exaggerations?

Ask the farmworkers who are still waiting for growers to bargain in good faith and sign contracts. Ask the farmworkers who've been fired from their jobs because they spoke out for the union. Ask the farmworkers who've been threatened with physical violence because they support the UFW.

These tragic events forced farmworkers to declare a new international boycott of California table grapes. That's why we are asking Americans once again to join the farmworkers by boycotting California grapes.

The Louis Harris poll revealed that 17 million American adults boycotted grapes. We are convinced that those people and that good will have not disappeared.

That segment of the population which makes our boycotts work are the Hispanics, the Blacks, the other minorities and our allies in labor and the church. But it is also an entire generation of young Americans who matured politically and socially in the 1960s and '70s—millions of people for whom boycotting grapes and other products became a socially accepted pattern of behavior.

If you were young, Anglo and on or near campus during the late '60s and early '70s, chances are you supported farmworkers.

Fifteen years later, the men and women of that generation are alive and well. They are in their mid–30s and 40s. They are pursuing professional careers.

Their disposable income is relatively high. But they are still inclined to respond to an appeal from farmworkers. The union's mission still has meaning for them.

Only today we must translate the importance of a union for farmworkers into the language of the 1980s. Instead of talking about the right to organize, we must talk about protection against sexual harassment in the fields. We must speak about the right to quality food—and food that is safe to eat.

I can tell you that the new language is working; the 17 million are still there. They are responding—not to picket lines and leafleting alone, but to the high-tech boycott of today—a boycott that uses computers and direct mail and advertising techniques which have revolutionized business and politics in recent years.

We have achieved more success with the boycott in the first 11 months of 1984 than we achieved in the 14 years since 1970.

South of the Sacramento River in California, Hispanics now make up more than 25 percent of the population. That figure will top 30 percent by the year 2000.

In light of these trends, it is absurd to believe or suggest that we are going to go back in time—as a union or as a people!

Today, the growers are like a punch-drunk old boxer who doesn't know he's past his prime. The times are changing. The political and social environment has changed. The chickens are coming home to roost—and the time to account for past sins is approaching.

I am told, these days, why farmworkers should be discouraged and pessimistic: The Republicans control the governor's office and the White House. They say there is a conservative trend in the nation.

Yet we are filled with hope and encouragement. We have looked into the future and the future is ours!

History and inevitability are on our side. The farmworkers and their children—and the Hispanics and their children—are the future in California. And corporate growers are the past!

Those politicians who ally themselves with the corporate growers and against the farmworkers and the Hispanics are in for a big surprise. They want to make their careers in politics. They want to hold power 20 and 30 years from now.

But 20 and 30 years from now—in Modesto, in Salinas, in Fresno, in Bakersfield, in the Imperial Valley, and in many of the great cities of California—those communities will be dominated by farmworkers and not by growers, by the children and grandchildren of farmworkers and not by the children and grandchildren of growers.

These trends are part of the forces of history that cannot be stopped. No person and no organization can resist them for very long. They are inevitable.

Once social change begins, it cannot be reversed.

You cannot uneducate the person who has learned to read. You cannot humiliate the person who feels pride. You cannot oppress the people who are not afraid anymore.

Our opponents must understand that it's not just a union we have built. Unions, like other institutions, can come and go.

But we're more than an institution. For nearly 20 years, our union has been on the cutting edge of a people's cause—and you cannot do away with an entire people; you cannot stamp out a people's cause.

Regardless of what the future holds for the union, regardless of what the future holds for farmworkers, our accomplishments cannot be undone. "La Causa"—our cause—doesn't have to be experienced twice.

The consciousness and pride that were raised by our union are alive and thriving inside millions of young Hispanics who will never work on a farm!

Like the other immigrant groups, the day will come when we win the economic and political rewards which are in keeping with our numbers in society. The day will come when the politicians do the right thing by our people out of political necessity and not out of charity or idealism.

That day may not come this year. That day may not come during this decade. But it will come, someday!

And when that day comes, we shall see the fulfillment of that passage from the Book of Matthew in the New Testament, "That the last shall be first and the first shall be last."

And on that day, our nation shall fulfill its creed—and that fulfillment shall enrich us all.

Thank you very much.

LARRY KRAMER
(1935–)

Acting Up
MARCH 10, 1987

We have little to be proud of this Gay Pride Week.

Founder of the Gay Men's Health Crisis (GMHC) and ACT UP, Larry Kramer was one of the first gay activists to draw attention to the AIDS epidemic. Notoriously off-putting and known for his inflammatory language, Kramer unleashed his shocking tactics to draw attention to "the plague" that was killing thousands of gay men in the 1980s: He dumped the ashes of a young friend onto the South Lawn of the White House, and he helped wrap Senator Jesse Helms's North Carolina home in a condom. Rodger McFarlane, one of Kramer's former lovers, explained, "When it comes to being an [ass], Larry is a virtuoso with no peer. Nobody can alienate people quicker."

That said, Kramer's antics were often fruitful and contributed to great progress in the gay movement. The GMHC, which was formed at a meeting in Kramer's Greenwich Village home, became one of the most effective mouthpieces for gay advocacy, with chapters in cities across the country. Within two days of its founding, the GMHC had the first AIDS hotlines in the world. Kramer's ACT UP attacked the National Institutes of Health (NIH) and the Food and Drug Administration (FDA) for their unnecessarily lengthy approval time for experimental drugs. Dr. Anthony Fauci of the NIH later credited ACT UP for "putting medical treatment in the hands of patients, changing medicine in this country, and getting drugs to more people faster."

Larry Kramer was born in Bridgeport, Connecticut. He attended Yale University, and shortly thereafter went to work as a screenwriter for movie studios (he wrote the screenplay for the movie musical *Lost Horizon*). Kramer has since penned dozens of articles, two autobiographical AIDS plays, and several books, including the novel *Faggots*.

This speech—delivered to a crowd of 250 at the Gay and Lesbian Community Center in New York—highlighted the work of GMHC and ACT UP, the burgeoning AIDS crisis, and the desperately slow pace of FDA approval for experimental drugs.

We have little to be proud of this Gay Pride Week.

One by one, we are being picked off by the enemy.

They are killing us.

I don't think you are going to like what I am going to say. It is the last time I am going to say it. I'm making a farewell appearance. I am not overly tired. I am certainly not suffering from burnout. I have a lot of piss and vinegar left in me—too much, in fact. No, I'm not tired.

Not physically tired, at any rate. I am, of course, as are you, very tired of many things. I am tired of what they are doing to us. I am tired of what *they* aren't doing for us. I am tired of seeing so many of my friends die—I'm exceptionally tired of that, as I know you are too.

I'm also tired of people coming up to me on the street and saying, "Thank you for what you're doing and saying." They mean it as a compliment, I know. But now I scream back, "Why aren't you doing it and saying it, too?" Why are there so few people out there screaming and yelling? You're dying too!

I'm telling you they are killing us! We are being picked off one by one, and half the men reading this could be dead in five years, and you are all still sitting on your asses like weaklings, and therefore we, the gay community, are not strong enough and our organizations are not strong enough and we are going to die for it!

I have come to the terrible realization that I believe this gay community of ours has a death wish and that we are going to die because we refuse to take responsibility for our own lives.

Yes, most of all, I'm tired of you. I'm tired of the death wish of the gay community. I'm tired of our colluding in our own genocide. I'm tired of you, by your own passivity, actively participating in your own genocide.

How many of you have given a thousand dollars or more at any one time to any gay organization or gay charity? Ten thousand?

How many of you have left anything in your wills to anything gay?

How many of you have spent at least one hour a week volunteering for a gay organization? Ten hours?

And if you don't like any of the gay organizations, how many of you have spent how much time to make any of them better? Instead of just bitching them into further weakness? Or helped them raise money to make themselves better?

How many of you have bothered to consider that by helping to raise $80,000 a year, you could fund a lobbyist in Washington to fight for us all year long—to join with a network of other gay lobbyists, paid for by groups in other cities, so that we could have as many lobbyists as General Motors or the

National Rifle Association or the National Council of Churches or the American Medical Association, all of whom get what they want?

Is it such a big deal to get a group together to raise $80,000 to save your lives? . . .

How many of you have written consistently or even irregularly to an elected official or testified at an official hearing on the subject of AIDS, or regarding treatment, or official lethargy in this city and state and country?

How many of you really trust the NIH to be capable of coordinating research around a crisis of this scope?

How many of you even know what the NIH is, or how important it is in your life? And that your very own life is in its hands? You didn't know that, did you? That your very own life is in the hands of an agency you don't know anything about.

How many of you believe there is sufficient education to contain what is happening?

How many of you have children? How many of you have spoken to a school board about sex education?

How many of you have had sex with more than one person in the last ten years?

How many of you have protested actively against mandatory testing?

How many of you are willing to face up to the fact that the FDA is fucked up, the NIH is fucked up, the CDC [Centers for Disease Control] is very fucked up—and that, entering the seventh year of what is now a pandemic, the boys and girls running the show at these organizations have been unable to make whatever system they're operating work?

How long are you prepared to wait for these systems to work?

How long are you prepared to wait before our own AIDS organizations provide us with adequate information on available treatments?

How many hours and days are you prepared to spend on the phone attempting, in vain, to find out what is going on where and how it's doing and why your dying friends can't get it immediately?

How many of you believe you have no responsibility to take action on any of these matters?

How many of you need to die or become infected before you feel you can take action on why every single branch of government in charge of AIDS, both local and federal, is dragging its ass?

What's the number of dead friends at which you can decide to stop just sitting quietly like the good little boys and girls we were all brought up to be—and start taking rude, noisy, offensive political action? One? Ten? One hundred?

It always amazes me when I tell people they have power, and they answer me, "Power? Me? What power?" How can you be so conservative, dumb, blind? You know what is going on better than anybody, and yet you are silent you constantly, consistently, and continuously sit on your collective asses and refuse to use your power.

Your voice is your power! Your collective voices! Your group power! Your political power! Your names all strung together on one long list is your power. Your bank accounts are your power, if you weren't all so devastatingly stingy when it comes to funding anything gayer than a Halloween costume. Your bodies are your power, your living bodies all strung together in one long line that reaches across this country and could reach to the moon if we only let it.

You know that this country is not responding on a national political level or a local political level, and yet you sit by along with everyone else and watch our men being picked off one by one by one by one by one.

No one is in charge of this pandemic, either in this city or this state or this country! It is as simple as that. And certainly no one who is compassionate and understanding and knowledgeable and efficient is even anywhere near the top of those who are in charge. Almost every person connected with running the AIDS show everywhere is second-rate. I have never come across a bigger assortment of the second-rate in my life. And you have silently and trustingly put your lives in their hands. You—who are first-rate—are silent. And we are going to *die* for that silence.

You know, it's not even a question of government funding anymore. For six long years we fought so hard to get the money. Finally Congress has appropriated masses of money. Can you believe me when I tell you that it is not being spent? Two years ago, nineteen official AIDS treatment centers, called ATEUs (AIDS Treatment Evaluation Units), were set up by the NIH—and they still aren't being utilized beyond a fraction of their humane possibilities and intentions. One year ago, the NIH was given $47 million just for testing new AIDS drugs—*and they aren't spending it!* Why didn't we know that? Where have we been for these long two years? Why didn't we know that this precious, precious time—during which how many dear friends of ours died—was being thrown out in the garbage because we didn't get on the phone and inquire politely: "Please, sirs, can you tell me what you're doing with all that nice money Congress gave you last May?" How could we have been so lazy and irresponsible—and *trusting?* We, of all people in this world, should know better, and know how not to trust. Where were our gay leaders? Where were all our AIDS organizations? Where were our people in Washington? Where was I? For I blame myself more than I blame anyone else. God fucking damn it, I trusted too!

When I found out about three months ago that $47 million was actually lying around not being used when I knew personally that at least a dozen drugs and treatments just as promising as AZT and in many cases much less toxic were not being tested and were not legally available to us, I got in my car and drove down to Washington. I wanted to find out what was going on. Like most people, I have no notion of how the system works down there, who reports to whom, which agency is supposed to do what. What I found out sent me into as profound a depression as I have been in since this epidemic started.

My first meeting was at the White House, with the President's Domestic Policy Adviser, Gary Bauer, who advises Ronald Reagan on AIDS. I asked him if ignoring AIDS was intentional. He answered me that he had not seen enough evidence that the Black Plague was going on yet. He was particularly interested to hear from me that the current evidence indicates that the gay male population of the major cities is on its way to becoming totally exposed to the virus. He asked me if I thought female-to-male transmission was as potent as male-to-male. I said the statistics were about the same. He said his advisers told him otherwise. I asked him if gay people who were AIDS experts could be on the President's Commission, and he told me No. I asked him why the President had refused to put anyone in charge—to appoint an AIDS czar? He told me the President *was* the AIDS czar. I asked him why the President had not only not read Surgeon General Koop's AIDS report, or the National Academy of Science's AIDS report—both of which were then over six months old and both of which beg for immediate, all-out action—but he hadn't even met with Koop personally, his own Surgeon General, and he answered me that the chain of command dictates that, in matters of health, the President talks only to his Secretary of Health and Human Services, Dr. Otis R. Bowen. It turns out that Dr. Koop has absolutely no power; his position is simply that of figurehead. They do not like what he is saying, and I think that if you listen to what he is beginning to say now, you will see that Dr. Koop is being pulled back into line.

What the fuck is going on here? Are they actually afraid they might learn something that might save us?

Research at NIH? I have not space to go into the gory details. Let me just say that the research rivalries in and among all the institutes at NIH could make a TV series to rival "Dynasty" and "Falcon Crest" in competitiveness, hostility, selfishness, and greed.

Now you know why NIH stands for Not Interested in Homosexuals.

What the fuck is going on here, and what the fuck are you doing about it?

If I use gross language—go ahead, be offended—I don't know how else to reach you, how to reach everybody. I tried starting an organization: I cofounded GMHC, which becomes more timid as it becomes richer day by day. I tried writing a play. I tried writing endless articles in the *Native* and *The New York Times* and *Newsday* and screaming on "Donahue" and at every TV camera put in front of me. I helped start ACT UP, a small bunch of too few very courageous people willing to make rude noises. I don't know what else to do to wake you up!

I will tell you something else to try to wake you up: If AIDS does not spread out widely into the white, non-drug-using, heterosexual population, as it may or may not do, then the white, non-drug-using population is going to hate us even more—for scaring them, for costing them a fucking fortune, for our "lifestyle," which they will say caused this. AIDS will stay a disease of blacks and Hispanics and gays, and it will continue to be ignored, it will be ignored even more.

The straight world is scared now because they're worried it's going to happen to them. What if it doesn't? Think about that for a while. If all this lethargy is going on now, think what will happen then—just as you are coming down with it and facing death.

Who is fighting back in any and all of this? Twenty-four million gay men and lesbians in this country, and who is fighting back? We have a demonstration at the White House and we have three hundred people and we think we're lucky! We get our pictures in all the magazines and newspapers for one or two days and we feel real proud. Sixty thousand Catholics march in Albany. Two hundred fifty thousand Jews march in New York against the treatment of Soviet Jews. One million people march for nuclear disarmament.

What does it take to get you off your fucking asses?

"You want to die, Felix? Die!" That's a line from *The Normal Heart*. In his immense frustration, Ned Weeks yells it at his dying lover. That's how I feel about all of you.

I am telling you they are killing us and we are letting them!

Yes, I am screaming like an hysteric. I know that. I look and sound like an asshole. I told you this was going to be my last tirade and I am going to go out screaming so fucking rudely that you will hear this coarse, crude voice of mine in your nightmares. You are going to die and you are going to die very, very soon unless you get up off your fucking tushies and fight back!

Unless you do—you will forgive me—you deserve to die.

I never thought I would come to say anything like that. Nobody *deserves* to die.

I recently spoke at a *Village Voice* AIDS Forum in New York on a panel with Dr. Ron Grossman, who has one of the largest gay practices in New York. "Larry," he said to me, "our most outrageous early pronouncements are short of the mark. And so have been our efforts. We are so *behind*."

AIDS is our holocaust. Tens of thousands of our precious men are dying. Soon it will be hundreds of thousands. AIDS is our holocaust and Reagan is our Hitler. New York City is our Auschwitz.

"Holocaust" is another word for "genocide."

"Genocide" is a word I hear myself and others using more and more frequently. You don't hear it as much as you hear words like "mandatory testing" or "no sex education in the schools" or "no condom ads on TV."

Why doesn't everybody realize that all the screaming and yelling going on about "education" and "mandatory testing" is one whale of a red herring?

⌒

Our leaders—such as they are—their energies are consumed fighting these battles against mandatory testing and for better education—and no one is fighting the NIH for drugs and increased protocol testing and faster research. I am telling you that there are drugs and treatments out there that can prolong the quality of our lives and you are not getting them and no one is fighting for them and these drugs and treatments are caught up in so much red tape that they are strangled in the pipeline, and the Reagan administration knows this, knows all this, and does nothing about untangling the red tape, and half the gay men here can die because of it.

Yes, by our own passivity we are actively colluding with, and participating in, our own genocide.

We are allowing ourselves to be knocked off one by one. Half the gay men here could be dead in five years.

Our gay organizations are weak and still don't work with each other, and our AIDS organizations have all been co-opted by the very systems they were formed to make accountable and you all sit by and allow it to happen when it's your lives that are going down the tubes.

Politicians understand only one thing: Pressure. You don't apply it—you don't get anything. Simple as that.

And it must be applied day by week by month by year. You simply can't let up for one single second. Or you don't get anything. Which is what is happening to us.

For six years I have been trying to get the gay world angry enough to exert this pressure. I have failed and I am ashamed of my failure. I blame myself—somehow I wasn't convincing enough or clever enough or cute enough to break through your denial or self-pity or death wish or self-destruction or whatever the fuck is going on. I'm very tired of trying to make you hear me.

I'm shutting up and going away. The vast majority of the gay world will not listen to what is so simple and plain. That there are so few voices as strident as mine around this country is our tragedy. That there is not one single gay leader who has any national recognition like Gloria Steinem or Cardinal O'Connor or Jerry Falwell or Jesse Jackson is also our tragedy. Why is that? Why does every gay spokesperson finally just collapse under the apathy of trying to make you listen—and failing, failing utterly.

Don't you ask yourselves quite often the Big Question: Why am I still alive? Untouched? At some point I did something the others did. How have I escaped?

Don't you think that obligates you to repay God or fate or whomever or whatever, if only your conscience, for this miraculous fact: I am still alive. I must put back something into this world for my own life, which is worth a tremendous amount. By not putting back, you are saying that your lives are worth shit, and that we deserve to die, and that the deaths of all our friends and lovers have amounted to nothing.

I can't believe that in your heart of hearts you feel this way. I can't believe you want to die.

Do you?

Virginia Apuzzo
(1941–)

Creating Change
November 20, 1988

*Do we really want to be a movement
for social change in this society?*

Born in the Bronx, New York, Virginia Apuzzo has dedicated her career to advancing gay rights, both in and out of the workplace. In 1997 Apuzzo became the highest-ranking openly gay official in the federal government. Before serving as an assistant to President Bill Clinton, she was a deputy secretary in the Department of Labor and executive director of the National Gay and Lesbian Task Force—the oldest and largest gay and lesbian civil rights organization in the United States. In 1980, at the Democratic National Convention, her helped coauthor the first gay and lesbian rights plank of a major party's platform. In recognition of her commitment to gay rights, she was honored with the Outstanding Public Service Award in 1996.

In this 1988 keynote address to the National Gay and Lesbian Task Force Conference, Apuzzo addressed the burgeoning AIDS crisis and the importance of several critical policy initiatives, including a federal gay and lesbian civil rights bill, federal hate crimes legislation with protections for sexual orientation, recognition of same-sex partnerships, and the right to spousal benefits and foster care. Beyond that, she urged her compatriots to consider the importance of a coordinated gay social movement, no different from the black and women's movements, with equal standing in the eyes of business, government, courts, and society as its goal. She also challenged activists to continue to press the government to promote gay and lesbian rights, and to provide the necessary resources, in the form of committed movement leaders and members, to strengthen the community.

IT SEEMS THAT it was never necessary to stake out the future quite as much as it is in this age of AIDS. In the past we believed that somehow we would have one.

It would be foolish to think that the experiences we have all shared around illness and death haven't had an impact on this community. But however profound our losses, our hope must exceed our grief. If we are to address the future with any seriousness, we cannot deny that our first order of business is to affirm our belief in our future.

Prior to the AIDS crisis, the white-male-dominated gay movement had an agenda that was largely libertarian. It saw government as having the capacity to protect its members from discrimination and sought that protection. The agenda was often summed up as "getting government off our backs and ... out of our bedrooms."

At the beginning of the AIDS crisis, we had behind us a decade of political activity which had focused on government as a wall of resistance. We studied that wall until we knew its every feature—but not what was on the other side.

I think we can agree that there has been a transformation that has taken place with regard to the agenda of the movement, namely the way the community has come to see the role of government in the lives of its members.

With the onslaught of aids we continue to experience a significant political transformation. The concerns that we have been raising over the last several years are not code words for special interest items. We have spoken to matters related to the insurance industry, to the health care industry.

We have raised questions related to the role of schools in the face of the most threatening health crisis of our time, and we have insisted that the intransigence of our religious institutions not be permitted to cost the lives of their members.

We have raised for public repudiation the posture of a renegade Justice Department that would have conspired in the discrimination of those disabled by AIDS. Our position on the question of the HIV test, insurance, and employment, framed in the larger context of predicative tests, touches millions who are at risk for everything from Huntington's chorea and diabetes to hepatitis B.

Ours has been a call aimed at the very posture of government toward its citizens.

Our ability to make the essential linkages to other groups in our society on whom these issues also impinge will determine the extent to which we will complete the political transformation of the community—from an issue to a constituency.

But there is more, much more.

If I could place a single question at the top of the agenda and ask the community to consider it before doing anything else, my question would be: Do we really want to be a movement for social change in this society?

Unless and until that question is squarely faced we will bicker about tactics and strategy:

We will be divided by differing objectives

We will be cut off from significant alliances.

Unless and until we address this question we will be high on the rhetoric of our diversity . . . and low on coming to grips with how it does, in fact, separate us: black and white, male and female, rich and poor.

Unless and until we confront the implications of this question, we will see our movement as a series of events, and not a process; we will read these events as signposts with no agreement on where we are going or how to get there.

Unless and until we recognize the importance of this question we run the risk of having the most fundamental meaning of our movement consigned to a nostalgic footnote in history.

Coming from the Bronx, I had to learn that politics and power isn't about tough-talking Damon Runyon characters with small IQs and big hearts—although I confess to having met a few.

It tries instead to define what you can and cannot do while you are alive.

Who you can and cannot be with some level of relaxed assurance.

It is all of the social and economic limits which must be pushed beyond artificial and self-serving boundaries.

It is every limitation you will ever have to confront or may ultimately succumb to.

For some it is possibly a limitation that could rob you of your capacity to rail against limitations.

It is serious stuff.

It is therefore somewhat understandable that some would approach it making all kinds of assurances that what is being sought will not undermine the system, not rock the boat or upset the apple cart.

In my opinion, that's a mistake. A big mistake.

If we affirm our intention to be a movement for social change, we must get right to the heart of the matter and recognize that calling ourselves family, seeking to secure spousal benefits, giving birth to our own children and seeking to provide foster care for the children of others is, quite simply, one of the most radical demands we make on the larger society.

———⌒〜———

I daresay that as significant as the litany of needs is that this community has *a legitimate right to demand* . . . items like . . .

A federal lesbian and gay rights bill including housing, employment and accommodations.

Immigration reform.

A federal bias crime bill that includes sexual orientation.

A sane AIDS program with the resources and compassion needed to finally address this epidemic.

And yet, each law or program cited can be won without ever challenging heterosexism at its core.

And each must be won.

But after we have tallied up the score—victory upon victory—we will still be looking down the barrel of heterosexism. Unless we address this issue we will continue to pursue our legitimacy at the expense of our liberation.

If the division of the sexes and a heterosexual vision of what reality is are the principles by which this society defines itself, to ask it to embrace a feature of its humanity which runs counter to itself is to be a participant in a genuine revolution.

To prevail is to have brought major change.

Consider the fact that one of the many things we share with the feminist movement is, not surprisingly, the same enemies for the same reasons. They strive to establish the norm and everything beyond that norm is fringe.

It is not a stupid strategy.

The fewer the options available to members of the women's movement or the gay and lesbian movement, the greater the homogeneity in society. The greater the degree of sameness that exists, the greater the penalty for those who refuse to be homogenized.

If the issue of our definition of relationships and family is as seminal as it appears, then it cannot be left to be fought solely in a political arena. Like any successful strategy for social change, it must be pursued on multiple fronts.

Major corporations have been approached with regard to personnel policies of non-discrimination in employment. In the context of the AIDS crisis they have been approached with regard to corporate giving.

But we have yet to see the potential of a coordinated . . . campaign to make corporate America be part of the solution and not part of the problem where the lives of lesbians and gay men are concerned.

There are at least four major areas that could be outlined as having promise:

Pursuing personnel policies with regard to non-discrimination in employment. Much progress has been made here; more needs to be made.

Corporate giving in two areas: One with regard to political candidates they support and the other with regard to gay and lesbian community projects that minimally parallel priorities in the corporations' existing patterns of giving.

And, finally, spousal benefit programs on a non-discriminatory basis.

A change of this magnitude would require education; I would begin with the professional personnel officers associations, giving workshops at conferences and conventions, working with legal organizations to develop model programs, and getting a maximum level of dialogue going in business journals and op-ed pages.

It would require an understanding of the opposition and not simply a dismissal of that opposition. It would require a willingness to analyze the opposition to determine how best to prevail in light of it.

It would require us entering the power-dominated world of corporate America with some grasp of what the coin of the realm is in that world.

If the division of the sexes and a heterosexual vision of what reality is are the principles by which this society defines itself, to ask it to embrace a feature of its humanity which runs counter to itself is to be a participant in a revolution.

That's a choice we will have to consider confronting.

Finally, we have been fighting the good fight and there have been some significant victories. Perhaps the most significant is the ever increasing number of us daring to live our lives visibly and with dignity as a 24 hour a day, 7 day a week rebuke to the myths, the lies and the distortions being peddled by the tinhorn moralists of the '80s.

We are not about to retreat now. We will use every resource we have, call upon every commitment made to us to respond to the threats that stalk our community: The ill and the dying, the tens of thousands whose lives have been stalled by fear, the victims of violence, the thousands who will die of alcohol- and substance-related deaths.

When we come together to speak with one voice, it must be with an agenda that does not permit this imperfect system to do what it does so very well. Namely, it cannot be permitted to simply shift the populations it selects to ignore.

In that spirit, let me close with a message I have repeated throughout the country—from the march on Washington to the smallest college gatherings.

From the San Francisco freedom day rally to this year, when New Hampshire had its first lesbian and gay pride day celebration:

Let us wed our promises to labor, each in our own way, for a community restored to health.

Let us pledge never to allow convention to rob us of our just outrage at indifference to the dignity and value of human lives.

Let us resolve that ours is a watch—a kind of tour of duty—that will not end with the passage of a lesbian and gay civil rights bill, though such a bill must be passed.

Ours is a watch that will not end with the treatment or cure for AIDS—though we will rejoice as never before.

Ours is a watch that must be vigilant, vigilant for as long as ignorance can bully . . . for as long as justice is frail.

Harry Hay

(1912–)

What Gay Consciousness Brings

June 26, 1991

We suggest that the Colonialized Racial and
Sexual Minorities can rise from their knees to their feet in
reclaiming their own appreciation of self-love.

Harry Hay is often hailed as the founder of the modern gay liberation movement. Born in England and raised in California, Hay studied drama at Stanford University and became an active member in the Communist Party in the 1930s. At that time, homosexuals were still considered "social deviants"; anti-gay laws and discriminatory policies discouraged homosexuals from organizing around, or even publicly admitting, their sexual preference.

Like others, Hay suppressed his own gay identity, even marrying a woman whom he had met at Communist Party meetings. In 1948, however, he courageously surfaced from "hiding" and formed an underground organization devoted to the rights of gays and lesbians; it was still illegal at the time for gays to assemble. Hay argued that gays, like blacks, were an oppressed cultural minority.

Two years later, Hay, along with four others, secretly created the Mattachine Society, an outgrowth of Hay's original group. Its name was borrowed from a Medieval French term for male dancers who only performed in public wearing masks. By 1953 the society had more than 2,000 members and a widely distributed newsletter. In many ways, it served as the catalyst for the American gay rights movement, encouraging homosexuals to wear their sexual identity with pride.

Although Hay had left the Communist Party years earlier, he was later persecuted for his participation, arguably because of the party's support for gay and lesbian issues. Consequently, he chose to distance himself from the Mattachines to avoid drawing negative attention to its effort. Undeterred in his commitment, Hay continued to be an outspoken force outside the organization, advancing the idea that gays and lesbians were a cultural minority—a theme now central to the gay liberation movement.

In this 1991 address to a community audience in San Francisco, California, Harry Hay recounted the history of the gay rights movement, emphasizing the importance of both maintaining autonomy and building coalitions with other oppressed groups.

MY YEARS AS A RADICAL Community Organizer in California, and more specifically in Los Angeles, prepared me to figure out how to set up a group in which Gay Brothers and Sisters would feel safe and secure from the witch-hunts and publicized entrapments that threatened our lives and livelihoods daily in the 1930s, 1940s, and 1950s. They taught me also how to safeguard our thoughts and actions from the probings and ferretings out of the local Vice Squad who, like their Federal counterpart, the Red Squad, prowled our back-alleys, pressured our neighbors to tell tales, listened in on our phone conversations, and even steamed open our mail.

During the first Mattachine Society years of 1951 to 1953, I projected the concept, drawn from my years as a Marxist teacher, that we Gays and Lesbians constituted a "Cultural Minority." To the majority of the new members who flocked in from October of 1953 on, the "Cultural Minority" concept was anathema! To this second wave of Homosexual Middle-Class Respectables, "We were absolutely the same as everybody else except for a minor sexual variation," and "Homosexuals had absolutely nothing in common with each other except for their sexual inclinations." Yet, by 1969—when a positive Gay Identity had been firmly established, Mattachine's most significant achievement, in contrast to the negative self-deprecating, self-demeaning, bitchy, back-biting hetero-gone-wrong or hetero-turned-pervert that we all had been socialized into perceiving ourselves as being since time immemorial—the concept of ourselves as a "Cultural Minority" was almost universally regarded as one that had been central to our Homophile Community's thinking since the year one!

The Stonewall Rebellion of 1969 transformed our positive Gay identity from the single person to the collective. And with that came the beginning of gay and lesbian groups expanding their functions to include political activity on an ongoing basis. Of course, there had been dozens of political actions between 1951 and 1969: entrapment cases openly fought in the courts and won; a U.S. Supreme Court case won; a motorcade in L.A.; openly advertised professional conferences in mainline hotels; protest demonstrations in L.A. and San Francisco; open forums on Berkeley's Telegraph Avenue; open dialogues on radio and TV; and polite picket lines in Philadelphia. But while such sporadic actions necessarily cleared the ground for future actions, they didn't touch to life the Gay Consciousness of the huge majority of the homophiles still hiding away, still buried alive under the ancient negativity.

However, Stonewall's inevitable consequence was the simultaneous light-ing off of the dozens of powder-trains by now previously laid by the twenty years of such sporadic efforts, and in dozens of cities suddenly groups of us gays and lesbians no longer had difficulty conceiving of ourselves as political cultural minorities with basic civil rights, presumably guaranteed by the U.S. Constitution, that were being denied us. The Mattachine Society experience, with its several dimensions of touching to life this positive Gay Identity and launching the concept of ourselves as a Cultural Minority, plus Stonewall illu-minating politically the material dimensions of the Cultural Minority Collective, transformed the shape and substance of Gay Consciousness.

It is a truism of natural selection that no negative trait (and as you recall, a neg-ative trait is one that does not reproduce itself) ever appears in a given species millennia after millennia after millennia unless it in some way serves the sur-vival of that species. . . .

Frederick Douglass, speaking of the three-hundred-year struggle of the Afro-American slaves to win back the Freedom they had been so viciously robbed of, said the longest, the most frightening, the most terrifying distance on the road to Freedom that each Slave had to travel—alone and with only his or her soul as guide—was the immeasurable distance from his knees to his feet! And, oh, . . . we queers also know about that dreadful and terrifying distance, from closet-crouching in denial or self-loathing, to that almost unendurable wrenching rise to our feet, in the moment of "coming out," with only the dream in our hearts to guide us.

But—differently from the slaves who thought they needed only to discover and forge the political route to Freedom across the Mason-Dixon line—we gays and lesbians, we queer folk, . . . have an additional responsibility to the larger Community of which we are a part. . . . There are two roads to Freedom and they both must be traversed! We queers have had to discover it through the agony and heart-break of twice patterning our gay and lesbian movement on hetero-imitative behaviors that do not bespeak us. After Stonewall, gay liberation was indeed a rebellion against the hetero-male-oriented systems of laws—but the rebellion itself developed in terms of het-ero-male-oriented cultural values. Within five years the dominant gay assimi-lationist culture had gutted it just as they had gutted the homophile movement twenty years before.

In 1979, I called the radical faeries to recognize that since we are not het-eros, we gays had no business imitating them. I called upon my faerie broth-ers to tear off the hetero-imitative conformities with which they've been spiritually crippling themselves by adopting them or adapting to them. At faerie gatherings and faerie workshops we've begun to recover our own *not*-man values, our beautiful *un*-Hetero ways of perceiving—so long obscured when not indeed temporarily obliterated by police or state torture, and by Church-sponsored public burnings and autos-da-fé of both medieval and modern holy inquisitions. Little by little we have begun to redeem and redevelop our own not-man values of self-love, self-esteem, and self-affirmation. We are re-discovering our own faerie way to rise from our knees to our feet! And—this year—the younger generations of queer nation are joining with us.

What we queers have learned through terror and tears, . . . is very clear. The hetero-male imperialist dominators, Anglo-European and Israeli alike, clearly hold their colonialized minority communities in the thrall of slavery still—spiritual slavery! Their shackles, which we today call racism, continue to deny those Communities held in bondage the necessary access to the spirit redemptions, grounded in their own ethnic symbols and values, that those communities must have to finally be enabled to rise to their feet in spiritual freedom!

Among the really first-class facilities the imperialist dominators lovingly maintain for keeping spiritual shackles in place—for instance—are the three state-approved organized religions: Judaism and its offshoots, Islam and Christianity. Christianity, particularly, and Judaism both have served willingly as shackles, by each requiring that the particular colonialized folk's universal need to "live in the spirit of community love and compassion" be expressed solely in the symbols and values, as well as language, of the dominator's own system—even to the total denial, even obliteration, of the folk's own tradi-tional core of heart and soul. Between these three—Islam, Judaism, and Christianity—the re-sprouting, re-budding, and re-blooming of new shoots of self-love, self-esteem, and self-affirmation are kept firmly subdued.

We queers can tell you black or Chicano or Asian hetero brothers and sis-ters precisely what this shackling of the spirit and of the heart is like because you folks continue to do the same to us! Even as gay spirit could hardly have been expected to launch and fly on hetero-centric wings, so also any given Afrocentrism, or whatever combination of non-Anglo-ethnic-centrism speaks for you—that "being and becoming" spirit that moves to redeem traditional cores of self-love, self-esteem, and self-affirmation—cannot be expected to launch and soar successfully on Eurocentric pinions. If, by our example of how we radical faeries and queer nations have reclaimed our own very un-hetero values of self-love, self-esteem, and self-affirmation, we can inspire the spiritu-ally still-indentured colonialized minority Communities to invent similar ways to rise from their white-imitative servitude to stand once more in joyously reclaimed centric self-affirmation—no longer in the values and symbols of the dominators, but in terms of what they, as Separate Cultures, have to contribute to the betterment of everybody—what a triumph of the Human Spirit that could be!

We suggest that the colonialized racial and sexual minorities can rise from their knees to their feet in reclaiming their own appreciation of self-love because we queers, against every combination of tyranny the hetero oppressors could devise, have done it. Among the several contributions we bring to you, the first is our example . . . and our courage!

To the Marxist left, we queers have to say "thanks"—for the spiritual tools and concepts you furnished, which got us launched on our long walk, with particular credit to that strut in the definition of a national minority, "a common psychological make-up manifested in a community of culture." It fitted us to a "T." To you, we radical faeries bring our insights. One of Marx's great formulations was his vision of the ultimate Communist relationship: "From each according to his abilities, to each according to his needs." As the radical faeries see it, this may well be one of the very first political appreciations of compassion, the human dimension totally missed—to their ultimate disaster and defeat—by the hetero-male-dominated second and third internationales.

With all this, we have to say that we queers, having won our autonomy with no help from anybody, shall continue to maintain that autonomy. We shall be happy to walk with any group so long as we and they remain in a loving-sharing consensus. But the moment the consensus breaks, exercising our ancient prerogatives to totally self-reliant independence—we faeries vanish! If you want us to re-appear, you shall have to make the first move to re-establish the loving-sharing consensus.

ANITA HILL
(1956–)

Anita Hill v. Clarence Thomas
OCTOBER 11, 1991

Telling the world is the most difficult experience of my life,
but it is very close to having to live through the
experience that occasioned this meeting.

In 1991 President George Bush appointed Clarence Thomas to the United States Supreme Court, replacing Justice Thurgood Marshall, an advocate and long-term ally of civil rights. Like Marshall, Thomas was African American, but his appointment drew the immediate ire of civil rights activists and organizations. In his previous service on the bench and in the federal government, Thomas had amassed a deeply conservative record, especially on social issues like affirmative action and reproductive choice.

As part of the U.S. Senate confirmation process, the Judiciary Committee held several days of hearings to assess Thomas's character and qualifications both inside and outside the courtroom. During this process, a law professor at the University of Oklahoma, Anita Hill, came forward with allegations that Thomas had sexually harassed her while they worked together at the Department of Education and the Equal Employment Opportunity Commission. Hill's testimony sparked a firestorm of protest from women's groups across the country; civil rights leaders from all backgrounds took to the airwaves in support of Hill and in opposition to Thomas. After nearly a week of highly charged testimony and media attention, the Senate confirmed Thomas in a vote of 52–48.

It has since been argued that Hill's testimony, and her willingness to come forward on the issue of sexual harassment, ushered in a new era for women in corporate and political America. In 1992, a record number of women ran for—and captured—seats in public office. This excerpt is from Hill's testimony before the Senate Judiciary Committee.

Mr. Chairman, Senator Thurmond, members of the committee.

My name is Anita F. Hill, and I am a professor of law at the University of Oklahoma. I was born on a farm in Okmulgee County, Oklahoma, in 1956. I am the youngest of 13 children.

I had my early education in Okmulgee County. My father, Albert Hill, is a farmer in that area. My mother's name is Irma Hill. She is also a farmer and a housewife.

My childhood was one of a lot of hard work and not much money, but it was one of solid family affection as represented by my parents. I was reared in a religious atmosphere in the Baptist faith, and I have been a member of the Antioch Baptist Church in Tulsa, Oklahoma, since 1983. It is a very warm part of my life at the present time.

For my undergraduate work, I went to Oklahoma State University and graduated from there in 1977. . . . I graduated from the university with academic honors and proceeded to the Yale Law School, where I received my J.D. degree in 1980.

Upon graduation from law school, I became a practicing lawyer with the Washington, D.C., firm of Wald, Hardraker & Ross. In 1981, I was introduced to now-Judge Thomas by a mutual friend.

Judge Thomas told me that he was anticipating a political appointment, and he asked if I would be interested in working with him.

He was in fact appointed as assistant secretary of Education for civil rights. After he was, after he had taken that post, he asked if I would become his assistant, and I accepted that position.

In my early period there, I had two major projects. The first was an article I wrote for Judge Thomas' signature on the education of minority students. The second was the organization of a seminar on high-risk students, which was abandoned because Judge Thomas transferred to the EEOC, where he became the chairman of that office.

During this period at the Department of Education my working relationship with Judge Thomas was positive. I had a good deal of responsibility and independence. I thought he respected my work and that he trusted my judgment.

After approximately three months of working there, he asked me to go out socially with him. What happened next, and telling the world about it, are the two most difficult things—experiences of my life.

It is only after a great deal of agonizing consideration and sleepless nights that I am able to talk of these unpleasant matters to anyone but my close friends.

I declined the invitation to go out socially with him and explained to him that I thought it would jeopardize at—what at the time I considered to be a very good working relationship. I had a normal social life with other men outside the office. I believed then, as now, that having a social relationship with a person who was supervising my work would be ill-advised. I was very uncomfortable with the idea and told him so.

I thought that by saying no and explaining my reasons, my employer would abandon his social suggestions. However, to my regret, in the following few weeks, he continued to ask me out on several occasions.

He pressed me to justify my reasons for saying no to him. These incidents took place in his office or mine. They were in the form of private conversations, which not—would not have been overheard by anyone else.

My working relationship became even more strained when Judge Thomas began to use work situations to discuss sex. On these occasions he would call me into his office for reports on education issues and projects, or he might suggest that because of the time pressures of his schedule we go to lunch to a government cafeteria.

After a brief discussion of work, he would turn the conversation to a discussion of sexual matters. His conversations were very vivid. He spoke about acts that he had seen in pornographic films involving such matters as women having sex with animals and films showing group sex or rape scenes.

He talked about pornographic materials depicting individuals with large penises or large breasts involving various sex acts. On several occasions, Thomas told me graphically of his own sexual prowess.

Because I was extremely uncomfortable talking about sex with him at all, and particularly in such a graphic way, I told him that I did not want to talk about this subject. I would also try to change the subject to education matters or to non-sexual personal matters, such as his background or his beliefs.

My efforts to change the subject were rarely successful.

Throughout the period of these conversations, he also from time to time asked me for social engagements. My reaction to these conversations was to avoid them by eliminating opportunities for us to engage in extended conversations.

This was difficult because, at the time, I was his only assistant at the Office of Education—or Office for Civil Rights. During the latter part of my time at the Department of Education, the social pressures, and any conversation of his offensive behavior, ended. I began both to believe and hope that our working relationship could be a proper, cordial and professional one.

When Judge Thomas was made chair of the EEOC, I needed to face the question of whether to go with him. I was asked to do so, and I did.

The work itself was interesting, and at that time it appeared that the sexual overtures which had so troubled me had ended.

I also faced the realistic fact that I had no alternative job. While I might have gone back to private practice, perhaps in my old firm or at another, I was dedicated to civil rights work, and my first choice was to be in that field. Moreover, at that time, the Department of Education itself was a dubious venture. President Reagan was seeking to abolish the entire department.

For my first months at the EEOC, where I continued to be an assistant to Judge Thomas, there were no sexual conversations or overtures. However, during the fall and winter of 1982, these began again. The comments were random and ranged from pressing me about why I didn't go out with him to remarks about my personal appearance. I remember his saying that some day I would have to tell him the real reason that I wouldn't go out with him.

He began to show displeasure in his tone and voice and his demeanor and his continued pressure for an explanation. He commented on what I was wearing in terms of whether it made me more or less sexually attractive. The incidents occurred in his inner office at the EEOC.

One of the oddest episodes I remember was an occasion in which Thomas was drinking a Coke in his office. He got up from the table at which we were working, went over to his desk to get the Coke, looked at the can and asked, "Who has put pubic hair on my Coke?"

On other occasions, he referred to the size of his own penis as being larger than normal, and he also spoke on some occasions of the pleasures he had given to women with oral sex. At this point, late 1982, I began to feel severe stress on the job. I began to be concerned that Clarence Thomas might take out his anger with me by degrading me or not giving me important assignments. I also thought that he might find an excuse for dismissing me. In January of 1983, I began looking for another job. I was handicapped because I feared that if he found out, he might make it difficult for me to find other employment, and I might be dismissed from the job I had. Another factor that made my search more difficult was that there was a period—this was during a period—of a hiring freeze in the government.

In the spring of 1983, an opportunity to teach at Oral Roberts University opened up. I participated in a seminar, taught an afternoon session in a seminar at Oral Roberts University. The dean of the university saw me teaching and inquired as to whether I would be interested in further pursuing a career in teaching beginning at Oral Roberts University. I agreed to take the job, in large part because of my desire to escape the pressures I felt at the EEOC due to Judge Thomas.

When I informed him that I was leaving in July, I recall that his response was that now I would no longer have an excuse for not going out with him. I told him that I still preferred not to do so. At some time after that meeting, he asked if he could take me to dinner at the end of the term. When I declined, he assured me that the dinner was a professional courtesy only and not a social invitation. I reluctantly agreed to accept that invitation but only if it was at the very end of a working day.

On, as I recall, the last day of my employment at the EEOC in the summer of 1983, I did have dinner with Clarence Thomas. We went directly from work to a restaurant near the office. We talked about the work I had done, both at Education and at the EEOC. He told me that he was pleased with all of it except for an article and speech that I had done for him while we were at the Office for Civil Rights. Finally he made a comment that I will vividly remember. He said that if I ever told anyone of his behavior that it would ruin his career. This was not an apology, nor was it an explanation. That was his last remark about the possibility of our going out or reference to his behavior.

It is only after a great deal of agonizing consideration that I am able to talk of these unpleasant matters to anyone except my closest friends, as I've said before. These last few days have been very trying and very hard for me, and it hasn't just been the last few days this week.

It has actually been over a month now that I have been under the strain of this issue.

Telling the world is the most difficult experience of my life, but it is very close to having to live through the experience that occasioned this meeting. I may have used poor judgment early on in my relationship with this issue. I was aware, however, that telling at any point in my career could adversely affect my future career, and I did not want early on, to burn all the bridges to the EEOC.

As I said, I may have used poor judgment. Perhaps I should have taken angry or even militant steps, both when I was in the agency or after I left it. But I must confess to the world that the course that I took seemed the better, as well as the easier, approach.

I declined any comment to newspapers, but later, when Senate staff asked me about these matters, I felt I had a duty to report. I have no personal vendetta against Clarence Thomas. I seek only to provide the committee with information which it may regard as relevant.

It would have been more comfortable to remain silent. It took no initiative to inform anyone—I took no initiative to inform anyone. But when I was asked by a representative of this committee to report my experience, I felt that I had to tell the truth. I could not keep silent.

DAVID MIXNER
(1946–)

The Story of Self-Hatred
MARCH 27, 1993

We are willing to do anything except return to the slavery of self-hatred and low self-esteem.

A well-known corporate and political strategist, gay-rights activist David Mixner has lodged himself on the front lines and in the planning rooms of American social and political movements since 1969, when he helped organize the largest protest against the Vietnam War. During the 1992 presidential campaign, Mixner served as an adviser to his old friend candidate Bill Clinton and, as a liaison to the gay community, he organized the first gay fundraiser for a White House candidate.

After the election, Mixner, in demonstrating his fealty to gay issues, protested President Clinton's "don't ask, don't tell" policy regarding gays in the military, to the point that he landed himself in a California jail cell. Even his old friend, former Clinton adviser George Stephanopoulos, couldn't talk him into suppressing his viewpoint. Mixner later patched his relationship with Clinton, helping shape other policies, including the passage of federal hate-crimes laws and anti-bias employment legislation. Outside the political arena, Mixner has also been an active force in the fight against HIV/AIDS and has lectured and published widely.

In this 1993 speech, David Mixner discussed coming to terms with his own sexual identity. He addressed the impact the AIDS crisis has had on his life, his friends, and the gay and lesbian community. Delivered in the midst of debate over gays in the military, he also urged newly elected President Clinton to provide solid support for gay and lesbian rights in the wake of the homophobic conservative backlash.

BROTHERS AND SISTERS,

It is rare that I have the opportunity to speak so urgently among people for whom I have so much love. It is difficult to speak truth and know that it might bring pain between old friends. But today I must . . .

Because for us, truth is our sword. For us, our unity in numbers is our army. For us, our AIDS dead have inspired in us courage and determination that we ourselves did not know existed.

We now get to prepare for the battle that we have long sought. A national debate that will eventually lead to our freedom. A national debate that no longer treats us as a fringe sideshow in American politics but as an emerging and powerful civil rights movement. The future of the next generations of lesbians and gays will be decided by us—not by weak leaders—not by ballot box terrorism—not by religious fanatics who use our freedom as a tool to build their bank accounts—but rather by our strength and our courage.

History will not present us with a more historical movement than now. Each one of us will be judged by future generations by our actions in the next several months and years. If, as a family, we rise to the challenge, we truly have the opportunity to change years of oppression into a future filled with hope.

Where do we begin? Where do we find such courage? How do we build the commitment and determination that will last us through these difficult and challenging years?

We begin with our gayness. We find courage in who we are. We build our commitment by a determination that not one more generation of gays and lesbians will ever have to suffer the pangs of discrimination and self-hatred. We will no longer deny our young their dreams.

I am often asked why it is so important for me to publicly and repeatedly declare my sexuality. As I stand here among the leaders of our church, I want you to know who I am. I am a spiritual person. Each morning I pray before I begin my day. In my prayers I thank God for making me a gay person. I thank God for allowing me one more day to join my brothers and sisters in battle. I ask God for the strength to join with you in fighting for our freedom and I ask my God to give me the time to see our young celebrate in that freedom.

You see I used to be ashamed. I wanted to kill myself. I deferred my dreams and adapted to a life offering less of myself to this world instead of more. I felt alone and alienated and I felt terribly afraid. Then because of the actions of a few brave drag queens, I saw strength and hope. I started to dream again. I felt pride. I felt your love and support. I could say I am gay and proud—not without fear—but I could say it.

Then came AIDS. Death and devastation. Our lives became hospital rooms, home-care delivery systems, life support machines, and funerals. I buried 189 of my friends. I fought so that in their illness they would not be persecuted by our own government. I once again felt despair and lost hope. We grew weary and wondered if those years of fleeting liberation in the 1970s were all that we would know of freedom. We joined together in the streets, in the voting booths, in our service centers and in our churches to support each other and to fight back.

Then came President Clinton.

Allow me to be frank and honest about our President. Our journey together as a community with the President has been an intoxicating one. We have found once again our united voice. We have discovered our own power. We raised money, walked precincts and begged our families, employers and friends to join us in ending our twelve years of darkness. We started to believe in ourselves again. We dreamed again of a future.

He was elected. He proceeded to keep his promises, not to us a special interest group, but to us as Americans who wanted to participate fully in our society, who at last would be allowed to contribute our skills and talents as an open and free people.

In this process of keeping his promise to us, he encountered what we experience every day of our lives—outright bigotry and homophobia! The voices of the past rose to deny us our moment of freedom. Military leaders are fighting to keep ancient apartheid laws on the books and to resist ending fifty years of repression and persecution. They frighten our neighbors with the big lie. They paint pictures that contain only dark colors. They resort to the same bigoted arguments that have been used for centuries to deny every emerging minority their freedom and equal rights. They sought the cover of legitimacy in Armed Forces Chairperson Sam Nunn. Let me be clear about Senator Nunn. Let us educate those people, including some in the Administration, that this is not an enlightened man. Listen to me carefully. Sam Nunn is our George Wallace. He is an old-fashioned bigot who will abuse his power to deny us our freedom. His hatred runs so deep that he is willing to jeopardize the nation's economic hopes in order to deny freedom to millions. His anger is so fierce that he will focus his energy on stopping us from serving our country while the world around him in Russia and Bosnia falls to pieces. This man does not deserve the respectability that he has been accorded by so many. He has chosen hate over love . . . fear over enlightenment . . . and division over unity. We will not quake in his presence. We will not fear him. We will not give him the power to determine our future.

This brings us back to our President. We were proud to stand by his side during this last campaign. We wept when he mentioned the words gay and lesbian at the convention and AIDS on election night. We pinched ourselves in disbelief when he came and gave a gay rights speech in Los Angeles. We were filled with hope and dreams when the poet at the inauguration dared to speak our name. But for the President, too—his moment has arrived.

Mr. President, our friend, hear us carefully. Only our total freedom will do. There can be no further compromises with our dreams, our rights and our futures. An Executive Order issued *without* moral authority and decisive lead-

ership is only a piece of paper. An Executive Order issued *with* moral authority and decisive leadership is history. Now is the time that will decide if you
will sit with the great emancipator Abraham Lincoln as a man who freed millions or if you will go down in history as a man who, for political expediency,
negotiated our freedom away in the backrooms of Congress. It is your choice.
We have made ours. We will fight however long it takes to be free. Will you
join us in creating a debate steeped in morality and not fear; one that appeals
to the best that this nation has to offer, not the worst; and one where your
leadership will enlighten, not distort? It is your call. Now is the time . . . not
June 15, not July 15, not next year when it will be too late . . . but NOW!

Mr. President, do not give dignity to false compromises. Do not embrace
the Vatican approach to homosexuality. What kind of freedom is it when you
ask us to either remain silent or, if we do speak of our sexuality, give up the
right to practice it in the privacy of our own homes. This is unacceptable.

Mr. President, do not negotiate our freedom away. Separate assignments
and separate units is no more than old-fashioned segregation. No rhetoric can
hide the fact that separating a whole group of American citizens because of
who they are is nothing more than segregation. Bigotry that wears a uniform
is nothing more than a uniform with a hood. Segregation is morally repugnant to us and we will never, ever accept segregation as a sign of progress.

Mr. President, you can make our road to freedom easier. You can speak to
this nation of unity, of our unused talents and skills and of our suffering. You
can educate Senators. You can provide the moral high ground that Senator
Nunn is stealing from us. You can provide decisive leadership, courage and
most of all our freedom. But make no mistake—with or without you, we will
be free. We *will* win and we *will* prevail.

Mr. President, do not underestimate our determination and our courage.
We are willing to lose our jobs for freedom. We are willing, if necessary, to go
to jail. We are willing to give our last cent for freedom. We are willing to do
anything except return to the slavery of self-hatred and low self-esteem.

My friends, in closing, don't forget what it used to be like. So many of our
friends who could share with us the horrible oppression of self-hatred have
passed on—but each of us here knows it. We know of the past lies to our families and friends . . . we know of the fear at work . . . we know of deferring
our dreams . . . we know of being ashamed of those we loved the most . . . we
know of the attempted suicides, and we know what each and every one of us
had to overcome to even be here in this room. We can't go back to that. We
can't retreat at the first sound of battle. We must join together to fight and—
make no mistake about it—to win.

Thank you very much.

LANI GUINIER
(1950–)

Seeking a Conversation on Race
JUNE 4, 1993

I hope we can learn some positive lessons from this experience,
lessons about the importance of a public dialogue on race.

Born in 1950, Lani Guinier attended Radcliffe College at Harvard and
then Yale Law School, where she first met Bill Clinton. After clerking
for a federal district judge in Michigan, she was a special assistant in
the Civil Rights Division of the Justice Department. From there, she
worked on groundbreaking voting-rights cases at the NAACP before
joining the law faculty at the University of Pennsylvania. In 1998 she
became the first tenured black female professor at Harvard Law
School. Guinier has written extensively on civil rights and women's
issues.

On June 4, 1993, Professor Guinier delivered these words at the
opening of a press briefing for reporters. Until just the night before,
Guinier had been newly-elected president Bill Clinton's nominee to
head the Civil Rights Division, where she had worked some twenty
years before. As soon as Clinton announced Guinier's nomination, conservatives relentlessly attacked her academic writings, while also making fun of her hair, her name, and her ideas. They dubbed her "the
quota queen" for her supposed support for voting districts shaped to
guarantee black majorities—known as "race-conscious districting." An
inflammatory op-ed piece in the *New York Times* wrongly claimed that
Guinier supported "segregating black voters in black majority districts."
In truth, Guinier favored "proportional representation," a race-neutral
system to apportion seats of governing bodies based on the percentage
of the votes each party receives.

The White House asked Guinier not to speak out publicly until her
Senate confirmation hearing. For civil rights and women's rights advocates, a Senate hearing would have been a "magic moment" to draw
national attention to the challenges ahead. Instead, Clinton withdrew
the nomination without waiting for a Senate hearing, seeking instead
to distance himself from Guinier and the political firestorm. He refuted
any detailed knowledge of Guinier's work, and even labeled some of
her ideas "anti-democratic." At the same time, he advised Guinier, a

longtime friend, "You will emerge, in any event, as a public voice." The President's decision not to go forward with the nomination was extremely controverisal in the civil rights community, which attacked him for abandoning his nominee without a fight. Guinier used these remarks to decry the political vitriol that doomed public dialogue on race. Noting that the two had been friends for decades, Guinier claimed that the president was well aware of her scholarship.

⸻

HAD I BEEN ALLOWED to testify in a public forum before the United States Senate, I believe that the Senate would also have agreed that I am the right person for this job, a job some people have said I have trained for all my life.

I would like to thank all the Americans, those who have known me all my life and those who have only just heard of me, for their support and encouragement. I am blessed with many loyal friends, fine colleagues, dedicated allies, and a wonderful husband and son. Their support has helped me to endure this process with some measure of dignity, and I am grateful.

I deeply regret that I shall not have the opportunity for public service in the Civil Rights Division. I am greatly disappointed that I have been denied the opportunity to go forward to be confirmed and to work closely to move this country away from the polarization of the last twelve years, to lower the decibel level of the rhetoric that surrounds race, and to build bridges among people of goodwill to enforce the civil rights laws on behalf of all Americans. In particular, I had been excited about the possibility of working closely with Attorney General Janet Reno, a woman of outstanding integrity, a woman of principle, a woman whose vision of a more just society has been an inspiration to us all. In many ways it is her example of strength and courage that has inspired me and has allowed me to remain true to my principles in the difficult days following the announcement of my nomination on April 29 [1993].

I have always wanted to be a civil rights lawyer. My father's experience at Harvard College in 1929, as he recounted it to me, was an early lesson in the indignity and inhumanity of racism. My father was denied any financial aid on the grounds that one black student had already been awarded a full scholarship. He was not allowed to live in the dormitories on the grounds that no black, except the relative of a United States senator, had ever resided [there]. He was the victim of a racial quota, a quota of one. I have never been in favor of quotas. I could not be, knowing my father's experience. My commitment to civil rights, to democratic fair play, to cross-racial coalition building, were all forged in the crucible of those memories.

I have been fortunate to have had the opportunity to pursue my ideals as a civil rights lawyer, first as a Civil Rights Division attorney and special assistant to Drew Days when he was head of the division in the Carter administration, and later as counsel for the NAACP Legal Defense Fund, where I litigated many cases and lost only two. In all my work I have been inspired by the civil rights movement of the 1960s, by the Voting Rights Act of 1965, and by the amendments to that act which I worked with Congress to produce in 1982, with the vision of those amendments of an integrated legislature in which all of its members work together for the common good.

I have been fortunate to have many heroes and mentors, heroes like Dr. Martin Luther King Jr., Justice Thurgood Marshall, and Judge Constance Baker Motley; mentors like Judge Damon Keith, Solicitor General Drew Days, former Ford administration transportation secretary William T. Coleman, and Elaine Ruth Jones, director counsel of the NAACP Legal Defense and Educational Fund. These are people who committed their hearts, their considerable intellectual energy, and their professional lives to a vision of a just society, a society in which America makes good on her promise to be a true, generous, and inclusive democracy.

I have always believed in democracy, and nothing I have ever written is inconsistent with that. I have always believed in one person, one vote, and nothing I have ever written is inconsistent with that. I have always believed in fundamental fairness, and nothing I have ever written is inconsistent with that. I am a democratic idealist who believes that politics need not be forever seen as "I win, you lose," a dynamic in which some people are permanent monopoly winners and others are permanent excluded losers. Everything I have written is consistent with that.

I hope that what has happened to my nomination does not mean that future nominees will not be allowed to explain their views as soon as any controversy arises. I hope that we are not witnessing the dawning of a new intellectual orthodoxy in which thoughtful people can no longer debate provocative ideas without denying the country their talents as public servants. I also hope that we can learn some positive lessons from this experience, lessons about the importance of public dialogue on race, in which all perspectives are represented and in which no one viewpoint monopolizes, distorts, caricatures, or shapes the outcome.

Although the president and I disagree about his decision to withdraw my nomination, I continue to respect the president. We disagree about this, but we agree about many things. He believes in racial healing and so do I. Last year in an interview with Bill Moyers, then candidate Bill Clinton was asked, "Is there one thing on which you would not compromise?" He answered, without flinching, "Yes—racial equality." I believe that he and Attorney General Janet Reno will use the opportunity of this presidency to act on that commitment, to act affirmatively to move this country forward, to work with and for all Americans to go beyond the polarization and divisiveness of the past few years and the poison of racism that has so infected our society.

There are real problems affecting real people in this country, people who are still the victims of unlawful discrimination on the basis of their race, their ethnicity, their gender, their sexual orientation, or their disability. I hope that despite the unfairness of the way that I have been treated by the political process that people will, nevertheless, work within that system to resolve the more important unfairness that others continue to suffer in their daily lives. We have made real progress toward Dr. Martin Luther King's vision of a society in which we are judged by the content of our character, not by the color of our skin, but we are not there yet, and we need real presidential leadership, action, not just words, to heal the racial hemorrhaging and to realize Dr. King's dream, which is my dream, too.

Thank you.

WILLIAM J. CLINTON
(1946–)

The Freedom to Die
NOVEMBER 13, 1993

King . . . would say . . . "I did not fight for the right of Black
people to murder other Black people with reckless abandon."

A son of the segregated South, William Jefferson Clinton was raised in
Hope, Arkansas, in the early years of the civil rights movement. Despite
his early exposure to racial discrimination and segregation up close,
Clinton's own experiences, and his family's influence, helped him
develop a different understanding than many of his peers. Beginning at
a young age, his mother and grandfather emphasized the importance of
equality, impressing on him the idea that all men were indeed "created
equal" regardless of their color. Clinton carried his knowledge and
experience first to Georgetown University, Yale Law School, and then
Oxford University, before seeking public office. In 1976 he was elected
governor of Arkansas; less than two decades later, he was sworn in as
president of the United States.

During his tenure in the White House, Clinton worked tirelessly to
advance issues important to minority communities: He appointed an
unprecedented number of African Americans to high-level government
posts; supported a "mended" affirmative action program; encouraged
minority home ownership; and introduced public-private partnerships
to bring new investment and jobs into hard-pressed communities.
Thanks largely to his efforts, both legislative and symbolic, the president
enjoyed an unprecedented level of support from people of color.
Author Toni Morrison even called him "the first black President."

In what is often considered the most powerful civil rights speech of
his presidency, Clinton traveled to Memphis, Tennessee, on November
13, 1993, to address 5,000 African-American ministers at the Church of
God of Christ. Speaking extemporaneously from the pulpit where
Martin Luther King, Jr., delivered his last sermon, relying largely on the
notes he had scribbled on his speech, Clinton decried the violence
plaguing African-American communities, comparing the current state
of the black community to the goals King had fought for decades earlier. He called on black ministers to celebrate King's legacy by rising up
to the challenges King had posed from that very pulpit. Evoking bibli-

cal themes, Clinton also addressed the contemporary social and spiritual issues confronting people of color in the 1990s—and offered his personal commitment to advancing racial equality. The power of Clinton's speech was not only in the rhetoric itself, but also in the risk of a white democratic leader directly highlighting the problem of black-on-black violence. The president listenened to a saxophonist play "Amazing Grace" before being introduced as "Bishop Clinton."

BY THE GRACE OF GOD and your help, last year, I was elected President of this great country. I never dreamed that I would ever have a chance to come to this hallowed place where Martin Luther King gave his last sermon. I ask you to think today about the purpose for which I ran and the purpose for which so many of you worked to put me in this great office. I have worked hard to keep faith with our common efforts—to restore the economy, to reverse the politics of helping only those at the top of our totem pole and not the hard-working middle class or the poor, to bring our people together across racial and regional and political lines, to make a strength out of our diversity instead of letting it tear us apart, to reward work and family and community, and try to move us forward into the 21st Century.

I have tried to keep faith. Thirteen percent of all my presidential appointments are African Americans and there are five African Americans in the Cabinet of the United States—two-and-a-half times as many as have ever served in the history of this great land.

I have sought to advance the right to vote with the Motor-Voter Bill supported so strongly by all the churches in our country. And next week, it will be my great honor to sign the Restoration of Religious Freedoms Act—a bill supported widely by people across all religions and political philosophies, to put back the real meaning of the Constitution, to give you and every other American the freedom to do what is most important in your life—to worship God as your spirit leads you.

But, what I really want to say to you today, my fellow Americans, is that . . . unless we do something about crime and violence and drugs that is ravaging the community, we will not be able to repair this country.

If Martin Luther King—who said, "Like Moses, I am on the mountain top and I can see the Promised Land, but I'm not going to be able to get there with you. But we will get there"—if he were to re-appear by my side today and give us a report card on the last 25 years, what would he say?

You did a good job, he would say, voting and electing people who formerly were not electable because of the color of their skin. You have more political power—and that is good. You did a good job, he would say, letting people who have the ability to do so, live wherever they want to live, go wherever they want to go in this great country.

You did a good job, he would say, elevating people of color into the ranks of the United States Armed Forces to the very top or into the very top of our government. You did a very good job. He would say, You did a good job creating a Black middle class of people who really are doing well, and the middle class is growing more among African Americans than among non-African Americans. You did a good job in opening opportunity.

But he would say, I did not live and die to see the American family destroyed. I did not live and die to see 13-year-old boys get automatic weapons and gun down nine-year-olds just for the kick of it. I did not live and die to see young people destroy their own lives with drugs and then build fortunes destroying the lives of others. That is not what I came here to do.

I fought for freedom, he would say, but not for the freedom of people to kill each other with reckless abandonment, not for the freedom of children to have children and the fathers of the children to walk away from them and abandon them, as if they don't amount to anything. I fought for people to have the right to work, but not to have whole communities and people abandoned. This is not what I lived and died for.

My fellow Americans, he would say, I fought to stop white people from being so filled with hate that they would wreak violence on black people. I did not fight for the right of black people to murder other black people with reckless abandonment.

The other day, the Mayor of Baltimore, a dear friend of mine, told me a story of visiting the family of a young man who had been killed—18 years old—on Halloween. He always went out with little-bitty kids so they could trick-or-treat safely. And across the street from where they were walking on Halloween, a 14-year-old-boy gave a 13-year-old boy a gun and dared him to shoot the 18-year old-boy—and he shot him dead.

In Washington, DC, where I live—your nation's capitol, the symbol of freedom throughout the world—look how that freedom is being exercised. The other night, a man came along the street and grabbed a one-year-old child and put the child in his car. The child may have been the child of the man. And two people were after him and they chased him in the car and they just kept shooting with reckless abandonment—knowing that baby was in the car. And they shot the man dead, and a bullet went through his body into the baby's body and blew the little booty off the child's foot.

The other day on the front page of our paper, the nation's capitol—Are we talking about world peace or world conflict? You know, a big article on the front page of the *Washington Post* about an 11-year-old child planning her funeral. "These are the hymns I want sung. This is the dress I want to wear. I know I'm not going to live very long." That is not the freedom—the freedom to die before you're a teenager is not what Martin Luther King lived and died for.

More than 37,000 people die from gunshot wounds in this country every year. Gunfire is the leading cause of death in young men. And now that we've all gotten so cool that everybody can get a semi-automatic weapon, a person shot now is three times more likely to die than 15 years ago, because they're likely to have three bullets in them. A hundred-and-sixty-thousand children stay home from school every day because they are scared they will be hurt in their school. The other day, I was in California at a town meeting, and a handsome young man stood up and said, "Mr. President, my brother and I, we don't belong to gangs. We don't have guns. We don't do drugs. We want to go to school. We want to be professionals. We want to work hard. We want to do well. We want to have families. And we changed our school, because the school we were in was so dangerous. So, when we showed up to the new school to register, my brother and I were standing in line, and somebody ran in the school and started shooting a gun, and my brother was shot down standing right in front of me at the safer school." The freedom to do that kind of thing is not what Martin Luther King lived and died for. Not what people gathered in this hallowed church for the night before he was assassinated in April of 1968. If you had told anybody who was here in that church on that night that we would abuse our freedom in that way, they would have found it hard to believe. And I tell you, it is our moral duty to turn it around.

And now, I think, finally, we have a chance. Finally, I think, we have a chance. We have a pastor here from New Haven, Connecticut. I was in his church, with Reverend Jackson, when I was running for President, on a snowy day in Connecticut, to mourn the deaths of children who had been killed in that city. And afterward, we walked down the street for more than a mile in the snow. Then, the American people were not ready. People would say, "Oh, this is a terrible thing, but what can we do about it?" Now, when we read that foreign visitors come to our shores and are killed at random in our fine state of Florida, when we see our children planning their funerals, when the American people are finally coming to grips with the accumulated waste of crime and violence and the breakdown of family and community and the increase in drugs and the decrease in jobs, I think, finally, we may be ready to do something about it.

And there is something for each of us to do. There are changes we can make from the outside in—that's the job of the President and the Congress and the governors and the mayors and the social service agencies. And then, there are some changes we're going to have to make from the inside out, or the others won't matter. That's what that magnificent song was about, isn't it?

Sometimes, there are no answers from the outside in. Sometimes, all of the answers have to come from the values and the stirrings and the voices that speak to us from within.

So, we are beginning. We are trying to pass a bill to make our people safer, to put another 100,000 police officers on the streets, to provide boot camps instead of prisons for young people who could still be rescued, to provide more safety in our schools, to restrict the availability of these awful assault weapons, to pass the Brady Bill and at least require people to have their criminal background checked before they get a gun, and to say, if you're not old enough to vote and you're not old enough to go to war, you ought not to own a handgun and you ought not to use one unless you're on a target range.

We want to pass a health care bill that will make drug treatment available for everyone. And we also have to do it—we have to have drug treatment and education available to everyone, and especially those who are in prison, who are coming out.

———

We cannot—I submit to you—repair the American community and restore the American family until we provide the structure, the values, the discipline, and the reward that work gives.

———

So, I say to you, we have to make a partnership—all the government agencies, all the business folks. But where there are no families, where there is no order, where there is no hope, where we are reducing the size of armed services because we have won the Cold War, who will be there to give structure, discipline, and love to these children? You must do that and we must help you. The scripture says, You are the salt of the earth and the light of the world," that, "If your light shines before men, they will give glory to the Father in Heaven." That is what we must do. That is what we must do. How would we explain it to Martin Luther King if he showed up today and said, Yes, we won the Cold War. Yes, the biggest threat that all of us grew up under— Communism and nuclear war—Communism is gone; nuclear war receding. Yes, we developed all of these miraculous technologies. Yes, we all got a VCR in our home. It's interesting. Yes, we get 50 channels on the cable. Yes, without regard to race, if you work hard, play by the rules, you get into a service academy or a good college, you'll do just great. How would we explain to him all these kids getting killed and killing each other? How would we justify the things that we permit that no other country in the world would permit? How could we explain that we gave people the freedom to succeed and we created conditions in which millions abuse that freedom to destroy the things that make life worth living and life itself? We cannot.

And so, I say to you today, my fellow Americans, you gave me this job, and we're making progress on the things you hired me to do. But unless we deal with the ravages of crime and drugs and violence, and unless we recognize that it's due to the breakdown of the family, the community, and the disappearance of jobs, and unless we say, Some of this cannot be done by government because we have to reach deep inside to the values, the spirit, the soul, and the truth of human nature, none of the other things we seek to do will ever take us where we need to go.

So, in this pulpit, on this day, let me ask all of you in your heart to say, We will honor the life and the work of Martin Luther King. We will honor the meaning of our church. We will somehow, by God's grace, we will turn this around. We will give these children a future. We will take away their guns and give them books. We will take away their despair and give them hope. We will rebuild the families and the neighborhoods and the communities. We won't make all the work that has gone on here benefit just a few. We will do it together by the grace of God.

SISTER SOULJAH
(1964–)

We Are at War
1994

Racism is a system of power and in the absence of power
you cannot be considered a racist.

Sister Souljah earned a place on the political landscape in 1992 when her comments on the Los Angeles riots set off a firestorm of controversy. A rap singer capable of using incendiary rhetoric, Souljah told a *Washington Post* reporter, "If black people kill black people every day, why not have a week and kill white people?" She went on to call the riots a "form of war," arguing that those affected by the riots should not cooperate with the government or law enforcement officials. Later that year, in a speech to Reverend Jesse Jackson's Rainbow PUSH Coalition, then presidential candidate Bill Clinton attacked Souljah's comments, calling them hate driven and racist—and not too dissimilar from those of former Ku Klux Klan member David Duke. In turn, Clinton's poll numbers shot right up, and journalists from around the country praised him for standing up to Souljah. Sister Souljah, however, went on the offensive, criticizing Clinton and defending her views in speech after speech.

Born Lisa Williamson in the Bronx, Souljah lived on and off the welfare system until high school, when she received scholarships to both Cornell and Rutgers universities. An opinionated activist, writer, and musician, she contended that blacks are systematically denied access to academic, economic, and political opportunity—all the result of a vicious cycle of racism. In 1994, after President Clinton was elected, Sister Souljah delivered this speech at Cheyney State University—in yet another effort to dispel her critics. With measured rhythm and defiant prose, she challenged black Americans to better their own situation by embracing spirituality, self-confidence, and especially education.

I REALIZE THAT most of you have become acquainted with me through a 30-second sound bite, or a 3-second sound bite on the news, and there have been a lot of confusing things that have been said. And so what I am hoping will happen this evening is that we will have an opportunity to dialogue with one another, so that I can hear some of the questions that are on your mind, and I can answer them as responsibly as possible.

Whenever I speak at a University the first thing that I try to clarify is who I am, because I cannot allow the American media to define you to me, or me to you. I am Sister Souljah, and that is spelled S-O-U-L-J-A-H. Soul meaning the essence of all things, and Jah, meaning God. Sister Souljah meaning a spiritual warrior for that which is right and correct for our people.

I was born in the Bronx, in New York City, and have been involved in a lot of the government programs that were produced for African people in this country, whether it was the welfare system, the section 8 housing system, the free lunch, free cheese, free breakfast, forced bussing, all of the programs that came out of the so-called "great society" which emerged in the late-'60s early-'70s. And the reason why I say that is because a lot of brothers and sisters have emerged from families that have been trapped in the welfare system, or in the cycle of poverty, but we have a habit of, when we get to college we try to front like we don't know anything about that stuff. So, when I say that I was a part of the welfare system, or the section 8 housing system, or the financial aid system, I say that so you can understand that those systems and those programs do not define you or your family. They were put in place for us because our ancestors fought and died, so that we would have the opportunity to have these programs so that we could emerge as strong, and comprehensive, and confident young adults.

. . . When they tell you that I am just a rapper with a big mouth, and a bad attitude, you should be aware of the fact that I have been very well educated in the topics that I am talking about.

. . . When I talk about our people, I do so not because I am ignorant, or illiterate, but because I am well-studied, and well-experienced in the area and because I have a fundamental love for our people, and I think that we deserve much better than we've encountered in the United States of America.

⌒

In Africa, the older women in the society took the younger women, and taught them what is the definition of womanhood. You could not just be a woman simply because you were 18 or 19 years old. The older women had to train you—how to judge a man, how to evaluate whether a man is valuable, how to judge yourself, how to control your power, how to control the society, how to control your man. But see in America, we get confused, because we don't want to be African so we don't know any of those definitions, so instead, you got sisters running around talking about, "Yeah, that's my man," but all they got is his beeper number. Never been to his house, never met his mamma, don't even know his real name, but that's "your man," right.

You see, in an African society they taught you that to be a woman is to be a powerful thing, but in America on the television, they teach you that to be a woman is to be cute and stupid. . . . We begin to judge African men, by the size of their wallet, and the kind of car they're driving, instead of the strength of their character.

. . . You see, but if you were an African woman, you would be taught that the first thing that you do is communicate, to try to understand what is the nature of the man that you're dealing with, what are his goals and objectives in life? What does he value, and consider precious, where is he moving, and does that have anything to do with where you're going? Communication to find out where he is, and what he's involved in. You meet his mother and his father to see what situation he has emerged from, not to judge him by the money that he has in his pocket, but to look at the situation so you know exactly what you're dealing with. . . .

In an African society, a man is taught the definition of being a man. It wasn't that you were a man just because you're 18 or 19 years old, or just because you attend Cheyney State University. You were a man if you have established a spiritual connection to the creator to teach you to value life, and to value a force that is greater than yourself. That you are a man if you can protect your woman, and provide for your woman. That you are a man if you produce your children, and claim the children that you produce. That you are not a man until you gain total mastery and discipline over your lower self, which means that you are not controlled by Saint Ives, malt liquor, drugs, crack, sex, or any foreign substance. And any young African man who could not meet that criteria would never be able to emerge from the manhood society with a level of respect and power. And he would cause shame on his family.

But in America, because we as African people in America don't want to be African, most of our young brothers struggle to try to understand what manhood means, which is why you have most of them making the mistake of thinking that to be a man is to be a gangster, to be a man is to shoot another brother that looks just like you to show you who is the punk and who's the chump, and who's the macho guy, something they saw in some old Italian movie. You got brothers thinking that to be a man has something to do with the size of their penis or how many sisters they can destroy on a daily basis.

Why am I going over these definitions? Because so many people don't know these definitions, and in the absence of knowing these definitions, you will have continual chaos, and you will not understand why you are a confused individual, and you will also be powerless.

When I say we are at war, a lot of people become confused. They think it means that Sister Souljah supports violence, and guns, and military opposition, and things of that nature. The thing that you should understand about war is war is not a voluntary state of existence. What that means is somebody, or some group of people, or some state, or some race, or some nation of people can declare war on you without your permission. So you can be at war not because you want to be, not because you're war-like people, not because you want to fight back, but because some alien force has declared war upon you. How do you recognize the conditions of a war? A state of war exists anytime anybody or any institution, or any family, or any group tries to take from you that which is rightfully yours, your right to life, your ability to think freely, your ability to celebrate and know your culture, your ability to control the economics of your community, your ability to eat, and live, and love, your ability to express yourself, and your ability to move freely in the society.

Now, when I tell black students that we are at war, they think that I'm radical and dramatic, but I try to use some very simple examples.

. . . [O]ne of the conditions of white racism is that white people are considered superior, which means that they own and rule everything so they have a right to be anywhere. Black people are considered inferior, which means that they are controlled and dominated so they don't have the right to be everywhere, only the places that were reserved for them, which we know are the inferior pieces of geography. We are at war.

. . . Well, listen, this has nothing to do with whether you love America. It has something to do with whether America loves you. . . .

⟶

What happens in the absence of the participation of strong African women? What happens is social chaos. What do I mean by social chaos? O.K., if there are four African women here to every one African man, now, we're in a dead and heated competition. None of the four African women wants to admit that there is a political and economic and military problem in America, because that's too much work, and involves too much study. And so one goes and gets a bra and some leggings and she says, "I'm going to wear this today." And the other one says, "I bet you I can top that, I'm going to wear my bra and my panties outside." And the clothes just start to disappear, until the whole campus is in a state of chaos. Brothers are saying, "Well god-damn, man, I want to be a man. I want to control my lower desires but these women are absolutely butt naked." And sisters walk around getting an attitude when brothers look at them in their bra and panties out on the lawn.

⟶

To the brothers, I say, you know that we are at war because you know that you suffer as African men. But many of you, instead of being men and meeting the challenge, tend to exploit African women and take advantage of the numbers, and you use your taking advantage of African women as an excuse, or as a mis-definition of manhood. But in the same way that the African woman imitates the white woman, the African man does the same thing to the white man, and so you begin to measure your manhood by how many women you make cry, how many women you destroy, how many women you got sweatin' you, which has nothing to do with the development of your mind, your commu-nity, or the protection of the African society. We are at war.

Many people say that Sister Souljah is a racist. Let me assure you that there is no such thing as a black racist. There is no such thing. "Black racism" and "reverse racism" are terms that were developed by intellectual white think-tanks in political circles to get you as African young people to feel guilty about discussing what has happened to you as African people in America. So when you start to discuss slavery, or the effects of slavery, or the effects of 500 years of domination, what they do is say, "Oh, you're a racist." When you react to the ugly things that they do or say to us, they say, "Oh, you're a racist." That is to get you to feel guilty about discussing, or organizing, or taking issue with the condition of African people in this country.

So what happens is you find a lot of young African students across the country who are very apologetic about discussing African issues. When they're talking about it they say, "You know, like I'm not a racist or anything, you know. I don't hate white people. You know I'm not that kind of person. I just feel that, you know I'm not a racist. I just wanted to explain that I'm not a racist." And the discussion loses its pull because they're so guilty and concerned about proving to white people and to black people that they're not racist, that they're scared to address and deal with the issue of racism and its effects on the community.

But everybody in here knows that racism has affected you as an individual because when one white person enters the room, it affects how you think, how you behave, how you talk, how you look, and how comfortable you feel as an individual. Some people become self-conscious about their hair. Some people develop an accent that just simply does not come from their commu-nity. Some people lose all of their cultural nuances and are like, you know, like . . . because they don't feel comfortable about being African in the presence of European white people.

Racism is a system of power. What does that mean? That a system of power means that you as an African woman, or you as an African man could go to any state in this country and the system will protect white privilege, white power, white jobs and white economics, and you will be a non-factor in that equation. Not only will it happen anyplace in the country, it will also happen anyplace in the entire world. So there's no such thing as a black racist, because none of you in here, and no African leader in this country, and no African leader in the Caribbean, or Latino America or the continent of Africa has the power to invade one white country. No African person in this country has the power to order white children to go to a black school and learn about black people all day and never study themselves. No black person has the power to determine whether your black husband, or brother or father has a job, and will continue to have a job or any type of power in this system, and no black system or police force anyplace in this country or anyplace in the world has the power to go into the white community and savagely beat their men and be completely excused for it in this system of justice. Racism is a system of power and in the absence of power you cannot be considered a racist—therefore there is no such thing as black racism.

Reverse racism means that if reverse racism exists, somewhere in this society, some group of African people took a ship and went to Europe, packed the white people into the ship, raped their mothers, sold their fathers, killed their babies, and perpetuated violence on them for 500 years, made it illegal for them to read, to write, to assemble, to think, to speak their own language, or wear their own clothes, or worship their own gods. You and I both know that nowhere in this society have African people been allowed to do that, or even try to do that, or even wanted, as a collective to do that. There is no such thing as reverse racism.

What is a state of accommodation? A state of accommodation exists anytime you have become so comfortable with the system of racism that you begin to accept it as being a normal way of life. A state of accommodation exists when black mothers take their little black children to school, and the class is 90% black, and 10% Latino, and it's a white teacher. A state of accommodation exists when there's a historically African university and African people in the community don't support it, so they become enslaved to government funding. A state of accommodation exists anytime African men begin to desire, date, sleep with, and marry white women, instead of their own African females. A state of accommodation exists anytime African people in this country believe that they're part of a Democratic Party that doesn't include them in the equation of power or even address the issues of African concerns. That is a state of accommodation, when you become so lazy and relaxed and accepting of racism that you think it's normal for you to be deprived and powerless and lazy and backwards. That's a state of accommodation.

I want to move to the area of solutions. The reason why I went over the definitions is so that you can really clarify some of the personal problems that you have in your life. And when I say that, I say that based on experience, and having had problems in my own life, and being a solution-orientated person always trying to look at what I could have done more effectively to avoid some of the problems, and being a loving person, wanting to share the mistakes that I've made with you so that you can avoid making those mistakes and improve the quality of life of African people. Understand that when I say "I," in the African tradition, I mean "we," and "we" is "us," and "us" is "them," and they are you, and you and I, and we're all in this thing together.

⸺⁓

. . . What we need to do is change the type of conversation in the groups that we have. Sisters, we need to stop discussing who's pregnant, whose baby is it, who got the abortion, who didn't get the abortion, who got the weave, whose hair is real, where she got her hair done, where she got her nails done, where she got her lipstick from. And we need to begin talking about businesses, and how 7 or 8 or 9 or 10 friends can get together and organize something.

⸺⁓

When I decided to make music my career, I began to say, I can create a character, Sister Souljah, and market that character to African people in America so that every young African woman could have a better option than a naked whore on television, as to what they wanted to be like. I could develop an image of an African woman that was strong and knowledgeable and comprehensive, to let every other African woman know that that's what we used to be in our original essence. And I could develop a character that would demand and command respect from African men so that they would know that they have to stop calling us skeezers and ho'es, and sluts, and boots, and all the other things that they describe us as, and I made a business out of that. . . .

⸺⁓

There are two more points that I have. One of the components of manhood that I mentioned is that men have to be able to protect their community. To the brothers in this audience, I would like to say that we cannot depend on the American police force to protect African men. What that means is that African men in America have got to become more aware of developing a way to defend ourselves and our communities. The only way this discussion will be made possible is if we stop fronting on one another. If brothers continue to embrace a white-minded sense of macho-ism where they can't even look at each other, much less talk to each other, where they judge each other by Ralph Polo, and some other freak, or faggot from Paris; if that becomes the criteria by which you judge the next black man, what will happen is that you will never have the discussion of how vulnerable and naked you and he actually are in the society that does not love you, does not honor you, and will never ever protect you. Brothers have to be big enough to drop the front and embrace one another. . . .

⸺⁓

The point becomes that we as African people are spiritual. We don't have to necessarily go to a church or a mosque or a temple. We can if we'd like to. It is not mandatory, but it's nice if we do. But you all have a voice in your mind that teaches you, and tells you the difference between right and wrong, the difference between fake and real. So when you go home tonight, and you're laying in your bed, and you're thinking to yourself, ask yourself, are you for real? Do you know the difference between right and wrong? What have you done to improve your quality of life, and the quality of life of your people? Have you become so accepting of mediocre performance that you no longer even strive for excellence? Have you become so common with misusing and abusing your body, and giving yourself up so freely, that you're no longer concerned about being righteous? Remember that the only power that we can draw as righteous people is through righteous deeds and a righteous God. We cannot draw strength from evil deeds because they return and smack you in the face. So while you think you're striving for what is right, everything that you're adding up on a negative bill is coming back to you, and hindering your ability to move forward, which is why so many people are confused about why they keep trying and there are no results. There are not going to be any results if you are not living a righteous life.

And so I'm asking you just as I challenge myself, and I say all of these things out of love, because I have not reached any level of perfection but challenge you to challenge yourself to do what is right, to be a stronger person, to take a stand, to speak up, to prepare your mind, and to honor your spirit, and love your people. Thank you.

COLIN POWELL
(1937–)

Rejecting Racial Hatred
MAY 14, 1994

As the world goes forward, we cannot start going backward.
African-Americans have come too far . . . to take a
detour into the swamp of hatred.

In April 1994, in a speech at the predominantly black Howard University, Khalid Abdul Muhammad attacked what he called the sins of white people, with a particular focus on the alleged evils of Jewish Americans. One of Louis Farrakhan's top lieutenants in the Nation of Islam, Muhammad was cheered by more than 1,500 students and community members—causing an outcry in the academy and in the national press. In the wake of controversy, the president of the university and others were forced to tender their resignations.

Three weeks later, General Colin Powell walked into the firestorm, agreeing to speak at the university's commencement ceremony. The son of Jamaican immigrants, Powell was raised in the South Bronx, attended City College of New York, and entered the United States Army, where he went on to serve for thirty-five years. Powell quickly ascended the military hierarchy, achieving the rank of four-star general—the highest rank ever held by an African American in the U.S. armed forces. Powell's confidence and ability were superb—and others recognized it; he was tapped as an aide to Reagan defense secretary Casper Weinberger and later as national security adviser. In 1989 President George Bush named Powell chairman of the Joint Chiefs of Staff, the most powerful military position in the world. In that post, he oversaw the Persian Gulf War, earning vast accolades, including the Congressional Gold Medal. Most recently he was named secretary of state by President George W. Bush. With these credentials in hand, Powell addressed the Howard community, excoriating anti-Semitism and racial and ethnic hatred, but stressing the importance of free speech.

THE REAL CHALLENGE in being a commencement speaker is figuring out how long to speak.

The graduating students want a short speech, five to six minutes and let's get it over. They are not going to remember who their commencement speaker was anyway. P-O-W-E-L-L.

Parents are another matter. Arrayed in all their finery they have waited a long time for this day, some not sure it would ever come, and they want it to last. So go on and talk for two or three hours. We brought our lunch and want our money's worth.

The faculty member who suggested the speaker hopes the speech will be long enough to be respectable, but not so long that he has to take leave for a few weeks beginning Monday. So the poor speaker is left figuring out what to do. My simple rule is to respond to audience reaction. If you are appreciative and applaud a lot early on, you get a nice, short speech. If you make me work for it, we're liable to be here a long time.

You know, the controversy over Howard's speaking policy has its positive side. It has caused the university to go through a process of self-examination, which is always a healthy thing to do. Since many people have been giving advice about how to handle this matter, I thought I might as well too.

First, I believe with all my heart that Howard must continue to serve as an institute of learning excellence where freedom of speech is strongly encouraged and rigorously protected. That is at the very essence of a great university and Howard is a great university.

And freedom of speech means permitting the widest range of views to be present for debate, however controversial those views may be. The First Amendment right of free speech is intended to protect the controversial and even outrageous word, and not just comforting platitudes, too mundane to need protection.

Some say that by hosting controversial speakers who shock our sensibilities, Howard is in some way promoting or endorsing their message. Not at all. Howard has helped put their message in perspective while protecting their right to be heard. So that the message can be exposed to the full light of day.

I have every confidence in the ability of the administration, the faculty and the students of Howard to determine who should speak on this campus. No outside help needed, thank you.

I also have complete confidence in the students of Howard to make informed, educated judgments about what they hear.

But for this freedom to hear all views, you bear a burden to sort out wisdom from foolishness.

There is great wisdom in the message of self-reliance, of education, of hard work, and of the need to raise strong families. There is utter foolishness, evil, and danger in the message of hatred, or of condoning violence, however cleverly the message is packaged or entertainingly it is presented. We must find nothing to stand up and cheer about or applaud in a message of racial or ethnic hatred.

I was at the inauguration of President Mandela in South Africa earlier this week. You were there too by television and watched that remarkable event. Together, we saw what can happen when people stop hating and begin reconciling. DeKlerk the jailer became DeKlerk the liberator, and Mandela the prisoner became Mandela the president. Twenty-seven years of imprisonment did not embitter Nelson Mandela. He invited his three jail keepers to the ceremony. He used his liberation to work his former tormentors to create a new South Africa and to eliminate the curse of apartheid from the face of the earth. What a glorious example! What a glorious day it was!

Last week you also saw Prime Minister Rabin and PLO Chairman Arafat sign another agreement on their still difficult, long road to peace, trying to end hundreds of years of hatred and two generations of violence. Palestinian authorities have now begun entering Gaza and Jericho.

In these two historic events, intractable enemies of the past have shown how you can join hands to create a force of moral authority more powerful than any army and which can change the world.

Although there are still places of darkness in the world where the light of reconciliation has not penetrated, these two beacons of hope show what can be done when men and women of goodwill work together for peace and for progress.

There is a message in these two historic events for us assembled here today. As the world goes forward, we cannot start going backward.

African-Americans have come too far and we have too far yet to go to take a detour into the swamp of hatred.

We, as a people who have suffered so much from the hatred of others, must not now show tolerance for any movement or philosophy that has at its core the hatred of Jews or anyone else.

Our future lies in the philosophy of love and understanding and caring and building up, not of hatred and tearing down.

We know that. We must stand up for it and speak up for it!

We must not be silent if we would live up to the legacy of those who have gone before us from this campus.

I have no doubt that this controversy will pass and Howard University will emerge even stronger, even more than ever a symbol of hope, of promise, and of excellence. That is Howard's destiny!

You face "Great Expectations." Much has been given to you and much is expected from you. You have been given a quality education, presented by a distinguished faculty who sit here today in pride of you. You have inquiring minds and strong bodies given to you by God and by your parents, who sit behind you and pass on to you today their still unrealized dreams and ambitions. You have been given citizenship in a country like none other on earth, with opportunities available to you like nowhere else on earth, beyond anything available to me when I sat in a place similar to this thirty-six years ago.

What will be asked of you is hard work. Nothing will be handed to you. You are entering a life of continuous study and struggle to achieve your goals.

A life of searching to find that which you do well and love doing. Never stop seeking. I want you to have faith in yourselves. I want you to believe to the depth of your soul that you can accomplish any task that you set your mind and energy to. I want you to be proud of your heritage. Study your origins. Teach your children racial pride and draw strength and inspiration from the cultures of our forebears.

Not as a way of drawing back from American society and its European roots. But as a way of showing that there are other roots as well. African and Caribbean roots that are also a source of nourishment for the American family tree. To show that African-Americans are more than a product of our slave experience. To show that our varied backgrounds are as rich as that of any other American—not better or greater, but every bit as equal.

Our black heritage must be a foundation stone we can build on, not a place to withdraw into.

I want you to fight racism. But remember, as Dr. King and Dr. Mandela have taught us, racism is a disease of the racist. Never let it become yours. White South Africans were cured of the outward symptoms of the disease by President Mandela's inauguration, just as surely as black South Africans were liberated from apartheid.

Racism is a disease you can help cure by standing up for your rights and by your commitment to excellence and to performance. By being ready to take advantage of your rights and the opportunities that will come from those rights. Never let the dying hand of racism rest on your shoulder, weighing you down. Let racism always be someone else's burden to carry.

As you seek your way in the world, never fail to find a way to serve your community. Use your education and your success in life to help those still trapped in cycles of poverty and violence.

Above all, never lose faith in America. Its faults are yours to fix, not to curse.

America is a family. There may be differences and disputes in the family, but we must not allow the family to be broken into warring factions. From the diversity of our people, let us draw strength and not cause weakness.

Believe in America with all your heart and soul and mind. It remains the "last best hope of Earth." You are its inheritors and its future is today placed in your hands.

Go forth from this place today inspired by those who went before you. Go forth with the love of your families and the blessings of your teachers. Go forth to make this a better country and society. Prosper, raise strong families, remembering that all you will leave behind is your good works and your children.

Go forth with my humble congratulations. And let your dreams be your only limitations. Now and forever.

Thank you and God bless you. Have a great life!

RAUL YZAGUIRRE
(1939–)

The Two Faces of American Immigration
MAY 31, 1994

*The fact is that immigrants are not a net burden to the
United States taxpayer but a net contributor.*

Founded in 1968, the National Council of La Raza (NCLR) aimed to
foster cohesion and a common network among more than 150 commu-
nity-based Hispanic groups in the United States. At the helm of NCLR
for nearly twenty-five years, Raul Yzaguirre has been a public and powerful voice for Latino cultural unity, technical assistance, and civil and
economic rights—championing, among other causes, Latino immigration, citizenship, and voter registration. Raised in the Rio Grande Valley
of South Texas and a graduate of George Washington University,
Yzaguirre was only fifteen when he organized a youth branch of the
American GI Forum—a group for Hispanic-American veterans. In 1964
he founded the National Organization for Mexican American Services,
out of which grew the NCLR. *Hispanic* magazine declared in 1992 that
he was at "the center of the Hispanic leadership stage."

In this address to Mercy College in White Plains, New York,
Yzaguirre addressed the negative image and inequitable treatment of
Hispanic Americans. Citing solidarity as the instrument for economic
and political progress, he equated the plight of Hispanics with that of
all American immigrant groups over the nation's long history.

~~~

AMERICA IS OF TWO MINDS when it comes to immigrants. On the one
hand, we are proud of our immigrant heritage, symbolized by that great
American icon known as the Statue of Liberty. Yet public opinion, going back as
far as the early 1800s, has been decidedly against each new wave of immigrants.

Every American, including American Indians, are immigrants or descendants of immigrants. Newcomers to our land are "Americans by choice";
indeed, our very existence as a nation is based on that heritage.

Yet we are witnessing a wave of immigrant-bashing that mimics the most
shameful episodes in our history. During the 1850s and through the Civil War,

the so-called Know-Nothing party campaigned successfully on an explicitly racist and anti-immigrant platform, and what is disconcerting is that *exactly* the same rhetoric used at that time is prevalent today.

Just this past month, the following "contest" played on a radio station in the state of Michigan. Now try to imagine all the bells and whistles and the appropriate jingles and background music and listen to this as you would be listening to a radio program:

Some are giving away trips to Mexico City, but we are bringing Mexico to *you!* That's right! We are giving away Mexicans—real, live Mexicans! Ay carramba!

We'll be smuggling illegal aliens across the border in the wheel-well of a station van, and then we'll give one to *you!* Imagine—your own personal Mexican! They'll wash your car, clean your house, pick your crops, anything you want. Because if they don't, you'll have them deported!

Adios, amigos. Be the fifth caller when you hear this sound (the sound of a mooing cow) and win a Mexican!

Bathing and delousing of Mexicans is winner's responsibility. Station assumes no liability for infectious diseases carried by Mexicans.

Celebrate Cinco de Mayo in your own home every day with your own Mexican!

How should we interpret these kinds of public remarks? Is it OK to talk about—even in jest—people owning people? Whatever the intent, we know from past history that the first step in oppressing a people is to dehumanize them and/or to demonize them.

And that is exactly what we did to the new Americans that came from Germany, from Ireland, from Italy, from China and Japan, from Hungary. And that is what we did to Jews who came from all over Europe. Anti-immigration legislation specifically aimed at these groups has either passed or nearly passed in our past.

I hasten to add that there are well-meaning Americans who believe in more restrictionist immigration policies who are neither racist nor xenophobic. Some Americans are honestly worried about the total population of this nation and about our collective ability to accommodate differences in culture and language. Others truly believe that immigrants cost the taxpayer additional burdens.

These are reasonable concerns that can be addressed by the facts. And the facts are that the number of foreign-born in the United States as a percentage of our population is not any higher than it has been in our past. The fact is that today's new Americans are assimilating faster than previous immigrants. The fact is that immigrants are not a net burden to the United States taxpayer but a net contributor, a significant contributor.

Yet we should all be worried about continued undocumented immigration and about exploitation of human beings—be they documented, undocumented, immigrant, or native-born.

We also know that economic security fuels our worst fears and brings out our meanest instincts. During every single recession, and especially during the Great Depression, the United States implemented policies that should bring shame to all of us. While precise figures are hard to come by, we can confidently estimate that well over one million legal immigrants and American citizens have been illegally and unjustly deported during economic downturns.

Today, we are witnessing a replay of history. Politicians from both parties are scapegoating immigrants for our economic and social problems. Apparently there is a great deal of political capital in demonizing immigrants.

Regretfully, there are few statesmen willing to stand tall and bring reason and decency to this debate.

We need leaders like my own personal hero, President Harry Truman. He stood up to Congress and vetoed a racist immigration bill, and he sent the following message to Congress and to the American people, and let me quote:

> The idea behind this policy [referring to the quota system] was, to put it boldly, that Americans with English or Irish names were better people and better citizens than Americans with Italian or Greek or Polish names. . . . Such a concept is utterly unworthy of our traditions and our ideals. It violates the great political doctrine of the Declaration of Independence that "all men are created equal". . . . It is incredible to me that, in this year of 1952, we should again be enacting into law such a slur on the patriotism, the capacity, and the decency of a large part of our citizenry.

Well, now we're here in 1994, and today we are not only slurring the decency of people, we are questioning their very humanity.

Thank you, have a great life, and God bless.

LOUIS FARRAKHAN
(1933–)

A Million Men Marching On
OCTOBER 17, 1995

We're not here to tear down America.
America is tearing itself down.

Minister Louis Farrakhan, born Louis Eugene Wilcott in Boston, Massachusetts, abandoned a promising career as a musician and entertainer to follow in the footsteps of Elijah Muhammad and Malcolm X as a leader of the Nation of Islam. During his time as an entertainer, Farrakhan was called "the charmer," and though he can no longer be heard swooning to the lyrics of calypso on the airwaves, the charismatic timbre of his voice has been at least partly responsible for the Nation of Islam's success in more than eighty cities across the United States, Great Britain, and Ghana. Since the late 1970s, following in the tradition, once promulgated by Booker T. Washington and Marcus Garvey, of emphasizing economic empowerment, community, and education, Farrakhan has sought to consolidate the African-American community's political and social gains.

But his gospel has also been a polarizing force, drawing the ire of ethnic and religious groups. He has been branded a racist, separatist, sexist, and anti-Semite. Farrakhan called Jews, Arabs, Koreans, and Vietnamese "bloodsuckers . . . because they took from our community and built their community." Countless leaders have decried his firebrand comments and repeated calls for black power.

As expected, civil rights leaders were wary when Farrakhan called for "a million sober, disciplined, committed, dedicated, inspired black men to meet in Washington in a day of atonement." Still, more than half a million men took Farrakhan up on his challenge, boarded buses and trains from across the country, and met in Washington on October 17, 1995 for a twelve-hour rally on a crisp, fall day. Leaders from the Anti-Defamation League to the president of the United States hit the airwaves in protest of the "Million Man March," not of its call for family unity and responsibility, but of Louis Farrakhan and the following two-hour speech—delivered from the Capitol steps, just a stone's throw from the Lincoln Memorial. The *New York Times* later critiqued his remarks as "convoluted," "rambling," and filled with "arcane references to the Bible, numerology, and . . . sulfurous interpretations of history."

〰〰〰

ABRAHAM LINCOLN was the 16th President of these United States and he was the man who allegedly freed us.

Abraham Lincoln saw in his day, what President Clinton sees in this day. He saw the great divide between black and white. Abraham Lincoln and Bill Clinton see what the Kerner Commission saw 30 years ago when they said that this nation was moving toward two Americas—one black, one white, separate and unequal. And the Kerner Commission revisited their findings 25 years later and saw that America was worse today than it was in the time of Martin Luther King, Jr. There's still two Americas, one black, one white, separate and unequal.

Abraham Lincoln, when he saw this great divide, he pondered a solution of separation. Abraham Lincoln said he never was in favor of our being jurors or having equal status with the whites of this nation. Abraham Lincoln said that if there were to be a superior or inferior, he would rather the superior position be assigned to the white race. There, in the middle of this mall is the Washington Monument, 555 feet high. But if we put a one in front of that 555 feet, we get 1555, the year that our first fathers landed on the shores of Jamestown, Virginia, as slaves.

In the background is the Jefferson and Lincoln Memorial, each one of these monuments is 19 feet high.

Abraham Lincoln, the sixteenth president. Thomas Jefferson, the third president, and 16 and three make 19 again. What is so deep about this number 19? Why are we standing on the Capitol steps today? That number 19—when you have a nine you have a womb that is pregnant. And when you have a one standing by the nine, it means that there's something secret that has to be unfolded.

Right here on this mall where we are standing, according to books written on Washington, D.C., slaves used to be brought right here on this Mall in chains to be sold up and down the eastern seaboard. Right along this mall, going over to the White House, our fathers were sold into slavery. But, George Washington, the first president of the United States, said he feared that before too many years passed over his head, this slave would prove to become a most troublesome species of property.

Thomas Jefferson said he trembled for this country when he reflected that God was just and that his justice could not sleep forever. Well, the day that these presidents feared has now come to pass, for on this mall, here we stand in the capital of America. And the layout of this great city, laid out by a black man, Benjamin Banneker. This is all placed and based in a secret Masonic rit-ual. And at the core of the secret of that ritual is the black man. Not far from here is the White House.

And the first president of this land, George Washington, who was a grand master of the Masonic order, laid the foundation, the cornerstone of this capi-tol building where we stand. George was a slave owner. Now, the President spoke today and he wanted to heal the great divide. But I respectfully suggest to the President, you did not dig deep enough at the malady that divides black and white in order affect a solution to the problem.

And so, today, we have to deal with the root so that perhaps a healing can take place.

Now, this obelisk at the Washington Monument is Egyptian and this whole layout is reminiscent of our great historic past, Egypt. And if you look at the original Seal of the United States, published by the Department of State in 1909. Gaylord Hunt wrote that late in the afternoon of July 4, 1776, the Continental Congress resolved that Dr. Benjamin Franklin, Mr. John Adams, and Mr. Thomas Jefferson be a committee to prepare a device for a Seal of the United States of America.

In the design proposed by the first committee, the face of the Seal was a coat of arms measured in six quarters. That number is significant. Six quarters, with emblems representing England, Scotland, Ireland, France, Germany and Holland, the countries from which the new nation had been peopled. The eye of providence in a radiant triangle and the motto "E Pluribus Unum" were also proposed for the face of the Seal. Even [though] the country was popu-lated by so-called Indians and black slaves were brought to build the country, the official Seal of the country was never designed to reflect our presence, only that of the European immigrants. The Seal and the Constitution reflect the thinking of the founding fathers, that this was to be a nation by white people and for white people. Native Americans, blacks, and all other non-white peo-ple were to be the burden bearers for the real citizens of this nation.

For the back of the Seal the committee suggested a picture of Pharaoh sit-ting in an open chariot with a crown on his head and a sword in his hand, passing through the divided waters of the Red Sea, in pursuit of the Israelites. And, hovering over the sea was to be shown a pillar of fire in a cloud, expres-sive of the divine presence and command.

And raised from this pillar of fire were to be shown, beaming down on Moses standing on the shore, extending his hand over the sea, causing it to overwhelm Pharaoh.

The motto for the reverse was, "Rebellion To Tyrants Is Obedience To God." Let me say it again. Rebellion is obedience to God. Now, why did they mention Pharaoh? I heard the President say today E Pluribus Unum—out of many, one.

But in the past, "out of many comes one" meant out of many Europeans come one people. The question today is, out of the many Asians, the many Arabs, the many Native Americans, the many Blacks, the many people of color who populate this country: Do you mean for them to be made into the one?

If so, truth has to be spoken to justice. We can't cover things up. Cover them over. Give it a pretty sound to make people feel good. We have to go to the root of the problem. Now, why have you come today?

You came not at the call of Louis Farrakhan, but you have gathered here at the call of God. For it is only the call of Almighty God, no matter through whom that call came, that could generate this kind of outpouring. God called us here to this place. At this time. For a very specific reason.

And now I want to say, my brothers—this is a very pregnant moment. Pregnant with the possibility of tremendous change in our status in America and in the world. And although the call was made through me, many have tried to distance the beauty of this idea from the person through whom the idea and the call was made.

Some have done it mistakenly. And others have done it in a malicious and vicious manner. Brothers and sisters, there is no human being through whom God brings an idea that history doesn't marry the idea with that human being, no matter what defect was [in] that human being's character.

⌒

When you say, "Farrakhan, you ain't no Moses, you ain't no Jesus, and you're not no Muhammad. You have a defect in your character."

Well, that certainly may be so, however, according to the way the Bible reads, there is no prophet of God written of in the Bible that did not have a defect in his character. . . .

So today, whether you like it or not, God brought the idea through me and he didn't bring it through me because my heart was dark with hatred and anti-Semitism, he didn't bring it through me because my heart was dark and I'm filled with hatred for white people and for the human family of the planet. If my heart were that dark, how is the message so bright, the message so clear, the response so magnificent?

So we stand here today at this historic moment. We are standing in the place of those who couldn't make it here today. We are standing on the blood of our ancestors. We are standing on the blood of those who died in the middle passage, who died in the fields and swamps of America, who died hanging from trees in the South, who died in the cells of their jailers, who died on the highways and who died in the fratricidal conflict that rages within our community. We are standing on the sacrifice of the lives of those heroes, our great men and women that we today may accept the responsibility that life imposes upon each traveler who comes this way.

We must accept the responsibility that God has put upon us, not only to be good husbands and fathers and builders of our community, but God is now calling upon the despised and the rejected to become the cornerstone and the builders of a new world.

And so, our brief subject today is taken from the American Constitution. In these words, Toward a more union. Toward a more perfect union.

Now, when you use the word "more" with "perfect," that which is perfect is that which has been brought to completion. So when you use "more perfect," you're either saying that what you call perfect is perfect for that stage of its development but not yet complete. When Jefferson said, "toward a more perfect union," he was admitting that the union was not perfect, that it was not finished, that work had to be done. And so we are gathered here today not to bash somebody else.

We're not gathered here to say, all of the evils of this nation. But we are gathered here to collect ourselves for a responsibility that God is placing on our shoulders to move this nation toward a more perfect union. Now, when you look at the word "toward," it means in the direction of, in furtherance or partial fulfillment of, with the view to obtaining or having shortly before coming soon, eminent, going on in progress. Well, that's right. We're in progress toward a perfect union. Union means bringing elements or components into unity.

It is something formed by uniting two or more things. It is a number of persons, states, et cetera, which are joined or associated together for some common purpose. We're not here to tear down America. America is tearing itself down. We are here to rebuild the wasted cities. What we have in the word "toward" is motion. The honorable Elijah Muhammad taught us that motion is the first law of the universe. This motion which takes us from one point to another shows that we are evolving and we are a part of a universe that is ever evolving.

We are on an evolutionary course that will bring us to perfect or completion of the process toward a perfect union with God. In the word "toward" there is a law and that law is everything that is created is in harmony with the law of evolution, change. Nothing is standing still.

It is either moving toward perfection or moving toward disintegration. Or under certain circumstances doing both things at the same time. The word for this evolutionary changing affecting stage after stage until we reach perfection, in Arabic it is called Rhab. And from the word "Rhab" you get the Rhaby, or teacher, one who nourishes a people from one stage and brings them to another stage. Well, if we are in motion, and we are, motion toward perfection, and we are, there can be no motion toward perfection without the Lord, who created the law of evolution.

And [the Lord] is the master of the changes. Our first motion then must be toward the God who created the law of the evolution of our being. And if our motion toward him is right and proper, then our motion toward a perfect union with each other and government and with the peoples of the world will be perfected. So let us start with a process leading to that perfect union must first be seen. Now, brothers and sisters, the day of atonement is established by God to help us achieve a closer tie with the source of wisdom, knowledge, understanding and power.

We are a wounded people but we're being healed, but President Clinton, America is also wounded. And there's hostility now in the great divide between the people. Socially the fabric of America is being torn apart and it's black against black, black against white, white against white, white against black, yellow against brown, brown against yellow. We are being torn apart. And we can't gloss it over with nice speeches, my dear Mr. President.

Sir, with all due respect, that was a great speech you made today. And you praised the marchers and they're worthy of praise. You honored the marchers and they are worthy of honor. But of course, you spoke ill indirectly of me, as a purveyor of malice and hatred.

I must hasten to tell you, Mr. President, that I'm not a malicious person, and I'm not filled with malice. But, I must tell you that I come in the tradition of the doctor who has to point out, with truth, what's wrong. And the pain is that power has made America arrogant. Power and wealth has made America spiritually blind and the power and the arrogance of America makes you refuse to hear a child of your slaves pointing out the wrong in your society.

And so, the eighth stage is perfect union with god. And in the Koran, it reads: "Oh soul that is at rest, well pleased with thy lord and well pleasing." Oh, brothers, brothers, brothers, you don't know what it's like to be free. Freedom can't come from white folks. Freedom can't come from staying here and petitioning this great government. We're here to make a statement to the great government, but not to beg them. Freedom [can] come from no one but the God who can liberate the soul from the burden of sin. And this is why Jesus said "Come unto me," not some who are heavy laden, "but all that are heavy laden, and I will give you rest."

I want to wash in the river of Jordan and the river that you see and the sea that is before us and behind us and around us.

It's validation. That's the mainstream. You're out of touch with reality. A few of you in a few smoke-filled rooms, calling that the mainstream while the masses of the people, white and black, red, yellow, and brown, poor and vulnerable are suffering in this nation.

America. America, the beautiful. There's no country like this on the earth. And certainly if I lived in another country, I might never have had the opportunity to speak as I speak today. I probably would have been shot outright and so would my brother Jesse and so would . . . Reverend Al Sampson and the wonderful people that are here.

But because this is America you allow me to speak even though you don't like what I may say. Because this is America, that provision in the constitution for freedom of speech and freedom of assembly and freedom of religion, that is your saving grace.

Because what you're under right now is grace. And grace is the expression of divine love and protection which God bestows freely on people.

And yet I point out the evils of black people like no other leader does, but my people don't call me anti-black, because they know I must love them in order to point out what's wrong so we can get it right to come back into the favor of God!

But, let me say in truth, you can't point out wrong with malice. You can't point out wrong with hatred. Because, if we point out wrong with bitterness and hatred, then the bitterness and the hatred becomes a barrier between you and the person whom you hope to get right, that they might come into the favor of God.

. . . The other is fratricidal conflict, drugs and dope and violence and crime. But we've had enough now. This is why you're in Washington today. We've had enough. We've had enough distress, enough affliction. We're ready to bow down now. If my people who are called by my name would just humble themselves and pray, and seek my face, and turn from their wicked ways, then will I hear from heaven, forgive their sins, heal their land.

You are ready now to climb out of your furnace of affliction. You are ready now to accept the responsibility, oh, not just of the ghetto. God wants to purify you and lift you up, that you may call America and the world to repentance. Black man, you are a master builder, but you got hit in the head.

The Democratic Party has for its symbol a donkey. The donkey stands for the unlearned masses of the people. But the Democratic Party can't call them asses no more. You got them all tied up, but you're not using. The donkey is tied up. But can you get off today? No, I can't get off, I'm tied up. Somebody on your donkey? Well, yeah. I got a master. He rides me like the Master rode Balaam's ass, you know. But, hail, the ass is now talking with a man's voice. And the ass wants to throw the rider off, because he got a new rider today.

If anybody ask you, tell them the Master has need. Look at you. Oh, I don't know what the number is. It's too much for me to count. But I think they said it's a million and a half, or two. I don't know how many. But you know, I called for a million. When I saw the word go out my mouth, I looked at it. I said, Oh, my God! It just came out of my mouth. I didn't know. And after it came out, I said, Well I got to go with it. And, I'm so glad I did. People told me you better change that figure to one more realistic. And I should have changed it to the Three Million Man March.

⌇

A woman, remember the nine, means somebody pregnant, with an idea. But, in this case, its a woman pregnant with a male child destined to rule the nations with a rod of iron. God is standing over her womb, and this child will be like the day sun, and he will say, "I am the light of the world." Hands coming out of that sun, come unto me all ye that are heavy laden. I'm gonna give you rest, but I'm gonna give you life, because I am the resurrection and the life, and if you believe in me, though you are dead, yet shall you live again.

You're dead, black man. But if you believe in the God who created this sun of truth and of light with 19 rays, meaning he's pregnant with God's spirit, God's life, God's wisdom. Abraham Lincoln's statue, 19 feet high, 19 feet wide. Jefferson, 19 feet high, and the third president, 19. Standing on the steps of the Capitol, in the light of the sun. Offering life to a people who are dead.

⌇

I'm not telling you I'm a psychiatrist, but I do want to operate on your head. White supremacy is the enemy of both white people and black people because the idea of white supremacy means you should rule because you're White; that makes you sick. And you've produced a sick society and a sick world. The founding fathers meant well, but they said, "toward a more perfect union." So the Bible says, we know in part, we prophesy in part, but when that which is perfect is come, that which is in part shall be done away with.

So either, Mr. Clinton, we're going to do away with the mind-set of the founding fathers. You don't have to repudiate them like you've asked my brothers to do me. You don't have to say they were malicious, hate-filled people. But you must evolve out of their mind-set. You see, their minds [were] limited to those six European nations out of which this country was founded. But you've got Asians here. How are you going to handle that? You've got children of Africa here. How are you going to handle that?

You've got Arabs here. You've got Hispanics here. I know you call them illegal aliens, but hell, you took Texas from them by flooding Texas with people that got your mind. And now they're coming back across the border to what is northern Mexico, Texas, Arizona, New Mexico, and California. They don't see themselves as illegal aliens. I think they might see you as an illegal alien. You have to be careful how you talk to people. You have to be careful how you deal with people. The Native American is suffering today. He's suffering almost complete extinction. Now, he learned about bingo. You taught him. He learned about black jack. You taught him. He learned about playing roulette. You taught him. Now he's making a lot of money. You're upset with him because he's adopted your ways. What makes you like this? See, you're like this because you're not well. You're not well. And in the light of today's global village, you can never harmonize with the Asians. You can't harmonize with the islands of the Pacific.

You can't harmonize with the dark people of the world who outnumber you 11 to one if you're going to stand in the mind of white supremacy. White supremacy has to die in order for humanity to live.

Now, oh, I know. I know. I know it's painful, but we have to operate now, just, just take a little of this morphine and you won't feel the pain as much. You just need to bite down on something, as I stop this last few minutes, just bite down on your finger. Listen, listen, listen, listen, white supremacy caused you all, not you all, some white folk, to try to rewrite history and write us out. White supremacy caused Napoleon to blow the nose off of the Sphinx because it reminded you too much of the Black man's majesty.

White supremacy caused you to take Jesus, a man with hair like lambs wool and feet like burnished brass and make him white. So that you could worship him because you could never see yourself honoring somebody black because of the state of your mind. You see, you, you really need help. You'll be all right. You'll be all right. You will be all right. Now, now, now, you painted the Last Supper, everybody there white.

My mother asked the man that came to bring her the Bible. He said, "Look there, the pictures in the Bible. You see, Jesus and all his disciples are at the Last Supper"—my mother in her West Indian accent said, "You mean ain't nobody Black was at the Last Supper?"

And the man said, "Yes, but they was in the kitchen." So now you've whitened up everything.

Any great invention we made you put white on it, because you didn't want to admit that a Black person had that intelligence, that genius. You try to color everything to make it satisfactory to the sickness of our mind.

So you whitened up religion, Farrakhan didn't do that. You locked the Bible from us, Farrakhan didn't do that. Your sick mind wouldn't even let you bury us in the same ground that both of us came out of. We had to be buried somewhere else, that's sick. Some of us died just to drink water out of a fountain marked white. That's sick. Isn't it sick?

You poisoned religion. And in all the churches, until recently, the master was painted white. So you had us bowing down to your image. Which ill-affected our minds. You gave us your version of history. And you whitened that up. Yes, you did. Yes, you did.

You are a white Shriner. The black Shriner don't integrate the shrine. Why don't you black Shriners integrate the shrine? Because in the shrine, you are the essence of the secret. They don't want you there. They'll have to tell the world, it's you we been thinking about all along.

Now, white folks see the reason you could look at the O.J. Simpson trial, in horror, and the reason black folk rejoiced had nothing to do with the horror of the tragedy. Black folk would never rejoice over the slaughter of Ron Goldman and Nicole Brown Simpson.

Black folk saw that with compassion. Many black folk grieve over that reality. You say, "O.J. sold out." No, he didn't sell out. He was drawn out.

Black folk that got talent, they all grow up in the "hood." When we first sing, we sing in these old raunchy night clubs in the hood.

When we play sandlot ball, we play it in the hood. But when you spot us, you draw us out. You say, "That Negro can run. Look at how high he jumps." So you give us a scholarship to your university. But the blacks who are in college, who play basketball for you, who play football for you, who run track for you, you disallow them to get involved with black students and the suffering of black students on all-white campuses. You hide them away. Give them privileges. Then they find themselves with your daughter.

Then you take them into the NBA, the NFL, and they become megastars. Or in the entertainment field, and when they become megastars, their association is no longer black. They may not have a black manager, a black agent, a black accountant. They meet in parties, in posh neighborhoods that black folk don't come into. So their association becomes white women, white men, and association breeds assimilation. And if you have a slave mentality, you feel you have arrived now, because you can jump over cars, running in airports, playing in films.

I'm not degrading my brother, I love him. But he was drawn out. He didn't sell out, he was drawn out. Michael Jackson is drawn out. Most of our top stars are drawn out. And then, when you get them, you imprison them with fear and distrust. You don't want them to speak out on the issues that are political, that are social. They must shut their mouths or you threaten to take away their fame, take away their fortune, because you're sick. And the president is not gonna point this out. He's trying to get well. But he's a physician that can't heal himself.

I'm almost finished. White supremacy has poisoned the bloodstream of religion, education, politics, jurisprudence, economics, social ethics and morality.

And there is no way that we can integrate into white supremacy and hold our dignity as human beings, because if we integrate into that, we become subservient to that. And to become subservient to that is to make the slave master comfortable with his slave. So, we got to come out of her, my people. Come out of a system and a world that is built on the wrong idea. An idea that never can create a perfect union with God.

The false idea of white supremacy prevents anyone from becoming one with God. White people have to come out of that idea, which has poisoned them into a false attitude of superiority based on the color of their skins. The doctrine of white supremacy disallows whites to grow to their full potential. It forces white people to see themselves as the law or above the law. And that's why [Mark] Fuhrman could say that he is like a god. See, he thinks like that, but that idea is pervasive in police departments across the country. And it's getting worse and not better, because white supremacy is not being challenged.

And I say to all of us who are leaders, all of us who are preachers, we must not shrink from the responsibility of pointing out wrong, so that we can be comfortable and keep white people comfortable in their alienation from God. And so, white folks are having heart attacks today because their world is coming down. And if you look at the Asians, the Asians have the fastest growing economies in the world. The Asians are not saying, bashing white people. You don't find the Asians saying the white man is this, the white man is that, the white man is the other.

He don't talk like that. You know what he does? He just relocates the top banks from Wall Street to Tokyo. He don't say, I'm better than the white man. He just starts building his world and building his economy and challenging white supremacy. I saw a young 14-year-old Chinese girl the other day play the violin.

———

Black man, you don't have to bash white people, all we gotta do is go back home and turn our communities into productive places. All we gotta do is go back home and make our communities a decent and safe place to live. And if we start dotting the black community with businesses, opening up factories, challenging ourselves to be better than we are, white folk, instead of driving by, using the "N" word, they'll say, look, look at them. Oh, my God. They're marvelous. They're wonderful. We can't, we can't say they're inferior anymore. But every time we drive-by shoot, every time we carjack, every time we use foul, filthy language, every time we produce culturally degenerate films and tapes, putting a string in our women's backside and parading them before the world, every time we do things like this we are feeding the degenerate mind of white supremacy, and I want us to stop feeding that mind and let that mind die a natural death.

And so, to all the artists that are present, you wonderful gifted artists, remember that your gift comes from God. And David the Psalmist said, "Praise Him on the timbrel, praise Him on the lute, praise Him on the harp, praise Him in the sultry, praise in the song, praise him in the dance, let everything be a praise of God."

So, when you sing, you don't have to get naked to sing. Demonstrate your gift, not your breast. Demonstrate your gift, not what is between your legs. Clean up, black man, and the world will respect and honor you. But you have fallen down like the prodigal son, and you're husking corn and feeding swine.

Filthy jokes. We can't bring our children to the television.

We can't bring our families to the movies because the American people have an appetite like a swine. And you are feeding the swine with the filth of degenerate culture. We got to stop it.

We're not putting you down, brothers, we want to pick you up so, with your rap, you can pick up the world. With your song, you can pick up the world. With your dance, with your music, you can pick up the world.

And so America, if your conscience is afflicted because God is lashing you, don't just start with the constitution, Mr. President. Start with the evil of slavery because that's the root of the problem.

And you can't solve the problem, Mr. President, unless we expose the root. For when you expose the root to the light, then the root will die. The tree will die. And something new can come to birth. And so to the whites of this nation, except you be born again, you cannot see the kingdom of God. But can I return back into my mother's womb for the second time? No. You can't do that. But this old mind of white supremacy has to die in order that a new mind might come to birth.

Go back, join the NAACP if you want to, join the Urban League, join the All African People's Revolutionary Party, join us, join the Nation of Islam, join PUSH, join the Congress of Racial Equality, join SCLC—the Southern Christian Leadership Conference—but we must become a totally organized people and the only way we can do that is to become a part of some organization that is working for the uplift of our people.

We must keep the local organizing committees that made this event possible, we must keep them together. And then all of us, as leaders, must stay together and make the National African American Leadership Summit inclusive of all of us.

. . . [W]e must continue to reach out for those that have condemned this, and make them to see that this was not evil, it was not intended for evil, it intended for good. Now, brothers, moral and spiritual renewal is a necessity. Every one of you must go back home and join some church, synagogue or temple or mosque that is teaching spiritual and moral uplift. I want you, brothers— there's no men in the church, in the mosque.

The men are in the streets and we got to get back to the houses of God. But preachers, we have to revive religion in America.

We have to revive the houses of God that they're not personal thiefdoms of those of us who are their preachers and pastors. But we got to be more like Jesus, more like Muhammad, more like Moses and become servants of the people in fulfilling their needs.

Brothers, when you go home, we've got to register eight million eligible but unregistered brothers, sisters. So you go home and find eight more like yourself. You register and get them to register. Should I register as Democrat? Should I register as a Republican? Should I register as independent?

If you're an independent, that's fine. If you're a Democrat, that's fine. If you're a Republican, that's OK. Because in local elections you have to do that which is in the best interest of your local community. But what we want is not necessarily a third party, but a third force.

———

We're no longer going to vote for somebody just because they're black. We tried that. We wish we could. But we got to vote for you, if you are compatible with our agenda.

———

And we want to show them that never again will they ever disrespect the black community. We must make them afraid to do evil to us and think they can get away with it.

———

Now atonement goes beyond us. I don't like this squabble with the members of the Jewish community. I don't like it. The honorable Elijah Muhammad said in one of his writings that he believed that we would work out some kind of an accord. Maybe so. Reverend Jackson has talked to the 12 presidents of Jewish organizations and perhaps in the light of what we see today, maybe it's time to sit down and talk. Not with any preconditions. You got pain. Well, we've got pain, too. You hurt. We hurt, too.

———

How many of you will adopt one black man in prison and make him your pal, your brother for life. Help him through the incarceration. Well, go to the chaplain of that jail and say you want to adopt one inmate. Start writing to that person, visiting that person, helping that person. And since so many of us have been there already, we know what they suffer. Let's help our brothers and sisters who are locked down.

Is that agreeable, Black man? Now, brothers, I want you to take this pledge. When I say "I," I want you to say "I," and I'll say your name. I know that there's so many names, but I want you to shout your name out so that the ancestors can hear it.

Take this pledge with me. Say with me please, "I," say your name, "pledge that from this day forward I will strive to love my brother as I love myself. I," say your name, "from this day forward will strive to improve myself spiritually, morally, mentally, socially, politically, and economically for the benefit of myself, my family, and my people. I," say your name, "pledge that I will strive to build business, build houses, build hospitals, build factories, and then to enter international trade for the good of myself, my family, and my people. I," say your name, "pledge that from this day forward I will never raise my hand with a knife or a gun to beat, cut, or shoot any member of my family or any human being, except in self-defense."

"I," say your name, "pledge from this day forward I will never abuse my wife by striking her, disrespecting her, for she is the mother of my children and the producer of my future. I," say your name, "pledge that from this day forward I will never engage in the abuse of children, little boys, or little girls for sexual gratification. But I will let them grow in peace to be strong men and women for the future of our people. I," say your name, "will never again use the 'B' word to describe my female, but particularly my own black sister."

"I," say your name, "pledge from this day forward that I will not poison my body with drugs or that which is destructive to my health and my well-being. I," say your name, "pledge from this day forward, I will support black newspapers, black radio, black television. I will support black artists, who clean up their acts to show respect for themselves and respect for their people, and respect for the ears of the human family."

Now, let us not be conformed to this world, but let us go home transformed by the renewing of our minds and let the idea of atonement ring throughout America.

That America may see that the slave has come up with power. The slave [has] been restored, delivered, and redeemed. And now call this nation to repentance. To acknowledge her wrongs. To confess, not in secret documents, called classified, but to come before the world and the American people as the Japanese prime minister did and confess her faults before the world because her sins have affected the whole world. And perhaps, she may do some act of atonement, that you may forgive and those ill-affected may forgive, that reconciliation and restoration may lead us to the perfect union with thee and with each other. We ask all of this in your Holy and Righteous Name, Allah akbar. Allah akbar. Allah akbar. That means God is great.

Turn to your brother and hug your brother and tell your brother you love him and let's carry this love all the way back to our cities and towns and never let it die, brothers. Never let it die.

Yuri Kochiyama

(1922–)

Consciousness Is Power

November 3, 1995

Consciousness-raising is pertinent for power . . . used for building
trust and goodwill domestically and internationally.

Since her time as a young woman in a Japanese-American internment camp during World War II, Yuri Kochiyama has been a dedicated fighter against injustice. During the war, with her family interned at a camp in Arkansas, Kochiyama witnessed black oppression firsthand—and recognized its striking parallels to Asian discrimination. In 1960 she moved to Harlem and quickly became immersed in the mainstream civil rights movement. With her six children by her side, Kochiyama joined the struggles of the Harlem community, including a fight for more traffic lights to increase pedestrian safety and equal education for black children in public schools. Thereafter, she became a radical, nationalist, and ardent advocate of the Black Panthers—building a bridge between their mission and the Japanese-American cause for reparations. In all, for nearly half a century, Kochiyama has championed the rights of Japanese Americans and lobbied for other humanitarian causes, including nuclear disarmament and the rights of international prisoners.

On November 3, 1995, Kochiyama addressed the annual Asian American Convocation at Brown University in Providence, Rhode Island. In her remarks, she outlined the history of the Asian-American movement in the context of the broader American civil rights movement. Kochiyama also encouraged young Asian Americans to embrace and celebrate their heritage and work toward parity across racial lines.

———

WHEN WE THINK of the question of how Asian Americans can fit into this society, we must be conscious that, although this is supposed to be an open and democratic society, there is a polarization by race and class. What issues Asian/Pacific Islanders should be concerned about are issues that pertain to them, like affirmative action, immigrant rights, anti-Asian violence, or more so, racial violence to anyone; and homophobia in the Asian community. Of course, there are dozens of other issues.

In regard to priorities, each of our lives are different. Thus, our priorities are different. For some, it may be an aging grandparent that must be cared for, or hanging on to a part-time job while trying to finish college; paying back a debt or loan; or taking care of one's own health problem. We are, each, accountable to our own priorities.

The question of who are our allies and who are the "opposition" is a political question. I am referring to who are the allies for Asian/Pacific Islanders as a group? Who would oppose issues important to us? Asians, themselves, are divided by class, perhaps more than by ethnicity. Thus, to answer, it must be analyzed and answered by which class of Asians do we support? If our concern is for those at the bottom, the newly arrived immigrants, and those who are marginalized, our allies are the progressives who believe in equality, justice, and human rights.

Our opposition is the government and those in power if we are measuring by what is happening today with budget cuts in human services. Where you stand as both an Asian or/and as an individual is pertinent. Hopefully, with consciousness-raising, your/our decision will side with those in greatest need.

How do we measure this society, and the general lot of Asians and Asian Pacific Americans? You, as students, can be good judges for you can study and research into the history of this country, the most powerful and richest nation in the world, with the highest living standard, with abundant technical mechanisms accessible, and with a large percent of students in higher education. But find out also how America became so powerful, and was it through inclusion or exclusion? And what about slavery?

There are pockets of poverty in the U.S. comparable to the Third World, and "Americans" who are not only impoverished, but powerless and dispossessed. Visibly, there are two Americas: one predominantly white with a more comfortable style of living and with unlimited opportunities; and the other, areas of people of color, sometimes living in [a] ghetto atmosphere, with high unemployment, homelessness, drug-affliction, lack of health care, poorly run schools, an unusually high rate of their men in prison, and a relatively small enrollment in colleges. This most often happens in Black and Latino communities, and also in Hawai'i. What does that say for America?

And how do we measure the Asians? We are not a monolithic entity. We are many different ethnic people. We are Asian immigrants, Asian American, part Asian, Amer-Asian, Asian national, Asian adoptee (mostly Korean), and a Korean category that calls itself "1.5." We are divided by class, religion, culture, language, and political affiliation. But because of racism and discrimination inherent in this society, despite our differences, we are, not just thrust together as Asians, but considered as "outsiders," foreigners, and "not quite Americans." As Asians, we have been victims of racial violence all over the country. We must support one another, protect one another, and see ourselves as part of our

Asian-American family. We must also see all peoples of color in the same light; also all who have been discriminated, the Jews, the Arabs, the lesbians and gays.

No wonder, consciousness-raising is so pertinent to struggle for a more just world. It is a "doing together" kind of thing; sharing with one another; learning in concert with others. It is to raise the consciousness of a group, or masses of people; not just one person or select people. Consciousness for Asian Americans must be a consciousness of Asian America—the whole panorama of Asian/Pacific people, as well as the broader America of diverse peoples which has been polarized by racism and classism. Our consciousness must embrace the whole gamut of all Asian ethnic peoples; consciousness of each of our history, culture, language; and why we are in America. We came at different times; some for economic reasons; some for political reasons; some as people seeking opportunities, or joining their families; or others, as refugees escaping oppression. Despite historical contradictions, we have more in common than differences to separate us. Some of us were born here, and yet have sometimes felt as strangers in our own land. Some even were incarcerated in concentration camps because we were considered enemy aliens during World War II. The reality of our commonality should bring Asians together, yet be flexible enough to understand that we must transcend race, color, religious and class differences if we are to bridge gaps that separate people in America from each other.

Vietnam revealed to the Western world in the '60s that though they were a peasant country, they were willing to tackle the mightiest military and economic power in the world when the U.S. transgressed into Vietnam, purportedly to save democracy. But it was more to stop Communism, their choice of a national ideology, but something America demonized. Vietnam won by ousting the U.S. military from their soil. Again, consciousness was their power. Under the guidance and inspiration of Ho Chi Minh, a nation was spurred to fight a David and Goliath battle, a Goliath who had already influenced a part of Vietnam to the U.S. side. The Vietnamese patriots, however, knew what they were fighting for. They were not going to let another foreign power rule them and take away their natural resources. They stopped France and Japan. Now it was the U.S. that was attempting to do the same. But the Vietnamese freedom fighters knew what they were fighting for. They were willing to make the sacrifice. Independence meant more than life. And though three million Vietnamese died and the nation became impoverished, Vietnam is still independent. To the Asian American students of the '60s and '70s, watching in awe through the television and becoming involved in protesting the war, an awakening took place. It was consciousness-raising for Asian/Pacific American students—a learning experience about imperialism, colonialism, and chauvinism.

It is also food-for-thought for Asians to launch some effort for Asian/Pacific unity of all Asian ethnic groups. Asian Americans do need to raise consciousness about each other and work in solidarity with each other [so] that we will never be pitted against each other. But actually, the Asian/Pacific movement from its inception has been Pan-Asian, which has been its greatest strength. We have always been a Pan-Asian entity. But because in the late '60s and early '70s, there were limited Asian groups in the movement (mostly just Chinese, Japanese, Filipinos, some Koreans and Vietnamese), there seemed to be certain Asian national chauvinism. But since the mid-'70s, with the increasing numbers of Southeast Asians (Cambodians, Hmong, Laotian, Thais) and South Asians (East Indians, Pakistanis, Indonesians, Malaysians and others from that area) becoming involved, there is now a broader, more diversified, stronger, more political span of Asian/Pacific representation. In those early movement days, fighting for ethnic studies; protesting the Vietnam War; learning about "identity crisis," Third World unity, political ideologies, and community involvement [all were] a period of growing up and bonding and finding that there was a wonderful, close-knit movement family.

The Pan-Asian/Pacific American movement marched, leafleted, petitioned, held forums, and often joined with Blacks, Latinos, American Indians, and progressive whites. They organized many consciousness-raising programs. They engaged in affirmative action struggles to open doors for people of color or the marginalized or discriminated. In later years, for lesbians and gays. Students fought hard against the conservative forces that became more prevalent. To break down the walls, climb over the barriers, unlock the doors of racism, was the concerted effort of thousands of Asian/Pacific Americans and other ethnics of the prior generation.

But what is happening today? Affirmative action is being contested, and may be going, going, gone—unless it is fought for again. It is your generation that must sustain it, save it. The new immigrant Asian groups need affirmative action just as Asians 30, 40, 50 years ago needed it. Don't let affirmative action die! Revive it! Fight for it! Despite opposition from some Asians, themselves, who are speaking out against it, think of the Asians at the bottom of the economic ladder who need help; who need doors to be kept open for education, housing, jobs; who need opportunities that can change their lives.

Consciousness-raising is power. The Black Panthers did it. The Young Lords did it. The American Indian Movement did it. The white anti-imperialists did it. And so did all the Asian groups, whether it was I Wor Kuen in New York's Chinatown, the Asian American Political Alliance at Columbia University, the Triple A (Asian Americans for Action) in New York mid-town, the Red

Guards in San Francisco, the I-Hotel group in San Francisco's Manila Town, the Vietnamese Students for National Liberation, or Korean student activists.

Consciousness-raising accomplished many things in the past: It helped Asians and Asian/Pacific Americans learn about themselves; their history and culture, the life of their foreparents in America; their difficulties and how they coped with them. They learned of the racism their foreparents experienced; also how Asian mothers and fathers worked long hours in the laundries, garment factories, and restaurants on the West Coast; in fish canneries and vegetable farms; lumber yards and produce markets; on pineapple and sugar plantations in Hawai'i; gardening in California or domestic work in New York. The students of the '60s and '70s came to realize how they got into colleges and universities through the sacrifice and often back-breaking labor of their parents.

Today, young Asian Americans like yourselves are earning degrees in every professional field. Life has changed from the kind of lives of the generations before. But consciousness-raising is still key to learn of the past; also it should be a requirement, not just to succeed or survive, but to be part of the humanity that needs participation for change. The great historian and writer Franz Fanon gave an important message in the '60s to activists world-wide. He said: "Each generation must out of its relative obscurity, discover its mission, and fulfill it."

For you young Asian American students, or students in general of any background, who are searching, who have the idealism and enthusiasm, and a natural love for all peoples—fight against racism, chauvinism and imperialism. Fight against polarization of peoples and communities, but understand and respect liberation or sovereignty struggles where peoples in such struggles need the autonomy and privacy of organizing their own fight. Your role can be that [of] supporters. You can also support political prisoners—most of whom are Black, Puerto Rican, and American Indian. The world you will help develop will surely be more understanding, harmonious, and just with equal opportunities; where human dignity and human rights become accessible to all. Leave new footsteps for those following after you.

Remember that consciousness is power. Consciousness is education and knowledge. Consciousness is becoming aware. It is the perfect vehicle for college students. Consciousness-raising is pertinent for power, and be sure that power will not be abusively used, but used for building trust and goodwill domestically and internationally. Tomorrow's world is yours to build.

BARNEY FRANK
(1940–)

Protecting Same-Sex Marriage
JULY 12, 1996

I find it implausible that two men deciding to commit themselves to each other threatens the marriage of people a couple of blocks away.

Born in Bayonne, New Jersey, in 1940, Barney Frank is the most famous openly gay congressman of his time. Frank became politically active while a student at Harvard and in the 1960s joined the civil rights movement in Mississippi. Upon his graduation in 1962, Frank familiarized himself with the local Boston political scene, where—after working for one year as an administrative assistant for Massachusetts representative Michael J. Harrington—Frank strongly believed he could never be an elected official, because he was gay. Yet in 1972 he ran for—and won—a seat in the Massachusetts legislature. After serving in local politics for twelve years, he was elected to the U.S. House of Representatives in 1981, one of the few liberals elected to Congress that year. Frank has since proved to be one of the brightest and most energetic defenders of civil rights issues in the past twenty years.

This excerpt from the *Congressional Record* of July 12, 1996, highlights the debate over a core gay-civil-rights issue—extending those same protections enjoyed by heterosexual married couples to homosexual couples. Frank argued against proposed federal legislation designed to countermand laws passed by the state of Hawaii that legalize gay marriage. As he pointed out, Republicans, long the party of state's rights in the twentieth century, had attempted to violate Hawaii's rights to pass its own legislation concerning marriage. That said, it was Democratic President Bill Clinton who signed the Defense of Marriage Act into law in 1997, handing Frank and the gay movement an unfortunate defeat.

─────

MR. CHAIRMAN, first a word on this amendment. What this amendment aims at is the anti–States' rights portion of this bill. This bill has been grossly misadvertised in several ways. One, it says that it is a defense of marriage, and I will return to that. But it is a defense against a nonattack.

Nothing in what Hawaii is about to say, namely probably sometime late next year or early in 1998 allowing same-sex marriages, nothing in that by any rational explanation would impinge on marriages between men and women. Nothing whatsoever.

The factors that erode marriages, the factors that lead to divorce, the factors that lead to abandonment and spousal abuse, none of them have ever been attributed to, in any significant degree, same-sex marriage.

Now, let me talk a little bit personally. We have had some personal talks. I would feel uncomfortable if I thought I was up here advocating something that I thought would be directly benefiting me.

I should say that Herb Moses, the man I live with, already has my pension rights. He has exactly the same pension rights I have. Zero. I do not pay into the pension. I am not a member of the congressional pension system, so Herb already has those pension rights.

That is not what I am talking about. I am talking about people less well favored in society than I and other Members. I am talking about working people, people who are working together, pooling their incomes, as many Americans do that today in difficult situations and economic circumstances, trying to get back, and feeling a strong emotional bond to each other, deciding they would like to pool their resources in a binding legal way. Hawaii says: We allow you to do that. This bill says: We overrule Hawaii. This bill says there will be no States' rights here.

. . . I want to be particularly clear now. People talk about their marriages being threatened. I find it implausible that two men deciding to commit themselves to each other threatens the marriage of people a couple of blocks away. I find it bizarre.

KWEISI MFUME
(1948–)

A Shining and Powerful Dream
JULY 13, 1997

Whether it is the repugnant act of burning churches in the dark or
desecrating synagogues, . . . or demonstrations against
immigrants, . . . tolerance, once again, has become a dirty word.

Born Frizzel Gray and nicknamed "Pee Wee," Kweisi Mfume took
his current name after his great aunt visited Ghana, sometime after his
twenty-third birthday. Raised in an impoverished Baltimore, Maryland,
community, Mfume had been a high-school dropout and teenage
father. He later said that his new name, which translates as "conquering
son of kings" was "part of my whole life process to remake my life at
the time."

In "remaking" himself, Mfume returned to college, graduating
magna cum laude from Morgan State University. At Morgan he was
active in student politics, edited the college newspaper, and headed the
Black Student Union. He stayed there after graduation, teaching political science and communications, and shortly after was elected to
Baltimore's city council.

With fire in his belly and his popularity on the rise, Mfume was
elected to the U.S. Congress, where he immediately took up the civil
rights cause, rising to the chairmanship of the Congressional Black
Caucus. After a decade of service, Mfume ended his tenure to become
the president of the National Association for the Advancement of
Colored People—the oldest, largest, and strongest civil rights organization in the United States. At the NAACP, building on the legacy of
founding father W.E.B. Du Bois, he has worked tirelessly on an agenda
geared toward political empowerment, educational excellence, and
economy development.

On July 13, 1997, at the NAACP's Eighty-eighth Annual
Convention, Mfume discussed these priorities with ebullience, urging
his fellow African Americans to reject gradualism, place faith in themselves, and work toward immediate change.

THANK YOU VERY MUCH. . . .

I know it's been a long morning. But some of the nights that we suffer through are longer than this. I pray today that those of you who are here who are white will understand the indignity that some of us feel as a result of racism, discrimination and preconceived stereotypes. And we pray that you will be just as indignant. I pray that those of you who are here today, no matter how small your number, who are Hispanic or Latino, Native American or Asian, that you will further understand as we do the need to embrace the concept of coalition even when some in your number and some in our number choose to go their separate ways. And I pray that those of you who are here who are of African ancestry understand as we must the real need to get beyond blame, to get beyond excuse and to once again start doing for ourselves.

Twenty-nine years ago, after two weeks of rioting and civil unrest, the Kerner Commission, appointed by Lyndon Baines Johnson, warned in its report that our nation was moving towards "two societies—one black, one white, separate and unequal." How cynical can one be? America has always been two societies. The master-slave ontology and the doctrine of white supremacy which pre-existed before the republic was founded have made and kept this nation of two societies. That was not where we were headed; that was regrettably where we were then, and in many respects, where we are now.

This nation did not become hypocritical on the matter of race beginning with 1997, for to speak the truth, it was conceived in hypocrisy. Even before the republic was founded, it compromised the moral claim and the moral principles articulated in the Declaration of Independence and in the Preamble to the Constitution, and in all other documents that they issue to justify their revolution against tyranny, having subjected human beings, our ancestors, to a bondage of the flesh as well as a bondage of the spirit.

Everything that the founding fathers claimed for humanity in the name of morality, they contradicted in their attitude towards and in their treatment of the descendants of Africa and the native inhabitants of this land. They spoke with the voice of Jacob, but they moved with the hand of Esaw. The enslavement of the Negro, the extermination of the Indian, and the annexation of the Hispanic made the birth of the American Nation an a conception conceived in hypocrisy, dedicated . . . to the twisted proposition that white men were somehow superior to non-white men and therefore entitled to enslave them, oppress them, and destroy them.

The hypocrisy painted in our nation's beginnings lingered on. It has formed and shaped the American character and the American conscientiousness on the issue of race and skin color. But NAACP, it is not so much the hypocrisy of the past that should concern us now as much as it is the hypocrisy of the present. We have grown in two short centuries from a band of impoverished colonies to become the strongest, the wealthiest, the most powerful, the most influential nation on the face of the Earth.

It is a national tragedy and a national disgrace that after 200 years of progress the goals of racial justice are receding, not advancing. After 200 years, where is the justice in health care when infant mortality rate, heart disease, hypertension, and other ailments continue to drive mortality and morbidity tables in our communities? After 200 years, where is the justice in education when the doors to our colleges and universities are being locked and closed in a concept that goes against the grain of equal opportunity, when some of our most promising students find themselves as nomads, wandering around with no place to go? After 200 years, where is the justice that we worked for and bled for, when a black assistant secretary of education, dancing to somebody else's music, calls for an end of race-based scholarships, as if he got to where he was all by himself? After 200 years, where is economic justice when African-ancestored Americans, Asians and Latinos and Native Americans are condemned to the bottom of the pay scale and government abandons its commitment to affirmative action and employment and education?

No, that check that we read about, that check that was so articulately stated for all of us by Martin Luther King at a mall in Washington, the check that was to be for liberty and equality was drawn on a bank account whose funds had been withdrawn by a new congressional majority that speaks platitudes about doing better but persists in doing worse.

I would hope that word goes out to my former colleagues who were seated here that the bankrupt policies of the new federalism [are] spawning a national environment that encourages discrimination and repudiates opportunity. I wish they'd stayed a little longer so that they might understand what our position is. For we recognize as an organization that our charge has been renewed by an old plague in America, a plague that has resurfaced, Madam Chair, with great abandon—it is a national scourge of insensitivity and intolerance.

Whether it is the repugnant act of burning churches in the dark or desecrating synagogues, whether it is increased violence from malicious groups, bombing attacks on federal buildings, or demonstrations against immigrants simply because they happen to be black and brown and do not speak as we do, tolerance, once again, has become a dirty word. We've lost, as a nation, our ability to be tolerant in terms of one's race, in terms of one's religion, and in terms of one's gender. We have created in many respects an ugly part of America that still loves too little and hates too much. Jim Crow, Sr., is dead, but Jim Crow, Jr., is alive and well.

Hate crimes, hate radio, hate speech and hate groups are attempting to divide this nation as never before. In an era of smaller vision, rampant apathy, and celebrated mediocrity, we so desperately need those who will stand up and speak out against that which is wrong and to stand up and embrace that which is right. We desperately need to mean it when we say that racism, sexism and anti-Semitism are wrong; to know as a matter of critical fact that black bigotry can be just as cruel as white bigotry; [to] know in our heart of hearts that union bashing, gay bashing, and immigrant bashing deplete us as a nation. They don't move us to some sort of golden heritage, some sort of golden era.

Thus, our challenge is to accept the fact that the road less traveled, the road that all of you are on, the one that no one else wants to embark upon, the road less traveled, is in fact the road less certain, but it is the road that beckons us anyway. We know instinctively and without equivocation better than most in this country that we can't quarantine bigotry; we can't banish it to some hillside far removed from society. Prejudice is something that people learn, usually at an early age. In fact, it is the fear of something unusual, something different from ourselves that inspires those in our society who hate us to recognize that they are in the process of hating themselves, that fear locks them into a glass house of racial indifference.

We don't want any special privileges. All we want is equal access and equal opportunity.

And I am mindful of the hour, but let me say this, because I get tired of having to stand up like you have to stand up in your communities around the country and defend your patriotism, defend your love of America simply because you question that which is wrong. I get tired of those who suggest how somehow that because our branches want to speak out and demonstrate and petition for the redress of their grievances that they are somehow less than full-fledged Americans. Let me say to the hate mongers around this country and remind others who listen that I don't know what else African ancestors must do to exhibit our faith in the American dream or in the American possibility.

～

I would say to you as I begin to slowly wrap things up that although we have crossed many rivers, we still have yet another river to cross. The gate to the American mainstream remains yet a bridge that resolves itself into discussions on the discussions, proposals on the proposals, studies on the studies. And then another Plan B for the Plan A that failed. We want to be real clear, particularly to the elected representatives. We want to make sure that the message is reported properly to the rest of the nation. These people are not here today by accident. We're going to start politically involving ourselves in such a way that we're going to be like an old cold—we're just never going to go away. Like a cold, they won't have a cure because what we want people to know is that all we're asking for is a fair and an equitable return on the black dollar. Jobs are not enough! Listen to me! As I said before, full employment was never the legitimate struggle of the liberation movement. Jobs are important, but jobs are not enough! In full development, which is what we want, full employment is inherent. But in employment, full development is not inherent. We want full development.

The last twenty years, we have concentrated on the public sector and rightfully so. We've made our case in the courts, state legislatures, on Capitol Hill and before corporations. But in 1997, we must focus anew, my friends, also on corporate America. We've got some friends in the corporate community. They're seated around us; you see them over and over again; they start looking like family members. They're there because they continue to push and cajole and jump up and down until somebody pays them attention because they're jumping up and down for us. But they are the minority.

<hr/>

. . . [F]or people who have suffered, endured and survived three centuries of slavery, oppression, deprivation, degradation, denial and disprivilege, we must stand tall and fight back. We must do it because we have before us a Welfare Reform Bill that punishes children for the sexual transgressions of their parents. Under the guise of the welfare reform, it eliminates Aid to Families with Dependent Children. Why is it important? It is important for us to fight back because hypertension, stroke, cancer, and cardiovascular disease can send you to askew in a disproportionate manner mortality and morbidity tables in our communities.

Why is it important? It is important because a company named Texaco, because the Rodney King of corporate America, because of the existence of tapes which proved what many of you have known all along . . . that racism exists at the highest level. Why is it important? It is important because five white women recruits in a place called Aberdeen had the nerve to stand forward with the NAACP and distill their stories of coercion by Army investigators hell-bent on changing charges of consensual sex into rape, hell-bent on prosecuting seemingly only black drill sergeants in an army that has gone astray. Why is it important? It is important because 13-year-old Leonard Clark lay comatose for almost three weeks in a Chicago Hospital, beaten nearly to death just because he happened to ride his bike in the wrong neighborhood, and because he happened to be black. Why is it important? It is important because even with a green jacket, for the racists of the world, Tiger Woods was just another black face. To them he was just another nigger.

We must reply that we still have a shining and powerful dream given by a shining and powerful God. When we hear that new version of an old song that speaks of gradualism, when we are told to wait for tomorrow or the next tomorrow, for the next election or the next generation, we must reply as Martin King did from an old Birmingham jail that "now is the time." Now has always been the time. And so we go believing today not in newspapers, we go believing today not in the pontificators; we go believing not in the politicians or in the government, but believing in ourselves and our mighty God that has brought us a mighty long way. We go believing as James Russell Lowell said,

> *Though the cause of evil prosper,*
> *Yet it is Truth alone as strong. . . .*
> *I can see around her throne,*
> *troops of beautiful tall angels*
> *to shield her from no wrong . . .*
> *Truth forever on the scaffold,*
> *Wrong forever on the throne,*
> *Yet that scaffold sways the future,*
> *And behind the dim unknown,*
> *Standeth God within the shadows,*
> *Keeping a watch above his own.*

If you are like the young and restless, sitting out there on the edge of night, and waiting in general hospital as the world turns, through the days of our lives . . . If the NAACP is not your guiding light, then you need not search for tomorrow because you will not see another world.

HILLARY RODHAM CLINTON
(1947–)

Seneca Falls: 150 Years Later
JULY 16, 1998

The women at Seneca Falls were silenced by someone else. Today,
women, we silence ourselves. We have a choice. We have a voice.

Since her days growing up in Chicago, Hillary Rodham Clinton has
been a recognized champion of women and children. After attending
Wellesley College and Yale Law School, she joined the staff of the
House Judiciary Committee, then investigating Watergate, taught criminal law, and was selected to direct the Legal Services Corporation in
Arkansas. The *National Law Journal* named her one of its hundred most
influential lawyers in America in 1988 and again in 1991. As the wife
of Governor Bill Clinton, Hillary became a national voice on the
Children's Defense Fund, and a leading activist for human rights, education, and health care reform in Arkansas. In the White House, she
continued her work on behalf of women, children, and the poor both
at home and abroad; her controversial statement at the 1994 United
Nations Fourth World Conference on Women in Beijing that "human
rights are women's rights—and women's rights are human rights" drew
worldwide praise. Since 2001, Clinton has carried her message to New
York State, where she now serves as a United States Senator—the first
first lady to hold that distinction.

In this July 16, 1998, address at the 150th anniversary of the first
Women's Rights Convention in Seneca Falls, New York, Clinton celebrated the birth of the modern women's movement by calling on
women to more aggressively participate in the continuing fight for
equality. To a crowd of 16,000, in ringing rhetoric, she encouraged her
audience to think back 150 years and consider the incredible fortitude
necessary for America's foremothers, like Susan B. Anthony and Lucretia
Mott, to speak out for women's rights. Clinton pointed to these
women's accomplishments as inspiration for continued advocacy of
women's full equality—from equal pay to an end of domestic violence.

I WOULD LIKE YOU to take your minds back a hundred and fifty years.
Imagine if you will that you are Charlotte Woodward, a nineteen-year-old

glove maker working and living in Waterloo. Every day you sit for hours sewing gloves together, working for small wages you cannot even keep, with no hope of going on in school or owning property, knowing that if you marry, your children and even the clothes on your body will belong to your husband. But then one day in July 1848, you hear about a women's rights convention to be held in nearby Seneca Falls. It's a convention to discuss the social, civil, and religious conditions and rights of women. You run from house to house and you find other women who have heard the same news. Some are excited, others are amused or even shocked, and a few agree to come with you, for at least the first day. When that day comes, July 19, 1848, you leave early in the morning in your horse-drawn wagon. You fear that no one else will come; and at first, the road is empty, except for you and your neighbors. But suddenly, as you reach a crossroads, you see a few more wagons and carriages, then more and more all going towards Wesleyan Chapel. Eventually you join the others to form one long procession on the road to equality.

Who were the others traveling that road to equality, traveling to that convention? Frederick Douglass, the former slave and great abolitionist, was on his way there, and he described the participants as "few in numbers, moderate in resources, and very little known in the world. The most we had to connect us was a firm commitment that we were in the right and a firm faith that the right must ultimately prevail." In the wagons and carriages, on foot or horseback, were women like Rhoda Palmer. Seventy years later, in 1918, at the age of one hundred and two, she would cast her first ballot in a New York state election.

Also traveling down that road to equality was Susan Quinn, who at fifteen will become the youngest signer of the Declaration of Sentiments. Catharine F. Stebbins, a veteran of activism starting when she was only twelve going door to door collecting anti-slavery petitions. She also, by the way, kept an anti-tobacco pledge on the parlor table and asked all her young male friends to sign up. She was a woman truly ahead of her time, as all the participants were. I often wonder, when reflecting back on the Seneca Falls Convention, who of us—men and women—would have left our homes, our families, our work to make that journey one hundred and fifty years ago.

Think about the incredible courage it must have taken to join that procession. Ordinary men and women, mothers and fathers, sisters and brothers, husbands and wives, friends and neighbors. And just like those who have embarked on other journeys throughout American history, seeking freedom or escaping religious or political persecution, speaking out against slavery, working for labor rights, these men and women were motivated by dreams of better lives and more just societies. At the end of the two-day convention, one hundred people, sixty-eight women and thirty-two men, signed the Declaration of Sentiments that you can now read on the wall at

Wesleyan Chapel. Among the signers were some of the names we remember today: Elizabeth Cady Stanton and Lucretia Mott, Martha Wright and Frederick Douglass and young Charlotte Woodward. The "Seneca Falls 100," as I like to call them, shared the radical idea that America fell far short of her ideals stated in our founding documents, denying citizenship to women and slaves.

Elizabeth Cady Stanton, who is frequently credited with originating the idea for the Convention, knew that women were not only denied legal citizenship, but that society's cultural values and social structures conspired to assign women only one occupation and role, that of wife and mother. Of course, the reality was always far different. Women have always worked, and worked both in the home and outside the home for as long as history can record. And even though Stanton herself had a comfortable life and valued deeply her husband and seven children, she knew that she and all other women were not truly free if they could not keep wages they earned, divorce an abusive husband, own property, or vote for the political leaders who governed them. Stanton was inspired, along with the others who met, to rewrite our Declaration of Independence, and they boldly asserted, "We hold these truths to be self-evident that all men and women are created equal." "All men and all women." It was the shout heard around the world, and if we listen, we can still hear its echoes today. We can hear it in the voices of women demanding their full civil and political rights anywhere in the world. I've heard such voices and their echoes from women, around the world, from Belfast to Bosnia to Beijing, as they work to change the conditions for women and girls and improve their lives and the lives of their families. We can even hear those echoes today in Seneca Falls. We come together this time not by carriage, but by car or plane, by train or foot, and yes, in my case, by bus. We come together not to hold a convention, but to celebrate those who met here one hundred and fifty years ago, to commemorate how far we have traveled since then, and to challenge ourselves to persevere on the journey that was begun all those many years ago. We are, as one can see looking around this great crowd, men and women, old and young, different races, different backgrounds. We come to honor the past and imagine the future. That is the theme the President and I have chosen for the White House Millennium Council's efforts to remind and inspire Americans as we approach the year 2000. This is my last stop on the Millennium Council's tour to Save America's Treasures—those buildings, monuments, papers, and sites—that define who we are as a nation. They include not only famous symbols like the Star Spangled Banner and not only great political leaders like George Washington's revolutionary headquarters, or creative inventors like Thomas Edison's invention factory, but they include also the women of America who wrote our nation's past and must write its future.

Women like the ones we honor here and, in fact, at the end of my tour yesterday, I learned that I was following literally in the footsteps of one of them, Lucretia Mott, who, on her way to Seneca Falls, stopped in Auburn to visit former slaves and went on to the Seneca Nations to meet with clan mothers, as I did. . . .

Because we must tell and retell, learn and relearn, these women's stories, and we must make it our personal mission in our everyday lives, to pass these stories on to our daughters and sons. Because we cannot—we must not—ever forget that the rights and opportunities that we enjoy as women today were not just bestowed upon us by some benevolent ruler. They were fought for, agonized over, marched for, jailed for, and even died for by brave and persistent women and men who came before us.

Every time we buy or sell or inherit property in our own name—let us thank the pioneers who agitated to change the laws that made that possible. Every time we vote, let us thank the women and men of Seneca Falls, Susan B. Anthony and all the others, who tirelessly crossed our nation and withstood ridicule and the rest to bring about the 19th Amendment to the Constitution.

Every time we enter an occupation—a profession of our own choosing— and receive a paycheck that reflects earnings equal to a male colleague, let us thank the signers and women like Kate Mullaney, whose house I visited yesterday in Troy, New York.

Every time we elect a woman to office—let us thank ground-breaking leaders like Jeannette Rankin and Margaret Chase Smith, Hattie Caraway, Louise Slaughter, Bella Abzug, Shirley Chisholm—all of whom proved that a woman's place is truly in the House, and in the Senate, and one day, in the White House, as well. And every time we take another step forward for justice in this nation—let us thank extraordinary women like Harriet Tubman, whose home in Auburn I visited yesterday, and who escaped herself from slavery and then risked her life, time and again, to bring at least two hundred other slaves to freedom as well.

Harriet Tubman's rule for all of her underground railroad missions was to keep going. Once you started—no matter how scared you got, how dangerous it became—you were not allowed to turn back. That's a pretty good rule for life. It not only describes the women who gathered in Wesleyan Chapel in 1848, but it could serve as our own motto for today. We, too, cannot turn back. We, too, must keep going in our commitment to the dignity of every individual—to women's rights as human rights. We are on that road of the pioneers to Seneca Falls; they started down it 150 years ago. But now, we too, must keep going. . . . Those who came here also understood that the convention and the Declaration were only first steps down that road. What matters most is what happens when everyone packs up and goes back to their families and communities. What matters is whether sentiment and resolutions, once made, are fulfilled or forgotten. . . .

⟶

I know how much change I have seen in my own life. When I was growing up back in the fifties and sixties, there were still barriers that Mrs. Stanton would have recognized—scholarships I couldn't apply for, schools I couldn't go to, jobs I couldn't have—just because of my sex. Thanks to federal laws like the Civil Rights Act of 1964, and Title IX, and the Equal Pay Act, legal barriers to equality have fallen.

. . . Because the work of the Seneca Falls Convention is, just like the work of the nation itself, never finished so long as there remain gaps between our ideals and reality. That is one of the great joys and beauties of the American experiment. We are always striving to build and move toward a more perfect union, that we on every occasion keep faith with our founding ideals, and translate them into reality. So what kind of future can we imagine together? If we are to finish the work begun here—then no American should ever again face discrimination on the basis of gender, race, or sexual orientation anywhere in our country.

If we are to finish the work begun here—then $0.76 in a woman's paycheck for every dollar in a man's is still not enough. Equal pay for equal work can once and for all be achieved. If we are to finish the work begun here—then families need more help to balance their responsibilities at work and at home. In a letter to Susan B. Anthony, Elizabeth Cady Stanton writes, "Come here and I will do what I can to help you with your address, if you will hold the baby and make the pudding." Even then, women knew we had to have help with child care. All families should have access to safe, affordable, quality child care. If we are to finish the work begun here—then women and children must be protected against what the Declaration called the "chastisement of women," namely, domestic abuse and violence. We must take all steps necessary to end the scourge of violence against women and punish the perpetrator. And our country must join the rest of the world, as so eloquently Secretary Albright called for on Saturday night here in Seneca Falls, "Join the rest of the world and ratify the convention on the elimination of discrimination against women." If we are to finish the work begun here—we must do more than talk about family values, we must adopt policies that truly value families—policies like a universal system of health care insurance that guarantees every American's access to affordable, quality health care. Policies like taking all steps necessary to keep guns out of the hands of children and criminals. Policies like doing all that is necessary at all levels of our society to ensure high-quality public education for every boy or girl no matter where that child lives. If we are to finish the work begun here—we must ensure that women and men who work full-time earn a wage that lifts them out of poverty and all workers who retire have financial security in their later years through guaranteed Social Security and pensions. If we are to finish the work begun here—we must be vigilant against the messages of a media-driven consumer culture that convinces our sons and daughters that what brand of sneakers they wear or cosmetics they use is more important than what they think, feel, know, or do.

And if we are to finish the work begun here—we must, above all else, take seriously the power of the vote and use it to make our voices heard. What the champions of suffrage understood was that the vote is not just a symbol of our equality, but that it can be, if used, a guarantee of results. It is the way we express our political views. It is the way we hold our leaders and governments accountable. It is the way we bridge the gap between what we want our nation to be and what it is. But when will the majority of women voters of our country exercise their most fundamental political right? Can you imagine what any of the Declaration signers would say if they learned how many women fail to vote in elections? They would be amazed and outraged. They would agree with a poster I saw in 1996. On it, there is a picture of a woman with a piece of tape covering her mouth and under it, it says, "Most politicians think women should be seen and not heard. In the last election, 54 million women agreed with them."

One hundred and fifty years ago, the women at Seneca Falls were silenced by someone else. Today, women, we silence ourselves. We have a choice. We have a voice. And if we are going to finish the work begun here we must exercise our right to vote in every election we are eligible to vote in. Much of who women are and what women do today can be traced to the courage, vision, and dedication of the pioneers who came together at Seneca Falls. Now it is our responsibility to finish the work they began. Let's ask ourselves, at the two hundredth anniversary of Seneca Falls, will they say that today's gathering also was a catalyst for action? Will they say that businesses, labor, religious organizations, the media, foundations, educators, every citizen in our society came to see the unfinished struggle of today as their struggle? Will they say that we joined across lines of race and class, that we raised up those too often pushed down, and ultimately found strength in each other's differences and resolved in our common cause? Will we, like the champions at Seneca Falls, recognize that men must play a central role in this fight? How can we ever forget the impassioned plea of Frederick Douglass, issued in our defense of the right to vote? How can we ever forget that young legislator from Tennessee by the name of Harry Burns, who was the deciding vote in ratifying the 19th Amendment. He was planning on voting "no," but then he got a letter from his mother with a simple message. The letter said, "Be a good boy, Harry, and do the right thing." And he did! Tennessee became the last state to ratify, proving that you can never ever overestimate the power of one person to alter the course of history, or the power of a little motherly advice. Will we look back and see that we have finally joined the rest of the advanced economies by creating systems of education, employment, child care, and health care that support and strengthen families and give all women real choices in their lives?

At the two hundredth anniversary celebration, will they say that women today supported each other in the choices we make? Will we admit once and for all there is no single cookie cutter model for being a successful and fulfilled woman today, that we have so many choices? We can choose full-time motherhood or no family at all or like most of us, seek to strike a balance between our family and our work, always trying to do what is right in our lives. Will we leave our children a world where it is self-evident that all men and women, boys and girls are created equal? These are some of the questions we can ask ourselves. Help us imagine a future that keeps faith with the sentiments expressed here in 1848. The future, like the past and the present, will not and cannot be perfect. Our daughters and granddaughters will face new challenges which we today cannot even imagine. But each of us can help prepare for that future by doing what we can to speak out for justice and equality for women's rights and human rights, to be on the right side of history, no matter the risk or cost, knowing that eventually the sentiments we express and the causes we advocate will succeed because they are rooted in the conviction that all people are entitled by their creator and by the promise of America to the freedom, rights, responsibilities, and opportunity of full citizenship. That is what I imagine for the future. I invite you to imagine with me and then to work together to make that future a reality. Thank you all very much.

AFTERWORD

The struggle for civil rights can be at times lonely and exhausting, particularly in periods when complacency eclipses reality. But I have always been energized by reflecting on the remarkable moments of accomplishment won by many of the men and women included in this anthology—when the barriers were even more resistant. The words in this book—these "ripples of hope"—are instructive; they demonstrate how much we have accomplished together and how far we still have to go.

When speaking in public, I often describe the progress of the American civil rights movement as three steps forward, two steps backward. We have traveled a long way since Abraham Lincoln emancipated the slaves, Sojourner Truth declared "Ain't I a Woman?", Martin Luther King, Jr., died in the cause of civil rights, and César Chávez gave his all in demanding equal rights for farm workers. Today, more African Americans and Hispanics are enrolled in college than ever before. It is no longer unusual to see women CEOs, pundits, and professors at major universities. Black home ownership is at an all-time high, and poverty is at an all-time low. But as far as we have come, many of the same obstacles that have always impeded our progress still stand in our way.

Women of any race or national origin and African-American men can register to vote without paying poll taxes or passing literary tests. Yet today, many African Americans, Latinos, and persons with disabilities are still kept from exercising their right to vote. Today, people of color have the legal right to eat at any lunch counter in America and take a seat at conference tables in many major corporations. Yet most women and blacks still earn but a portion of what their white contemporaries make, and those who enter white-collar professions are often limited in how far they can break through the proverbial glass ceiling.

Today, Hispanic- and Asian-American workers can organize—without the overt threat of violence—on the farm or factory floor. But even today, rampant jingoism keeps immigrants and migrant labor at the margins. Today in most cities, blacks, whites, gays, and heterosexuals live together under the same roof. Many gay couples can even adopt children. However, in most places same-sex unions are still outlawed, preventing lifelong couples from enjoying spousal benefits.

Today, minorities and women cannot be legally excluded from attending any school or university alongside white students; they can study to be physicians, astronauts, and lawyers. Yet, many of the most prestigious public colleges and universities maintain irrational barriers to the entry of African Americans and Latinos. Further, neighborhoods and schools in the United States remain segregated, if not in law then in fact. People of color also lack equal access to health care, and mortality rates among black infants are markedly higher than those among whites.

The speeches in this collection are an apt portrayal of this continuing civil rights struggle; they chronicle the movement's great progress, but they also bring to life the unfortunate reality that the goal of equal opportunity for all remains elusive. I know that Josh Gottheimer, while compiling this collection, had in mind the need to remember what the civil rights movement has accomplished, and what remains undone. He sought, as I always have, to engage the interests of others who share his passion for social justice.

As one of my students at the University of Pennsylvania, Josh demonstrated a burning interest in civil rights—not just their history but their future. He wrote his thesis on women and equal employment opportunity and continued his research at Oxford. Josh then had the rare opportunity to take the ideals he forged as an academic and apply them to his work at the White House.

The past is indeed prologue. I urge all Americans—young and old—to read these speeches, for they contain important lessons for future generations of freedom fighters, who, like their forbears, must take their place in the struggle. It has always been true that each generation must make its own dent in the wall of injustice.

MARY FRANCES BERRY

Geraldine R. Segal Professor
American Social Thought
University of Pennsylvania

Chairperson United States
Commission on Civil Rights

August 2002

CREDITS

Virginia Appuzo, "Creating Change" (November 20, 1988, San Francisco, Keynote at the National Gay and Lesbian Task Force Conference) from *Lesbian Herstory Archives, Special Collection*. Reprinted with the permission of Virginia Appuzo.

Stokely Carmichael, "Black Power" (October 1966, University of California, Berkeley). Reprinted with the permission of Mabel Carmichael.

César Chavéz, "Breaking Bread for Progress" (March 10, 1968) from United Farm Workers papers, Wayne State University, and "We Organized" (November 9, 1984, San Francisco, Commonwealth Club of California). TM/© 2002 the César E. Chavéz Foundation by CMG Worldwide www.cmgww.com.

Hillary Rodham Clinton, "Seneca Falls: 150 Later" (July 18, 1998). Reprinted with the permission of The Honorable Hillary Rodham Clinton.

W. E. B. Du Bois, "A Negro Nation Within a Nation" (June 26, 1934). Reprinted with the permission of David G. Du Bois and The W. E. B. Du Bois Foundation.

Louis Farrakhan, "A Million Men Marching On" (October 17, 1995). Reprinted with the permission of The Honorable Minister Louis Farrakhan and *Final Call*.

Betty Friedan, "The Real Sexual Revolution" (1969, Chicago, First National Conference for the Repeal of Abortion Laws). Reprinted as "Abortion: A Woman's Civil Right" from *It Changed My Life* (New York: Random House, 1976). Copyright © 1976 by Betty Friedan. Reprinted with the permission of Curtis Brown, Ltd.

Marcus Garvey, "A Separate Nation" (June 17, 1923) from Amy Jacques Garvey, *The Philosophy and Opinions of Marcus Garvey* (Dover, Mass.: The Majority Press, 1986). Reprinted with the permission of Marcus Garvey, Jr.

Rodolfo "Corky" Gonzalez, "Chicano Nationalism: Fighting for *La Raza*" (November 13, 1969, Haywood, California). Reprinted with the permission of Rodolfo Gonzalez.

Lani Guinier, "Seeking a Conversation on Race" (June 4, 1993). Reprinted with the permission of Professor Lani Guinier.

José Angel Gutiérrez, "A Chicano Defined" (November 12, 1970, University of Texas). Reprinted with the permission of the author.

Harry Hay, "What Gay Consciousness Brings" (June 26, 1995, San Francisco) from *Radically Gay: Gay Liberation in the Words of Its Founder*, edited by Will Roscoe. Copyright © 1996 by Harry Hay and Will Roscoe. Reprinted with the permission of Beacon Press, Boston.

INDEX